THE PENGUIN DICTIONARY OF ARCHITECTURE

John Fleming was born in 1919 and was educated at Rugby School and Trinity College, Cambridge. His main interests are eighteenth-century art and architecture, especially British and Italian. In 1961 he published *Robert Adam and His Circle in Edinburgh and Rome*, which was awarded the Bannister Fletcher Prize and the Alice Davis Hitchcock Medal. He is completing a second volume on Robert Adam, and his account of the Rococo style is to be published in the Pelican *Style and Civilization* series.

Hugh Honour was born in 1927 and was educated at the King's School, Canterbury, and St Catharine's College, Cambridge. After working in the British Museum he became assistant director of the Leeds City Art Gallery. Since 1954 he has lived in Italy. He published *Chinoiserie: The Vision of Cathay* in 1961 and *The Companion Guide to Venice* in 1965. He has specialized in later Italian sculpture and is writing a biography of Canova and a general book on Romanticism. His *Neo-Classicism* has already been published in the *Style and Civilization* series. He has collaborated with John Fleming in the recently published *Penguin Dictionary of Decorative Arts*.

Sir Nikolaus Pevsner, who was born in 1902 and educated at Leipzig, is Emeritus Professor of the History of Art, University of London, and an Honorary Fellow of St John's College, Cambridge. He is an Honorary D.Litt. and has five other honorary degrees. He is a member of the Historic Buildings Council, the Royal Fine Art Commission and the Advisory Board on Redundant Churches. He was knighted in 1969.

Since its inception he has edited the *Pelican History of Art*. His numerous publications include over forty volumes of *The Buildings of England*, *An Outline of European Architecture*, *Pioneers of Modern Design* and *The Englishness of English Art*.

THE PENGUIN DICTIONARY OF
ARCHITECTURE

JOHN FLEMING, HUGH HONOUR
NIKOLAUS PEVSNER

DRAWINGS BY DAVID ETHERTON

PENGUIN BOOKS

Penguin Books Ltd, Harmondsworth, Middlesex, England
Penguin Books, 625 Madison Avenue, New York, New York 10022, U.S.A.
Penguin Books Australia Ltd, Ringwood, Victoria, Australia
Penguin Books Canada Ltd, 2801 John Street, Markham, Ontario, Canada L3R 1B4
Penguin Books (N.Z.) Ltd, 182–190 Wairau Road, Auckland 10, New Zealand

—

First published in 1966
Reprinted 1967, 1969, 1970,
Second edition 1972
Reprinted 1974, 1976, 1977 (twice), 1978, 1979

—

—

Made and printed in Great Britain
by Richard Clay (The Chaucer Press) Ltd,
Bungay, Suffolk
Set in Monotype Bembo

FOREWORD

This edition is considerably larger than its predecessor and the authors are indebted to many friends for suggestions and corrections, especially to L. D. Ettlinger, John Harris, John Shearman, Sir John Summerson, and Nicholas Taylor.

As before, the dictionary is the work of three authors. Sir Nikolaus Pevsner wrote the entries about medieval and nineteenth- and twentieth-century architects, also the European and American national entries and most of the stylistic entries. He was assisted by Sabrina Longland in connection with definitions of medieval terms, and by Enid Caldecott in connection with modern technical terms. The rest was written jointly by John Fleming and Hugh Honour, who would like to acknowledge the help and advice they received from Ralph Pinder-Wilson (Middle Eastern and Indian entries) and from Peter Swann (China and Japan).

The authors will be most grateful to readers who inform them of errors in the text.

A

AALTO, Alvar (1898–1976) an important modern architect, and certainly pre-eminent in his native Finland. Started neo-classically, in a typically Scandinavian idiom, *c.* 1923–5, and turned to the INTERNATIONAL MODERN with his excellent Library at Viipuri (1927–35), Convalescent Home at Paimio (1929–33), and factory with workers' housing at Sumila (1936–9, with large additions of 1951–7). He possessed a strong feeling for materials and their characters, which, Finland being a country of forests, inspired him to use timber widely. He also invented bent plywood furniture (1932). Timber figured prominently in his Finnish Pavilion at the Paris Exhibition of 1937 and in the Villa Mairea at Noormarkku (1938). Aalto's most original works date from after the Second World War. By then he had evolved a language entirely his own, quite unconcerned with current clichés, yet in its vigorous display of curved walls and single-pitched roofs, in its play with brick and timber, entirely in harmony with the international trend towards plastically more expressive *ensembles*. The principal works are a Hall of Residence at the Massachusetts Institute of Technology, Cambridge, Mass. (1947–9), with a curved front and staircases projecting out of the wall and climbing up diagonally; the Village Hall at Säynätsalo (1951); the Pensions Institute at Helsinki (1952–7), a more straightforward job; the church at Imatra (1952–8), on a completely free plan; and the Hall of Culture at Helsinki (1958).

ABACUS. The flat slab on the top of a CAPITAL: in Greek Doric a thick square slab; in Greek Ionic, Tuscan, Roman Doric and Ionic, square with the lower edge moulded; in Corinthian and Composite with concave sides and the corners cut off. *See figure 64.*

ABADIE, Paul, *see* VAUDREMER.

ABBEY, *see* MONASTERY.

ABUTMENT. Solid masonry placed to counteract the lateral thrust of a VAULT or ARCH. *See figure 4.*

ACANTHUS. A plant with thick, fleshy, scalloped leaves used on carved ornament of Corinthian and Composite CAPITALS and on other mouldings. *See figure 1.*

Fig. 1. Acanthus.

ACROPOLIS. The citadel of a Greek city, built at its highest point and containing the chief temples and public buildings, as at Athens.

ACROTERIA. Plinths for statues or ornaments placed at the apex and ends of a PEDIMENT; also, more loosely, both the plinths and what stands on them. *See figure 2.*

ADAM, Robert (1728–92), the greatest British architect of the later C18, was equally if not more brilliant as a decorator, furniture designer, etc., for which his name is still a household word. He is comparable in his chaste and rather epicene elegance with his French contemporary SOUFFLOT, but without Soufflot's chilly solemnity. He was a typically hard-headed Scot, canny and remorselessly ambitious, yet with a tender, romantic side to his character as well. Both facets were reflected in his work, which

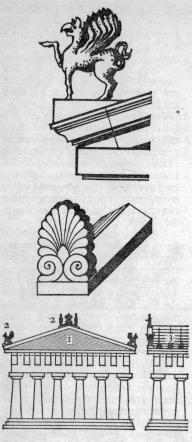

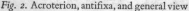

Fig. 2. Acroterion, antifixa, and general view

Key:

1. Pediment   2. Acroterion   3. Antifixa

oscillates between a picturesque version of neo-classicism and a classicizing version of neo-Gothic. His work has an air of unceremonious good manners, unpedantic erudition, and unostentatious opulence which perfectly reflects the civilized world of his patrons. Appreciating that it would be bad manners, and bad business, to make any violent break with established

traditions, he devised a neo-classical style lighter and more gaily elegant than that of the Palladians who preceded or the Greek Revivalists who succeeded him. He avoided startling innovations such as the Greek Doric for classical buildings or the picturesquely asymmetrical for Gothic ones. He answered the current demand for a new classicism by enlarging the repertory of decorative motifs and by a more imaginative use of contrasting room plans derived largely from Imperial Roman Baths. In his cunning variation of room shapes and in his predilection for columned screens and apses to give a sense of spatial mystery, no less than in his neo-Gothic castles – so massively romantic outside and so comfortably classical within – he answered the taste for the picturesque. He became the architect *par excellence* to the Age of Sensibility, as BURLINGTON had been to the English Augustan period. His influence spread rapidly all over England and beyond, as far as Russia and America. His output was enormous, and only the unlucky Adelphi speculation robbed him of the fortune he would otherwise have made.

His father William Adam (1689–1748) was the leading architect of his day in Scotland and developed a robust, personal style based on VANBRUGH, GIBBS, and the English Palladians, e.g., Hopetoun House, near Edinburgh (1721 etc.) and Duff House, Banff (1730–9). His brothers John (1721–92) and James (1732–94) were also architects, and all three trained in their father's Edinburgh office: Robert and James attended Edinburgh University as well. Robert Adam's early work is no more than competent, e.g., Dumfries House (designed 1750–4). His genius emerged only after his Grand Tour (1754–8), most of which was spent in Rome studying Imperial Roman architecture under CLÉRISSEAU, with whom he also surveyed Diocletian's palace at

Split in Dalmatia (later published by him as *Ruins of Spalatro*, 1764).

In 1758 he settled in London, where he was joined by his brother James after a similar Grand Tour with CLÉRISSEAU (1760–3). The columnar Admiralty Screen, London (1759–60), gave immediate proof of his ability and originality, but all his other early commissions were for the internal transformation of old houses or the completion of houses already begun by other architects. Nevertheless, his style rapidly matured, and the interiors of Harewood House (1758–71), Kedleston Hall (1759 etc.), Syon House (1760–9), Osterley Park (1761–80), Luton Hoo (1766–70), Newby Hall (1767–85), and Kenwood (1767–9) are perhaps his masterpieces of interior design. His meticulous attention to detail is revealed no less in the jewel-like finish of the painted decorations and very shallow stucco work than in the care he lavished on every part of each room from the carpets to the keyhole guards. No previous architect had attempted such comprehensive schemes of interior decoration. Although individual decorative motifs are often small in scale they are woven together with such skill that the general effect is rarely finicking, and although the same artistic personality is evident in each room the effect of a series is never monotonous. They perfectly illustrate those qualities for which he and James expressed their admiration in the introduction to their *Works in Architecture* (1773; 2nd vol. 1779; 3rd vol. 1822): movement or 'rise and fall, the advance and recess and other diversity of forms' and 'a variety of light mouldings'. His neo-classicism is most evident in the planning of Syon with its varied geometric shapes (basilican hall, rotunda, projected central Pantheon, etc.), and on the south front of Kedleston, modelled on a Roman triumphal arch.

His originality and ingenuity in planning culminated in his London houses of the 1770s – e.g., 20 St James's Square, 20 Portman Square – in which, however, the decoration became increasingly shallow and linear, tending towards the flippancy and frippery for which he was much criticized towards the end of his life.

Between 1768 and 1772 he and James embarked on their most ambitious enterprise, the Adelphi, a vast palatial group of houses on the banks of the Thames (now destroyed). Unfortunately the speculation failed and they were saved from bankruptcy only by the expedient of a lottery and by loans from their elder brother John in Edinburgh.

Partly as a result of the Adelphi fiasco the quality of Robert Adam's work declined sharply after 1775. But it recovered amazingly during the last decade of his life under the stimulus of large commissions in Edinburgh – the General Register House (begun 1774 and completed, with modifications, after his death), the University (begun 1789, completed by W. H. Playfair to modified designs 1815–34, the dome added by Rowand Anderson in 1887), and Charlotte Square (designed 1791). The entrance front to the University is his most monumental building and perhaps his masterpiece as an architect. To the same period belong most of his sham castles, e.g., Culzean Castle (1777–90) and Seton Castle (1789–91), which were much in advance of their date. His earlier neo-Gothic style, e.g., the interiors of Alnwick Castle (c. 1770, now destroyed), had been similar in its sophisticated elegance to his neo-classical style. Now he developed a much bolder manner. At Culzean he took full advantage of a dramatic site on the Ayrshire coast for a martial display of round towers and battlements embracing rooms of feminine delicacy inside. The charm of the place lies in this contrast, which would have been greatly relished by the c18 Man of

9

Sensibility, who could here enjoy the chilling horror of storms at sea from an eminently safe and civilized interior.

ADDORSED. An adjective applied to two figures, usually animals, placed symmetrically back to back; often found on CAPITALS.

ADOBE. Unburnt brick dried in the sun, commonly used for building in Spain and Latin America, also in New Mexico, e.g., Santa Fé.

ADYTUM. The inner sanctuary of a Greek temple whence oracles were delivered; also, more loosely, any private chamber or sanctuary.

AEDICULE. Properly a shrine framed by two columns supporting an ENTABLATURE and PEDIMENT, set in a temple and containing a statue; but also, more loosely, the framing of a door, window, or other opening with two columns, piers or pilasters supporting a gable, lintel, plaque, or an entablature and pediment.

AEOLIC CAPITAL, see ORDER.

AFFRONTED. An adjective applied to two figures, usually animals, placed symmetrically facing each other; often found on CAPITALS.

AGGER. Latin term for the built-up foundations of Roman roads; also sometimes applied to the banks of hillforts or other earthworks.

AGORA. The open space in a Greek or Roman town used as a market-place or general meeting-place, usually surrounded by porticos as in a FORUM.

AICHEL, Giovanni Santini (1667-1723). A Bohemian architect of Italian extraction born in Prague but trained in Italy, he also visited England and Holland. He worked sometimes in a Baroque (derived from BORROMINI and GUARINI), sometimes in a neo-Gothic style. His speciality was the latter, a carpenter's Gothic, gay, naïve, and very personal, with a predilection for star-shaped forms (derived from Borromini) in his elegant and airy vaulting: e.g., Marienkirche, Kladrau (1712-26), the churches at Seelau (began 1712) and St John

Nepomuk on the Green Mountain near Saar (1719-22). But he was a freak, and had no influence or followers at all.

AISLE. Part of a church, parallel to, and divided by piers or columns – or in rare cases by a screen wall – from the nave, choir, or transept. See figure 10.

ALAN OF WALSINGHAM. Sacrist of Ely Cathedral at the time when the new Lady Chapel was begun (1321) and the tower over the Norman crossing collapsed (1322) and was replaced by the celebrated octagon. From the documents it is almost certain that the bold idea of replacing the square crossing tower by a larger octagon was his.

ÁLAVA, see JUAN DE ÁLAVA.

ALBERTI, Leone Battista (1404-72). Playwright, musician, painter, mathematician, scientist, and athlete as well as architect and architectural theorist, he came nearer than anyone to the Renaissance ideal of a 'complete man'. Aristocratic by temperament, he was the first great dilettante architect. He confined himself to designing, and had nothing to do with the actual building of his works. But his few buildings are all masterpieces, and his *De re aedificatoria* (1452, fully published 1485) is the first architectural treatise of the Renaissance. It crystallized current ideas on proportion, the orders, and ideal (symbolic) town planning. But though he began with theory his buildings are surprisingly unpedantic and undogmatic. They progressed from the nostalgically archaeological to the boldly experimental. Perhaps his dilettante status allowed him greater freedom than his professional contemporaries. He designed only six buildings and saw only three of them completed. To some extent he was indebted to BRUNELLESCHI, whom he knew personally and to whom (among others) he dedicated his treatise *Della pittura* (1436), but whereas Brunelleschi's buildings were elegantly linear his were massively plastic. Architectural beauty he defined as 'the harmony and concord of all the parts achieved in such a manner that nothing could be added, or taken away, or altered except for the worse' and ornament as 'a kind of additional brightness and improvement of Beauty'. By ornament he meant the classical vocabulary of orders, columns, pilasters, and architraves. which he always used correctly and grammatically but frequently out of context, e.g., his columns always support architraves (not arches), but are frequently merely decorative and without real structural purpose. His most notable and influential achievement was the adaptation of classical elements to the wall architecture of the Renaissance.

The illegitimate son of a Florentine exile, he was probably born in Genoa. Educated in the humanist atmosphere of Padua, he later studied law at Bologna university and visited Florence for the first time in 1428. In 1431 he went to Rome, where he joined the Papal civil service which apparently allowed him ample time for both travel and the cultivation of his various talents. As Papal inspector of monuments (1447–55) he 'restored' and radically altered the C5 circular church of S. Stefano Rotondo, Rome. His first independent work appears to have been the façade of Palazzo Rucellai, Florence, executed by Bernardo ROSSELLINO by 1460. With rusticated walls articulated by three superimposed orders of pilasters (Ionic and Corinthian very freely interpreted), it is indebted to Brunelleschi's Palazzo di Parte Guelfa. But it has certain novelties, e.g., square-headed door-cases, a vast cornice instead of eaves, and double windows with pilasters and a central column supporting an architrave beneath the rounded cap. The exquisite adjustment of the proportions distinguishes the palace from that designed and built in emulation of it at Pienza by Rossellino. In 1450 he was com-

missioned to transform the Gothic church of S. Francesco, Rimini, into a memorial to the local tyrant Sigismondo Malatesta, his wife, and courtiers. It was subsequently called the Tempio Malatestiano. He designed a marble shell to encase the old building, the front freely based on a Roman triumphal arch (symbolizing the triumph over death), the side walls pierced by deep arched niches each containing a sarcophagus. The front was never finished, and it is now difficult to visualize how he intended to mask the upper part of the old Gothic façade. As it stands it is a magnificent fragment, one of the noblest and most poignant evocations of the grandeur, *gravitas*, and decorum of Roman architecture. His next work was another addition to a Gothic church, the completion of the façade of S. Maria Novella, Florence (1456–70). Entirely coated with an inlay of different coloured marbles, it owes as much to the C11–12 church of S. Miniato, Florence, as to any Roman building, though the central doorway is derived from the Pantheon. But the whole design is based on a complex geometrical arrangement of squares, and is thus the first instance of the use of HARMONIC PROPORTIONS in the Renaissance. The upper part of the façade is in the form of a pedimented temple front linked to the sides by great scrolls which were to be much copied in later periods. It was commissioned by Giovanni Rucellai whose name is inscribed across the top with typical Renaissance confidence. For the same patron he designed the exquisite, casket-like little marble-clad shrine of the Holy Sepulchre (1467) and perhaps also the Cappella Rucellai, Florence, in which it stands.

S. Sebastiano (1460) and S. Andrea (1470), both at Mantua, are the only buildings which he designed entire. For S. Sebastiano he chose a centralized Greek cross plan and designed the massively austere façade as a pilastered temple front approached up a wide flight of steps. But he broke the entablature with a round-headed window (derived from the Roman arch of Tiberius at Orange, *c.* 30 B.C.) and increased its severity by reducing the pilasters from six to four. This alteration and his complete rejection of columns marks his increasing tendency to stray from correct classical usage in the creation of a more logical wall architecture. The church was completed, with further alterations, after his death. At S. Andrea his plans were carried out more faithfully, though the dome he designed to cover the crossing was never executed. The façade is a combination of a pedimented temple front and a triumphal arch, with shallow pilasters in place of columns and a deep central recess framing the main door. Inside he abandoned the traditional aisle structure for a barrel-vaulted nave flanked by side chapels. Interior and exterior are carefully integrated. The sides of the nave, with pilastered solids and arched recesses alternating, repeat the rhythmical pattern and the triumphal arch of the façade on exactly the same scale. These two buildings herald a new and less archaeological attitude to antiquity. They reach forward from the Early to the High Renaissance and even beyond.

ALBINI, Franco (b. 1905). Studied and lives at Milan. His interior of the Palazzo Bianco Museum at Genoa and of the treasury of Genoa Cathedral (1951 and 1954) establish him as one of the most brilliant display architects of the century. His principal building is the Rinascente department store in Rome (1961).

ALEIJADINHO (António Francisco Lisboa, 1738–1814). The greatest Brazilian sculptor and architect. A mulatto (illegitimate son of a Portuguese architect), he worked in the rich goldmining province of Minas Gerais, and combined barbarically rich and contorted sculptural decoration with the more dignified architectural forms of traditional Lusitanian church design. His masterpieces are São Francisco, Ouro Preto (1766–94), and the monumental scenic staircase in front of Bom Jesus de Matozinhos, Congonhas do Campo (1800–5).

ALESSI, Galeazzo (1512–72). The leading High Renaissance architect in Genoa. Born in Perugia and trained in Rome where he was much influenced by MICHELANGELO, he settled in Genoa by 1548. He was adept at turning difficult sloping sites to advantage, and made great play with monumental staircases, colonnades, and courtyards on different levels. His several palaces, notably Villa Cambiaso (1548), Palazzo Cambiaso (1565, now Banco d'Italia), and Palazzo Parodi (1567), set the pattern for Genoese domestic architecture. He also built the imposing S. Maria di Carignano, Genoa (1552), based on BRAMANTE's design for St Peter's.

ALFIERI, Benedetto (1700–67), a Piedmontese nobleman (uncle of the poet), began as a lawyer, turned to architecture, and succeeded JUVARRA as royal architect in Turin (1739). He was largely employed in completing Juvarra's work in Palazzo Reale, Turin, and elsewhere. His main independent building is the vast parish church at Carignano (1757–64), with a severe façade and very rich interior on a peculiar kidney-shaped plan. He also designed the noble W. portico at Geneva Cathedral in a surprisingly radical classicizing style (1752–6).

ALGARDI, Alessandro (1595–1654). Born in Bologna but settled in Rome, best known as a sculptor, representing the sobriety of Bolognese classicism in opposition to BERNINI. His reputation as an architect rests on the Villa Doria-Pamphili in Rome of which he had the general direction, though it seems to have been designed by G. F. Grimaldi.

ALMONRY. The room in a MONASTERY in which alms are distributed.

ALTAR. A structure on which to place or sacrifice offerings to a deity. In Greece and Rome altars took many different forms. The Christian altar is a table or slab on supports consecrated for celebration of the sacrament; usually of stone. In the Middle Ages portable altars could be of metal. After the Reformation communion tables of wood replaced altars in England.

ALTAR-TOMB. A post-medieval term for a tomb resembling an altar with solid sides but not used as one. *See* TOMB-CHEST.

ALTAR FRONTAL, *see* ANTEPENDIUM.

AMADEO, Giovanni Antonio (1447–1522). Born in Pavia, and primarily a sculptor, he was working at the Certosa there by 1466; then he worked in Milan (MICHELOZZO's Portinari Chapel in S. Eustorgio), where he encountered the Early Renaissance style. The immediate result was the Colleoni Chapel (1472–6) attached to S. Maria Maggiore, Bergamo – based on the Portinari Chapel but encrusted with Renaissance ornamentation in Gothic profusion. He designed the lower storey of the façade of the Certosa outside Pavia (1474) in a similar manner. From 1500 onwards he worked on Milan Cathedral (retardataire Gothic in style).

AMBO. A stand raised on two or more steps, for the reading of the Epistle and the Gospel; a prominent feature in medieval Italian churches. Sometimes two were built, one for the Epistle and one for the Gospel, on the south and north sides respectively. After the C14 the ambo was replaced by the PULPIT.

AMBULATORY. A semicircular or polygonal aisle enclosing an APSE or a straight-ended sanctuary; originally used for processional purposes.

AMMANATI, Bartolomeo (1511–92), was primarily a Mannerist sculptor. His architectural masterpiece is the very graceful Ponte S. Trinità, Florence (1567–70, destroyed 1944 but rebuilt). With VIGNOLA and VASARI he played some part in designing Villa Giulia, Rome (1551–5). He enlarged and altered Palazzo Pitti, Florence (1558–70), building the almost grotesquely over-rusticated garden façade (1560). He completed Palazzo Grifoni, Florence (1557) and supervised the building of MICHELANGELO's vestibule stairway in the Laurenziana, Florence. Outside Florence, he designed the Tempietto della Vittoria, near Arezzo (1572). In Lucca he designed part of the Palazzo Provinciale (1578) with a handsome Serlian loggia.

AMPHIPROSTYLE. The adjective applied to a temple with porticos at each end, but without columns along the sides.

AMPHITHEATRE. An elliptical or circular space surrounded by rising tiers of seats, as used by the Romans for gladiatorial contests, e.g., the Colosseum, Rome.

ANATHYROSIS. The smooth marginal dressing of the outer contact band of a masonry joint, the central portion being left roughened and sunk so as to avoid contact.

ANCONES. 1. Brackets or CONSOLES on either side of a doorway, supporting a CORNICE. 2. The projections left on blocks of stone, such as the drums of a column, to hoist them into position.

ANGLO-SAXON ARCHITECTURE, *see* ENGLISH ARCHITECTURE.

ANGULAR CAPITAL. An IONIC capital with all four sides alike, and the volutes turned outwards as in a Corinthian capital. A C16 innovation, probably due to SCAMOZZI and frequently employed until the late C18 when rejected as incorrect.

ANNULET, *see* SHAFT-RING.

ANSE DE PANIER, *see* ARCH.

ANTA. A PILASTER of which the base and CAPITAL do not conform with the ORDER used elsewhere on the building; it is usually placed at the ends of the projecting walls of a portico.

ANTECHURCH (or FORECHURCH). An appendix to the west end of a church, resembling a porch or a NARTHEX, but several bays deep and usually consisting of nave and aisles.

ANTEFIXAE. Ornamental blocks on the edge of a roof to conceal the ends of the tiles. *See figure 2.*

Fig. 3. Anthemion and palmette

ANTELAMI, Benedetto (active 1177–1233), a sculptor and probably an architect. Attributed to him are the Parma Baptistery (begun in 1196), the cathedral of Borgo San Donnino (1179 etc., chiefly 1214–18) and S. Andrea at Vercelli. This church already has features pointing in the direction of the French Gothic. The transition from Romanesque to Gothic is obvious in his sculpture.

ANTEPENDIUM. A covering for the front of an altar, usually of metal or fabric.

ANTHEMION. Ornament based on the honeysuckle flower and leaves, common in Greek and Roman architecture. *See figure 3.*

ANTHEMIUS OF TRALLES. Geometrician and theorist rather than architect, he is known for sure to have designed only one building, but that among the greatest in the world: Hagia Sophia, Constantinople (A.D. 532–7). The dates of his birth and death are unknown. Born at Tralles in Lydia, he came of a Greek professional middle-class family; his father was a physician. In 532 Justinian chose him to design the new church of Holy Wisdom (Hagia Sophia) to replace a predecessor which had been burnt in riots. This vast undertaking was completed in the incredibly brief period of five years, to the gratification of Justinian

who claimed to have surpassed Solomon. Anthemius described architecture as 'the application of geometry to solid matter', and his great work with its dome 107 ft in diameter is remarkable as a feat of engineering (even though the dome collapsed in 558). But it is also much more, for by the cunning use of screened aisles and galleries around the central area of the church he concealed the supports of the dome which thus seems to float above the building, creating an atmosphere of mystery emphasized by the contrast between the light central space and the dark aisles. He was assisted by ISIDORE OF MILETUS.

ANTIS, IN, *see* PORTICO.

ANTOINE, Jacques-Denis (1733–1801). A leading architect in the reign of Louis XVI. His masterpiece is the Mint, Paris (designed 1768, begun 1771) – huge, solemn, and very Roman, though he did not visit Italy until 1777. He used Paestum Doric for the peristyle of the Hôpital de la Charité, Paris (*c.* 1785), but his other works are less sternly neo-classical.

ANTONELLI, Alessandro (1798–1888). Professor of Architecture at Turin from 1836 till 1857. His most famous works are the crazily high, externally classical and internally iron-supported towers of the so-called Mole Antonelliana at Turin (originally intended as a synagogue and about 550 ft high) and of the cathedral of Novara (about 420 ft high). The former was designed in 1863, the latter in 1840.

APEX STONE. The top stone in a GABLE end, sometimes called the *saddle stone*.

APOLLODORUS OF DAMASCUS (active A.D. 97–130). Born in Syria, he went to Rome and became official architect to Trajan (A.D. 97–117), accompanying him on his military campaigns and designing or inspiring almost all the buildings erected under him. His first recorded work is the stone-and-wood bridge over the Danube at Dobreta (A.D. 104). But his masterpieces were naturally in Rome itself: an odeon circular in plan (probably that built by Domitian in the Campus Martius), the Baths of Trajan, and Trajan's Forum. The latter, with its imposing axial planning and subtle play of symmetry, illustrates his style, a brilliant compromise between the Hellenistic and the pure Roman traditions. He also planned the markets at the extreme end of the Quirinal hill, and was probably involved in work at the port of Rome (Fiumicino) and at Civitavecchia. The triumphal arches at Ancona and Benevento have been attributed to him. Though he was on less happy terms with Hadrian, he collaborated with him on at least one project, and dedicated to him his treatise on the construction of engines of assault, *Poliorketa*. But, according to Dio Cassius, Hadrian banished him from Rome in about A.D. 130, and later condemned him to death because of his harsh criticism of the Temple of Venus and Rome.

APOPHYGE. The slight curve at the top and bottom of a column where the SHAFT joins the CAPITAL or base.

APPLIED COLUMN, *see* ENGAGED COLUMN.

APRON. A raised panel below a window-sill, sometimes shaped and decorated.

APSE. A vaulted semicircular or polygonal termination, usually to a chancel or chapel. *See figure 10.*

APTERAL. An adjective describing a classical-style building with columns at the end, but not along the sides.

AQUEDUCT. An artificial channel for carrying water, usually an elevated masonry or brick structure; invented by the Romans.

ARABESQUE. Intricate and fanciful surface decoration generally based on geometrical patterns and using combinations of flowing lines, tendrils, etc., and classical vases, sphinxes, etc.

ARAEOSTYLE. With an arrangement of columns spaced four diameters apart. *See also* DIASTYLE; EUSTYLE; PYCNOSTYLE; SYSTYLE.

ARCADE. A range of arches carried on PIERS or columns, either free-standing or blind, i.e., attached to a wall.

ARCH. *Anse de panier* is a French term for an arch whose curve resembles that of the handle of a basket; also called *basket arch*. It is formed by a segment of a large circle continued left and right by two segments of much smaller circles.

Basket arch or *three-centred arch, see above.*

Discharging arch, see relieving arch.

A *drop arch* is pointed with a span greater than its radii.

An *elliptical arch* is a half ellipse from a centre on the springing line.

Equilateral arch, see pointed arch.

A *four-centred* or *depressed arch* is a late medieval form – a pointed arch of four arcs, the two outer and lower ones springing from centres on the SPRINGING LINE, the two inner and upper arcs from centres below the springing line.

A *horseshoe arch* is often found in Islamic buildings; it can be either a pointed or a round horseshoe.

A *lancet arch* is pointed, with radii much larger than the span.

An *ogee arch* is pointed and usually of four arcs, the centres of two inside the arch, of the other two outside; this produces a compound curve of two parts, one convex and the other concave. Introduced *c.* 1300 this arch was popular throughout the late Middle Ages and in England especially in the early C14.

A *pointed arch* is produced by two curves, each with a radius equal to the span and meeting in a point at the top; also called an *equilateral arch*.

A *relieving arch* is usually of rough construction placed in a wall, above an arch or any opening, to relieve it of much of the superincumbent weight; also called a *discharging arch*.

A *segmental arch* is a segment of a circle drawn from a centre below the springing line.

A *shouldered arch* consists of a lintel

connected with the jambs of a doorway by corbels. The corbels start with a concave quadrant and continue vertically to meet the lintel.

A *stilted arch* has its springing line raised by vertical *piers* above the IMPOST level.

A *strainer arch* is one inserted, in most cases, across a nave or an aisle to prevent the walls from leaning.

A *Tudor arch* is a late medieval pointed arch whose shanks start with a curve near to a quarter circle and continue to the apex in a straight line. *See figure 4.*

ARCHER, Thomas (1668–1743). The only English Baroque architect to have studied continental Baroque at first hand. His buildings are unique in England in showing an intimate appreciation of BERNINI and BORROMINI. He came of good family and made a four-year Grand Tour after Oxford, returning home about 1693. A Whig, he was successful at Court and in 1703 obtained the lucrative post of Groom Porter. His buildings date between then and 1715, when he acquired the even more profitable post of Controller of Customs at Newcastle, whereupon he gave up architecture. The north front of Chatsworth (1704–5) and the garden pavilion at Wrest Park (1711–12) are his best surviving

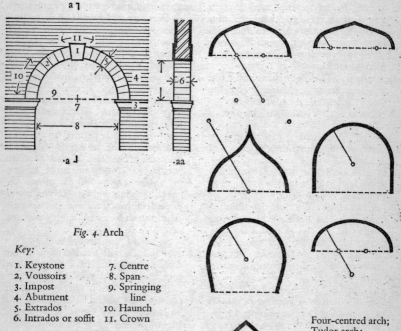

Fig. 4. Arch

Key:

1. Keystone
2. Voussoirs
3. Impost
4. Abutment
5. Extrados
6. Intrados or soffit
7. Centre
8. Span
9. Springing
   line
10. Haunch
11. Crown

Four-centred arch;
Tudor arch;
Ogee arch;
Stilted arch;
Horseshoe arch;
Basket arch;
Lancet arch

secular buildings, but his reputation rests mainly on his three churches – Birmingham Cathedral (1710–15); St Paul, Deptford, London (1712–30); and St John, Smith Square, London (1714–28), with its spectacular and much-maligned towers. Heythrop House, Oxon, was his most grandiloquent effort but it was burnt down and rebuilt 1870.

ARCHITECTS' CO-PARTNERSHIP. A group of English architects born about 1915–17. Their principal works include: a factory at Bryn Mawr in Wales (1949); a range of students' sets for St John's College, Oxford (1956–9); a range of sets for King's College, Cambridge (1960–2); a school at Ripley, Derbyshire (1958–60) and other schools; housing at Ikoyi, Lagos (1957–9); and the Biochemistry Building, Imperial College, London (1961–4).

ARCHITRAVE. The lowest of the three main parts of an ENTABLATURE; also, more loosely, the moulded frame surrounding a door or window (if this frame turns away at the top at right angles, rises vertically and returns horizontally, forming a shoulder, it is called a *shouldered architrave*). See *figures 39, 42, and 64.*

ARCHITRAVE-CORNICE. An ENTABLATURE from which the FRIEZE is elided.

ARCHIVOLT. The continuous architrave moulding on the face of an arch, following its contour; also the INTRADOS or under-side of an arch.

ARCUATED. A term applied to a building dependent structurally on the use of arches or the arch principle, in contrast to a TRABEATED building.

ARENA. The central open space of an AMPHITHEATRE; also, more loosely, any building for public contests or displays in the open air.

ARISS, John, the first professional architect in North America, emigrated from England in or shortly before 1751, when he advertised in the *Maryland Gazette* as being 'lately from Great Britain' and ready to undertake 'Buildings of all Sorts and Dimensions ... either of the Ancient or Modern Order of Gibbs, Architect'. Unfortunately his work is unrecorded, but some of the finer Virginian houses were probably designed by him, e.g., Mount Airey, Richmond County (1755–8); they are English Palladian, with Gibbsian overtones.

ARK, *see* ECHAL.

ARNOLFO DI CAMBIO. A Florentine sculptor and mason of the later C13 (d. 1302?). Assistant of Nicola PISANO in 1266, he is already called a *subtilissimus magister* in 1277. He signed works of decorative architecture and sculpture combined in 1282, 1285, and 1293. The architectural forms used are truly Gothic, aware of French precedent, and include trefoil-headed and trefoil-cusped arches. In 1296 the new cathedral of Florence was begun; Arnolfo was master mason. His design is recognizable in the nave and aisles, but the present centralizing east end with its three polygonal apses is Talenti's, though it only enlarged and pushed considerably farther east the east end as intended by Arnolfo, perhaps under the influence of Cologne. It is curious that Arnolfo, in the earliest source referring to him (though as late as *c.* 1520), is called a German. Several other buildings have been attributed to Arnolfo, among them, with convincing arguments, S. Croce (begun 1295) and the Florentine Badia (begun 1284).

ARRIS. A sharp edge produced by the meeting of two surfaces.

ARRUDA, Diogo (active 1508–31). The leading practitioner of the MANUELINE STYLE in Portugal. His main work is the nave and chapterhouse of the Cristo Church, Tomar (1510–14), with its almost surrealist sculptured decoration: sails and ropes around the circular windows, mouldings of cork floats threaded on cables, buttresses carved with patterns of coral and seaweed. His brother Francisco (active 1510–47) was mainly a military architect, but built the exotic, almost Hindu, tower at Belem (1515–20).

ART NOUVEAU. The name of a shop opened in Paris in 1895 to sell objects of modern, i.e., non-period-imitation, style. The movement away from imitation of the past had started in book production and textiles in England in the 1880s (see MACKMURDO), and had begun to invade furniture and other furnishings about 1890. Stylistically, the origins lay in the designs of William MORRIS and the English Arts and Crafts. One of the principal centres from 1892 onwards was Brussels (see HORTA, van de VELDE). In France the two centres were Nancy, where in Émile Gallé's glass Art Nouveau forms occurred as early as the 1880s, and Paris. Art Nouveau forms are characterized by the ubiquitous use of undulation like waves or flames or flower stalks or flowing hair. Some artists kept close to nature, others, especially van de Velde, preferred abstract forms as being a purer expression of the dynamics aimed at. The most important representative of Art Nouveau in America is Louis C. Tiffany (1848–1933), in Germany Hermann Obrist (1863–1927) and August Endell (1871–1925). In architecture by far the greatest is GAUDÍ. It has rightly been pointed out that Art Nouveau has a source and certainly a parallel in the paintings and graphic work of Gauguin, Munch, and some others. The climax in Britain, and at the same time the beginning of the end, is the work of Charles R. MACKINTOSH of Glasgow, in whose architecture and decoration the slender curves and the subtle opalescent colours of Art Nouveau blend with a new rectangular crispness and pure whiteness of framework. Vienna took this up at once, and found from it the way into the twentieth-century emphasis on the square and the cube (see LOOS, HOFFMANN and LECHNER).

ARUP, Ove (b. 1895). Studied Philosophy before graduating in Engineering in Copenhagen in 1922. Engaged first in civil engineering and then became involved in architecture, working with Lubetkin in London to produce Highpoint, the Penguin Pool and Finsbury Health Centre, where he applied new ideas of concrete construction and pioneered the use of load-bearing concrete walls. His own consulting practice has become known for its fresh approach to the solution of difficult structural problems, and he has collaborated closely with leading architects in England and overseas, notably with Utzon for Sydney Opera House (1956–73). A parallel partnership of architects and engineers, led by Philip Dowson, Ronald Hobbs and others, was formed in 1963. This multi-professional team aims to practise close collaboration between professions. It has been responsible for Point Royal, Bracknell, buildings for Corpus Christi, Cambridge, and Somerville, Oxford, the Mining and Metallurgy Departments at Birmingham University and the buildings for CIBA at Duxford, and Smith, Kline & French at Welwyn.

ASAM, Cosmas Damian (1688–1739) and Egid Quirin (1692–1750), were brothers who always worked together as architects though sometimes separately as decorators (Cosmas Damian was a fresco-painter and Egid Quirin a sculptor). Sons of a Bavarian fresco-painter, they did not emerge from provincial obscurity until after visiting Rome (1712–14), where they seem to have admired the juicier C17 Italians and remained essentially Baroque rather than Rococo architects. They decorated many important churches (e.g., Weingarten; Einsiedeln; St Jacobi, Innsbruck; Osterhofen; Freising Cathedral; St Maria Victoria, Ingolstadt; Aldersbach), but designed or partially designed only four, in which, however, they carried to unprecedented lengths the melodramatic effects of concealed lighting, spatial illusionism, and other tricks which they had picked up in Rome. Their emotionalism is seen at its wildest in the fantastic *tableau vivant* altar-pieces at Rohr (1717–26) and Weltenburg (1716–21). They attempted something better in St John Nepomuk, Munich (1733–38), a church which is attached to their house and was entirely paid for by them. It is known as the Asamkirche. This is a tiny but sensational church, a masterpiece of German Baroque in which architecture and decoration are successfully combined to achieve an intense atmosphere of religious fervour. Their last work, the Ursulinenkirche, Straubing (1738–41), is almost equally good.

ASHBEE, Charles Robert (1863–1942). More a social reformer than an architect. His model was MORRIS. In 1888 he founded his Guild and School of Handicraft in the East End of London. The guild moved into the country, to Chipping Campden, in 1902. The First World War killed it. His best architectural designs are two houses in Cheyne Walk, London (1899).

ASHLAR. Hewn blocks of masonry wrought to even faces and square edges and laid in horizontal courses with vertical joints, as opposed to rubble or unhewn stone straight from the quarry.

ASPLUND, Gunnar (1885–1940), the most important Swedish architect of the twentieth century, started in the Scandinavian classicism first developed by the Danes; his principal work in that style is the Stockholm City Library (1920–8) with its high circular reading room rising as a drum above the rest of the *ensemble*. With his work for the Stockholm Exhibition of 1930 he changed to the Central European Modern, but instead of treating it in the relatively massive manner then current, he lightened up his forms by means of thin metal members, much glass, and some freer forms of roof, etc., thereby endowing the style with a grace and translucency which had a great international impact. But Asplund was never demonstrative or aggressive. His buildings always observe a noble restraint. The finest of them are the extension of the Town Hall of Göteborg (1934–7), with its beautifully transparent courtyard, and the Stockholm Crematorium (1935–40), which may well be called the most perfect example of genuine C20 monumentality and religious architecture in existence.

ASPRUCCI, Antonio (1723–1808). A notable early neo-classical architect in Rome. His masterpiece is the interior of Villa Borghese, Rome (1777–84), and the elegant temples, sham ruins, and other follies in the park.

ASSYRIAN AND SUMERIAN ARCHITECTURE. As early as the fourth millennium the Sumerians in the Euphrates delta had evolved a complex architecture. The main material was brick: techniques included the arch, the dome, and the vault (though the latter appears to have been used only for underground burial chambers). Having solved these basic problems of construction, architects applied themselves to decoration. An astonishing proof of their ability is provided by the great ZIGGURAT temple of the Uruk period (late fourth millennium) at Warka (Biblical Erech), where the surface was decorated with a mosaic of red-, black-, and buff-coloured terracotta cones arranged in geometrical patterns. The façades were further articulated by a succession of decorative buttresses – a device that was to distinguish sacred buildings in Mesopotamia until Hellenistic times. The temple of Al 'Ubaid near Ur, built by King A-annipaddi, *c.* 2600 B.C., shows that by this date painted and relief decorations were used not merely as ornaments but to emphasize the structure. But perhaps the most remarkable of these early constructions is the vast ziggurat at Ur, built in the C22 B.C. – an extremely sophisticated building with dramatic staircases ascending to the shrine on top and with every line subtly curved to correct optical illusions. The principles of this architecture were taken over by the Assyrians of northern Mesopotamia towards the end of the second millennium. So far as may be judged from the excavated sites (unfortunately their great cities at Nineveh and Nimrud yield little for the student of architecture), the Assyrians were unable to make any technical advances of importance on the Sumerians, but they demanded effects of greater grandeur with lavish use of brilliant colour and much sculpture in the round as well as in relief. The Palace of Sargon at Khorsabad reveals that they achieved their effects of splendour by the multiplication of units rather than by bold over-all designing.

ASTRAGAL. A small moulding circular in section, often decorated with a bead and reel enrichment. *See figures 5 and 42.*

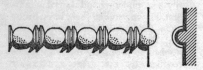

Fig. 5. Astragal

ASTYLAR. A term applied to a façade without columns or pilasters.

ATLANTES. Supports in the form of carved male figures, used especially by German Baroque architects instead of columns to support an ENTABLATURE. The Roman term is *telamones*. *See also* CARYATID.

ATRIUM. 1. In Roman domestic architecture, an inner court open to the sky and surrounded by the roof. 2. In Early Christian and medieval architecture, an open court in front of a church; usually a colonnaded quadrangle.

ATTACHED COLUMN, *see* ENGAGED COLUMN.

ATTIC BASE. The base of an IONIC column consisting of two large rings of convex mouldings (the lower of greater diameter) joined by a spreading concave moulding, used in Athens in the C5 and C4 B.C.

ATTIC STOREY. 1. A storey above the main ENTABLATURE of a building and in strictly architectural relation to it, as, e.g., in Roman triumphal arches. 2. Also, more loosely, the space within the sloping roof of a house or the upper storey of a building if less high than the others.

AUMBRY (or AMBRY). A cupboard or recess used to keep sacred vessels in.

AUSTRIAN ARCHITECTURE. Austria originated in the Ostmark (Eastern Marches) established in 803 by Charlemagne after he had subdued the Bavarians in 788. When the Hungarian invasion had been halted (955), the Ostmark was renewed and remained in the hands of the Babenberg dynasty from 976 to 1246. After that Austria passed to the Habsburgs. The archbishopric of Salzburg was created in 789; additional bishoprics came much later: Gurk in 1070, Seckau in 1218, and Vienna only in 1480.

Of pre-Romanesque architecture in Austria little is known. Salzburg Cathedral (767–74) was, according to excavations, nearly 200 ft long and had a straightforward Early Christian basilica plan with one apse. The Romanesque style is an interesting mixture of elements from Bavaria and Lombardy, although West Germany (especially Hirsau, the centre of Cluniac architecture for Germany) and even France also play a part. Bavarian influence means basilican churches with pillars (Hirsau stood for columns – see St Paul im Lavanttal in Austria), no transepts, and three parallel apses, while Lombardy was the source of much of the best decoration; it is to be found at Klosterneuburg (1114–33), Gurk (1140s–c. 1200; crypt of a hundred marble columns), Millstatt, and even the portal of St Peter at Salzburg (*c.* 1240). Another source of ornament was Normandy (zigzag, etc.) via Worms, Bamberg, and Regensburg – see St Stephen, Vienna; St Pölten; and the Karner at Tulln. Karners are bone-houses with chapels, centrally planned, and they are an Austrian speciality. The largest church of the C12 was Salzburg Cathedral as rebuilt in 1181 etc. It was as long as Old St Peter's in Rome, and had double aisles, round towers over apses in the end walls of the transepts, two (older) west towers, and an octagonal crossing tower.

Cistercian colonization was actively pursued in Austria, and Viktring (built 1142–1202) is indeed an early and faithful follower of Fontenay, the earliest preserved house in France; it has, for example, the pointed tunnel vaults of Fontenay. On the other hand Heiligenkreuz (begun *c.* 1150–60) has rib vaults with heavy square ribs, a Lombard characteristic. Heiligenkreuz received a choir in 1295, of the hall type. This is of course fully Gothic, and hall churches are characteristic of the German Late Gothic. The hall choir was suggested by an earlier Cistercian hall choir in Austria: Lilienfeld (1202–30), also nearly entirely Gothic. This is an extremely early case of the hall elevation and one which established Austria as one of the sources of German hall churches. Zwettl, also Cistercian, received its splendid hall choir with ambulatory and low radiating chapels much later (1343–83). From here influences again reached out to South and South-west Germany. The friars, the most active order of the later C13 and the C14, went in for halls too.

The principal achievement of the C14 and C15 is of course St Stephen in Vienna, not a cathedral originally. The hall chancel is of 1304–40, the glorious south tower of 1359–1433. Connections in the early C14 were principally with Bohemia (Vienna) and Bavaria (Franciscan Church,

Salzburg, 1408 etc.; by Hans STET-HAIMER). Developments in architecture in the later C15 and early C16 were as great and important as they were in sculpture: intricate vaults, with star, net, and even rosette motifs, are characteristic, and culminate in the stucco ribs with vegetable details of Laas (*c.* 1515–20) and Kötschach (1518–27) in Carinthia. Supports may be twisted piers (Salzburg Castle, 1502) or even tree-trunk piers (Bechyně Castle, just across the Moravian border). The first secular buildings are also of these late years: the Bummerlhaus at Steyr (1497), the Goldenes Dachl at Innsbruck (completed 1500), and the Kornmesserhaus at Bruck on the Mur (1499–1505). The arcading here suggests Venetian influence.

But Italian influence was very soon to mean something quite different from the Gothic of the Kornmesserhaus. The portal of the Salvator Chapel in Vienna of just after 1515 is entirely Lombard Renaissance and must be the work of a sculptor from there. Similar works, especially funerary monuments, picked up the new forms at once. In architecture the next examples are the portal of the Arsenal at Wiener Neustadt (1524) and the elegant courtyard of the Portia Palace at Spital (*c.* 1540); a comparison of this with the much heavier courtyard of the Landhaus at Graz (1556–65; by Domenico dell'Allio) shows a characteristic development. The stage after this is represented by the courtyard of the Schallaburg near Melk (1572–1600) with caryatids, etc. – what would in Britain be called Elizabethan. On the whole, Austria is less rich in first-rate Renaissance buildings than Bohemia. The Hofkirche at Innsbruck (1553–63) is a Gothic hall, though with slender columns instead of piers. The only fully Italian building in the ecclesiastical field is Salzburg Cathedral, by Santino SOLARI, with two west towers and a crossing dome, and this is of 1614–34. The cathedral, the Archiepiscopal Palace, and the Franciscan church show a very complete development of Italianate C17 stucco decoration.

In Vienna a remarkable number of churches were built and rebuilt, but they appear minor when one measures them by the achievements of the Austrian Baroque of c. 1690–1730. The great names are first the theatrical designer and engineer Lorenzo Burnacini (1636–1707), who designed the wildly Baroque Trinity Monument on the Graben in 1687; then Domenico MARTINELLI (1650–1718) of the two Liechtenstein palaces of the 1690s; and then FISCHER VON ERLACH and HILDEBRANDT. Little need be said about them here – of Fischer's brilliant centralizing church plans at Salzburg (Trinity, 1694–1702; Collegiate, 1694–1707), heralded by those of Gaspare ZUCCALLI of 1685; of his Karlskirche in Vienna with its fantastic Trajan's Columns; of his restrained and courtly decoration; and of Hildebrandt's brilliant spatial interlocking and his fiery decoration (Upper Belvedere, Vienna, 1714–24). Meanwhile the great abbeys in the country were as busy rebuilding as the towns and the nobility: Melk (1702–14; by PRANDTAUER); St Florian (1686–1708; by CARLONE and then Prandtauer); Göttweig (1719 etc.; by Hildebrandt); Klosterneuburg (1730 etc.; by d'Allio). Particularly splendid are the libraries in the abbeys (Altenburg, 1740; Admont, c. 1745).

The Louis XVI or Robert ADAM style of the later C18 is represented in Vienna by the Academy of the Sciences (1753; by Jadot de Ville Issey) and the Josephinum (1783; by Canevale). The Gloriette, a large-scale eye-catcher in the park of Schönbrunn by Ferdinand von Hohenburg, is, in spite of its early date (1775), in a neo-Cinquecento style. Neo-Grecian at its most severe are the Theseustempel (1819) and the Burgtor (1821), both by NOBILE (the latter originally designed by CAGNOLA).

C19 historicism is in full swing with the perfectly preserved Anif Castle near Salzburg (1838 etc.), the church of Altlerchenfeld, Vienna (1848–61; by Eduard van der Nüll) in neo-Romanesque, and the Arsenal (1849–56; by Förster and others), also in a neo-Romanesque style. Shortly after, Vienna established herself as one of the centres of historicism on a grand scale with the abolition of the fortress walls of inner Vienna and the making of the Ringstrasse (begun 1859). Along this wide green belt a number of majestic public buildings were erected in various period styles: the Votivkirche (1856 etc.; by von Ferstel), in Gothic; the Opera (1861 etc.; by van der Nüll and Siccardsburg), in free Renaissance; the Town Hall (1872 etc.; by Ferdinand von Schmidt), in symmetrical Gothic; the Museums (1872 etc.; by SEMPER and Hasenauer), in Renaissance to Baroque; the

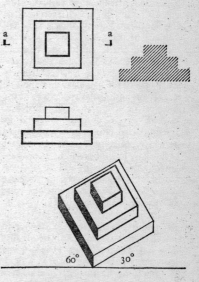

Fig. 6. Axonometric projection. Plan; Section aa; Elevation

Academy (1872 etc.; by Theophil von Hansen), in Renaissance; the Parliament (1873 etc.; also by von Hansen), in pure Grecian; the Burgtheater (1873 etc.; again by Semper and Hasenauer), in Renaissance; the University (by Ferstel), in a mixed Italian and French C16 style; and, finally, the Neue Hofburg (1881 etc.; by Semper and Hasenauer), again in Renaissance. There are also large blocks of flats as parts of the monumental, strung-out composition.

Vienna was one of the most important centres in the whole world when it came to abandoning historicism and creating a new idiom for the C20. The leaders were Otto WAGNER, whose Postal Savings Bank (1904) is remarkably fresh and enterprising, his pupil OLBRICH, whose Secession (1898) blazed the trail – though more towards ART NOUVEAU than towards the C20 – and the two even younger men, HOFFMANN and LOOS. When the C20 style began to settle down and be accepted in the mid-twenties, a mild variety of it was applied to the many blocks of working-class flats, some of them vast, which the municipality of Vienna erected.

AXONOMETRIC PROJECTION. A geometrical drawing showing a building in three dimensions. The plan is set up truly to a convenient angle, and the verticals projected to scale, with the result that all dimensions on a horizontal plane and all verticals are to scale, but diagonals and curves on a vertical plane are distorted. *See figure 6.*

AZTEC ARCHITECTURE, *see* MESO-AMERICAN ARCHITECTURE.

AZULEJOS. Glazed pottery tiles, usually painted in bright colours with floral and other patterns, much used on the outsides and insides of Spanish, Portuguese, and Central and South American buildings.

B

BAGUETTE (or BAGNETTE). A small
moulding of semicircular section, like
an ASTRAGAL; also a frame with a
small BEAD MOULDING.

BÄHR, Georg (1666–1738). The leading
Baroque architect in Dresden. He began as a carpenter and in 1705 became
Ratszimmermeister (master carpenter
to the city) in Dresden. But he had
already begun to study mechanics (he
invented a *camera obscura* and a mechanical organ) and his first building was
begun the same year, the parish church
of Loschwitz (1705–8) on an elongated
octagonal plan. Two Greek cross plan
churches followed, at Schmiedeberg
(1713–16) and Forchheim (1719–26)
both in the Erzegebirge. His masterpiece was the Frauenkirche in Dresden
(1726–43: destroyed 1944), by far the
grandest Protestant church in Germany. Bähr's first design for it dates
from as early as 1722, a Greek cross
plan with octagonal galleries, deriving
from VISCARDI's Mariahilfkirche at
Freystadt (1700–08). But in 1726 this
design was revised in favour of a
square ground plan with a circular arrangement of piers, with angle turrets
flanking the dome on all four sides.
The dome was also re-designed to
increase its height and pitch, thus
producing a very bold silhouette.
The interior resembled a centrally
planned theatre with curving galleries
and a richly decorated organ (by
Gottfried Silbermann 1732–6) as the
main feature. The Dreikönigskirche
in Dresden Neustadt (1732–9) originally designed by PÖPPELMANN was
supervised by Bähr.

BAILEY. An open space or court of a
stone-built castle; also called a *ward*.
See also MOTTE-AND-BAILEY.

BAKER, Sir Herbert (1862–1946), was
born in Kent and remained an English

countryman. Baker's most interesting
work belongs to South Africa. He
went out early, gained Cecil Rhodes's
confidence, and built Groöte Schuur
for him in 1890 in the traditional
Dutch Colonial idiom, and later private houses in Johannesburg, some
very successful in an Arts and Crafts
way (Stonehouse, 1902). His most
prominent buildings were the Government House and Union Buildings in
Pretoria (1905 onwards and 1910–13).
Side by side with his friend LUTYENS
he was called in at New Delhi, and
was responsible there for the Secretariat Buildings and the Legislative
Building (1912 etc.). His style is
as imperially classical as Lutyens's, but
much weaker, less original, and less
disciplined. This is especially evident
in his later London buildings (Bank of
England, 1921; India House, 1925;
South Africa House, 1930). He was
more at ease where he could use a less
elevated style and display a great
variety of materials. This is why the
War Memorial Cloister at Winchester
College (1922–4) is one of his most
successful buildings.

BALCONY. A platform projecting
from a wall, enclosed by a railing or balustrade, supported on
brackets or columns or cantilevered
out.

BALDACHIN or BALDACCHINO. A
canopy over a throne, altar, doorway,
etc. It may be portable, suspended from
a ceiling, projecting from a wall or
free-standing on columns or other
supports. *See also* CIBORIUM.

BALISTRARIA. In medieval military
architecture, the cross-shaped opening
in BATTLEMENTS and elsewhere for
the use of the crossbow.

BALLFLOWER. A globular three-petalled
flower enclosing a small ball; a decora-

tion in use in the first quarter of the CI4. *See figure 7.*

Fig. 7. Ballflower

BALLOON FRAMING. A method of timber-frame construction used in the U.S.A. and Scandinavia: the STUDS or uprights run from sill to eaves, and the horizontal members are nailed to them.

BALLU, Théodore (1817–85). French architect. His best-known building is Holy Trinity, Paris (1863–7), a design in the Early Renaissance of Italy and France.

BALTARD, Louis-Pierre (1764–1846). French architect. He built the Law Courts at Lyon (1836–41) which, with its long row of giant Corinthian columns, is a belated representative of the Empire style. Baltard taught first at the École Polytechnique, then at the École des Beaux Arts.

BALTARD, Victor (1805–74). French architect. His most famous work is – or, as one must say now, was – the Market Hall of Paris (1852 etc.), all glass and iron. His church St Augustine (1860–71) is externally a domed building of the Early French Renaissance but internally proclaims its iron construction.

BALUSTER. A short post or pillar in a series supporting a rail or COPING and thus forming a *balustrade. See figure 79.*

BALUSTRADE, *see* BALUSTER.

BANDED COLUMN. *See* RUSTICATED COLUMN.

BAPTISTERY. A building for baptismal rites containing the font; often separate from the church.

BAR TRACERY, *see* TRACERY.

BARBICAN. An outwork defending the entrance to a castle.

BARELLI, Agostino (1627–79). Born in Bologna, where he designed the Thea-

tine church of S. Bartolomeo (1653), he later introduced the Italian Baroque style to Bavaria. He designed the Theatine church of St Cajetan, Munich (1663, completed by Enrico ZUC-CALLI), on the model of S. Andrea della Valle, Rome. He also built the squarish central block of the electoral palace at Nymphenburg outside Munich (1663), completed by EFFNER in 1717–23.

BARGEBOARDS. Projecting boards placed against the incline of the gable of a building and hiding the ends of the horizontal roof timbers; sometimes decorated. *See figure 8.*

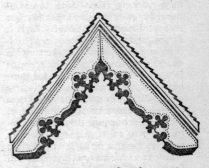

Fig. 8. Bargeboards

BAROQUE ARCHITECTURE. The architecture of the CI7 and part of the CI8. It is characterized by exuberant decoration, expansive curvaceous forms, a sense of mass, a delight in large-scale and sweeping vistas, and a preference for spatially complex compositions. According to the number of these and kindred qualities present, a building or a national style of architecture may be called Baroque. The term applies fully to the CI7 in Italy and to the CI7 and part of the CI8 in Spain, Germany, and Austria, but with limitations to the CI7 in France (LE VAU, Versailles), the CI8 in Italy (FONTANA, JUVARRA), and the late CI7 and early CI8 in England (WREN, HAWKS-MOOR, VANBRUGH, ARCHER). For all these latter cases the term Baroque

Classicism has been adopted to denote that they are instances of the Baroque tempered by classical elements. This is especially evident in England, where the swelling forms of Baroque plans and elevations were never favoured. *See also* ENGLISH ARCHITECTURE, FRENCH ARCHITECTURE, GERMAN ARCHITECTURE, ITALIAN ARCHITECTURE, SPANISH ARCHITECTURE.

BARREL VAULT, *see* VAULT.

BARRY, Sir Charles (1795–1860). The most versatile of the leading Early Victorian architects, an excellent planner and an energetic, tough, and hard-working man. With some inherited money he travelled in 1817–20 through France, Italy, Greece, Turkey, Egypt, and Palestine, studying buildings and doing brilliant sketches. In 1823 he won the competition for St Peter's, Brighton, and then for some years did 'pre-archaeological' Gothic churches, i.e., an inventive rather than a correct interpretation of the style. In 1824 he designed the Royal Institution of Fine Arts in Manchester – Grecian this time – and he followed this up with the Manchester Athenaeum (1836). But the Travellers' Club in London (1829–31) was Quattrocento, and this meant the start of the neo-Renaissance for England. With the Reform Club of 1837 his Renaissance turned Cinquecento, and with Bridgewater House (1847) a free, not to say debased, Cinquecento. This development from the reticent to the spectacular and from low to high relief permeates his work in general – see, now in the Northern Renaissance field, the development from Highclere (1837), itself far busier than his early work, to the Halifax Town Hall (1859–62), which is asymmetrical and a jumble of motifs. It was completed by Barry's son Edward M. Barry (1830–80), who built the Charing Cross and Cannon Street Hotels.

But Sir Charles's *magnum opus* is, of course, the Houses of Parliament, won in competition in 1835–6 and begun in 1839; it was formally opened in 1852. Its ground plan is functionally excellent, its façade to the Thames still symmetrical in the Georgian way, but its skyline completely asymmetrical and exceedingly well balanced, with its two contrasting towers and its flèche. Most of the close Perpendicular detail and nearly all the internal detail is by PUGIN, who was commissioned by Barry for the purpose.

BARTIZAN. A small turret projecting from the angle on the top of a tower or parapet. *See figure 9.*

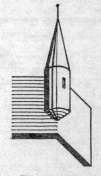

Fig. 9. Bartizan

BASEMENT. The lowest storey of a building, usually below or partly below ground level or, if beginning at ground level, of less height than the storey above.

BASEVI, George (1794–1845), was articled to SOANE. In 1816–19 he was in Italy and Greece. His first buildings are Grecian, but his best-known building, the Fitzwilliam Museum at Cambridge (begun 1836), already shows the trend towards classical harmony becoming, with clustered giant columns and a heavy attic, more dramatic and indeed Baroque. It is the same trend which distinguishes the Beaux Arts style in France from the Empire style. Early in his career (*c.* 1825), Basevi also designed Belgrave

Square (minus the corner mansions) and a number of country houses in various styles.

BASILICA. A church divided into a nave and two or more aisles, the former higher and wider than the latter, lit by the windows of a CLERESTORY, and with or without a gallery. *See figure 10.* In Roman architecture, a

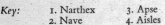

Fig. 10. Basilica

Key: 1. Narthex 3. Apse
      2. Nave   4. Aisles

basilica was a large meeting-hall, as used in public administration. The term indicated function and not form, but Roman basilicas were often oblong buildings with aisles and galleries and with an apse opposite the entrance which might be through one of the longer, or one of the shorter, sides. Early Christian churches evolved from Roman basilicas of this type (not from pagan religious architecture). By the C4 the Christian basilica had acquired its essential characteristics: oblong plan; longitudinal axis; a timber roof, either open or concealed by a flat ceiling; and a termination, either rectangular or in the form of an apse.

BASKET ARCH, *see* ARCH.

BASTION. A projection at the angle of a fortification, from which the garrison can see and defend the ground before the ramparts.

BATTER. The inclined face of a wall.

BATTLEMENT. A PARAPET with alternating indentations or EMBRASURES and raised portions or *merlons*; also called *crenellation. See figure 18.*

BAUDOT, Anatole de (1834–1915). A pupil of LABROUSTE and VIOLLET-

LE-DUC. His St Jean de Montmartre in Paris (1894–1902) is the first building where all the structural members, including the vaulting ribs, are of exposed reinforced concrete. Yet the character remains Gothic. It can be called the most successful demonstration of the union of old and new advocated by Viollet-le-Duc in his *Entretiens.*

BAUHAUS. The Grand-Duke of Saxe-Weimar had founded a school of arts and crafts at Weimar in 1906. He appointed Van de VELDE to the directorship – a very progressive move; for Van de Velde believed in teaching in workshops rather than studios. When Van de Velde left Germany, he suggested GROPIUS as his successor, and Gropius took over in 1919. He re-organized the school and called it the Bauhaus. According to its first manifesto the school was to teach crafts, and all artists and architects were to work together towards the great goal of 'the building of the future'. The manifesto was enthusiastic in tone and had on its cover an Expressionist vision of a cathedral, a woodcut by Feininger. This first phase of the Bauhaus, inspired by MORRIS and sustained by the Expressionist mood of post-war Germany, did not last long. The aim now became industrial design, and stark cubic simplicity replaced the Expressionism. This fundamental change of programme was accelerated by lectures which Theo van Doesburg (1883–1931) gave in 1922, and by the appointment of Moholy Nagy (1895–1946) in 1923. The result was a memorandum by Gropius issued in 1924 and called *Art and Technology – A New Unity.* However, in the same year, political changes led to the dissolution of the Bauhaus. At that moment the Burgomaster of Dessau in Anhalt offered the school a new field of activity. A new building was designed by Gropius and built in 1925–6. In 1926 the Bauhaus received recognition as the State School of Art of Anhalt. This seemed to secure the future. A department of architecture was established, and Hannes Meyer became its head. One year later, in 1928, Gropius resigned and suggested Hannes Meyer as his successor. Meyer was politically far more radical than Gropius. He organized the department of architecture, but was dismissed for political reasons in 1930. His successor was MIES VAN DER ROHE. However, the growth of National Socialism in Anhalt led to his dismissal and, in 1932, to the closure of the school. Mies tried to carry on in Berlin, converting the school into a private enterprise. But in 1933 that also was closed by the Nazis.

The Bauhaus is the most important school of art of the C20. Its most significant achievement was that to the very end artists and craftsmen, and in the end architects, too, worked together. As the start of the Bauhaus the *Vorkurs*, as built up by Johannes Itten, comprised them all. The intention of the *Vorkurs* was to stimulate a theoretically and practically sound sense of form and colour. Later the Bauhaus became the only art school in which designs for industrial products were developed. Moreover, Gropius's own style of architecture became almost automatically a symbol of the programme of the school. But, when all is said, the most impressive fact about the Bauhaus is that Gropius succeeded in keeping together in a happy co-operation such dissimilar artists as Kandinsky, Feininger, Klee and Schlemmer.

BAUTISTA, Francisco (1594–1679). A Spanish Jesuit priest who built churches for his order in Madrid and Toledo. That in Madrid, S. Isidro el Real (1629), is the most interesting, based on the plan of the Gesù in Rome, with a somewhat severe façade. The church had considerable influence in Spain.

BAY. A vertical division of the exterior or interior of a building marked not by walls but by fenestration, an order, buttresses, units of vaulting, roof compartments, etc.

BAY LEAF GARLAND. Classical decorative motif used to enrich TORUS mouldings, etc. *See figure 11.*

Fig. 11. Bay leaf garland

BAY WINDOW. An angular or curved projection of a house front filled by fenestration. If curved, also called a *bow window*. If on an upper floor only, called an *oriel* or *oriel window*.

BEAD MOULDING. A small cylindrical moulding enriched with ornament resembling a string of beads; used in the Romanesque period.

BEAD AND REEL. *See* ASTRAGAL.

BEAKHEAD. A Norman decorative motif consisting of a row of bird, animal, or human heads biting a ROLL MOULDING. *See figure 12.*

Fig. 12. Beakhead moulding

BED MOULDING. A small moulding between the CORONA and the FRIEZE in any ENTABLATURE.

BEEHIVE HOUSE. A primitive structure, circular in plan and built of rough stones set in projecting courses to form a dome. Prehistoric examples, called *nuraghi*, have been found in Sardinia, and others of later date in Ireland and Scotland. They are still inhabited in South-east Italy (Apulia), where they are called *trulli*. The finest example of beehive construction is the tomb called the 'Treasury of Atreus' at Mycenae (C13 B.C.).

BEER, Michael (d. 1666). He was born at Au in the Bregenzerwald and was the founder of the Vorarlberger school of architects which included, besides the Beer family, the MOSBRUGGER family and the THUMB family. The latter intermarried with the Beer family. The long series of buildings by this school, mostly for Benedictine monasteries in S. W. Germany and Switzerland, was eventually to mark the triumph of German over Italian elements in S. German Baroque architecture (i.e., over the domination of such Italians as ZUCCALLI and VISCARDI from the Grisons). Michael Beer is known to have worked at the abbey church at Kempten until 1654 and he was probably responsible for its design which attempted a fusion of the longitudinal and centralized types of church. It has a curious, large-domed octagon between nave and chancel. His son Franz Beer (1659–1726) became one of the leading architects of the Vorarlberg school. He began at Obermarchtal abbey church where he and Christian THUMB took over after the death of Michael THUMB in 1690. The influence of the Thumbs is still evident in his next building, Kloster Irsee (1699–1704). But he achieved an individual style and also great elegance and lightness at the abbey church at Rheinau in Switzerland (1704–11) where he emphasized verticality by setting the galleries well back from the pilaster ends of the internal buttresses which typify the Vorarlberg type of church. His style culminated in the Cistercian abbey church of St Urban in the Canton of Lucerne (1711–15) and at the Benedictine abbey church at Weingarten (1715–23) though his responsibility at the latter is uncertain. (He refused to direct the building operations, and the design was probably a collaboration with Johann Jakob Herkommer (1648–1717) and perhaps also Caspar MOSBRUGGER.) In 1717 he reconstructed the Premonstratensian abbey church at Weissenau near Ravensburg. Two plans (unexecuted) for the abbey church at Einsiedeln are attributed to him. His eldest daughter married Peter THUMB. Johann Michael Beer (1696–1780) designed the choir and E. façade at the abbey church at St Gallen (1760–69) and Ferdinand Beer (1731–89) designed the administrative block of the monastery at St Gallen.

BEHRENS, Peter (1868–1940), started as a painter but after 1890 was attracted by design and the crafts, under the direct or indirect influence of the teachings of MORRIS. He designed typefaces, was one of the founders of the Vereinigte Werkstätten at Munich, and for them designed table glass among other things. In 1900 Ernst Ludwig, Grand Duke of Hesse, called him to Darmstadt (see OLBRICH). The house he designed for himself there in 1901 is original, vigorous, and even ruthless. In 1907 he was appointed architect and consultant to the A.E.G. (General Electricity Company) in Berlin, and designed for them factories, shops, products, and even stationery. The factories are among the earliest anywhere to be taken seriously architecturally and designed without any recourse to period allusions. For more representational jobs he used a more representational style which has been called a 'scraped classicism' (offices in Düsseldorf for Mannesmann, 1911–12; German Embassy, St Petersburg, 1911–12). After the First World War his style paid tribute first to the then current Expressionism (offices for I. G. Farben, Höchst, 1920–4), then to the International Modern (warehouse for the State Tobacco Administration, Linz, Austria, 1930). In 1925 he designed 'New Ways', 508 Wellingborough Road, Northampton – the earliest example of the C20 style in England. (The house incorporates a room designed by MACKINTOSH in 1907.)

BÉLANGER, François-Joseph (1744–
1818). The most elegant Louis XVI
architect and the leading French landscape gardener. Trained in Paris, he
visited England in 1766. The following
year he joined the Menus Plaisirs and
in 1777 designed his masterpiece, the
exquisite neo-classical Bagatelle in the
Bois de Boulogne, Paris, which he
built for the king's brother in sixty-
four days to win a bet with Marie
Antoinette. The garden, laid out between 1778 and 1780, was the most
famous *jardin anglais* of the period. It
was followed in 1784 by the *jardin
anglo-chinois* at another of his pavilions,
the Folie Saint James at Neuilly, and in
1786 by the last of his great landscape
gardens, Méréville. He also designed
the exquisite pavilion in the garden
of the Hôtel de Brancas, Paris (1771)
and some interiors of great elegance,
e.g., Hôtel de Mlle Desvieux, Paris
(1788). In 1803 he designed a remarkable glass and iron dome for the Halle
aux Blés in Paris to replace the no less
remarkable glass and wood dome of
Legrand and Molinos of 1782.

BELFAST ROOF, *see* ROOF.

BELFRY. Generally the upper room or
storey in a tower in which bells are
hung, and thus often the bell-tower
itself, whether it is attached to or stands
separate from the main building. Also
the timber frame inside a church
steeple to which bells are fastened.
Derived from the old French *berfrei*
(= tower), the word has no connection
with 'bell'.

BELGIAN ARCHITECTURE. In the
Middle Ages the Southern Netherlands belonged to the archdiocese of
Cologne; hence Romanesque building
drew its inspiration chiefly from Germany. The earliest building of major
importance, St Gertrude at Nivelles
(consecrated 1046), is, side by side with
St Michael at Hildesheim, the best-
preserved Ottonian church in the
German orbit. The former St John
at Liège was built to a central plan like
Charlemagne's church at Aachen, the
former Liège Cathedral had a west as
well as an east chancel, St Bartholo-
mew, also at Liège, has a typically
German unrelieved façade block with
recessed twin towers (cf. especially
Maastricht), and the cathedral of
Tournai has a trefoil east end (i.e.,
transepts with apsidal ends) on the
pattern of St Mary in Capitol at
Cologne; its group of five towers
round the crossing may also be derived from Cologne.

Tournai had a great influence on the
Early Gothic architecture of France
(Noyon, Laon): the east end was rebuilt *c.* 1242, no longer on a German
pattern but on that of such High
Gothic cathedrals as Soissons and
Amiens. The Gothic style in present-
day Belgium was, in fact, imported
from France; borrowings also occurred from Normandy and Burgundy, and as in other countries the
Cistercians were among the pioneers.
Orval of the late C12 is still Transitional, Villers (1210–72) is fully Gothic,
as are the principal church of Brussels,
Ste Gudule (begun before 1226, the
façade C15), the beautiful chancel of St
Martin at Ypres (1221 etc.), and
Notre Dame at Tongres (1240 etc.).
Later Gothic architecture in the
Southern Netherlands first drew
mainly on French inspiration, dominant at Hertogenbosch (*c.* 1280–1330)
and in the chancel of Hal in the C14.
But in the C15 Belgium, admittedly
influenced by French Flamboyant as
well as German 'Sondergotik', developed a splendid style of her own.
The principal buildings are Notre
Dame at Antwerp (completed 1518),
St Rombaut at Malines, St Peter
at Louvain (1425 etc.), and the
Sablon Church at Brussels. Characteristic features are complicated lierne
vaults of German derivation, proud
towers – that of Antwerp 306 ft high,
that of Malines about 320 ft and intended to be about 530 ft – and exceedingly elaborate Flamboyant fitments, such as rood screens.

The most spectacular castle is that of Ghent (inscribed 1180), with its oblong keep and its many towers along the curtain wall. But the sphere in which Belgium is in the forefront of European building is the town halls and guild halls of her prosperous towns. The Cloth Hall at Ypres (C13–C14), 440 ft long, is the grandest such building in all Europe, and there is the town hall of Bruges (tower c. 1280–1482, 350 ft high), then, ornately and lacily decorated, those of Brussels (1402 etc.), Louvain (1447 etc.), Ghent (1517), and Oudenarde (1527). Interiors were as rich as exteriors – see, for example, the magnificent chimney-piece in Courtrai Town Hall (1526). The names of the master masons are now mostly known: the family of the Keldermans is the most familiar. There are also plenty of medieval town houses preserved; Romanesque buildings are mostly in stone (Tournai), Gothic most often in brick and frequently with crow-stepped gables (as early as the C13).

The Renaissance appeared in occasional motifs in paintings as early as 1500 and was more widely represented after 1510. The most important date for the promotion of the Renaissance spirit is 1517, when Raphael's cartoons for tapestries in the Sistine Chapel reached Brussels, where the tapestries were to be made. In the same year the Stadtholderess Margaret of Austria had additions built to her palace at Malines in the Renaissance style. Their relative purity is exceptional; the usual thing in the twenties and thirties is a happy-go-lucky mixing of Renaissance with traditional motifs, sometimes quite restrained (The Salmon, Malines, 1530–4), but mostly exuberant (The Greffe, Bruges, with its fabulous chimneypiece, 1535–7; the courtyard of the former Bishop's Palace, Liège, 1526). In churches the Renaissance was confined to details; the proportions and the vaults remained Gothic (St Jacques, Liège, 1513–38). A very influential element in architectural decoration was introduced in Antwerp in the forties and spread all over Northern Europe – the combination of STRAPWORK, inspired by Fontaine-bleau, and grottesche, inspired by ancient Roman excavations. Cornelis FLORIS and later Hans Vredeman de VRIES (d. after 1604) were its most eminent practitioners.

But Floris also designed the Antwerp Town Hall (1565 etc.), and this, though provided with a big, dominating gable in the northern style, is in its motifs entirely developed from BRAMANTE and SERLIO, i.e., the Italian (and French) Cinquecento. The former Granvella Palace in Brussels (c. 1550) is also classical Cinquecento. However, the Jesuits, in their churches, clung to the Gothic well into the C17; an exception is St Charles Borromeo at Antwerp (1615–21), with a broad Mannerist façade and a tunnel-vaulted interior with arcades on columns in two tiers. True C17 architecture came in under the influence of Italy and France (domes such as Notre Dame de Montaigu, 1609 etc.; St Pierre, Ghent, 1629 etc.; Notre Dame de Hanswyck, Malines, 1663 etc.), and after c. 1650 developed into a characteristic Belgian Baroque, inspired largely by Rubens. Church façades are without towers and covered with sumptuous and somewhat undisciplined decoration (St Michael, Louvain, 1650–66; St John Baptist, Brussels, 1657–77; St Peter, Malines, 1670–1709). Typical of the situation about 1700 are the houses round the Grand' Place in Brussels built after the bombardment of 1695 and with their gables basically still rooted in the Belgian past.

Of the C18 and early C19 little need be said; this period was dominated by French classicism (Royal Library, Brussels, c. 1750; Palais des Académies, Brussels, 1823–6). But in the later C19 Belgium found the way back to an exuberant Baroque. Poelaert's cyclopean Palais de Justice, Brussels (1866 etc.), is one of the most Baroque buildings of its time in Europe, though Poelaert could also work in a wild Gothic (Laeken Church, 1854, etc.). A generation later Belgium for the first time in her architectural history, and only for a few years, proved herself a pioneer; this was when attempts were being made to establish ART NOUVEAU as a viable architectural style. By far the most important architect in this movement was Victor HORTA of Brussels, and the key buildings are No. 6 rue Paul Emile Janson (designed 1892), the Hôtel Solvay (1895 etc.), and the Maison du Peuple (1896 etc.), all of them with much of the undulating-line ornament of Art Nouveau, but also with a daring use of iron both externally and internally. Henri van de VELDE, though Belgian, belongs to international rather than Belgian Art Nouveau.

BELL GABLE, *see* BELLCOTE.

BELLCOTE. A framework on a roof to hang bells from; also called a *bell gable*.

BELVEDERE, *see* GAZEBO.

BEMA. The Greek word means a speaker's tribune or a platform. 1. Raised stage for the clergy in the apse of Early Christian churches. 2. In Eastern usage, a space raised above the nave level of a church, which is shut off by the ICONOSTASIS and contains the altar. 3. In synagogues, the elevated pulpit from which are read the Pentateuch and Torah. Rabbinical authorities differ over its correct position: Maimonides (1204) maintains that the centre is correct, so does Moses Isserles of Cracow (C16), but Joseph Karo (1575) prescribed no fixed place. In modern times it has often been moved forward near the Ark for practical reasons. It is usually wooden and rectangular, and sometimes has a curved front and back, also open sides approached by steps.

BENCH-ENDS, *see* PEW.

BENEDETTO DA MAIANO (1442–97). He was the younger brother of GIULIANO DA MAIANO and collaborated with him at the Fini chapel in the Collegiata in S. Gimignano (1468). Though primarily a sculptor, he designed two Early Renaissance masterpieces of architecture: Palazzo Strozzi, Florence (begun 1489 in collaboration with Cronaca (Simone del Pollaiuolo) 1454–1508) and the portico of S. Maria delle Grazie in Arezzo (1490–91). Palazzo Strozzi, a vast pile of uniform rusticated masonry from the ground to the gargantuan projecting cornice, derives from MICHELOZZO's Palazzo Medici-Riccardi. (It was completed by Cronaca who designed the noble cortile.) The portico of S. Maria delle Grazie in Arezzo is supremely elegant and airy, very different in feeling from the exterior of Palazzo Strozzi.

BENTLEY, John Francis (1839–1902). A pupil of Henry Clutton. Converted to Catholicism in 1861, he set up on his own in 1862. After a number of years spent mostly on designs for church furnishings and on additions and alterations, he built the Convent of the Sacred Heart at Hammersmith (1868 onwards) with a scrupulous simplicity and near-bareness; the serried chimneys are particularly impressive. Wider success came much later. Among the most memorable buildings are Holy Rood, Watford, a rich Gothic church, but also most intelligently thought out (1887 etc.), and St Francis at Bocking, Essex (1893). In 1894 he was commissioned to design Westminster Cathedral in London. The style here is Byzantine, the material brick with ample stone dressings and concrete for the domes. No iron is used: Bentley called it 'that curse of modern construction'. The campanile, asymmetrically placed, is the tallest church tower in London. The interior is superbly large in scale and extremely sparing in architectural detail, although according to Bentley's intention it should have been covered with mosaics and slabs of variegated marble (and this is gradually being done). However. Philip WEBB admired it bare as it was, BERLAGE, Hendrik Petrus (1856–1934), studied at the Zürich Polytechnic, and then worked under CUYPERS. The building that made him famous, and is indeed a milestone in the development of Dutch architecture away from C19 historicism, is his Amsterdam Exchange (begun 1897). It does not mark a break with the past, but the treatment of period forms, derived from the Romanesque as well as the C16, is so free and the detail so original that it amounted to a profession of faith in an independent future. Specially characteristic are certain chunky, rather primeval details and others that are jagged and almost Expressionist. Berlage's style, indeed, prepared the way for the Expressionism of the so-called School of Amsterdam (see OUD). Berlage designed one building for England, the office building for Messrs Muller in Bury Street, London (1910–14). His last major work, the Municipal Museum in The Hague (1919–34), is less personal in style and rather reflects that of DUDOK.

BERM. The level area separating ditch from bank on a hill-fort or barrow.

BERNINI, Gianlorenzo (1598–1680). The dominating figure in Roman Baroque art. Primarily a sculptor, like MICHELANGELO, he was almost as universal a genius, being painter and poet as well as architect. He was born in Naples of a Neapolitan mother and Florentine father, Pietro Bernini, a late Mannerist sculptor of the second rank. The family settled in Rome c. 1605. Bernini spent the whole of his working life there, and no other city bears so strong an imprint of one man's vision and personality. His buildings and sculpture perfectly express the grandeur, flamboyance, and emotionalism of the Counter-Reformation. He was already famous as a sculptor by the age

of twenty, but his long and uniformly successful career as an architect began with the election of Urban VIII (Barberini) in 1624. He was appointed architect to St Peter's five years later. But most of his important buildings belong to his middle age, mainly during the pontificate of Alexander VII (Chigi, 1655–67). By then his fame was so great that Louis XIV begged him to come to Paris to enlarge the Louvre. Unlike his neurotic contemporary and rival BORROMINI, he was well-balanced and extrovert in temperament, polished and self-assured in manner. Yet he was devout and deeply religious: an ardent follower of Jesuit teaching, he regularly practised the Spiritual Exercises of St Ignatius. He combined to an exceptional degree a revolutionary artistic genius with the organizing ability of a man of affairs.

His first commissions (1624) were for the renovation of S. Bibiana and the baldacchino in St Peter's. Though interesting as an experiment, S. Bibiana suffers from a lack of assurance most uncharacteristic of its author and in striking contrast to the daringly original baldacchino (1624–33) he erected under Michelangelo's dome in the centre of St Peter's. With its gigantic bronze barley-sugar columns, buoyant scrolls, and dynamic sculpture, this showy masterpiece is the very symbol of the age – of its grandeur, luxury, and lack of restraint. And by its glorification of the twisted columns used in Constantine's basilica and traditionally connected with the Temple of Jerusalem it celebrates the continuity of the Church and its triumph over the Reformation.

Various other commissions followed: the façade and staircase of Palazzo Barberini, the remodelling of Porta del Popolo, the Cornaro Chapel in S. Maria della Vittoria. In the latter polychrome marbles, exaggerated perspective, and every trick of lighting and scenic illusion are exploited to heighten the dramatic effect of his marble group of the Ecstasy of St Teresa, placed as if behind a proscenium arch above the altar. But not until he was almost sixty did he get the chance to show his skill as a designer of churches, first at Castelgandolfo (1658–61), then at Ariccia (1662–4), and, finally and most brilliantly, at S. Andrea al Quirinale in Rome (1658–70), which perfectly realizes his conception of a church as a unified architectural setting for the religious mysteries illustrated by the sculptural decoration.

Of his two great secular buildings in Rome, Palazzo di Montecitorio (1650 onwards) and Palazzo Odescalchi (1664 onwards), the latter is by far the more important. It is composed of a richly articulated central part of seven bays with giant composite pilasters, between simple rusticated receding wings of three bays, and marks a decisive break with Roman tradition. It was very influential and became the model for aristocratic palaces all over Europe. Unfortunately, the composition was ruined by later alterations and enlargements. His gift for the monumental and colossal found supreme expression in the Piazza of St Peter's (1656 onwards). The conception is extremely simple and extremely original – an enormous oval surrounded by colonnades of free-standing columns with a straight entablature above. This not only helped to correct the faults of MADERNO'S façade by giving it an impression of greater height but expressed with overwhelming authority and conviction the dignity, grandeur, and majestic repose of Mother Church. Bernini himself compared his colonnades to the motherly arms of the church 'which embrace Catholics to reinforce their belief'. The Piazza was to have been enclosed by a third arm, unfortunately never built, and the intended effect of surprise and elation on passing through the colonnades has now been idiotically destroyed by opening up the via della Conciliazione. The free-standing colonnades of the Piazza have been widely copied, from Greenwich to Leningrad. Bernini's last great work, the Scala Regia in the Vatican (1663–6), epitomizes his style – his sense of scale and movement, his ingenuity in turning an awkward site to advantage, his mastery of scenic effects (optical illusions, exaggerated perspectives, concealed lighting), and his brilliant use of sculpture to dramatize the climaxes of his composition. He here achieved the perfect Baroque synthesis of the arts.

BERTOTTI-SCAMOZZI, Ottavio (1719–90), the leading Palladian-Revival architect in Italy, built numerous houses in and around Vicenza, notably Palazzo Pagello-Beltrame (1780) and Palazzo Franceschini (1770, now the Questura), distinctly neo-classical versions of PALLADIO. He is more important as the editor of Palladio's work: *Le fabbriche e i disegni di Andrea Palladio raccolti e illustrati* (1776–83) and *Le terme dei Romani, disegnate da A. Palladio* (1797).

BÉTON BRUT. 'Concrete in the raw', that is, concrete left in its natural state when the FORMWORK has been removed. Sometimes special formwork is used to show clearly the timber graining on the concrete surface.

BIANCO, Bartolommeo (c. 1590–1657), a leading Baroque architect in Genoa, was born in Como, but was working in Genoa by 1619 when he began Palazzo Durazzo-Pallavicini. His best building is the University (1630–6), where he took full advantage of a steeply sloping site to produce a masterpiece of scenic planning with dramatic staircases and colonnaded courtyards on four levels.

BIBIENA, see GALLI DI BIBIENA.

BILLET. A Romanesque moulding consisting of several bands of raised short cylinders or square pieces placed at regular intervals. See figure 13.

BLIND (or BLANK) TRACERY. Tracery applied to the surface of walls, wood

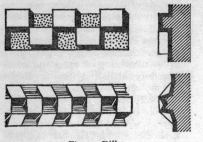

Fig. 13. Billet

panels, etc., in Gothic buildings. *See also* ARCADE.

BLOCK CAPITAL, *see* CAPITAL.

BLOCKING COURSE. In classical architecture, the plain course of stone surmounting the CORNICE at the top of a building; also a projecting cornice of stone or brick at the base of a building.

BLONDEL, Jacques-François (1705–74). A minor architect (not related to Nicolas-François Blondel) but also a very influential writer and theorist. He ran his own school of architecture in Paris from 1743 until he became Professor at the Académie royale de l'Architecture in 1762. Conservative in taste he exalted the French tradition as exemplified by MANSART and PERRAULT and thus paved the way for Neo-classicism (*see* CLASSICISM). His publications include *De la Distribution des Maisons* ... (1783); *L'Architecture française* (1752–6) known as the 'Grand Blondel' of which only four of the projected eight volumes appeared; *Discours sur la nécessité de l'étude de l'architecture* (1754) and *Cours d'Architecture* (1771–7) which contains his public lectures and the substance of his teaching. The last two volumes were published posthumously by his pupil PATTE. Of his buildings nothing survives except three sides of the Place d'Armes at Metz.

BLONDEL, Nicolas-François (1617–86), engineer and mathematician, was more interested in the theory than the practice of architecture. He expounded the rigidly classical and rationalist doctrines of the French Academy in his *Cours d'architecture* (1675, augmented ed. 1698). The Porte St Denis, Paris (1671), is his best surviving building.

BLUM, Hans (fl. 1550). Blum published the most influential German treatise on the orders: *Quinque Columnarum exacta descriptio atque delineatio* ... (Zurich 1550) and thus provided German architects with their first grammar to the classical language of architecture. It was based on SERLIO and often reprinted. Later editions (*Ein kunstrych Buoch von allerley Antiquiteten* ... Zurich c. 1560, *Warhafte Contrafacturen etlich alt u. schoner Gebauden* ... Zurich 1562) contain designs by Blum for churches, triumphal arches, etc. An English edition appeared in 1608.

BOASTED WORK. Stonework roughly blocked out preparatory to carving; also masonry finished with a boaster chisel.

BÖBLINGER. A family of South German masons of which the two most important members were Hans Senior and Matthäus. Hans (d. 1482) was a journeyman at Konstanz in 1435, then became foreman under Matthäus ENSINGER at St Mary, Esslingen, and in 1440 master mason of this church. Matthäus (d. 1505) was one of Hans's sons and was probably trained in Cologne. He was later at Esslingen with his father, and then at Ulm where, after three years, he became master mason of the Minster (1480). He was successor there to Ulrich and Matthäus Ensinger, and replaced Ulrich's design for the west tower with one of his own. His steeple was completed in 1881–90 and became the highest church tower in Europe (530 ft). However, Matthäus had to resign from the post and leave the town after cracks had appeared in the tower. He was called to a number of other places for consultation or to provide designs and supervise.

Thieme and Becker's *Künstler-Lexikon* mentions eight more members of the family.

BODLEY, George Frederick (1827–1907), was of Scottish descent and George Gilbert SCOTT's first pupil (1845–c. 1850). Mostly but not exclusively a church architect, he always worked in the Gothic style; in his earlier works he was influenced by the French C13, later by English models. His style is as competent and knowledgeable as Scott's, but distinguished by a never-failing taste and by abundant and elaborate details, including the choice of those who were to do furnishings and fitments. An early patron of MORRIS, he also started C. E. Kempe on his career. Among his earliest works are St Michael, Brighton (1859–61); St Martin, Scarborough (1861–2); All Saints, Cambridge (1863–4). In 1869 he went into partnership with Thomas Garner (1839–1906), another pupil of Scott's; the partnership lasted till 1898, though after 1884 the partners designed and supervised jobs individually. Among their most lavish works is Holy Angels, Hoar Cross, Staffordshire (1871–7). St Augustine, Pendlebury (1874), on the other hand, is one of the most monumental by virtue of its simplicity; instead of aisles, it has passages through internal buttresses, a motif derived from Albi and Spain and often repeated by the younger generation. Perhaps the noblest of all Bodley's churches is that of Clumber (1886–9), now standing forlorn in the grounds of the demolished mansion. Bodley also designed the chapel of Queen's College, Cambridge (1890–1), and buildings for King's College, Cambridge (1893). Among his pupils were C. R. Ashbee and Sir Ninian Comper.

BODT, Jean de (1670–1745). A Huguenot who left France after the revocation of the Edict of Nantes in 1685, was trained as an architect in Holland and after working for a time in England settled in 1698 in Berlin where he soon became the most important architect after SCHLÜTER. In 1701 he built the Fortuna Portal of the Potsdam Stadtschloss (retained by KNOBELSDORFF in his rebuilding of 1744) and completed NERING's Arsenal in Berlin (c. 1706) and Parochialkirche, modifying both designs. In about 1710 the E. front of Wentworth Castle, Yorkshire, was built to his designs for the Earl of Strafford. (The Earl of Strafford was ambassador to the King of Prussia 1706–11.) In 1728 he settled in Dresden where he was appointed Superintendent of the Royal Works and thus was in charge of PÖPPELMANN's work at the Japanisches Palais. But all his own ambitious projects for buildings in Dresden and elsewhere in Saxony remained on paper.

BOFFRAND, Gabriel Germain (1667–1754), the greatest French Rococo architect, began as a sculptor, studying under Girardon in Paris (1681), but soon turned to architecture. He became the pupil and later the collaborator of J. H. MANSART. He was very prolific and made a large fortune, mainly by the speculative building of Parisian *hôtels* (e.g., Hôtels de Montmorency, 1712; de Seignelay, 1713; de Torcy, 1714), but he lost the bulk of it in the Mississippi Bubble of 1720. Like his contemporary de COTTE he had great influence outside France, especially in Germany (e.g., on the Residenz, Würzburg). His virtuosity is well seen in the Hôtel de Montmorency, Paris, built round an oval court with rooms of various shapes and sizes, including a pentagon. The elevations, as always with Boffrand, are of the utmost simplicity and reticence, while the interior is of course very luxurious. His finest interior is probably that of the pavilion he added (c. 1737–40) to the Hôtel de Soubise (now the Archives Nationales), Paris. His Rococo ideal of elegant informality and sophisticated simplicity was realized in his Château de Saint Ouen, a brilliant and original conception consisting of a tiny Trianon-like pavilion of three rooms, set in a spacious courtyard formed by the guests' apartment, offices, stables, etc. He published *Livre d'architecture contenant les principes généraux de cet art* in 1745.

BOILEAU, Louis-Auguste (1812–96). French architect. One of the first to use iron construction in church architecture. His only familiar work is St Eugène in Paris (1854–5), earlier than BALTARD's St Augustine and VIOLLET-LE-DUC's defence of iron in the *Entrétiens*. However, earlier still than St Eugène is the Ste Geneviève Library by LABROUSTE. St Eugène was the model for the church of Vésinet (1863). Boileau also wrote a book on the use of iron in architecture.

BOISERIE. French for wainscoting or panelling, but applied more strictly to C17 and C18 panelling elaborately decorated with shallow-relief carvings.

BOLECTION MOULDING. A moulding used to cover the joint between two members with different surface levels. It projects beyond both surfaces. *See figure 14.*

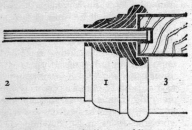

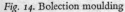

Fig. 14. Bolection moulding

Key:
1. Bolection moulding
2. Panel
3. Frame

BOND, *see* BRICKWORK.

BONNET TILE. A curved tile used for joining plain tiles along the HIPS of a roof.

BORROMINI, Francesco (1599–1667). The most original genius of Roman High Baroque architecture and the jealous rival of his almost exact contemporary BERNINI. A late starter, lonely, frustrated, and neurotic, he eventually committed suicide. Born at Bissone on Lake Lugano, the son of a mason, he began humbly as a stonecutter, went to Rome in his early twenties, and remained there for the rest of his life. Befriended by his distant relation MADERNO, he found employment as a stone-carver at St Peter's, mainly on decorative *putti*, festoons, etc. After Maderno's death (1629) he continued under Bernini, later becoming his chief assistant and occasionally contributing to the designs both at St Peter's and at Palazzo Barberini. But their relationship was uneasy. Himself a first-rate craftsman, Borromini despised Bernini's technical shortcomings; Bernini's success rankled. The two men parted for good in 1633 when Borromini's great opportunity came with the commission for S. Carlo alle Quattro Fontane. Despite its miniature size, S. Carlo (1638–46) is one of the most ingenious spatial compositions ever invented and displays Borromini's mastery of his art and revolutionary disregard for convention. The oval plan, emphasized by the honeycomb dome, is based on geometric units (equilateral triangles), but the swaying rhythm and sculptural effect of the undulating walls and restless, intertwined plastic elements produce an almost voluptuous effect. The concave-convex-concave façade was added in 1667. S. Carlo was quickly followed by S. Ivo della Sapienza (1642–60). Borromini's triangular planning system here produced a star-hexagon, which he worked out vertically with dynamic effect. The fantastic dome culminates in an extraordinary ZIGGURAT-like spiral feature.

His style reached its zenith at S. Ivo. Later buildings were either left unfinished or inhibited by complexities of site or by his having to take over plans by previous architects. Unfinished works include S. Maria dei Sette Dolori (*c.* 1655–66); the interior remodelling of S. Giovanni in Laterano (1646–9), which still lacks the intended nave vaulting; and S. Andrea delle Fratte (1653–65), where the dome is still without its lantern though the drum-like casing and three-storey tower outdo even S. Ivo in fantasy. At S. Agnese in Piazza Navona (1653–7) he took over from Carlo RAINALDI, changing the character of his interior designs by seemingly minor alterations and completely redesigning the façade on a concave plan. The dramatic grouping of high drum and dome framed by elegant towers is one of his best and most typical compositions, though he was dismissed as architect before its completion. An awkward site cramped his style at the Oratory of St Philip Neri (1637–50), remarkable mainly for its ingenious dual-purpose façade uniting chapel and monastic buildings. His domestic architecture is fragmentary but no less startling – *trompe l'œil* arcade at Palazzo Spada, river front and loggia at Palazzo Falconieri, grand *salone* at Palazzo Pamphili, and the library at the Sapienza. The latter was the prototype of many great C18 libraries.

He became increasingly unorthodox, and his last work, the Collegio di Propaganda Fide (*c.* 1660), shows a remarkable change of style towards monumentality and austerity, the capitals, for example, being reduced to a few parallel grooves. Its façade in via di Propaganda – heavy, oppressive, nightmarish – is unlike anything before or since. Reproached in his own day for having destroyed the conventions of good architecture, Borromini had little immediate influence in Italy except superficially in ornamentation. (His revolutionary spatial concepts were to bear abundant fruit later on in Central Europe.) His style was too personal and eccentric, especially in its combination of Gothic and post-Renaissance elements. His Gothic affinities were noted by his contemporaries (e.g., Baldinucci), and indeed they went beyond a partiality for medieval features such as the SQUINCH, for his geometrical system of planning and emphasis on a dynamic skeleton brought him close to the structural principles of Gothic. Yet his blending of architecture and sculpture and his voluptuous moulding of space and mass tie him to the Italian anthropomorphic tradition.

BOSS. An ornamental knob or projection covering the intersection of ribs in a vault or ceiling; often carved with foliage. *See figures 15 and 85.*

Fig. 15. Boss

BOULLÉE, Étienne-Louis (1728–99). A leading neo-classical architect, he probably had more influence than LEDOUX, though he built little (the Hôtel Alexandre, Paris, 1766–8, is the most interesting survivor), and his treatise on architecture remained unpublished until as recently as 1953, for he had many and important pupils, such as J. N. L. DURAND who wrote the most influential treatise of the Empire period. His best designs date from the 1780s and 1790s and are, if anything, even more megalomaniac than Ledoux's – e.g., a 500-ft-high spherical monument to Newton – and they are also, like Ledoux's, expressive or *parlantes* in intention despite their apparently abstract, geometrical simplicity. In his treatise he pleads for a felt, as much as reasoned, architecture, and for character, grandeur, and magic.

BOW WINDOW, *see* BAY WINDOW.

BOWSTRING ROOF, *see* ROOF.

BOWTELL. A term in use by the C15 (e.g., William of Worcester's notes; mason's contracts) for a convex moulding. A form of ROLL MOULD-ING usually three-quarters of a circle in section; also called *edge roll*. *See figure 16.*

Fig. 16. Bowtell

BOX. A small country house, e.g., a shooting box. A convenient term to describe a compact minor dwelling, e.g., a rectory.

BOX-FRAME. A box-like form of con-crete construction, where the loads are taken on cross walls. This is suit-able only for buildings consisting of repetitive small cells, such as flats or hostels. Sometimes called *cross-wall* construction. *See figure 17.*

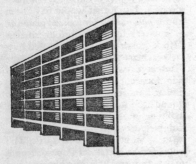

Fig. 17. Box-frame

BOX-PEW, *see* PEW.

BRACE, *see* ROOF.

BRACKET. A small supporting piece of stone or other material, often formed of scrolls or VOLUTES, to carry a projecting weight. *See also* CORBEL.

BRAMANTE, Donato (Donato di Pas-cuccio d'Antonio, 1444–1514). The first of the great High Renaissance architects. He began under the shadow of ALBERTI and MICHELOZZO, and was profoundly influenced by LEO-NARDO DA VINCI, from whom he derived his interest in centrally-planned churches. In Rome he evolved a classic style of imposing monumen-tality which was to have a deep and lasting effect on the development of Italian architecture. PALLADIO de-clared that he 'was the first who brought good architecture to light'. He was born near Urbino, where he probably met the leading artists at the humanist court of Federigo da Monte-feltro, Piero della Francesca, and FRANCESCO DI GIORGIO, to whom he presumably owed his interest in the problems of perspective. He is first recorded in 1477 painting perspective decorations on the façade of Palazzo del Podestà, Bergamo, and he later (1481) made a drawing which was engraved as a perspective model for painters. He entered the service of Duke Ludovico Sforza *c.* 1479, for whom he worked at Vigevano as both decorative painter and architect. His first building of importance is S. Maria presso S. Satiro, Milan (begun 1482). Here he encased the tiny C9 Cappella della Pietà in a drum decorated with niches flanked by slender pilasters, and crowned it with a rather chunky octagonal lantern. He entirely rebuilt the rest of the church on a Latin cross plan. Alberti's influence is apparent in the design for the façade (never com-pleted), the use of shallow pilasters on the side wall and the barrel-vaulted nave. There was no room for a chancel so he feigned one in *trompe l'œil* paint-ing and relief (still deceptive if seen from the right spot). Above the crossing he built a dome with coffered interior, the first since Roman times. He also built an octagonal sacristy, very richly decorated with carvings. In 1488 he was appointed consultant to Pavia Cathedral but only the crypt was carried out according to his proposals. He designed a centrally planned east end for the Gothic church of S. Maria delle Grazie, Milan, spacious and airy internally, but with a lavish use of elegant but rather finicking carving on the exterior of the apses and the sixteen-sided drum which encases the dome (though much of this ornament may have been added without the warrant of his designs). For S. Ambrogio, Milan, he designed the Canons' Cloister (1492, only one wing built) and a further group of four cloisters (1497, two completed after 1576 to his plans). In the Canons' Cloister he used slender Corinthian columns with high friezes and boldly projecting impost blocks, and four columns in the form of tree trunks with the stumps of sawn-off branches protruding from the cylinders.

In 1499 the French invasion of Lombardy and the fall of the Sforzas forced him to flee to Rome, then the artistic centre of Italy. Apart from some frescoes, his first work in Rome was a cloister at S. Maria della Pace (1500), astonishingly different from anything he had previously designed. It has sturdy piers and attached Ionic columns derived from the Colosseum on the ground floor, and an open gallery on the first with alternate columns and piers supporting not arches but an architrave. The effect is wholly Roman in its quiet gravity. He became still graver and more Roman in his next building, the circular Tempietto of S. Pietro in Montorio, Rome (1502), the first great monument of the High Renaissance, which has a majestic solemnity belying its small size. Surrounded at the base by a Tuscan Doric colonnade with a correct classical entablature, it has no surface decorations apart from the metopes and the shells in the niches. It was intended to have been set in the centre of a circular peristyle which would have provided the perfect

spatial foil to its solidity, for it is conceived in terms of volume rather than space, like a Greek temple. Here the Renaissance came closer to the spirit of antiquity than in any other building.

The election of Pope Julius II in 1503 provided Bramante with a new and wholly congenial patron who commissioned him to draw up a vast building plan for the Vatican and St Peter's. A range of buildings later incorporated in the Cortile di S. Damaso was promptly begun, with three tiers of superimposed arcades. Though massive, this was relatively modest in comparison with the scheme for the Cortile del Belvedere, a huge courtyard on three levels measuring about 950 ft by 225 ft, flanked by arcaded buildings, with a theatre at the lower end and a museum for classical antiquities with a central exedra closing the upper court. Work began at the museum end, but only the first storey was completed to his designs (much altered later). The only one of his works in the Vatican which survives intact is the handsome spiral ramp enclosed in a tower of the Belvedere (c. 1505). For St Peter's he proposed a church that would have been the *ne plus ultra* in centralized planning – a Greek cross with four smaller Greek crosses in the arms, roofed by a vast central dome as large as the Pantheon's with four smaller domes and four corner towers, all standing isolated in an immense *piazza*. The foundation stone was laid in 1506 and building was begun but little was completed before the Pope's death in 1513 brought all work to a halt. The choir for S. Maria del Popolo, Rome (1505–9), is small in scale but grand in conception, with a massively coffered vault and shell-capped apse. He also designed and began Palazzo Caprini (1514, later altered out of recognition), with a heavily rusticated basement and five pedimented windows between coupled half-columns on the upper floor, a design which was to be widely imitated. The house was later acquired by RAPHAEL, who inherited his position as leading architect in Rome.

BRATTISHING. An ornamental cresting on the top of a screen or cornice usually formed of leaves, Tudor flowers, or miniature battlements.

Fig. 18. Battlements

BRAZILIAN ARCHITECTURE. Brazil was settled by the Portuguese early in the C16 and remained a Portuguese colony till 1807. The country became an independent empire in 1822, and a republic in 1889. Architecture during the colonial centuries remained dependent on Portugal; one of the earliest Baroque churches is S. Bento at Rio of 1652. The centres of the Baroque, however, are S. Salvador de Bahia and the towns of Minas Gerais, where gold was discovered in the late C17. At Bahia the Terceiros Church of 1703 is exuberantly CHURRIGUERESQUE; so is the decoration of the church of S. Francisco (1708 etc.). The architectural climax of Brazilian Baroque, however, is Ouro Preto near Belo Horizonte, with its many churches of the second half of the C18, mostly with two façade towers and elongated central plans. To the same group belongs the church of Bom Jesus at Congonhas do Campo (1777): sculpture here and in several of the Ouro Preto churches is by ALEIJADINHO.

A revulsion from the Baroque came only after 1815. French artists immigrated, including A. H. V. Grandjean de Montigny (1776–1850), who finished the Customs House at Rio in 1820. A little later, but still French Classical, is the theatre at Recife by Louis Vauthier (*c.* 1810–77), and the rather more American-Colonial-looking theatre at Belém do Pará (1868–78) with its attenuated giant portico. The neo-Baroque is best illustrated by the opera house at Manáus of 1890–6.

While all this had been first colonial and then peripheral, Brazil became one of the leading countries of the world in architecture after the Second World War. The Modern Movement had been introduced by the white cubic houses built from 1928 onwards by Gregori Warchavchik, who published his *Manifesto on Modern Architecture* in 1925. LE CORBUSIER visited Brazil briefly in 1929, and again in 1936, in connexion with the proposed new Ministry of Education at Rio. The building was begun to an amended plan by a group of young Brazilian architects in 1937. Among them were both Lucio COSTA and Oscar NIEMEYER, now the most famous Brazilian architects. Niemeyer is especially important for his early buildings at Pampulha, a club, a dance hall, and a casino of 1942, and a church of 1943. They are the earliest buildings in any country resolutely and adventurously to turn away from the international rationalism then just being accepted by progressive authorities and clients in most countries. Instead, Niemeyer introduced parabolic curves in elevation, a tower with tapering sides, passages under canopies snaking their way from one building to another, a pair of monopitch roofs slanting downward to where they meet. Other architects whose names have become familiar are Marcelo and Milton Roberto, Affonso Reidy, and Rino Levi.

Lucio Costa's name became a household word overnight when in 1956 he won the competition for the plan of Brasilia, the new capital of Brazil (*see* COSTA). The principal buildings there are by Niemeyer: the hotel, the brilliant president's palace, the palaces of the three powers, and the ministry buildings. Niemeyer's centrally planned cathedral is not yet completed.

BREASTSUMMER, *see* BRESSUMER.

BRESSUMER. A massive horizontal beam, sometimes carved, spanning a wide opening such as a fireplace. Also the principal horizontal rail in a timber-framed house. *See figure 83.*

BRETTINGHAM, Matthew (1699–1769), was undistinguished, but had a large practice and built Holkham Hall to KENT's designs. He later claimed to have designed it himself. Few of his own works survive; Langley Park is probably the best. In London he designed several important town houses: Norfolk House (1747–56, demolished 1938), York House, Pall Mall (1760–67, demolished) and No. 5, St James's Square (1748–51). His son Matthew (1725–1803) was also an architect, equally successful and equally undistinguished.

BREUER, Marcel, was born at Pécs in Hungary, 1902. He studied at the BAUHAUS from 1920. In 1925 he was put in charge of the joinery and cabinet workshop, and in that year designed his first tubular steel chair. He went to London in 1935, to Harvard in 1937, and was in a partnership with GROPIUS 1937–40. His independent practice in America started effectively only after the Second World War. He was first commissioned to design private houses in New England. A sympathy with natural materials (rubble, timber), derived perhaps from his Bauhaus days, had already been apparent in some of his work in England. In the last twenty years his practice has spread to other countries (Bijenkorf, Rotterdam, with Elzas, 1953; Unesco, Paris, with Zehrfuss and NERVI, 1953), and his style has followed the rather less rational and more arbitrary trend of architecture in general (Abbey of St John, Collegeville, Minnesota, 1953 and the Lecture Hall for New York University on University Heights, Bronx, N.Y., 1961).

BRICKWORK. A *header* is a brick laid so that the end only appears on the face of the wall, while a *stretcher* is a brick laid so that the side only appears on the face of the wall.

English bond is a method of laying bricks so that alternate courses or layers on the face of the wall are composed of headers or stretchers only: *Flemish bond* is a method of laying bricks so that alternate headers and stretchers appear in each course on the face of the wall. *Heading bond* is composed of headers only. *See figure 19.*

English bond

Flemish bond

Fig. 19. Brickwork

BRISE-SOLEIL. A sun-break or check; now frequently an arrangement of horizontal or vertical fins, used in hot climates to shade the window openings.

BROACH SPIRE, *see* SPIRE.

BROACH-STOP, *see* STOP-CHAMFER.

BRODRICK, Cuthbert (1822–1905). A Yorkshire architect whose capital work is the Leeds Town Hall (1853–8), a grand edifice with a many-columned dome, influenced by COCKERELL and of course WREN. More original is his Leeds Corn Exchange (1861–3), elliptical in plan, Italian Renaissance in style, and with little in the way of enrichment. He also did the wondrously big and heavy Grand Hotel at Scarborough in a style paying tribute to the then fashionable French Renaissance (1863–7), and the Town Hall of Hull (1862–6).

BRONGNIART, Alexandre-Théodore (1739–1813), a prominent neo-classical architect, was born in Paris and trained under J.-F. BLONDEL. In 1765 he began his very successful independent practice, designing the theatre at Caen (destroyed) and the Hôtel de Montesson, Paris. For his private houses he adopted a graceful and unpedantic neoclassical style, the nearest equivalent in architecture to the sculpture of Clodion, who was several times employed to decorate them (e.g., Hôtel de Condé, Paris, designed 1780). But for the Capuchin convent in the Chaussée d'Antin, now Lycée Condorcet (1780–82, façade rebuilt 1864), he developed a much more severe manner, designing a colonnade of Paestum Doric columns for the cloister. In 1804 he was entrusted with the new cemetery of Père-Lachaise in Paris and its *jardin anglais* layout was very influential. His last important work was the Paris Bourse, an appropriately grandiose Corinthian building in the Imperial Roman style (begun 1807, altered and enlarged 1895).

BROOKS, James (1825–1901). A Gothic-Revival church architect whose directness of approach is comparable to BUTTERFIELD's; but where Butterfield is obstinate and perverse, Brooks excels by a simplicity which LETHABY called big-boned. His favourite material was stock brick, his favourite style that of the early C13 with lancet windows and apse. His principal churches are all in London: first a group in the poor north-eastern suburbs (St Michael, Shoreditch, 1863; Holy Saviour, Hoxton, 1864; St Chad, Haggerston, 1867; St Columba, Haggerston, 1867); and then, a little more refined, three individual masterpieces, among the best of their date in the country: the Ascension, Lavender Hill, 1874; the Transfiguration, Lewisham, 1880 (recently mutilated by the insertion of a *mezzanine* floor above the arcades); and All Hallows, Gospel Oak, 1889. The latter was intended to be vaulted throughout.

BROSSE, Salomon de (1571–1626), was born at Verneuil where his maternal grandfather Jacques Androuet DU CERCEAU was building the *château*. His father was also an architect. He settled in Paris *c*. 1598, and was appointed architect to the Crown in 1608. Unlike his relations in the Du Cerceau family and his predecessor BULLANT he conceived architecture in terms of mass and not merely of surface decoration. This plastic sense is evident in his three great *châteaux* of Coulommiers (1613), Luxembourg (1613–14, but enlarged and altered C19), and Blérancourt (1619). The latter is the finest, and was revolutionary in its day, being a free-standing symmetrical block designed to be seen from all sides. In 1618 he began the Palais du Parlement at Rennes, to which his feeling for sharply defined masses and delicacy of classical detail gives great distinction. His frenchified classicism is epitomized in the façade of St Gervais, Paris (1623), which combines VIGNOLA's Gesù scheme with DELORME's frontispiece at Anet with three superimposed orders. He was the most notable precursor of François MANSART, whom he anticipated in some ways.

BROWN, Lancelot (nicknamed Capability, 1716–83). The architect of several Palladian country houses, e.g., Croome Court (1751–2) and Claremont House (1770–2). But he is much more important as a landscape gardener. In 1740 he became gardener at Stowe where he worked on KENT's great layout, and in 1749 he became a consulting landscape gardener. Very soon he developed an artfully informal manner and devised numerous parks with wide expanses of lawn, clumps of trees, serpentine lakes, which provided a perfect setting for the neo-Palladian country seat. Nature was not fettered, as in the formal schemes of LE NÔTRE, but tamed, and a thick planting of trees served both to conceal the bounds of the idyllic park and to protect it from the unimproved landscape beyond. His probably apocryphal remark on his lake at Blenheim, 'Thames, Thames you will never forgive me,' sums up his attitude. His parks were less an alternative to the formal garden than an alternative to nature which proved irresistibly appealing not only in England but also on the Continent. His best surviving parks are: Warwick Castle (*c.* 1750), Croome Court (1751), Bowood (1761), Blenheim (1765, much altered), Ashburnham (1767), Dodington Park (1764), and Nuneham Courtenay (1778).

BRUANT, Libéral (*c.* 1635–97), built the Hôtel des Invalides in Paris (1670–7), notable for the Roman gravity of its arcaded courts, and the highly original Salpêtrière Chapel in Paris (*c.* 1670). He was a greatly gifted architect who never achieved the success he merited.

BRUCE, Sir William (d. 1710), introduced the classical style into Scotland. He came into prominence after the Restoration, for which he had vigorously intrigued, and was rewarded with the lucrative Clerkship to the Bills (1660). He was created baronet 1668, and in 1671 appointed King's Surveyor and Master of Works in Scotland. His work at Holyrood House, Edinburgh (1671 onwards), is frenchified but still rather gauche. Kinross House (1685) and Hopetoun House (1698–1702) are more accomplished in the PRATT tradition.

BRUNEL, Isambard Kingdom (1806–59). The son of Sir Marc Isambard Brunel (1769–1849), who had been born in Normandy, had worked in the French Navy, then as city engineer in New York, and had settled in England in 1799; his most famous English work is the Thames Tunnel from Wapping to Rotherhithe (1824–43). The son was educated in Paris and trained in his father's office. In 1829 he designed the Clifton Bridge at Bristol, one of the noblest of English suspension bridges. He was also responsible for the Great Western line from London to Bristol, including the Box Tunnel. His best-known bridge is the Saltash Bridge, opened in 1859. He also built ships (the *Great Western*, which took only fifteen days to America, and the even larger *Great Eastern*) and in addition, docks (Bristol, Monkwearmouth).

BRUNELLESCHI, Filippo (1377–1446), the first Renaissance architect and one of the greatest, as elegant and refined as Botticelli and as springlike. Far less dogmatic and antiquarian than his immediate successors, e.g., ALBERTI and MICHELOZZO, he was less concerned with the revival of antiquity than with practical problems of construction and the management of space. He, more than anyone else, was responsible for formulating the laws of linear perspective, and a preoccupation with the linear conquest of space characterizes his architecture. In his buildings the horizontals are marked by thin lines which seem to follow the guides of a perspective framework, while the verticals, columns, and fluted pilasters have a spidery, linear attenuation.

Born in Florence, he began as a goldsmith and sculptor, joining the Arte della Seta in 1398, then working for a goldsmith in Pistoia (silver altar, Pistoia Cathedral, *c.* 1399), and competing in 1401–2 for the second bronze door of the Florence Baptistery (he tied with Ghiberti but refused to collaborate with him). In 1404 he was admitted as a master to the Goldsmiths' Guild, and in the same year his advice was sought about a buttress for the cathedral in Florence. Sometime after 1402 he made his first visit to Rome, with Donatello, to study antique sculpture. He continued as a sculptor for a while, but gradually turned his attention exclusively to architecture. In 1415 he repaired the Ponte a Mare at Pisa; in 1417 he advised on the projected dome of Florence Cathedral. His first major works, all in Florence, date from 1418 onwards – a domed chapel in S. Jacopo sopr'Arno (destroyed), the Barbadori Chapel in S. Felicità (partly destroyed), the Palazzo di Parte Guelfa (much altered, but the prototype Early Renaissance palace), and S. Lorenzo. While these were in progress he began, in 1420, to build his masterpiece, the dome of Florence Cathedral, and in 1419 the Ospedale degli Innocenti in Florence.

At S. Lorenzo he began with the sacristy (finished 1428), a cube roofed by a very elegant dome with narrow ribs radiating from the central lantern, a type of construction he called *a creste e vele* (with crests and sails), which neatly expresses its appearance of canvas stretched over the quadrant ribs. The whole interior is painted white, while taut bands of grey *pietra serena* outline the main architectural members; this is the first instance of this strikingly effective decorative scheme. The church itself he designed as a basilica, adding shallow transepts and also chapels attached to the side aisles. But he drew his inspiration not from Imperial Rome so much as the Tuscan Romanesque or proto-Renaissance of the CII–12.

He was commissioned to build the cathedral dome in partnership with Ghiberti who gradually slipped out of the picture. The dome is Gothic in outline with elegantly curved white ribs springing up to the centre, but it is essentially Renaissance in its engineering technique – herringbone brickwork in the Roman manner. The skeleton was completed in 1436, and a further competition held for the lantern – won this time by Brunelleschi alone. He designed the exquisite marble octagon which is perhaps the most successful part of the whole composition. In 1438 he designed the semicircular tribunes with shell-capped niches and coupled Corinthian columns which stand beneath the drum.

The Ospedale degli Innocenti, Florence (designed 1419, built 1421–44), is often claimed as the first Renaissance building. It consists of an arcade of slender, even spindly, Corinthian columns with blue-and-white glazed terracotta plaques between the arches, and a first floor with widely spaced pedimented windows above the centre of each arch. The wide spacing of the arches harks back to CII and CI2 Tuscan work, but the detail is distinctly Roman.

In 1429 he began the Pazzi Chapel in the cloister of S. Croce, Florence. The plan is more complex than that of the S. Lorenzo Sacristy: an atrium in the ratio of 1 : 3, the main building 2 : 3, and a square chancel. The interior decoration is more forceful than S. Lorenzo, with virile semicircular arcs of *pietra serena*, Corinthian pilasters, and, in the spandrels, glazed terracotta reliefs. The façade is odd, closer to the tribune of a basilica than a temple portico – slender Corinthian columns supporting a blank attic storey with shallow carved rectangular panels and coupled pilasters. It seems likely that this construction, which looks uncomfortably flimsy from the side, was intended to be continued round the whole cloister. In 1433 he went again to Rome for further study of antiquity, the immediate result of which was S. Maria degli Angeli, Florence, his most archaeological design, though unfortunately building stopped after three years and only the lower parts of the walls remain. It was the first centrally planned church of the Renaissance (an octagon with eight chapels surrounding the central space, sixteen-sided outside with flat walls and deep niches alternating). At S. Spirito, Florence (begun 1436), he reverted to the basilican Latin cross plan, but gave it an entirely new centralized emphasis by running an aisle round the whole church (the west section never built). Once again the proportions are straightforward – an arrangement of cubes, half cubes, and double cubes – creating that balance and feeling of tranquil repose which was among the chief aims of Renaissance architects.

45

The classical ornamentation is correct and vigorous though sometimes employed in a slightly unorthodox fashion. Several other works have been attributed to him, notably the centre of Palazzo Pitti, Florence, which he may have designed shortly before his death. Though astylar it is clearly an Early Renaissance building, with its massive rusticated stonework inspired by Roman work and with proportions governed by a simple series of ratios.

Brunelleschi became the first Renaissance architect almost by accident. He seems to have been drawn towards ancient Rome less for aesthetic than for practical, engineering reasons. An eclectic empiricist, he hit by instinct on those ideas which were to be developed by his successors. Perhaps his greatest merit was to have preserved Early Renaissance architecture from the dry pedantry of archaeology and revivalism.

BRUTALISM. A term coined in England in 1954 to characterize the style of LE CORBUSIER at the moment of Marseille and Chandigarh, and the style of those inspired by such buildings: in England STIRLING & GOWAN; in Italy Vittoriano Viganò (Istituto Marchiondi, Milan, 1957); in America Paul RUDOLPH; in Japan Maekawa, TANGE, and many others. Brutalism nearly always uses concrete exposed at its roughest (BÉTON BRUT) and handled with overemphasis on big chunky members which collide ruthlessly.

BUCRANE (or BUCRANIUM). In classical architecture, a sculptured ox-skull, usually garlanded, often found in the METOPES of a Doric frieze. *See figure 20.*

Fig. 20. Bucranium

BULFINCH, Charles (1763-1844), came of a wealthy, cultivated Boston family. He graduated at Harvard and was, on his European journey in 1785-7, advised by JEFFERSON. His principal works are the Beacon Monument (1789) in Boston, a Doric column, 60 ft high; the State House at Hertford, Conn. (1792); the State House in Boston (1793-1800); and the Court House, also in Boston (1810). They are perhaps the most dignified American public buildings of their time. In Boston extensive street planning and the building of terraces of houses with unified façades was also done under Bulfinch's chairmanship. In his church plans (Holy Cross, Boston, 1805; New South Church, Boston, 1814) he was influenced by WREN, in his secular work by CHAMBERS and ADAM. From 1817 to 1830 Bulfinch was in charge of work on the Capitol in Washington.

BULLANT, Jean (c. 1520/25-78). His early, rather pedantic classical style is based on DELORME and the study of antiquity (he visited Rome c. 1540-5), but it rapidly acquired Mannerist complexities and, finally, in his late works for Catherine de' Medici, showed a fantasy similar to that of his rival DU CERCEAU. Much of his work has been destroyed. His additions to the Château of Écouen are early and illustrate his characteristically pedantic accuracy in classical details and no less characteristic misunderstanding of the spirit that stood behind them, as witness his most unclassical use of the colossal order. Mannerist features are striking in his bridge and gallery at Fère-en-Tardenois (1552-62) and in the Petit Château at Chantilly (c. 1560). Of his work for Catherine de' Medici only his additions to Chenonceaux survive – the western arm of the forecourt and gallery over the bridge (c. 1576). He published *Reigle générale d'Architecture* (1563) and *Petit Traicté de Géométrie* (1564).

BULLET, Pierre (1639–1716), a pupil of F. BLONDEL, began in the classical academic tradition and did not display much originality until towards the end of his career at the Hôtels Crozat and d'Évreux in the Place Vendôme, Paris (1702–7). Built on irregular corner sites, they foreshadow the freedom and fantasy of Rococo architects in the shape and disposition of rooms.

BUNGALOW. A single-storey house. The term is a corruption of a Hindustani word, and was originally given to the light dwellings with verandas erected mainly for the British administrators. So many of these have been built in England by unqualified designers that certain areas have been opprobriously called 'bungaloid growths'.

BUNNING, James Bunstone, see LABROUSTE.

BUNSHAFT, Gordon, see SKIDMORE, OWINGS & MERRILL.

BUON or BON, Giovanni (c. 1355–c. 1443) and Bartolomeo (c. 1374–c. 1467), were father and son, and the leading sculptor–builders in early C15 Venice. They are known to have worked at S. Maria dell'Orto (1392), the Ca' d'Oro (1427–34), and the Porta della Carta of the Doge's Palace (1438–42). They were probably responsible for the design as well as the carved decorations.

BUONTALENTI, Bernardo (c. 1536–1608). Florentine Mannerist architect, painter and sculptor, and also a prolific designer of masques, fire-works (hence his nickname 'delle Girandole') and other entertainments for the Tuscan Grand Ducal court. He was even more sophisticated and stylish than his contemporary AMMANATI, e.g., the fantastic *trompe l'œil* altar steps in S. Stefano (1574–6), the perverse Porta delle Suppliche at the Uffizi (c. 1580), and the grottoes in the Boboli Gardens (1583–8), all in Florence. But this preciosity and sense of fantasy was necessarily restrained in his major works of which the most notable are the Villa di Artimino at Signa (1594), the *galleria* and *tribuna* of the Uffizi (c. 1580), the façade of S. Trinità (1592–4) and the Fortezza del Belvedere (1590–95), all in Florence, and the Loggia de Banchi in Pisa (begun 1605). He also produced a fantastic design for the façade of the cathedral at Florence (1587) and carried out much engineering work for the Grand Duke, notably at the harbour of Leghorn and a canal between Leghorn and Pisa (1571–3). His grand-ducal villa at Pratolino (1569–75) was destroyed in the C19.

BURGES, William (1827–81), trained in engineering, then in the offices of Blore and M. D. WYATT. He travelled in France, Germany, and Italy, and was always as interested in French as in English Gothic forms. In 1856, he won, with Henry Clutton (1819–93), the competition for Lille Cathedral, but in the event the building was not allotted to them. In 1859 he added the east end to Waltham Abbey, where for the first time the peculiar massiveness and heavy-handedness of his detail come out. He was a great believer in plenty of carved decoration, and specialized much less in ecclesiastical work than the other leading Gothic Revivalists. His principal works are Cork Cathedral (1862–76), still in a pure French High Gothic; the substantial addition to Cardiff Castle (1865); the remodelling of Castle Coch near Cardiff (c. 1875); the Harrow School Speech Room (1872); and his own house in Melbury Road, Kensington (1875–80). Hartford College, Connecticut, was also built to his designs (1873–80).

BURGHAUSEN, Hans von, see STETHAIMER.

BURLINGTON, Richard Boyle, 3rd Earl of (1694–1753), was the patron and high priest of English PALLADIANISM and a gifted architect in his own right. He first visited Italy in 1714–15, but his conversion to Palladianism came after his return to

London, which coincided with the publication of CAMPBELL's *Vitruvius Britannicus* and LEONI's edition of Palladio's *Four Books of Architecture*. He immediately replaced GIBBS with Campbell as architect of Burlington House and set out once more for Italy to study the master's buildings at first hand. He returned (1719) with his protégé William KENT, and for the next thirty years dominated the architectural scene in England. The widespread fashion for Palladio was largely due to his influence. He financed Kent's *Designs of Inigo Jones* (1727) and in 1730 published Palladio's drawings of Roman *thermae*. But there was a marked difference between his own and his followers' interpretation of the master. For him Palladianism meant a return to the architecture of antiquity as explained and illustrated by Palladio and he avoided, whereas his followers blindly accepted, all the non-classical and Mannerist features in the master's style. Cold, intellectual, and aristocratic, he was described by Pope as a 'positive' man, and both the strength and weakness of Palladianism derive from his obsessive, puritanical urge to preach absolute classical standards – those just and noble rules which were in due course to 'Fill half the land with imitating fools' (Pope). His fastidious but dogmatic character is equally evident in his buildings, which became increasingly dry and pedantic. They have a staccato quality – an over-articulation or overemphasis of individual features – which suggests a formula-loving mind. His *œuvre* appears to have consisted in about a dozen buildings designed mostly for himself or friends, beginning in 1717 with a garden pavilion – the Bagno – at Chiswick, where he later built his best-known work, the ornamental villa based on Palladio's Rotonda (*c.* 1725). His only other important works to survive are the Dormitory, Westminster School, London (1722–30, rebuilt 1947), Northwick Park,

Worcs. (1730), and the Assembly Rooms, York (1731–2, refronted 1828). This latter is an exact model of Palladio's Egyptian Hall, based on VITRUVIUS. In addition to his independent work, he may be credited as part author of several buildings by his protégé Kent, notably Holkham Hall.

BURN, William, *see* SHAW.

BURNHAM, Daniel H. (1846–1912), came of an old Massachusetts family. His father moved to Chicago, and there, after several false starts, the son went into an architect's office, where he met J. W. ROOT. The two went into partnership, an ideal pair: Root was poetic and versatile, Burnham practical and a skilled administrator. Burnham and Root have an important share in the evolution of the so-called Chicago School. Their best-known buildings are the Monadnock Block (1889–91), still a load-bearing masonry structure, though severely direct and unornamented; the Masonic Temple (1891), with its twenty-two storeys the tallest building in the world at the time it was built and with a complete steel skeleton (as introduced slightly before by HOLABIRD & ROCHE); and the Flat-iron Building in New York (1902). Burnham was made Chief of Construction for the World's Columbian Exposition in Chicago, which took place in 1893. Buildings were designed by HUNT, MCKIM, Mead and WHITE, C. B. Atwood, POST, SULLIVAN, and others. The most monumental of them were classical and columnar, and this demonstration of Beaux Arts ideals cut short the life of the Chicago School. Later Burnham concentrated more and more on town and area planning: his plans for the District of Columbia (1901–2) are the start of comprehensive town planning in America. They were followed by the plan for Chicago (1906–9) and many others.

BURTON, Decimus (1800–81). The son of James Burton (1761–1837), a successful big London builder. As early as 1823 he designed the Colosseum in Regent's Park with a dome larger than that of St Paul's and a Greek Doric portico. It housed a panorama of London. In 1825 he began the Hyde Park Improvements which included the Hyde Park Corner Screen. He designed several housing estates (e.g., at Tunbridge Wells, 1828 etc.), the centre of Fleetwood (1835 etc.), the great Palm Houses at Chatsworth (with PAXTON) and Kew (with R. Turner), many villas (including several in Regent's Park), the Athenaeum, London (1829–30), and a number of country houses.

BUSH-HAMMERING. A method of obtaining an even, rough texture on concrete after it has set, by using a bush-hammer with a specially grooved head which chips the surface.

BUTTERFIELD, William (1814–1900), a High-Church Gothic-Revivalist, was aloof in his life (a bachelor with a butler) and studious in his work. The peculiar aggressiveness of his forms – one jarring with the other – and of his colours – stone and multicoloured brick in stripes or geometrical patterns – was tolerated by the purists of the Cambridge Camden movement and their journal *The Ecclesiologist*, partly because he was their personal friend (he drew much for the *Instrumenta Ecclesiastica* of 1847), partly because he must have had a great power of conviction. His earliest church (and parsonage) of importance was Coalpit Heath (1844). This was followed by St Augustine's College, Canterbury, quieter than most of his work. The eruption of his fully developed personal style came with All Saints, Margaret Street, London (1849–59), a ruthless composition in red brick of church and accessory buildings on three sides of a small courtyard. The steeple is slender, noble, North German Gothic, and asymmetrically placed. St Matthias, Stoke Newington, London, followed in 1850–2 – yellow

brick, with a nave crossed by two transverse arches; then St Alban's, Holborn, London, in 1863; Keble College, Oxford, in 1867–75; the Rugby School buildings in 1870–86; and many others. Nearly all his work, apart from that for colleges and schools, was ecclesiastical. An exception is the robustly utilitarian County Hospital at Winchester (1863). His early cottages (c. 1848–50) are also remarkably free from historicism. They are the pattern for WEBB's Red House.

BUTTRESS. A mass of masonry or brickwork projecting from or built against a wall to give additional strength.

Angle buttresses. Two meeting at an angle of 90° at the angle of a building.

Clasping buttress. One which encases the angle.

Diagonal buttress. One placed against the right angle formed by two walls, and more or less equiangular with both.

Flying buttress. An arch or half-arch transmitting the thrust of a vault or roof from the upper part of a wall to an outer support or buttress.

Setback buttress. A buttress set slightly back from the angle. *See figure 21.*

BYZANTINE ARCHITECTURE. The culmination of Early Christian architecture. This style developed after A.D. 330 when Constantine established the Imperial capital at Byzantium (renamed Constantinople) on the Bosphorus. The arts in Rome were then at a low ebb, but no efforts were spared to make the new capital as traditionally Roman as possible. Such a building as the aqueduct of Valens differs little from those built in the West during the previous 300 years. But gradually a new and original style emerged. Classical concepts, such as the ORDERS, were no longer observed; classical detail of all kinds was coarsened and the lush relief decorations popular in Rome were abandoned in favour of flat, rather lacy ornaments. Early C5

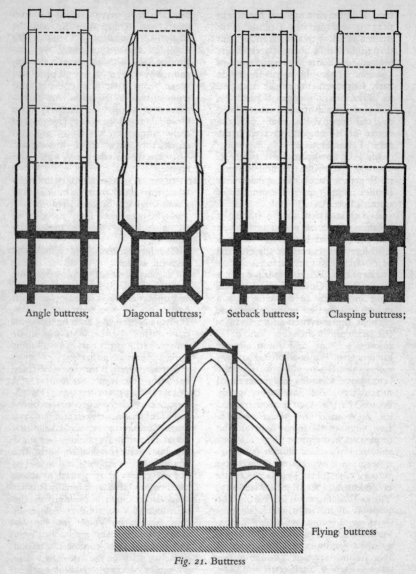

Angle buttress;   Diagonal buttress;   Setback buttress;   Clasping buttress;

Flying buttress

Fig. 21. Buttress

churches in Cilicia (e.g., Kandirli and Cambazli), built in a mixture of Syrian and Roman styles, suggest that some of the new influences came from the East. The later c5 church of St John in Studion, Constantinople, also shows a tendency to depart from classical precepts. Yet classicism, or at least a desire to recapture the splendours of the classical past, was to remain a force of recurrent importance throughout Byzantine art, especially in the secular arts where the taint of paganism probably mattered less to early Christians. Very little is known of Byzantine domestic architecture, but recent excavations have revealed that the Imperial Palace in Constantinople was among the greatest buildings of its time.

In the c5 two forms of church were evolved: the BASILICA and the centrally planned church reserved for the shrines of martyrs. The latter, called *martyria*, were usually built on a Greek cross plan and were domed – the combination of a dome with a square base being a Byzantine introduction from the Near East. It was the achievement of c6 architects to combine these two forms of church and to create interiors in which a wholly unclassical play of void and solid, dark and light, produced an effect of mystery which is perhaps the most striking feature of the Byzantine church. The outstanding masterpiece of Byzantine church architecture, Hagia Sophia, Constantinople (built A.D. 532–7 by ANTHEMIUS OF TRALLES and ISIDORE OF MILETUS), shows this quality to perfection. But it was the mathematical and intellectual rather than the emotive qualities of Hagia Sophia that impressed contemporaries. 'Through the harmony of its measurements it is distinguished by indescribable beauty,' wrote Procopius. The same author commented that 'a spherical-shaped Tholos standing upon a circle makes it exceedingly beautiful'. At this time mathematics was considered the highest of the sciences, and Anthemius was a notable mathematician who believed that architecture was 'the application of geometry to solid matter'.

By the c9 symbolism began to play a greater part in Byzantine church architecture. The church was now regarded as a microcosm of all earth and sky, as the setting of Christ's life on earth, and at the same time as the image of the liturgical year. This complex triple symbolism was expressed in painted or mosaic decorations where the very colours used had an emblematic significance. The mystique of numbers also found reflection in church design. To the Byzantine these intellectual concepts were as important as the air of mystery created by screens and galleries dividing the well-lit central area from those surrounding it. The typical Byzantine church plan of a Greek cross inscribed in a square and capped by a central dome (evolved in the c7) provided a perfect background for the display of this elaborate painted or mosaic decoration.

As early as the c5 the Byzantine style began to influence architecture in Italy, especially Ravenna (S. Giovanni Battista, S. Croce, and the so-called Mausoleum of Galla Placidia). The basilican S. Apollinare in Classe, Ravenna (c. 536–50), and the octagonal S. Vitale, Ravenna (c. 526–47), are among the greatest and least altered of all Byzantine buildings. Though erected by Byzantine architects, and probably by Byzantine masons as well, both reveal slight Western peculiarities, notably in the decoration of the exterior. Later, Western buildings began to show more radical departures from Byzantine precedents – e.g., S. Marco, Venice, with its very rich marble-clad exterior.

No new developments were made after the c9. The types of plan evolved – notably the very popular Greek cross inscribed in a square – were repeated endlessly. After the c11 the beauty of their forms tended to be masked by an overabundance of painted decoration. But many fine churches were built, especially in Greece (Hosios Lukas in Phocis; Holy Apostles, Salonika; the Panagia in Athens) and as late as the c13 and c14 in Serbia (Gracanica and Ljuboten).

C

CABLE MOULDING. A Romanesque moulding imitating a twisted cord. *See figure 22.*

Fig. 22. Cable moulding

CABLED FLUTING, *see* FLUTING.

CAGNOLA, Marchese Luigi (1762–1833). A neo-classical architect who played a leading role in the Napoleonic transformation of Milan, designing the severe Ionic Porta Ticinese (1801–14) and the much richer Arco della Pace (1806–38). He also designed a Pantheon-like parish church at Ghisalba (*c.* 1830), a fantastic campanile crowned with CANEPHORAE supporting a dome at Urgnano (*c.* 1820), and his own many-columned Grecian villa Inverigo (begun 1813).

CAISSON. 1. An air chamber, resembling a well, driven down to a firm foundation stratum in the soil and filled with concrete. It is used for construction below water (e.g., for the piers of a bridge) or on waterlogged ground. 2. A sunken panel in a flat or vaulted ceiling.

CALDARIUM. The hot-room in a Roman bath.

CALLICRATES was the leading architect in Periclean Athens, and with ICTINUS designed the Parthenon (447–442 B.C.). He probably designed and built the exquisite little Ionic temple of Athena Nike on the Acropolis, Athens (448–after 421 B.C.). He also built the south and central portion of the Long Walls from Athens to Piraeus, and perhaps restored part of the city walls.

CAMARÍN. A small chapel behind and above the high altar in Spanish churches. It is usually visible from the nave. The earliest example is in the church of the Desamparados in Valencia (1647–67).

CAMBER. To curve (a beam) either by sawing or by bending, so that the middle is higher than the ends. This is a good remedy for sagging tie-beams (*see* ROOF), as it gives them a slightly arched form.

CAMBODIAN ARCHITECTURE, *see* KHMER ARCHITECTURE.

CAME. A metal strip used for LEADED LIGHTS.

CAMERON, Charles (*c.* 1740–1812), was born in Scotland, visited Rome *c.* 1768, and published *The Baths of the Romans* in 1772. Nothing more is known of him until he was summoned to Russia in about 1774 by Catherine the Great, and lived there for the rest of his life. For Catherine he decorated several apartments in RASTRELLI's palace at Tsarskoe Selo (now Pushkino) near Leningrad (1780–85), and also designed the Agate Pavilion and Cameron Gallery there. For the Grand Duke Paul he built the great palace at Pavlovsk (1780–96) and the circular Doric peripteral Temple of Friendship (destroyed) in the English Park – the first of its kind in Russia. In about 1787 he was superseded as architect-in-chief by his pupil Brenna, and when Catherine died in 1796 he was dismissed altogether from royal service. But he stayed on in Russia, building for private patrons, e.g., the Rasumovski Palace at Batourin in the Ukraine (1799–1802, unfinished). He returned to favour after the death of Paul I, and in 1805 designed the naval hospital and barracks at Kronstadt. He was an admirer and close follower of Robert ADAM, especially in interior decoration, though lacking his finesse.

CAMPANILE. The Italian word for a bell-tower, usually separate from the main building. The earliest surviving Italian campanili are at Ravenna – circular and probably of c9. The earliest recorded campanile was square and was attached to St Peter's in Rome. It went back to the mid-c8.

CAMPBELL, Colen (1673–1729). Little is known about him until 1715 when he published the first volume of *Vitruvius Britannicus* and built Wanstead House (now demolished), which became the model for large English Palladian country houses. With Baldersby Park, Yorks (1720–21) he initiated the neo-Palladian villa. He was probably responsible for Lord BURLINGTON's conversion to PALLADIANISM and was commissioned to remodel Burlington House, London (1718–19). Mereworth Castle (1722–5) is perhaps the best of the English versions of Palladio's Rotonda design. Houghton Hall (1721, executed with modifications by Ripley) is enormous and imposing, but Ebberston Lodge near Scarborough (1718) and Compton Place, Eastbourne (1726–7), are more elegant and refined.

CAMPEN, Jacob van (1595–1657). A wealthy and erudite painter-architect and the leading exponent of Dutch PALLADIANISM, an unpretentious, placid and economic form of classicism characterized by its use of brick mixed with stone and its straightforward, almost diagrammatic use of pilasters. He studied in Italy and probably knew SCAMOZZI who certainly influenced him greatly, rather more indeed than Palladio. Van Campen's style is epitomized in his masterpiece the Mauritshuis, The Hague (1633–35), entirely Palladian in plan, with giant Ionic pilasters raised on a low ground floor and supporting a pediment, crowned with a typically Dutch

hipped roof rising in a slightly concave line from the eaves. His great Town Hall in Amsterdam (now the Royal Palace: 1648–55), built entirely of stone, is heavier but very imposing – the grandest of all town halls. More original is the Nieuwe Kerk in Haarlem (1645) of the Greek-cross-in-square type. He also designed the Coymans house on the Keizersgracht, Amsterdam (1625), the earliest example of Palladianism in Holland, the Noordeinde Palace, The Hague (1640) and the Accijnhuis and theatre in Amsterdam (1637). With Christian Huygens he was responsible for the general conception of decoration by Jordaens and others in POST's Huisten-Bosch. His domestic style had great influence through his followers Pieter Post, Arend van 's-Gravesande and Philip Vingboons. And it was later introduced into England by Hugh MAY and others.

CANCELLO. In Early Christian architecture, a latticed screen or grille separating the choir from the main body of a church.

CANDELA, Felix (b. 1910), was born in Spain but lives in Mexico. He is one of the most resourceful concrete engineers of the age and is also important architecturally. He was inspired initially by TORROJA. Among his most significant works, both in Mexico City, are the Church of Our Lady of Miracles (1953–5), an extreme example of mid-century Expressionism, and in collaboration with the architect José Gonzáles, the Radiation Institute (1954), which is a tiny four-legged shed with a paraboloid roof only about 1 in. thick at the ridge. Later buildings by Candela are the Chapel of the Missionaries of the Holy Spirit at Coyoacán (1956, with Enrique de la Mora) with a simple saddle-shaped canopy on rough stone walls; the restaurant at Xochimilco (1958, with Joaquín Alvarez Ordóñez) placed in the water gardens like an eight-petalled flower of paraboloids; the

Market Hall at Coyoacán (1956, with Pedro Ramírez Vásquez and Rafael Mijares) with the mushroom-shaped umbrellas which Candela has since used at the John Lewis warehouse, Stevenage, England (1963, with Yorke, Rosenberg and Mardall).

CANDID, Peter; or Peter de Wit or de Witte (1548–1628). Mannerist painter and architect, born in Bruges. He was the son of a Flemish sculptor, Elias de Witte, with whom he went to Florence *c.* 1573. He studied painting in Italy, perhaps under VASARI, and worked as a painter both in Florence and Rome. In 1586 he settled in Munich under the patronage of Duke Wilhelm V and Maximilian I who had already attracted thither Friedrich SUSTRIS and the Mannerist sculptor Hubert Gerhard. Candid was probably involved as an architect in the later stages of the building of the Munich Residenz though nothing is known about this for certain.

CANEPHORA. A sculptured female figure carrying a basket on her head.

CANOPY. A projection or hood over a door, window, tomb, altar, pulpit, niche, etc.

CANTERBURY, *see* MICHAEL OF CANTERBURY.

CANTILEVER. A horizontal projection (e.g., a step, balcony, beam or canopy) supported by a downward force behind a fulcrum. It is without external bracing and thus appears to be self-supporting. *See figure 23.*

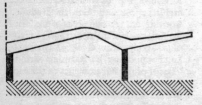

Fig. 23. Cantilever beam

CAP. The crowning feature of a windmill, usually a domical roof; also an abbreviation for CAPITAL.

CAPITAL. The head or crowning feature of a column.

Aeolic capital. See ORDER.

Bell capital. A form of capital of which the chief characteristic is a reversed bell between the SHAFT or NECKING and the upper moulding. The bell is often enriched with carving.

Crocket capital. An Early Gothic form, consisting of stylized leaves with endings rolled over similar to small VOLUTES.

Cushion capital. A Romanesque capital cut from a cube, with its lower parts rounded off to adapt it to a circular shaft; the remaining flat face of each side is generally a LUNETTE. Also called a *block* capital.

Protomai capital. A capital with half-figures, usually animals, projecting from its four corners.

Scalloped capital. A development of the block or cushion capital in which the single lunette on each face is elaborated into one or more truncated cones.

See also STIFF-LEAF; WATER-LEAF; *and, for capitals in classical architecture,* ORDER. *See figures 24 and 64.*

CARATTI, Francesco (d. 1677), was born at Bissone near Como, and went in 1652 to Prague, where he became the leading architect. His masterpiece is the Czernin Palace (begun 1668), with a row of thirty giant attached Corinthian columns and a rusticated basement which breaks forward to provide bases for the columns and bulges out into a central porch. The strong chiaroscuro created by the projections makes this façade one of the most exciting of its time. He also built the Mary Magdalen Church, Prague (begun 1656), and the E. wing of the palace at Roudnice (1665).

CARLONE, Carlo Antonio (d. 1708), is the most important member of a large family of Italian artists working in Austria and South Germany. His masterpiece is the richly stuccoed interior of the Italianate Priory Church

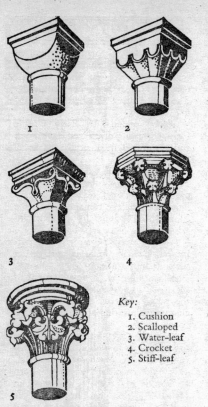

Key:

1. Cushion
2. Scalloped
3. Water-leaf
4. Crocket
5. Stiff-leaf

Fig. 24. Capital

of St Florian (1686–1705). Other works include the Jesuitenkirche zu den Neun Chören der Engel, Vienna (1662), with a rather secular street façade, and the charming little pilgrimage church of Christkindl (begun 1706), which was finished by PRANDTAUER, who was much indebted to Carlone.

CAROLINGIAN ARCHITECTURE takes its name from Charlemagne (King from 768, Emperor 800–14), and his descendants and the style extends in time from the late C8 into the C10, and in space through those countries which formed part of Charlemagne's Empire, especially France, Germany, and the Netherlands. Anglo-Saxon architecture in England and Asturian architecture in Spain stand outside this style, which is composite and the result of conflicting trends in these formative centuries of Western civilization. Charlemagne himself promoted a renaissance of Roman – i.e., Constantinian – Christianity. This is evident in poetry, in script, in illumination, and also in the plans and elevations of certain churches which follow Early Christian examples (St Denis, Fulda, etc.). But indigenous characteristics also make themselves felt and point forward to the ROMANESQUE. In this category are prominent towers, strongly stressed west ends and east ends (Centula, plan for St Gall), and also heavier, more massive members. The most spectacular building preserved from Charlemagne's time is the cathedral of Aachen. *See also* GERMAN ARCHITECTURE, FRENCH ARCHITECTURE.

CARR, John (1723–1807). A late and provincial exponent of PALLADIANISM, working mainly in Yorkshire. He began life as a mason in his father's quarry near Wakefield, and in his twenties built Kirby Hall to the design of Lord BURLINGTON and Roger MORRIS. He was later associated with Robert ADAM in the building of Harewood House (begun 1759). From then onwards he designed and built many large country houses. He was unoriginal, but could be refined and dignified in a quiet way, e.g., Denton Park (*c.* 1778) and Farnley Hall (*c.* 1786). His largest and perhaps his best work is the Crescent at Buxton (1779–84), where he very successfully combined the younger WOOD's invention of the monumental residential crescent with the arcaded ground floor surmounted by giant pilaster order used by Inigo JONES at Covent Garden.

CARREL (or CAROL). A niche in a cloister where a monk might sit and work or read; sometimes applied to BAY WINDOWS.

CARTOUCHE. An ornamental panel in
the form of a scroll or sheet of paper
with curling edges, usually bearing an
inscription and sometimes ornately
framed.

CARYATID. A sculptured female figure
used as a column to support an entablature or other similar member, as
on the Erechtheum. The term is also
applied loosely to various other
columns and pilasters carved wholly
or partly in the form of human figures:
ATLANTES (male caryatids), CANE-
PHORAE (females carrying baskets on
their heads), HERMS (three-quarter-
length figures on pedestals), Telamones (another name for Atlantes),
and TERMS (tapering pedestals merging at the top into human, animal, or
mythical figures). *See figure 25.*

CASEMATE. A vaulted room, with EM-
BRASURES, built in the thickness of the
ramparts or other fortifications, and
used as a barracks or battery, or both.

CASEMENT. 1. The hinged part of a
window, attached to the upright side
of the window-frame. 2. The wide
concave moulding in door and
window JAMBS and between COM-
POUND columns or piers, found in
Late Gothic architecture. The term
was in use by the middle of the C15
(William of Worcester's notes).

CASEMENT WINDOW. A metal or
timber window with the sash hung
vertically and opening outwards or
inwards.

CASINO. 1. An ornamental pavilion or
small house, usually in the grounds of
a larger house. 2. In the C18 a dancing
saloon, today a building for gam-
bling.

CASSELS, Richard (*c.* 1690–1751). A
German who settled in Ireland *c.* 1720
and became the leading architect of
his day in Dublin. His surviving works
conform to English PALLADIANISM,
without any trace of his foreign origin:
e.g., Tyrone House (1740–5) and
Leinster House (1745) in Dublin, and
his two great country houses, Carton
(1739) and Russborough (1741).

Fig. 25. Caryatid

CASTELLAMONTE, Carlo Conte di (1560–1641), was trained in Rome. He became architect to the Duke of Savoy in 1615 and played a large part in developing the city plan of Turin, where he designed Piazza S. Carlo (1637) and several churches. He began Castello di Valentino, Turin (1633), completed in the French style with a high hipped roof (1663) by his son Amadeo (1610–83), who succeeded him as court architect.

CASTELLATED. Decorated with BATTLEMENTS.

CASTLE. A fortified habitation. The planning and building of castles is primarily directed by the necessities of defence; it rarely extends as a whole into architecture proper, though certain features may. In the earlier Middle Ages the principal elements of castles were the donjon or KEEP and the hall in France and England, the Bergfrid and the Palas in Germany. The keep is a tower spacious enough to act as living quarters in time of war for the lord or governor and the garrison; the Bergfrid is a tower of normal proportions; the Palas is the hall-range. The earliest dated donjon is at Langeais (c. 990), the earliest surviving major hall at Goslar (mid CII).

England built some hall-keeps, i.e., keeps wider than they are high (Tower of London). In France and Italy in the early C13 Roman precedent led to symmetrical compositions with angle towers and a gatehouse in the middle of one side. Some castles of Edward I in Britain took this over, and where in the late Middle Ages castles were still needed (south coast, Scottish border), they were often symmetrically composed. The rule in Britain at this time, however, was that castles could be replaced by unfortified manor houses. Towards the end of the Middle Ages the spread of fire-arms changed the castle into the fortress, with low BASTIONS for mounting cannon and no towers.

Fortress Elements

Casemate. Vaulted chamber in a bastion for men and guns.

Cavalier. Raised earth-platform of a fortress used for look-out purposes or gun placements.

Counterscarp. The face of the ditch of a fortress sloping towards the defender.

Demi-Lune, see Half-Moon.

Glacis. The ground sloping from the top of the rampart of a fortress to the level of the country around.

Half-Moon. Outwork of a fortress, crescent-shaped or forming an angle.

Hornwork. Outwork of a fortress with two demi-bastions.

Ravelin. Similar to a *Half-Moon.*

Redoubt. Small detached fortification.

Scarp. The side of the ditch of a fortress sloping towards the enemy.

Sconce. Detached fort with bastions.

CATHEDRA. The bishop's chair or throne in his cathedral church, originally placed behind the high altar in the centre of the curved wall of the APSE.

CATHEDRAL. Bishop's church, from CATHEDRA.

CAULCOLE. The stalk rising from the leaves of a Corinthian capital and supporting one of the VOLUTES.

CAVALIER. In military architecture, a raised earth-platform of a fortress, for look-out purposes or gun placements.

CAVETTO MOULDING. A hollow moulding, about a quarter of a circle in section. *See figure 26.*

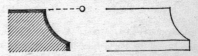

Fig. 26. Cavetto moulding

CELL. One of the compartments of a groin or rib VAULT, in the Romanesque period usually of plastered rubble, in the Gothic period of neatly coursed stones; the earliest known example is St Denis of 1140–4. Also called a *web.*

CELLA. The main body of a classical temple (containing the cult image), as distinct from the portico, etc.

CELURE. The panelled and adorned part of a wagon roof (*see* ROOF) above the ROOD or the altar.

CENOTAPH. A monument to a person or persons buried elsewhere.

CENTERING. Wooden framework used in arch and vault construction; it is removed (or 'struck') when the mortar has set.

CHAIR-RAIL (or DADO-RAIL). A moulding round a room to prevent chairs, when pushed back against the walls, from damaging their surface.

CHALET. A Swiss herdsman's hut or mountain cottage. The term is now loosely applied to any house built in the Swiss style.

CHALGRIN, Jean François Thérèse (1739–1811). A pupil of BOULLÉE and Rome scholar (1758–63). He began in the rather epicene neo-classical manner then current (e.g., in the work of SOUFFLOT), and reintroduced the basilican plan in his St Philippe-du-Roule, Paris (designed pre-1765, built 1772–84), which was very influential. But his masterpiece, the Arc de Triomphe, Paris (1806–35), is more Romantic–Classical in the style of Boullée, with its imperial symbolism and megalomaniac scale. He did not live to see it finished, and the sculptural decoration by Rude and others gives it a distinctly C19 appearance. He rebuilt the Odéon, Paris, in 1807, following the original designs by Joseph Peyre and Charles DE WAILLY.

CHAMBERLIN, POWELL & BON. A London partnership, the members of which were born about 1920. The partners won the competition in 1952 for a City of London housing estate round Golden Lane, and this extensive scheme is not completed yet. They built a fine warehouse at Witham in Essex (1953–5) and an excellent school (Bousfield School, London) in 1952–6. Their building for New Hall,

Cambridge (begun 1960), is decidedly *outré* in its forms as the most recent work of the partnership tends to be. Their largest job in progress at present is for Leeds University.

CHAMBERS, Sir William (1723–96), the greatest official architect of his day in England, was born in Göteborg, Sweden, the son of a Scottish merchant. At sixteen he joined the Swedish East India Company and for nine years made voyages to India and China. His architectural training began in 1749 in Paris under J.-F. BLONDEL, and was continued in Italy from 1750 until 1755, when he settled in London. He was an immediate success. His appointment (1756) as architectural tutor to the Prince of Wales established him in royal favour, and he became successively Architect to the King, jointly with Robert ADAM (1760), Comptroller (1769), and Surveyor General (1782). He was the first treasurer of the Royal Academy and took a leading part in its foundation. In 1770 the king allowed him to assume a knighthood on receiving the Order of the Polar Star from the King of Sweden.

His career was that of a supremely successful official and his buildings are extremely competent; fastidious in ornament, impeccable in the use of orders, but rather academic, despite his famous Pagoda in Kew Gardens, and much less spectacular than those of his rival Robert Adam. His style is scholarly but eclectic, based on English PALLADIANISM smoothed out and refined by the neo-classicism of SOUFFLOT and his contemporaries, whom he had known in Paris and with whom he afterwards kept in touch. Usually best on a small scale, his scholarly finesse is well illustrated by two of his earlier works, the Casino at Marino, Dublin (1757–69), an exemplary combination of strictly classical elements to fit a Greek cross plan, and the Pagoda at Kew (1757–62), in which he aspired to similar archaeological accuracy in another manner. He was notable for his staircases, e.g. Gower House, London (*c.* 1769, destroyed), Melbourne House, London (*c.* 1772, destroyed) and Somerset House, London. His country houses are neo-Palladian in plan and composition – e.g., Lord Bessborough's villa, now a school, at Roehampton (*c.* 1760) and Duddingston House, Edinburgh (1762–4) – while the Strand façade of his largest and best-known work, Somerset House, London (1776–86), is a conscious imitation of a Palladian composition by Inigo JONES on the site. The courtyards and river façade display more vivacity and originality, and some of the interior decoration equals anything by Adam for elegant refinement particularly in the Strand block in which some rooms represent the earliest examples of a mature Louis XVI style in England. Though never as fashionable as Adam, he exerted great influence both as official head of his profession and through his numerous pupils. His *Treatise on Civil Architecture* (1759) became a standard work.

CHAMFER. The surface made when the sharp edge or ARRIS of a stone block or piece of wood, etc., is cut away, usually at an angle of 45° to the other two surfaces. It is called a *hollow chamfer* when the surface made is concave.

CHANCEL. That part of the east end of a church in which the main altar is placed; reserved for clergy and choir. From the Latin word *cancellus*, which strictly means the screen that often separated it from the body of the church. The term more usually describes the space enclosed and is applied to the whole continuation of the nave east of the CROSSING.

CHANCEL ARCH. The arch at the west end of a CHANCEL.

CHANTRY CHAPEL. A chapel attached to, or inside, a church, endowed for the celebration of Masses for the soul

of the founder or souls of such others as he may order.

CHAPTERHOUSE. The place of assembly for abbot or prior and members of a monastery for the discussion of business. It is reached from the CLOISTERS, to whose eastern range it usually belongs, and in England is often polygonal in plan. *See figure 61.*

CHATRI. In Hindu architecture, an umbrella-shaped dome. *See figure 27.*

Fig. 27. Chatri

CHEQUER-WORK. A method of decorating walls or pavements with alternating squares of contrasting materials (e.g., stone, brick, flint) to produce a chessboard effect.

CHEVET. The French term for the east end of a church, consisting of APSE and AMBULATORY with or without radiating chapels.

CHEVRON. A Romanesque moulding forming a zigzag; so called from the French word for a pair of rafters giving this form. *See figure 28.*

Fig. 28. Chevron

CHIAVERI, Gaetano (1689–1770). Late Baroque architect, born in Rome but worked mainly in N. Europe – St

Petersburg (1717–27), Warsaw and Dresden (c. 1737–48). His masterpiece was the Hofkirche in Dresden (begun 1738, badly damaged 1944), a Roman Catholic church intended to rival the grandeur of BÄHR's Lutheran Frauenkirche. It has a very elegant campanile with an open-work top section which provided the perfect foil to the solidity of Bähr's dome, as did also the exterior of the church itself with its rhythmically advancing and receding walls crowned by numerous statues. Chiaveri provided plans for the river front of the royal palace in Warsaw (1740, only partly adopted) and somewhat theatrical designs for a royal palace in Dresden (c. 1748, not executed). He published a volume of engraved designs: *Ornamenti diversi di porte e finestre* (1743–4).

CHICAGO SCHOOL, *see* BURNHAM; HOLABIRD & ROCHE; JENNEY; ROOT; SULLIVAN; UNITED STATES ARCHITECTURE.

CHICAGO WINDOW. A window occupying the full width of a bay and divided into a large fixed sash flanked by a narrow movable sash on each side, as in the Marquette Building by HOLABIRD & ROCHE (1894) and SULLIVAN's Carson Pirie & Scott Store (1899–1904) in Chicago.

CHIMNEY BAR. The bar above the fireplace opening which carries the front of the CHIMNEY-BREAST.

CHIMNEY-BREAST. The stone or brick structure projecting into or out of a room and containing the flue.

CHIMNEY-PIECE, *see* MANTELPIECE.

CHIMNEY SHAFT. A high chimney with only one flue.

CHIMNEY-STACK. Masonry or brickwork containing several flues, projecting above the roof and terminating in chimney-pots.

CHINESE ARCHITECTURE. Except for pagodas, Chinese buildings have always been of wood, and thus very few examples of temples and none of private houses or palaces survive from before the Ming dynasty (1368–1644).

Our knowledge of earlier buildings derives from paintings and low-reliefs. The loss is less grave than it would be in the West since Chinese traditionalism permitted little change in architectural principles or practice over the centuries. Excavations of neolithic sites reveal that from the beginning Chinese architecture was based on the column and that walls were used as protective screens rather than as structural members. Masonry vaults were used to roof tombs as early as the Han dynasty (206 B.C.–A.D. 220), but were not otherwise employed until the Yüan dynasty (1280–1368), when city gates were often vaulted. Temple roofs were invariably constructed of beams, whose length determined the width of the building.

Apart from some bridges (e.g., the Great Stone Bridge at Chao Hsien, Hopei, of C6) and some Buddhist cave temples of the C5 and C6 – which can hardly be described as architecture, despite their decoratively carved doorways and interiors – the earliest buildings of importance to survive in China are the pagodas erected in the T'ang dynasty (618–906). The form was introduced with Buddhism from India but soon modified. They are usually on a square plan with successive storeys of diminishing width: decorations are derived from the structural elements of wooden architecture. The most notable surviving example is the Wild Goose Pagoda, Ch'ang-an, Shensi (701–5). Hexagonal or octagonal plans were preferred during the Sung period (960–1279), when the classic type was evolved – a tall tower of uniform width with roofs marking each storey. Stone and brick were the materials used, but decorations continued to be derived from wooden buildings, especially the prominent and richly carved brackets. Many-storeyed pagodas of this type continued to be built until the C19, with few alterations save in the increasing elaborateness of the brightly coloured decorations. A fine example of the Sung dynasty is the South Pagoda at Fang-shan, Hopei (1117): a much prettified late example is the C18 Marble Pagoda in the Western Hills near Peking.

The earliest wooden building of importance to survive is the relatively small mid-C9 main hall of the temple Fo-kuang-ssu on Wu-t'ai-shan, which already foreshadows the essential elements of Chinese temple and palace architecture – columnar construction, with roofs of curving lines and wide eaves supported on intricately carved brackets. It is of one storey, as were all Chinese buildings except pagodas, though a purely decorative attic might occasionally be added to houses or palaces. The prototype of such buildings is already seen in the low-reliefs of the Han dynasty. Present-day Peking is a monument to the building mania and grandiose taste of the Ming. The Imperial City and the Forbidden City, with their rigidly symmetrical plans, gaily coloured palace pavilions and temples, though somewhat altered in later epochs, are a vast and imposing complex of courtyards, curving roofs, and white marble balustrading. The best preserved architectural group of the period is the Chih-hua-ssu temple, Peking, completed in 1444.

In the early C18 the Imperial Summer Palace, Yüan-ming-yüan (destroyed), was built under Jesuit influence in an imitation of Italian Baroque style. But this was a unique instance of Western influence; the traditional style persisted throughout the C19 and the drum-shaped Hall of Annual Prayers in the Temple of Heaven, Peking, one of the best-known Chinese buildings, was built as late as 1896. A change came after the Republican revolution of 1911, and European styles were adopted (e.g., the lecture hall of Nanking University in a pidgin-English neo-Georgian style). In the 1920s there was a so-called Chinese renaissance, when Chinese decorative features were applied to otherwise European-style buildings: the Municipal Government Building, Shanghai (1930), is among the worst examples, the Chung Sheng Hospital, Shanghai, (1937), among the best. Since 1949 the INTERNATIONAL MODERN style has won increased support. The Chinese preference for single-storey buildings has been abandoned in favour of tall blocks, though these are limited to nine storeys in Peking for aesthetic reasons.

CHINOISERIE. European imitations or evocations of Chinese art which first appeared in the C17, became very popular in the C18 – especially in England, Germany, France, and Italy – and lingered on into the C19. Numerous PAGODAS were built in Europe. Of the larger buildings in the style the tea-house at Potsdam (1754–7), the pavilion at Drottningholm, Sweden (1763–9), the Palazzina La Favorita, Palermo (1799), and the interior of the Royal Pavilion, Brighton (1802–21), are the most important.

CHOIR. The part of a church where divine service is sung.

CHURRIGUERA, José Benito de (1665–1725). The eldest of three architect brothers, the others being Joaquín (1674–1724) and Alberto (1676–1750). They came of a family of Barcelona sculptors specializing in elaborately carved retables and began in this way themselves; hence their peculiar architectural style with its lavish piling up of surface ornamentation, now known as the Churrigueresque style. Some of its more fantastic and barbaric features may have been inspired by native art in Central and South America. José Benito settled early in Madrid as a carver of retables (e.g., Sagrario in Segovia Cathedral) and did not turn architect until 1709, when he laid out the town of Nuevo Baztán, the most ambitious and original urban scheme of its period in Spain. His brother Joaquín's best works date from the next decade, e.g., the patio of the Colegio de Anaya and Colegio de

Calatrava at Salamanca. The youngest brother, Alberto, was the most talented, but did not emerge as an architect in his own right until after the death of his two elder brothers. The Plaza Mayor at Salamanca (begun 1729) is his first great work. San Sebastian, Salamanca, followed in 1731, but seven years later he left Salamanca and resigned as architect in charge. His last works are small but among his best: e.g., the parish church at Orgaz (1738) and the portal and façade of the church of the Assumption at Rueda (1738–47).

CHURRIGUERESQUE STYLE. The lavish, over-decorated style named after the Churriguera family, though the term is often extended to include all the more florid, Late Baroque architecture in Spain and Spanish America, especially Mexico. Pedro de RIBERA and Narciso TOMÉ were its best practitioners in Spain where it was popular mainly in Castille.

CIBORIUM. A canopy raised over the high altar. It is normally a dome supported on columns. *See also* BALDACHIN.

CIMBORIO. The Spanish term for a LANTERN admitting light over a crossing tower (*see* CROSSING) or other raised structure above a roof.

CINCTURE. A small convex moulding round the SHAFT of a column.

CINQUEFOIL, *see* FOIL.

CIRCUS. 1. In Roman architecture a long oblong building with rounded ends and with tiered seating on both sides and at one end. 2. In the C18 a circular or nearly circular range of houses. 3. In modern town planning a circular road or street junction.

CITADEL. In military architecture, a fort with from four to six bastions. It was usually sited at a corner of a fortified town but connected with it, e.g., Lille or Arras.

CLADDING. An external covering or skin applied to a structure for aesthetic or protective purposes. *See also* CURTAIN WALL.

CLAPBOARD. In the U.S.A. and Canada the term for WEATHERBOARD.

CLAPPER BRIDGE. A bridge made of large slabs of stone, some built up to make rough PIERS and other longer ones laid on top to make the roadway.

CLASSICISM. A revival of or return to the principles of Greek or (more often) Roman art and architecture. The word 'classic' originally signified a member of the superior tax-paying class of Roman citizens. It was later applied, by analogy, to writers of established reputation; and in the Middle Ages it was extended to all Greek and Roman writers and also to the arts of the same period, though always with an implication of 'accepted authority'. The various classical revivals were thus attempts to return to the rule of artistic law and order as well as evocations of the glories of ancient Rome. Although most phases of medieval and later European art have to some extent been influenced by antiquity, the term 'classicism' is generally reserved for the styles more consciously indebted to Greece and Rome.

The first of these revivals was the CAROLINGIAN *renovatio* of the C8–9 – a politically, no less than aesthetically, inspired return to late Imperial Roman art and architecture. The Tuscan C11 Proto-Renaissance represents a somewhat similar attempt to revive Roman architectural forms. The few monuments produced under it exerted considerable influence on the earliest works of BRUNELLESCHI and thus the initial phase of the RENAISSANCE proper. But from the C16 onwards the Renaissance reinterpretation of antiquity was to exert almost as much influence on classicizing architects as antiquity itself. For it was during the Renaissance that writers began to evolve a classical theory of architecture based largely on the confused and confusing treatise of VITRUVIUS which had been rediscovered in

1414. Throughout the C17 architectural theory remained essentially classical, though practising architects often paid no more than lip-service to it. But there was a practical as well as a theoretical return to classical standards in late C17 France (notably in the work of PERRAULT and MANSART). And in early C18 England such architects as Colen CAMPBELL, Lord BURLINGTON, and William KENT led a return to classicism by way of Inigo JONES and PALLADIO. This PALLADIANISM has sometimes been interpreted as the first phase of the late C18 neo-classical movement.

This movement, generally referred to as Neo-classicism, began in the 1750s as a reaction against the excesses of the late BAROQUE and ROCOCO and as a reflection of a general desire for established principles based on laws of nature and reason. In art and architecture these also embodied the 'noble simplicity and calm grandeur' which Winckelmann regarded as the prime qualities of Greek art. Fresh attention was given to surviving antique buildings in Europe and Asia Minor. PIRANESI's etchings inspired a new vision of Roman architecture, emphasizing its formal and spatial qualities. Classically 'incorrect' motifs were rejected in favour of those more archaeologically correct. But the mere copying of Greek and Roman buildings was rarely practised and never recommended. Theorists like LAUGIER and LODOLI demanded rational architecture based on first principles, not one which imitated Roman grandeur.

These new ideas were bound up with a nascent primitivism – a belief that architecture, like society, had been at its purest and best in its simplest and most primitive form. This led to an appreciation of the severity of Greek DORIC, made possible by the publications of James STUART and others and by the discovery of the early Doric temples in Sicily and at Paestum – though for the more fundamentalist architects (e.g., C. A. Ehrensvärd in Sweden) even the latter were insufficiently plain, sturdy and masculine. It also led to the creation of an architecture of pure geometrical forms – the cube, pyramid, cylinder and sphere – which found its most extreme expression in the designs of BOULLÉE, LEDOUX and GILLY, and in buildings by SOANE in England, LATROBE in the U.S. and ZAKHAROV in Russia. But if few late C18 architects took neo-classical principles to their logical conclusion equally few remained entirely immune to them.

Neo-classical buildings are solid and rather severe. Decoration, including classical enrichments, is restrained and sometimes eliminated altogether. The orders are used structurally rather than ornamentally, with columns supporting entablatures and not merely applied to the walls. Volumetric clarity is emphasized both internally and externally by unbroken contours. The Baroque organic principle by which a façade is unified by interlocking its various parts (so that the wings flow out of the central block and the main storey into those above and below) is rejected in favour of an inorganic one by which the masses are rigidly defined and, sometimes brutally, juxtaposed.

In the early C19 these severe neo-classical ideals were abandoned in favour of styles richer in decoration, more picturesque in composition and more literary in their allusions to the past. In France, under the Empire, the richly luxurious and dramatically expressive Roman Imperial style was revived as propaganda for the régime. Architects once more played for effect rather than sought to express visually a high intellectual ideal. Thus the classical tradition survived, in Europe and the U.S. and in various European colonies in Asia and Africa, throughout the C19, but simply as a form of revivalism – whether Greek, Roman or Renaissance (*see* GREEK REVIVAL). And although many individual buildings in these styles are of high quality (notably those by BARRY, SMIRKE, PLAYFAIR, STRICKLAND, SCHINKEL, KLENZE, HITTORF, etc.) they show little further development. Ironically enough, the leading tenets of the neo-classicists (logical construction, truth to materials, etc.) were taken up and developed in an anti-classical way by the architects of the GOTHIC RE-VIVAL.

CLERESTORY (or CLEARSTORY). The upper stage of the main walls of a church above the aisle roofs, pierced by windows; the same term is applicable in domestic building. In Romanesque architecture it often has a narrow wall-passage on the inside.

CLÉRISSEAU, Charles-Louis (1721–1820). A French neo-classical draughtsman and architect who exerted a wide influence through his pupils and patrons, William CHAMBERS, Robert and James ADAM, and Thomas JEFFERSON. He also provided designs (not executed) for Catherine the Great. His own buildings are uninspired, e.g., the Palais de Justice, Metz (1776–89).

CLERK, Simon (d. *c.* 1489). Master mason of Bury St Edmunds Abbey from 1445 at the latest, and also of Eton College, *c.* 1455–60 (in succession to his brother John), and King's College Chapel, Cambridge, from 1477 to 1485. Of his work at Bury nothing survives; at Eton and Cambridge he continued work, that is, he did not initiate, and so his style remains unknown to us. He is named here as an example of the way distinguished masons were given responsibility in several places.

CLOCHER. The French term for a bell-tower.

CLOISTER VAULT. The American term for a domical VAULT.

CLOISTERS. A quadrangle surrounded by roofed or vaulted passages connecting the monastic church with the domestic parts of the MONASTERY; usually south of the NAVE and west of the TRANSEPT. *See figure 61.*

CLUSTERED PIER, *see* COMPOUND PIER.

COADE STONE. Artificial cast stone invented and successfully marketed in the 1770s by Mrs Eleanor Coade, and later by Coade & Sealy of London. It was widely used in the late C18 and early C19 for all types of ornamentation.

COATES, Wells (1895–1958). An English architect, memorable chiefly for his Lawn Road Flats in Hampstead, London (1933–4), one of the pioneer works in England in the massive concrete INTERNATIONAL MODERN style of the thirties.

COB. Walling material made of clay mixed with straw, gravel and sand.

COCKERELL, Charles Robert (1788–1863), son of S. P. COCKERELL, studied under his father and assisted Sir Robert SMIRKE. From 1810 to 1817 he was abroad, first in Greece, Asia Minor, and Sicily, then in Italy. Keenly interested in archaeology, he was excellent at classical and modern languages; in Greece he worked on the discoveries of Aegina and Phigaleia. However, Cockerell combined his passion for Greek antiquities with a great admiration for WREN, and the result is a style which is the English parallel of the Paris Beaux Arts style of about 1840: grander than before, fond of giant orders and sudden solecisms, yet still firmly disciplined. Cockerell is an architects' architect, and PUGIN hated him passionately. Among his buildings the following only can be referred to: the Cambridge University (now Law) Library (1836–42) with its splendid coffered tunnel vault; the Taylorian (Ashmolean) Building in Oxford (1841–5); various branch buildings for the Bank of England, whose architect he became in 1833 (e.g., those in Manchester and Liverpool, both begun in 1845); and a number of insurance office buildings (e.g., the Liverpool & London and Globe Insurance, Dale Street, Liverpool of 1855-7). He was Professor of Architecture at the Royal Academy, the recipient of the first Gold Medal of the Royal Institute of British Architects, and a member of the academies of Paris, Rome, Munich, Copenhagen, etc. He also wrote on the iconography of the west front of Wells Cathedral.

COCKERELL, Samuel Pepys (1754-1827), began in TAYLOR's office along with NASH. He acquired numerous surveyorships – Admiralty, East India Company, St Paul's, Foundling Hospital, etc. – but is remembered for his fantastic country house, Sezincote (1803), the first Indian-style building in England. Elsewhere he showed French influence of an advanced kind, e.g., west tower of St Anne's, Soho, London. In 1792 he restored Tickencote church in the Norman style, thus anticipating C19 restorations.

CODUCCI, Mauro (c. 1440-1504), a leading architect in late C15 Venice, was born at Lenna near Bergamo, and had settled in Venice by 1469. Like his rival LOMBARDO he achieved (though rather less successfully) a synthesis between the Renaissance and Veneto-Byzantine style with its rich surface decoration and mysterious spatial effects. His earliest known work is S. Michele in Isola (1469), the first Renaissance church in Venice, with a façade derived from ALBERTI's Tempio Malatestiano but capped by a semicircular pediment of Veneto-Byzantine inspiration. Between 1480 and 1500 he completed S. Zaccaria, with its very tall façade on which columns and niches are piled up on one another, and with classical ornament in most unclassical profusion. He was more restrained in S. Giovanni Crisostomo (1497-1504), the first

centrally planned church in Venice (cross-in-square). His main domestic building is Palazzo Vendramin-Calergi (c. 1500), with round-headed windows and rich marble cladding. He also designed the clock-tower and Procuratie Vecchie in Piazza S. Marco (1496-1500).

COFFERING. Decoration of a ceiling, a vault, or an arch SOFFIT, consisting of sunken square or polygonal ornamental panels. *See also* CAISSON *and* LACUNAR.

COLLAR-BEAM, *see* ROOF.

COLONIA, Juan, Simón, Francisco, *see* SIMÓN DE COLONIA.

COLONNADE. A row of columns carrying an entablature or arches.

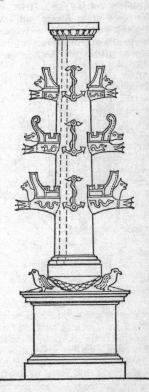

Fig. 29. Columna rostrata

COLOSSAL ORDER. Any ORDER whose columns rise from the ground through several storeys, sometimes called a giant order.

COLUMN. An upright member, circular in plan and usually slightly tapering; in classical architecture it consists of base, SHAFT, and CAPITAL. It is designed to carry an ENTABLATURE or other load, but is also used ornamentally in isolation. *See figure 64.*

COLUMNA ROSTRATA (or ROSTRAL COLUMN). In Roman architecture, an ornamental column decorated with ships' prows to celebrate a naval victory. *See figure 29.*

COMMON RAFTER, *see* ROOF.

COMMUNION TABLE, *see* ALTAR.

COMPOSITE ORDER, *see* ORDER.

COMPOUND PIER. A pier with several SHAFTS, attached or detached, or demi-shafts against the faces of it; also called a *clustered* pier. *See figure 30.*

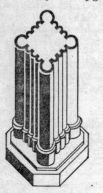

Fig. 30. Compound pier

CONCH. A semicircular niche surmounted by a half-dome.

CONCRETE. Cement mixed with coarse and fine aggregate (such as pebbles, crushed stone, brick), sand, and water in specific proportions. In some form it has been used for more than two thousand years, especially by the Romans. The discovery of Portland Cement in 1824 led to the great developments during the C19, and its use in structures of all kinds has largely revolutionized the shape of building today. *See also* PRECAST, PRESTRESSED, and REINFORCED CONCRETE.

CONFESSIO. In early medieval churches a subterranean chamber or recess located below or near the altar and sheltering a relic.

CONSOLE. An ornamental bracket with a compound curved outline and usually of greater height than projection. *See* ANCONES, BRACKET, CORBEL, MODILLION.

CONURBATION. A term used in town planning to denote a group of towns linked together geographically, and possibly by their function, e.g., the towns of the Black Country or the Potteries. The word was first used by Patrick GEDDES about 1910.

COPING. A capping or covering to a wall, either flat or sloping to throw off water.

CORBEL. A projecting block, usually of stone, supporting a beam or other horizontal member. *See figure 69.*

CORBEL TABLE. A range of CORBELS running just below the eaves; often found in Norman buildings.

CORBELLING. Brick or masonry courses, each built out beyond the one below like a series of corbels, to support a BARTIZAN, CHIMNEY-STACK, projecting window, etc.

CORBIE STEPS (or CROW STEPS). Steps on the COPING of a gable, used in Flanders, Holland, North Germany and East Anglia, and also in C16 and C17 Scotland.

CORDEMOY, J. L. de. An early Neo-classical theorist about whom very little is known except that he was a priest (prior of St Nicholas at La Ferté-sous-Jouars) and was not, as is sometimes said, identical with L. G. de Cordemoy (1651–1722). His *Nouveau traité de toute l'architecture* (1706) was the first to preach truth and simplicity in architecture and to insist that the purpose of a building should be expressed in its form. His ideas anticipated and probably influenced those of LAUGIER and LODOLI.

CORDON. In military architecture, the rounded stone moulding or band below the parapet of the revetment of the rampart, going all round the fort.

CORINTHIAN ORDER, *see* ORDER.

CORNICE. In classical architecture, the top, projecting section of an ENTABLATURE; also any projecting ornamental moulding along the top of a building, wall, arch, etc., finishing or crowning it. *See figures 42 and 64.*

CORONA. The vertical-faced projection in the upper part of a CORNICE, above the BED MOULDING and below the CYMATIUM, with its SOFFIT or under-surface recessed to form a drip.

CORPS DE LOGIS. The French term for the main buildings as distinct from the wings or pavilions.

CORTILE. The Italian term for a courtyard, usually internal and surrounded by ARCADES.

CORTONA, Pietro Berrettini da (1596–1669), painter and architect, second only to BERNINI in the history of Roman Baroque art, was born at Cortona, the son of a stone mason. Apprenticed to the undistinguished Florentine painter Commodi, he went with him to Rome *c.* 1612 and settled there. He can have received only superficial training in architecture, if any at all. First patronized by the Sacchetti family, for whom he designed the Villa del Pigneto (1626–36, now destroyed), he was soon taken up by Cardinal Francesco Barberini and his cultivated circle. Thereafter he had architectural and pictorial commissions in hand simultaneously. His first important building, SS. Martina e Luca, Rome (1635–50), is also the first great, highly personal, and entirely homogeneous Baroque church, conceived as a single plastic organism with a single dynamic theme applied throughout. It is notable especially for the pliable effect given to the massive walls by breaking them up with giant columns: these are not used to define bays or space, as they would have been by a Renaissance architect, but to stimulate the plastic sense. The decoration is extremely rich, even eccentric (e.g., the wildly undulating forms of the dome coffering), with here and there Florentine Mannerist traits. In contrast to Bernini he excluded figure sculpture entirely; he also excluded colour and had the interior painted white throughout.

His use of concave and convex forms in the façade of S. Maria della Pace, Rome (1656–7), is typically Baroque. More original is his application of theatre design to the *piazza*: he treated it as an auditorium, the side entrances being arranged as if they were stage doors and the flanking houses as if they were boxes. The gradual elimination of Mannerist elements from his style and his tendency towards Roman simplicity, gravity, and monumentality are apparent in the façade of S. Maria in Via Lata, Rome (1658–62). Comparison between his early and late works, notably the dome of S. Carlo al Corso, Rome (begun 1668), illustrates his remarkable progress from eccentricity and complexity, with effervescent decoration, to serene classical magnificence. Most of his grander and more ambitious schemes remained on paper (Chiesa Nuova di S. Filippo, Florence; Palazzo Chigi, Rome; Louvre, Paris). Though equally great as painter and architect he said that he regarded architecture only as a pastime.

COSMATI WORK. Decorative work in marble with inlays of coloured stones, mosaic, glass, gilding, etc., much employed in Italian Romanesque architecture, especially in and around Rome and Naples, C12–13. Roman marble workers of this period were known collectively as the Cosmati from the name Cosma, which recurs in several families of marble workers.

COSTA, Lucio, born 1902 at Toulon in France. Brazilian architect, planner, and architectural historian (in which capacity he works in the Commission for Ancient Monuments). An example of his excellent architectural work is the block of flats in the Eduardo Guinle Park at Rio (1948–54). As a planner he suddenly rose to fame by winning the competition for Brasilia, the new capital (Nova-Cap) of Brazil, in 1957. The plan is a formal one, yet not at all formal in the Beaux Arts sense. It has the shape of a bow and arrow or a bird, the head being the square with the two houses of parliament and the parliamentary offices, the tail being the railway station. Close to this are sites for light industry; nearer the head, but on the way along the straight monumental axis towards the station, follows the quarter of hotels, banks, theatres, etc., which lies at the junction of body and wings. The long curved wings (or the bow proper) are for housing; this area is divided into large square blocks, called *superquadre*, each with its freely arranged high slabs of flats, schools, church, etc.

COTTAGE ORNÉ. An artfully rustic building, usually of asymmetrical plan, often with a thatched roof, much use of fancy WEATHERBOARDING, and very rough-hewn wooden columns. It was a product of the picturesque cult of the late C18 and early C19 in England: an entire village of such cottages was built by NASH at Blaise Hamlet (1811). It might serve merely as an ornament to a park or as a lodge or farm labourer's house, but several, intended for the gentry, were built on a fairly large scale. Papworth's *Designs for Rural Residences* (1818) includes numerous designs.

COTTE, Robert de (1656–1735), an early Rococo architect, was instrumental in the diffusion abroad, especially in Germany, of French architectural and decorative fashions. He began under his brother-in-law J. HARDOUIN-MANSART, who established him professionally and whom he eventually succeeded as *premier architecte* (1709). His Parisian *hôtels* date from 1700 onwards, the most notable among those that survive being the Hôtel de Bouvallais (*c.* 1717) and the redecoration of François Mansart's Hôtel de la Vrillière, in which the gallery (*c.* 1719) is a Rococo masterpiece. He also worked extensively outside Paris (e.g., Palais Rohan, Strasbourg), and was frequently consulted by German patrons, for extensions to the *château* at Bonn and for Schloss Clemensruhe at Poppelsdorf, for example; but his designs or advice were not always accepted (e.g., at Schloss Brühl, Schloss Schleissheim, and the Residenz at Würzburg).

COUPLED ROOF, *see* ROOF.

COVARRUBIAS, Alonso de (1488–1570), was a mason and decorative sculptor in a limpid, playful Early Renaissance style, though for structural members he still adhered to the Gothic tradition. He appears first as one of the nine consultants for Salamanca Cathedral in 1512, a sign of remarkably early recognition. From 1515 he did decorative work at Sigüenza. The church of the Piedad at Guadalajara (1526) is now in ruins, but the Chapel of the New Kings at Toledo Cathedral (1531–4) survives complete and is a delightful work. The fine staircase of the Archbishop's Palace at Alcalá is of *c.* 1530, the richly tunnel-vaulted Sacristy at Sigüenza of 1532–4. Covarrubias was master mason of Toledo Cathedral and architect to the royal castles (1537 etc.); see the courtyard of the Alcázar at Toledo.

COVER FILLET. A moulded strip used to cover a joint in panelling, etc.

COVING. 1. The large concave moulding produced by the sloped or arched junction of a wall and ceiling. 2. In the case of ROOD SCREENS the concave curve supporting the projecting ROOD LOFT.

COWL. A metal covering, like a monk's hood, fixed over a chimney or other vent, and revolving with the wind to improve ventilation.

CRADLE ROOF, *see* ROOF.

CREDENCE. A small table or shelf near the altar, on which the Sacraments are placed.

CRENELLATION, *see* BATTLEMENT.

CREPIDOMA. The stepped base of a Greek temple.

CRESCENT. A concave row of houses. It was invented by John WOOD the younger at the Royal Crescent, Bath (1761–5); John CARR followed with his Crescent at Buxton (1779–84) which combined Wood's invention of a monumental residential crescent with an arcaded ground floor.

CREST, CRESTING. An ornamental finish along the top of a screen, wall, or roof; usually decorated and sometimes perforated.

CRETAN AND MYCENAEAN ARCHITECTURE. Excavations have revealed the earliest examples of European architecture at Knossos and Phaestos in Crete. Although many of the discoveries are of controversial significance, and most of the proposed reconstructions are unconvincing, enough survives to reveal certain general characteristics. At both Knossos and Phaestos there were elaborate palaces, richly coloured and decorated with selinite revetments, destroyed in the (probably seismic) catastrophe of *c.* 1700 B.C. which marks the first break in Cretan history. The palaces built to replace them were more carefully integrated with the surrounding landscapes; they had hanging gardens, cool courtyards, and colonnaded walks. Planning seems to have been wilfully asymmetrical, and long corridors linked a bewildering series of tiny rooms with the grand MEGARA and pillared halls. Decorations proliferated, and both interiors and exteriors were boldly and brightly painted in a manner which must have been almost jazzy. Another dramatic destruction occurred *c.* 1400 B.C.; shortly afterwards Crete came under Mycenaean control.

The Mycenaeans of the Greek mainland developed their architecture under Cretan influence. They adopted the Cretan *megaron* and also the *tholos* or BEEHIVE tomb, of which the best surviving example is the so-called 'Treasury of Atreus' at Mycenae (C15 B.C.). But between 1400 and 1200 B.C., when the Mycenaeans held the upper hand in the Greek world, they produced an architecture of greater monumentality and sophistication. The great cyclopean walls surviving at Mycenae and Tiryns reveal their engineering abilities. They developed the fortified acropolis as the civic and religious centre of the city. They began to use stone sculpture (e.g., the Lion Gate at Mycenae) as well as painting for decoration and, for especially fine rooms, incrustations of alabaster and lapis lazuli. But their most important achievement was in monumental planning. Abandoning the haphazard systems of the palaces at Knossos and Phaestos, they enhanced the majestic impact of the acropolis at Mycenae by arranging a succession of courtyards, staircases, and rooms on a single axis. The Mycenaeans were overthrown and their buildings destroyed by incursions from the North in the C12 B.C., but three Cretan-Mycenaean architectural elements – the *megaron*, the acropolis, and the axial plan – were destined to survive in GREEK ARCHITECTURE.

CRINKLE-CRANKLE WALL. A serpentine or continuously snake-like curving or undulating wall.

CROCKET. A decorative feature carved in various leaf shapes and projecting at regular intervals from the angles of spires, PINNACLES, canopies, gables, etc., in Gothic architecture. *See figure 31.*

CROCKET CAPITAL, *see* CAPITAL.

CROSS VAULT, *see* VAULT.

Fig. 31. Crocket

Key: 1. Finial 2. Crocket

CROSS WINDOW. A window with one MULLION and one TRANSOM. *See figure 32.*

Fig. 32. Cross window

CROSSING. The space at the intersection of the nave, chancel, and transepts of a church; often surmounted by a crossing tower.

CROW STEPS, *see* **CORBIE STEPS.**

CRUCKS. Pairs of large curved timbers used as the principal framing of a house. They take the place of both posts of the walls and rafters of the roof.

CRYPT. In a church, a chamber or vault beneath the main floor, not necessarily underground, and usually containing graves or relics. *See also* CONFESSIO. The term Ring Crypt is used for semi-circular corridor crypts below the apse of a church. They are early medieval and the first seem to belong to the late c6 (St Peter's in Rome).

CRYPTOPORTICUS. In Roman architecture, an enclosed gallery having walls with openings instead of columns; also a covered or subterranean passage.

CUPOLA. A DOME, especially a small dome on a circular or polygonal base crowning a roof or turret.

CURTAIL STEP. The lowest step in a flight, with a curved end which projects beyond the newel.

CURTAIN WALL. 1. A non-load-bearing wall which can be applied in front of a framed structure to keep out the weather. There are now many types, manufactured from a variety of materials such as aluminium, steel, and glass; sections may include windows and the spaces between. *See figure 33.* 2. In medieval architecture the outer wall of a castle, surrounding it and usually punctuated by towers or BASTIONS.

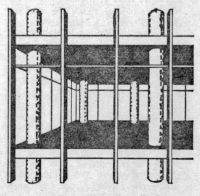

Fig. 33. Curtain wall

CURVILINEAR TRACERY, *see* TRACERY.

CUSHIONED FRIEZE. A frieze with a convex profile, also called a pulvinated frieze.

CUSP. Projecting points formed at the meeting of the FOILS in Gothic TRACERY, etc. *See figure 46.*

CUTWATER. The wedge-shaped end of a pier of a bridge, so constructed to break the current of water.

CUVILLIÉS, François (1695–1768). One of the most accomplished Rococo architects. Though he derived inspiration from the French Rococo, his decoration is much more exuberant than anything in France. His masterpiece, the Amalienburg in the park of Nymphenburg near Munich, has an easy elegance and gossamer delicacy which makes it the supreme secular monument of the Rococo. Born at Soignies-en-Hainaut, he entered the service of the exiled Elector Max Emanuel of Bavaria in 1708. As court dwarf, he travelled in the Elector's train through France, and in 1714 accompanied him on his return to Munich. Too small for the army, he began by working as a military architect and showed such promise that he was sent to Paris (1720–4) to study under J.-F. BLONDEL. In 1725 he was appointed Court Architect in Munich with EFFNER. For the Elector's brother he replaced SCHLAUN as architect at Schloss Brühl near Cologne (1728) and designed the beautiful little house of Falkenlust in the park. His first work in Bavaria was the decoration of the Reiche Zimmer in the Residenz, Munich (1729–37, partly destroyed). In 1733 he provided designs for the abbey church of Schäftlarn and for Palais Königsfeld (now the Archbishop's Palace), Munich. His next work was the Amalienburg (1734–9). It is a single-storey building with a large circular room in the centre which makes the garden façade curve outwards gracefully. The carved wood and silvered decorations in the main rooms are of exquisite refinement and the colour schemes are remarkably subtle – a cool watery blue background in the centre, citron yellow in one of the side rooms, and straw yellow in the other. In 1747 he provided plans for Wilhelmstal, near Kassel (erected by C. L. du Ry). His last major work was the Residenztheater, Munich (1751–3; partly destroyed 1944, restored 1958), one of the last insouciant extravaganzas of the Rococo, liberally decorated with exquisitely carved *putti*, caryatids, swags, trophies of musical instruments, and those frothy cartouches which characterize the style. In 1767 he completed the façade of the Theatine church of St Cajetan in Munich. He published a *Livre de cartouches* in 1738.

CUYPERS, Petrus Josephus Hubertus (1827–1921), the most important Dutch architect of the C19, studied at the Antwerp Academy and in 1850 became City Architect at Roermond. In 1852 he set up a workshop there for Christian art. In 1865 he went to Amsterdam, where he built his two most famous buildings, both in the Dutch brick Renaissance, and both restrained and without the exuberance of others working in the Northern Renaissance styles. The two buildings are the Rijksmuseum (1877–85) and the Central Station (1881–9). But the majority of Cuypers's works are neo-Gothic churches. It is hard to single out a few from the large total: they might be St Catharina, Eindhoven (1859); St Wilibrordus and Sacred Heart, both Amsterdam (1864–6 and 1873–80); St Bonifatius, Leeuwarden (1881); St Vitus, Hilversum (1890–2); and Steenbergen (1903). Cuypers also restored and enlarged the castle of Haarzuylen (1894–6).

CYCLOPEAN MASONRY. In pre-classical Greek architecture, masonry composed of very large irregular blocks of stone; also any polygonal masonry of a large size. *See figure 73.*

CYMA RECTA. A double-curved moulding, concave above and convex below, also called an *ogee moulding*. *See figures 34 and 42.*

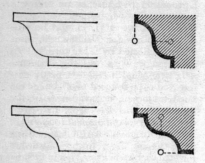

Fig. 34. Cyma recta; cyma reversa

CYMA REVERSA. A double-curved moulding, convex above and concave below; also called a *reverse ogee moulding. See figures 34 and 42.*

CYMATIUM. The top member of a CORNICE in a classical ENTABLATURE.

CZECHOSLOVAK ARCHITECTURE. In the Middle Ages architecture in Bohemia and Moravia formed part of German architecture. The oldest Christian buildings date from the C10 (Rotunda, Hradshin, Prague, excavated). The principal Romanesque buildings of the C12 and early C13 are St George at Prague, the crypt of Doksany and Strahov Abbey in Prague. At Třebič in the mid-C13 French Gothic influence begins to make itself felt. Its climax is Prague Cathedral, begun in 1344 by Matthias of Arras and inspired by Narbonne. It was continued after Matthias' death in 1353 by Peter PARLER from Swabia, and his work is the architectural parallel to Charles IV's great epoch in Bohemian history. Charles made Prague the capital of the Empire, added large, boldly planned areas to the city, and built not far from Prague his castle Karlstejn (1348–67). Peter Parler represents a stylistic link

with South Germany which was never to snap. With the flowing tracery in its windows, the complicated rib vaults, the flying ribs and the superb portrait heads on the triforium, Prague Cathedral blazed the trail for the architecture of the C15 and early C16 in Germany and Austria. Peter Parler was also the architect of the chancel of Kolin, added to a hall nave of *c.* 1280 – the first in Bohemia, and of course derived from Germany. Parler also began the cathedral-like church of Kutná Hora. Yet another important church of Charles' time is the octagonal Karlov church in Prague.

Of the other Late Gothic churches the most notable are those of Třeboň, Cesky Krumlov Olomouc, Košice, Plzeň, Most (Brüx) of 1517, and finally Louny (Laun) of 1529 etc. by Benedict Rieth.

For by then Benedict RIETH had reached his full maturity. His (though begun by M. Rajsek) are also the fabulously intertwined vaults of Kutná Hora, but his centre was of course Prague. On the Hradshin a predecessor, in the 1480s, had done the amazing oratory in the cathedral with its intricate decorative ribs in the form of branches and twigs. This may or may not be by Rajsek. Rieth's *magnum opus* is the Vladislav Hall on the Hradshin. This, begun *c.* 1487, combines another intertwined vault with windows of pure Italian Renaissance forms and other details in an insouciant mixture of Latest Gothic and Renaissance.

The last years of the C15 are an early date for Renaissance features in the East, later, it is true, than the years of King Matthias in Hungary, but earlier than the earliest pieces in Poland – and indeed in Austria and Germany. Only one generation later Italians (Paolo della Stella and others) built the Belvedere (1537 etc.) in the Hradshin gardens in the purest and most elegant Cinquecento style. It is of a precociousness as astonishing as

Rieth's work. However, with the one exception of Hvězd (Stern) near Prague, a star-shaped hunting-lodge of 1555 with exquisite wholly Italian stucco decoration, it remained alone, and the common development is more similar to the German and the Polish so-called Renaissance. The number of buildings and such features as portals is great. The Schwarzenberg Palace on the castle hill has shaped gables and diamond-cut ashlar blocks (1545 etc.), the Tennis Court on the Hradshin (1565–8, by B. Wolmut) rich sgraffito decoration. The same technique of decoration appears in a house of 1555 at Telc whose crazy gable is reminiscent of Poland. Among the most characteristic features are colonnaded courtyards, in two or even three tiers (Bučovice, Velké Losiny).

Count Waldstein, the ambitious general, led architecture back to the Italian grandeur and simplicity with his vast palace in Prague and especially its Loggia corresponding in height to three storeys of the palace (1623–34, by Andrea Spezza and others). Vienna has nothing to compare with it, but the two largest palaces of the second half of the c17 are in the same vein as contemporary work in Vienna (and Hungary). They are the Lobkowicz Palace at Roudnice (1652) and the Czernin Palace in Prague (1664), both by Francesco CARATTI. The Czernin Palace is twenty-nine windows wide and four storeys high, with no pavilions or other projections, but with the heaviest diamond rustication on the ground floor and serried attached giant columns above. The change from this massed display to the splendidly curvaceous Bohemian c18 style was due to two members of the Bavarian DIENTZENHOFER family: Christoph and Kilian Ignaz. Christoph's principal work is the church of St Niklas on the Kleinseite (Malá Strana) at Prague (1708 onwards). The source of the style is GUARINI,

who designed a church near Prague, and there are also close relations to HILDEBRANDT's work. The most characteristic features of Christoph Dientzenhofer's churches are façades curving forward and backward, interlocked oval spaces inside, and skew-or three-dimensional arches. A particularly bold motif is the diagonally set façade towers of Kilian Ignaz Dientzenhofer's St John Nepomuk on the Rock (1730). Among domestic buildings there is much influence from FISCHER VON ERLACH in the early c18 (Liblice by Alliprandi, 1699 etc.). A layout of exceptional boldness was that of Kuks, built from 1707 onwards for Count Sporck. A palace, no longer extant, faced a vast block of almshouses across a valley in which was a race-course, and extremely Baroque sculpture adorns the terrace of the almshouses and extends into the dense woods near by. The most interesting architect of these years was AICHEL or Santini with his remodellings of Gothic churches in a queer Baroque-Gothic all his own, though inspired by Rieth and BORROMINI.

The best examples of the turn to Neo-Classicism are the extensive Palladian mansion of Kačina (by C. F. Schuricht, 1802 etc.) and the beautiful Saloon of the Rohan Palace at Prague (by L. Montoyer, 1807). The style carries on to the colonnade, the baths, etc. of the Chotek gardens at Kroměříz (Kremsier) of the 1830s and 1840s. Little needs singling out between 1850 and 1900, foremost the National Theatre and the Rudolfinum of 1868 etc. and 1876 etc., both in Prague and both by J. Zitek and J. Schulz. Both are Italianate, the theatre richer, the Rudolfinum more restrained and refined.

For the c20 the names of J. Gočar and J. Chochol deserve record. In c. 1910–14 they designed in a weird Expressionist or Cubist way. The Modern Movement, inspired by

Germany, was going strong already before 1930. The Office of the Administration of Pensions by Havlíček and Honzik, designed in 1928, is as good as the best German work. So is the Electricity Company building of 1926 by A. Beneš and J. Křiž with its large, glazed inner courtyard. Only a few years later is the plan for Zlín (now Gottwaldov), the town of the Bata shoe factory. The style continues without much deviation in recent housing, office buildings and factories all over the country.

D

DADO. 1. In classical architecture, the portion of a PLINTH or PEDESTAL between the base and CORNICE; also called a *die*. *See figure 66*. 2. In modern architecture, the finishing of the lower part of an interior wall from floor to waist height.

DAGGER. A TRACERY motif of the Decorated style: a lancet shape, rounded or pointed at the head, pointed at the foot, and cusped inside. *See figure 35*.

Fig. 35. Dagger

DAIS. A raised platform at one end of a medieval hall, where the head of the house dined with his family circle.

DANCE, George (1741–1825), son of George Dance senior (d. 1768, architect of the Mansion House, London, 1739–52), went at seventeen to Italy for seven years with his brother Nathaniel, the painter, winning a gold medal at Parma in 1763 with some surprisingly advanced neo-classical designs. His early buildings are equally original and advanced, and might almost suggest an acquaintance with his more *avant-garde* French contemporaries, LEDOUX and BOULLÉE, because of his use of the elements of architecture as a means of expression rather than of abstract geometrical design. His first building after his return from Italy was the exquisitely pure and restrained All Hallows, London Wall (1765–7). This was followed by his daring and highly imaginative Newgate Prison, London (1769–78, demolished), the most original and dramatic building of its period in England. His ability appears to have

been quickly recognized, despite his unorthodoxy, for he was elected a founder member of the Royal Academy in 1768. His later buildings show no decline in originality or imagination: indeed, some of them anticipate SOANE – e.g., the Council Chamber of London Guildhall (1777, destroyed), in which the dome was treated like a parachute with fine lines radiating from the glazed opening in the centre, and the library of Lansdowne House, London (1792, completed by SMIRKE), which was lit by concealed windows in the semi-domed *exedrae* at either end of the long flat-vaulted room. After the turn of the century his style became increasingly austere and at Stratton Park (1803–4) and the College of Surgeons, London (1806–13), he foreshadowed the Greek Revival of SMIRKE and WILKINS. But his principal artistic legatee was his pupil Soane. (His unorthodoxy was exhibited in such works as the neo-Gothic S. front of the Guildhall, London (1788–9) and the Tudor Gothic exterior of Ashburnham Place, Sussex (1813–17, refaced 1853).

DANCING STEPS. Shaped steps on a turn, the tapered end being widened to give a better foothold; also called *Danced stairs* or *Balanced winders*.

DANISH ARCHITECTURE, *see* SCANDINAVIAN ARCHITECTURE.

DAVIS, Alexander Jackson (1803–92) was born in New York, joined Ithiel Town (1784–1844) as a draughtsman and became his partner in 1829. Town had already designed the Connecticut State Capitol with a Greek Doric portico in 1827. The partners now designed more capitols of the same type, but with domes a little incongruously rising over the middle of the longitudinal blocks (Indiana, 1831;

North Carolina, 1831; Illinois, 1837; Ohio, 1839). They are among the grandest of the Greek-Revival buildings in America. Their United States Custom House, New York (1833–42, now the Federal Hall Memorial Museum) should also be mentioned. But Davis could also do collegiate Gothic (New York University, Washington Square, 1832 etc.) and other versions of Gothic, and was versed in the cottage style too. At the same time he was interested in modern materials – he did an iron shop-front as early as 1835 – and was in fact an exceptionally versatile designer. He was one of the founders of the American Institute of Architects and of the villa estate of Llewellyn Park, New Jersey (1857).

DE SANCTIS, Francesco (1693–1740), designed the Spanish Steps in Rome (1723–5), the vast and fabulous external Baroque stairway of elegant, curvilinear design, mounting from Piazza di Spagna to S. Trinità dei Monti; a masterpiece of scenic town planning.

DE WAILLY, Charles (1730–98). Notable Louis XVI architect trained under BLONDEL, SERVANDONI and at the French Academy in Rome (1754–6). His talent ranged from interiors of a somewhat theatrical opulence (salone of Palazzo Spinola, Genoa, 1772–3) to the austerity of his most celebrated building, the Odéon in Paris (1779–85), designed in collaboration with Marie-Joseph Peyre (1730–85). It was twice burnt but little altered in rebuilding (1807 and 1818). De Wailly's later work is even more severe: château Montmusard near Dijon, the château de Rocquencourt (1781–6) and various private houses in Paris.

DECASTYLE. Of a PORTICO with ten fronted columns.

DECKER, Paul (1677–1713). German Baroque architect famous for his book of engraved designs: Fürstlicher Baumeister, oder: Architectus civilis (1711, 2nd edition with supplementary plates 1716). He worked under SCHLÜTER in Berlin from 1699, later settled in Nuremberg and finally, in 1712, in Bayreuth. Little is known of his work and he appears to have built nothing of importance. But his magnificent and fantastic designs, illustrating the most extravagant type of Baroque architecture and decoration (the latter derived from Berain through Schlüter) had considerable influence on later German and Austrian architecture, e.g., FISCHER VON ERLACH. Decker's posthumous Architectura Theoretica-Practica (1720) is a handbook to ornament.

DECORATED STYLE, see ENGLISH ARCHITECTURE.

DEINOCRATES, a Hellenistic architect, contemporary with Alexander the Great, appears to have been the architect, with Paeonius, of the temple of Artemis at Ephesus (c. 356 B.C.). He is credited with the town plan of Alexandria and various other important undertakings, some of them rather fanciful, e.g., the project to transform Mount Athos into a colossal statue of the king, holding in one hand a city and in the other a huge cup into which the mountain streams would be gathered and then cascade into the sea.

DELAFOSSE, Jean Charles (1734–91). French architect known mainly for his ornamental designs in a rather ponderous version of the Louis XVI style, with much use of heavy swags and chunky Greek frets. Two of the houses he built in Paris survive – Hôtel Titon and Hôtel Giox (nos. 58 and 60 rue du Faubourg-Poissonnière) of 1776–80, both discreetly decorated with his favourite type of ornament.

DELORME, Philibert (1500/15–1570), who was born in Lyon, the son of a master mason, went to Rome for three years, probably 1533–36, where he moved in high diplomatic-humanist circles but entirely misunderstood the point of Italian architecture. He was nothing if not original and as utterly French as his friend and admirer Rabelais. His buildings are notable for their ingenuity and sometimes outrageous experimentation. Almost everything he built has been destroyed, except for parts of Anet (Diane de Poitiers's house) and the tomb of Francis I in St Denis (begun 1547). The frontispiece of Anet (begun before 1550, now in the École des Beaux Arts, Paris) is a good example of his style, correct in detail and rather more monumental than that of his contemporary LESCOT. The chapel (1549–52) and entrance front (*c.* 1552) are still *in situ*. He had a great influence on the development of French architecture, partly through his books, *Nouvelles Inventions* (1561) and *Architecture* (1567), the most practical architectural treatise of the Renaissance, containing a complete manual on the erection of a house. The decorative part of the screen in St Étienne-du-Mont, Paris, with its pierced balustrades and spiral staircase (*c.* 1545), is probably by Delorme.

DEMI-COLUMN (or HALF-COLUMN). A column half sunk into a wall; a type of ENGAGED COLUMN, to be distinguished from a PILASTER.

DEMILUNE. In military architecture, a detached crescent-shaped or triangular outwork, built in the moat.

DENTIL. A small square block used in series in Ionic, Corinthian, Composite, and more rarely Doric CORNICES. *See figures 42 and 64.*

DIACONICON. In Byzantine architecture, a room attached to or enclosed in a church; in Early Christian times, utilized for the reception of the congregation's offerings and serving as archive, vestry and library; later used only for the latter functions (also, a sacristy).

DIAPER WORK. All-over surface decoration composed of a small repeated pattern such as lozenges or squares. *See figure 36.*

DIAPHRAGM ARCH. A transverse arch (*see* VAULT) across the nave of a church, carrying a masonry gable. Diaphragm arches divide wooden

Fig. 36. Diaper work

roofs into sections and were probably used to prevent fire spreading.

DIASTYLE. With an arrangement of columns three diameters apart. *See also* ARAEOSTYLE; EUSTYLE; PYCNOSTYLE; SYSTYLE.

DIE. The part of a PEDESTAL between the plinth and the cornice, also called the dado. *See figure 66.*

DIENTZENHOFER, Christian or Christoph, *see* DIENTZENHOFER, Kilian Ignaz.

DIENTZENHOFER, Georg (d. 1689). The eldest member of an important Bavarian family of Baroque architects. His main works are the Cistercian abbey church at Waldsassen (1685–1704, with A. Leuthner); the nearby pilgrimage church at Kappel (1685–9), built on an unusual trefoil plan with three minaret-like towers to symbolize the Trinity; and the façade of St Martin, Bamberg (1681–91).

DIENTZENHOFER, Johann (1663–1726), the son of Georg, studied first in Prague then in Italy (1699–1700). His Italianate cathedral of Fulda (1704–12) reflects BORROMINI's remodelling of S. Giovanni in Laterano. His most impressive church is that of the Benedictine abbey of Banz (1710–18), where his brother Leonhard (d. 1707) had built the conventual buildings; it has a complex ground plan based on a series of ovals and derived perhaps from GUARINI. His masterpiece is Schloss Pommersfelden, one of the largest and finest of German Baroque palaces, built in the remarkably short period of seven years (1711–18), with vastly imposing staircase (for which the patron, Lothar Franz von Schönborn, sought the advice of HILDEBRANDT and also contributed ideas of his own), marble hall, gallery, hall of mirrors, and numerous richly stuccoed apartments.

DIENTZENHOFER, Kilian Ignaz (1689–1751), the most distinguished member of the Dientzenhofer family, was the son of Christian or Christoph (1655–1722, a brother of Johann, who settled in Prague, where he built several churches, notably St Niklas on the Kleinseite, 1703–11, and St Margeretha, Břevnow, 1708–15). Trained first under his father, then under HILDEBRANDT, Kilian Ignaz soon became the leading Baroque architect in Prague. His style is sometimes a little theatrical, and he makes much play with contrasting concave and convex surfaces. His first independent building is the pretty little Villa Amerika, Prague (1720), with an almost Chinese roof in two tiers and very elaborate window surrounds. He also built the Palais Sylva-Tarouca, Prague (1749), on a much larger scale. His originality is best seen in his churches: the Thomaskirche, Prague (1723), with its intentionally jarring details; St Johann Nepomuk am Felsen, Prague (1730), with diagonally set towers on either side of the façade, a device he used again at St Florian, Kladno (c. 1750). His many other churches are notable for the variety of their Baroque plans – a circle at Nitzau, pure oval at Deutsch-Wernersdorf, an elongated octagon with straight sides at Ruppersdorf, and with convex inner and concave outer sides at Hermsdorf (near Hallstadt) and star shaped for the Chapel of St Mary of the Morning Star above Wockersdorf. He added a bold dome and towers to his father's St Niklas (1737–52). At the abbey church of Unter-Rotschow (1746–7) he showed for the first time a tendency towards classical restraint.

DIOCLETIAN WINDOW, see THERMAL WINDOW.

DIPTERAL. A term applied to a building with a double row of columns on each side.

DISCHARGING ARCH, see ARCH.

DISTYLE IN ANTIS. In classical architecture, a PORTICO with two columns between pilasters or ANTAE.

DODECASTYLE. Of a PORTICO with twelve frontal columns.

DOG-LEG STAIRCASE, see STAIR.

DOGTOOTH. Early English ornament consisting of a series of four-cornered stars placed diagonally and raised pyramidally. See figure 37.

Fig. 37. Dogtooth

DOME. A vault of even curvature erected on a circular base. The section can be segmental, semicircular, pointed, or bulbous.

If a dome is to be erected on a square base, members must be interpolated at the corners to mediate between the square and the circle. They can be pendentives or squinches. A pendentive is a spherical triangle; its curvature is that of a dome whose diameter is the diagonal of the initial square. The triangle is carried to the height which allows the erection on its top horizontal of the dome proper. A squinch is either an arch or arches of increasing radius projecting one in front of the other, or horizontal arches projecting in the same manner. If squinches are placed in the corners of the square and enough arches are erected on them they will result in a suitable base-line for the dome. In all these cases the dome will have the diameter of the length of one side of the square. It can be placed direct on the circular base-line, when this is achieved, or a drum, usually with windows, can be interpolated. If the dome has no drum and is segmental, it is called a saucer dome.

Another method of developing a dome out of a square is to take the diagonal of the square as the diameter of the dome. In this case the dome starts as if by pendentives, but their curvature is then continued without any break. Such domes are called *sail vaults*, because they resemble a sail with the four corners fixed and the wind blowing into it.

A *domical vault* is not a dome proper. If on a square base, four webs (CELLS) rise to a point separated by GROINS (*see* VAULT). The same can be done on a polygonal base.

An *umbrella, parachute, pumpkin* or *melon dome* is a dome on a circular base, but also divided into individual webs, each of which, however, has a base-line curved segmentally in plan and also curved in elevation. *See figure 38.*

DOMICAL VAULT, *see* VAULT.

DOMUS. In Roman architecture, a house for a single well-to-do family, as distinct from the huts or tenements of the poor and the apartment houses (INSULAE) of the middle class.

DONJON, *see* KEEP.

DOOR, *see figure 39.*

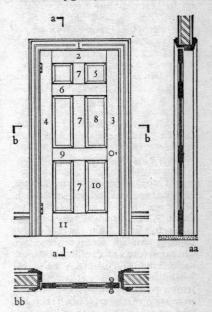

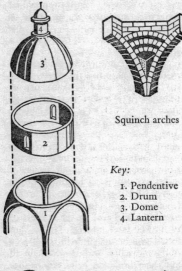

Squinch arches

Key:
1. Pendentive
2. Drum
3. Dome
4. Lantern

Sail vault; Domical vault; Umbrella dome

Fig. 38. Dome

Fig. 39. Door

Key:
1. Architrave
2. Top rail
3. Shutting stile
4. Hanging stile
5. Top panel
6. Frieze rail
7. Muntin
8. Middle panel
9. Lock rail
10. Bottom panel
11. Bottom rail

DORIC ORDER, *see* ORDER.

DORMER WINDOW. A window placed vertically in a sloping roof and with a roof of its own. The name derives from the fact that it usually serves sleeping quarters. Also called a LU-CARNE.

DORTER, *see* MONASTERY.

DOSSERET. The French term for an additional high block or slab set on top of an ABACUS and placed between it and the SPANDREL of the arch above; also called a *super-abacus*. Common in Byzantine work, and found in some Romanesque buildings. *See* IMPOST BLOCK, *see also figure 40.*

Fig. 40. Dosseret

Key: 1. Dosseret   2. Capital

DOTTI, Carlo Francesco (*c.* 1670–1759). A leading Late Baroque architect in Bologna. His sanctuary of the Madonna di S. Luca, Bologna (1723–57), is a masterpiece of dramatic grouping, with a domed church built on an elliptical plan and a boldly undulating colonnade sweeping out from the main façade.

DOUBLE-FRAMED ROOF, *see* ROOF.

DOWNING, Andrew Jackson (1815–52), the son of a nurseryman and from the beginning an enthusiast for landscape and plants, became America's leading writer on landscape gardening, cottages, and country houses, America's REPTON or LOUDON. His chief writings are *A Treatise on the Theory and Practice of Landscape Gardening*, 1841; *Cottage Residences*, 1842; *Notes about Buildings in the Country*, 1849; and *The Architecture of Country Houses*, 1850. For architectural commissions he was in partnership with Calvert Vaux (1824–95).

DRAGON BEAM, *see* OVERHANG.

DRAVIDIAN ARCHITECTURE, *see* INDIAN AND PAKISTANI ARCHITECTURE.

DRESSINGS. Stones worked to a finished face, whether smooth or moulded, and used around an angle, window, or any feature.

DRIP. A projecting member of a cornice, etc., from which rainwater drips and is thus prevented from running down the face of the wall below.

DRIP-JOINT. A joint between two pieces of metal on a roof, acting as a water conductor and preventing water from penetrating between the metal.

DRIPSTONE, *see* HOOD-MOULD.

DROP. The lower projecting end of a newel (*see* STAIR).

DROP ARCH, *see* ARCH.

DROP ORNAMENT. A carved ornament in the form of a pendant.

DROP TRACERY. A border of pendant tracery on the SOFFIT of a Gothic arch.

DROPS. English term for GUTTAE.

DRUM. A vertical wall supporting a DOME or CUPOLA; it may be circular, square, or polygonal in plan. Also the cylindrical blocks of stone that make up a column.

DU CERCEAU. A family of French architects and decorators. Jacques Androuet the elder (*c.* 1515–*c.* 1590) was the founder of the dynasty; he is, and always was, more famous for his engravings than for his buildings, none of which survives. The châteaux of Verneuil and Charleval were probably the best. But he was essentially an inventor of ornament, not an architect, and indulged in the most wanton and grotesque designs, generally in a Late Mannerist style. His first *Livre d'architecture* (Paris, 1559) reveals his personal vein of fantasy and lack of refinement. It had considerable influence, and some of the more practical designs may even have been built. But he was best known for his *Les plus excellents bastiments de France* (1576–79). His son Jean Baptiste (*c.* 1545–*c.* 1590) succeeded LESCOT as architect at the Louvre in 1578. In 1584 he became *Architecte ordinaire du roi* but had to leave Paris the following year as a Protestant refugee. He provided designs for the Pont Neuf, Paris (1578) and may have designed the Hôtel d'Angoulême, Paris (1584). His younger brother Jacques II (1550–1614) was, with Louis MÉTEZEAU, the favourite architect of Henry IV. He became *Architecte du roi* in 1594 and probably designed the pavilions of the Place des Vosges, Paris. Baptiste's son Jean (*c.* 1590–after 1649) became *Architecte ordinaire du roi* in 1617. He built the *escalier en fer de cheval* at Fontainebleau (1634) and designed two of the most typical Louis XIII Parisian hôtels – the Hôtel Sully (1625–9) and the Hôtel de Breton-ville (1637–43). They are both remarkable for the richness of their elaborately carved decoration – sculptural friezes, pediments with scrolls and masks, and allegorical figures in niches.

DUDOK, William Marinus (b. 1884), was architect to the small town of Hilversum near Amsterdam from 1916. He designed many schools and other public buildings, and his style appears to be complete as early as 1921 (Dr Bavinck School, Public Baths): exposed brick; asymmetrical compositions of rectangular blocks, usually with a tower; long bands of low windows. The style reached its climax with the Hilversum Town Hall of 1928–30, internationally one of the most influential buildings of its date. Of Dudok's later buildings, the Utrecht Theatre (1938–41) and the Royal Dutch Steel Works at Velsen (Ijmuiden, 1948) are the most notable.

DURAND, Jean-Nicolas-Louis (1760–1834), was probably the most widely influential architectural theorist of the early C19, not only in France but also in Germany. He was trained partly under BOULLÉE and partly under the civil engineer Rodolphe Perronet (1708–94, designer of the Pont de la Concorde, Paris). He built little (Maison La Thuile, Paris, 1788, destroyed in C19) but was employed on festival decorations during the Revolution and submitted numerous projects for public buildings to the Convention. In 1795 he was appointed professor of architecture at the new École Polytechnique, which replaced and was modelled on the royal school of military engineering, retaining this post until 1830. He published in 1800 *Recueil et parallèle des édifices en tout genre* in which public buildings of various periods and countries (including non-European) were illustrated according to his theory of modular proportions. But his major work is the two-volume *Précis et leçons d'architecture* (1802–5, frequently reprinted and translated into German) in which he stated a rationalist ideal of utilitarian functionalism. 'One should not strive to make a building pleasing, since if one concerns oneself solely with the fulfilment of practical requirements, it is impossible that it should not be pleasing', he wrote. 'Architects should concern themselves with planning and with nothing else.' Yet he abandoned neither the use of historical ornament nor the principle of strictly symmetrical planning.

DUTCH ARCHITECTURE. The oldest preserved buildings in the Northern Netherlands belong to the CAROLINGIAN fringe. They are the WESTWORK of St Mary at Maastricht and the Valkhof Chapel at Nijmegen which was built in strict imitation of Charlemagne's palace chapel at Aachen. The ROMANESQUE style proper appears first at Deventer, St Peter at Utrecht and the more impressive abbey church of Susteren (*c.* 1060 etc.), the latter clearly dependent on Werden and Essen. A little later is the grand westwork of St Servatius at Maastricht, again German in type. Even more patent is the German origin of the trefoil-shaped early C12 chancel of Rolduc (Cologne). The mature and late Romanesque of the Rhineland is represented by St Mary at Maastricht and the splendid Roermond Abbey, begun as late as 1219–20. It was Cistercian but shows nothing of the Cistercian architectural customs. Its nearest parallel is at Neuss, and, just as in such churches of the Rhineland, a general Romanesque mood is combined with French Early Gothic motifs.

The GOTHIC style was accepted late. The cathedral of Utrecht was begun in 1254. Its style is derived from that of Soissons via the chancel of Tournai only completed in 1255. The vaulting pattern of ambulatory and radiating chapels shows the dependence. The smaller Buur Church at Utrecht has the French High Gothic type of piers and was started shortly after 1253. Halls were occasionally built on Westphalian pattern (Zutphen), but the type of the major later medieval churches, the large number and size of which testifies to the prosperity of Holland, is basilican and remarkably simple, with an inner elevation of arcade and clerestory divided by no more than a triforium, a blind triforium or a narrow wall passage. To this type belong the major churches of Breda, Delft (New Church), Dordrecht, Haarlem, The Hague (Great Church), Leiden, all begun in the late C14. The New Church at Amsterdam followed later. All these churches have an ambulatory, but the majority leave out the radiating chapels. Some have very large transepts. The Great Church at The Hague has a specially airy hall nave, which continued inspiring architects into the C17. The only church of richly decorated interior and exterior is St John at Hertogenbosch, started again in the late C14. Of other typical features of the Dutch Gothic the widespread use of brick must be remembered, also with patterns in the façade (as in North Germany) and the great prominence of Late Gothic west steeples with pretty and daring openwork details (Utrecht Cathedral C14; Zierikzee 1453 etc. mostly destroyed;

Amersfoort St Mary later C15; Rhenen 1492 etc.).

Concerning secular architecture the earliest noteworthy structures are the circular castles or enclosures of Leiden, Egmond, Teilingen, etc. They are of the late C11 and C12, and some have had as their centre a keep. The most spectacular secular building is the Great Hall of the Binnenhof at The Hague, built in the second half of the C13 and more akin to Westminster Hall than to Continental great halls. For the late Middle Ages the lively façades of some town halls (Middelburg, 1452 etc.) and houses with stepped gables are characteristic.

Holland has some fine Early Renaissance monuments of the 1530s built by Italians, notably the tower of Ijsselstein church (1532–5 by Alessandro Pasqualini of Bologna) and the courtyard of Breda castle (1536 etc. by Tommaso Vincidor also of Bologna). Buildings such as the town halls of Nijmegen (c. 1555) and The Hague (1564–5) show how the new Renaissance motifs are absorbed into the native traditions. Soon, however, out of tradition and the enjoyment of the multifariousness of available Renaissance motifs and the modifications and distortions they were capable of, a gay, boisterous national style with ornate gables and extensive play with brick and stone mixtures was developed. It culminates in the work of Lieven de KEY at Haarlem (Meat Hall 1602–3, tower New Church 1613) and in Leiden (Town Hall 1594) and the churches by Hendrik de KEYSER in Amsterdam which are extremely interesting for their centralizing Protestant plans. This style, as exemplified by buildings like the Kloveniersdoelen at Middelburg (of c. 1607–10), had immense influence along the German seaboard as far as Gdansk (Danzig) and in Denmark. Architects from the Netherlands are found in most of these places.

At the same time as in England and

France classical restraint replaced these 'Jacobean' displays. The first signs of a change were Honselersdijk of 1621–c. 1630 and Rijswijk of 1630, both inspired from France and both by unknown architects. But at a time between these two country houses of the Stadholder Jacob van CAMPEN began his activity, and his are the most important classical buildings in Holland. His earliest is the Coymans House at Amsterdam (1624), and in the thirties and forties plenty more outstanding classical buildings appeared, especially van Campen's Mauritshuis at The Hague (1633), his magnificent Amsterdam Town Hall, now Royal Palace (1648 etc.), and his Nieuwe Kerk at Haarlem (1645). Other architects also contributed to this noble and restrained style: Pieter POST with the Weigh-House at Leiden (1657) and the Town Hall of Maastricht (1659) with its splendid entrance hall, Arend van s-GRAVESANDE with the octagonal Mare Church at Leiden (1638–48), Adriaan Dorsman with the round Lutheran church at Amsterdam (1668–71) and Justus VINGBOONS with the ambitious Trippenhuis at Amsterdam (1662), built as a private house for two brothers. Altogether no other town in Europe is as rich as Amsterdam in prosperous private houses. They allow us to see the whole development from the time of de Keyser into the late C18.

With the late C17 French influence became paramount not only in painting but also in architecture. The finest examples are William of Orange's Het Loo of c. 1685–7 by J. Roman and the French refugee Daniel MAROT, the beautiful town hall of Enkhuisen of 1686–8 by S. Vennecol, and then such remarkably ambitious private (or formerly private) houses as the Middelburg Library of 1733 (by J. P. van Baurscheidt Jun. of Antwerp), the Royal Library at The Hague of 1734–6 (by Marot) and Felix Meritis at Amsterdam. The latter, by J. Otten

Husly, is of 1778 and hence on the way to neo-classicism. The Pavilion at Haarlem for Henry Hope, the banker, followed in 1785–8. The best early neo-classical church is St Rosalia at Rotterdam of 1777–9 (by Jan Giudici). This is on the pattern of the palace chapel of Versailles, while the ballroom in the Knuiterdijk Palace at The Hague of the 1820s (by Jan de Greef) is on the pattern of the Vitruvian Egyptian Hall and of its English imitators.

The first third of the C19 was unquestioningly classical and more or less Grecian (Scheveningen, Pavilion 1826; Leeuwarden, Law Courts 1846). Then about 1840 neo-Gothic made a late start (Catholic Church Harmelen 1838, Gothic Hall behind the Kneuterdijk Palace The Hague 1840, Riding School The Hague 1845, former station Rotterdam 1847). Concurrently neo-Romanesque appears, though more rarely (Coolsingel Hospital Rotterdam 1842 etc.). As in other countries the Gothic soon turns from the romantic to the archaeologically accurate, and the best examples of this serious-minded Gothicism are the churches by CUYPERS. But Cuypers's fame is his large neo-1600 buildings, clearly disposed and resourcefully detailed (Rijksmuseum and Station Amsterdam, 1877 etc. and 1881 etc.).

From there a way into the C20 was found by the brilliant and typically Dutch BERLAGE. His Exchange at Amsterdam of 1897 etc. is in style transitional between historicism and the C20. From Berlage, whose detail tends to be arty-crafty and often very curious, one line went to J. M. van der Mey's crazy Shipping Palace at Amsterdam (of 1912–16) and then to the Expressionism of Piet Kramer and Michael de Klerk; another line went into the rationalism of the International Modern (OUD). Cubistic but fantastic is Gerrit RIETVELD's Schroeder house at Utrecht of 1925, cubic and rational and extremely well grouped the buildings of DUDOK. Oud's work during and after the Second World War represents a turn away from rationalism which took place in other countries as well. The most noteworthy Dutch achievement after the Second World War is the rebuilding of the centre of Rotterdam.

DWARF GALLERY. A wall-passage with small arcading on the outside of a building; usual in Romanesque architecture, especially in Italy and Germany.

E

EAMES, Charles (b. 1907). A universal artist. He designed furniture (the famous Eames Chair of 1940–41, developed in collaboration with Eero SAARINEN), he made films (Black Top, 1950), he made toys, organized exhibitions and built his own house at Santa Monica in California (1949). The house had a great success among architects. Windows and doors were prefabricated standard items, ordered from a manufacturer's catalogue. Yet, with these standard elements Eames succeeded in achieving a light, grid-like effect of Japanese finesse. The metal frames are filled in with transparent and translucent glass and stucco.

EARLY ENGLISH, see ENGLISH ARCHITECTURE.

EASTER SEPULCHRE. A recess with TOMB-CHEST, usually in the north wall of a CHANCEL; the tomb-chest was designed to receive an effigy of Christ for Easter celebrations.

EAVES. The underpart of a sloping roof overhanging a wall.

ECHAL. In a synagogue, the fitting enclosing the Ark or cupboard in which are kept the rolls of the Law; often of wood. An ornate example of the C18 exists in London at Bevis Marks, in the form of a large tripartite REREDOS.

ECHINUS. An OVOLO MOULDING below the ABACUS of a Doric CAPITAL. See figure 64. Also the moulding, covered with egg and dart, under the cushion of an IONIC capital.

EFFNER, Joseph (1687–1745), born in Munich, was the son of the chief gardener to Max Emanuel, Elector of Bavaria, who sent him to be trained as an architect in Paris under BOFFRAND (1706–15). In 1715 he was appointed Court Architect. He was in Italy in 1718. Between 1719 and 1725

he completed ZUCCALLI's Schloss Schleissheim and designed the magnificent monumental staircase. He also completed Agostino BARELLI's Schloss Nymphenburg outside Munich (1717–23), converting Barelli's Italianate villa into a German Baroque palace, and adding several exquisite little pavilions in the park; the Pagodenburg (1716, classical exterior with chinoiserie interior), the Roman Badenburg (1718), and the precociously picturesque Magdalenklause (c. 1726). At the Munich Residenz he was in charge of the new Grottenhof from 1715 onwards where the sparkling Ahnengalerie or Gallery of Ancestors (1726–31) was presumably designed by him. On Max Emanuel's death in 1726 he was succeeded as court architect by CUVILLIÉS and his only later building of note is the Preysing Palace in the Residenzstrasse in Munich (1727–34).

EGAS, Enrique de (d. probably 1534), was the son either of Hanequin of Brussels, who built the upper parts of the towers of Toledo Cathedral and the Portal of the Lions (1452), or of Egas Cueman, Hanequin's brother, who was a sculptor and died in 1495. In 1497 Enrique became master mason of Plasencia Cathedral – where work, however, soon stopped and was later continued by JUAN DE ÁLAVA and FRANCISCO DE COLONIA – and in 1498 of Toledo Cathedral. Enrique's masterpieces are the hospitals of Santiago (1501–11), Toledo (1504–15), and Granada (begun 1504 and soon abandoned), where the North Italian Early Renaissance appears early and at its most delightful. He was consulted at the Seo of Zaragoza in 1500, and at Seville Cathedral in 1512, 1523, 1529, and 1534. He was also connected with the designs for the Royal Chapel at Granada (begun *c.* 1504), and was the designer of Granada Cathedral (begun 1523, but soon turned Renaissance from Enrique's Gothic by Diego de SILOE).

EGG AND DART (or EGG AND TONGUE). An OVOLO MOULDING decorated with a pattern based on alternate eggs and arrow-heads. *See figure 41.*

Fig. 41. Egg and dart

EGYPTIAN ARCHITECTURE. As Herodotus pointed out, the ancient Egyptians regarded the dwelling-house as a temporary lodging and the tomb as a permanent abode. Houses were built of clay, sometimes but not always in the form of baked bricks; tombs and temples reproduced the elements of this domestic architecture on the grandest possible scale and in the most durable materials. Thus the bundles of papyrus stalks used as supports in mud huts were transformed into the majestic carved stone papyrus columns of the temples. No efforts were spared to secure the permanence of the tombs and their attendant temples by such devices as the use of the living rock and the steep BATTER of walls to resist earthquake shocks. The result is an architecture of inhuman, impersonal, and to this day daunting monumentality. Features peculiar to ancient Egyptian architecture include the PYRAMID, the OBELISK, the steeply battered PYLON, the symbolical lotus column, and incised relief decoration without any structural relevance.

The earliest large-scale work in stone is the funeral complex at Saqqara, built by the architect IMHOTEP for King Zoser, founder of the third dynasty (*c.* 2650–2600 B.C.) – a vast stepped pyramid almost 200 ft high, surrounded by a columned processional hall and other buildings to provide a habitation for the dead king and a realistic stage-setting for ritual, all enclosed by a niched limestone wall. The stepped pyramid was superseded by the regular pyramid, of which the most famous examples are at Giza, built for kings of the fourth dynasty (*c.* 2600–2480 B.C.). The collapse of the Old Kingdom (*c.* 2000 B.C.) created the first break in the history of ancient Egyptian architecture. There was a temporary revival in the period of the Middle Kingdom (1991–1650 B.C.): earlier styles were slightly simplified and less durable materials were used (as in the pyramid of Sesostris I at Lisht). But not until the New Kingdom period (1570–1085 B.C.) were great buildings once again erected. The most notable monuments are the mortuary temple of Queen Hatshepsut at Deir el Bahari (*c.* 1480 B.C.), with its pillared halls, colonnades, and gigantic ramps connecting the different levels; the magnificent temple of Amon at Karnak (*c.* 1570–1085 B.C.); and the many-columned temple of Amon-Mut-Khons at Luxor (*c.* 1570–1200 B.C.), with its succession of rooms of diminishing size and increasing gloom. The final revival took place under the rule of the Ptolemies, whom Alexander the Great had established on the Egyptian throne. Numerous temples survive from this period (323–30 B.C.), still built in the traditional manner but slightly more elegant and less crushingly inhuman, e.g., the temple of Horus at Edfu and the temples on the island of Philae. For later architecture in Egypt *see* HELLENISTIC ARCHITECTURE and ISLAMIC ARCHITECTURE.

EGYPTIAN HALL. A hall with an internal PERISTYLE as derived by PALLADIO from VITRUVIUS. It was especially popular with Neo-Palladian architects, e.g., Lord BURLINGTON's Assembly Rooms in York. It has no direct connection with Egyptian architecture.

EIERMANN, Egon (1909–70), was a pupil of POELZIG. By concentrating on industrial buildings, Eiermann managed to carry the INTERNATIONAL MODERN of the thirties through the Nazi years in Germany. Of his many post-war factories one of the finest is at Blumberg (1951). His international fame was established by the German Pavilion at the Brussels Exhibition of 1958, a perfect blend of crisp, clear, cubic, transparent blocks and their grouping in a landscape setting. The solution to the problem of grouping the new Kaiser-Wilhelm Gedächtniskirche at Berlin (1959–62) with the dramatic neo-Romanesque ruin of the old is more questionable. Other recent buildings of special importance are the offices of the Essener Steinkohlen-Bergwerke, Essen (1958–60); the wholesale warehouses, etc., for Messrs Neckermann at Frankfurt (1958–61); and the German Embassy in Washington (1961–3).

EIFFEL, Gustave (1832–1923), the French engineer, is famous chiefly for the Eiffel Tower built for the Paris Exhibition of 1889. At 1010 ft, the Tower was the highest building in the world until the Chrysler and then the Empire State Buildings were erected in New York. The Eiffel Tower in its immensely prominent position in the centre of Paris marks the final acceptance of metal, in this case iron, as an architectural medium. Eiffel's iron bridges are technically and visually as important as the Eiffel Tower (Douro, 1876–7; Garabit Viaduct, 1880–4). He was also engineer to the Bon Marché store in Paris (1876), and to the Statue of Liberty in New York, both of which have remarkable iron interiors.

EIGTVED, Nils (1701–54). Danish Rococo architect famous for the Amalienborg in Copenhagen, the finest C18 urban group outside France. Trained in Dresden and Warsaw under Karl Friedrich PÖPPELMANN (1725–33), he also visited Paris and Rome before settling in Copenhagen in 1735. As court architect he laid out an entire new section of the city with the octagonal Amalienborg (1750–54) and its four palaces set diagonally as its centre. He designed the Frederiks church on axis with it but his designs were greatly altered in execution. His Rococo interiors (1734 onwards) in the royal palace of Christiansborg were destroyed in 1794.

ELEVATION. The external faces of a building; also a drawing made in projection on a vertical plane to show any one face (or elevation) of a building. See figure 6.

ELIAS OF DEREHAM or DURHAM (d. 1245) was Canon of Salisbury and Wells and a confidant of Archbishops Hubert Walter and Stephen Langton, Bishop Jocelyn of Wells, Bishop Hugh of Lincoln, Bishop Poore of Salisbury, and Bishop des Roches of Winchester. He was present at the sealing of Magna Carta and at the translation of the relics of Thomas à Becket in 1220. He was, in addition, in charge of the King's Works at Winchester Castle and Clarendon Palace, and 'a prima fundatione rector' of Salisbury Cathedral. Rector sounds like administrator rather than designer, but he was also paid for making a vessel for Salisbury Cathedral and is called artifex in connection with the new shrine of Thomas à Becket; so he was certainly something of an artist, and it is likely that he was, like ALAN OF WALSINGHAM a hundred years later, a man capable also of designing buildings and of discussing details constructively with the master masons.

ELIZABETHAN AND JACOBEAN ARCHITECTURE, see ENGLISH ARCHITECTURE

ELL. In the U.S.A. a single-storey lean-to wing containing a kitchen. Ells were added in the C17 to WEATHERBOARDED, timber-framed buildings in New England.

ELLIPTICAL ARCH, see ARCH.

ELLIS, Peter (1804–84). A Liverpool architect now famous as a pioneer of the modern office building. His Oriel Chambers in Water Street, Liverpool, of 1864, with its façade glazed throughout in the form of angular oriels separated by very slender mullions, foreshadows the Chicago skyscraper of twenty years later. The back is almost entirely of glass, cantilevered out in front of the frame, itself of cast iron with brick arches. The back of his office block, No. 16 Cook Street, Liverpool (1866), is even more advanced, consisting of a wall and spiral staircase entirely of glass except for the thinnest of iron mullions.

ELMES, Harvey Lonsdale (1813–47). The son of James Elmes (1782–1862), architect and writer, a champion of the Elgin Marbles, of Keats, and of Wordsworth. James wrote on prison reform, and in 1823 edited the life and works of Wren. Harvey was a pupil of his father, and 1836 won the competition for St George's Hall, Liverpool. Even though, in its grouping and its massing of columns, it is no longer of Grecian purity, the building is convincedly classical. It was completed brilliantly by C. R. COCKERELL after Elmes's death from consumption.

ELY, see REGINALD OF ELY.

EMBRASURE. A small opening in the wall or PARAPET of a fortified building, usually splayed on the inside.

ENCAUSTIC TILES. Earthenware tiles glazed and decorated, much used in the Middle Ages and in Victorian churches for flooring.

ENCEINTE. In military architecture, the main enclosure of a fortress, surrounded by the wall or ditch.

ENFILADE. The French system of aligning internal doors in a sequence so that a vista is obtained through a series of rooms when all the doors are open. They are usually placed close to the windows. The arrangement was introduced c. 1650 and became a feature of Baroque palace planning.

ENGAGED COLUMN. A column attached to, or partly sunk into, a wall or PIER; also called an *applied column* or *attached column*. See also DEMI-COLUMN.

ENGEL, Carl Ludwig (1778–1840). German but active from 1815 in Finland. He knew SCHINKEL's work and had lived several years in St Petersburg. These are the two sources of his neo-classical style. His main buildings are the Senate (1818–22), the Old Church (1826), the University (1818–32), the Cathedral (1830–40) and the University Library (1836–44) all at Helsinki. The cathedral is strictly centrally planned, a Greek cross with four porticos outside, a quatrefoil inside. Above the centre is a tall dome. The university library has two splendid oblong reading-rooms with detached giant columns all round.

ENGLISH ARCHITECTURE. The Romans left England in 410. No datable document of English architecture exists of before the C7, but excavations have proved in places as distant from one another as Tintagel and Llantwit Major in Cornwall and Whitby in Yorkshire that early monastic establishments were of the Egyptian coenobitic type with separate detached huts clustered round a centre with the church and probably a refectory. At Abingdon it must have been the same, and Nendrum is an Irish example. The type reached England via Ireland. Of the same C7 are also the earliest surviving churches. They fall into two groups, one in the South-east, characterized by apses and a triple arcade dividing the choir from the nave, the other in the North, with long, tall, narrow nave and straight-ended chancel: the first group includes St Pancras and St Martin at Canterbury, Reculver, and Bradwell-on-Sea; the latter, Monkwearmouth, Jarrow, and Escomb. None of these has aisles, but instead they have side chambers, called *porticus*. Towers did not exist, but there were west porches.

Between the two groups stand Brixworth in Northamptonshire, larger than the others and with aisles, and Bradford-on-Avon in Wiltshire. But the typically Anglo-Saxon decoration of Bradford, with its pilaster-strips, flat blank arches, triangles instead of arches – the whole applied like the timbering of timber-framed work – is as late as the C10 and is indeed the most prominent decorative feature of later Anglo-Saxon architecture. Towers seem to have made their appearance in the C10 too; they are either at the west end or placed centrally between nave and chancel. Highly decorated examples are to be found at Earls Barton and Barton-on-Humber. Transepts also appear, and aisles become a little more frequent. That churches of timber which must have been the rule in the earliest centuries still went on as late as the C11 is proved by Greensted in Essex which can be dated c. 1013. Many churches of the later C11 have Anglo-Saxon side by side with Norman motifs; the mixture is called the *Saxo-Norman overlap*.

What is called Norman architecture in England is not the art of Normandy but that brought by William the Conqueror to England, i.e., really what on the Continent is called Romanesque. The Norman style in fact begins just before the Conquest, with Westminster Abbey as rebuilt by Edward the Confessor. This is a close parallel to such buildings in Normandy as Jumièges, Mont St Michel, and the churches of Caen: internally with arcade, gallery (ample or small, with large or subdivided openings towards the nave), CLERESTORY, and open timber roof; externally with two façade towers and a square crossing tower (Canterbury, Southwell). The volume of building was enormous. Nearly every cathedral and abbey church was rebuilt, and most of the bishops and abbots came from Normandy. But apart from the system of Normandy, there are also interesting

variations of divers origin: the mighty single west tower of Ely on the pattern of Germany; the giant niches of the façades of Tewkesbury and Lincoln, also on German patterns; the gallery tucked in below the arch of the arcade (Jedburgh); and the giant round piers of Tewkesbury and Gloucester, perhaps on a Burgundian pattern (as at Tournus). Ornament is prevalently geometrical (zigzag, CRENELLATION, chain, reel and similar motifs). Figure sculpture is rarely concentrated on the portals as in the French royal domain (York, chapterhouse of St Mary); its connections are rather with the West of France and with Lombardy.

In only one respect does England appear to lead in the European Romanesque style; in the vaulting of Durham Cathedral. For while England has no parallel to the mighty tunnel vaults of so many French naves and the groin vaults of so many German naves, Durham was rib-vaulted from the beginning (1093), and hers seem to be the earliest rib vaults not only of northern Europe but possibly of Europe altogether. While it may be that some of the elementary rib vaults of Lombardy are in fact of earlier date, those of Durham are without question infinitely more accomplished, and they and their descendants in France (Caen, St Étienne; Beauvais) led to the triumphant adoption of rib vaulting at St Denis and in the whole Gothic style, first in France and then everywhere.

The Gothic style reached England first by means of the Cistercian Order. Its first English buildings of c. 1130–60, however, though provided with pointed arches, have Burgundian Cistercian sources of a Romanesque kind, and where rib vaults first appear, they are derived from Durham rather than France. Cistercian churches go Gothic very gradually about 1160–80 (Roche), and a few non-Cistercian churches take part in this development (Ripon). But the real, the only fully convinced, beginning of Gothic architecture in England is the E. end of Canterbury Cathedral, begun by William of Sens in 1175 and brought to completion in 1185 by William the Englishman. Sens and Paris Cathedrals are the precursors, the retrochoir at Chichester and the nave of the Temple Church the immediate successors. Also immediately follows the retrochoir at Winchester, a hall choir, and this form was liked in England (on the pattern of Anjou churches), as it reappears at Salisbury, the Temple and Barking Abbey.

But real, thoroughly English Gothic, i.e., the so-called Early English style, begins with Wells *c.* 1180 and Lincoln 1192. Here there is more stress on horizontals than in France, there are straight E. walls (not radiating chapels), and the details also keep right away from the central French development. The chancel of Lincoln in particular with its crazy vault has no French parallel and begins a distinguished series of figured vaults which precedes those of any other country. The first star vaults are in the Lincoln nave, and the acme of this system is Exeter of the late C13. Less original but equally impressive are Salisbury of 1220–*c.* 70 and the E. transept of Durham.

Durham Cathedral lies on the castle hill and late C11 as well as C12 domestic parts survive. Altogether, although English castles are primarily castles with keeps, like the French donjons (the Tower in London, Colchester, Rochester, etc.), these keeps were not normally used domestically, but great halls, chapels, etc. were also built. A reform of the defensive system was brought about by the Crusades, in England as (a little earlier) in France. Emphasis was now laid on the defence not of one tower but of the whole wall with its many smaller towers, and often even on more than one concentric wall, on the pattern ultimately of the walls of Constantinople. Such castles are Dover, the Tower of London and the splendid late C13

castles of Wales (Conway, Caernarvon, Harlech, Beaumaris).

In church architecture the late C13 marks the change from the Early English to the Decorated style. This lasted into the second half of the C14, and is characterized first and foremost by the OGEE, a double or S-curve, which occurs chiefly in arches and in the TRACERY of windows. The other main characteristic is a maximum of decoration covering surfaces (e.g., in foliage DIAPERS) and encrusting arches, gables, etc.; the leaves are not naturalistic but stylized, with nobbly forms reminiscent of certain seaweeds. Spatially the Decorated style favours the unexpected vista, especially in diagonal directions. Principal works are the east parts of Bristol Cathedral (begun in 1298) and Wells Cathedral (*c.* 1290–*c.* 1340), the Lady Chapel and the famous Octagon at Ely (1321–53), and screens (Lincoln), funerary monuments (Edward II, Gloucester Cathedral; Percy Tomb, Beverley), stalls (Exeter), etc. No other country has anything as novel, as resourceful and as lavish as the English Decorated style, though when a similar direction was taken by Peter PARLER at Prague, it is likely that English influence played a determining part. The start at Prague was in 1353.

At that time, however, England was already turning her back on the Decorated. The Perpendicular style, beginning in London *c.* 1330 and reaching a full climax in the Gloucester chancel in 1337–57, is the very reverse of the Decorated. Perpendicular is characterized by the stress on straight verticals and horizontals, by slender, vertically subdivided supports and large windows, by window tracery with little fantasy and inventiveness. The signature tune is the panel motif, which is simply arched but with the arch cusped. This occurs in rows and tiers everywhere in the tracery, and almost as frequently in blank-wall decoration. In vaulting the Perpendicular first favours LIERNE VAULTS, therein following the inventions of the Decorated, and later FAN VAULTS, introduced about 1350–60 either in the cloisters at Gloucester or in the chapterhouse at Hereford. For the Early Perpendicular the chancel of Gloucester Cathedral is the most important work; for the time about 1400 the naves of Canterbury (c. 1375 etc.) and Winchester (c. 1360 etc., but mostly c. 1394 etc.), for the Late Perpendicular St George's Chapel at Windsor (1474 etc.), King's College Chapel at Cambridge (1446 etc. and 1508–15) and the chapel of Henry VII at Westminster Abbey (1502 etc.) and its predecessor, the chancel vault of Oxford Cathedral (c. 1478 etc.). But for the Perpendicular style parish churches are as significant as the major buildings so far noted. The grandest of these are in Suffolk and Norfolk, in Somerset (especially towers), and in the Cotswolds, demonstrating the riches which the wool and cloth trade made for the middle class. The Perpendicular style, once it had been established, went on without major changes for 250 years, and it can be argued that the Elizabethan style in England is more Perpendicular than it is Renaissance.

It was in Henry VII's Chapel that the first works in England in the Italian Renaissance style were put up, the tombs of the Lady Margaret and Henry VII by Pietro Torrigiani of Florence (1511 etc.). Henry VIII and his court favoured the new style which was impressively promoted in the crafts by Holbein's designs. But the Renaissance in England remained till about 1550 a matter of decoration, and it was coarsened as soon as it fell into native hands. The Protector Somerset in Somerset House was the first to understand Italian or rather by then French Renaissance principles more fully, and from Somerset House the Elizabethan style proceeded. It combines the symmetry of façades, as

the Renaissance had taught it, and Renaissance details, with Netherlandish decorative motifs (STRAPWORK) and the Perpendicular belief in very large windows with MULLIONS and TRANSOMS. Longleat (mainly 1568 etc.) is the first complete example: others are Burghley House (1560s–1580s), Montacute (c. 1590 etc.), Wollaton (1580–88) and Hardwick (1591–7). The first fifteen years of the reign of James I brought no change. Among the principal buildings are Hatfield (1608–12), Audley End (1603 etc.), Bramshill (1605–12). Plans of houses are often of E or H shape, if they do not have internal courtyards as the largest have. Windows are usually very large and may dominate the walls. Gables, straight or curved in the manner of the Netherlands, are frequent. Wood and plaster decoration is rich and often over-extravagant. Ecclesiastical architecture was almost at a standstill, and even the ample Jacobean-looking church furnishings are usually Jacobean only in style but as late as the 1630s.

By then the greatest revolution in English architecture had, however, already taken place, the revolution achieved by Inigo JONES. His Queen's House at Greenwich was begun in 1616, his Banqueting House in Whitehall in 1619. Jones's strictly Palladian classicism was continued by John WEBB, Sir Roger PRATT, and Hugh MAY. Another contributing factor was the domestic architecture of Holland, which influenced England first in a semi-classical form with Dutch gables. The Jones style was too pure and exacting to find favour immediately outside the most cultured circles. The universal acceptance of classical architecture came only with the time of WREN, but in domestic building the so-called Wren type of house – quite plain, with a middle pediment, a pedimented doorway, and a hipped roof – is not a creation of Wren. Stuart churches are a rarity.

They also become more frequent only at the time of Wren and are largely the result of the Fire of London. They are of a wide variety of plans, longitudinal or central or a synthesis of the two, and also of a wide variety of elevational features, especially in the steeples. The range of forms used by Wren is immense. It goes from the noble classical simplicity of the dome of St Paul's to the dramatic Baroque of the west towers of St Paul's and of Greenwich and the Hampton Court plans, to the brick domesticity of Kensington Palace and even to the Gothic Revival of a few of the city churches.

HAWKSMOOR, Wren's favourite pupil, and the ingenious VANBRUGH followed Wren's lead in working towards a synthesis of Baroque and Gothicism or a general Medievalism. The creation of picturesque landscaping in England about 1715–20 is closely allied to this medievalism which was much stronger than in any other country. The fact that the architects of the generation after Vanbrugh and Hawksmoor returned to the Palladianism of Jones is only at first sight a contradiction. Palladian houses and picturesque grounds must be seen as the two sides of the same coin. The architects in question are men such as Colen CAMPBELL, Lord BURLINGTON, and KENT (the latter, however, much inspired by the Vanbrugh style as well). GIBBS continued rather in the Wren vein: he is chiefly remembered for his churches, which had much influence in America as well as in England. Palladianism ruled until modified by the more elegant and varied style of Robert ADAM, but essentially the Palladian tradition maintained its hold until the 1820s (NASH's Regent's Park terraces).

Georgian architecture is classical in its major exteriors; but on the smaller domestic scale it still has the sensible plainness of the QUEEN ANNE style. Interiors are more elaborate than exteriors; here also Palladianism was the rule at first, but it was handled with greater freedom and verve. A brief phase of ROCOCO followed about the middle of the century: then the enchantment of Robert Adam's delicate decoration captured nearly everybody. Grecian interiors were rare until about 1820, but Victorian licence and exuberance are already heralded in certain Regency interiors (Brighton Pavilion).

But Victorian architecture is not all licence and exuberance. At the other end of the scale is the respect for the past, a historicism taken very seriously, as a matter of religious or social responsibility. The licence is usually paramount in domestic, the seriousness in ecclesiastic architecture. Not that historicism did not dominate domestic architecture too, but there it was taken in a less demanding way. Victorian church architecture is almost entirely Gothic, though in the 1840s there was a passing fashion for neo-Norman and neo-Early-Christian or neo-Italian-Romanesque (T. H. WYATT, Wilton). The revived Gothic was treated as a rule correctly (SCOTT); but some of the very best (PEARSON) were able to allow themselves freedom within the Gothic *ensemble*. The Gothic phase most readily imitated was first Perpendicular (Houses of Parliament), then from *c.* 1840 onwards, thanks chiefly to PUGIN, the so-called Second Pointed or Middle Pointed, i.e., the style of *c.* 1250–1300, and then from the seventies onwards, again Perpendicular (BODLEY). At the end of the century historicism began to break down, and Norman SHAW could use domestic C17 elements in a church (St Michael, Bedford Park) and Sedding yet freer, but always sensitively handled, elements.

In secular architecture the possibility of using Gothic side by side with Classical had already been handed down from Wren and Hawksmoor *via* the Rococo Gothic of Horace Walpole's Strawberry Hill and the romantic Gothic of WYATT's Fonthill. Other styles had also occasionally been tried, though not seriously (CHINOISERIE, also the Indian of the Brighton Pavilion). But Gothic was given publicly the same weight as Classical only with BARRY's Houses of Parliament (1835 etc.). At the same time Barry introduced a neo-Quattrocento (Travellers' Club) and neo-Cinquecento (Reform Club) and a neo-Elizabethan (Highclere, 1837). So by *c.* 1840 a wide range of historical possibilities was accepted. To them in the late fifties the French Renaissance with its prominent pavilion roofs was added.

Quite separate from all this was the great engineering development. England had been first in the Industrial Revolution (and the size of the new mansions and size and frequency of the new churches bear witness to England's unprecedented industrial and consequently commercial prosperity). The first iron bridges belong to England (TELFORD, BRUNEL), and the largest iron and glass conservatories (PAXTON, BURTON). In BUNNING's Coal Exchange (1846–9) iron and glass first appeared with architectural ambitions, and only two years after its completion Paxton's Crystal Palace was entirely of iron and glass, the whole 1800 ft length of it. But iron and glass in architecture remained after that confined to exhibition buildings, train sheds, and, on the fringe of architecture, to warehouses and office buildings. The functional self-sufficiency of these new materials and the shunning of over-decoration which followed from their convinced use, however, made them unpopular with the High Victorian architects. But from 1877 onwards William MORRIS fought publicly for simplicity, for truth to materials and against over-decoration, though he did so in a militant anti-industrial spirit. Hence those who were convinced by Morris's teachings were less attracted by an alliance with industry and commerce than by an application of Morris's principles to the human scale of domestic architecture. The leaders were Morris's friend Philip WEBB and the more richly endowed Norman SHAW. They, from the sixties onwards, built houses for a small section of the middle class which were fresher and aesthetically more adventurous than anything done at the same time abroad. Working-class architecture, on the other hand, i.e., housing provided by manufacturers and then by trusts (Peabody Trust), remained grim and was only humanized when HOWARD's garden city principle had begun to be applied to factory housing (Port Sunlight, Bournville). About 1900 England was still leading both in the planning conception of the garden suburb and in the architecture of the so-called Domestic Revival. This, in the work of VOYSEY, and the early work of LUTYENS, was beginning to move out of historicism towards a greater independence of period motifs and towards that simplicity and directness which in the commercial field had already been achieved by the CHICAGO SCHOOL.

However, as soon as radical innovation became the demand of the most go-ahead architects, England ratted. The revolution remained in the hands of, apart from the Chicago School, French, German and Austrian architects, and England re-joined the party of the progressives again only very occasionally in the later 1920s, a little more frequently in the 30s (FRY, YORKE, GIBBERD, TECTON), and wholeheartedly only after the Second World War. Two phases must be distinguished for the last twenty years, the INTERNATIONAL MODERN and the new individualism and expressionism (and BRUTALISM) sparked off by LE CORBUSIER's buildings at Marseille and Ronchamp. The former phase has its acme in housing, where the English tradition of landscaping made such a triumph as Roehampton possible, and also in schools, built to fixed modules from prefabricated parts and grouped with the same trained sense of landscape. For the latter phase see LASDUN, MARTIN, SHEPPARD and others. *See also* GOTHIC REVIVAL *and* GREEK REVIVAL.

ENSINGER. A family of South German masons: the two most important members are Ulrich and Matthäus. Ulrich von Ensinger (d. 1419) was sufficiently distinguished by 1391 for the cathedral authorities at Milan to want to consult him; he refused the invitation. In 1392 he became master mason for Ulm Minster (begun 1377). He changed plan and elevation boldly and designed the west tower with its splendid porch. The upper parts of the tower were built to a changed design by Matthäus BÖBLINGER. In 1394 Ulrich went after all to Milan, but was not satisfied or able to convince the authorities, and so left in 1395. In 1399, in addition to his job at Ulm, he was put in charge of the continuation of the west tower at Strassburg. Here it was he who started the single tower instead of the two originally projected and built the enchanting octagon stage. The spire, however, is by his successor Johann HÜLTZ. He also worked at Esslingen from *c.* 1400 onwards, and probably designed the west tower which was carried out (and probably altered) by Hans BÖBLINGER.

Ulrich had three sons who became masons. One of them is Matthäus (d. 1463), who first worked under his father at Strassburg, then became master mason at Berne, where he designed the new minster in 1420-1. From Berne he also undertook the job of master mason at Esslingen, but was replaced there in 1440 by Hans Böblinger. From 1446 he was master mason at Ulm. Of his sons three were masons.

ENTABLATURE. The upper part of an ORDER, consisting of ARCHITRAVE, FRIEZE, and CORNICE. *See figures 42 and 64.*

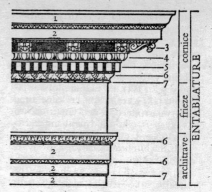

Fig. 42. Entablature: Corinthian

Key:

1. Cyma recta   5. Dentils
2. Fascia   6. Cyma reversa
3. Modillions   7. Astragal
4. Ovolo

ENTASIS. The very slight convex curve used on Greek and later columns to correct the optical illusion of concavity which would result if the sides were straight. Also used on spires and other structures for the same reason.

ENTRESOL, *see* MEZZANINE.

EQUILATERAL ARCH, *see* ARCH.

ERDMANNSDORF, Friedrich Wilhelm Freiherr von (1736–1800). Neo-classical architect inspired by the English neo-Palladians, then fashionable at Frederick the Great's Potsdam, rather than by Palladio himself. He decided to become an architect when travelling in England in 1763. His work is elegant and polite, very different from the radical and severe neo-classicism of his exact contemporary LEDOUX. In 1765–6 he travelled in Italy with his patron the Duke of Anhalt and met both Winckelmann and CLÉRISSEAU. He also visited England again. On his return to Germany he built the neo-Palladian palace at Wörlitz (1768–73). His later buildings in Dessau have all been destroyed: the Schlosstheater (1777), Schloss Georgium (*c.* 1780) and the Stables and Riding School (1790–91).

ERWIN VON STEINBACH (d. 1318) is one of the most famous medieval architects, because Goethe wrote his prose poem on Strassburg Cathedral, and especially its façade and steeple, round Erwin's name. According to an early inscription (which is not beyond suspicion), Erwin did indeed begin the façade in 1277. Documents refer to him under 1284 (?), 1293, and 1316. But during that time the steeple was not reached anyway, and even the lower part of the façade presupposes two changes of design. It is most likely that the happily preserved drawing for the façade known as B is Erwin's.

ESCARP or SCARP. In military architecture, the bank or wall immediately in front of and below the rampart. It is often the inner side of the fosse or ditch.

ESTÍPITE. A type of PILASTER tapering towards the base, extensively used in Spanish post-Renaissance architecture.

ETRUSCAN ARCHITECTURE. The main building materials were wood, rubble, clay (sometimes baked); stone was used only for the foundations of temples and secular buildings, for fortifications, and for tombs. As the Romans were anxious to erase all memory of the Etruscans very few of their buildings survive above ground level. Their most notable surviving constructions are city walls dating from C6 to C4 B.C. (Tarquinia, Chiusi, Cortona, etc.) – sometimes with hand-some if rather heavy arched gateways – though most of these are later (e.g., Falerii Novi, c. 250 B.C.; Perugia, c. 100 B.C.). After C5 B.C. temples were built on a plan derived from Greece, but with rather widely spaced, stocky, wooden, unfluted columns, wooden beams, and richly modelled terracotta facings and ACROTERIA applied to them. Underground tombs were usually hewn out of the living rock; their interiors were very elaborately painted and occasionally decorated with stucco reliefs (e.g., Tomb of the Stucchi, Cerveteri, C3 B.C.).

EULALIUS designed the Church of the Holy Apostles, Constantinople (536–45, destroyed), the prototype Greek cross-plan church with five domes. It inspired S. Marco, Venice, and St Front, Périgueux.

EUSTYLE. With an arrangement of columns two and a quarter diameters apart. See also AEROSTYLE; DIASTYLE; PYCNOSTYLE; SYSTYLE.

EXEDRA. In classical architecture, a semicircular or rectangular recess with raised seats: also, more loosely, any APSE or niche or the apsidal end of a room or a room opening full width into a larger, covered or uncovered space.

EXTRADOS. The outer curved face of an arch or vault. See figure 4.

EYE-CATCHER. A decorative building, such as a sham ruin, usually built on an eminence in an English landscape park to terminate a view or otherwise punctuate the layout. See also FOLLY.

F

FACING. The finishing applied to the outer surface of a building.

FAN VAULT, *see* VAULT.

FANLIGHT. 1. A window, often semicircular, over a door, in Georgian and Regency buildings, with radiating glazing bars suggesting a fan. 2. Also, less commonly, the upper part of a window hinged to open separately.

FANZAGO, Cosimo (1591–1678), was born at Clusone near Bergamo, but settled in 1608 in Naples where he became the leading Baroque architect. Trained as a sculptor, he also worked as a decorator and painter, and was interested less in planning than in decoration. His exuberant style is epitomized in the fantastic Guglia di S. Gennaro (1631–60), and in such effervescent façades as those of S. Maria della Sapienza (1638–41), S. Giuseppe degli Scalzi (*c.* 1660), and his vast unfinished Palazzo Donn'Anna (1642–4). His earlier buildings are more restrained and elegant, e.g., the arcades of the Certosa di S. Martino above Naples (1623–31).

FASCIA. A plain horizontal band, usually in an ARCHITRAVE, which may consist of two or three fasciae oversailing each other and sometimes separated by narrow mouldings. *See figures 42 and 64.*

FENESTRATION. The arrangement of windows in a building.

FERETORY. A shrine for relics designed to be carried in processions; kept behind the high altar.

FESTOON. A carved ornament in the form of a garland of fruit and flowers, tied with ribbons and suspended at both ends in a loop; commonly used on a FRIEZE or panel and also called a *swag. See figure 43.*

FIELDED PANEL. A panel with a plain raised central area.

Fig. 43. Festoon

FIELDSTONE. The American word for rubble.

FIGINI, Luigi (born 1903) and POLLINI, Gino (born 1903). Figini and Pollini in 1926 established with Terragni (1904–41) and a few others the Gruppo Sette, the first Italian group with an uncompromisingly modern programme. Their best-known works were done for Olivetti's at Ivrea (headquarters building 1948–50). The church of the Madonna dei Poveri at Milan (1952–6) shows the development from the rational International Style of the thirties to the freer forms of the second half of the century.

FIGUEROA, Leonardo de (*c.* 1650–1730), the creator of the Sevillian Baroque style, was the first to make use of the cut-brick construction in white or yellow walls surrounded with red trim so intimately associated with the city. His style is rich in an abundance of glazed tiles, patterned columns, SALOMÓNICAS, ESTÍPITES, tassels, foliated brackets, undulating cornices, statues of saints and caryatids and mermen. All his works are in Seville: e.g., Hospital de Venerables Sacerdotes (1687–97); Magdalena Church (1691–1709); Salvador Church (1696–1711); and the very ornate west entrance to S. Telmo (1724–34). S. Luis, the richest and finest Baroque church in Seville (1699–1731), is usually attributed to him. His son Ambrosio (1700–75) maintained his style in Seville (S. Catalina, 1732; chapel of the Cartuja,

1752–8; and Sacrament chapel in El Arahal, 1763–6), and the family tradition was carried on over the threshold of the neo-classical period by his grandson Antonio Matías (*c*. 1734–96?), who built the elegant campanile at La Palma del Condado (1780).

FILARETE, Antonio Averlino (*c*. 1400–69), built little but played an important part in the diffusion of the Early Renaissance style. Born in Florence, he adopted the Greek name Filarete (lover of virtue) fairly late in life. He began as a sculptor and executed a bronze door for St Peter's (1443) in Rome. In 1451 he was commissioned by Francesco Sforza to build the Ospedale Maggiore in Milan, which he designed on a very elaborate symmetrical plan. He built only the first storey of the central block, a sturdy basement carrying an elegant Brunelleschian arcade. While in Milan he completed his *Trattato d'architettura*, which VASARI called the most ridiculous book ever produced; it circulated widely in manuscript but was not printed until the C19. Based partly on ALBERTI, it is important mainly for its designs of ideal and hopelessly impracticable buildings and the elaborate plan for an ideal city, 'Sforzinda', which was to be blessed with every amenity, including a ten-storey tower of Vice and Virtue, with a brothel on the ground floor and an astronomical observatory on the top.

FILLET. A narrow, flat, raised band running down a shaft between the flutes in a column or along an arch or a ROLL MOULDING; also the uppermost member of a CORNICE, sometimes called a *listel*. *See figure 44*.

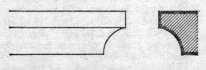

Fig. 44. Fillet

FINIAL. A formal ornament at the top of a canopy, gable, pinnacle, etc.; usually a detached foliated FLEUR-DE-LIS form. *See figure 31*.

FINNISH ARCHITECTURE. Although Finland lies between Sweden and Russia, Eastern inspiration remained very sporadic right down to the beginning of the C19. The principal influence came throughout the centuries from Sweden and North Germany. Nothing exists that is older than the C13, and the earliest buildings are village churches. Brick soon became the favourite material – apart of course from wood. In the village churches detail is elementary. The only large church is the cathedral of Turku (Åbo) which dates from the C14. Star vaults and ornamented brick gables came from Germany, detached wooden campanili (such as also exist in England) from Sweden. The extremely copious wall-paintings have their parallel in Sweden too.

Gothic plan types survived very long, and there is no Early Renaissance decoration. The turn to a classical style came only with the C17, and then again on Swedish patterns. The best early example is the manor house of Sarvlax of 1619, with giant pilasters already of a classical kind. Then in the late C17 the churches – being all Protestant – adopted cruciform and other central plans, again in connection with Swedish patterns (St Katharine, Stockholm). Wood, however, remained the favourite material.

The first climax of Finnish architecture came immediately after the country had become Russian. Helsinki was made the capital in 1812, and a plan for a new centre was made in 1817 (by J. A. Ehrenstrom). Thus C19 Helsinki is a planned town with streets as wide as in the Russian provinces and a large central square. The main buildings around this square are all the work of C. L. ENGEL. They are in a neo-classical idiom mixed of SCHINKEL and Petersburg elements.

They culminate in the Cathedral of 1830–40. But even as late as 1848 a large church in the country was still built of wood (Kerimaki).

The second climax falls into the years between *c.* 1850 and *c.* 1910. They are the years of a national romanticism. Like Sweden, like Russia, like Hungary, Finland looked to a romanticized and very colourful past for inspiration. Axel Gallén, the painter, (and of course Sibelius) are the best known representatives of this trend. In architecture it is exemplified by the National Museum at Helsinki, by SAARINEN, Lindgren and Gesellius (1901 etc.) and Tampere Cathedral of 1902–7 by Lars Spronck (1870–1956). They are quite irregular in outline, use assorted motifs of the past freely and emphasize boldly local materials. Saarinen won the competition for the Helsinki Station, and this (1906–14) is a blend of a rational plan with motifs partly curvaceous and fantastical and partly (already) rectangular. The latter motifs come close to those used in the same years by OLBRICH and BEHRENS.

Finland achieved independence at last in 1917. AALTO was nineteen then and the much less known Erik Bryggman (1891–1955) twenty-six. A mere twelve years later Aalto had, with the Paimio Sanatorium and the Viborg Library (Viborg was taken away from Finland by Russia in 1940), achieved international fame within the current Central European modern style. But Aalto was not just one of many. His strong personality had come through already by 1937, and in his work from 1947 onwards he is one of the leaders of a style of free curves, unexpected skylines, bold rhythms of glass and windowless walls. He likes to use timber and hard red brick. Side by side with him there are others, first Bryggman whose Cemetery Chapel at Turku of 1939 is as bold and novel as anything by Aalto himself, and then a younger generation led by V. Rewell

(1910–64; Toronto City Hall). Three more of the best in Finland are T. Toiviainen, A. Ervi and K. & H. Siren. The place to see the high standard of present-day Finnish architecture at its most concentrated is Tapiola outside Helsinki, a 'new town' of *c.* 17,000 inhabitants.

FISCHER, Johann Michael (1692–1766), the most prolific of South German Rococo architects, built no less than twenty-two abbeys and thirty-two churches. Though less gifted than his contemporaries NEUMANN and ZIMMERMANN, he had great sensitivity to spatial relationships and could obtain monumental effects. His masterpiece is the Benedictine abbey church at Ottobeuren (1744–67), with a fine soaring façade and magnificently rich interior frothing with effervescent decoration. The smaller church at Rott-am-Inn (1759–63) shows a tendency towards greater restraint and provides a perfect setting for the statues by Ignaz Günther. Other works include St Anne, Munich (1727–39), on an oval plan; the abbey church at Diessen (1732–9); the church at Berg-am-Laim (1737–43); the Benedictine abbey at Zwiefalten (1740–65), even larger than Ottobeuren and still richer inside; and finally, the Brigittine abbey church at Altomünster (1763–6).

FISCHER VON ERLACH, Johann Bernhard (1656–1723), a leading Baroque architect in Austria, was more restrained and intellectual than his rival HILDEBRANDT, but also more courtly and traditional. Born near Graz, he began as a sculptor and stucco worker, then went to Italy probably in 1674 and perhaps received some training in architecture under Carlo FONTANA in Rome. In 1685 he settled in Vienna. There he was eventually appointed Court Architect in 1704. His first building of note is Schloss Frain in Moravia (1690–94), with an imposing oval hall. Italian influence, especially that of BORROMINI, is very evident in his three churches in Salzburg, the Dreifaltig-keitskirche (1694-1702), Kollegien-kirche (1694-1707), and Ursulinen-kirche (1699-1705). His masterpiece, the Karlskirche in Vienna (begun 1716), is a unique design with no antecedents and no successors, but his Roman memories are again quite explicit, notably in the opening theme of a Pantheon portico framed by a couple of Trajan's columns, expressive of his conscious striving after imperial grandeur. His secular buildings include the façade and monumental staircase, with its monumental AT-LANTES, of the Stadtpalais of Prinz Eugen, Vienna (1695-8); the Palais Batthyány-Schönborn, Vienna (c. 1700); the Palais Clam Gallas, Prague (1707-12); the Palais Trautson, Vienna (1710-16); and finally, the Hofbiblio-thek in the Hofburg, Vienna, which he began the year of his death (1723) and which was finished by his son Joseph Emanuel (1693-1742). This library is one of the most imposing interiors in Europe and illustrates his imperial manner at its grandiloquent best. He assumed the title 'von Erlach' on being knighted by the Emperor. His wide scholarship found expression in his *Entwurf einer historis-chen Architektur* (published Vienna 1721), which was the first architectural treatise to include and illustrate Egyptian and Chinese buildings, and which thus exerted a great influence on various later architectural exoticisms.

FLAMBOYANT. The late Gothic style in France. In Flamboyant TRACERY the bars of stonework form long wavy divisions.

FLANK. In military architecture, the side of a BASTION returning to the courtine from the face.

FLÈCHE. A slender spire, usually of wood, rising from the RIDGE of a roof; also called a *spirelet*.

FLEUR-DE-LIS. French for lily-flower; originally the royal arms of France.

FLEURON. A decorative carved flower or leaf.

FLIGHT. A series of stairs unbroken by a landing.

FLITCROFT, Henry (1697-1769), was a protégé of Lord BURLINGTON, who procured him various posts in the Office of Works, where he eventually succeeded KENT as Master Mason and Deputy Surveyor. He was known as 'Burlington Harry'. Competent but uninspired, he was little superior to the 'imitating fools' who, according to Pope's prophecy, followed Lord Burlington's just and noble rules. His colossal west front at Wentworth Woodhouse (1735 etc.), the longest façade in England, illustrates the empty pomposity into which PALLA-DIANISM declined: Woburn Abbey is equally derivative (c. 1747). His town houses are more successful, notably 10 St James's Square, London (1734). St Giles-in-the-Fields, London (1731-3), is an unflattering imitation of St Martin-in-the-Fields.

FLORIS, Cornelis (1514/20-75). Primarily a sculptor and ornamentalist but also the leading Mannerist architect in the Southern Netherlands. He visited Rome c. 1538. The tall, grave and classicizing Antwerp Town Hall (1561-6) is his masterpiece. Other notable works include the House of the German Hansa, Antwerp (c. 1566) and the rood screen in Tournai Cathedral (1572). His style was widely diffused (and debased) by the engravings of Hans Vredeman de VRIES.

FLÖTNER or FLETTNER, Peter (c. 1485-1546). German Renaissance architect, sculptor, goldsmith and an influential ornamental designer. He published at Nuremberg innumerable engraved designs for furniture, arabesques, etc. In 1518 he was working at the Fugger chapel in St Anna, Augsburg, and later travelled in Italy before settling in Nuremberg in 1522. His rather fanciful version of the Renaissance style can be seen in the fountain in the market-place at Mainz (1526), but his masterpiece as an architect was the Hirschvogelsaal in

Nuremberg (1534, destroyed), the earliest and perhaps most accomplished example of Renaissance domestic architecture in Germany.

FLUSH BEAD MOULDING. An inset bead or convex moulding, its outer surface being flush with adjacent surfaces. *See figure 45.*

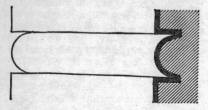

Fig. 45. Flush bead moulding

FLUSHWORK. The decorative use of KNAPPED FLINT in conjunction with dressed stone to form patterns, such as TRACERY, initials, etc.

FLUTING. Shallow, concave grooves running vertically on the SHAFT of a column, PILASTER, or other surface; they may meet in an ARRIS or be suspended by a FILLET. If the lower part is filled with a solid cylindrical piece it is called *cabled fluting. See figure 64.*

FLYING BUTTRESS, see BUTTRESS.

FOIL. A lobe or leaf-shaped curve formed by the CUSPING of a circle or an arch. The number of foils involved is indicated by a prefix, e.g., trefoil, multifoil. *See figure 46.*

FOLIATED. Carved with leaf ornament.

FOLLY. A costly but useless structure built to satisfy the whim of some eccentric and thought to show his folly; usually a tower or a sham Gothic or classical ruin in a landscaped park intended to enhance the view or picturesque effect.

FONTAINE, Pierre François Léonard (1762–1853), the son and grandson of architects, became Napoleon's favourite architect and was largely responsible, with his partner PERCIER, for the creation of the Empire style. He studied in Paris under A. F. Peyre, then in Rome 1786–90. Percier joined him in Paris the following year, and they remained together until 1814. Their decorative style is well illustrated at Malmaison, where they worked for Napoleon from 1802 onwards, Joséphine's tented bedroom being completed in 1812. They extended the north wing of the Louvre to the Tuileries, and built the beautifully detailed Arc du Carrousel (1806–7) between the Tuileries and the Grande Galerie. Their joint works also include the rue de Rivoli, Paris (1801); the fountain in the Place Dauphine, Paris (1802); and much restoration and decoration at the royal *châteaux* (Fontainebleau, Saint-Cloud, Compiègne, Versailles) and at the Louvre, notably the Salle des Cariatides. Their influence spread rapidly throughout Europe mainly by means of their publications: *Palais, maisons, etc., à Rome* (1798) and especially their

i: Detail of flowing tracery showing elaborate use of cusping

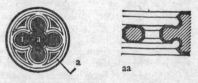

ii: Foil (aa: cusp in section)

Fig. 46

Recueil de décorations intérieures (1801). The most notable of Fontaine's independent works are the restoration of the Palais Royal, Paris (1814–31, including the Galerie d'Orléans), and the Hôtel-Dieu, Pontoise (1823–7).

FONTANA, Carlo (1634–1714), was born near Como but settled in Rome *c.* 1655. He began as assistant to CORTONA, RAINALDI, and BERNINI, working under the latter for ten years. His accomplished but derivative style is best seen in the façade of S. Marcello al Corso, Rome (1682–3), and in the many chapels he built in Roman churches: Cappella Cibo in S. Maria del Popolo (1683–7); baptismal chapel in St Peter's (1692–8). Less successful is the Jesuit church and college at Loyola in Spain. He restored and largely rebuilt SS. Apostoli, Rome (1702), and completed Bernini's Palazzo di Montecitorio, Rome, including the main entrance (1694–7). His secular buildings are undistinguished, e.g., Palazzo Spreti, Ravenna (1700), and Ospizio di S. Michele, Rome (1700–3). By industry and perseverance he became undisputed leader of his profession in Rome and was largely responsible for the classicizing, bookish academicism into which the Baroque style declined. He had an enormous influence all over Europe through his numerous pupils who included FISCHER VON ERLACH and HILDEBRANDT in Austria, GIBBS in England, and PÖPPELMANN in Germany.

FONTANA, Domenico (1543–1607), was born near Lugano, settled in Rome *c.* 1563, and became architect to Sixtus V (1585–90). His *magnum opus* is the Lateran Palace in Rome (1586), which displays his dry and monotonous style. He assisted Giacomo della PORTA in building the dome of St Peter's. In 1592 he settled in Naples, where he was appointed 'Royal Engineer' and obtained many large commissions including the Royal Palace (1600–2).

FORECHURCH, *see* ANTECHURCH.

FORMERET. In a medieval VAULT, the rib against the wall, known also as a *wall rib*.

FORMWORK. Commonly called *shuttering*, this is the temporary form that 'wet' concrete is poured into; it is constructed of braced timber or metal. When the formwork is removed, the concrete is found to have the texture of the material imprinted upon its surface. The formwork may be re-used if the type of construction is suitable, as in walls or repeating floor BAYS.

FORTRESS, *see* CASTLE.

FORUM. In Roman architecture, a central open space usually surrounded by public buildings and colonnades: it corresponds to the Greek AGORA.

FOSSE. A ditch or moat, whether dry or wet, used in defence.

FOYER. The vestibule or entrance hall of a theatre.

FRAMED BUILDING. A structure whose weight is carried by the framework instead of by load-bearing walls. The term includes modern steel and RE-INFORCED CONCRETE structures, as well as TIMBER-FRAMED (half-timbered) buildings. In the former the frame is usually encased within a FACING (or CLADDING) of light material; in the latter the infilling may be of WATTLE AND DAUB or of brick.

FRANCESCO DI GIORGIO MARTINI (1439–1501/2), a leading Early Renaissance theorist, wrote a treatise which, though not printed until the C19, exerted considerable influence, especially on LEONARDO DA VINCI, who owned a copy of it. He was born in Siena, the son of a poultry dealer, and trained as a sculptor and painter. Before 1477 he moved to Urbino and entered the service of Federigo da Montefeltro, who employed him as a medallist and military engineer. He wrote *c.* 1482 his *Trattato di architettura civile e militare*, based partly on VITRUVIUS (whom he translated or had translated) and ALBERTI, but showing a more practical attitude to the problems of architectural symbolism. Much of it is devoted to church planning: he produces a symbolic rationalization of the church with a long nave and centralized east end, and he also deals with the placing of the altar in a centralized church or tribune, stating the case for a central position to symbolize God's place in the universe, and for a peripheral position to symbolize his infinite distance from mankind.

His work as an architect is poorly documented. He probably contributed to the design of Palazzo Ducale, Urbino (perhaps the exquisitely beautiful loggia looking out over the surrounding hills). In 1485 he provided a model for the Latin cross church of S. Maria del Calcinaio, Cortona (completed 1516), a masterpiece of Early Renaissance clarity, harmony, and repose. He also provided a design for the austerely simple Palazzo del Comune, Jesi (1486; but much altered). Many other works have been attributed to him: S. Maria degli Angeli, Siena; S. Bernardino, Urbino; and Palazzo Ducale, Gubbio. He was also renowned as a designer of fortifications and war machinery.

FREESTONE. Any stone that cuts well in all directions, especially fine-grained limestone or sandstone.

FRENCH ARCHITECTURE. The earliest Christian buildings in France, such as the baptisteries of Fréjus, Mélas, Aix and Marseille Cathedral, all dating from the C5, are of the same Early Christian type as baptisteries of that century in Italy and other Mediterranean countries. The origin of the plan types is Imperial Roman. Of the Merovingian period the two most interesting buildings are the so-called crypt of Jouarre near Meaux and the baptistery of St Jean at Poitiers. The former was not a crypt at all, but an attachment to a church. It was much changed in the C11 and C12, but the columns and the coarsely sub-Roman capitals are probably of the late C7. St Jean is also essentially of the C7, and still has a pediment of Roman descent, but a group of oddly triangular and semicircular windows. Chronicles tell us of more civilized and more Italo-Early-Christian buildings (Tours, Clermont Ferrand, both C5) with aisles, columns, transepts and apses. Such buildings must have continued or been revived in the Carolingian age. However, nothing of any ambition has survived. Germigny-des-Prés is tiny, though with its central plan of Byzantine origin (via Spain?) interesting enough. The excavations at St Denis have revealed a building of Early Christian type there, with aisles, transepts and apse. It was consecrated in 775. In 790–99 Centula (St Riquier) was built. All we know of it is deduced from texts and parallels with other buildings. It was of revolutionary novelty in plan and elevation, with a WESTWORK, nave and aisles, transepts, a chancel and an apse, and with towers of identical details, perhaps of timber, over the W. as well as the E. crossings. They were flanked by round stair turrets. The result must have been as proud and as lively as any of the later German Romanesque cathedrals on the Rhine.

The Romanesque style can be said to have started in the C10, when two new types of plans were evolved, both to become Romanesque standard and both devised to allow for the placing of more altars. One is connected with the second building of Cluny Abbey, the centre of a much-needed monastic reform. This was consecrated in 981 and had chancel aisles flanking the E. apse, and moreover apsidal chapels on the E. sides of the transept. In contrast to this so-called staggered plan is the plan with ambulatory and radiating chapels which seems to have been derived from such a crypt as that of St Pierre-le-Vif at Sens and to have been adopted in the late C10 or anyway about 1000. Early examples are Tournus and Notre Dame de la

Couture at Le Mans. The building to popularize it all over present-day France was, it seems, St Martin at Tours. From here it became one of the distinguishing features of a small but important group of late CII to early CI2 churches in the country. They are or were St Martial at Limoges, St Sernin at Toulouse and to a lesser degree St Foy at Conques. Their other characteristics are transepts with aisles and, in elevation, galleries and tunnel vaults.

The vaulting of the main spaces of churches was a practical as well as an aesthetic need. A stone vault increases security against fire when a church is struck by lightning, and at the same time creates a spatial unity which a timber ceiling on stone walls can never achieve. Yet most French churches before the later CII had timber ceilings (St Remi at Reims 1005–49, Jumièges in Normandy c. 1040–67, St Étienne and Ste Trinité at Caen begun c. 1060–65). The great exception to the rule is the fascinating church of Tournus in Burgundy which has early CII vaults of such a variety and used in such a variety of ways that it appears to us a laboratory of vaulting. There are tunnel vaults longitudinal and transverse, groin vaults and half-tunnels.

Tournus has a separate forechurch or antechurch, two-storeyed, aisled and of three bays in depth. Such an antechurch, though single-storeyed, had already been done at Cluny and was repeated when in 1088 a new church was begun at Cluny. This was, with its antechurch and its two pairs of E. transepts, to be the largest church of Europe, c. 600 ft long. In elevation it differed from the Tours–Toulouse type. It had a blind triforium, clerestory windows and a pointed tunnel vault. Pointed arches are by no means an invention of Gothic builders. The details at Cluny and otherwise in Burgundy show signs of an appreciation of the Ancient Roman remains in

the area. Autun Cathedral, consecrated in 1132, has much in common with Cluny. Vézelay on the other hand is inspired by the Rhineland. It has no gallery or triforium and groin instead of tunnel vaults.

Tunnel vaults are the most usual system of vaulting in Romanesque France. The regions to which we must now turn have them as their standard. They are Auvergne (Clermont-Ferrand, Issoire), similar to the Tours–Toulouse type, but more robust in detail and built with the local volcanic materials, Poitou with HALL CHURCHES of steep and narrow proportions (the finest by far is St Savin), and Provence (Arles, St Paul-trois-Châteaux), also tall and narrow but with clerestory lighting. Provençal churches are often aisleless. Where they have aisles, groin vaults or half-tunnels are used.

Exceptions to this standard are two regions, Normandy and the Angoumois and Périgord. The former was slow in taking to major vaulting. After the Conquest anyway the weight of Norman activity and ambition shifted to England, and here at the end of the CII rib-vaulting was introduced, a technically superior form of groin-vaulting (Durham). The churches of Caen took it over about 1115–20 in sexpartite forms. The Angoumois and Périgord on the other hand placed their faith in vaults of a different type, inspired, it seems, by Byzantium – either direct or via Venice. They kept away from aisles, and put on their solid outer walls domes on PENDENTIVES. Cahors, Angoulême and Périgueux are the foremost examples. Angers Cathedral, begun c. 1145, is of this type too, but in its details it is unmistakably Gothic, though a Gothic deliberately different from that of the Royal France which was the Angevins' enemy.

The Gothic of Royal France, i.e., the Gothic sooner or later for most of Europe, begins at St Denis and Sens about 1140. It is characterized by the combining of pointed arch and rib vault into a system of great logic and structural ingenuity. St Denis moreover has an ambulatory and chapels of a suppleness which makes all Romanesque E. ends appear elementary additions of separate parts. Both St Denis and Sens have two-tower façades. This motif which became Gothic standard is derived from such Norman buildings as St Étienne at Caen, just as the rib vault with the sophisticated profiles of St Denis had its origin in Norman architecture. St Denis also possessed the first of the Gothic figure portals, with column-like figures standing erect in the jambs. At St Denis they are not preserved, but they are at Chartres in the W. front where they date from *c.* 1145–50.

The great Early Gothic cathedrals are Sens, *c.* 1140 etc.; Noyon, *c.* 1150 etc.; Laon, *c.* 1160 etc.; Paris, 1163 etc. They have the sexpartite rib vaults of Caen and show a development to higher proportions, thinner members, larger openings, and less inert wall. At Noyon and Laon CROCKET capitals begin to appear, a symbol of the resilience and freshness of the Early Gothic style. Noyon and Laon have four-tier elevations inside, i.e., galleries as well as triforia. This represents a quickening of rhythm and a further opening of the wall.

Chartres, as rebuilt from 1194, turned Early Gothic into High Gothic. Its quadripartite rib vaults, tall arcades, tall clerestory windows, flying buttresses, and its replacement of the gallery by a low triforium band all convey a sense of greater coherence, a yet quicker rhythm and yet more open walling. The system created at Chartres was taken over for the rebuilding of the cathedrals of Reims (1211 etc.) and Amiens (1220 etc.), and the abbey church of St Denis (1231 etc.), with the scale and the daring of slender supports and large openings

ever increasing, until Beauvais reached a height of *c.* 155 ft. Bar TRACERY started at Reims; so did naturalistic foliage, the convincing concomitant of the High Gothic mood. Of the major cathedrals of these years, only Bourges stands apart, a very individual synthesis of conservative Early Gothic with the most boldly High Gothic elements. The greatest subtlety and refinement but also a first step away from High Gothic clarity appear in St Urbain at Troyes of 1262 etc. and St Nazaire at Carcassonne of *c.* 1270 etc. The later C13 cathedrals built as a sign of the spreading of royal power to the South and the West followed the lead of Reims and Amiens. Only in a few provinces did regional features manage to hold their own. Thus Poitou and also Anjou persisted with hall churches, even if their proportions and their spatial feeling changed in the Gothic direction. In the South a type established itself, probably on a Catalan pattern, with high proportions and chapels between internal buttresses instead of aisles (Albi, 1282 etc.).

The greatest part of the C14 in France was a period of less architectural progress, and this changed only gradually after about 1375, when Flamboyant tracery began to establish itself – more than two generations after flowing tracery had become the standard in England. The Flamboyant Style, as the French call it, i.e., French Late Gothic, got a firm foothold only in the C15, although even then it remained more a matter of decoration than of plan and elevation. The richest province is Normandy (Caudebec, St Maclou Rouen, Pont Audemer). Other principal churches are Abbeville, Notre Dame de l'Épine near Châlons, the chancel of Moulins in Burgundy, the Trinité at Vendôme, St Nicolas-du-Port in Lorraine and the transept of Sens.

Castle building is first characterized by the KEEP or donjon, turning very early from square or oblong to round or rounded. In consequence of the experience of eastern fortification during the Crusades the keep was given up about 1200 and systems were designed instead where defence is spread along the whole CURTAIN WALL, which is sometimes doubled and has many towers. Shortly after 1200 (Louvre, Dourdan) this new system was occasionally regularized and made into a symmetrical composition of four ranges with angle towers round a square or oblong courtyard. In the course of the C15 the manor house or country house (Plessis-lès-Tours, 1463–72) began to replace the castle. The Flamboyant style created many splendid and ornate public and private buildings in the towns, such as the Law Courts of Rouen (1499–1509) and, the finest of all private houses, the House of Jacques Cœur at Bourges (1443 etc.).

The Renaissance arrived early in France, but in a desultory way. Italians were working in Marseille in 1475–81. Odd Quattrocento details in painting occur even earlier. They also appear in architectural decoration (Easter Sepulchre, Solesmes, 1496). The earliest examples of a systematic use of Quattrocento pilasters in several orders is Gaillon (1508). With François I full acceptance of such motifs as this is seen at Blois (1515 etc.) and in other *châteaux* along the Loire. The most monumental of them is Chambord (1519 etc.), a symmetrical composition with a square main building having an ingenious double-spiral staircase in the centre and tunnel-vaulted corridors to N., S., W. and E. with standard lodgings in the corners. The largest of the *châteaux* of François I is Fontainebleau (1528 etc.), and here, in the interior (Gallery of François I, 1532 etc.), Mannerism in its most up-to-date Italian form entered France. By the middle of the C16 France had developed a Renaissance style of her own, with French characteristics and architects. The most important of them

were LESCOT, who began the rebuilding of the Louvre in 1546, and DELORME. Delorme introduced the dome and proved himself an ingenious technician as well as a creator of grand compositions (Anet, c. 1547 etc.). BULLANT at Écouen (c. 1555 etc.) appears as Delorme's equal. His use of giant columns, internationally very early, had a great influence on France.

The wars of religion shook France so violently that little on a large scale could be built. The palace of Verneuil (begun c. 1565) was built slowly, while the palace of Charleval (begun 1573) was abandoned very soon. Both are by the elder DU CERCEAU, and both show an overcrowding of the façades with restless and fantastical detail. The typically French pavilion roofs make their appearance here. Another example of the restlessness of these years is the town hall at Arras (1572).

With Henri IV things settled down. His principal contributions are *places* in Paris, i.e., town planning rather than palace architecture. The Place des Vosges (1605 etc.) survives entirely, the Place Dauphine fragmentarily, and the Place de France, the first with radiating streets (an idea conceived under Sixtus V in Rome), was never built. The elevations are of brick with busy stone DRESSINGS, a style which remained typical up to about 1630 (earliest part of Versailles, 1624). Henri IV's ideas on *places* as focal points of monumental town planning were taken up enthusiastically under Louis XIV and Louis XV, and reached their climax in the Paris of Napoleon III (Louis XIV: Place des Victoires, Place Vendôme, layout of Versailles).

The leading architects under Louis XIV were at the start François MANSART and LE VAU, then PERRAULT and Jules HARDOUIN-MANSART. François Mansart (like Corneille in literature and Poussin in painting) guided France into that classical style to which she remained faithful till beyond 1800, though it looks as if Salomon de BROSSE, the important architect under Louis XIII, had in his last work, the Law Courts at Rennes (begun 1618), preceded Mansart. Mansart is of the same fundamental importance in *châteaux* (Blois, 1635 etc.), town *hôtels* (Vrillière, 1635 etc.; Carnavalet, 1655), and churches. In church architecture de Brosse had started on tall façades crowded with Italian columns (St Gervais, 1616). Mansart toned them down to something closer to the Roman Gesù pattern, and he established the dome as a feature of ambitious Parisian churches (Visitation, 1632; Minimes, 1636). His grandest church is the Val-de-Grâce begun in 1645 and continued by LEMERCIER. But Lemercier had preceded Mansart in the field of major domed churches: his Sorbonne church with its remarkably early giant portico of detached columns was begun in 1635. Le Vau was more Baroque a designer than Mansart, as is shown by his liking for curves, and particularly for ovals, externally and internally. His first Paris house is the Hôtel Lambert (*c.* 1640 etc.), his first country house Vaux-le-Vicomte (1657–61), with its domed oval central saloon, where Louis XIV's team of Le Vau, Lebrun (the painter) and LE NÔTRE appeared together for the first time.

In 1665 Louis XIV called BERNINI to Paris to advise him on the completion of the Louvre. But Bernini's grand Baroque plans were discarded in favour of Perrault's elegant, eminently French façade with its pairs of slender columns and straight entablature in front of a long loggia (1667–70). The King's architect during Louis XIV's later years was Hardouin-Mansart. He was not a man of the calibre of the others, but he was a brilliant organizer, and it fell to him vastly to enlarge and to complete Versailles (1678 etc.). The magniloquent grandeur of the interiors is his but also the noble simplicity of the Orangery and the informal layout of the Grand Trianon (1687). He also designed the truly monumental St Louis-des-Invalides (1680–91). In Mansart's office the Rococo was created by younger designers (Pierre Lepautre) about 1710–15. It became essentially a style of interior decoration. Otherwise the difference between the C17 and C18 *hôtel* or country house is greater finesse and delicacy of detail, a more cunning planning of cabinets and minor rooms, and a decrease in scale. The most impressive major work of the mid century is perhaps the planning and building of the new centre of Nancy by HÉRÉ (1753 etc.).

From the middle of the C18 onwards France turned to Classicism, first by some theoretical writings (Cochin, 1750, LAUGIER, 1753), then in actual architecture too. A moderate, still very elegant classicism prevails in the work of GABRIEL (Place de la Concorde, 1755 etc., Petit Trianon 1763 etc.). More radical is SOUFFLOT's Panthéon (1757 etc.) with its exquisite dome (inspired by Wren's St Paul's) resting on piers of Gothic structural daring, its Greek-cross shape and its arms accompanied by narrow aisles or ambulatories, the separation from the arms being by columns carrying straight lintels. The last quarter of the C18 saw even more radical endeavours towards architectural reform. They were made mostly by young architects back from the French Academy in Rome. There they found inspiration not only in classical Antiquity but even more in its bewitching interpretation by PIRANESI. One such was M. J. Peyre (1730–85) whose influential *Œuvres d'Architecture* came out in 1765. But the most influential of all – BOULLÉE – had not been in Rome. His Hôtel de Brunoy of 1772 belongs to the earliest examples of the new simplicity and rectangularity. Others are the Mint (1771–7) by J.-D. ANTOINE (1733–1801), the Hôtel de Salm (1782) by Pierre Rousseau (*c.*

1750–1810), and CHALGRIN's brilliant St Philippe-du-Roule of 1772–84. But Boullée's influence was exerted less by what he built than by the drawings he made for a future book. They and LEDOUX's buildings at Arc-et-Senam and in Paris together with his published drawings represent a new radicalism of form and at the same time a megalomania of scale. Boullée's most influential follower was J. N. L. DURAND (1760–1834), not because of his buildings but because of the publications which came out of his lecture courses at the École Polytechnique. They were used abroad as much as in France (see, e.g., SCHINKEL). Durand's two books were issued in 1800 and 1802–9. But the most successful architects of the years of Napoleon's rulership were PERCIER and FONTAINE. In their works and in e.g., the Bourse (1807) by A. T. BRONGNIART (1739–1813), the façade of the Palais Bourbon (1803–7) by B. Poyet (1742–1824) and the Madeleine (1816–32) by P. A. VIGNON (1763–1828) the style of Boullée and Ledoux became less terse and demanding and more rhetorical and accommodating. Side by side with this classical development from Revolution to Empire runs the development of Romanticism in the form of the *jardin anglais* and its furnishings. Examples are the Bagatelle by BÉLANGER of 1778 and the part of Versailles where Marie-Antoinette's Dairy was built in 1782–6 by Richard MIQUE (1728–94).

The interaction between classical and Gothic went on in the C19. The grand chapel of Louis XVIII at Dreux was built classical in 1816–22, but enlarged Gothic in 1839. Ste Clotilde (1846 etc.) by F. C. GAU is serious neo-Gothic; so is Notre Dame de Bon Secours outside Rouen (1840–7) by J. E. Barthélemy (1799–1868), and in the 1840s also VIOLLET-LE-DUC began his highly knowledgeable if drastic restorations. Medieval scholarship reached its acme with his publica-

tions. Meanwhile HITTORF completed St Vincent-de-Paul (1824 etc.) in a classical turning Early Christian. His later work is in a free Italianate, and in his two circuses of 1839 and 1851 he used glass and iron domes. The understanding among architects of what role iron could play was wider in France than in Britain. LABROUSTE's Ste Geneviève Library of 1843–50 is of a very pure and refined Italian Renaissance outside but has its iron framework exposed inside. Viollet-le-Duc in his *Entretiens* pleaded for iron, and already before their publication, in 1854–5, L.-A. BOILEAU (1812–96) had built St Eugène essentially of iron.

Concerning façades rather than structure, the French Renaissance was now added to the *répertoire*, first in the enlargements of the Louvre by Louis Visconti and H.-M. LEFUEL (1852 etc.) then in the façade of St Augustin by Victor BALTARD (1805–74). The church (1860–67) again has iron inside. Shortly after, the full Baroque triumphed in GARNIER's Opéra of 1861–74. Those less ready for lush displays now rediscovered the Romanesque (VAUDREMER, 1864 etc.; Abadie, Sacré Coeur 1874 etc.) and with this sparked off the style of RICHARDSON in America and with it the great rise of American architecture.

But while Paris remained leading in the development of iron and steel (Halles des Machines and Eiffel Tower, both for the exhibition of 1889), in architecture proper she produced nothing to emulate the English Domestic Revival or the American Chicago School. France came into her own again only about 1900 with the ART NOUVEAU structures of GUIMARD and the pioneer designs of PERRET and Tony GARNIER. From them the way was open to the INTERNATIONAL MODERN of the 1920s in the hands of LE CORBUSIER, Robert Mallet Stevens (born 1886) and André Lurçat (born 1892). Jean PROUVÉ (born 1901) is today the most interesting French experimenter in structure.

FRENCH WINDOW. A long window reaching to floor level and opening in two leaves like a pair of doors.

FRET. A geometrical ornament of horizontal and vertical straight lines repeated to form a band, e.g., a *key pattern*. *See figure 47.*

Fig. 47. Fret

FREYSSINET, Eugène (1879–1962). One of the leading concrete designers of his generation. His fame rests principally on the two airstrip hangars at Orly (1916). They were of parabolic section, with a transversely folded surface and over 200 ft high. They were destroyed in 1944. Freyssinet also designed important concrete bridges.

FRIEZE. 1. The middle division of an ENTABLATURE, between the ARCHITRAVE and CORNICE; usually decorated but may be plain. *See figures 42 and 64.* 2. The decorated band along the upper part of an internal wall, immediately below the cornice.

FRISONI, Donato Giuseppe (1683–1735). He was born at Laino, between Como and Lugano, and began as a stucco-worker. In this capacity he was employed in 1709 on the vast palace at Ludwigsburg. In 1714 he succeeded the previous architect there (Johann Friedrich Nette) and became responsible for the final form of the palace with its imposing central block crowned with a double-curving hipped roof and turret. He also designed the elegant small banqueting house, Favorite, on the hill opposite (begun 1718). But perhaps his major achievement is the town plan of Ludwigs-

burg, very unusual for its integration of the palace and its garden with a regular system of streets.

FRONTISPIECE. The main façade of a building or its principal entrance BAY.

FRY, Maxwell (b. 1899). One of the pioneers in England of the INTERNATIONAL MODERN of the 1930s. His early buildings are private houses, dating from 1934 onwards. From 1934 to 1936 he was in partnership with GROPIUS. The most important outcome of this is the Impington Village College (1936). Of the major post-war work of the firm (now Fry, Drew & Partners), university and other buildings for Nigeria (Ibadan University College; Co-operate Bank, Ibadan, 1947–61), housing at Chandigarh (1951–4) and the new main offices for Pilkington's at St Helens (1961–4) must be mentioned.

FUGA, Ferdinando (1699–1782), was born in Florence and died in Naples. But his principal works are all in Rome, e.g., Palazzo della Consulta (1732–7), the façade of S. Maria Maggiore (1741–3), and Palazzo Corsini (1736 onwards), in which his sophisticated Late Baroque style is seen at its elegant best. In 1751 he settled in Naples, where he received several important commissions (Albergo de' Poveri, Chiesa dei Gerolamini), but his early virtuosity had by then faded into a tame classicism and his late works are notable mainly for their size.

FULLER, Richard Buckminster (b. 1895). After working in a variety of commercial jobs, he started work in 1922 on structural systems for cheap and effective shelter, light in weight as well as quick to erect and capable of covering large spans. The result was his *geodesic domes* developed after the Second World War. They have been made by him on the SPACE-FRAME principle in many different materials: timber, plywood, aluminium, paper board, PRESTRESSED CONCRETE, and even bamboo. The largest is at Baton Rouge, Louisiana: it has a diameter of 384 ft and was built in 1958.

FUNCTIONALISM. The creed of the architect or designer who holds that it is his primary duty to see that a building or an object designed by him functions well. Whatever he wishes to convey aesthetically and emotionally must not interfere with the fitness of the building or the object to fulfil its purpose.

G

GABLE. The triangular upper portion of a wall at the end of a pitched roof. It normally has straight sides, but there are variants. A crow-stepped or corbie-stepped gable has stepped sides. A Dutch gable has curved sides crowned by a pediment, *see figure 48*. A hipped gable has the uppermost part sloped back. A shaped gable has multi-curved sides, *see figure 48*.

Shaped gable   Dutch gable

Fig. 48. Gable

GABLET. A decorative motif in the form of a small gable, as on a buttress, above a niche, etc.

GABRIEL, Jacques-Ange (1698–1782). The greatest C18 architect in France and perhaps in Europe. His genius was conservative rather than revolutionary: he carried on and brought to its ultimate perfection the French classical tradition of François MANSART, by-passing, as it were, the Rococo. He resembled his great contemporary Chardin in his solid unostentatious good taste, which reached its highest pitch of refinement in small intimate buildings such as his Hermitage or Pavillon de Pompadour at Fontaine-bleau (begun 1749) and in his great masterpiece, the Petit Trianon in the park at Versailles (1761–8). His father was a successful architect, Jacques Gabriel (1667–1742), who builts everal good Parisian hôtels, notably the Hôtel Peyrenne de Moras (now the Musée

Rodin), and the Place Royale at Bordeaux (begun 1728), a masterpiece of Rococo urbanism. In 1735 he succeeded de COTTE as *Premier Architecte* and Director of the Academy. Jacques-Ange Gabriel was trained in Paris under his father and never went to Italy. He worked under and with his father for the Crown, and in due course succeeded him as *Premier Architecte*. In this position he built exclusively for the king, Louis XV, and Mme de Pompadour. Additions and alterations to the various royal palaces – Fontainebleau, Compiègne, Versailles – took up most of his time, but they lack inspiration, though the theatre and the projected reconstruction of the Marble Court at Versailles are extremely elegant. His largest commissions outside Versailles were for the École Militaire, Paris (1751–88), and the layout of the Place de la Concorde, Paris (1755 etc.); while the two great palaces (Hôtel de Crillon and Ministère de la Marine, 1757–75) flanking his rue Royale – their façades with screens in the style of PERRAULT's great east front of the Louvre – are his most successful buildings on a monumental scale. The Pavillon Français, Versailles (1750), the small hunting-boxes or Pavillons de Butard (1750) and de la Muette (1753–4) and the Petit Château at Choisy (1754–6) foreshadow the civilized intimacy of his masterpiece. The Petit Trianon may owe something to the sober dignity of English PALLADIANISM, but the extreme elegance and refinement of this perfectly proportioned cubical composition is wholly French and achieves a serenity and distinction different in kind and quality from any other contemporary building.

GADROONED. Decorated with convex curves; the opposite of fluted (*see* FLUTING).

GALILEE. A vestibule or occasionally a chapel, originally for penitents and usually at the west end of a church. Sometimes called a NARTHEX or PARADISE.

GALILEI, Alessandro (1691–1737), born in Florence and trained there, went to England in 1714, but failed to attract any commissions. In 1731 he won the competition for the façade of S. Giovanni in Laterano, Rome, with a somewhat tight, severely classical design (executed 1733–6). He also designed the elegant Corsini Chapel in S. Giovanni in Laterano (1732–5) and the façade of S. Giovanni dei Fiorentini, Rome (1734).

GALLERY. In church architecture, an upper storey over an aisle, opening on to the nave. Also called a *tribune* and often, wrongly, a TRIFORIUM. Found as an exterior feature with continuous small open ARCADING in medieval Italian and German churches, and sometimes called a DWARF GALLERY.

GALLETING. Inserting into mortar courses, while still soft, small pieces of stone, chips of flint, etc., sometimes for structural but usually for decorative reasons.

GALLI DA BIBIENA. The leading family of QUADRATURA painters and theatrical designers in early C18 Italy. They came from Bibiena near Bologna. Several members of the family were spirited draughtsmen and accomplished painters of *trompe l'œil* architecture; a few were architects as well. Ferdinando (1657–1743) designed the church of S. Antonio Abbate, Parma (1712–16), with a very effective double dome. One of his sons, Giuseppe (1696–1757), worked as a theatrical designer in Vienna and in Dresden (1747–53) and in 1748 designed the wonderfully rich interior of the theatre at Bayreuth; while another son, Antonio (1700–74), designed

several theatres in Italy, of which only two survive: Teatro Comunale, Bologna (1756–63), and Teatro Scientifico, Palazzo dell'Accademia Virgiliana, Mantua. A third son, Alessandro (1687–1769), became Architect-General to the Elector Palatine in Mannheim, where he built the opera house (1737, destroyed) and began the fine Jesuit church (1738–56). The very elaborate stage designs by members of the family may have exerted some influence on JUVARRA and PIRANESI.

GAMBREL ROOF, *see* ROOF.

GANDON, James (1743–1823). A pupil of CHAMBERS, he became the leading neo-classical architect in Dublin. He was of French Huguenot descent and his work is sometimes surprisingly advanced and close to his *avant-garde* French contemporaries, e.g., Nottingham County Hall (1770–72) of which the façade survives. In 1781 he went to Dublin to supervise the construction of the Custom House on the Liffey (completed 1791, interior destroyed 1921). But his masterpiece is the Four Courts, also on the Liffey, where he took over from T. Cooley (1786–1802, interior destroyed 1922). Also in Dublin are his portico of the Bank of Ireland (1785) and the King's Inns (begun 1795 but later enlarged). He published, with J. Woolfe, two supplementary volumes to *Vitruvius Britannicus* in 1769 and 1771.

GARDEN CITY or GARDEN SUBURB. See HOWARD, Sir Ebenezer. The first garden suburbs in England were Port Sunlight and Bournville, but the finest English specimen is the Hampstead Garden Suburb in London, started in 1906. In Germany the most interesting is that planned by Richard Riemerschmid (1868–1957) at Hellerau near Dresden and begun in 1909.

GARDEROBE. Wardrobe. Also the medieval name for a lavatory.

GARGOYLE. A water spout projecting from a roof, or the PARAPET of a wall or tower, and carved into a grotesque figure, human or animal.

GARNER, Thomas, *see* BODLEY.

GARNIER, Charles (1825–98), won the Grand Prix of the Academy in 1848, and went to Rome in the same year and to Athens in 1852. Back in Paris in 1854, he worked under BALLU. In 1861 he won the competition for the Opéra, and the building was completed in 1875. Prominently placed in one of HAUSSMANN's many grand *points de vue*, it is the most splendid incarnation of the Second Empire. The exterior, the ample staircase, the glittering foyer are frankly Baroque, and openly endeavour to beat the Baroque at its own game. At the same time Meyerbeer, Wagner, Verdi could not be heard in more sympathetic surroundings, since the building is most intelligently planned for its particular purpose of combining a setting for opera with a setting for social display. The same is true, in its own intentionally more meretricious way, of the Casino at Monte Carlo (1878), which, needless to say, had a universal influence in Romance countries on light-hearted resort architecture. Garnier's own villa at Bordighera (1872), with its asymmetrically placed tower, is Italianate and not Baroque.

GARNIER, Tony (1869–1948). When he gained the Prix de Rome in 1899 and duly went to Rome, he spent much of his time not measuring and studying ancient buildings, but working on the designs for a Cité Industrielle. These designs were submitted in 1904, exhibited, and finally published in 1917. They represent a completely new approach to town planning, in radical opposition to the academic principles of town planning as taught by the École des Beaux Arts, principles of symmetry and imposed monumentality. Garnier instead gave himself a site that was imaginary and yet realistic, since it resembled the country near his native Lyon: he decided that his town should have 35,000 inhabitants, located industry, railway lines, station, town centre, and housing, and related them

rationally to each other. Moreover, he proposed that all the buildings should be made essentially of CONCRETE. He designed small houses of a quite novel cubic simplicity placed among trees, and some major buildings with the large CANTILEVERS which RE-INFORCED CONCRETE had just begun to make possible, with glass and concrete roofs, etc. In 1905 Garnier was called by the newly elected mayor, Édouard Hérriot, to Lyon to be municipal architect. He built the slaughterhouse in 1909–13, the stadium in 1913–16.

GÄRTNER, Friedrich von (1792–1847), the son of an architect, studied at the Munich Academy, then for a short time with WEINBRENNER, and after that in Paris with PERCIER and FONTAINE. In 1815–17 he was in Italy, and in 1818–20 in Holland and England. After that he held a chair at the Munich Academy. On a second journey to Italy in 1828 he was introduced to King Ludwig I of Bavaria, and from then was, side by side and in competition with KLENZE, the king's favourite architect. Gärtner's speciality was what the Germans call the *Rundbogenstil*, the style of round arches, be they Italian Romanesque or Italian Quattrocento: it is said that it was King Ludwig rather than Gärtner who favoured this post-classical style. In Munich Gärtner built the Ludwigskirche (1829–40), the State Library (1831–40), and the University (1835–40), all three in the Ludwigstrasse, and at its south end the Feldherrenhalle, a copy of the Loggia dei Lanzi in Florence (1840–4) and an essay in the Tuscan Gothic. In 1835–6 Gärtner was in Athens, where he designed the palace of the new king, a son of Ludwig.

GAU, Franz Christian (1790–1853) was born in Cologne, went to Paris in 1810, and in 1815 with a Prussian grant to Rome, where he became a friend of the Nazarenes (Overbeck, Cornelius, etc.). In 1818–20 he was in Egypt and Palestine, but returned to Paris in

1821. Gau was more widely known during his lifetime as an Egyptian scholar than as an architect. Yet his Ste Clotilde (1846–57; completed by BALLU) is the one outstanding neo-Gothic church in Paris. The style is a rich High Gothic, the façade has two towers with spires like St Nicaise at Reims, and the roof construction is of iron.

GAUDÍ, Antoni (1852–1926), was born at Reus (Tarragona), where his father was a coppersmith and pot- and kettle-maker. So he grew up acquainted with metals, and it is not surprising that the savagery of his ornamental invention appeared first in metal railings and gates. Nor was the architecture of the building for which these were designed – the Casa Vicens at Barcelona – tame or imitative in the sense of C19 historicism. The house, built in 1878–80, is in fact a nightmarish farrago of Moorish and Gothic elements; indeed, Moorish and Gothic – and in addition, it seems, Moroccan – are the sources of Gaudí's style. The Casa Vicens was followed in 1883–5 by El Capricho, a house at Comillas in Northern Spain – equally crazy and less dependent on any past style.

In 1883 Gaudí was put in charge of the continuation of a large church in Barcelona, the Sagrada Familia, begun as a conventional neo-Gothic building. He did the crypt in 1884–91 and began the transept façade in 1891. By then he had been taken up by Count Güell, an industrialist who remained his faithful patron. His town house, the Palacio Güell, dates from 1885–9, and here there first appeared the parabolic arches and the wild roof excrescences which were to become part of Gaudí's repertoire. But far more fiercely extravagant than anything he or any architect had done before were the designs for the chapel of Sta Coloma de Cervelló which Gaudí began to build in 1898 for one of Count Güell's estates: it was never completed. It has an entirely free, asymmetrical, jagged plan, with pillars set at a slant, warped vaults, an indescribable interplay of exterior and interior, and ostentatiously crude benches. For the Parque Güell, a park at Barcelona, begun in 1900, similar motifs were used, and in addition the snakily undulating back of a long seat running along the sides of a large open space was faced with bits of broken tile and crockery in arbitrary patterns as effective as any invented by Picasso (who lived at Barcelona during these very years, 1901–4).

In 1903 Gaudí began the upper part of the transept of the Sagrada Familia. The lower part had gradually reached an ever freer interpretation of Gothic motifs, but the turrets at the top defeated comparison with anything architectural from the past or the present. Instead, comparisons with termite hills or with crustaceous creatures come at once to mind. The ceramic facing is similar to that in the Parque Güell. Aesthetically as surprising and socially more so than any earlier building are Gaudí's two blocks of luxury flats, the Casa Batlló and the Casa Milá (both begun 1905); for here was acceptance by wealthy Barcelonians of Gaudí's unprecedented architecture. The façades undulate, rise and fall, and are garnished with fantastical top excrescences and sharp, piercing, aggressive wrought-iron balconies. Moreover, the rooms have no straight walls, no right angles. The principles behind ART NOUVEAU (see HORTA, MACKINTOSH, MACKMURDO, van de VELDE), usually confined to decoration and mostly two-dimensional decoration, could not well be pushed to a further architectural extreme.

GAZEBO. A small look-out tower or summerhouse with a view, usually in a garden or park but sometimes on the roof of a house; in the latter case it is also called a *belvedere*.

GEDDES, Sir Patrick (1854–1932). If Raymond UNWIN was the greatest British town-planner of his day in practice, Geddes was the greatest in town-planning theory, a theory which he established in the present much-widened sense of the word, with emphasis laid on the necessity of preliminary surveys, on 'diagnosis before treatment', and on the dependence of acceptable town planning on sociological research bordering on biological work. Geddes was, in fact, a trained biologist and zoologist though he never took a degree. He was Professor of Botany at Dundee from 1889 to 1918, and of sociology at Bombay from 1920 to 1923. He was knighted shortly before his death. His principal work on town planning is *City Development* (1904).

GENELLI, Christian, *see* GILLY.

GEOFFREY DE NOIERS (active *c*. 1200), was called *constructor* of the choir of St Hugh at Lincoln Cathedral (begun 1192). The term may mean only supervisor, but more probably he is the designer of this epoch-making building. The design is, in spite of Geoffrey's name, entirely English, not merely in its proportions and the curious layout of the east chapels, but especially in its vault, the earliest vault whose ribs make a decorative (and a very wilful) pattern rather than simply express their function.

GEORGIAN ARCHITECTURE, *see* ENGLISH ARCHITECTURE.

Georgian architecture is classical in its major exteriors; but on the smaller domestic scale it still has the sensible plainness of the QUEEN ANNE style. Interiors are more elaborate than exteriors; here also Palladianism was the rule at first, but it was handled with greater freedom and verve. A brief phase of ROCOCO followed about the middle of the century: then the enchantment of Robert Adam's delicate decoration captured nearly everybody. Grecian interiors were rare until about 1820, but Victorian licence and exuberance are already heralded in certain Regency interiors (Brighton Pavilion).

GERBIER, Sir Balthazar (1591?–1667), a Dutch-born Huguenot who settled in England in 1616, was courtier, diplomat, miniaturist, and pamphleteer as well as architect. He almost certainly designed the York Water Gate, Victoria Embankment Gardens, London (1626–7). Nothing else by him survives.

GERMAN ARCHITECTURE. We know more about early German churches now than we did thirty years ago. Until then there was the rotunda of St Mary on the Würzburg fortress and the traces of the grand basilica of St Boniface at Fulda, both eighth century and both of Early Christian inspiration. Excavations have now told us of small aisleless churches with straight-ended chancels, much as in Northern England.

But all this is small fry compared with Charlemagne's buildings, especially the happily preserved palace chapel of Aachen and the large abbey church of Centula (St Riquier) only known from descriptions and derivations. Aachen was a palace of the Emperor, Ingelheim was another. Both were spacious, axially planned, and apparently aware of Imperial Roman plans. The large Aachen chapel dedicated in 805 is externally a polygon of sixteen sides, and internally has an ambulatory round an octagonal centre; above the ambulatory is a gallery and on top of the octagon a domical vault. Details are amazingly pure in the Roman tradition, as indeed is so much – script, poetry, illumination – that issued from the Emperor's circle. This applies also, e.g., to the curious gatehouse of Lorsch Abbey. At Aachen the most original feature is the westwork, and as for Centula, consecrated in 799, all is original – a WESTWORK with a tower repeating the shape of the crossing tower, transepts emanating from the crossing, and transept-like wings off the westwork, a chancel and an apse. As original is the vellum plan for St Gall Abbey, datable to about 820. This has a west as well as an east apse and a pair of round campanili, the earliest church towers of which we have a record.

Centula can be called the pattern from which the German Romanesque style derived. The years of development are the late CIO – with the west-work of St Pantaleon in Cologne, consecrated in 980, and the nunnery church of Gernrode of 961 etc. At St Michael in Hildesheim of c. 1001–33 the Romanesque style is complete. Its climax is the great cathedrals and abbeys of the Rhineland dating from the mid CII to the early CI3: Speier c. 1030 etc., Mainz 1081 etc., Maria Laach 1093 etc. and Worms c. 1175 etc. Internationally speaking the mid CII was the time of the great superiority of the work in the Empire over work in England, Italy and most parts of France, as it was the time of the Salians, the most powerful of the emperors. The principal buildings are the following: the hall-range of the palace of Goslar of c. 1050 not matched anywhere, Speier Cathedral already mentioned, with its ruthlessly grand inner elevation and the groin vaults which the nave received about 1080–90, the first major vault in Germany. The decoration is inspired by Northern Italy, the elevational system is probably inspired by the Roman basilica of Trier. Trier Cathedral is another of the masterpieces of these years – a length-ening of a centrally planned Roman building. The west front has the first so-called dwarf gallery, i.e., an arcaded wall-passage, earlier than any in Italy. But the most coherent major building of these years is St Mary-in-Capitol at Cologne, built on a trefoil plan for the east end and with tunnel vaults. The details are very severe – BLOCK CAPITALS e.g., as had been introduced at St Pantaleon and at Hildesheim. Beneath is a crypt of many short columns; Speier has an-other. The trefoil east end became the hallmark of the Romanesque school

of Cologne. Cologne before the Second World War had more Roman-esque churches than any other city in Europe. They go on into the early CI3, when motifs tend to get fanciful and decoration exuberant – baroque, as it has been called. The west end of Worms, completed c. 1230, shows this at its most outré, but it also shows that now the French Gothic began to make its mark.

But we cannot leave the Roman-esque without referring to a develop-ing liking for HALL CHURCHES in Westphalia (Kirchlinde c. 1175) and also in Bavaria (Waldersbach c. 1175) and to the style promoted by the Congregation of Hirsau, i.e., the German Cluniacs. Their churches are not much like French Cluniac churches. The main church at Hirsau was begun in 1082; specially good other Hirsau-type churches are Alpirs-bach and Paulinzella, the latter of 1112–32. The Hirsau type had an antechurch (like Cluny) with two west towers, nave arcades with columns, mostly with plain block capitals, and two slim towers over the east bays of the aisles.

Now for the relation to the Gothic in France which had been created there about 1135–40. Germany did not take notice of it until about 1200 with Gelnhausen (c. 1200–1230), the 'PARA-DISE' of the abbey church of Maul-bronn (c. 1210–20), St Gereon at Cologne (1219 etc.) and Limburg on the Lahn (consecrated 1235). The result here is a mixture, resourceful and entertaining, but impure and not guided by any understanding of what Gothic architecture really is about. That changed suddenly and very dramatically with St Elizabeth at Marburg started in 1235, the church of the Virgin at Trier started a few years later (a centrally planned build-ing making ingenious use of French elements) and Cologne Cathedral started in 1248. St Elizabeth with its rib vaults and bar-tracery presupposes

Reims started in 1211, but with its trefoil east end derived from Cologne. The church after a change of plan was built as a HALL CHURCH, and that is a motif of Westphalian derivation. It became the hallmark of the Late Gothic in Germany. Cologne Cathedral is French in general and particular. Amiens and Beauvais are closest to it. It was to be the largest and the highest of all High Gothic cathedrals, but only the east end was built, and that was consecrated only in 1322. The rest is mostly C19.

To proceed with German Gothic development one must watch for the spread of the hall church. One group is hall chancels of Austrian abbeys – Lilienfeld (consecrated 1230), Heiligenkreuz (consecrated 1295) and Zwettl (begun 1343). Meanwhile Westphalia turned from Romanesque to Gothic halls (Osnabrück 1256–92, nave Münster c. 1267 etc.). Halls also established themselves in Northeast and East Germany and especially in the architecture of the Friars. An early example (c. 1240) is the Frankfurt Blackfriars.

The full maturity of the German hall church is reached in South Germany from 1351, the date when the chancel of Schwäbisch Gmünd was begun, probably by Heinrich PARLER, and through the C15 into the C16. The architects spreading this Late Gothic style were the PARLER family, with Peter, the greatest, who in 1353 became the Emperor Charles IV's architect of Prague Cathedral and introduced here complicated rib vaults and incidentally amazing portrait sculpture (in the triforium). A Michael Parler worked at Ulm, a Johann was called to Milan, another Johann appears at Freiburg, but the fantastic spire with its filigree tracery all over is earlier than that Parler. Altogether we hear of more architects' names now (see ENSINGER, BÖBLINGER, HEINZELMANN) and also of the statutes of masons' lodges. There are many outstanding Late Gothic parish churches in South Germany and Austria, such as St Martin at Landshut (and the Salzburg Greyfriars) by Hans STETHAIMER, Nördlingen (1427 etc.), Dinkelsbühl (1448 etc.), Amberg (1420 etc.), the Frauenkirche in Munich (1468 etc.) and the chancel of St Lorenz in Nuremberg (1445 etc.). Nor is North Germany poor in Late Gothic hall churches.

But the pride of North Germany is its brick town halls such as those of Lübeck and Stralsund and the overwhelming one, mainly of the late C14, at Torun (Thorn) in the territory of the Prussian Knights. Their castles are as overwhelming, especially the C14 Malbork (Marienburg).

Altogether Germany is rich in Late Gothic secular buildings. At the castle at Meissen rebuilding of 1471–c.85 demonstrates the transition from castle to palace. So does, on an even grander scale, the work of Benedict RIETH on the Hradchin at Prague. The Vladislas Hall was begun c. 1487. Its curvaceous rib vaults are the acme of German Late Gothic fantasy.

But the Vladislas Hall also has motifs of the Italian Renaissance. The infiltration started in fact earlier in Bohemia, Hungary and Poland than in Germany. In Germany Dürer and Burkmayr used Renaissance detail elegantly in 1508, and in 1509 the Fuggers of Augsburg founded a chapel in that city which was intended to look North Italian as an ensemble. In the second quarter of the C16 much decoration à la Como or Pavia can be found (Georgentor, Dresden 1534). Ensembles however remained rare – the purest is part of the palace of Landshut (1536) inspired by GIULIO ROMANO. Soon in any case purity was no longer the ideal. As the wholly national Elizabethan style emerges in England, so does the so-called German Renaissance in Germany, with gables, stubby columns and coarse, more Flemish than Italian, decoration. Examples are the Leipzig and Rothenburg Town Halls (1556 etc. and 1572 etc.), the former Lusthaus in Stuttgart (1580–93), the Plassenburg near Kulmbach (1559 etc.), the Pellerhaus in Nuremberg (1605). There are, however, also some more internationallooking buildings, i.e., buildings of French (Schloss Aschaffenburg, 1605–14) or Flemish (Ottheinrichsbau, Heidelberg, 1556 etc.; Town Hall portico, Cologne, 1569–70) or Italian inspiration (St Michael, Munich, 1583 etc.). The most original churches about 1600 are Protestant and North German, those of Wolfenbüttel (1607 etc.) and Bückeburg (1613 etc.). With Renaissance all this has little to do.

Just as in England with Inigo Jones, a true understanding of the High Renaissance came only after 1600 and even then very rarely. The key work is Elias HOLL's Augsburg Town Hall of 1615–20. But then – and this singles out Germany – the Thirty Years' War interrupted this organic development.

It left the country devastated and impoverished, and when building again became possible, the situation in the country – and indeed taste – had changed. The most important architectural events took place in the Catholic South, and the source of inspiration was Italy, and at first even the architects were Italian, as, e.g., BARELLI and ZUCCALLI who built the Theatinerkirche in Munich (1663–88). About 1700 Germans replaced the Italians. Of the first generation are SCHLÜTER who built the Palace and the Arsenal in Berlin, the great FISCHER VON ERLACH in Vienna and PÖPPELMANN of the Zwinger in Dresden (1709 etc.). All three were born about 1660. HILDEBRANDT in Vienna was a little younger. While Fischer von Erlach, despite his ingenious plans with their centralizing tendencies and their ovals, is a classicist at bottom, Hildebrandt represents the BORROMINI and GUARINI party in Europe, as do the DIENTZENHOFERS

in Franconia and Bohemia (Johann: Banz 1710–18; Christoph: Břevnov near Prague 1708–15; Kilian Ignaz: the two St Nicholases Prague 1730s). The Fischer–Hildebrandt antinomy is equally patent in Dresden, but here it is a Catholic–Protestant antinomy: BÄHR's Protestant Frauenkirche of 1725 etc., the town church v. CHIAVERI's Catholic church of 1738 etc., the court church.

As for other Northern centres Frederick the Great's early Sanssouci at Potsdam (1745–7) looked to Rococo France (even if not with such abandon as CUVILLIÉS's Amalienburg at Nymphenburg near Munich of 1734–9), his later buildings, including the Gothic Nauener Gate at Potsdam of 1755, to England. The Rhineland naturally looked to France, but even there – Brühl, Bruchsal – in the end the greatest German architect of the century won.

He is, needless to say, Balthasar NEUMANN, and his masterworks are the Episcopal Palace of Würzburg (1720–44), still in some elements guided by Hildebrandt, and the splendid churches of Vierzehnheiligen (1743 etc.) and Neresheim (1745 etc.). Neumann lived at Würzburg, i.e., in Franconia. The three greatest Bavarian church builders were ASAM, ZIMMERMANN and FISCHER, all born between 1685 and 1695. The Asam brothers, also painters and sculptors, are the most Italian – influenced by Borromini, and rich in their brown and gold decoration (Weltenburg, St John Nepomuk Munich). J. M. Fischer (Ottobeuren, Zwiefalten, Rott) is all large and light in colours and ingenious in planning as well. Zimmermann is primarily remembered – rightly so – for the Wies Church (1745–54). There were two Zimmermann brothers as well, the other being a painter, and the *unisono* of all the arts is of course one of the most characteristic features of the Baroque. The great abbeys of South Germany and even more Austria show that in all their sumptuous parts (see e.g., Melk, St Florian, Klosterneuburg).

No wonder then that the total reaction against the Rococo was a Protestant and a North German initiative. Friedrich GILLY in Berlin came from Huguenot stock. He never visited Italy, but he visited Paris and London. What London meant to him we do not know, but Paris meant the most radical innovators of Europe – the Odéon, the Théâtre Feydeau, the rue des Colonnes. Gilly died too young to build more than negligibly, but his designs for a National Monument to Frederick the Great and for a National Theatre prove him to be one of the few architects of genius of the period.

SCHINKEL was his pupil, again one of the greatest of the period in all Europe, less brilliantly endowed perhaps, but of rare competence and as resourceful as Gilly. He started as a painter, especially as a theatrical painter, in the romantic vein. His design of 1810 for a mausoleum for Queen Louise is Gothic. When after Napoleon's defeat building started again, he built in a pure but highly original Grecian. The Old Guard House, the Theatre, the Old Museum (all in Berlin and all designed in 1816–22) are among the noblest of the Greek Revival anywhere. He became Superintendent of Building in Prussia and his influence stretched far, even into Scandinavia and Finland. Later in life he experimented with more original forms – centrally planned churches, façades of public buildings of exposed brick and functional bareness (Academy of Building of 1832–5, designs for a library and a bazaar). When he visited England in 1826, his principal interest was industrial products and the new huge mills.

KLENZE, Schinkel's opposite number in Bavaria, was more accommodating but equally resourceful. His œuvre already comprises the full historicism of the nineteenth century;

the Greek Glyptothek and Walhalla, the Quattrocento and Cinquecento parts of the Royal Palace, the Early Christian of the church of All Saints, the originality of the Hall of Liberation above Kelheim. As for C19 historicism Germany made the Rundbogenstil one of her specialities. In the Italian Renaissance vein SEMPER did such beautiful buildings as the Dresden Gallery (1847 etc.) and the Dresden Opera. The difference between the first and the second Opera (1837 etc. and, after a fire, 1871 etc.) is that between C19 neo-Renaissance and neo-Baroque. The neo-Baroque appeared at its best in Paul Wallot's Houses of Parliament (1884 etc.). Compare then the Parliament with Ludwig von Hoffmann's Supreme Court at Leipzig (1887 etc.), and you will get a first idea of the development from ornateness to simplicity.

Germany was indeed one of the leading countries in overcoming historicism and establishing the new functional style of the C20. The key works are Peter BEHRENS's of c. 1904–14, buildings including the famous factories for the AEG and also their industrial products. For his Austrian colleagues see AUSTRIAN ARCHITECTURE. Behrens's pupils were GROPIUS and MIES VAN DER ROHE. Gropius's *magnum opus* remains the BAUHAUS building at Dessau, Mies's greatest work was done after his emigration to Chicago. Other leaders in the so-called INTERNATIONAL MODERN were Max Berg of the Centennial Hall at Wroclaw (Breslau) of 1913 – the first (apart from bridges) to take into account the possibilities of arcuated concrete – and MENDELSOHN of the Einstein Tower of 1918–20.

But the Einstein Tower is pre–the-International–Modern of Mendelsohn. It belongs to that Expressionism which for a brief moment even Gropius and Mies fell victim to. Most convincedly Expressionist in the years about 1920 were POELZIG (Grosses Schauspielhaus Berlin 1919), Häring (Garkau farm buildings 1923) and SCHAROUN.

Scharoun's is an interesting case. His Expressionism disqualified him for the years of International Modern. Only when the neo-sculptural, individualistic, chunky-concrete style of the fifties and sixties replaced the disciplined, often neutral International Modern – and Germany was late in making the change set off originally by LE CORBUSIER – did Scharoun come into his own. The Berlin Philharmonic Hall of 1956–63 is supreme proof. Frey Otto with his brilliant suspended roofs is now continuing in this neo-Expressionism. EIERMANN led the other, the Miesian side. He died in 1970.

GIANT ORDER, see COLOSSAL ORDER.

GIBBERD, Sir Frederick (b. 1908). One of the first in England to accept the INTERNATIONAL MODERN style of the 1930s (Pulman Court, Streatham, London, 1934–5). His best-known works after the Second World War are the plan and some of the chief buildings for the New Town of Harlow (1947 etc.); the Lansbury Market at Poplar, London (1950–1); and the buildings for London Airport (1950 etc.).

GIBBS, James (1682–1754). The most influential London church architect of the early C18. In contrast to his predominantly Whig and neo-Palladian contemporaries, he was a Scot, a Catholic, and a Tory with Jacobite sympathies, and had the unique advantage of training under a leading Italian architect, Carlo FONTANA. Born in Aberdeen he went to Rome c. 1703 to study for the priesthood, but left the Scots College after a year. He stayed on in Rome until 1709, and appears to have studied painting before turning to architecture. His first building, St Mary-le-Strand, London (1714–17), is a mixture of WREN and Italian Mannerist and Baroque elements.

Rather surprisingly, he was then taken up by Lord BURLINGTON, though only to be dropped in favour of Colen CAMPBELL, who replaced him as architect of Burlington House. He had no further contact with the neo-Palladians and remained faithful to Wren and his Italian masters, although he absorbed into his eclectic style a few Palladian features. St Martin-in-the-Fields, London (1722–6), is his masterpiece, and was widely imitated, especially in its combination of temple-front portico and steeple rising from the ridge of the roof. The monumental side elevations of recessed giant columns and giant pilasters have windows with his characteristic GIBBS SURROUND.

His best surviving secular buildings are outside London: the Octagon, Twickenham (1720); Sudbrooke Park, Petersham (c. 1720); Ditchley House (1720–5); and the Senate House (1722–30) and King's College Fellows' Building at Cambridge (1724–49). Several of these display his ebulliently Italian Baroque style of interior decoration at its sumptuous best. His last and most original building, the Radcliffe Library, Oxford (1737–49), is unique in England in showing the influence of Italian Mannerism. He exerted great influence both in Britain and in America through his *Book of Architecture* (1728), one of the plates from which probably inspired the White House in Washington.

GIBBS SURROUND. The surround of a doorway or window consisting of alternating large and small blocks of stone, quoinwise, or of intermittent large blocks; sometimes with a narrow raised band connecting up the verticals and along the face of the arch. Named after the architect James GIBBS though used by other architects, e.g. PALLADIO, CAMPBELL. *See figure 49.*

GIL DE HONTAÑÓN, Juan (d. 1526), and Rodrigo (d. 1577), father and son. Juan is the designer of the last two Gothic cathedrals of Spain, Salamanca

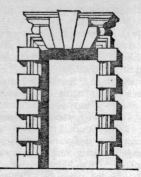

Fig. 49. Gibbs surround

and Segovia: at Salamanca he was consulted in 1512 (with eight others) and made master mason; at Segovia he started the new building in 1525. An earlier work of his is the cloister of Palencia Cathedral (begun 1505). He was consulted in 1513 for Seville Cathedral and designed the new lantern, etc., also still Gothic (1517-19).

Rodrigo appears first in 1521 at Santiago, probably as an assistant of JUAN DE ÁLAVA; then, in 1526, as one of the five architects consulted on the projected vast collegiate church of Valladolid (the others are his father, his master, FRANCISCO DE COLONIA, and Riaño). He was master mason at Astorga Cathedral (1530 etc.), where he built the nave; at Salamanca Cathedral (1537 etc.), where the transepts must be his; at the cloister of Santiago (1538 etc.), where he followed Álava; at Plasencia Cathedral (1537 or 1544), where the contributions of various masons are obscure; and at Segovia Cathedral (1563 etc.), where the east end is his. His finest secular work is the PLATERESQUE façade of Alcalá University (1541-53). He also wrote a book on architecture which is known only at second-hand.

GILBERT, Cass (1859-1934). He designed the Woolworth Building in New York (1913) which until 1930 was the highest building in America (*c.* 260 m.). With its Gothic details it still belongs to Historicism.

GILL, Irving John (1870-1936). American architect, working – after a training period in Chicago under SULLIVAN – in California. He started his own practice at San Diego in 1896. His early buildings belong to the SHINGLE STYLE, but later he created his own style, emphatically cubic and with large concrete blocks. It is the Spanish Missions Style of California that must have inspired him. The Dodge House of 1916 at Los Angeles illustrates this idiom of his. It is curiously similar to the most advanced European work of the same years.

GILLY, Friedrich (1772-1800), came of a French Huguenot family which had moved to Berlin in 1689, and was the son of the architect David Gilly. In spite of his neo-classical convictions he started as a Gothic enthusiast, drawing the Marienburg in West Prussia (1794). The king bought one of the drawings and gave young Gilly a four-year travel grant which, because of the war, he could not take up. In 1796 the idea of a national monument for Frederick the Great was revived. The king had died in 1786, and in the following year the monument had first been suggested: Christian Genelli at once submitted a Greek Doric temple, a very early case of faith in Grecian ideals (*but see* LEDOUX and SOANE). Gilly now designed a great funerary precinct and in its centre, raised on a high platform, a much larger Greek Doric temple – a Parthenon for the Prussian king. The precinct is strikingly original and strikingly severe in its forms. It is true that Gilly leant on the most recent work of young Parisian architects and their model PIRANESI (e.g., in the tunnel-vaulted triumphal arch), but the absolutely unmoulded cubic shapes are all his.

The year after, he took up his grant, but went to France and England instead of Italy: what he drew in Paris shows the sympathies already indicated by the monument. On his return in 1798 Gilly was made Professor of Optics and Perspective at the newly founded Academy of Architecture. In the same year he did his design for a national theatre for Berlin; in spite of certain motifs derived from Paris it is perhaps the most unimitative design of the age. It seems easier to reach the C20 from this unrelieved geometrical shape than from anything between Gilly and 1890. The functions of the various parts of the building are made perfectly clear, and the semicircular front in particular, taken from Legrand and Molinos's Théâtre Feydeau (which Gilly drew in Paris), was handed by him to Moller (Theatre, Mainz, 1829), and from there reached SEMPER.

GIOCONDO, Fra (c. 1433–1515). A Dominican friar, born in Verona. His main building is the Palazzo del Consiglio, Verona (1476–93), with its elegant Renaissance arcade and its two-light windows on the first floor placed in a Gothic manner above the columns. He was in Paris 1495–1505. In 1511 he published the first illustrated edition of VITRUVIUS. Appointed architect to St Peter's with RAPHAEL, he produced a very elaborate plan (unexecuted).

GIOTTO DI BONDONE (c. 1266–1337) was appointed master mason to the cathedral and city of Florence in 1334 on account of his fame as a painter. His architectural work was limited to the campanile of the cathedral, which he began in that year. The design was altered after his death.

GIULIANO DA MAIANO (1432–90). He was the elder brother of BENEDETTO DA MAIANO. He began as a wood-carver (choirstalls in Pisa Cathedral, cupboards in New Sacristy, Florence Cathedral, 1463–5) but later worked mainly as an architect and was appointed architect to Florence Cathedral from 1477 until his death. He helped to diffuse the Early Renaissance style of BRUNELLESCHI and MICHEL-

OZZO throughout Tuscany and beyond to the Marches and Naples. He designed the chapel of S. Fina in the Collegiata at S. Gimignano (1468), Palazzo Spannochi, Siena (c. 1473) and Palazzo Venier, Recanati (1477, much altered later). His masterpiece is the cathedral of Faenza (1474–86). At Naples he designed the Palazzo di Poggio Reale (c. 1488, destroyed) and the quadrangular Porta Capuana (c. 1485) and, probably, the Piccolomini, Terranova and Tolosa chapels in the Chiesa di Monteoliveto, Naples.

GIULIO ROMANO (Giulio Pippi or Giulio Giannuzzi, 1492/9–1546), who was born in Rome, began as both painter and architect in the classical shadow of RAPHAEL, but soon developed a strongly personal and dramatically forceful Mannerist style. His first building, Palazzo Cicciaporci-Senni, Rome (1521–2), is in the tradition of BRAMANTE and Raphael but with significant variations, e.g., columns resting on a bold string course which appears to have swallowed up their bases, and tall oblong panels instead of pilasters, connected neither to an entablature nor to a base. In 1524 he went to work for Federigo Gonzaga at Mantua, where all his most notable buildings were constructed. Palazzo del Te (1526–31) was designed for Federigo's honeymoon and as a summer villa. One storey high, it is built around an enormous courtyard and looks on to a garden terminated by a semicircular pilastered colonnade. Much in the plan derives from ancient Rome by way of Raphael's Villa Madama, but the careful interrelation of house and garden is new. Still more revolutionary were the façades: one of them smooth, with the SERLIAN MOTIF repeated as a blind arcade towards the garden; the others excessively rough with irregular rustication, Tuscan columns, massive keystones and wilfully misused classical details (the centre triglyph of each intercolumniation looks as if it had slipped out of place). He decorated the interior with frescoes, mainly of an erotic nature. One room gives a key to his strange personality: it has only one door and no windows and the walls and ceiling are painted to represent the Fall of the Titans, so that the shape of the room is entirely effaced and the visitor finds himself engulfed in a cascade of boulders and gigantic nude figures some 14 ft high.

On the façade of his own house in Mantua (c. 1544) he again indulged in a truculently licentious misuse of classical detail, but this time with a different intention. It is elegantly aloof and sophisticated instead of oppressive and neurotic. For the Palazzo Ducale, Mantua, he designed the Cortile della Cavallerizza (c. 1544), with coupled twisted columns on the first floor and one wing pierced by arches and square windows to afford a view across a near-by lake. He also designed Mantua Cathedral (1545), with double aisles supported by sturdy Corinthian columns whose repeated drum-beat monotony draws the visitor towards the high altar – another instance of his preoccupation with the effect a building would make rather than with the perfection of its form. With him the history of Expressionism in architecture begins.

GLACIS. In military architecture, the ground sloping from the top of the parapet of the covered way till it reaches the level of the open country, so that every part of it can be swept by the fire of the ramparts.

GODEFROY, Maximilien (c. 1760–1833). French *émigré* architect who introduced Parisian NEO-CLASSICAL ideals to the U.S. He was trained in Paris where he knew the painter J.-L. David and probably LEDOUX. His chief works are the advanced neo-classical Unitarian Church in Baltimore (1807, interior destroyed) and the Commercial and Farmer's Bank in Baltimore (1810) of which only the doorway survives. His masterpiece is the Battle Monument in Baltimore (designed 1810, built 1814–27), the first great civic monument in the U.S. and a precursor of MILLS's Washington Monuments in Baltimore and Washington. But Godefroy's neo-classical ideals did not prevent him from indulging in neo-Gothic, e.g., the chapel of St Mary's Seminary, Baltimore (1807).

GONDOUIN or Gondoin, Jacques (1737–1818). French neo-classical architect trained under J.-F. BLONDEL and at the French Academy in Rome (1761–64), then travelled in Holland and England. His masterpiece is the École de Médecine in Paris (1769–75) designed as a temple of Aesculapius. The street façade is in the form of an Ionic colonnade (correctly Greek in detail) with a triumphal arch motif in the centre giving access to a square court on the far side of which a Corinthian portico leads into the semicircular anatomy theatre covered by a half Pantheon-dome. The building also included a small hospital, library, laboratories, etc. Monumental in design and practical in plan it is one of the finest and most advanced public buildings of its period anywhere. The anatomy theatre became the prototype for the Chamber of Deputies in the Palais Bourbon (1795–7 but rebuilt 1828–33) and for many later legislative buildings including LATROBE's House of Representatives in the Capitol at Washington. Gondouin established a successful private practice but was ruined by the Revolution and went into hiding. Under the Empire he re-emerged and designed the column in the Place Vendôme, Paris (completed 1810), first of the giant columns to be erected in the early C19 from Baltimore to Leningrad.

GOPURA. The elaborate high gateway to South Indian temples, characteristic of Hindu architecture. *See figure 50.*

GOTHIC ARCHITECTURE. The architecture of the pointed arch, the RIB VAULT, the FLYING BUTTRESS, the

Fig. 50. Gopura

walls reduced to a minimum by spacious arcades, by GALLERY or TRIFORIUM, and by spacious CLERESTORY windows. These are not isolated motifs; they act together and represent a system of skeletal structure with active, slender, resilient members and membrane-thin infilling or no infilling at all. The motifs are not in themselves Gothic inventions. Pointed arches had existed in ROMANESQUE Burgundy, Southern France, and also Durham. Rib vaults had existed in Durham too; and the principle of flying buttresses as half-arches or half-tunnel vaults under the roofs of aisles or galleries above aisles is also found in French and English Romanesque. Even the verticalism of Gothic churches is only rarely more pronounced than that of, say, St Sernin at Toulouse or Ely (both Romanesque churches). The earliest completely Gothic building is the lower part of

the east end of St Denis Abbey, dating from 1140–4. For the development of the style in France and then in all other countries, *see* FRENCH; ENGLISH; GERMAN; SPANISH; etc.

GOTHIC REVIVAL. The movement to revive the Gothic style belongs chiefly to the late C18 and the C19. Before the late C18 it must be distinguished from the Gothic Survival, an unquestioning continuation of Gothic forms, which is of course largely a matter of out-of-the-way buildings. Of major buildings mostly churches are concerned, and St Eustache in Paris and the chapel of Lincoln's Inn in London were completed well within the C17. By then, however, the new attitude of Revival had also appeared – the conscious choice of the Gothic style in contrast to the accepted current style. The first cases are those of the finishing of Gothic buildings, cases of Gothic for the sake of conformity (flèche, Milan Cathedral; façade, S. Petronio, Bologna), but soon the choice was also made for new buildings, though rarely before *c.* 1720. Then cases multiply, at least in England (HAWKSMOOR), and with Horace Walpole's Strawberry Hill (*c.* 1750–70) the Gothic Revival became a fashion. It affected France and Germany in the later C18, and a little later also Italy, Russia, America, etc. With the growth of archaeological knowledge, the Gothic Revival became more competent but also more ponderous. For churches Gothic remained the accepted style well into the C20. Of public buildings, the epoch-making one was the Houses of Parliament in London (1834 etc.): other major examples are the Town Hall in Vienna, the Houses of Parliament at Budapest, the Law Courts in London, the University at Glasgow.

GRAND ORDER, *see* COLOSSAL ORDER.

GRAVESANDE, Arent van 's (d. 1662). A follower of van CAMPEN and a leading exponent of Dutch classicism. His style was already well developed in his earliest known building, the Sebastiaansdoelen in The Hague (1636). His mature work is all in Leyden where he was municipal architect – the Cloth Hall (1639), the Bibliotheca Thysiana and his masterpiece the Marekerk (1638–48), an octagonal domed church with Ionic columns supporting the drum of the dome. He later began a variant of this design in the Oostkerk at Middelburg (1646).

GREEK ARCHITECTURE. Commenting on the buildings on the Acropolis at Athens, Plutarch remarked: 'They were created in a short time for all time. Each in its fineness was even then at once age-old; but in the freshness of its vigour it is, even to the present day, recent and newly wrought.' No better description of the aims and achievements of Greek architects has ever been written. Their ambition was to discover eternally valid rules of form and proportion; to erect buildings human in scale yet suited to the divinity of their gods; to create, in other words, a classically ideal architecture. Their success may be measured by the fact that their works have been copied on and off for some 2,500 years and have never been superseded. Though severely damaged, the Parthenon remains the most nearly perfect building ever erected. Its influence stretches from the immediate followers of its architects to LE CORBUSIER. Greek architecture was, however, predominantly religious and official. Whereas temples and public buildings were of the greatest magnificence, private houses seem to have been fairly simple single-storey affairs, built of cheap materials.

Although the technique of constructing arches was known to the Greeks and the materials used for building temples, after the C6 B.C., were normally stone or marble, their architecture was TRABEATED and preserved many of the techniques of wooden construction. A deep respect for tradition led them to preserve as decorative elements in their stone buildings many of the constructional elements of wooden ones: TRIGLYPHS representing the end of cross beams, GUTTAE the pegs used for fastening them, and METOPES the space between them. They derived much from other Mediterranean civilizations – the plan of the temple from Crete by way of Mycenae, the columnar form from Egypt, the capital from Assyria.

But the Doric temple form evolved in the late C7 B.C. was as original as it was typically Greek in its bold simplicity, unity of design, and use of decoration to emphasize (never to mask) structure. The earliest Doric temple to survive is that of Hera at Olympia (before 600 B.C.); it originally had wooden columns which were gradually replaced in stone. Fragments from the temple at Korkyra, Corfu (c. 600 B.C.), reveal that sculpture was already used for the pediments. Other notable early Doric temples include the Temple C at Selinunte in Sicily (mid C6 B.C.), the so-called Basilica at Paestum (c. 530 B.C.), and the temple of Zeus Olympios at Agrigento in Sicily (c. 500–470 B.C.). In all these the columns are rather stocky and primitive-looking, partly because their smooth stucco coverings have flaked off. Much greater refinement marks the temple of Hephaistos, Athens (c. 449–444 B.C.). The summit was reached at the Parthenon (447–438 B.C.), with its perfect proportions and nicely balanced relation of sculpture to architecture. Here, as in other Doric temples, great pains were taken to correct optical illusions by the subtle use of ENTASIS. The temple to Athena Nike (448–421 B.C.) and the Erechtheum (421–406 B.C.), also on the Acropolis, reveal a tendency towards the exquisite; and the latter, with its graceful Ionic capitals and wonderful CARYATIDS, also points towards a new appreciation of architectural movement.

A desire for richer ornamentation was manifested by the Mausoleum of Halicarnassus (355–330 B.C.), where the role of the sculptor was greater than that of the architect. The final stage of Greek architectural development may be illustrated by the Choragic Monument of Lysicrates, Athens (335–334 B.C.), of an almost over-bred elegance which seems to anticipate the C18, when, indeed, it became the most popular of all Greek monuments.

Although the main Greek achievement was in the evolution of the Doric temple, many other types of religious buildings were of great beauty. The grandest were the theatres, notably that of Dionysus under the Acropolis in Athens (C5 B.C., but much altered) and that at Epidaurus (c. 350 B.C.), which reveal as perfect a command of acoustics as of visual effects. Theatres of this type were much imitated, especially in Asia Minor, during the HELLENISTIC period. *See also* CRETAN AND MYCENAEAN ARCHITECTURE.

GREEK CROSS. A cross with four equal arms.

GREEK KEY, *see* FRET.

GREEK REVIVAL. Greek as against Roman architecture became known to the West only about 1750–60. It was at first regarded as primitive and imitated by only a few architects. The earliest example is a garden temple at Hagley by 'Athenian' STUART (1758). A Grecian fashion began only in the 1780s. Among the earliest believers in the positive value of the simplicity and gravity of the Greek C5 were LEDOUX and SOANE. The Greek Revival culminated in all countries in the 1820s and 1830s, even, with the HANSENS, in Athens itself. (*See also* GILLY, SCHINKEL, SMIRKE, WILKINS, STRICKLAND, HAMILTON, PLAYFAIR, etc.)

GROIN. The sharp edge formed by the intersection of vaulting surfaces.

GROIN VAULT, *see* VAULT.

GROPIUS, Walter (1883–1969).

Studied at the Colleges of Technology of Berlin and Munich. He received his introduction to the C20 problems of architecture and the responsibilities of the architect in the office of Peter BEHRENS, who believed in the architect's duty to provide well-designed buildings for working in, and also well-designed everyday products. He spent the years 1907–10 with Behrens. The outcome of this was that Gropius, as soon as he had established a practice of his own (1910), submitted a memorandum to a powerful potential client on the mass-producing of housing and equipment. One year later he built, with Adolph Meyer (1881–1929), the Fagus factory at Alfeld, one of the earliest buildings in any country to be in full command of the elements of architecture which were to constitute the INTERNATIONAL MODERN style: glass CURTAIN WALLING, unrelieved cubic blocks, corners left free of visible supports. For the Werkbund Exhibition at Cologne in 1914, Gropius produced, also with Adolphus Meyer, a Model Factory and Office Building, equally radical in its statement of new principles. Apart from Behrens, Frank Lloyd WRIGHT was now a source of inspiration; for two publications about him had appeared in Berlin in 1910 and 1911. On the strength of the Werkbund Exhibition building, Henri van de VELDE, then head of the School of Arts and Crafts at Weimar, advised the Grand Duke to make Gropius his successor. Gropius accepted and, when the First World War was over, settled down at Weimar to convert the school into a completely new establishment, for which he coined the name BAUHAUS (House of Building). This name alludes to Gropius's conviction that, as with the medieval cathedral, the building ought to be the meeting-place of all arts and crafts teaching; all should work towards this ultimate unity. He also believed that all artists should be familiar with crafts, and that the initial training of artists and craftsmen should be one and the same – an introduction to form, colour, and the nature of materials. This part of the teaching programme, first worked out by Johannes Itten, was known as the Basic Course (*Vorkurs*).

Gropius, in the first years of the Bauhaus, was propelled by the ideas of William MORRIS on the one hand, by the enthusiasm of the Expressionists on the other. There are, indeed, a few works by him belonging to these first years which are entirely Expressionist in style, notably the jagged concrete monument to those killed in the March Rising (1921) and the large log-house for the timber manufacturer Adolf Sommerfeld (1921–2), the latter equipped by Bauhaus staff and students. But then in 1923, stimulated by contacts with the Dutch group of De Stijl (led by Theo van Doesburg), Gropius returned to the ideals of his early years. The Bauhaus turned from emphasis on craft to emphasis on industrial design, and Gropius's own style followed once again the line laid down by the Fagus factory. The principal monument of this change is the Bauhaus's own new premises at Dessau (1925–6), functionally planned and detailed. Other important designs of these flourishing years in Germany are those for a Total Theatre (1926) and the long slabs of 'rational' housing for Siemensstadt (1929).

The rising tide of National Socialism killed the Bauhaus, but Gropius had already left it in 1928. After Hitler assumed power, Gropius left Germany and, following a short spell of partnership with Maxwell FRY in London (1934–7) – the most influential outcome of which was the Impington Village College near Cambridge – he went to Harvard. The Impington College is the first of a type of informally grouped school buildings which after the Second World War has focused international attention on England. At Harvard Gropius's principal job was once again teaching. In accordance with his faith in cooperative work he started his own firm as the Architects' Collaborative – a group of younger men working with him in full freedom. Of the achievements of this cooperative the Harvard Graduate Centre (1949) and a block of flats for the Berlin Hansa Quarter (Interbau Exhibition, 1957) may be mentioned. Foremost among Gropius's later work is the United States Embassy at Athens (1957–61).

GROTESQUE. Fanciful ornamental decoration in paint or stucco, resembling ARABESQUE and used by the Romans on walls of buildings which, when discovered, were underground (i.e., in 'grottoes'), hence the name. It consists of medallions, sphinxes, foliage, etc., and was much used by painters and decorators from RAPHAEL onwards, especially during the C18.

GROTTO. An artificial cavern, usually with fountains and other water-works, and decorated with rock- and shell-work. It was especially popular in the C18.

GUARINI, Guarino (1624–83), was born in Modena and was a Theatine father, well known as a philosopher and mathematician, before he won fame as an architect. (He expanded Euclid and even foreshadowed Monge in his learned *Placita philosophica* of 1665.) Since he was first a mathematician and second an architect, his complex spatial compositions are sometimes difficult to understand by eye alone. But they are as exhilarating intellectually as artistically. All his important surviving buildings are in Turin, where he spent the last seventeen years of his life. His admiration of BORROMINI is very obvious in Collegio dei Nobili (1678) and Palazzo Carignano (1679), especially the latter with its oval saloon and undulating façade in the style of S. Carlo alle Quattro Fontane. To inflate Borromini's miniature church to palatial grandiloquence was daring enough, yet his originality had already carried him even farther in the Cappella della SS. Sindone (1667–90) and in S. Lorenzo (1668–87). Both churches are crowned with fantastic and unprecedented cone-shaped domes. That of SS. Sindone is built of superimposed segmental arches that diminish in span as they ascend, the abstract geometric poetry of this free construction being emphasized by the diaphanous light which filters through the grids. The S. Lorenzo dome is equally unusual: it is composed of interlocking semicircular arches forming an octagon on a circular drum. The inspiration for this odd conception may have come from Hispano-Moresque architecture, perhaps from the similar dome in the mosque of al Hakim at Cordova (A.D. 965). Guarini's structural ingenuity was not confined to domes, and his other experiments, notably those with banded vaults and diagonal, forward-tilted, or three-dimensional arches, were to be very influential in Germany and Austria. None of his important buildings outside Turin has survived: e.g., SS. Annunziata and Theatine Palace in Messina (1660); Ste Anne-la-Royale, Paris (1662 onwards); St Mary of Altötting, Prague (1679); and S. Maria Divina Providencia, Lisbon. His influence was greatly increased by his *Architettura civile*, published posthumously in 1737: engravings from it were known from 1668 onwards.

GUAS, Juàn (d. 1496). A Spanish mason of French descent, probably the designer of S. Juan de los Reyes at Toledo (1476 etc.). Towards the end of his life Guas was master mason of Segovia and Toledo Cathedrals. It is likely that the wildly Late Gothic façade of S. Gregorio at Valladolid is his (1487–96).

GUÊPIÈRE, Pierre-Louis-Philippe de la (*c.* 1715–73). French architect who, alongside PIGAGE, introduced Louis XVI taste and standards into Germany. In 1750 he published *Recueil de projets d'architecture* and in the same year was summoned to Stuttgart where he succeeded Leopoldo Retti as *Directeur des bâtiments* in 1752 and designed the interiors of Retti's Neues Palais (destroyed). His masterpieces are the small and exquisite La Solitude (1763–7) outside Stuttgart and Mon Repos (1764–7) near Ludwigsburg. The interior of the latter was partially modified *c.* 1804 in an Empire style. He returned to France in 1768 but built nothing of note there. His designs for the Hôtel de Ville at Montbéliard were executed after his death with considerable alterations. He published *Recueil d'esquisses d'architecture* in 1762.

GUILLOCHE. A pattern of interlacing bands forming a plait and used as an enrichment on a moulding. *See figure 51.*

Fig. 51. Guilloche

GUIMARD, Hector (1867–1942), was professor at the École des Arts Décoratifs from 1894 to 1898. He is the best of the French ART NOUVEAU architects. At the beginning of his career (in 1893) he was influenced, it seems, by HORTA. His most remarkable building is the block of flats called Castel Bérenger in Paris (1894–8). The use of metal, faïence, and glass-bricks is bold and inventive, though the exterior is of less interest. On the other hand his Métro stations (1899–1904) are nothing but exterior – open metal arches in extreme Art Nouveau shapes – a daring thing for an architect to design, and perhaps an even more daring thing for a client to accept.

GUMPP, Johann Martin (1643–1739). The most important member of a family of architects working in Innsbruck where he was Hofkammerbaumeister and a pioneer exponent of the Baroque. His main works are the

Fugger-Welsberg palace (1679–80), the remodelling of the old Government House (1690–92) and the Spitalkirche (1700–1701). His son Georg Anton (1682–1754) followed him as master mason to the Innsbruck court and was responsible for the boldly unconventional Landhaus (1725–8).

GUTTAE. Small drop-like projections carved below the TENIA under each TRIGLYPH on a Doric ARCHITRAVE. *See figure 64.*

H

HADFIELD, George (*c.* 1764–1826), was born in Leghorn and trained at the Royal Academy Schools, London, winning the Gold Medal in 1784 and studying in Italy 1790–1. In about 1794 he went to America and was appointed in 1795 to supervise the construction of the new Capitol in Washington, replacing Stephen Hallet. He disapproved of the design (by Thornton) and Hallet's revisions, but the radical alterations he suggested, such as the introduction of a colossal order, were not approved and he was dismissed in 1798. He continued to practise in Washington and impressed his neo-classical taste on the new city, e.g., the City Hall, United States Bank, Fuller's Hotel, Gadsby's Hotel, Van Ness's mausoleum, and Arlington House (*c.* 1803–17) whose imposing Paestum portico is one of the most splendid examples of the Greek Revival in America.

HAGIOSCOPE, *see* SQUINT.

HALFPENNY, William (Michael Hoare, d. 1755). His only surviving buildings of note are Holy Trinity, Leeds (1722–7) and the Redlands Chapel, Bristol (1740–43), but he published some twenty architectural manuals for country gentlemen and builders which were enormously successful and influential. His designs are mostly Palladian but also include some rather ham-fisted attempts at Rococo sophistication, CHINOISERIE, GOTHIC REVIVAL, etc. *A New and Compleat System of Architecture* (1749) and *Rural Architecture in the Chinese Taste* (*c.* 1750) are among the best of his books.

HALF-TIMBERING, *see* FRAMED BUILDING *and* TIMBER-FRAMING.

HALL CHURCH. A church in which nave and aisles are of approximately equal height.

HAMILTON, Thomas (1784–1858), was the leading GREEK REVIVAL architect in Edinburgh alongside W. H. PLAYFAIR. His masterpiece is the Royal High School, Edinburgh (1825–9). It is as forceful and dramatic – and as accomplished – as any Greek Revival building anywhere. But he was never able to repeat this success and his later work lacks impetus, e.g., the Assembly Rooms, Ayr (1827–30), the Dean Orphanage, Edinburgh (1831–3), the Burns Monument on Calton Hill, Edinburgh (1830) and the ingenious, refined but unconvincing Physicians' Hall, Edinburgh (1843–6).

HAMMERBEAM, *see* ROOF

HANSEN, Theophil von (1813–91). A Danish architect who became a leading exponent of C19 Historicism in architecture, specializing in Italian Renaissance but equally at home with Greek Revival and Venetian Byzantine. He was trained in Copenhagen and travelled to Berlin, Munich, Italy and Greece and settled there, in Athens, for eight years (1838–46). His elder brother Hans Christian Hansen (1803–83) had been in Athens since 1833, became the Royal Architect and built Athens University (1839–50) in an appropriate Greek Revival style. Theophil Hansen's buildings in Athens, also Greek Revival, date from some years later – the Academy (1859–87) and Library (1885–92). In 1846 he had settled in Vienna where he spent the rest of his life. In 1851 he married the daughter of Ludwig Förster, with whom he had collaborated on the Army Museum in the Arsenal in Vienna (1850) and who was mainly responsible for the Ring and the consequent urban development in Vienna. Hansen designed several of the more prominent public buildings on or near the Ring: Heinrichshof (1861-3, destroyed 1945); Musikverein (1867-9); Stock Exchange (1874-7); Academy of Art (1872-6); Parliament (1873-83).

HARDOUIN-MANSART, Jules (1646-1708), the grand-nephew of François MANSART, by whom he may have been trained, owed more to LE VAU, whose grand manner he and Lebrun brought to perfection in the Galerie des Glaces at Versailles. He understood perfectly the artistic needs of Louis XIV's court and excelled as an official architect, being competent, quick, and adaptable. (He was appointed Royal Architect in 1675, *Premier Architecte* in 1685, and *Surintendant des Bâtiments* in 1699.) His meteoric career aroused jealousy, and Saint-Simon accused him of keeping tame architects in a backroom to do all his work for him. He was certainly lucky in having such gifted assistants as Lassurance and Pierre Le Pautre, but he had real ability himself and a vivid sense of the splendour and visual drama required for a royal setting. From 1678 onwards he was in charge of the vast extensions to Versailles. These were disastrous externally, for he filled in the central terrace of Le Vau's garden façade and trebled its length. The stables, orangery, Trianon, and chapel are more successful (the latter being finished by Robert de COTTE). His Baroque tendencies reached their height in the Invalides Chapel in Paris (1680-91), while the Place Vendôme (1698 etc.) illustrates his genius for the spectacular in town planning. Towards the end of his life, notably in a number of rooms at Versailles, Trianon, and Marly, which were redecorated under his direction in the 1690s, he veered away from Baroque splendours towards a lighter and more elegant style which marks the first step towards the Rococo.

HARDWICK, Philip (1792-1870). He stopped practising in the course of the 1840s. His son and grandson were also architects. In 1815 he was in Paris, and he spent 1818-19 in Italy. His *œuvre* does not seem to have been large, but it is of high quality and varied interest. His most famous building was Euston Station, with its majestic Greek Doric propylaea (1836-9) which became famous when it was infamously destroyed by the British Transport Commission. The station building was quite independent of the propylaea, whose spiritual function was that of a worthy introduction to that miracle of human ingenuity, the London-to-Birmingham railway. The range of stylistic possibilities open to Hardwick was great, and he was remarkably good at all of them: a monumentally plain, strictly utilitarian classicism of brick and short Tuscan columns for the St Katherine's Dock warehouses (1827-8); an at the time most unusual restrained English Baroque for the Goldsmiths' Hall (1829-35); Jacobean for Babraham Hall, Cambridgeshire (1831); and a convincing and unaffected Tudor for Lincoln's Inn Hall and Library (1842-5). On the latter, PEARSON was assistant, and it is possible that the refined detailing is his; at all events, the building is effortlessly convincing and has no longer the character of romantic make-believe of early C19 Tudor imitations.

HARLING. The Scots term for ROUGH-CAST.

HARMONIC PROPORTIONS. A system of proportions relating architecture to music. The Ancients discovered that if two cords are twanged the difference in pitch will be one octave if the shorter is half the length of the longer, a fifth if one is two thirds of the other, and a fourth if the ratio is $3:4$. It was therefore assumed that rooms or whole buildings whose measurements followed the ratios $1:2$, $2:3$, or $3:4$ would be harmonious. Early Renaissance architects, notably ALBERTI, seized on this discovery as the key to the beauty of Roman architecture and also to the harmony of the universe. The idea was further developed by PALLADIO who, with the aid of Venetian musical theorists, evolved a far more complex scale of proportions based on the major and minor third – 5:6 and 4:5 – and so on.

HARRISON, Peter (1716–75). The only architect of distinction in pre-Revolutionary America. Born in England, he emigrated in 1740, and settled in Newport, Rhode Island, as a trader in wines, rum, molasses, and mahogany. He presumably taught himself architecture but quickly acquired competence in the Palladian style, as his first work shows – Redwood Library, Newport (1749–58), a timber building imitating rusticated stone. Other buildings show Gibbsian influence: King's Chapel, Boston (1749–58); Synagogue, Newport (1759–63). But he returned to Inigo JONES and the English Palladians for inspiration in his later works: Brick Market, Newport (1761–72), and Christ Church, Cambridge, Mass. (1760). He settled in New Haven, Conn., in 1761, and became Collector of Customs there in 1768, suffering some persecution in his later years as a loyalist and government official.

HASENAUER, Karl von, see SEMPER.

HAUSSMANN, Baron Georges-Eugène (1809–91). A Protestant from Alsace who became a lawyer and civil servant. He was ruthless, canny, and obstinate. Napoleon III made him Prefect of the Seine Department in 1853 and entrusted to him his sweeping plans for city improvement. Haussmann kept the post till 1870, and did as much as, or perhaps more than, the emperor expected. Haussmann's improvements follow the traditional principles of French town planning as established by Henri IV and developed by Louis XIV, and finally – Haussmann's direct model – by the so-called Artists' Plan of 1797: long straight boulevards meeting at *rond-points* are the principal motifs. It is often said that Haussmann made these boulevards to obtain good firing-lines in case of a revolution, but he was at least as much guided by traffic considerations (e.g., the connecting of railway stations) and was without doubt also passionately devoted to vistas towards monuments or monumental buildings such as the Arc de Triomphe or the Opéra.

HAVILAND, John (1792–1852). American architect. He was a pupil of James ELMES and went to live at Philadelphia in 1816. In 1818–19 he brought out *The Builder's Assistant*, the first American book to illustrate the ORDERS of columns. His *magnum opus* is the Eastern Penitentiary at Cherry Hill, Philadelphia (1821–9), much imitated in Europe. It has battlements, whereas Haviland's Institute for the Deaf and Dumb (1824) has classical features and The Tombs in New York (1836–8), Law Courts and Prison, in one, is neo-Egyptian.

HAWKSMOOR, Nicholas (1661–1736), the most original of English Baroque architects except VANBRUGH, came from a family of Nottinghamshire farmers. At eighteen he became WREN's amanuensis and was closely associated with him at Greenwich Hospital and other buildings until his death. Vanbrugh also found him an able assistant and employed him from 1690 onwards, notably at Castle Howard and Blenheim Palace. Indeed, he became more than just an assistant to both Wren and Vanbrugh, though it is impossible now to assess how much they owed to him. His independent works have great originality, and only his dour, capricious character and lack of push denied him greater opportunities and worldly success. Vigorous, odd, bookish, yet massively plastic in feeling, his style is a highly personal Baroque amalgam of Wren, classical Rome, and Gothic. Like Vanbrugh, but unlike Wren, his passion was for dramatic effects of mass, and he has been criticized for heaviness as a result. He began working on his own *c.* 1702 at Easton Neston, a compact rectangular building with a giant order all round; it combines Wren's grandeur and urbanity, and in some details foreshadows Vanbrugh. In 1711 he was appointed Surveyor under the Act for Building Fifty New Churches, and the six he designed himself form the bulk of his *œuvre*. All of them are minor masterpieces: St Anne's, Limehouse (1712–24), with its medieval steeple in classical dress; St Mary Woolnoth (1716–27), with its square within a square plan; St George's, Bloomsbury (1720–30), the most grandiose and least odd of all his buildings; and Christchurch, Spitalfields (1723–39), as perverse and megalomaniac as anything by Vanbrugh. His other buildings are only slightly less notable – the quadrangle and hall at All Souls', Oxford (1729), and the west towers of Westminster Abbey (1734), all in his neo-Gothic manner; and finally, the grim and austere circular Doric mausoleum at Castle Howard (1729), where he returned to Rome and BRAMANTE for inspiration.

HEADER, *see* BRICKWORK.

HEINZELMANN, Konrad (d. 1454), was at Ulm in the 1420s. He was called to Nördlingen in 1429 as master mason to design and build the church of St George, then to Rothenburg in 1428 to work on the church of St Jakob. In 1439 he went to Nuremberg, and there designed and began the beautiful chancel of St Lorenz.

HELIX. A spiral motif, especially the inner spiral of the volute of a Corinthian capital.

HELLENISTIC ARCHITECTURE. The style developed in the Hellenistic kingdoms created out of the empire conquered by Alexander the Great (356–323 B.C.). The tendency towards greater elegance and elaboration in small buildings (e.g., Choragic Monu-

ment of Lysicrates, Athens) and a more richly sculptural and monumental style for large ones (e.g., Mausoleum of Halicarnassus and the Ionic temple of Artemis at Ephesus), already evident in early C4 GREEK ARCHITECTURE, was accelerated. The greatest Hellenistic city was Alexandria, laid out on a regular grid plan with numerous vast and very splendid buildings, none of which survives. The Ionic temple of Athena Polias, Priene (*c.* 335 B.C.), and of Artemis Leukophryene at Magnesia by HERMOGENES (*c.* 130 B.C.) are representative of the style. Doric temples were still built, but the columns became much more slender and motifs from the Ionic order were introduced, as in the Temple of Hera Basileia at Pergamum (*c.* 150 B.C.). The richer Corinthian order was more to the taste of the new civilization: at Athens the great Olympeion (begun 174 B.C., though not completed until A.D. 131) is the first Corinthian building on the grand scale, and provides a piquant contrast to the sober solemnity of the Parthenon on the Acropolis above it.

Many of the finest Hellenistic buildings are civic rather than religious: the Bouleuterion at Miletus (174–65 B.C.) and various colonnaded walks like the recently restored Stoa in the Athenian AGORA (*c.* 150 B.C.). Military engineering was brought to a new height of efficiency and many forts and walls, with handsome crisply cut masonry and sometimes with arched gateways, survive both in Greece and in Asia Minor (e.g., Priene). Excavations have revealed that private houses were built on a much grander scale than before.

The Hellenistic style survived the conquest of Asia Minor by the Romans; indeed, Imperial Roman architecture may be regarded as its logical development. The main buildings of the two great Syrian sites, Baalbek (the very rich Temple of

Bacchus, courts, and portico, c. A.D. 120–200) and Palmyra (Temple of the Sun, c. A.D. 1; Temple of Baal, A.D. 131), are predominantly Hellenistic in feeling, though their vaults, arches, and domes are typically Roman.

HELM ROOF, *see* ROOF.

HENNEBIQUE, François (1842–1921). One of the pioneers of concrete architecture. He first used REINFORCED CONCRETE in 1879. His most important patents are of 1892. In 1894 he built at Viggen in Switzerland the first bridge of reinforced concrete, in 1895 at Roubaix the first grain elevator. His concrete and glass factories begin in 1894. For an exhibition at Geneva in 1896 he built a cantilevered concrete staircase, and for a small theatre at Morges in 1899 cantilevered galleries. In a small theatre at Munich in 1903 he was allowed to leave the concrete frame exposed. His own crazy concrete villa at Bourg-la-Reine dates from 1904.

HENRY OF REYNS, Master of the King's Masons to Windsor Castle in 1243, and later to Westminster Abbey. He was dead, it seems, by 1253. This means he was King's Master Mason when Westminster Abbey was begun and so was probably its designer. Reyns sounds temptingly like Reims, and Reims Cathedral is, in fact, the stylistic source of much at Westminster (tracery, the wall-passages in the east chapels), together with work at Amiens, Royaumont and the Sainte Chapelle in Paris, only just completed when the abbey was begun. However, there are other features, such as the large gallery and the ridge-rib of the vault, which are entirely English and may make it more likely that Henry was an Englishman who had worked at Reims. Judging by style, Henry may also have designed the King's Chapel at Windsor Castle (built c. 1240).

HÉRÉ DE CORNY, Emmanuel (1705–63). The architect of the Place Royale (Place Stanislas) in Nancy, the finest example of Rococo urbanism anywhere. He was trained under BOFFRAND in Paris but returned c. 1740 to Nancy to become architect to Stanislas Leszczynski, ex-king of Poland, for whom all his work was carried out – Hôtel des Missions Royales (1741–3), Château de Malgrange (1743), Place Royale (1752 onwards, with the Place de la Carrière leading into the Hemicycle) and the Place d'Alliance, all in Nancy. The Place Royale owes much to the superb ironwork by Lamour. Héré published his works in *Recueil des plans*, etc. (1750) and *Plans et élévations de la Place Royale de Nancy* (1753).

HERLAND, Hugh (d. c. 1405). Carpenter in the king's service probably from c. 1350, and in charge of the king's works in carpentry from 1375, when William Herland, presumably his father, died. His *magnum opus* is the hammerbeam roof of Westminster Hall, done in the 1390s; it has a span of about 67 ft. He also worked for William of Wykeham (with WILLIAM OF WYNFORD) at New College, Oxford, and probably at Winchester College.

HERM. Originally, a rectangular pillar terminating in a head or bust (usually of Hermes), used to mark boundaries, etc. in ancient Greece. The form was adopted by Renaissance and Post-Renaissance architects for decorative purposes. [*See also* TERM.]

HERMOGENES (*fl. c.* 130 B.C.). Architect and apparently the most influential architectural theorist of the Hellenistic period. He was probably born at Priene where he designed an altar. Critical of the Doric ORDER, because 'the distribution of the triglyphs and metopes is troublesome and unharmonious', he designed two important Ionic temples – that of Dionysos at Teos and the large pseudodipteral temple of Artemis Leukophryne at Magnesia on the Meander. He commented on these works in writings which are lost but were known to and quoted by VITRUVIUS.

HERRERA, Juan de (*c.* 1530–97), travelled abroad, mainly in Italy, from 1547 to 1559. He was appointed to succeed Juan Bautista de TOLEDO at the Escorial in 1563, though he did not design any additions until after 1572: the infirmary and chapel (1574–82) were his main contributions. But his majestic if sometimes rather solemn and Italianate style is best seen at the Palace of Aranjuez (1569), at the Exchange at Seville (1582), and in his designs for Valladolid Cathedral (*c.* 1585), which were only partly executed but had enormous influence, e.g., on Salamanca, Mexico, Puebla, and Lima Cathedrals.

HERRINGBONE WORK. Stone, brick, or tile work in which the component units are laid diagonally instead of horizontally. Alternate courses lie in opposite directions, forming a zigzag pattern along the wall-face.

HEWN STONE. The American term for ASHLAR.

HEXASTYLE. Of a portico with six frontal columns.

HILDEBRANDT, Johann Lukas von (1668–1745). The leading Baroque architect in Austria alongside FISCHER VON ERLACH, he was born in Genoa, the son of a captain in the Genoese army and an Italian mother. Italian always remained his first language. He studied with Carlo FONTANA in Rome before settling in Vienna. He was appointed Court Architect in 1700 and knighted by the emperor in 1720. He succeeded Fischer von Erlach as First Court Architect in 1723. His style is lighter than SCHLÜTER's and more Italianate than Fischer von Erlach's, livelier too and homelier, with typically Viennese charm. He much admired GUARINI, as his early (1699) Dominican church at Gabel in North Bohemia shows. It has Guarini's characteristic three-dimensional arches and a complicated and imaginative Guarinesque plan (concave corners hidden by convex balconies etc.). The influence of BOR-ROMINI is evident in much of the carved decoration of his masterpiece, the Lower and Upper Belvedere in Vienna, built for Prince Eugene (the former completed 1714/15, the latter built 1720–23). His secular buildings are notable for their oval and octagonal rooms (Palais Schwarzenberg in Vienna, begun 1697; Summer Palace Ráckeve in Hungary, 1701–2; Palais Starhemberg-Schönborn in Vienna, 1706–17) and for their ingeniously planned and spacially dramatic ceremonial staircases (Palais Daun-Kinsky of 1713–16 and the Upper Belvedere in Vienna, Schloss Mirabell in Salzburg of 1713–16 and his addition to the Palais Harrach in Vienna of 1727–35). In 1711 he was consulted about the great staircase at Johann DIENTZENHOFER's Pommersfelden Palace and added the three-storey gallery there. From 1720–23 and again from 1729–44 he collaborated with NEUMANN on the rebuilding of the Residenz at Würzburg, contributing the designs for the lavishly decorated upper part of the central pavilion facing the gardens and the interiors of the Imperial hall and chapel. Though primarily a secular architect Hildebrandt built several churches including the Church of the Seminary at Linz (1717–25) with its boldly *mouvementé* façade, the parish church of Gollersdorf (1740–41) and probably the Piaristenkirche in Vienna (plan dated 1698, begun 1716 but later modified by K. I. DIENTZENHOFER), octagonal in plan and bright, rhythmical and Borrominesque inside.

HIP. The external angle formed by the meeting of two sloping roof surfaces. *See* ROOF *and figure 70.*

HIPPED ROOF, *see* ROOF.

HIPPODAMOS OF MILETUS (*fl. c.* 500 B.C.). Town-planner, political theorist and philosopher interested in the problem of urbanism. According to Aristotle (*Politics*), he originated the art of town planning and devised an ideal city to be inhabited by ten thousand citizens, divided into three classes (soldiers, artisans and husbandmen) and with the land also divided into three parts (sacred, public and private). The gridiron plan associated with his name had been in use since the C7 B.C. in Ionia though not in Attica. And his social ideas were hardly forward looking. But he seems to have been the first to appreciate that a town plan might formally embody and clarify a rational social order. He taught the Athenians the value of having a clear, regular and strictly functional town plan instead of the haphazard layouts of archaic Greek towns. He lived in Athens and became a friend of Pericles whose social ideas he appears to have shared. Though not an architect and never in charge of the actual construction of any town, he was probably responsible for the layout of Piraeus (founded by Themistocles c. 470 B.C.) on a gridiron system with a formal, enclosed AGORA as its central feature. He possibly inspired the plan of Thourioi (founded 443 B.C.) as a Pan-Hellenic centre. The town plan of Rhodes has been less plausibly attributed to him. The gridiron plan was much used in the later classical and Hellenistic periods. Thanks to Aristotle he has influenced writers on urbanism since the Renaissance (e.g. Sir Thomas More in *Utopia*).

HITTORF, Jakob Ignaz (1792–1867), was born at Cologne, went to Paris in 1810 with GAU and placed himself under PERCIER. He then worked under BÉLANGER just at the time when the latter was busy with the glass-and-iron dome of the Corn Market. In 1819–23 Hittorf travelled in Germany, England, and Italy. After that, till 1848, he was Royal Architect. His first major building, executed with his father-in-law Lepère, is St Vincent de Paul (begun 1824), still with an Ionic portico, but Early Christian rather than classical inside, with its two superimposed orders and its open roof. The exterior already shows the change from the pure classical to the new, grander, more rhetorical classical of the École des Beaux Arts as it culminated in Hittorf's Gare du Nord (1861–5). He also did extensive decorative work; laid out the Place de la Concorde in its present form (1838–40); built two Circuses (des Champs Élysées, 1839; Napoléon, 1851) with iron-and-glass domes; and, with Rohault de Fleury and Pellechet, designed the Grand Hôtel du Louvre – all of which proves his interest in new functions and new materials. Hittorf also made a name as an archaeologist, chiefly by his discovery of the polychromy of Greek architecture (1830), a 'Victorian' discovery shocking to the older generation of Grecian purists.

HOBAN, James (c. 1762–1831), was born in Ireland, emigrated to America after the Revolution, and was advertising in Philadelphia in 1785. But he settled in South Carolina until 1792, designing the State Capitol at Columbia (completed 1791, burnt down 1865), based on L' ENFANT's designs for the Federal Hall in New York. But he is remembered chiefly for the White House, Washington, which he designed in 1792, basing the front on a plate in GIBBS's *Book of Architecture*. He may also have had Leinster House, Dublin, in mind, though the White House is not, as has been suggested, a mere copy. It was built 1793–1801, and Hoban also supervised its rebuilding after 1814 (completed 1829). He also designed and built the Grand Hotel (1793–5) and the State and War Offices (begun in 1818), Washington. He ended his life as a solid and much respected councillor of that city.

HOFFMANN, Josef (1870–1956), was a pupil of Otto WAGNER in Vienna and one of the founders of the Wiener Werkstätte (1903), based on the

William MORRIS conviction of the importance of a unity between architecture and the crafts. His style developed from ART NOUVEAU towards a new appreciation of unrelieved square or rectangular forms ('Quadratl-Hoffmann') – a change not uninfluenced by MACKINTOSH, whose furniture and other work had been exhibited by the Secession (*see* OLBRICH) in 1900. The Convalescent Home at Purkersdorf outside Vienna (1903) is one of the most courageously squared buildings of its date anywhere in the world, and yet it possesses that elegance and refinement of detail which is the Viennese heritage. With his Palais Stoclet in Brussels (1905–11) Hoffmann proved that this new totally anti-period style of unrelieved shapes could be made to look monumental and lavish by means of the materials used – in this case white marble in bronze framing outside, mosaics by Gustav Klimt inside. Hoffmann later built many wealthy villas, some Austrian Pavilions for exhibitions, and also some blocks of flats, but his chief importance lies in his early works.

HOLABIRD & ROCHE. William Holabird (1854–1923) went to West Point in 1873–5 and to Chicago in 1875, where he took an engineering job in the office of W. Le B. JENNEY. In 1880 he formed a partnership with Martin Roche. Their Tacoma Building (1886–7), following Jenney's Home Insurance and going decisively beyond it, established steel-skeleton construction for SKYSCRAPERS (in this case of twelve storeys) and with it the Chicago School style. Their Marquette Building (1894) has the same importance stylistically as the Tacoma Building has structurally. Its horizontal windows and its crisp, unenriched mouldings pointed the way into the C20.

HOLFORD, Sir William, was born 1907 in South Africa. The leading town-planner in England, he is also widely recognized abroad, as witness his report on the development of Canberra (1957–8) and his presence on the jury for Brasilia (1957). In England his most brilliant design is that for the precinct of St Paul's Cathedral in London (1955–6), now in course of execution, with some unfortunate modifications. He was also responsible for the post-war plan for the City of London (with Charles Holden, 1946–7).

HOLL, Elias (1573–1646). The leading Renaissance architect in Germany where he holds a position parallel historically to that of his exact contemporaries Inigo JONES in England and de BROSSE in France and to the slightly younger van CAMPEN in Holland. He came of a family of Augsburg masons who had risen to prominence under the Fuggers. He travelled in Italy, visiting Venice 1600–1601 and presumably studying PALLADIO and other Italian architects. In 1602 he was appointed city architect of Augsburg where he was responsible for a large building programme including houses, warehouses, guildhalls, market halls for the various trades, schools, gates and towers for the city walls, the arsenal and the town hall. As a Protestant he suffered from the religious wars and was out of office 1630–32 and finally dismissed in 1635. His first building after his nomination as city architect was the Arsenal, begun 1602. He believed in symmetry and classical proportions – e.g., St Anne's School (1613) with its high arcades encircling the court, regular fenestration, horizontal emphasis and remarkably well-designed classrooms lit from both sides; and the Hospital of the Holy Ghost (1626–30) which had high arcades encircling a court. But his masterpiece is the Town Hall (1615–20, damaged in Second World War but rebuilt), a handsome, simple, rather severe building, much in advance of anything previously built in Germany. His aim was, he said, 'to obtain a bolder, more heroic appearance' and he claimed it was well proportioned. His first, unexecuted, design for it was more advanced stylistically than that built and made much play with Palladian windows almost in the manner of Palladio's Basilica in Vicenza. As built it is distinctly German in its verticality, especially in the central section of the façade which contrasts strikingly with the more classically pure bays on either side. His work outside Augsburg was less important but includes additions to the Willibaldsburg at Eichstätt (1608) and, probably, the designs for the Schloss at Bratislava (Pozsony: Pressburg, 1632–49).

HOLLAND, Henry (1745–1806), began under his father, a Fulham builder, then became assistant to 'Capability' BROWN, whose daughter he married. His first independent work, Brooks's Club, London (1776–8), was quickly followed by his greatest, Carlton House, London, which he enlarged and altered for the Prince of Wales (1783–5, demolished). Also for the Prince of Wales he built the Marine Pavilion at Brighton (1786–7), later transformed into the Royal Pavilion by NASH. His style owed something to both CHAMBERS and ADAM, with various Louis XVI elements added. Though lacking originality, the refined taste and 'august simplicity' of his interior decoration approached French neo-classicism in elegance. His best country houses are Southill (1795) and Berrington Hall (1778). He laid out and built Hans Town, Chelsea (1771 etc.), but this has been largely rebuilt.

HOOD, Raymond (1881–1934). His McGraw-Hill Building in New York (1931) is one of the first skyscrapers designed in the INTERNATIONAL MODERN style. In his Daily News Building (1930) he stressed the closely set verticals, and this must have inspired the Rockefeller Center (begun 1931).

HOOD-MOULD. A projecting moulding to throw off the rain, on the face of a wall, above an arch, doorway, or window; can be called *dripstone* or *label. See also* LABEL-STOP *and figure 52.*

Fig. 52. Hood-mould

HORNWORK. In military architecture, an outwork of two demi-bastions connected by a curtain and joined to the main work by two parallel wings.

HORSESHOE ARCH, *see* ARCH.

HORTA, Baron Victor (1861–1947), a Belgian architect, studied in Paris in 1878–80, then at the Brussels Academy under Balat. He appeared in the forefront of European architecture with his Hôtel Tassel in the rue Paul-Émile Janson (designed 1892). This is the same year as that of van de VELDE's first exploration of ART NOUVEAU typography and design. The Hôtel Tassel is less startling externally, but its staircase with exposed iron supports, floral iron ornament, and much linear decoration on the wall is Art Nouveau architecture of the boldest. The Hôtel Tassel was followed by the particularly complete and lavish Hôtel Solvay (1895–1900); the Maison du Peuple (1896–9), with a curved glass-and-iron façade and much structural and decorative iron inside the great hall; the store L'Innovation (1901; destroyed); and several more private houses. Later Horta turned to a conventional classicism (Palais des Beaux Arts, Brussels, 1922–9).

HÔTEL. In France a town-house of which the standard design was

established by SERLIO's 'Grand
Ferrare' in Fontainebleau (1544–6),
i.e., a *corps-de-logis* with narrower
wings forming a courtyard which is
enclosed towards the street by a wall or
by a stable and kitchen block, broken
in the middle by the entrace door. The
best surviving early example is the
Hôtel Carnavalet in Paris by LESCOT
of *c.* 1545. It was usual to have a
garden or small park behind the *corps-
de-logis*. The latter often contained a
gallery on the first floor. MANSART's
Hôtel de la Vrillière, Paris (1635–45)
became the model for the classical
type of Parisian hôtel.

HOWARD, Sir Ebenezer (1850–1928),
started as a clerk in the City of
London, rose to be a valued shorthand
writer, and remained that nearly to the
end. During a stay of five years in
America (1872–7), he learned to know
and admire Whitman and Emerson,
and began to think of the better life
and how it could be made to come
true. In 1898 he read Edward
Bellamy's utopian work *Looking
Backward*, and this gave him the idea
of his lifetime: that of the garden city
which is an independent city and not
a suburb – this is important – and is
placed in the green countryside and
provided with countrified housing as
well as industry and all cultural
amenities. His book *Tomorrow* came
out in 1898, in 1899 the Garden City
Association was founded, in 1902 the
book was republished as *Garden Cities
of Tomorrow*, and in 1903 Letchworth
was started, to the design of Parker &
UNWIN. This was the earliest of the
garden cities and greatly influenced
the post-war SATELLITE TOWNS of
Britain. Howard was knighted in
1927.

HOWE, George (1886–1955). Designed
in collaboration with William Lescaze (1896–1967) the Philadelphia
Savings Fund Building (1932), one
of the first skyscrapers in the INTER-
NATIONAL MODERN style. Another
of the *incunabula* is Raymond HOOD's

McGraw-Hill Building in New York
(1931).

HUEBER, Joseph (1716–87). Late Rococo
architect working in Styria. The son
of a Viennese mason, he began as a
journeyman mason in Bohemia,
Saxony and Central and Southern
Germany. In 1740 he took over the
architectural practice of Giuseppe
Carlone in Graz on marrying his
widow. He built the handsome twin
towers of the Mariahilfkirche in Graz
(1742–4), the pilgrimage church on
the Weizberg, with an elaborate interior like a stage-set (1757–76) and
completed in 1774 the splendid library
which Gotthard Hayberger (1699–
1764) had designed for the Abbey of
Admont.

HÜLTZ, Johann (d. 1449), was master
mason of Strassburg Cathedral and as
such designed the openwork spire with
its fabulous spiral staircases. The work
was completed in 1439. Hültz was the
successor to Ulrich von ENSINGER,
who built the octagon (the stage below
the spire).

HUNGARIAN ARCHITECTURE. Medieval architecture in Hungary reflects
the events in various centres of the
West. Sometimes inspiration came
from one centre, sometimes from
more than one. As in other countries
the beginnings are tantalizing. A
building like Feldebrö of the C10
is mysterious in its stylistic pedigree.
It is a square in plan with three apses in
the middle of three sides. Should one
link it with Germigny-des-Prés?
Zalavár of the C9 has three parallel
E. apses like the contemporary buildings in Switzerland. The Romanesque
style is, as one would expect, most
closely linked with South Germany
and Austria and with Lombardy. The
latter appears most clearly in the grand
though over-restored cathedral of
Pécs with its four towers flanking the
W. and the E. end of the nave. The
splendid west portal of Ják has German
but also North Italian and even Norman elements. The abbey churches

of Ják, Lébény and Zsámbék are the most conspicuous Romanesque churches of German descent in Hungary. They have in common a relatively late date (first half C13), three E. apses, two W. towers and a W. gallery.

As in other countries the Cistercians and the Premonstratensians brought into Hungary a new plan and new details, all first developed in France. The finest buildings are of the C13. They are Bélapátfalva (founded in 1232), Pannonhalma, the latter (1217–24) not Cistercian, though Cistercian in style with sexpartite rib vaults, and Ócsa with polygonal instead of straight-ended E. chapels. Sexpartite rib vaults are a French Early Gothic feature, and the Gothic of, e.g., Noyon is also mixed with Romanesque especially Norman detail in the elegant chapel in the castle of Esztergom.

Of the High Gothic style Hungary possesses no major monument.

As for the Late Gothic, it is clearly dependent on South Germany and Austria. The churches are of the HALL type. They are high, with slender piers, sometimes without capitals, and they have complicated figured rib vaults. Examples are Sopron, Koloszvár, and Brassó (chancel). The friars built much in Hungary during these centuries.

Among the castles of Hungary three at least must be mentioned: Buda, where much restoration and reconstruction of the great halls and the chapel is taking place, Visegrád with its mighty keep of c. 1260, square with triangular projections on two opposite sides, and Diósgyör of the second half of the C14 which is oblong with an inner courtyard and four prominent angle towers.

Internationally speaking the most important phase in Hungarian architecture is that of King Matthias Corvinus (1458–90) and the decades after his death. The king was a patron of Mantegna, Verrocchio, Ercole Roberti, BENEDETTO DA MAIANO and

other Italians. His library of illuminated manuscripts in the Renaissance style is unparalleled north of the Alps, and he also favoured the new style in architecture. Earlier than in any country outside Italy – including even France – are the friezes from Buda Castle now in the Castle Museum and the well in Visegrád castle whose stepped terraces, still largely Gothic, are of great magnificence. In ecclesiastic art the Bakócz Chapel in Esztergom Cathedral, begun as early as 1507, is purely Italian.

After these years of enthusiasm Hungary settled down to a less adventurous later C16 and early C17. The fancy battlements and arcaded courtyards of houses are generally Eastern. The monuments of Turkish domination (mosques, minarets, baths and funerary chapels at Pécs, Eger, Budapest) look odd side by side with them. As a sign of the war against the Turks some fortresses were erected (Györ, etc.) by Italian engineers on the new Italian models. The Turkish occupation ended only in the late C17, and in the C18 Austrian and Bohemian Baroque held the stage. The most interesting buildings are the Eszterházy palace at Eisenstadt across the Austrian border (C. M. Carlone, 1663–72), Prince Eugene's delightful Ráckeve (Lucas von HILDEBRANDT, 1702) and then St Anne at Budapest (1740 etc.), the huge Eszterházy palace at Fertöd (1764 etc.) and the Lyceum at Eger (Jacob Fellner, 1765–85).

The turn away from the Baroque in the direction of Neo-classicism was taken early in Hungary. Vac Cathedral by Isidore Canevale is of 1767–72 and yet, with its giant portico of detached columns carrying a heavy attic and not a pediment and with its central dome and coffered vaults, would be highly remarkable even if it stood in Paris. Neo-classicism culminates in the immensely impressive cathedral of Esztergom (J. S. Pack and J. Hild, 1822 to c. 1850) with its central plan, its many-columned dome and its eight-column giant portico, and in the competent but more conventional neo-Greek work of Mihály POLLAK (National Museum, Budapest, 1836–45).

The climax of C19 eclecticism is the richly Italianate Opera at Budapest (M. Ybl, 1875–84) and the surprisingly late Gothic-Revival Houses of Parliament (I. Steindl, 1884–1902). The revolution against eclecticism which is commonly called ART NOUVEAU had in Ödön LECHNER an exceptionally brilliant representative. The Modern Movement set in as a branch of the style of the Vienna of HOFFMANN and LOOS (B. Lajta). At present the most interesting Hungarian work is in industrial architecture.

HUNT, Richard Morris (1827–95), came of a wealthy early Colonial family. They moved to Paris in 1843, and there Hunt joined LEFUEL's *atelier* and the École des Beaux Arts. He also worked on painting with Couture and on sculpture with Barye. He travelled widely before he was made an *inspecteur* under Lefuel on the Louvre in 1854. This first-hand knowledge of the French-Renaissance Revival he took back to America in 1855. He settled in New York and, side by side with his practice, ran an *atelier* on the Parisian pattern. But he returned to Europe again in the 1860s and only in 1868 finally came to rest. He designed the Tribune Building in New York (1873, one of the first with lifts), and then rich men's residences at Newport, in New York (W. K. Vanderbilt, 1878 onwards; J. J. Astor, 1893), and elsewhere (Biltmore, Ashville, N.C., 1890). The French Renaissance remained his favourite style. Hunt was also the designer of the Administration Building at the Chicago Exposition of 1893 and the façade of the Metropolitan Museum, New York (built in 1900–2). He was one of the founders of the American Institute of Architects.

HURTADO, Francisco (1669–1725), one of the greatest Spanish Baroque architects, was quite the most exuberantly rich. His work is confined to interiors, which are of a fantasy unparalleled in Europe. Born and educated in Cordova, he became a captain in the army and possibly visited Sicily. He may have designed the Victoria *camarín* above the Mausoleum of the Counts of Buenavista, Málaga (1691–3). Most of his work is in Granada, where he designed the relatively simple *sagrario* or Sacrament Chapel for the Cathedral (1704–5). The Sacrament Chapel of the Cartuja (1702–20), walled with marble, jasper, and porphyry and containing a marble tabernacle supported by red and black SALOMONICAS, is a masterpiece of polychromatic opulence. He called it 'a precious jewel', and claimed that there was nothing like it in all Europe. In 1718 he designed the very complex *camarín*, liberally decorated with grey-and-coral-coloured marble and lapis lazuli, for the Cartuja of El Paular, Segovia. He has also been credited with the design of the still more bizarrely rich sacristy of the Granada Cartuja (executed 1730–47), where the tendency to muffle the structure in a riotous welter of ornament is taken to its final extreme.

HYPAETHRAL. Without a roof, open to the sky.

HYPERBOLIC PARABOLOID ROOF. A special form of double-curved shell, the geometry of which is generated by straight lines. This property makes it

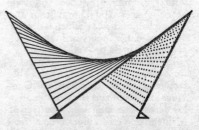

Fig. 53. Hyperbolic paraboloid

fairly easy to construct. The shape consists of a continuous plane developing from a parabolic arch in one direction to a similar inverted parabola in the other. *See figure 53*.

HYPOCAUST. The underground chamber or duct of the Roman system of central heating by means of air flues.

HYPOGEUM. An underground room or vault.

HYPOSTYLE. A hall or other large space over which the roof is supported by rows of columns giving a forest-like appearance.

HYPOTRACHELIUM. The groove round a Doric column between the SHAFT and the NECKING.

I

ICONOSTASIS. A screen in Byzantine churches separating the sanctuary from the nave and pierced by three doors; originally a lattice of columns joined by a decorated PARAPET and COPING. Since the C14–15 it has become a wooden or stone wall covered with icons, hence the name.

ICTINUS. The leading architect in Periclean Athens and one of the greatest of all time. With CALLICRATES he designed and built the Parthenon (447/6–438 B.C.), about which he later wrote a book, now lost, with Carpion. He was commissioned by Pericles to design the new Telesterion (Hall of Mysteries) at Eleusis, but his designs were altered by the three new architects who took over on the fall of Pericles. According to Pausanias he was also the architect of the Doric temple of Apollo at Bassae, begun after the Great Plague of 430 B.C.

IMBREX. In Greek and Roman architecture, a convex tile to cover the join between two flat or concave roofing tiles.

IMHOTEP. Ancient Egyptian high priest and chief minister to King Zoser (3rd dynasty, c. 2780–2680 B.C.), Imhotep later acquired a mythological character as a healing deity and also as an architect (originator of the use of stone as a building material). According to the 3rd-century Egyptian historian Manetho, the Greeks attached some importance to Imhotep as an architect because of the appearance of his name on the enclosure wall of the unfinished pyramid at Saqqara. As architect of the Saqqara complex Imhotep personifies an important phase in the development of Egyptian architecture. For here are found 'dummy' buildings in stone (simulating the more fragile materials used for actual habitations), all ranged round vast courtyards. Some of these buildings are mere façades with doors carved in relief. In the centre was a six stepped pyramid (the first of its type), a symbolical ladder to Heaven. Papyrus columns and channelled columns are among the other familiar features of Egyptian architecture which make their first appearance at Saqqara.

IMPLUVIUM. The basin or water cistern, usually rectangular, in the centre of an ATRIUM of a Roman house to receive the rain-water from the surrounding roofs. The term is also used, loosely, for the uncovered space in the atrium as well as the water cistern.

IMPOST. A member in the wall, usually formed of a projecting bracket-like moulding, on which the end of an arch rests. *See figure 4.*

IMPOST BLOCK. A block with splayed sides placed between ABACUS and CAPITAL.

INDENT. A shape chiselled out in a stone slab to receive a brass effigy.

INDIAN AND PAKISTANI ARCHITECTURE. Nearly all buildings surviving from before the C16 Moghul conquest of the Indian subcontinent (modern India and Pakistan) are religious. The earliest buildings known are those associated with the rise of Buddhism – cave temples hollowed out of rocky mountainsides, with elaborate façades and halls lined with massive pillars, as at Karli (80 B.C.) and Ajanta (C4–5 A.D.). The Buddhists also built stupas, sacred mounds erected over relics and surrounded by walls with richly carved gateways, as at Sanchi where the finest of several stupas dates from the C1 A.D. In form the stupa symbolized the universe, with the hemispherical dome of the mound representing the sky.

Hindu temples survive in considerable numbers, distributed over the subcontinent. All reveal a love of very rich carved figurative decoration, usually of a sensuous and often of an overtly erotic character. Temple groups consist of a tall vimana or shrine, a columned hall and some minor buildings within a walled enclosure pierced by elaborate gates. Styles differ according to district rather than period, the three main styles being Northern, Chalukyan, and Dravidian. The principal northern Hindu temples include the group in Orissa (800–1200); the Great Temple, Bhubanesvar (C9, but with many later additions); and the group of thirty at Khajuraho. They are distinguished by the cactus-like curving roof-cones of the vimanas. The later Chalukyan temples have vimanas built on star-shaped (rather than square) plans, and the points of the star are surmounted by spires clustering round the roof cone and giving it a lively vertical emphasis – e.g., the group of temples at Belur (C12). Some Dravidian temples are cut out of the rock but, unlike earlier rock-cut or cave temples (e.g., Ajanta), in such a way that they are free-standing with all façades exposed – e.g., the Raths at Mamallapuram near Madras (C8). Other Dravidian temples, such as that at Tanjore (C10), rise like stepped pyramids above square bases.

The Jain religion, an offshoot of Hinduism, produced numerous temples. One of the finest is the Temple of Vimala on Mount Abu (1032), with fantastically carved columns and beams inside. Of about the same date, the Great Sas Bahu temple appears like a mound of heavy decorative elements heaped on top of one another. Among later South Indian temples, that of Madura (C17) is perhaps the grandest.

Muslims from Afghanistan, who had made periodic incursions into India, established themselves in the north in the late C12 under the Ghorid Dynasty, who created a capital at Delhi. They brought with them the ISLAMIC style. As in other lands subdued by Islam, temples were speedily converted into mosques, e.g., at Ajmer where a Jain college was masked by a façade decorated with geometrical carvings and Kufic script (1192). In Delhi itself a vast mosque, the Qutbul-Islam (1193), was built with a high MINARET which was to be much imitated in later Islamic architecture. Many other mosques were built under the Pathan dynasty – Jami Masjid, Jaunpur (1438–78), the Adinah Mosque, Gaur (1358–89), Jami Masjid, Ahmadabad (1424) – with Islamic decorations slightly modified by Hindu styles.

But it was not until after the establishment of the Moghul dynasty (1526) as the rulers of the greater part of India that the great Islamic monuments were erected. Indians were normally employed as architects and consequently the Islamic style of Persia and the Mediterranean countries was considerably modified. Better materials were used – finely jointed stonework, various coloured marbles, incrustations of semi-precious and sometimes precious stones – and an appearance of greater monumentality was obtained. At the same time the decorations were finished with jewel-like precision, even a coarse material like sandstone being carved with a delicacy usually reserved for ivory. Lace-like patterns were wrought out of marble panels for MUSHRABEYEH WORK (elaborate grilles). Thus Moghul architecture attained a unique combination of monumentality on a vast scale with miniaturist delicacy of detail. The two great Moghul patrons were Akbar (1556–1605) and his grandson Shah Jahan. Akbar built the remarkable new city of Fatehpur-Sikri (1568–75) and moved his capital there from nearby Agra. It incorporates the beautiful tomb of Sheik Salim

Chisti, besides numerous pavilions. It was abandoned in 1585 and never reinhabited. Of Akbar's palace at Allahabad only the square audience hall with sixty-four columns has been preserved. Akbar's own tomb at Sikandara (1593–1613) is among the grandest in India – a massive red sandstone gateway inlaid with white marble opening into a garden which leads towards the tomb itself, a four-storey building encircled by an arcaded cloister and entered through a domed portal. Rich as they are, these monuments look almost severe in comparison with those built by Shah Jahan, most notably the Taj Mahal (1630–53) near Agra, the tomb of his favourite wife – grandiose in scale, exquisite in its opalescent colour and refinement of carved and inlaid detail, and perfectly balanced in its proportions and in the relationship of the mausoleum with its great bulbous dome to the four minarets standing out from its corners, to the mosque and hall on either side, and to the great gateway which is separated from it by a garden crossed by ornamental canals. Other notable buildings of Shah Jahan's reign include the palace (1639–48) and the Jami Masjid (1644–58) in Delhi, the Pearl Mosque (1646–53) and the Royal Palace (1636) in Agra, and the two marble pavilions on an artificial lake at Ajmer. In mosques and monuments the bulbous dome first made its appearance and the elegant CHATRI received its classic form for the crowning of a minaret. The palaces derive their beauty no less from their setting with gardens and water than from their architectural form and decoration. The works of the Moghul emperors were imitated by lesser potentates throughout India.

The British conquest of India introduced European styles, which were adopted for churches, administrative buildings, and town-houses in the main centres. Neo-Palladian and GREEK REVIVAL styles were pre-ferred until well into the C19 (Fort St George, Madras; Government House and Town Hall, Calcutta). But one of the most remarkable buildings is in the French C18 style, La Martinière, Lucknow (1795). In the Portuguese city of Goa, Iberian Baroque predominated. The last and largest notable monument of British rule was New Delhi, designed by Sir Edwin LUTYENS and Sir Herbert BAKER in an Imperial Roman style with occasional Moghul flourishes. The most noteworthy buildings erected since India and Pakistan achieved independence have been designed by LE CORBUSIER for Chandigarh.

INDUSTRIALIZED BUILDING. Ever since the prefabrication of the first brick, building materials have been industrial products; and ever since Thomas Cubitt in 1815 established a building firm in London which employed all trades on a permanent wage basis, industry has gradually replaced craftsmanship as the basis of European building. Until after 1945, however, the building industry was 'labour-intensive'; it could afford to employ large gangs of unskilled labourers to put up buildings quickly in a traditional way. Since 1945, a growing shortage of both skilled and unskilled labour, coupled with growing programmes of public housing and welfare building, has made it imperative to pre-fabricate as much as possible and thus minimize site work. It is this recent acceleration of technical development, making the industry 'capital-intensive', which is normally called Industrialized Building.

There had already been progress in mass-production of building parts long before 1945, from Abraham Darby's Iron Bridge at Coalbrookdale (1775–9) and Benyon, Bage & Marshall's iron-framed flax mill at Shrewsbury (1796) or Boulton & Watt's seven-storey cotton mill at Salford (1801) to Bunning's Coal Exchange in London (1847–9) and James Bogardus's repetitive cast-iron façades as well as frames (his own factory, 1848–9; Harper Brothers building, 1854). PAXTON's wholly prefabricated cast-iron and glass Crystal Palace for the 1851 Exhibition in London was the answer to a construction deadline of nine months, impossible to meet even with a massive labour force. Its linear descendant is the geodesic domes of Buckminster FULLER (Union Tank Car Co., Baton Rouge, Louisiana, 1958, 384 ft in diameter; U.S. Pavilion at Montreal Expo, 1967, *c.* 250 ft). This is built on the SPACE-FRAME principle which has been developed further by Jean PROUVÉ in France.

Even BARRY's Houses of Parliament in London (1839–52), an apparently craft-made building, had its bronze window-frames mass-produced by Hope's of Birmingham; and the metal window became a leitmotif of industrialized building. At GROPIUS's Fagus Works at Alfeld (1911), the structural grid was fully glazed; such window walling was used by LE CORBUSIER in the Salvation Army Citadel, Paris, and the Maison Clarté, Geneva (both 1932). In 1918 Willis Polk (1870–1924) gave the Hallidie Building at San Francisco a continuous 'CURTAIN WALL' of steel and glass which hung in front of the main frame – thus achieving a crucial separation of 'structure' from 'cladding', taken up by Gropius in the workshop wing of the Bauhaus (1925–6). Prefabricated curtain walling, often in aluminium, was made internationally acceptable by three New York skyscrapers: the United Nations Headquarters (1947–50, by Wallace K. Harrison and others, on an idea by Le Corbusier), the Lever Building (1950–52, by Gordon Bunshaft of SKIDMORE, OWINGS AND MERRILL) and the Seagram Building (1955–8 by MIES VAN DER ROHE and Philip JOHNSON). Mies had drawn a 'glass skyscraper' as early as 1920. Buckminster Fuller's Dymaxion

House project (1927) derived from the techniques of aircraft and vehicle building – its relevance is becoming apparent now that America makes more than twice as many caravans each year as static prefabricated homes. The early postwar 'prefabs' in Britain were fully made up in the factory (expensively, as production runs were not long enough); the London County Council Mobile Homes (1963–5) show how such short-life houses can continue to meet an emergency.

For permanent homes, however, Industrialized Building has meant the manufacture of systems of components which can be fitted together 'dry' on site (i.e., without 'wet' cement). For reasons of fire precaution, PRECAST CONCRETE has been generally preferred to steel for housing. Following the experimental work of PERRET and NERVI, systems of precast wall and floor panels have been developed in Russia, Scandinavia and France. Steel shuttering (rather than timber) has been used to minimize applied internal finishes by giving meticulously smooth surfaces, while various methods of moulding, blasting and tamping have given external surfaces a roughness, with the aggregate exposed, which is expected to weather attractively. Electrical conduits and other services can be inserted off the site, with preformed kitchens and bathrooms in so-called 'heart units'. Prefabrication is usually done in a special factory, close to the site. Its cost, and the cost of the expensive tower cranes necessary on site, have to be met by long and continuous production. Systems of 'battery casting' in special SHUTTERING on the site have proved more flexible for smaller housing areas. Leading concrete systems include Larsen-Nielsen and Jespersen in Denmark, Skaine in Sweden, Camus and Balency in France, Wates, Reema and Bison Wall Frame in Britain.

Light steel framing has been used

for schools, clinics and other single-storey structures. A British team under the Hertfordshire county architect, C. H. Aslin (1893–1959), developed a system of components from many manufacturers, on an 8 ft 3 in. grid (later altered to 2 ft 8 in.). A hundred Hertfordshire schools were built from 1946 to 1955, the year in which the CLASP (Consortium of Local Authorities Special Programme) system was developed by the then county architect of Nottinghamshire, (Sir) Donald Gibson (b. 1908). Subsequently, as Director-General of Research and Development at the Ministry of Public Building and Works, Gibson has helped to develop the NENK system for Army barracks, which has space frame roofing, and the SCOLA system for a Second Consortium of Local Authorities building schools.

Meanwhile the National Building Agency in Britain (chief architect, A. W. Cleeve Barr) has been attempting to rationalize the 'boom' in industrialized systems for housing, of which there were said in 1964 to be 284 in various stages of production – and at various levels of quality. Concrete panel systems have tended to be suitable only for high blocks of flats, often undesirable socially. For low houses, traditional methods have been systematically rationalized: repetitive brick crosswalls can be given a prefabricated infill of timber walls and floors, and precut timber frames (on the Canadian system) can be given an infill of made-up panels of brickwork. Reinforced plastic panels, with curved-cornered windows like those of a car, have been used by the Greater London Council at Walterton Road (1967). In the Scandinavian countries 'winter building' under temporary shelters, themselves prefabricated, has speeded production.

The main doubt about industrialized building systems is whether they are sufficiently flexible. From 1963

CLASP has been used to build the University of York, England (architects, Robert MATTHEW, Johnson-Marshall and Partners) for which non-loadbearing partition walls with good sound insulation have been devised; and in Germany, also from 1963, a sophisticated system of precast concrete beams and lightweight infill has been developed for the University at Marburg (chief architect, Kurt Schneider). Mexico's Federal Committee for School Planning (architect-chairman, Pedro Ramírez Vásquez) has conducted an outstanding programme of cheap school building, adapted to various heights and climates – generally in concrete with steel space-frame roofing. Meanwhile in the industrially most advanced country, the U.S.A., where industrialized methods have generally been used only to perfect finishes and crane-handling techniques for tall office blocks, English types of school design have been much improved in the steel framed SCSD system in California (1965; chief architect, Ezra Ehrenkrantz) by incorporating a sophisticated range of mechanical services in space-frame roofs. Ehrenkrantz is working (1967) on a system of student housing for the University of California.

The hope of many architects lies in Modular Co-ordination on an internationally agreed basis. It could make every prefabricated material available in related measurements, as a 'palette' from which designs could be flexibly composed. A key problem, however, is the variety of jointing at present necessary, from rigid all-welded joints to the neuter non-rigid types packed with plastic.

[NOTE. This entry has been contributed by Mr Nicholas Taylor – Eds.]

INGLENOOK. A recess for bench or seat built beside a fireplace, sometimes covered by the CHIMNEY-BREAST.

INTARSIA. A form of mosaic or inlay made up of different coloured woods, popular in c15–16 Italy especially for the decoration of studies and small rooms in palaces and for the choirs of churches.

INTERCOLUMNIATION. The space between columns measured in diameters. Vitruvius established five main ratios, 1½D. Pycnostyle, 2D. Systyle, 2¼D. Eustyle, 3D. Diastyle, 4D. Araeostyle, of which Eustyle is the commonest.

INTERNATIONAL MODERN. A term coined in America to refer to the new architectural style of the c20, as created before the First World War by such architects as WRIGHT, GARNIER, LOOS, HOFFMANN, GROPIUS, and as accepted, at least in progressive circles, first in Central Europe in the course of the twenties and then in other countries of Europe and in America from the late twenties onwards. The style is characterized by asymmetrical composition, unrelievedly cubic general shapes, an absence of mouldings, large windows often in horizontal bands, and a predilection for white RENDERING.

INTRADOS. The inner curve or underside of an arch; also called a soffit. See figure 4.

INWOOD, Henry William (1794–1843). The son of an architect (William Inwood, c. 1771–1843), with whom he designed his only building of note, St Pancras Church, London (1819–22), one of the great monuments of the GREEK REVIVAL in England. Every detail is faithfully copied from the Erechtheum, Tower of the Winds, Choragic Monument, and other famous Athenian buildings. Sometimes his archaeological material is rather recondite, but he always uses it with sensibility.

IONIC ORDER, see ORDER.

IRISH ARCHITECTURE. The most rewarding and original phase is that before the Normans, the phase of monastic communities where coenobites lived in round or square huts, stone-vaulted by pseudo-vaults of horizontally laid stones corbelled forward gradually. There were several oratories in such communities, tapering round towers and the glorious High Crosses. The most famous sites are Skellig Michael, Nendrum, Glendalough, Clonmacnois, and Monasterboyce. The buildings are mostly c10–11.

The Hiberno-Romanesque style has its most dramatic monument in Cormac's Chapel at Cashel (dated 1134); it has a tunnel-vaulted nave and a rib-vaulted chancel. There are plenty of monuments in the Norman style with only minor national characteristics. The Cistercians came in the 1140s, and the east end of Christ Church Cathedral, Dublin, shows their influence. The fully Gothic style in a wholly Early English version appears in the nave of Christ Church (connected with Wells and St David's) and the largely rebuilt St Patrick's Cathedral, also at Dublin. The most conspicuous Irish contribution to Gothic architecture is her friaries, mostly rurally sited; they have the tower between nave and chancel, which is also typical of English friaries.

Medieval architecture lasted into the c17. The English promoted such new towns as Londonderry, with its Gothic cathedral of 1628–33, and such houses as Carrick-on-Suir and Strafford's Jigginstown, both of the 1630s. Gothic gradually gave place to hipped roofs or parapets, and such buildings as Beaulieu and the Kilmainham Hospital of 1679 are entirely English in style. PALLADIANISM also bore an ample harvest in Ireland, the chief architects being Sir Edward Lovett PEARCE, Richard CASSELS, James GANDON, and Francis Johnston. Examples are Castletown; Parliament House, Dublin, by Pearce; Powerscourt by Cassels; the Customs House and the Four Courts, Dublin, by Gandon; the house of the Provost of Trinity College, Dublin; Caledon, by NASH; Townley Hall, and many others. Ireland is indeed exceedingly rich in Georgian houses, though for lack of a function they are rapidly decreasing. In Dublin very much is still preserved, and the city may well claim to be the finest major Georgian city in the British Isles. If any Victorian buildings are to be singled out, they would again have to be essentially English ones: Cork Cathedral by BURGES; Queen's University, Belfast, by Lanyon; and the Trinity College Museum by Deane & Woodward – all Gothic in style. The best architect today is Michael Scott, the best building up to date the new Library of Trinity College by Ahrends, Burton & Koralek, built in 1963–7.

ISIDORE OF MILETUS assisted AN-THEMIUS OF TRALLES in the building of Hagia Sophia, Constantinople (A.D. 532–7), and was, like him, a geometrician who turned his attention to architecture. He is not to be confused with a younger Isidore, who rebuilt the dome of Hagia Sophia in 558.

ISLAMIC ARCHITECTURE. The origins are very obscure. The Bedouin Arabs, who were the original followers of Mohammed and responsible for the first Islamic conquests in Syria, Palestine, and Persia, were a nomadic people who lived in tents. In the cities they conquered they began by converting old buildings, and Christian churches became MOSQUES; in Damascus a pagan temple transformed into a Christian church was incorporated in the Great Mosque (706–15). The earliest and one of the most beautiful of Islamic buildings is the Dome of the Rock, Jerusalem, built as a sanctuary (not as a mosque) on a circular plan (685–705), but much altered later, especially in 1561 when the exterior was cased in Persian tiles and the interior lined with marble). The first MINARETS were converted church towers in Syria, and that built at Kairouan, Tunisia (724–7), is modelled on such a tower. True to their nomadic origins the Umayyad rulers preferred desert residences to town palaces. Several survive as ruins – Qasr al-Hair (728–9); Mshatta near Amman, Jordan; and Qasr at-Tuba in the Wadi Ghadorf near Amman. In plan these groups of buildings were derived from Roman frontier stations. But both religious and secular buildings of the period incorporate elements which were to become distinguishing features of Islamic architecture: the horseshoe arch, tunnel vaults of stone and brick, rich surface decoration in carved stone, mosaic, and painting. During the Umayyad period the mosque took on its permanent architectural form, dictated by liturgical needs – minarets from which the faithful could be called to prayer; a wide courtyard with a central fountain for ablutions, with surrounding colonnades to give protection from the sun; a large praying chamber, marked externally by a dome (as a sign of importance) and internally by the mihrab or niche indicating the direction of Mecca, towards which the faithful must turn in prayer. The last survivor of the Umayyad dynasty became the founder of the Emirates at Cordova in Spain, where the early style of Islamic architecture was brought to perfection in the Great Mosque (786–990).

Under the Abbasids, who supplanted the Umayyads in 750, Persian influence began to dominate the Islamic world. The main achievements in architecture were the foundation of the new capital at Baghdad, built on a circular plan (762–7, now largely destroyed), and, slightly later, the smaller city of Raqqa, Syria, of which little survives except its richly decorated gateways. It was at this period that Islamic architecture began to depart radically from HELLEN-ISTIC and BYZANTINE conventions. An elaborate court etiquette, derived from Persia and contrary to Bedouin ideas of informality, was introduced, and palaces were designed for the new caliphs on more formal and grandiose lines, e.g., the palaces at Ukhaidir and Samarra in Iraq. These large buildings were run up very quickly: stone was abandoned in favour of brick and there was much use of decorative stucco. The main C9 achievements were the Great Mosque of Kairouan, Tunisia (836); the mosque of Bu Fatata, Susa, Tunisia (850–1); the Great Mosque of Samarra, Iraq, with its strange ZIGGURAT-like minaret (c. 850); and the very well preserved mosque of Ibn Tulun, Cairo (876–7). Building materials were usually rough but dressed with intricate geometrical or floral surface decorations in painted stucco, mosaic, glazed tiles, or shallow relief carving. Local traditions influenced the decorative style in various regions (*see* INDIAN AND PAKISTANI; PERSIAN; TURKISH ARCHITECTURE).

In the original nucleus of the Islamic world the most notable later mosques are those at Tabriz, Persia (1204), Cairo (Mosque of Sultan Barquq, 1384), and Isfahan, Persia (1585). Most of the earlier religious buildings, including the Masjid-el-Aksa and the Dome of the Rock in Jerusalem, were also altered and more richly decorated in these centuries. In southern Spain a local style of great opulence was developed: its principal monuments are the Giralda tower, Seville (1159), and the Alhambra, Granada (1309–54).

ISOMETRIC PROJECTION. A geometrical drawing to show a building in three dimensions. The plan is set up with lines at an equal angle (usually 30°) to the horizontal, while verticals remain vertical and to scale. It gives a more realistic effect than an AXONOMETRIC PROJECTION, but diagonals and curves are distorted. *See figure 54.*

ITALIAN ARCHITECTURE. Early Christian churches in Italy are mostly of the basilican type: nave and aisles separated by columns carrying arches or straight entablatures, and an apse, sometimes flanked by two subsidiary

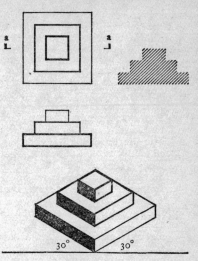

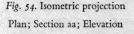

Fig. 54. Isometric projection

Plan; Section aa; Elevation

chambers. The best preserved of the type in Rome is S. Sabina of c. 425–30. Transepts are rare, but occur just in the most monumental churches: Old St Peter's (324–49, with double aisles; not preserved), S. Paolo fuori le Mura (late C5, also double aisles; rebuilt after a fire of 1823), S. Maria Maggiore (c. 430–40). Centrally planned buildings also exist, but they are not frequent. S. Giovanni in Laterano (mid–C5) is octagonal. The central plan is explained here by the fact that it is a baptistery, and for baptisteries a central plan is functionally advantageous. S. Costanza (first half C4), one of the most beautiful buildings, is circular, with an ambulatory, and here the explanation is that it was a mausoleum and for mausolea the ancient Roman tradition was a round plan.

Next to Rome Ravenna was the most important centre. It became the capital of the Roman West in 404, of Odoacer in 476 and of Theodoric in 493, and of the Byzantine bridgehead in Italy in 540. Here also the majority of the churches are basilican: e.g., S. Apollinare Nuovo of *c.* 510–20 and S. Apollinare in Classe of *c.* 550. More original and varied are the centrally planned buildings: S. Vitale, completed in 547 and entirely Byzantine with its complex and ingenious octagonal plan, the Mausoleum of Galla Placidia of *c.* 450 which is a Greek cross, and the two octagonal Baptisteries. The Mausoleum of Theodoric, as befitted this Gothic king, is much more massive. Moreover, it is of stone, whereas the other buildings are of brick. Characteristic features of these latter are external blank arcading or LESENES connected by a small frieze of blank arches, a motif which became typical of the North Italian Romanesque style. The earliest Italian CAMPANILI are also at Ravenna. They are circular and were probably a C9 addition. The earliest campanile of which we know is the square one once attached to St Peter's in Rome, and this went back to the mid-C8.

At least two Early Christian buildings not in Rome nor in Ravenna must be mentioned. One is S. Salvatore at Spoleto, of the late C4, with a complete façade, its details and those of the interior still strikingly Late Roman, but with an oval dome over the chancel which is a motif of Syria or Asia Minor. The other is S. Lorenzo at Milan, remodelled in the C16, but essentially of the late C5 and already exhibiting spatial subtleties as thrilling as those of S. Vitale. Milan possesses more early churches at least in substantial parts than had been known until recently.

The transition from Early Christian to Early Medieval is imperceptible in Italy. S. Agnese in Rome of *c.* 630 is still entirely Early Christian, but S. Maria in Domnica and S. Maria in Cosmedin of the early C9 are in plan and elevation not essentially different. Nor is S. Prassede, although the latter has a transept, like that at Fulda probably a self-conscious revertion to Constantinian greatness. S. Maria in Cosmedin has a hall crypt, one of the earliest ever. Both Cosmedin and Domnica end in three parallel apses, and this is so in the most important early C9 churches in North Italy too: Agliate and S. Vincenzo in Milan. But on the whole these and other North Italian churches continue the Early Christian type as well (Brescia S. Salvatore, Pomposa Abbey). Innovations are the square piers of e.g. Bagnacavallo and the small tunnel vaults of S. Maria in Valle at Cividale (which latter has also the finest early medieval sculpture in Italy). Cividale is extraordinary in plan as well, as is the interesting S. Maria at Cassino in the South, of *c.* 780–90, which introduces the Byzantine plan of the inscribed cross and has moreover groin and tunnel vaults and the three parallel apses.

It is not easy to decide where to start using the term Romanesque in Italy. The basilican plan, the columns of the arcades, the apse continuing the nave without a transept remain the Italian norm in the C11 and into the C12. The essential innovations in plan which France and Germany introduced in the late C10 and early C11 did not at once touch Italy and remained the exception even later. Ambulatories with radiating chapels for instance are rare (S. Antimo in Central and Aversa in South Italy), although vestigial ambulatories had occurred remarkably early (S. Stefano Verona, Ivrea Cathedral). The new elements which came in in the C11 seem to have been derived from the Empire. Montecassino of 1066 etc. had a transept, though one not projecting. It also still had the typically Italian three parallel apses. At Salerno Cathedral, consecrated in 1084, the transept stretches out beyond the aisle lines, and S. Nicola at Bari, the most important southern building (begun immediately after 1087), has transepts, alternating supports in the nave, a gallery, two W. towers placed in Norman fashion outside the aisle lines and the stumps of two E. towers as well. Such E. towers also occur, and here clearly under German influence, at S. Abbondio at Como, consecrated in 1095. S. Fedele at Como is later but still on a trefoil plan inspired by Cologne. S. Abbondio has no transept, but Aquileia of c. 1020 etc. already has, although for the rest it follows Early Christian tradition.

The C12 and the early C13 in Italy are hard to summarize. There is little of regional standards, at least in plans and elevations, though decorative motifs differ considerably from area to area. The great C12 cathedrals of the North Italian plain are truly Romanesque, though they also differ in many respects. But they have mostly alternating supports and galleries inside and the so-called dwarf galleries, small arcaded wall-passages, outside. Their towers are campanili, not integrated with the buildings themselves. Modena, begun in 1099, is the first, with a transept not projecting, and with the traditional three parallel apses. This is the same at S. Ambrogio in Milan with its solemn façade and its beautiful atrium. But the most important aspect of S. Ambrogio is the rib vaults with heavy ribs of plain rectangular section. This type occurs also in the South of France, and the several examples in Lombardy are probably all of the C12, i.e., later than the much more sophisticated ribs of Durham. The other principal North Italian cathedrals are Parma of after 1117, with a more German plan (far projecting transepts with apses and only one E. apse), Piacenza of c. 1120 etc., Cremona and Ferrara. A spectacular appendix to these North Italian cathedrals is their large, detached, octagonal baptisteries. The most famous of the Italian baptisteries, however, is in Central Italy, that of Pisa begun in 1153. Pisa Cathedral, exceptionally large, is exceptional in other

ways as well. It was started as early as 1063 (by Busceto) and has long aisled transepts with end-apses, a double-aisled nave and no vaults. The campanile, i.e., the leaning tower, arcaded in many tiers all round, was started in 1173. The same predilection for outer arcading in tiers is to be found at Lucca. Florence is different. Here already in the late C11 a movement arose which deserves the name Proto-Renaissance. It favoured ancient Roman motifs and has a graceful elegance unique in Romanesque Europe. The principal examples are the Baptistery, S. Miniato and SS. Apostoli, all in Florence, and the Badia at Fiesole, none of them exactly datable. A comparable interest in ancient Rome is found in and around Rome in the early C13 (façade, Città Castellana Cathedral, 1210; and façade, S. Lorenzo Rome by Vassalletto, 1220). An exception in Central Italy is the church of Chienti near Macerata which is on the Byzantine inscribed-cross plan.

The relations of the Italian Romanesque to Byzantium are manifold and interesting. The major monument, totally Byzantine, is of course St Mark's in Venice (1063 etc.) with a central plan and five domes. Domes were also placed over naves in a few major South Italian churches (Canosa Cathedral, 1071 etc; Molfetta Cathedral, c. 1160 etc.). The inscribed-cross plan appears here and there in different parts of Southern Italy, at Stilo, at Otranto (S. Pietro), at Trani (S. Andrea). The Byzantine elements in Sicilian architecture are fascinatingly overlaid with Saracen and Norman elements. The island had been under Byzantium from the C6, under Islam from 827, under the Normans from 1061. But during the years of the greatest Sicilian architecture, the country was one of the centres of the Hohenstaufen Emperors. The Norman motifs of Cefalù and Monreale Cathedrals (1131 etc. and 1166 etc.) are patent to English visitors. On the other hand the Martorana at Palermo (1143 etc.) is on the Byzantine inscribed-cross plan, and S. Cataldo in Palermo looks wholly Arabic. This applies even more to the royal palaces and pavilions such as the Ziza and the Cuba at Palermo.

Romanesque Italy has much of secular architecture to offer. Here only a few buildings can be referred to – some byzantinizing palaces of Venice (especially the Fondaco dei Turchi) and the equally byzantinizing CII Palazzo della Ragione at Pomposa, the slender towers of the nobility, especially famous those of San Gimignano and the two in the centre of Bologna, and the town halls of Como (1216), Orvieto and Massa Marittima. All these are of the C13.

But at that time the Gothic style had started on its Italian course. It had come, as in all countries, from France and, as in most countries, by means of the Cistercians (Fossanova 1187 etc., Casamari 1203 etc. with rib vaults, both in Lombardy, S. Galgano in Tuscany 1227 etc.). The collegiate church of S. Andrea at Vercelli of c. 1220 etc. is transitional between Italian Romanesque and French Gothic. The most original of the early Gothic buildings in Italy is S. Francesco at Assisi, begun in 1228 and, oddly enough, inspired by the French West and most probably Angers Cathedral. Another early French (Burgundian) inspiration explains the splendid castles of Frederick II in the South of Italy and in Sicily (Augusta; Maniace, Syracuse; Ursino, Catania) and especially Castel del Monte of c. 1240 etc., where French Gothic structure is fascinatingly mixed with ancient Roman detail used in a spirit of Renaissance. The plans of these castles are regular, mostly with angle towers, a plan introduced at the same time in France and thus continued in both countries (e.g., Ferrara 1389 etc.).

Altogether the Italy of the C13 and

C14 is rich in remarkable secular buildings, the public halls of Genoa, Orvieto and Piacenza, all C13 and all continuing the Romanesque type, the slightly later and less peacefully open town halls of Perugia (1283 f.), Siena (1288 etc.) and Florence (Palazzo Vecchio 1298 etc.), the Loggia dei Lanzi in Florence of 1376 with its strangely un-Gothic round arches, the Doge's Palace in Venice of 1309 etc., unique in size and composition, and some C14 palaces in Florence and Siena, and early C15 palaces in Venice (Ca' d'Oro, 1421–40). North Italian Late Gothic detail is more ornate, more Northern than that further South (Porta della Carta, Doge's Palace, c. 1440).

This Northern, trans-alpine character applies with much greater force to Milan Cathedral, begun in 1386 and the work of a mixture of masters from Lombardy, Germany and France, all fighting each other. The scale of Milan Cathedral incited the starting on a similar scale of the Certosa of Pavia (1396 etc., built slowly) and S. Petronio, the largest parish church of Bologna (1390 etc.). But meanwhile, i.e., in the C13 and earlier C14, the Gothic style had made progress everywhere in Italy. In Bologna itself the friars' church of S. Francesco in 1236 etc. started with a French ambulatory with radiating chapels. The friars otherwise built large but without an accepted system of plan or elevation. S. Francesco at Siena of 1326 etc. has no aisles and no vault, S. Croce in Florence, the Franciscan church there, of 1294 etc. (by ARNOLFO DI CAMBIO) has aisles and no vault. The E. ends of both are in the Cistercian tradition. The Frari (Franciscan) and SS. Giovanni e Paolo, Venice (Dominican; both C14) have aisles, high round piers and rib vaults. The airiness of these churches is fundamentally different from the spatial feeling of the French Gothic. This Italian-ness of Italian Gothic expresses itself most strongly in

S. Maria Novella in Florence (Dominican; 1278 etc.) and Florence Cathedral
(begun by Arnolfo in 1296). The arcades are much more generously
opened than in France so that nave and
aisles appear parts of one space and not
three parallel vessels. The measure of
each bay opening of the arcades is *c.*
64 ft; at Amiens it was *c.* 25 ft. The
campanile of Florence Cathedral (by
GIOTTO) is the finest of all Italian
Gothic campanili. The finest Gothic
façades are Siena (1284 etc. by GIO-
VANNI PISANO) and Orvieto (*c.* 1310
etc.). As against Florence Rome had
little to contribute. The only important
Gothic church is S. Maria sopra Minerva of *c.* 1280 etc.

For the introduction of the Renaissance also Florence took precedence
over Rome, however much the Renaissance masters owed to ancient Rome.
However, even that debt is less great
than C19 scholars assumed. It is certain
that BRUNELLESCHI in his churches
looked more to the Tuscan Proto-
Renaissance (*see above*) than to Imperial Rome. For Florence the date of
the conversion to the Renaissance is
c. 1420; for Venice, Milan and also
Rome it is a generation later. For Rome
ALBERTI, who was more in sympathy with the ancient Roman character in architecture than anyone else,
was instrumental in establishing the
Renaissance, though he had probably
nothing to do with the courtyard of
the Palazzo Venezia of *c.* 1470 which
was the first to take up the ponderous
motif of orders of attached columns to
separate arched openings such as the
Romans had used it for the Theatre of
Marcellus and the Colosseum. But on
the whole the Quattrocento prefers
arcades of slender columns carrying
arches, i.e., rather delicate members,
and a graceful lively decoration. Examples of the former are Brunelleschi's
earliest façade, that of the Foundling
Hospital in Florence (1419 etc.), and
such palace courtyards as that of
MICHELOZZO's Palazzo Medici in

Florence (1444 etc.) or the Ducal
Palace at Urbino (1460s), which also
has some of the most exquisite Quattrocento decoration. Palace façades,
especially in Tuscany, are still forbidding, in direct continuation of the
Trecento. Heavy rustication was
favoured (Palazzo Medici, Palazzo
Strozzi), though Alberti in his Palazzo
Rucellai (1446 etc.) used a more elegant
articulation by tiers of pilasters, and
this was taken up by the Cancelleria in
Rome (*c.* 1485 etc.). Church plans are
usually longitudinal: Brunelleschi's
with nave and aisles and slim arcades,
Alberti's S. Andrea at Mantua aisleless,
but with side-chapels, a system with a
great future. But both Brunelleschi
and Alberti and others as well (Giuliano da SANGALLO) favoured central
plans and developed them in a variety
of ways (Brunelleschi, S. Maria
degli Angeli, 1434 etc.; Alberti, S.
Sebastiano, Mantua, 1460 etc.; Sangallo, S. Maria delle Carceri, Prato,
1485 etc.).

Central Italians (MICHELOZZO,
FILARETE) had introduced the Renaissance to Milan in the 1450s, and at the
same time it appeared in Venice
(Arsenal portal, 1457). In contrast to
Central Italy, however, the North of
Italy went in for extremely busy
decoration of façades as well as interiors
(Verona and Brescia Town Halls,
Certosa of Pavia, Como Cathedral,
1470s to 1490s and after 1500). These
façades had considerable influence on
the Early Renaissance in trans-alpine
countries. Even BRAMANTE, in his
early years in Milan, used this rich and
playful decoration, though at S. Maria
presso S. Satiro it is rather Alberti (in
Mantua) who inspired him. Bramante
lived in Milan in the same years as
LEONARDO DA VINCI, but it is impossible to say what their relationship
was. Leonardo sketched architectural
ideas, but did not build. Nearly all his
church plans are of central types, and
he reached unprecedented complexities. Bramante clearly was attracted by

the same problem, even if none of the central churches of Lombardy can with certainty be ascribed to him (Lodi, Crema).

With Bramante's move from Milan to Rome in 1499 the High Renaissance was established, with more substantial and also more Roman forms and character (St Peter's, Belvedere Court Vatican, Palazzo Caprini). RAPHAEL (Villa Madama), PERUZZI (Villa Farnesina), and GIULIO ROMANO were Bramante's successors, but the latter two soon turned away from his style to Mannerism. The solecisms of Giulio's Palazzo del Té (1525 etc.) and his own house (1544), both at Mantua, are both eloquent and painful. At the same time MICHELANGELO designed in the Mannerist way (Medici Chapel and Laurentian Library, Florence, 1520s; exterior of St Peter's, 1546 etc.; and Porta Pia, Rome, 1561). Mannerism produced exquisite works (Farnese Palace, Caprarola, by VIGNOLA, 1547 etc.; Villa di Papa Giulio by Vignola, 1550 etc., Casino of Pius IV by LIGORIO, 1560, both Rome; Uffizi, Florence, by VASARI, 1550 etc.), as well as perverse ones (Casa Zuccari, Rome, 1590); but it never ruled unchallenged. In the north of Italy the Renaissance spirit was alive throughout the c16, as is demonstrated by buildings such as SANSOVINO's Library of S. Marco, Venice (1532 etc.) and Palazzo Corner, Venice (1532 etc.), SANMICHELI's palaces and city gates of Verona (1520s to 1550s), and PALLADIO's palaces inside and villas outside Vicenza. Though in the work of Palladio, especially his churches in Venice, Mannerist traits are easily discovered, most of his secular work must be classed as Renaissance. The problem of Vignola in Rome is similar, but whereas Palladio, where he is not Mannerist, belongs to the past, Vignola where he is not Mannerist, points forward to the Baroque.

There can be no doubt that Vignola's

Gesù (begun 1568) established a canon of church plan and elevation for the Baroque: chapels instead of aisles, transepts and a dome (S. Andrea della Valle, S. Carlo al Corso, etc.). The completion of St Peter's by MADERNO was also longitudinal. But the most interesting Baroque churches are those on central or elongated central plans. Vignola had used the oval as early as 1573, but it became a standard element only in the c17, varied inexhaustibly, especially by the greatest Roman Baroque architects BERNINI and BORROMINI. Bernini uses the oval transversely at S. Andrea al Quirinale, and RAINALDI uses a grouping of elements which gives the impression of a transverse oval at S. Agnese. The façade of this church, with its two towers and its concave centre, is by Borromini, whose façade of S. Carlino is even more complex in its use of concave and convex parts. There the interior carries the interaction of curves to the highest point it achieved in Rome, but the acme of spatial complications was reached by GUARINI at Turin. Bernini's work at St Peter's was concerned with decoration on the grandest scale (Baldacchino, Cathedra Petri) and with the forecourt in front of Maderno's façade. The elliptical colonnades and their splaying-out connection with the façade are aesthetically and from the planning point of view equally satisfying.

In the field of major urban planning Rome had already taken the lead in the late c16, when the long streets radiating from the Piazza del Popolo had been laid out. In secular architecture Rome contributed less, though the open façade of the Palazzo Barberini and the giant pilasters of Bernini's Palazzo Odescalchi had much influence. For Baroque palaces Genoa is the most interesting city.

As early as about 1700 Italy began to tone down the Baroque (FONTANA, then JUVARRA in Turin:

Superga, 1717 etc.; Palazzo Madama, 1718 etc.) and in the Veneto a Palladian revival took place (Scalfarotti's S. Simeone, Venice, 1718 etc.; Preti's Villa Pisani, Strà, 1735 etc.).

The C19 is more interesting in Italian architecture than most tourists realize. The neo-classical and especially neo-Greek style has produced much outstanding work. French influence is occasionally patent (S. Carlo Theatre, Naples, by Antonio Niccolini, 1810–44). The most monumental church is S. Francesco di Paola at Naples by Pietro Bianchi (1817–28). Neo-Greek masterpieces are JAPELLI's Caffè Pedrocchi at Padua of 1816–31, the Canova Temple at Possagno by SELVA of 1819–30, the Carlo Felice Theatre at Genoa by C. Barabino of 1827 etc., the Cemetery of Staglieno (1835) by the same, and the grandiose Cisternone at Livorno by P. Poccianti of 1829 etc. A curious anachronism is the use of the classical apparatus of forms in ANTONELLI's two monster towers at Novara and Turin in 1840 and 1863. In the sixties other styles had taken the place of the classical, a Super-Renaissance in MENGONI's Galleria in Milan (1861 etc.), a Lombardo-Gothic in the Milan Cemetery by C. Maciacchini (1863 etc.) and others. As in other Continental countries Neo-Baroque followed the Neo-Renaissance (Law Courts, Rome, by G. Calderini, 1888 etc.; University, Naples, by P. P. Quaglia, 1897 etc.), and Art Nouveau the Neo-Baroque. Italian Art Nouveau is inspired by Vienna in the work of Raimondo d'Aronco (Exhibition Palace, Turin, 1902); more original is that of SOMMARUGA (Palazzo Castiglioni, Milan, 1901).

The C20 style started with SANT'ELIA's dreams of skyscrapers, but the new international style did not make itself felt until the later C20 and did not get a chance of showing itself in buildings until after 1930 (G. Terragni, Casa del Fascio, Como, 1932 etc.). Today Italian architecture is characterized by much high talent (PONTI, ALBINI, FIGINI & POLILINI, Luigi Moretti) but a lack of unified direction. The most important contribution is that of NERVI to the structural and aesthetic problems of wide spans.

IXNARD, Michel d' (1726–95), a French early neo-classical architect, worked mainly in the Rhineland. Born at Nîmes and trained in Paris, he became architect to the Elector of Trier. His main work is the very large, severe, and rather heavy abbey church of St Blasien in the Black Forest (1764–84), with a Doric exterior and solemn Corinthian rotunda.

J

JACOBEAN ARCHITECTURE, *see*
ENGLISH ARCHITECTURE.

JACOBSEN, Arne (1902–71). His
style is the most refined and meticulous INTERNATIONAL MODERN,
was initially influenced by ASP-
LUND'S Stockholm Exhibition of
1930 and appeared as an International
Modern architect with work of 1931,
at a time when Copenhagen was reaching the climax of a classicism as
refined and meticulous in its own way
as Jacobsen's architecture was to be.
He built chiefly private houses and
housing until shortly before the
Second World War, when he was
also commissioned for work on a
larger scale. The Town Hall of
Aarhus (with Erik Møller, 1938–42)
has a concrete skeleton tower. Søl-
lerud, an outer suburb of Copenhagen,
got a town hall by Jacobsen in 1939–
42. The Munkegård School at Gen-
tofte, another outer suburb of Copenhagen, is characterized by the many
small play-yards between classrooms
(1952–6). The Town Hall of Rødovre,
yet another outer suburb of Copenhagen, is Jacobsen's most exquisite
public building (1955–6), entirely
unmannered, without any cliché or
gimmick, nothing really but the
formal apparatus of the International
thirties, yet handled with an unparalleled precision and elegance. The
same is true of his cylinder-boring
factory at Aalborg (1957) and the
S.A.S. Hotel at Copenhagen (1960; a
tower block on a podium of the Lever
House type, *see* SKIDMORE, OWINGS
& MERRILL). Recently St Catherine's
College at Oxford has been completed
to Jacobsen's designs. During the
fifties he also designed some fine and
original furniture and cutlery.

JADOT DE VILLE ISSY, Jean-Nicolas

(1710–61). He was trained in France
and became at an early age architect
to the Archduke Franz I of Lorraine
whom he accompanied to Vienna on
his marriage to Maria Theresa. He built
the Academy of Sciences and Letters
in Vienna (1753) and the menagerie at
Schönbrunn, both in an accomplished
Louis XV style: and he probably provided the plan for the royal palace in
Budapest (1749, greatly altered in the
C19). He also designed the Arco di S.
Gallo in Florence, erected to mark the
Archduke's accession to the Grand
Duchy of Tuscany in 1739.

JAMB. The straight side of an archway,
doorway, or window; the part of the
jamb which lies between the glass or
door and the outer wall-surface is
called a *reveal*.

JAMES, John (c. 1672–1746), built St
George's, Hanover Square, London
(1712–25), with its hexastyle portico
of free-standing giant Corinthian
columns and pediment. This idea was
quickly taken up by HAWKSMOOR
(St George's, Bloomsbury) and GIBBS
(St Martin-in-the-Fields). Wrickle-
marsh, Blackheath (1721), was his
masterpiece, but it was demolished,
like nearly all his work. He rebuilt
St Mary's Church, Twickenham, except for the W. tower (1713–15). He
published an English edition of Andrea
Pozzo's treatise on perspective in *c.*
1720.

JAPANESE ARCHITECTURE. The
earliest buildings are religious and
date from after the introduction of
Buddhism from China c. A.D. 550.
As in China the usual building material
was wood and the main structural
element the column. The principle of
the truss was never exploited, and thus
the width of buildings was controlled
by the lengths of timber available.

Walls were merely protective screens, sometimes of material as flimsy as paper or cardboard. Although dependent on China for many seminal ideas, the Japanese produced a truly distinctive architectural style, more delicate in decoration if less monumental in scale. They also paid greater attention to the relation of buildings to landscape, not merely by designing exquisite artfully naturalistic gardens but also by taking advantage of sloping hillside sites for picturesque stairways linking one temple building to another (e.g., the Kurodanji Temple, Kyoto).

Among the earliest surviving buildings of importance are those of the Buddhist monastery, the Horyuji (c7, but much altered), comprising a Buddha hall and pagoda with cloister-like enclosure, library, and c10 lecture hall. The pillared hall is the prototype Japanese temple. The pagoda is of five storeys, square in plan, with boldly projecting roofs above each floor, and crowned with a tall finial of metal rings and bells supported on a great central post about 100 ft high. Pagodas of this design remained popular throughout the centuries and a number of notable examples have survived. Temples maintained the general lines of the Horyuji, but with infinite variations in size and layout. Later periods showed a tendency to greater elaboration and sometimes to heaviness (e.g., Hokaiji Amidado, late c11). The Shinto shrines, some of which were rebuilt every few years, are much simpler than the Buddhist temples, and the oldest have thatched roofs of most elegant shape. Though they may be of little interest architecturally, their large and elaborately carved gateways are most impressive and some perpetuate the pre-Buddhist, indigenous Japanese style.

Houses are generally of simple design and of one storey. They are built on a rectangular plan rigidly controlled by a scale of proportion of which the basic unit is a mat measuring 6 ft × 3 ft. They are so designed that interior walls, usually of paper, may be moved to increase the size of rooms. Tea-houses, where the tea-drinking ceremony is performed, are like miniature private houses, set in beautifully planned gardens. Proportion, simplicity, and the eloquent use of natural materials are here all-important. The palace of the emperor at Kyoto consists of a group of pavilions distinguished from private houses only by larger and more elaborate roofs (like those of temples) and a different scale of proportions based on the imperial floor mat, which measured 7 ft × 3 ft 6 in.

One of the finest buildings is the c11 Byodo-in or 'Phoenix Hall' at Uji near Kyoto, originally erected as a villa beside a lotus lake but later transformed into a temple. This reflects influences from China of the Sung period, when elegance and grace were the artistic touchstone. As in all Japanese art, Chinese influences are often very strong, and Japan has preserved much of Chinese styles which have been destroyed on the mainland. Although most houses and temples are single-storey buildings, multi-storey houses are far less uncommon than in China: the soaring castle at Himeji (late c16) is of several storeys and possibly owes something to Western influence. Palaces and houses are generally distinguished less for their architecture than for their decorative fixtures – gilt metalwork applied to gable boards, brass caps affixed to the ends of projecting timbers, lacquer panels and wall paintings indoors – all wrought with exquisite artistry.

The westernization of Japan in the late c19 had a depressing influence on native architecture. But since the Second World War Japan has produced the most imaginative school of non-European architects, notably Junzo Sakakura, Kunio Maekawa, and Kenzo TANGE. They all go in for extremely massive concrete and bold, heavily fanciful forms.

JAPELLI, Giuseppe (1783–1852), a leading Italian romantic architect and landscape gardener, was a true eclectic of a type rare in Italy, able to work happily in a wide range of styles. Beginning at the Caffè Pedrocchi, Padua (1816), in a very elegant version of neo-classicism, he then turned to a severe manner derived from the astylar backs of Palladian villas – e.g., Villa Vigodarzere, Saonara (1817) – then to a bold Grecian style for the Doric slaughterhouse in Padua (1821, now the Istituto d'Arte). After a visit to France and England he added a neo-Gothic wing to the Pedrocchi (1837), and finally built the neo-Rococo Teatro Verdi, Padua (1847). His landscape parks are consistently in the English manner; most of them are in the Veneto (e.g., Saonara, Ca' Minotto, Rosà), but one of the finest was at Villa Torlonia, Rome (1840).

JEAN DE CHELLES. Architect of the south transept of Notre Dame in Paris (begun 1258). He died soon after. His successor and perhaps son, Pierre de Chelles, was still active in 1316, when he was called to Chartres Cathedral as a consultant.

JEAN D'ORBAIS. Probably the designer and first master mason of Reims Cathedral (begun c. 1211).

JEFFERSON, Thomas (1743–1826), legislator, economist, educationalist, and third President of the United States of America (1801–9), was also an able and immensely influential architect. The son of a surveyor, he inherited a considerable estate in Albemarle County, where in 1769 he chose a high romantic site for his own house, Monticello. He derived the plan from Robert MORRIS's *Select Architecture*, but modified it with reference to GIBBS and Leoni's edition of PALLADIO. It had porticos front and back and a great forecourt with octagonal pavilions at the corners and square pavilions terminating the wings. It is very carefully thought out, both in its planning, on which he had strong personal views, and in its adaptation of Palladian elements. He was interested in Palladio mainly as the interpreter of Roman villa architecture, and looked back to Antiquity for the 'natural' principles of his architectural theory. In 1785, while he was in Europe, he was asked to design the Virginia State Capitol for Richmond. With the help of CLÉRISSEAU, he produced a temple design based on the Maison Carrée (16 B.C.) at Nîmes, but Ionic instead of Corinthian and with pilasters in place of half-columns on the flanks and rear. The Virginia State Capitol (completed 1796 with the assistance of LATROBE) set a pattern for official architecture in the U.S.A. As Secretary of State to George Washington he played a leading part in planning the new federal capital in Washington from 1792 onwards. After he became President he entrusted Latrobe with the task of completing the new Capitol (1803, burnt 1814). Latrobe also assisted him with the University of Virginia, Charlottesville – a group of porticoed houses (each containing a professor's lodging and a classroom) linked by colonnades in a formal plan, with a great Pantheon at one end of the oblong composition (1817–26).

JENNEY, William Le Baron (1832–1907), was born in Massachusetts, studied at the École Centrale des Arts et Manufactures in Paris, was an engineer in the Civil War, and opened a practice in architecture and engineering in Chicago in 1868. In 1869 he published a book called *Principles and Practices of Architecture*. By far his most important building was the Home Insurance Building (1883–5), because its iron columns, iron lintels and girders, and indeed steel beams, prepared the way for the skeleton construction of the Chicago School (*see* HOLABIRD & ROCHE). Stylistically his work is of no value.

JETTY. The projecting floor-joists supporting the OVERHANG of a timber-framed building, sometimes called a *jettied storey*.

JIB DOOR. A concealed door flush with the wall-surface, painted or papered to correspond with the walls. The DADO and other mouldings are similarly carried across the door.

JOGGLE, JOGGLING. Masons' terms for joining two stones in such a way as to prevent them from slipping or sliding, by means of a notch in one and a corresponding projection in the other. It is often seen exposed on the face of a flat arch. If the joggle is concealed it is called a 'secret joggle'. *See figure 55.*

Fig. 55. Joggled joint

JOHNSON, Philip (b. 1906), lives in Connecticut. He became an architect only in middle age. His fame was first spread by the house he built for himself at New Canaan (1949) – very much in the style of MIES VAN DER ROHE – a cube with completely glazed walls all round. The siting is romantic, and perhaps in the years about 1950 one should already have been able to guess that Johnson would not remain faithful to Mies's principles. In the guest-house (1952) close to his own house vaults began to appear, inspired by SOANE, and the synagogue at Port Chester, New York (1956), made it clear that he would prefer variety, the unexpected effect, and elegance to the single-mindedness of Mies. Buildings of more recent years are the Amon Carter Museum at Fort Worth, Texas (1961), the Art Gallery for the University of Nebraska at Lincoln (1962), the New York State Theatre for the Lincoln Center in New York (1962–4), and the indianizing

shrine at New Harmony, Indiana (1960).

JOISTS. Horizontal timbers in a building, laid parallel to each other with their upper edges REBATED to receive the boards of a floor. The underside either forms the ceiling of the room below or has ceiling lathe nailed to it. In a large floor the main or *binding* joists are often crossed by smaller *bridging* joists which bear the floorboards. For a span exceeding about 15 ft, it was usual to insert one or more SLEEPERS to carry the joists, which would then run longitudinally.

JONES, Inigo (1573–1652), a genius far in advance of his time in England, imported the classical style from Italy to a still half-Gothic North and brought English Renaissance architecture to sudden maturity. He was the same age as Donne and Ben Jonson, and only nine years younger than Shakespeare. Born in London, the son of a Smithfield clothworker, he appears to have visited Italy before 1603, being then a 'picture-maker'. Not until 1608 is he heard of as an architect (design for the New Exchange in London), and his earliest known buildings date from later still. Meantime he had become a prominent figure at Court as a stage-designer for masques in the most lavish and up-to-date Italian manner. Many of his designs survive, of fantastic Baroque costumes and hardly less fantastic architectural sets, executed in a free, spontaneous style of draughtsmanship he had presumably picked up in Italy. In 1613 he went to Italy again, this time for a year and seven months, with the great collector Lord Arundel. He returned with an unbounded admiration for PALLADIO and a first-hand knowledge of Roman monuments unique in England at that date. (He met SCAMOZZI in Venice.)

From 1615, when he became Surveyor of the King's Works, until the Civil War in 1642 he was continuously employed at the various royal palaces. Immediately he built three startlingly novel buildings which broke uncompromisingly with the Jacobean past: the Queen's House, Greenwich (1616–18 and 1629–35); the Prince's Lodging, Newmarket (1619–22, now destroyed); and the Banqueting House, Whitehall, London (1619–22). The Queen's House is the first strictly classical building in England, though there was a long break in its construction (the foundations were laid in 1616, but the elevations and interior date from 1632–5). The Prince's Lodging, modest in size, set the pattern for the red-brick, stone-quoined, hipped-roof house with dormers, so popular later in the century. The Banqueting House is Jones's masterpiece; it perfectly expresses his conception of architecture – 'sollid, proporsionable according to the rulles, masculine and unaffected' – as well as his adoration of Palladio. But though every detail is Palladian it is not a mere imitation. Everything has been subtly transmuted and the result is unmistakably English: solid, sturdy, and rather phlegmatic. The Queen's Chapel, St James's Palace, London (1623–7), was also something new for England – a classical church, consisting of an aisleless parallelogram with a coffered segmental vault, a pedimented front, and a large Venetian window. Equally striking but more elaborate was the Bramantesque temple design he used for King James's hearse in 1625.

His principal buildings for Charles I have been destroyed, except for the Queen's House, Greenwich. This is an Italian villa sympathetically reinterpreted, whose chastity and bareness must have seemed daringly original. The upper-floor loggia is very Palladian, as is also the two-armed, curved open staircase to the terrace; but, as always with Jones, nothing is a direct copy. The proportions have been slightly altered and the general effect is long and low and very un-Italian. In-

side, the hall is a perfect cube and symmetry prevails throughout. Also to the 1630s belong his great Corinthian portico at Old St Paul's, transforming the medieval cathedral into the most Roman structure in the country, and Covent Garden, the first London square, of which the church and a fragment of the square survive, the latter rebuilt. The square was conceived as one composition, the houses having uniform façades with arcaded ground floors and giant pilasters above (perhaps influenced by the Place des Vosges, Paris). In about 1638 he also produced elaborate designs for an enormous Royal Palace in Whitehall. These reveal his limitations and it is perhaps fortunate for his reputation that they were never executed.

1642 brought his brilliant career at Court to an end. He was with the king at Beverley, but nothing more is heard of him until 1645. Although his property was sequestrated he was pardoned in 1646 and his estate restored. From then onwards he seems to have swum quite happily with the political tide, working for the Parliamentarian Lord Pembroke. The great garden front at Wilton House was for long thought to have been built by him at about this date, but is now known to have been designed by his assistant Isaac de Caus (c. 1632). It was badly damaged by fire c. 1647 and the famous state rooms therefore date from about 1649, by which time Jones was too old to give much personal attention; he put it in the hands of his pupil and nephew by marriage, John WEBB. Nevertheless, the celebrated double-cube room, perhaps the most beautiful single room in England, epitomizes his style of interior decoration – gravity and repose combined with great opulence of heavy and rather French classical detail. Innumerable buildings have been attributed to Jones, of which a few may have had some connection with him, notably the pavilions at Stoke Bruerne Park (1629–

35). Though profound, his immediate influence was confined to Court circles. In the early C18 he largely inspired the Palladian revival of BURLINGTON and KENT.

JUAN DE ÁLAVA (d. 1537), a Spanish master mason on the verge of Late Gothic and Early Renaissance, appears first as consultant at Salamanca Cathedral in 1512 (with eight others) and Seville Cathedral in 1513 (with three others), in the latter years as master to the newly restarted work at Plasencia Cathedral (first with Francisco de Colonia, see SIMÓN DE COLONIA, who soon quarrelled with him). Then we come across him as the designer of the cloister of Santiago Cathedral (1521 onwards) and finally as master mason to Salamanca Cathedral after the death of Juan GIL DE HONTAÑÓN in 1526. S. Esteban at Salamanca (1524 etc.) is also by him; this and the work at Plasencia round the crossing are perhaps his finest.

JUBÉ. The French name for ROOD SCREEN.

JUSSOW, Heinrich Christoph (1754–1825). He was born in Kassel, was given a classical education and then studied law at Marburg and Göttingen before joining the Landgräflichen Baudepartment under Simon Louis du RY in 1778. He later studied architecture in Paris under DE WAILLY and visited Italy and England (1784–8). He completed du Ry's Schloss Wilhelmshöhe outside Kassel and built numerous ornamental buildings in the Roman, Chinese and Gothic tastes in the park. Among these is his masterpiece, the picturesque castle Löwenburg (1793–8), much influenced by the English Gothic Revival and the most elaborate C18 essay in the genre anywhere on the Continent. Built on a dramatic hillside site and approached by drawbridge across a moat, it is amply provided with ramparts, towers and (originally) guards in medieval costumes.

JUTTING, see OVERHANG.

JUVARRA, Filippo (1678–1736), born in Messina of a family of silversmiths, is the greatest Italian C18 architect and a brilliant draughtsman. His elegant and sophisticated Late Baroque buildings are as typical of their period as Tiepolo's paintings and equally accomplished; they have a Mozartian gaiety and fecundity of decorative invention. Trained in Rome under FONTANA (1703/4–14), he first won fame as a stage-designer, and this theatrical experience was to leave a mark on nearly all his subsequent work.

In 1714 he was invited to Turin by Victor Amadeus II of Savoy, who appointed him 'First Architect to the King'. Apart from a trip to Portugal, London, and Paris in 1719–20, he remained in Turin for the next twenty years. His output was enormous, ranging from churches, palaces, country villas, and hunting-lodges to the layout of entire new city quarters in Turin – not to mention work as an interior decorator and designer of furniture and the applied arts. Of his churches the Superga (1715–27) and the chapel of the Venaria Reale (1716–21), both near Turin, are spectacular, the former being by far the grandest of all Italian Baroque sanctuaries, comparable with Melk in Austria and Einsiedeln in Switzerland. S. Filippo Neri (1715), S. Croce (1718 etc.), and the Carmine (1732–5, gutted during the war) in Turin are all very fine. His city palaces in Turin include Palazzo Birago della Valle (1716), Palazzo Richa di Covasolo (1730), and Palazzo d'Ormea (1730), while his work for the king is remarkable for the four great palaces and villas in or near Turin – Venaria Reale (1714–26), Palazzo Madama (1718–21), Castello di Rivoli (1718–21, but only partly executed), and his masterpiece Stupinigi (1719 etc.). In all these works he had the assistance of numerous highly skilled painters, sculptors, and craftsmen, who were summoned from all parts of Italy to execute his designs.

Though little development is discernible in his style, which is a brilliant epitome of current ideas rather than an original invention, it reached its fine flower in Stupinigi, especially in the great central hall whose scenic quality and skeletal structure suggest an influence from north of the Alps. In 1735 Juvarra was summoned to Spain by Philip V, for whom he designed the garden façade of S. Ildefonso near Segovia and the new Royal Palace in Madrid, executed with alterations after his death by G. B. SACCHETTI. He died suddenly in Madrid in January 1736.

K

KAHN, Louis, was born in 1901 on the Island of Ösel. He studied and lives at Philadelphia, and was internationally noticed only fairly late in life, first with the Yale University Art Gallery (with D. Orr, 1951–3), then with the Richards Medical Research Building of the University of Pennsylvania (1957–60). The Art Gallery has for its main exhibition space a SPACE-FRAME ceiling. The Medical Research Building has all ducts gathered in a number of sheer square towers projecting from and rising above the outer walls: the reason is said to be functional, but the effect is curiously dramatic and indeed aggressive – an original version of the so-called BRUTALISM which has come to the fore in the last fifteen years.

KAZAKOV, Matvey Feodorovich (1733–1812), the leading neo-classical architect in Moscow, began in the Baroque tradition but soon adopted an Imperial Roman style, perhaps under QUARENGHI's influence (he modified and completed Quarenghi's palace at Ostankino (Moscow) for Count Sheremetiev). He probably designed the rich Pashkov Palace, Moscow (1785–6). His main building is the Church of the Ascension of the Razumovski estate (1790–3). He also built the Petrovski Palace near Moscow (1775–82), a curious Gothic or rather Russian medieval revival fantasy.

KEEL MOULDING. A moulding whose outline is like the keel of a ship – a pointed arch in section. *See figure 56.*

KEEP. The principal tower of a castle, containing sufficient accommodation to serve as the chief living-quarters permanently or in times of siege; also called a *donjon*.

KENT, William (1685–1748), painter, furniture designer, and landscape

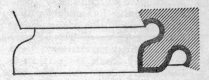

Fig. 56. Keel moulding

gardener as well as architect, was born in Bridlington of humble parents. He contrived to study painting in Rome for ten years and was brought back to London in 1719 by Lord BURLINGTON, whose friend and protégé he remained for the rest of his life. Whimsical, impulsive, unintellectual, in fact almost illiterate, he was the opposite of his patron – and as happy designing a Gothic as a classical building. Nevertheless, he allowed Burlington to guide his hand along the correct PALLADIAN lines in all his major commissions. His interior decoration is more personal, being, like his furniture, richly carved and gilt in a sumptuous manner deriving partly from Italian Baroque furniture and partly from Inigo JONES, whose Designs he edited and published in 1727.

He did not turn architect until after 1730, by which time he was well into his forties. His masterpiece Holkham Hall (1734 onwards, executed by BRETTINGHAM) was almost certainly designed largely by Burlington, whose hand is evident in the 'staccato' quality of the exterior and in the use of such typical and self-isolating features as the VENETIAN WINDOW within a relieving arch. The marble apsidal entrance hall, based on a combination of a Roman basilica and the Egyptian Hall of VITRUVIUS, with its columns, coffered ceiling, and imposing staircase leading up to the *piano nobile*, is one of the most impressive rooms in England. His lavishly gilt and damask-hung state apartments, elaborately carved and pedimented door-frames, heavy cornices, and niches for antique marbles epitomize the English admiration for Roman magnificence. The Treasury (1734), 17 Arlington Street (1741), and 44 Berkeley Square (1742-4), all in London, are notable mainly for their interior decoration, especially the latter, which contains the most ingenious and spatially exciting staircase in London. Esher Place, Surrey, was the best of his neo-Gothic works (wings, now demolished, and other alterations, *c.* 1730). His last building, the Horse Guards, London (1750-8), is a repetition of Holkham, with the unfortunate addition of a clock-tower over the centre: it was executed after his death by John VARDY. Through Burlington's influence Kent was appointed Master Carpenter to the Board of Works in 1726, and Master Mason and Deputy Surveyor in 1735. He is perhaps more important historically as a designer of gardens than as an architect. He created the English landscape garden, being the first to have 'leap'd the fence and seen that all nature is a garden'. This revolutionized the relation of house to landscape and led to less dramatic and forceful façades. From his time onwards the country house was designed to harmonize with the landscape, rather than to dominate and control it.

KENTISH RAG. Hard unstratified limestone found in Kent and much used as an external building stone on account of its weather-resisting properties.

KEY, Lieven de (*c.* 1560-1627), the first Dutch architect of note to work in the so-called 'Dutch Renaissance' style (similar to English Jacobean). He worked for some years in England before becoming municipal architect of Haarlem (1593), where he intro-

duced the characteristic colourful use of brick with stone dressings (horizontal bands of stone, stone voussoirs set singly in brick above windows, etc.). His masterpieces are the façade of the Leiden Town Hall (1597), the Weigh House, Haarlem (1598), the Meat Market, Haarlem (1602-3) and the tower of the Nieuwekerk, Haarlem (1613).

KEY PATTERN, *see* FRET.

KEYSER, Hendrick de (1565-1621), the leading architect of his day in Amsterdam, where he was appointed city mason and sculptor in 1595, worked in a style somewhat similar to English Jacobean. His plain utilitarian churches had great influence on Protestant church design in the Netherlands and Germany, especially his last, the Westerkerk in Amsterdam, built on a Greek cross plan (1620). His most important secular buildings are the Amsterdam Exchange (1608) and Delft Town Hall (1618). In domestic architecture he simplified and classicized the traditional tall, gable-fronted Amsterdam house, introducing the ORDERS and reducing the number of steps in the gables. His works were engraved and published by Salomon de Bray as *Architectura Moderna* (1631).

KEYSTONE. The central stone of an arch or a rib vault; sometimes carved. *See figure 4.*

KHMER ARCHITECTURE. Under strong Indian influence an architectural style known as Khmer was developed in Cambodia between C7 and C13. The main site is Angkor, a vast deserted city from which all structures built in perishable materials have disappeared, leaving only a widely distributed complex of about 400 stone-built and brick-built temples, tombs, walls, bridges, and embankments among a series of artificial lakes. These buildings are almost oppressively rich in figurative sculpture, with long galleries containing well-preserved low reliefs. The most important, Angkor Wat (early C12), perhaps the largest temple in the world (208 ft high and covering 20,000 sq. ft), typifies the Khmer style: enclosed within a vast galleried wall on a square plan, with towers at the corners. It rises up like a fantastic mountain (a symbolic representation of Mount Meru upon which the world rests), with a group of five gigantic towers all of a bulging Hindu profile.

KING-POST, *see* ROOF.

KIOSK. A light open pavilion or summerhouse, usually supported by pillars and common in Turkey and Persia. European adaptations are used mainly in gardens, as band-stands, for example, or for small shops selling newspapers.

KLENZE, Leo von (1784–1864), a North German, was a pupil of GILLY in Berlin, and then of DURAND and PERCIER and FONTAINE in Paris. He was architect to King Jérome at Cassel in 1808–13, and to King Ludwig I in Munich from 1816. Klenze was at heart a Grecian, but he was called upon to work in other styles as well, and did so resourcefully. His chief Grecian buildings are the Glyptothek, or Sculpture Gallery (1816–34) – the earliest of all special public museum buildings – and the Propylaea, both in Munich. The Propylaea was begun in 1846, a late date for so purely Grecian a design. Grecian also, strangely enough, is that commemorative temple of German worthies, the Walhalla near Regensburg (1830–42), which is in fact a Doric peripteral temple. But as early as 1816 Klenze did a neo-Renaissance palace (Palais Leuchtenberg), the earliest in Germany, even if anticipated in France. This was followed by the Königsbau of the Royal Palace (1826) – which has affinities with the Palazzo Pitti – and the freer, more dramatic Festsaalbau of the same palace (1833). In addition, Klenze's Allerheiligen Church, again belonging to the palace (1827), is – at the king's request – neo-Byzantine. *See also* GÄRTNER.

KLINT, P. V. Jensen (1853–1930), is famous chiefly for his Grundtvig Church at Copenhagen, won in competition in 1913 but, after further development of the design, begun only in 1921. With its steeply gabled brick façade, all of a stepped organ-pipe design, and with its interior, Gothic in feeling, it stands mid-way between the Historicism of the C19 and the Expressionism of 1920, a parallel in certain ways to BERLAGE's earlier Exchange. The surrounding buildings, forming one composition with the church, are of 1924–6. Klint's son Kaare (b. 1888) is one of the most distinguished of the brilliant Danish furniture designers.

KNAPPED FLINT. Flint split in two and laid so that the smooth black surfaces of the split sides form the facing of a wall. *See also* FLUSHWORK.

KNIGHT, Richard Payne (1750–1824), country gentleman and landscape-gardening theorist, began in 1774 to build Downton Castle for himself: rough, irregular (the plan is anti-symmetrical rather than asymmetrical), and boldly medieval outside, smooth, elegant, and distinctly neo-classical within, it is the prototype of the picturesque country house 'castle' which was to remain popular for half a century. In 1794 he published *The Landscape – a Didactic Poem* attacking 'Capability' BROWN's smooth and artificial style of landscape gardening. It was dedicated to Uvedale PRICE, who published a lengthy reply differing on points of detail. Knight's much longer *Analytical Enquiry into the Principles of Taste* (1805) examines the PICTURESQUE philosophically.

KNOBELSDORFF, Georg Wenzeslaus von (1699–1753). Court architect to Frederick the Great with whom he was on terms of close friendship and whose sophisticated, eclectic tastes he faithfully mirrored although they quarrelled over the designs for Sanssouci. He was a Prussian aristocrat and began his career in the army, but in 1729 resigned his Captain's commission to train as a painter. By 1733 he was already on friendly terms with Frederick (then Crown Prince) for whom he built a little circular temple of Apollo in his garden in the garrison town of Neu-Ruppin. Frederick then enabled him to visit Italy and after his return commissioned him to enlarge the old border house of Rheinsberg (1737). Immediately after Frederick's accession to the throne in 1740 Knobelsdorff was sent off to Dresden and Paris to prepare himself for more ambitious projects. He added a wing to Monbijou for the Queen Mother (1740–42) and a wing to Charlottenburg for the King (1742–6) with a very grand, rich, colourful interior plastered with Rococo motifs (partly destroyed in the Second World War). In 1741 he began the Berlin opera-house with a less exuberant interior and a severely Palladian exterior which owes much to English neo-Palladian models (burnt out 1843, renewed by K. F. Langhans; seriously damaged 1945 but now restored). While this was going forward he was appointed Surveyor General of Royal Palaces and Parks, Director in Chief of all buildings in the royal provinces, and a member of the Prussian Council of Ministers. In 1744 work began on the large Stadtschloss at Potsdam, colourful outside and in, and with one of the richest of all Rococo interiors (destroyed). He began Sanssouci, Potsdam, in 1745 in close collaboration with the King, who provided the general design. (Frederick's original sketch survives.) In 1746 he quarrelled with the King who dismissed him and thus ended his architectural career, though he made posthumous amends by writing the 'Éloge de Knobelsdorff' which was read at the Berlin Academy in 1753. (His sketch design for a palace for Prince Heinrich in Unter den Linden, Berlin, was built by J. Boumann, 1748–66. It is now the Humboldt University.)

KNÖFFEL, Johann Christoph (1686–1752). He was a contemporary in Dresden of CHIAVERI and LONGUELUNE and was much influenced by the French classicism of the latter. His Wackerbarth Palais, Dresden (1723–8, destroyed 1945) and Kurlander Palais, Dresden (1728–9, destroyed 1945) were elegant examples of restrained pilastered town architecture. In 1734 he became Oberlandbaumeister in Dresden and in 1737 began his masterpiece, the Brihl Palais (destroyed 1899). He rebuilt the large hunting-lodge, Hubertusberg, between 1743 and 1751 and completed his rival Chiaveri's Hofkirche in Dresden after Chiaveri returned to Rome in 1748.

KORB, Hermann (1656–1735). He began as a carpenter and was promoted architect by Duke Anton-Ulrich of Brunswick-Wolfenbüttel. He visited Italy in 1691, then supervised the construction of the schloss at Salzdahlum designed by Johann Balthasar Lauterbach (1660–94) – a vast building with features anticipating DIENTZENHOFER's Pommersfelden and HILDEBRANDT's Upper Belvedere, but of mainly timber construction faced to simulate stone (demolished 1813). Also of wood was the interesting library he erected at Wolfenbüttel (1706–10). It was centrally planned (on the advice of Leibniz) with an oval interior lit by windows in the dome. His only surviving building of note is the church of the Holy Trinity, Wolfenbüttel (1705) with two tiers of galleries creating an octagonal central space.

KREMLIN. A citadel or fortified enclosure within a Russian town, notably that in Moscow.

KRUBSACIUS, Friedrich August (1718–89). Architect and architectural theorist, author of Betrachtungen über den wahren Geschmack der Alten in der Baukunst (Dresden, 1747) attacking the Baroque style and reverting to the humanist idea that 'the noblest structure, man, the perfect proportions and graceful symmetry of his figure, were the first standards for architectural invention'. Though indebted to French theorists, he thought little of French architecture. He became Royal architect and in 1764 professor of architecture at the new Academy of Arts in Dresden. But in his buildings he remained faithful to the Baroque. The most notable were the Neues Schloss at Neuwitz (1766–75; destroyed) and the Landhaus in Dresden (1770–76; burnt out 1944).

L

LA VALLÉE, Simon (d. 1642). son of an architect, settled in Sweden in 1637, becoming royal architect in 1639. He designed the Riddarhus in Stockholm (1641/2) derived from de BROSSE's Palais Luxembourg in Paris. He was succeeded as royal architect by his son Jean (1620–96), who travelled and studied in France, Italy, and Holland between 1646 and 1649. He completed his father's Riddarhus (with Justus VINGBOONS who designed the façades), built the Oxenstjerna Palace, Stockholm (1650), which introduced the Roman *palazzo* style, and designed the Katherinenkirka, Stockholm (1656), on a centralized plan probably derived from de KEYSER, as well as various palaces in Stockholm (e.g., for Field-Marshal Wrangel) and country houses (Castle Skokloster).

LABEL, *see* HOOD-MOULD.

LABEL-STOP. An ornamental or figural BOSS at the beginning and end of a HOOD-MOULD.

LABROUSTE, Henri (1801–75), a pupil of VAUDOYER and Le Bas, won the Grand Prix in 1824, and was in Rome 1824–30. After his return he opened a teaching *atelier* which became the centre of rationalist teaching in France. His rationalism appears at its most courageous in the interior of his only famous work, the Library of Ste Geneviève by the Panthéon in Paris (1843–50). Here iron is shown frankly in columns and vault, and endowed with all the slenderness of which, in contrast to stone, it is capable. Labrouste's is the first monumental public building in which iron is thus accepted. The façade is in a nobly restrained Cinquecento style with large, even, round-arched windows, and there again, in comparison with the debased Italianate or the neo-Baroque

of Beaux Arts type which just then was becoming current, Labrouste is on the side of reason. The London architect, J. B. Bunning (1802–63), in his Coal Exchange of 1846–9, recently criminally demolished, was as bold in his use of iron, but as an architect was undeniably lacking in the taste and discipline of Labrouste. In the 1860s Labrouste also built the reading-room and the stack-rooms of the Bibliothèque Nationale, again proudly displaying his iron structure.

LACED WINDOWS. Windows pulled visually together vertically by strips, usually in brick of a different colour from that of the wall, which continue vertically the lines of the window surrounds. It was a popular motif *c.* 1720 in England.

LACUNAR. A panelled or coffered ceiling: also the sunken panels or COFFERING in such a ceiling.

LADY CHAPEL. A chapel dedicated to the Virgin, usually built east of the CHANCEL and forming a projection from the main building; in England it is normally rectangular in plan.

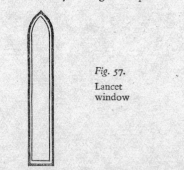

Fig. 57.
Lancet
window

LANCET WINDOW. A slender pointed-arched window, much used in the early C13. *See figure 57.*

LANGHANS, Carl Gotthard (1732–1808). German neo-classical architect famous for the Brandenburg Gate in Berlin (1788–91), his one important work and the first of the Doric ceremonial gateways that were to be built all over Europe in the early C19. The Brandenburg Gate is still C18 in its elegant and rather un-Grecian proportions. His later buildings were more ponderous and cubic, e.g., the Potsdam Theatre (1795) and the theatre in Gdańsk (Danzig) (1798–1801). He also did the theatre at Charlottenburg Schloss in Berlin (1788–91). His son Carl Ferdinand Langhans (1782–1869) worked under SCHINKEL in the 1830s but continued his father's style in the palace of Kaiser Wilhelm I in Berlin (1836, burnt out 1945 but now restored externally), the old Russian Embassy in Berlin (1840–41) and the theatre at Wrocław (Breslau) (1843).

LANGLEY, Batty (1696–1751), the son of a Twickenham gardener, published some twenty architectural books, mostly manuals for the use of country builders and artisans, e.g., *A Sure Guide to Builders* (1729); *The Builder's Compleat Assistant* (1738). But his fame rests on his *Gothic Architecture Restored and Improved* (1741) in which he formalized KENT's neo-Gothic into 'orders'. He built little, and none of his works survives.

LANTERN. A small circular or polygonal turret with windows all round, crowning a roof or dome. *See figure 38.*

LANTERN CROSS. A churchyard cross with lantern-shaped top; usually with sculptured representations on the sides of the top.

LASDUN, Denys (b. 1914), worked with Wells COATES 1935–7. From 1938 to 1948 he was a partner in TECTON. On the strength of his fertile imagination, his directness, and the force of his forms he has become one of the most impressive English architects of the post-war years. His principal buildings to date are flats at Bethnal Green, London (1956–9); luxury flats in St James's Place, London (1957–61); the Royal College of Physicians in Regent's Park, London (1960–64), Fitzwilliam House, Cambridge (1959 etc., not yet completed), and the buildings for the University of East Anglia at Norwich (1963 onwards).

LATIN CROSS. A cross with three short arms and a long arm.

LATROBE, Benjamin (1764–1820), the son of a Moravian minister in England, spent his boyhood and youth in England, in Germany, and again in England, where he worked under S. P. COCKERELL as an architect, and under Smeaton as an engineer. He must have been much impressed by SOANE's work. In 1795 he emigrated to America, where he was taken up by JEFFERSON and did the exterior of the Capitol at Richmond, Va. In 1798 he moved to Philadelphia, and there built the Bank of Pennsylvania and in 1800 the Water Works (the latter largely an engineering job). The architecture of these two buildings was resolutely Grecian – the first examples of the GREEK REVIVAL in America – the former Greek Doric, and the latter Ionic. Of the same year 1799 is Sedgeley, the earliest GOTHIC-REVIVAL house in America. In 1803 Latrobe was called in at the Capitol in Washington, and there did some of his noblest interiors, with much vaulting in stone. The work dated from 1803–11, but the majority had to be redone after the fire of 1814, so what one now sees is mostly of Latrobe's maturity. But his most perfect work is probably Baltimore Cathedral (1804–18). Its interior in particular, on an elongated central plan, with the shallow central dome and the segmental tunnel vaults is as fine as that of any church in the neo-classical style anywhere. Latrobe had at the beginning submitted designs in Gothic as well as classical forms, the Gothic being the earliest Gothic church design in America. Among his other buildings were the Baltimore Exchange (1816–20, destroyed 1904), the 'Old West' of Dickenson College, Carlisle, Pa. (after 1811) and the Louisiana State Bank, New Orleans (begun 1819). Latrobe was the first fully trained architect in the United States. Yet his engineering training made it possible for him, throughout his career, to work as well on river navigation, docks, etc. – a combination which was to become typical of American C19 architects. His pupils included MILLS, STRICKLAND and William Small.

LATTICE WINDOW. A window with diamond-shaped LEADED LIGHTS or with glazing bars arranged like an open-work screen: also, loosely, any hinged window, as distinct from a SASH WINDOW.

LAUGIER, Marc-Antoine (1713–69), was a Jesuit priest and outstanding neo-classical theorist. His *Essai sur l'architecture* (1753) expounds a rationalist view of classical architecture as a truthful, economic expression of man's need for shelter, based on the hypothetical 'rustic cabin' of primitive man. His ideal building would have free-standing columns. He condemned pilasters and pedestals and all Renaissance and post-Renaissance elements. His book put NEO-CLASSICISM in a nutshell and had great influence, e.g., on SOUFFLOT.

LAURANA, Luciano (*c.* 1420–79), was born in Dalmatia, and appeared in Urbino *c.* 1466 at the humanist court of Federigo da Montefeltro, which included Piero della Francesca and, later on, FRANCESCO DI GIORGIO. He was appointed architect of the Palazzo Ducale, Urbino (1468–72), for which he designed numerous chimney-pieces, doorcases, etc., of extreme refinement and elegance, anticipating and surpassing the C18 in delicacy. His masterpiece is the Florentine-style *cortile* in the Palazzo Ducale, with a light springy arcade of Corinthian columns echoed by shallow pilasters between the windows on the upper storey.

LAVES, Georg Friedrich (1788–1864), was a nephew of H. C. JUSSOW under whom he trained in Kassel. After travelling in Italy, France and England he settled in Hanover in 1814. During the next fifty years Hanover was to be transformed by his romantic GREEK REVIVAL style almost as impressively as were Berlin and Munich by his great contemporaries SCHINKEL and KLENZE. The Leineschloss, later Landtag (begun 1817), Wangenheim Palace (begun 1827) and the more Italianate Opera (1848–52) are his masterpieces, together with the layout of the Waterlooplatz (1855) and other new squares and streets. But Laves was also an inventive and remarkably forward-looking engineer and submitted a startling design for the 1851 Exhibition Hall in London to be constructed largely of iron railway-track. It was an early attempt at pre-fabrication.

LE BLOND, Jean-Baptiste Alexandre (1679–1719), a minor Parisian architect, is of importance mainly because he introduced the French Rococo style into Russia. His masterpiece is the vast Peterhof Palace, St Petersburg (1716, later enlarged), decorated with typically French elegance and civilized reticence.

LE BRETON, Gilles (*fl.* 1530). Master-mason who carried out Francis I's enlargements at the Château de Fontainebleau and presumably designed them. His only surviving works are the Porte Dorée, the N. side of the Cour du Cheval Blanc, and the now greatly mutilated portico and staircase in the Cour de l'Ovale (begun 1531). Le Breton's simple and austere classicism, in his later works, derived from SERLIO and was to have some influence on the next generation of French architects, notably LESCOT.

LE CORBUSIER, Charles-Édouard (Jeanneret) (1887–1966). Le Corbusier was born at La Chaux-de-Fonds in French Switzerland. He worked in PERRET'S office in Paris in 1908–9, then for a short time in that of BEHRENS in Berlin. Le Corbusier was the most influential and the most brilliant of C20 architects, of a fertility of formal invention to be compared only with Picasso's. But he was also restless and an embarrassingly superb salesman of his own ideas. It is no doubt relevant to an understanding of his mind and his work that he was an abstract or semi-abstract painter, comparable in some ways to Léger.

In Le Corbusier's early work three strains can be followed, continually interacting. One is the mass-production of housing (Dom-ino, 1914–15, Citrohan House, 1921; the abortive housing estate of Pessac, 1925). The second is town planning. Le Corbusier published and publicized a number of total plans for cities with a centre of identical skyscrapers, symmetrically arranged in a park setting, with lower building and complex traffic routes between. They are less realistic than GARNIER's Cité Industrielle of 1901, but far more dazzling (Ville Contemporaine, 1922; Plan Voisin, 1925; Ville Radieuse, 1935; plan for Algiers, 1930). The third strain of Le Corbusier's early thought tends towards a new type of private house, white, cubist, wholly or partly on PILOTIS, with rooms flowing into each other. The earliest is the villa at Vaucresson (1922). Many followed, including the exhibition pavilion of the Esprit Nouveau at the Paris Exhibition of 1925, with a tree growing through the building. The most stimulating and influential villas were probably those at Garches (1927) and Poissy (1929–31). In the same years Le Corbusier did some designs for major buildings: for the League of Nations at Geneva (1927; not executed) and the Centrosojus in Moscow (1928). The designs had a great effect on progressive architects everywhere. Of major buildings actually erected two must be referred to: the Salvation Army Hostel in Paris (begun 1929) with its long CURTAIN WALL; and the Swiss House in the Paris Cité Universitaire (1930–32), introducing a random-rubble baffle wall to contrast with the usual white-rendered concrete. In 1936 Le Corbusier was called to Rio de Janeiro to advise on the new building of the Ministry of Education which was subsequently executed by COSTA, NIEMEYER, Reidy (1909–64), and others. Their contribution has never been fully distinguished from his. In 1947 Le Corbusier was one of the group of architects to come to terms with the programme of the United Nations Headquarters in New York, and the Secretariat building, a sheer glass slab with solid, windowless end walls, is essentially his design.

At the same time, however, Le Corbusier began to abandon this rational smooth glass-and-metal style which until then he had been instrumental in propagating, and turned to a new anti-rational, violently sculptural, aggressive style which was soon to be just as influential. The first example is the Unité d'Habitation at Marseille (1947–52), with its heavy exposed concrete members and its fantastic roofscape. The proportions are worked out to a complicated system, called MODULOR, which Le Corbusier invented and pleaded for. The Unité was followed by another at Nantes (1953–5) and a third at Berlin (for the Interbau-Exhibition, 1956–8). Le Corbusier's most revolutionary work in his anti-rational style is the pilgrimage chapel of Ronchamp not far from Belfort (1950–4), eminently expressive, with its silo-like white tower, its brown concrete roof like the top of a mushroom, and its wall pierced by small windows of arbitrary shapes in arbitrary positions. In his villas the new style is represented by the Jaoul Houses (1954–6), whose shallow concrete tunnel vaults soon became an international cliché. Of yet later buildings the Philips Pavilion at the Brussels Exhibition of 1958 had a

HYPERBOLIC PARABOLOID ROOF, a form pioneered by M. Novitzki and the engineer Deitrich in the stadium at Raleigh, North Carolina (1950–53). At Chandigarh Le Corbusier laid out the town and built the extremely powerful Law Courts and Secretariat (1951–6), the influence of which proved to be strongest in Japan. At the same time he did some houses at Ahmedabad (1954–6) which, like the buildings of Chandigarh, are of excessively heavy, chunky concrete members. In 1957 Le Corbusier designed the Museum of Modern Art for Tokyo and the Dominican Friary of La Tourette (1957–60), a ruthlessly hard block of immense force. His last important building was the Carpenter Art Centre at Harvard.

LE MUET, Pierre (1591–1669), a *retardataire* Mannerist, published *Manière de bien bastir pour toutes sortes de personnes* (1623), an up-to-date version of DU CERCEAU's first book of architecture, containing designs suitable for different income groups but going farther down the social scale. His best surviving building is the Hôtel d'Assy, 58 rue des Francs-Bourgeois, Paris (1642). The Hôtel Duret de Chevrey (now part of the Bibliothèque Nationale) was for long attributed to him but is now known to be by Jean Thiriou. His later buildings, e.g., Hôtel Tubeuf, Paris (1650), are more classical but never entirely free of Mannerist traits.

LE NÔTRE, André (1613–1700), the greatest designer of formal gardens and parks, was the son of a royal gardener. He studied painting and architecture as well as garden design, and was appointed Contrôleur Général des Bâtiments du Roi in 1657. The enormous park at Versailles (1662–90), with its vast *parterres*, fountains, sheets of water, and radiating avenues, is his masterpiece. It extends the symmetry of LE VAU's architecture to the surrounding landscape and provides a perfect setting for the building. He began at Vaux-le-Vicomte (1656–61) and later worked at St Cloud, Fontainebleau, Clagny, Marly, and elsewhere, mostly for Louis XIV.

LE PAUTRE, Antoine (1621–c. 1682), designed the Hôtel de Beauvais in Paris (1654–after 1657), the most ingenious of all Parisian *hôtel* plans considering the awkward site. But he is best known for the engraved designs in his *Œuvres* (first published 1652 as *Desseins de plusieurs palais*) of vast and fantastic town and country houses, which far exceed his contemporary LE VAU in Baroque extravagance. His influence is evident in the work of WREN and SCHLÜTER.

LE QUEU, Jean-Jacques (1757–after 1825). French neo-classical fantasist of neurotic power. He was born in Rouen, visited Italy in the early 1780s, and worked mainly as an architectural draughtsman until the Revolution and then as a cartographer. None of his few buildings survives. His fame rests on his drawings (Bibliothèque Nationale, Paris) in which the designs and ideas of BOULLÉE and LEDOUX appear to have gone to his head – monument to Priapus, vast and megalomaniac towers, a dairy to be built in the form of a cow, houses composed of both Gothic and Antique motifs etc., with much use of phallic and other symbols. In them he broke away from all conventions of symmetry, stylistic purity, proportion and taste.

LE VAU, Louis (1612–70), the leading Baroque architect in France, was less intellectual and refined than his great contemporary MANSART. He was also less difficult in character and headed a brilliant team of painters, sculptors, decorators, gardeners, with whom he created the Louis XIV style at Versailles. He was a great *metteur-en-scène* and could produce striking general effects with a typically Baroque combination of all the arts. Born in Paris, the son of a master mason by whom he was trained, he first revealed his outstanding gifts in the

Hôtel Lambert, Paris (1642–4), where he made ingenious use of an awkward site and created the first of his highly coloured, grandiloquent interiors: the staircase and gallery are especially magnificent. In 1656–7 he built the Hôtel Lauzun, Paris, and in 1657 he was commissioned by Fouquet, the millionaire finance minister, to design his country house at Vaux-le-Vicomte. This is his masterpiece and by far the most splendid of all French *châteaux*. Here grandeur and elegance are combined in a manner peculiarly French, and no expense was spared. The *château* was built in about a year and the luxurious interior, decorated by Lebrun, Guérin, and others, and the gardens laid out by LE NÔTRE were finished by 1661. In the same year Fouquet was arrested for embezzlement, whereupon his rival Colbert took over his architect and artists to work for the king. Le Vau was commissioned to rebuild the Galerie d'Apollon in the Louvre (1661–2), decorated by Lebrun (1663). In 1667 he was involved (with PERRAULT) in the design of the great E. front of the Louvre in Paris. Work began on the remodelling of Versailles in 1669. Le Vau rose to the occasion, and his feeling for the grand scale found perfect expression in the new garden front. Unfortunately, this was ruined a few years later by HARDOUIN-MANSART's alterations and extensions, and nothing survives at all of the interiors he executed with Lebrun; these included the most spectacular of all, the Escalier des Ambassadeurs. In the Collège des Quatre Nations, Paris (now the Institut de France, begun 1661), which was built at the expense of Cardinal Mazarin, he came closer than any other Frenchman to the warmth and geniality of the great Italian Baroque architects. The main front facing the Seine is concave, with two arms curving forward from the domed centre-piece to end in pavilions. The sense of splendour both in planning

and decoration is no less typical than the occasional lack of sensitivity in the handling of detail.

LEADED LIGHTS. Rectangular or diamond-shaped panes of glass set in lead CAMES to form a window. In general use in domestic architecture until the C18.

LEAN-TO ROOF, *see* ROOF.

LECHNER, Ödön (1845–1914). One of the most interesting of all representatives of ART NOUVEAU architecture. He started (like Gaudí) in a free Gothic (town hall, Kecskemét, 1892, Museum of Decorative Art, Budapest, 1893–6) and developed towards a fantastic style with curvaceous gables and Moorish as well as folk-art connotations (Postal Savings Bank, Budapest, 1899–1902).

LEDOUX, Claude-Nicolas (1736–1806), began as a fashionable Louis XVI architect, patronized by Mme du Barry, and developed into the most daring and extreme exponent of neo-classicism in France. Only BOULLÉE among his contemporaries was his equal in imagination and originality, but most of Boullée's designs remained on paper. Neither was properly appreciated until recently. Despite its extreme geometrical simplicity their more advanced work is not abstract but expressive or *parlant*. Born at Dormans, Ledoux studied under J.-F. BLONDEL in Paris. He never went to Italy, though he was profoundly influenced by Italian architecture, especially by the cyclopean fantasies of PIRANESI. Though eccentric and quarrelsome, he was immediately and continuously successful and never lacked commissions. His first important buildings were the Hôtel d'Hallwyl, Paris (1766), the Château de Benouville (1770–77), and the Hôtel de Montmorency, Paris (1770–2), the last displaying his originality in planning on a diagonal axis, with circular and oval rooms.

In 1771 he began working for Mme du Barry and in the following year completed the Pavillon de Louve-ciennes, a landmark in the history of French taste. It was decorated and furn-ished throughout in the neo-classical style, the architectural treatment of the interior being confined to shallow pilasters, classical bas-reliefs, and delicate, honeycomb coffering. In 1776 he began the remarkable Hôtel Thélusson (demolished) in Paris, approached through an enormous triumphal arch leading into a garden laid out in the English landscape manner. This conception, in which the informality of the garden emphasized the stark simplicity and geometrical forms of the building, was repeated on a larger scale in the group of fifteen houses he built for the West Indian nabob Hosten in Paris (1792, demol-ished). They, too, were informally disposed in a landscape garden.

Success and official recognition appear to have stimulated rather than dulled his powers of invention, for his most advanced and original work dates from after he became an Acade-mician and Architecte du Roi in 1773. His masterpieces are the massive and rigidly cubic theatre at Besançon (1775–84, burnt out 1957), with its unpedimented Ionic portico and, inside, a hemicycle with rising banks of seats surmounted by a Greek Doric colonnade. Odder still is his saltworks at Arc-et-Senans (1775–9), some of which still survives in a dilapidated condition. It is the supreme expression of his feeling for the elemental and primeval. The glowering entrance portico is carved inside to emulate the natural rock out of which gushes water, presumably saline though also carved in stone. Even more extreme were the buildings he envisaged for his 'ideal city' of Chaux which were not, understandably, executed: one was to have been a free-standing sphere and another an enormous cylinder set horizontally.

His Paris toll-houses of 1785–9 are less extreme, but they illustrate the wide range of his stylistic repertoire. Of those that survive the most exicting is the Barrière de La Villette in Place de Stalingrad, consisting of a Greek cross surmounted by a cylinder – a very successful essay in pure architec-tural form. In 1783 he built a Salt Warehouse at Compiègne (only the massive arched façade survives) and in 1786 provided designs for a Palais de Justice and prison at Aix en Provence (not executed according to his de-signs). His career came to an end with the Revolution (he was imprisoned during the 1790s) and he spent his last years preparing his designs for publica-tion: *L'architecture considérée sous le rapport de l'art, des mœurs et de la légis-lation* (1804).

LEFUEL, Hector M. (1810–80), won the Grand Prix in 1839 and in the same year went to Rome. In 1854, at the death of Louis Visconti (1791–1853), he became chief architect to the Louvre, which Napoleon III had in 1851 decided to complete by large and elaborate links connecting it with the Tuileries. The neo-Renaissance fashion originated here and soon be-came international (cf. HUNT). Lefuel also designed the palace for the International Exhibition of 1855.

LEGRAND, J. B., *see* GILLY.

LEMERCIER, Jacques (*c.* 1585–1654), was the son of a master mason who worked at St Eustache, Paris. He studied in Rome *c.* 1607–14, bringing back to Paris the academic idiom of Giacomo della PORTA. Though he never quite succeeded in fusing this with his native French tradition, he ranks only just below MANSART and LE VAU in French classical architec-ture. If seldom inspired he was always more than competent. In 1624 he was commissioned by Louis XIII to plan extensions to the Louvre (the Pavillon de l'Horloge is the most notable of his additions), in harmony with LESCOT's work of the previous century. But his principal patron was Cardinal Riche-lieu, for whom he designed the Palais

Cardinal (Palais Royal), Paris (begun 1633); the Sorbonne, Paris (begun 1626); the *château* and church of Rueil and the *château* and town of Richelieu (begun 1631). Only a small domed pavilion of the office block survives from the enormous Château Richelieu, but the town still exists as laid out by Lemercier in a regular grid with houses of uniform design built of brick with stone quoins. As a designer of *hôtels* he was remarkably ingenious, and his solution at the Hôtel de Liancourt, Paris (1623), became a prototype which was followed by nearly all his successors. His church of the Sorbonne (begun 1635) is perhaps his finest work and is one of the first purely classical churches in France. His dome at the Val-de-Grâce, Paris, where he took over from Mansart in 1646, is also most dramatic and effective.

L'ENFANT, Pierre Charles (1754–1825), a French architect and engineer who served as a volunteer major in the American army during the War of Independence, designed the old City Hall in New York and the Federal House in Philadelphia, but is remembered mainly for having surveyed the site and made the plan for the new federal capital in Washington, a grandiose conception based in some respects on Versailles. He would probably have been given the commission to design the Capitol and other buildings in Washington had he not become unmanageable. He was dismissed in 1792.

LEONARDO DA VINCI (1452–1519). The greatest artist and thinker of the Renaissance. His wide-ranging mind embraced architecture as well as many other fields of human activity. Although he built little or nothing, he provided a model for the dome of Milan Cathedral (1487, not executed), and during his last years in France produced a vast scheme for a new city and royal castle at Romorantin (not executed). But his influence was great, especially on BRAMANTE, who took over his interest in centralized

churches. S. Maria della Consolazione at Todi (1508), begun by Cola da Caprarola, probably derived from one of his sketches by way of Bramante.

LEONI, Giacomo (*c.* 1686–1746), who was born in Venice, settled in England sometime before 1715, having previously been architect to the Elector Palatine. An apostle of PALLADIANISM, he published the first English edition of Palladio's *Works* (1715) and at Queensberry House, London (1721, reconstructed 1792), provided the prototype English Palladian town house In 1726 he published *The Architecture of L. B. Alberti.* His surviving buildings include Lyme Hall, Cheshire (1720–30); Argyll House, London (1723); and Clandon Park, Surrey (1731–5).

LESCOT, Pierre (1500/15–78). The son of a well-to-do lawyer, who gave him a good education. His only work to survive more or less intact is part of the square court of the Louvre (1546–51), which laid the foundations of French classicism. Essentially decorative, his style is very French and entirely lacks the monumentality of his Italian contemporaries. He had the great advantage of the sculptor Jean Goujon's collaboration, and his ornamental detail is therefore of the greatest refinement and delicacy. Though much altered, parts of his Hôtel Carnavalet, Paris (*c.* 1545–50), survive.

LESENE. A PILASTER without a base and capital often called a pilaster-strip and usually found on the exteriors of later Anglo-Saxon and early Romanesque churches. Although they were much used as decoration during the latter period, there is evidence in some Anglo-Saxon buildings to suggest that pilaster-strips as used by the Saxons were primarily functional. They served as bonding courses in thin rubble walls, and thus split up an unbroken expanse of wall, reducing cracking in the plaster and preventing longitudinal spread. The north nave wall at Breamore church shows long stones on end between flat stones, all clearly projecting some distance into the wall. This is a crude example of LONG AND SHORT WORK, but no claim can be made that the pilaster-strip and long and short work as used for QUOINS were evolved in any particular sequence. Other examples of the structural significance of the pilaster-strip are at Worth, where they are solid stone partitions, clearly of a piece with the long and short quoins, at Sompting and at Milborne.

LETHABY, William Richard (1857–1931), joined the office of Norman SHAW in 1877, became his trusted principal assistant, and set up on his own in 1889, helped on by Shaw. While he thus owed much to Shaw, as an artist and a thinker he owed more to MORRIS and Philip WEBB, on whom he wrote a book. He was as much an educator as a scholar and an architect, and indeed built very little. Foremost among his buildings are Avon Tyrrell in Hampshire (1891) and Melsetter on Orkney (1898), the church at Brockhampton in Herefordshire (1900–2) – probably the most original church of its date in the world – and the Eagle Insurance in Birmingham (1899), also of a startling originality, even if influenced by Webb. Lethaby was the chief promoter and the first principal of the London Central School of Arts and Crafts, which was established in 1894 on Morris's principles. It was the first school anywhere to include teaching workshops for crafts. Also in 1894, Lethaby (with Swainson) brought out a learned book on Hagia Sophia in Constantinople; in 1904 a general, very deeply felt book on medieval art; in 1906 and 1925 two learned volumes on Westminster Abbey; and in 1922 a collection of brilliant, convincedly forward-looking essays called *Form in Civilisation*.

LEVERTON, Thomas (1743–1824), the son of an Essex builder and not highly regarded in his own day, nevertheless designed some of the most elegant interiors in London, e.g., Nos. 1 and 13 Bedford Square (1780). His 'Etruscan' hall and other rooms at Woodhall Park (1778) are equally distinguished.

LIBERGIER, Hugues (d. 1263). A French master mason whose funerary slab is now in Reims Cathedral. He is called Maistre on it and is represented holding the model of the major parish church of Reims, St Nicaise, which he designed and began in 1231. He also has a staff, an L-square, and compasses.

LIERNE, *see* VAULT.

LIGHTS. Openings between the MULLIONS of a window.

LIGORIO, Pirro (*c.* 1500–83). Painter and archaeologist as well as architect. In 1550 he built the Villa d'Este, Tivoli, and laid out its wonderful formal gardens with elaborate fountains and water-works. His masterpiece is the exquisite little Casino di Pio IV (1558–62) in the Vatican gardens, Rome, one of the most elegant of Mannerist buildings. Also in the Vatican, he transformed the exedra in BRAMANTE's Cortile del Belvedere into a gargantuan niche.

LINENFOLD. Tudor panelling ornamented with a conventional representation of a piece of linen laid in vertical folds. One such piece fills one panel. *See figure 58.*

Fig. 58. Linenfold

LINTEL. A horizontal beam or stone bridging an opening.

LISSITSKY, Eleazar Markevich, called El (1890–1941). Russian painter, typographer, designer and theorist as well as architect, Lissitsky became the apostle of Contructivism in the West in the 1920s. He trained under Joseph OLBRICH at the College of Technology, Darmstadt (1909–14). In 1919 he became Professor of Architecture at Vitebsk where he evolved his PROUN idea (PROUN = 'For the New Art') which he described as an 'interchange station' between painting and architecture – an interplay between the pictorial and structural. His ideas probably owed something to both MALEVICH and TATLIN, then famous for his 1920 design for a spiral-shaped monument to the Third International. In 1920 Lissitsky designed his Lenin Tribune project which foreshadowed the prime Constructivist building, the Leningrad Pravda building projected by the VESNIN brothers in 1923. From 1922 until 1931 Lissitsky was in the West where he knew and influenced the de Stijl and other *avant garde* architects. His 'Proun Cabinet' for the 1923 Berlin exhibition has recently been reconstructed at Eindhoven (Stedelijk van Abbemuseum), and his 'Abstract Cabinet', created in 1926 for Dresden and in 1927 for Hannover and intended to 'allow abstract art to do justice to its dynamic properties', has now been reconstructed in the Landesmuseum in Hannover. His most ambitious and forward-looking design – the 1924 *Wolkenbügel* project (with Mart Stam) for office blocks in Moscow on upright or splayed legs straddling roads – never got off the drawing board. In 1939 he produced designs for the Soviet Pavilion restaurant at the New York World Fair.

LISTEL, *see* FILLET.

LODGE. The medieval term for the masons' workshop and living-quarters set up when a church, castle, or house was to be built. In the case of cathedrals and great abbeys it was often permanent, under a resident master mason, to maintain the fabric of the building.

LODOLI, Carlo (1690–1761). A Venetian priest and architectural theorist. His neo-classical and 'functional' ideas were published after his death by A. Memmo (*Elementi d'architettura lodoliana*, 1786), but they had been current for many years and were very influential, e.g., on Algarotti's *Saggio sopra l'architettura* (1753).

LOGGIA. A gallery open on one or more sides, sometimes pillared: it may also be a separate structure, usually in a garden.

LOMBARDO, Pietro (*c.* 1435–1515). A leading sculptor and architect in late C15 Venice. Though of exquisite sensitivity he stands outside the main development of Renaissance architecture. He was born at Carona in Lombardy, hence his name. He appears to have visited Florence before 1464, when he is first recorded working in Padua as a sculptor. Soon after 1467 he settled in Venice. Between 1471 and 1485 he designed and carved decorations for the chancel of S. Giobbe, Venice, a work of strongly Florentine character. His next and most important work was S. Maria dei Miracoli (1481–9), in which he successfully blended the Veneto-Byzantine and Renaissance styles – marble panelling inside and out and a Byzantine dome, combined with crisply carved Renaissance ornament. To give an illusion of greater size he resorted to various *trompe l'œil* devices which he repeated on a larger scale, but with less success, on the façade of the Scuola di S. Marco (1488–90, upper storeys completed by CODUCCI). He also introduced into Venice the large architectural sepulchral monument with a classical framework and abundance of classically inspired sculpture. Here he was much assisted by his sons Antonio (*c.* 1485–1516) and Tullio (*c.* 1455–1532). Various Venetian palaces have been attributed to Lombardo, notably Palazzo Dario (*c.* 1487).

LONG AND SHORT WORK. Saxon QUOINS, consisting of long stones on end between flat ones, all bonded into the wall. The chancel arch JAMBS at Escomb (C7 or 8) may have a bearing on the origin of the technique; it may also have been evolved simultaneously and in association with pilaster-strip work (*see* LESENE). It is the insertion of the large flat stones which makes long and short work such a good bonding technique for corners, as in many cases they extend practically through the thickness of the walls; the upright blocks alone are subject to diagonal thrust.

Superficially long and short work is of two kinds:

a. the 'upright and flat' type, where the full size of the horizontal stone is visible on both flanks;

b. the long and short strip quoin, where the horizontal stones have been cut back, making them flush with the upright blocks.

This was a refinement in the process of finding a solid cornering for stone buildings, but is not necessarily an indication of a later date (e.g., Deerhurst of the early C10 has the 'upright and flat' type). The method of construction is the same for both kinds.

LONGHENA, Baldassare (1598–1682), the only great Venetian Baroque architect, was born in Venice of a family of stone carvers and was trained under SCAMOZZI. In 1630 he won a competition for the design of the *ex voto* church of S. Maria della Salute, with which he was to be occupied off and on for the rest of his long life (it was not finally consecrated until 1687). Standing on an imposing site at the entrance to the Grand Canal, this church is a masterpiece of scenographic design, with a vast buoyant dome anchored by huge Baroque scrolls to an octagonal base, and a very complex façade which directs the eye through the main door to the high altar. The interior is conceived as a series of dramatic vistas radiating from the centre of the octagonal nave. Longhena realized a

similarly theatrical concept in the design of his imposing double staircase for the monastery of S. Giorgio Maggiore (1643–5), which had considerable influence on later architects. In the domestic field he was less adventurous: Palazzo Rezzonico (begun 1667) and Palazzo Pesaro (begun 1676) on the Grand Canal – both completed after his death – with heavily rusticated basements, abundance of carving, and deep recesses which dissolve the surface of the exterior in patterns of light and shade, are merely Baroque variations on SANSOVINO's Palazzo Corner. (G. Massari built the top floor of Palazzo Rezzonico in 1752–6.) A tendency towards wilful exaggeration of sculptural detail in these works reaches its fantastic peak in the little church of the Ospedaletto (1670–8), with a preposterously overwrought façade bursting with *telamones*, giant heads, and lion masks. He has been credited with numerous villas on the mainland, but none is of much interest.

LONGHI, Martino the younger (1602–60), the most important member of a family of architects working mainly in Rome, was the son of Onorio Longhi (1569–1619) and the grandson of Martino Longhi the elder (d. 1591). He continued his father's work on S. Carlo al Corso, Rome, and began S. Antonio de'Portoghesi, Rome (1638). His major achievement is the façade of SS. Vincenzo ed Anastasio, Rome (1646–50), a powerfully dramatic, many-columned composition in which Mannerist devices are used to obtain an overwhelming high Baroque effect of grandeur and mass.

LONGUELUNE, Zacharias (1689–1748). French-born painter–architect who collaborated with Matthaeus PÖPPELMANN in Dresden from 1715 onwards and in Warsaw from 1728 onwards on the designs for the vast new Saxon Palace. Very few of his own projects were executed but his grandiose designs, which embodied French classicist theory, exerted considerable influence both in Saxony and as far away as Poland and Denmark. He designed the formal park at Gross-Sedlitz (1726), additions to the Japanisches Palais in Dresden (1729 onwards) and the Blockhaus terminating the Hauptstrasse in Dresden Neustadt (1731) (burnt out 1945 but now under reconstruction).

LOOS, Adolf (1870–1933), was born at Brno in Moravia, studied at Dresden, spent three crucial years in the United States (1893–6), and then worked in Vienna, strongly influenced by the doctrines just then expounded by Otto WAGNER. From the very first his designs (Goldmann shop interior, 1898) refused to allow any decorative features or any curves. His most important buildings are private houses of between 1904 (house, Lake Geneva) and 1910 (Steiner House, Vienna). They are characterized by unrelieved cubic shapes, a total absence of ornament, and a love of fine materials. In his theoretical writings, or rather his journalism, he was a rabid anti-ornamentalist, an enemy therefore of the Wiener Werkstätten and HOFFMANN, and a believer in the engineer and the plumber. His famous article called *Ornament and Crime* came out in 1908. As an architect, however, he wavered. His office building in the Michaelerplatz (1910) has Tuscan columns, his design for the Chicago Tribune competition of 1923 is a huge closely windowed Doric column; but smaller domestic jobs, such as the house for the Dadaist Tristan Tzara in Paris (1926), remained faithful to the spirit of 1904–10. Loos was not a successful architect, but he was influential among some of the *avant-garde* in Europe.

LOUDON, John Claudius (1783–1843), was apprenticed to a landscape gardener in Scotland, and educated himself the hard way. He settled in London in 1803, and at once began writing on gardening and agriculture. He also took up farming, made money and lost it, travelled on the Continent (1814 as far as Moscow, 1819–20 in France and Italy). His *Encyclopaedia of Gardening* came out in 1822, an *Encyclopaedia of Agriculture* in 1825, an *Encyclopaedia of Plants* in 1829, and the architecturally important *Encyclopaedia of Cottage, Farm and Villa Architecture* in 1833. This is the standard book if one wants to see what ideals and what styles of the past English country-houses followed, chiefly in the 1840s. Loudon also started and edited the *Gardener's Magazine* (1826 etc.) and the short-lived *Architectural Magazine* (1834). He was an exceedingly hard worker, labouring under great physical disabilities, and making and losing large sums of money.

LOUIS, Victor (1731–1800). French neo-classical architect working in a somewhat florid style derived from ancient Rome and the city palaces (rather than the villas) of PALLADIO. Born in Paris, he was trained there and at the French Academy in Rome (1756–9). In 1765 he was called to Warsaw by Stanislas-Augustus but returned the next year without having built anything. His first work of importance is also his masterpiece, the theatre at Bordeaux (1775–80), a massive structure with a dodecastyle portico (without pediment) stretching the full length of the main façade. It contains a large stage, very grand auditorium and the most monumental staircase and foyer that had been realized up to that date. He did a certain amount of other work in and around Bordeaux (e.g., Hôtel Saige, now the Préfecture, Château de Bouilh). He also had an extensive practice in Paris where his main and perhaps most appealing work was the colonnades in the Palais Royal gardens (1780–85) and the adjoining Théâtre de la Comédie-Française (1786–90, rebuilt 1902). The original building had an iron and hollow-tile roof to reduce the danger of fires.

LOUVRE. 1. An opening, often with a LANTERN over, in the roof of a hall to let the smoke from a central hearth escape; either open-sided, or closed by slanting boards to keep out the rain. 2. One of a series of overlapping boards or slips of glass to admit air and exclude rain. *See figure 59.*

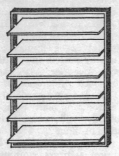

Fig. 59. Louvre

LOW SIDE WINDOW. A window usually on the south side of the chancel, lower than the others, possibly intended for communication between persons outside the chancel and the priest within; perhaps also for the sanctus bell to be heard outside the church.

LOZENGE. A diamond shape.

LUCARNE. 1. A small opening in an attic or a spire. 2. A DORMER WINDOW.

LUDOVICE, João Frederico (Johann Friedrich Ludwig, 1670–1752), the leading Late Baroque architect in Portugal, was born at Hall in Swabia, the son of a goldsmith whose craft he practised first in Rome (1697–1701) then in Lisbon. In about 1711 the King of Portugal commissioned him to build a small convent at Mafra. Gradually the size of the project was enlarged, and the building finally became one of the largest in Europe (built 1717–70). It includes a royal palace, a vast church, and conventual buildings for 300 monks. Mafra derives mainly from High Baroque Rome with a few South German and

Portuguese overtones: the church, liberally decorated with Italian statues, is especially impressive. His only other works of importance are the library of Coimbra University (1717–23) with a very rich *mouvementé* façade and the apse of Évora Cathedral (1716–46).

LUNETTE. A semicircular opening or TYMPANUM. The term can also be applied to any flat, semicircular surface.

LUTYENS, Sir Edwin (1869–1944), after a short time with George & Peto, was already in independent practice in 1889. In 1896 he designed Munstead Wood for Gertrude Jekyll, the gardener and garden designer who helped him in his career. A number of excellent country houses in the Arts and Crafts style followed (Deanery Garden, Sonning, 1899; Orchards, Godalming, 1899; Tigbourne Court, 1899; Folly Farm, Sulhampstead, 1905 and 1912), establishing Lutyens's originality and ability for coordinating forms. However, he was very early attracted by classicism, first of a William and Mary variety (Liberal Club, Farnham, 1894; Crooksbury, east front, 1899; Hestercombe Orangery, 1905), then of a grander neo-Georgian (Nashdom, Taplow, 1905) and a semi-Palladian, semi-English-Baroque 'Wrenaissance' (Heathcote, Ilkley, 1906). Lutyens shared to the full the imperial *folie de grandeur* of the Edwardian years, and this made him the ideal architect for the last crop of really spectacular English country houses (Lindisfarne Castle, 1903; Castle Drogo, 1910–30), and of course for New Delhi. His Viceroy's House (1913 onwards) has a genuine monumentality and a sense of grandiose display which Baker in his buildings for Delhi never achieved.

However, classicism bogged Lutyens down in the end. In spite of extreme care for details of proportion and oddly impish details into which his former originality retreated, his later commercial buildings – Britannic House (1920 etc.) and the Midland

Bank (1924 etc.) – stand outside the mainstream of European developments, whereas an earlier church by Lutyens such as St Jude's in the Hampstead Garden Suburb (1909–11) possessed a true originality and a sense of massing very rare in European ecclesiastical architecture of the time.

LYCH GATE. A covered wooden gateway with open sides at the entrance to a churchyard, providing a resting-place for a coffin (the word *lych* is Saxon for corpse). Part of the burial service is sometimes read there.

LYMING, Robert, carpenter, builder, and architect, designed the loggia and frontispiece of Hatfield House (1611). At Blickling Hall (*c.* 1625) he produced the last of the great Jacobean 'prodigy' houses in which Flemish ornamentalism and asymmetrical planning were completely anglicized.

M

MACHICOLATION. A gallery or PARA-PET projecting on brackets and built on the outside of castle towers and walls, with openings in the floor through which to drop molten lead, boiling oil, and missiles.

MACHUCA, Pedro (d. 1550), began as a painter, worked in Italy and returned to Spain in 1520. His masterpiece, the Palace of Charles V in the Alhambra at Granada (1527–68), is very Italian in the RAPHAEL–GIULIO ROMANO style; indeed, it is larger and more complete than any Bramantesque palace in Italy. But various Spanish or PLATERESQUE features crept into his design, e.g., the garlanded window frames.

MACKINTOSH, Charles Rennie (1868–1928), studied at the Glasgow School of Art at the time when Glasgow painting had suddenly turned from a provincial past to new forms of considerable interest to people in England and even on the Continent. In 1893 and the following years he, his friend McNair, and the two Macdonald sisters, Margaret (later Mrs Mackintosh, 1865–1933) and Frances (later Mrs McNair), designed graphic work and repoussé metalwork in an ART NOUVEAU way, inspired by The Studio (which started in London in 1893) and especially by Jan Toorop, the Dutchman. In 1896 Mackintosh won the competition for the new building of the Glasgow School of Art and erected a building inferior to none of its date anywhere in Europe or America – on a clear rational plan, with the basic external forms equally clear and rational (e.g., the studio windows), but with a centre-piece of complete originality and high fancifulness, influenced by VOYSEY, by the Scottish castle and manor-house tradi-tion, and even a little by the current English 'Wrenaissance'. The metalwork of the façade and much of the interior achieve a unification of the crisply rectangular with the long, delicate, languid curves of Art Nouveau. It is in this unique harmony that Mackintosh's greatness lies, and it explains the deep impression his furniture and furnishings made on Austrian architects when they became familiar with him, first through The Studio and then through an exhibition at the Secession (see OLBRICH) in 1900. The Viennese were abandoning Art Nouveau excesses for a clearer, saner style, and Mackintosh both inspired and confirmed them.

Mackintosh had fully evolved his style in his interior work by 1899 – white lacquered chairs and cupboards, erect, elegant, clearly articulated, and with wistfully curved inlays in metal and pink, mauve, or mother-of-pearl enamel. There was no one else who could combine the rational and the expressive in so intriguing a way. His capital works at or near Glasgow are the tea-rooms for Mrs Cranston (Buchanan Street, 1897 etc.; Argyle Street, 1897 and 1905; Sauchiehall Street, 1904; Ingram Street, 1901; c. 1906, and c. 1911), now alas mostly destroyed or disused; two houses (Windyhill, Kilmacolm, 1899–1901, and Hill House, Helensburgh, 1902–3); a school (Scotland Street, 1906); and the library wing of the School of Art (1907–9) with its sheer, towering outer wall and its bewitchingly complex interior. In 1901 he had won second prize in a German publisher's competition for the house of an art-lover (Baillie Scott came first), and this consolidated his reputation abroad.

However, he was not an easy man,

and his erratic ways alienated clients. In 1913 he left the firm (Honeyman & Keppie) in which he had been a partner since 1904. He moved to Walberswick, then to London, then after the war to Port Vendres, and finally back to London, painting highly original, finely drawn landscapes and still-lifes, but never recovering an architectural practice.

MACKMURDO, Arthur H. (1851–1942), came from a wealthy family and had plenty of leisure to evolve a style of his own. In 1874 he travelled to Italy with RUSKIN. About 1880 he seems to have built his first houses. In 1882 he founded the Century Guild, a group of architects, artists, and designers inspired by RUSKIN and MORRIS. The group began in 1884 to publish a magazine, *The Hobby Horse*, which anticipated some of the features of book design recovered by Morris from the medieval past in his Kelmscott Press of 1890. As early as 1883, in the design for the cover of his book on Wren's City churches, Mackmurdo introduced those long flame-like or tendril-like curves which nearly ten years later were taken up, especially in Belgium, as a basis for ART NOUVEAU. But while in such two-dimensional designs, including a number for textiles (*c.* 1884), Mackmurdo is the lone pioneer of Art Nouveau, the furniture he designed from 1886 onwards and a stand for an exhibition at Liverpool, also of 1886, established him as the forerunner of VOYSEY in clarity of structure, elegance, and originality in the sense of independence of the past. Specially characteristic, on the exhibition stand, are the long, tapering posts with a far-projecting flat cornice. In 1904 Mackmurdo gave up architecture; later he concentrated on economic thought and writing, his ideas being similar to those of Social Credit.

MADERNO, Carlo (1556–1629), was born at Capolago on Lake Lugano, and had settled in Rome by 1588, beginning as assistant to his uncle Domenico FONTANA. He was appointed architect of St Peter's in 1603, when he also completed the façade of S. Susanna, Rome, a revolutionary design with which he broke away from the current rather facile and academic Mannerism and established his own lucid, forceful, and intensely dynamic style. S. Susanna and the majestic dome of S. Andrea della Valle, Rome, are his masterpieces, though he is best known for his work at St Peter's, where he had the unenviable job of altering MICHELANGELO's centralized plan by adding a nave and façade. Work began in 1607, and the façade was finished by 1612. Its excessive length is due to the later addition of towers, of which only the substructures were built and which now appear to form part of the façade. His Confessio before the high altar and his elegant fountain in the *piazza* are more successful. His secular buildings include Palazzo Mattei, Rome (1598–1618), and Palazzo Barberini, Rome (1628 onwards), though the latter was almost entirely executed after his death by BERNINI, who made various alterations, notably to the main façade.

MAEKAWA, Kunio, *see* TANGE.

MAIANO, Benedetto da, *see* BENEDETTO DA MAIANO.

MAIANO, Giuliano da, *see* GIULIANO DA MAIANO.

MAILLART, Robert (1872–1940), a Swiss engineer, studied at the Zürich Polytechnic (1890–4), had jobs in various engineering firms, and then set up on his own (1902). He worked on the unexplored possibilities of REINFORCED CONCRETE, and in the course of that work arrived at a new aesthetic for concrete, using it to span by curves, rather than merely as a new means of building post-and-lintel structures. His Tavenasa Bridge (1905) is the first in which arch and roadway are structurally one. He built many bridges afterwards, all of them of a thoroughbred elegance: the one across the Salzinatobel has a span of nearly 300 ft (1929–30). In 1908 he also began experimenting with concrete mushroom construction, at a time when this was being done independently in the United States; the technique involves a post and a mushroom top spreading from it that are one inseparable concrete unit. Maillart's first building of mushroom construction was a warehouse at Zürich (1910).

MAITANI, Lorenzo, (d. 1330), was a Sienese sculptor and architect. He was called in to advise on Orvieto Cathedral in 1310 being then described as 'universalis caputmagister' which testifies to his celebrity as an architect. From then until his death he was in complete control of all work on the façade of Orvieto Cathedral, including the sculpture some of which is probably by him. Two drawings for the façade survive, the second being probably by Maitani (Opera del Duomo, Orvieto). In 1317 he was mentioned as working on a fountain at Perugia and in 1322 he was on the commission for the new Baptistery of Siena Cathedral.

MALEVICH, Kasimir (1878–1935). Though a painter, Malevich, like TATLIN and Gabo, designed in the mid-twenties pieces of fantastical architecture in the new modern, Constructivist manner. They were called Architectonics.

MANNERISM is in its primary sense the acceptance of a manner rather than its meaning. Now Mannerism has also become a term to denote the style current in Italy from MICHELANGELO to the end of the C16. It is characterized by the use of motifs in deliberate opposition to their original significance or context, but it can also express itself in an equally deliberate cold and rigid classicism. The term applies to French and Spanish architecture of the C16 as well (DELORME; the Escorial), but how far it applies to the Northern countries is contro-

versial. Principal examples in Italy are MICHELANGELO's Medici Chapel and Laurentian Library, GIULIO ROMANO's works at Mantua, VASARI's Uffizi at Florence, and other works by these architects and LIGORIO, AMMANATI, BUONTALENTI, etc. PALLADIO belongs to Mannerism only in certain limited aspects of his work.

MANOR HOUSE. A house in the country or a village, the centre of a manor. Architecturally the term is used to denote the unfortified, medium-sized house of the later Middle Ages.

MANSARD ROOF, see ROOF.

MANSART, François (1598–1666), the first great protagonist of French classicism in architecture, holds a position parallel to Poussin in painting and Corneille in drama. He never went to Italy, and his style is extremely French in its elegance, clarity, and cool restraint. Though of scrupulous artistic conscience he was unfortunately both arrogant and slippery in his business relationships, and his inability to make and keep to a final plan not unnaturally enraged his clients. As a result, he lost many commissions. For the last ten years of his life he was virtually unemployed. He was seldom patronized by the Crown and never by the great nobility; his clients belonged mainly to the newly rich bourgeoisie, who had the intelligence to appreciate and the money to pay for his sophisticated and luxurious buildings.

Born in Paris, the son of a master carpenter, he probably began under de BROSSE at Coulommiers. By 1624 he had already established himself as a prominent architect in the capital. His early work derives from de Brosse, with Mannerist overtones in the style of DU CERCEAU, but his individual style began to emerge at the Château de Balleroy (1626), where the harmonious grouping of massive blocks achieves an effect of sober monumentality. His first masterpiece, the

Orléans wing of the *château* at Blois (1635–8), would have been a grander and more monumental Palais Luxembourg had it ever been completed. Only the central block and colonnades were built. But these display to the full the ingenuity of planning, clarity of disposition, and purity and refinement of detail which distinguish his work. He also introduced here the continuous broken roof with a steep lower slope and flatter, shorter upper portion that is named after him. His style reached culmination at Maisons Lafitte (1642–6), the country house near Paris which he built for the immensely wealthy René de Longeuil, who apparently allowed him a completely free hand. (He pulled down part of it during construction in order to revise his designs!) It is his most complete work to survive and gives a better idea of his genius than any other. The oval rooms in the wings and the vestibule, executed entirely in stone without either gilding or colour, epitomize his suave severity and civilized reticence in decoration. His design for the Val-de-Grâce in Paris (*c.* 1645) is contemporary with Maisons Lafitte, but he was dismissed and replaced by LEMERCIER in 1646, when the building had reached the entablature of the nave and the lower storey of the façade. The conception appears to derive from PALLADIO's Redentore.

His other important buildings are Ste Marie de la Visitation, Paris (1632–4); the Hôtel de la Vrillière, Paris (begun 1635), wholly symmetrical and the model for the classical type of Parisian *hôtel*; the Hôtel du Jars, Paris (begun 1648, now destroyed), in which he developed a freer, more plastic disposition of rooms which was to be very influential. His last surviving work is his remodelling of the Hôtel Carnavalet in Paris (1655). He was consulted by Colbert in the 1660s in connection with the Louvre and a royal chapel at St Denis, but his designs were not executed.

MANSART, Jules Hardouin, *see* HARDOUIN-MANSART, Jules.

MANTELPIECE. The wood, brick, stone, or marble frame surrounding a fireplace, frequently including an overmantel or mirror above; sometimes called *chimney-piece*.

MANUELINE STYLE. An architectural style peculiar to Portugal and named after King Manuel the Fortunate (1495–1521). *See* PORTUGUESE ARCHITECTURE.

MAQSURAH. A screen or grille of wood in a mosque to protect and separate the imam from the crowd.

MARKELIUS, Sven (b. 1889), is a Swedish architect and town-planner. City architect and planner to the city of Stockholm 1944–54, Markelius laid out the new suburb of Vällingby. Vällingby is not a SATELLITE TOWN, as it is not meant to have a completely independent existence, but is of an exemplary plan combining a truly urban-looking centre with peripheral housing of both high blocks of flats and small houses (1953–9).

MAROT, Daniel (*c.* 1660–1752), was the son of a minor French architect Jean Marot (*c.* 1619–79), who is chiefly remembered for his volumes of engravings *L'architecture française* known as 'le grand Marot' and 'le petit Marot'. Born in Paris, Daniel emigrated to Holland after the Revocation of the Edict of Nantes (1685), becoming almost immediately architect to William of Orange. He developed an intricate style of ornamentation, similar to that of Jean Berain (see his *Nouvelles cheminées à panneaux de la manière de France*), and was involved among other things with the design of the audience chamber or Trêveszaal in the Binnenhof, The Hague (1695–8), and the interior decoration and garden design at Het Loo. He followed William to England and designed the gardens (Grand Parterre) and perhaps some of the furnishings and interior decoration at Hampton Court, but though he later described himself as 'Architect to the King of England' no buildings can be ascribed to him (Schomberg House, London, c. 1698, appears to have been strongly influenced by him). He died at The Hague, where he designed part of the Royal Library (1734–8) and Stadthuis (1733–9). He published his *Œuvres* in Amsterdam in 1715 but his main buildings date from the following years and are all in The Hague – the German Embassy (1715), the Hôtel van Wassenaar and the façade of the Royal Library (1734, wings by Pieter de Swart, 1761).

MARTIN, Sir Leslie (b. 1908), was Architect to the London County Council from 1953 to 1956, in succession to Sir Robert MATTHEW, and is now Professor of Architecture at Cambridge University. Under Martin the finest of all L.C.C. housing estates was built, that at Roehampton for a population of about 10,000. Some of the brightest young architects in England were at that time working in the L.C.C. office, and Martin gave them full scope. In the course of building the style of the scheme changed from one inspired by Sweden to that of LE CORBUSIER at Chandigarh, and Martin's own work in partnership with C. A. St J. Wilson has moved in the same direction – see, for example, the new building for Caius College, Cambridge (1960–2). Other recent work is College Hall, Leicester University (1958–61), and the outstandingly fine new Oxford libraries (1961–4).

MARTINELLI, Domenico (1650–1718), quadratura painter and architect errant, who travelled widely and played an important part in the diffusion of the Italian Baroque style north of the Alps, was born in Lucca and ordained priest, but this did nothing to interfere with his wandering artistic career. His masterpiece is the Stadtpalais Liechtenstein in Vienna (1692–1705), which introduced the elaborate triumphal staircase which was to become an essential feature of Viennese palace architecture. He also designed the large but simpler Gartenpalais Liechtenstein, Vienna (1698–1711), and probably the Harrach Palais, Vienna (c. 1690), as well as a house for Graf von Kaunitz, Austerlitz. It is said that he also worked in Warsaw, Prague, and Holland.

MARTYRIUM. A church or other building erected over a site which bears witness to the Christian faith, either by referring to an event in Christ's life or Passion, or by sheltering the grave of a martyr, a witness by virtue of having shed his blood.

MATHEY, Jean Baptist (c. 1630–c. 1695). He was probably born in Dijon and trained as a painter, but was then taken to Prague in 1675 as architect to the Archbishop and, despite much local opposition, began to work in a classicizing French manner very different from that practised by F. CARATTI and others in Prague. He built a country house at Troya (1679–96), the quietly handsome Toscana Palace in Prague (1689–90) and, in a more exuberant style, two churches which influenced FISCHER VON ERLACH – St Francis in Prague (1679–88) and the abbey church of St Josef Malá Straná (Kleinseite).

MATTHEW, Sir Robert (b. 1906), was Architect to the London County Council from 1946 to 1953, in the years in which the Council embarked on its exemplary housing and schools work. Matthew can be considered instrumental in establishing the progressive style of these buildings and the principles of variety in grouping, mixture of heights, and siting in landscape which have made the L.C.C. estates a pattern for the whole of Europe. Of recent buildings designed by the firm Robert Matthew, Johnson-Marshall & Partners the finest is New Zealand House, London (1958–63), while the most challenging is the Commonwealth Institute (1959–62), also in London, with its incorporation of the fashionable HYPERBOLIC PARABOLOID roof.

MAUSOLEUM. A magnificent and stately tomb. The term derives from the tomb of Mausolus at Halicarnassus.

MAY, Hugh (1622–84), the son of a Sussex gentleman and prominent among the virtuosi of the Restoration, imported the placid spirit of Dutch PALLADIANISM into England and helped, with PRATT, to establish the type of house later known, erroneously, as the 'Wren' type. Eltham Lodge, London (1663–4), is his only surviving work, a rectangular brick-built house with a central pediment and stone pilasters. He may also have designed Holme Lacy House, Hereford (begun 1673–4). His work at Windsor Castle (remodelling the Upper Ward including St George's Hall and the King's Chapel, 1675–83) was important but has been almost completely destroyed. It was the most fully developed example of a Baroque scheme of decoration in Northern Europe – achieved with the aid of the painter Verrio and the sculptor Grinling Gibbons.

MAYAN ARCHITECTURE, see MESO-AMERICAN ARCHITECTURE.

MAYBECK, Bernard R. (1862–1937). Active chiefly at Berkeley and San Francisco. His is a curious, highly original Stick Style. Wood was his favourite material. Examples are the Faculty Club on the Berkeley campus (1899) and the First Church of Christ Scientist at Berkeley (1910–12). The mixture of vernacular, Gothic and Japanese in this building is irresistible. Many private houses show the same qualities, the interiors often being yet more stimulating than the exteriors.

MCINTIRE, Samuel (1757–1811), was a self-trained architect of great ability and the outstanding example of the early American craftsman–builder tradition, though most of his work dates from after the end of the Revolutionary War. He was a wood-carver by trade and lived in Salem, Mass. With the help of Batty LANGLEY's and WARE's books and perhaps an edition of Palladio (which he owned at his death), he taught himself the PALLADIAN style, which he adopted for his first houses, e.g., Pierce-Nichols House (1782) in Salem. His most ambitious effort was Salem Court House (1785, now demolished) with superimposed orders and a dome. In the 1790s he came under the influence of BULFINCH, who provided the general design for his most important private house, the Derby Mansion (1795–9, demolished 1815) and from whom he picked up the ADAM style which he used in his later and finest houses (mostly destroyed, but there are rooms from them in the Boston and Philadelphia museums).

MCKIM, Charles Follen (1847–1909), studied first engineering at Harvard, then, in 1867–70, architecture in Paris at the École des Beaux Arts. On his return to the States he entered the office of H. H. RICHARDSON. When he set up his own practice, he went into partnership with W. R. Mead and a little later with Stanford WHITE. In 1878 they were all interested in Colonial architecture, a highly unusual thing at the time. To this was added almost at once a liking for the Italian Renaissance which was first introduced, it seems, by Joseph Merrill Wells, who entered the office in 1879 and died early, in 1890. The Italian Renaissance meant to them the High Renaissance, not the Baroque exuberance of classical motifs then current. A first proof of this new taste was the impressively restrained group of the Villard Houses in Madison Avenue (1882), the second the Boston Public Library (1887 etc.) with its façade by McKim, inspired by LABROUSTE's Ste Geneviève Library. McKim believed in interior enrichment on a grand scale, and for the library was able to call in Sargent and

Puvis de Chavannes. For the Chicago exhibition of 1893, McKim did the Agriculture Building.

Later jobs include the Germantown Cricket Club (1891), decidedly American Colonial; the lavish Madison Gardens (1891), Spanish with a tall tower reminiscent of Seville; the Washington Triumphal Arch in New York in the style of the Étoile; Columbia University in New York with its library rotunda (1893) inspired by the Pantheon in Rome and JEFFERSON's Charlottesville (1817–26); the Morgan Library in New York (1903); and the Pennsylvania Railway Station also in New York (1904–10), a grandiose scheme echoing Imperial Roman *thermae*. It was recently demolished.

MEGARON. A large oblong hall, especially in Cretan and Mycenaean palaces; sometimes thought to be the ancestor of the Doric temple.

MENDELSOHN, Erich or Eric (1887–1953). The boldness of Mendelsohn's vision of a sculptural architecture emerged early in his many small sketches for buildings that are not functionally determined but are highly expressive with their streamlined curves. In the years of German Expressionism at and after the end of the First World War, he was just once enabled actually to build such a vision (the Einstein Tower at Potsdam, 1919–20); but vigorous curves carried round corners also characterize his remodelling of the Mosse Building in Berlin (1921), and appear much tempered by the more rational spirit of the INTERNATIONAL MODERN style of the later twenties and the thirties in his excellent Schocken stores for Stuttgart (1926) and Chemnitz (1928). As expressive as the Einstein Tower, but in terms of multi-angular roof shapes instead of curves, is another early work of Mendelsohn's, a factory at Luckenwalde (1923). Mendelsohn visited the United States in 1924 and was understandably impressed by the expressive qualities

of the skyscrapers. Later Berlin buildings include the headquarters of the Metal Workers' Union (1929) and Columbushaus (1929–30). In 1933 Mendelsohn went to London and joined Serge Chermayeff. Joint work are the de la Warr Pavilion at Bexhill (1935–6) and No. 64 Old Church Street, Chelsea (1936). But in 1934 he moved on to Israel, and in 1941 finally settled in the United States. In Israel he built, among other things, the Hadassah University Medical Centre on Mount Scopus, Jerusalem (1936–8), in America the Maimonides Hospital at San Francisco (1946–50).

MENGONI, Giuseppe (1829–77). Architect of the Galleria Vittorio Emanuele in Milan, won in competition in 1861. It was built in 1864–7 (though work on the decoration continued until 1877), and is the largest, highest, and most ambitious of all shopping arcades. It is cruciform, and the buildings through which it runs take part in the free Renaissance design of the *galleria*. Especially impressive is the façade towards the Piazza del Duomo.

MERLON, *see* BATTLEMENT.

MESO-AMERICAN ARCHITECTURE. The architecture of the Mayan, Aztec and earlier civilizations in central America. The term Meso-American is applied to the area south of the Pánuco River and north of Panama, comprising part of modern Mexico, Honduras and Nicaragua. Nearly all the surviving Pre-Columbian buildings are religious and the most notable of them are pyramids. These differ from Egyptian pyramids in both form and function – they are flat topped and of varying plan (circular, oblong, square) and were conceived as artificial hills for the celebration of religious rites. The earliest is the pyramid of Cuilcuilco (C1–2) composed of four superimposed truncated cones of stone some 30 m. high but on a base of more than 100 m. diameter. Slightly later are the buildings at Teotihuacán (a great religious centre until the c6 when it was abandoned) with the very large Pyramid of the Sun (about 230 m. square and 60 m. high) of five receding storeys with a monumental staircase leading up the W. façade to the uppermost platform, the smaller and later Pyramid of the Moon (c5–6) and the Temple of Quetzalcoatl adorned with sculptured serpent heads and relief masks of the god Tlaloc. The form of the pyramid was taken over by the Mayan civilization which arose in the c4 at Uaxactún in the forest of Petén and vanished as mysteriously as it had come in the late c9 or early c10. Mayan pyramids are, however, higher in relation to the base. The Maya lived in city states distributed over a wide area – W. Honduras, Guatemala, British Honduras, the whole Yucatan peninsula and the Mexican states of Tabasco and Chiapas. Each appears to have had pyramids, temples and sanctuaries, courts for the ball game (which had a religious origin), and 'palaces', often of several storeys and containing many small ill-lit rooms unsuitable for human habitation and probably used as treasuries or for storage. They are all built of stone on stone terraces with a mortar composed of lime and sand, often with openings of triangular corbelled arches and narrow interior rooms roofed with corbelled vaults which make their first appearance early in the c4 at Uaxactún. Much use was made of monumental sculpture, often of very high quality – on lintels, wall-panels, borders of ramps beside the pyramid staircases – intricately carved in relief with representations of religious ceremonies, as on the 'palaces' at Uxmal (c9–10), Piedras Negras, Palanque, Yaxchilán and, at its richest, on the Casa de las Monjas at Chichen Itzá (c5–10) and the Codz-Pop or Palace of the Masks at Kabah (c9–10).

During the Mayan period the distinct culture of the Zapotecs emerged at Monte Alban where a whole hill was covered with somewhat severe undecorated terraces, platforms and buildings linked by great staircases. A striking contrast is provided by the contemporary Tajín, the centre of the so-called Totonac culture where numerous buildings in a great variety of forms and with much sculptured decoration were constructed between the c5 or c6 and the c13 when the place was abandoned.

By the c10 when these early civilizations had begun to falter groups of invaders collectively known as the Chichimecs began to arrive from the north. The most important of them, the Toltecs, founded the city of Tula where they built a grandiose pyramid dedicated to Tlahuizcalpantecuhtli, with savage sculptural decorations which include the first references to human sacrifice to be found in the region. They took over Chichen Itzá where they added to the earlier buildings the nine-storey pyramid called the Castillo, the Temple of the Jaguars, the Temple of the Warriors with a many-columned portico and the largest of all Meso-American ball courts.

The Toltec civilization was already in decline before the arrival of the Aztecs who settled on the island of Texcoco in 1325, and soon dominated the entire Meso-American area. They took over the architecture of their predecessors, their only original contribution being the double pyramid. Their capital city Tenochtitlán and their holy city Cholula with many pyramids and temples were entirely destroyed by the Spaniards immediately after the conquest. Of surviving Aztec buildings the most important is the double pyramid at Tenayuca with a monumental staircase up one side and a row of fiercely grimacing serpent heads projecting from the base on the other three sides. This pyramid appears to have been rebuilt every 52 years for the ceremony of the New Fire, which initiated each cycle of the Aztec calendar. The present one dates from *c.* 1450–1500. Other notable buildings include the Pyramid at El Tepozteco (*c.* 1502–20) constructed high on a rocky ridge and a complex of buildings hewn from the living rock at Malinalco (1476–1520). Although the bloodthirsty and warlike Aztecs expanded their empire, in quest of prisoners for human sacrifice as well as land, one subject group maintained cultural independence – the Mixtecs who occupied an area bordering the Pacific and roughly corresponding to the modern Mexican states of Oaxaca, Puebla and Guerrero. The only important Mixtec site is Mitla where there are no pyramids, only palaces, notably the Palace of the Columns decorated with finely cut geometrical reliefs which provide a striking contrast to the terrifying grotesques on Aztec and Toltec buildings.

MÉTEZEAU, Louis (1559/72–1615), was closely involved with the D U CER-CEAUS in Henry IV's improvements to Paris, notably the Place des Vosges (1603 onwards) and at the Louvre where he probably designed the S. façade of the Grande Galerie. He also assisted in the interior decoration of the Petite Galerie, the Salle des Antiques and the Grande Galerie (1601–8). He collaborated with Dupérac on the interior decoration of the Hôtel de Jean de Fourcy, Paris (1601). His brother Clément or Jacques Clément Métezeau (1581–1652) may have been a more important architect. He was transitional between de BROSSE and LE VAU. He designed the Place Ducale at Charleville (1610), the portail of Saint-Gervais, Paris (1616), the Orangerie du Louvre (1617), the Hôtel de Brienne (1630–32) and the Château de la Meilleraye (*c.* 1630). He worked with de Brosse at the Luxembourg in Paris *c.* 1615 and in 1611 was sent to Florence by Marie de Medici to make drawings of Palazzo Pitti in connection with it, though they do not appear to have been used by de Brosse.

METOPE. The square space between two TRIGLYPHS in the FRIEZE of a Doric order; it may be carved or left plain. *See figure 64.*

MEUTRIÈRE. In military architecture, a small loophole, large enough for the barrel of a gun or musket and through which a soldier might fire under cover.

MEWS. A row of stables with living accommodation above, built at the back of a town-house, especially in London. They are now nearly all converted into houses or 'mews flats'.

MEXICAN ARCHITECTURE, see MESO-AMERICAN ARCHITECTURE.

MEZZANINE. A low storey between two higher ones; also called an *entresol.*

MICHAEL OF CANTERBURY. A master mason working *c.* 1300, first at Canterbury for the cathedral, then in London, where he was the first master mason of St Stephen's Chapel (begun 1292) in the palace of Westminster and probably its designer. A Walter of Canterbury was in charge of work at the palace in 1322. A Thomas of Canterbury was working under him in 1324 and, in 1331, probably after Walter's death, was put in charge of work at St Stephen's Chapel. Thomas may have died in 1336.

MICHELANGELO BUONARROTI (1475-1564). Sculptor, painter, poet, and one of the greatest of all architects, he was the archetype of the inspired 'genius' – unsociable, distrustful, untidy, obsessed by his work, and almost pathologically proud – in fact, the antithesis of the Early Renaissance ideal of the complete man so nobly exemplified in ALBERTI and LEONARDO. Deeply and mystically religious, he was consumed by the conflicts and doubts of the Counter-Reformation. As in his life, so in his art, he rejected all the assumptions of the Renaissance and revolutionized everything he touched. Nowhere was his influence so profound or so enduring as in architecture. He invented a new vocabulary of ornament, new and dynamic principles of composition, and an entirely new attitude to space. His few dicta and his drawings reveal that he conceived a building as an organic growth and in relation to the movement of the spectator. He made clay models rather than perspective drawings, and appears to have eschewed the type of highly finished design which could be turned over to the builders ready for execution. He usually made considerable modifications as the building went up, and it is now impossible to tell exactly how his many incomplete works would have looked had he finished them or how he would have finally realized in stone those compositions which remained on paper – the façade of S. Lorenzo, Florence (1516), or the centrally planned S. Giovanni dei Fiorentini, Rome (1556–60).

His first work in architecture is the exterior of the chapel of Leo X in Castel Sant'Angelo, Rome (1514). In 1515 he received his first major commission, for the façade of BRUNELLESCHI's S. Lorenzo, Florence, which he conceived as an elaborate framework for more than life-size sculpture. In 1520, before his S. Lorenzo design was finally abandoned, he was commissioned to execute the Medici family mausoleum in the new sacristy of the same church, much of which was already built. He produced a revolutionary design in which, for the first time, the tyranny of the orders was completely rejected: windows taper sharply, capitals vanish from pilasters, tabernacles weigh down heavily on the voids of the doors beneath them. But the novelty of his design is less evident in this truculent misuse of the classical vocabulary than in the revolutionary conception of architecture which inspired it. He saw the wall not as an inert plane to be decorated with applied ornaments but as a vital, many-layered organism – hence the extraordinary form of the tabernacles with their strange elisions and recessions. The fact that he

developed this new conception while the sacristy was in course of construction accounts for its many inconsistencies. The work was brought more or less to its present state by 1534 but never completed.

In 1524 he was commissioned to design a library for S. Lorenzo, Florence – the famous Biblioteca Laurenziana (reading-room designed 1525, vestibule 1526). The site determined its awkward shape and also limited the thickness of the walls. But he turned both these limitations to good effect, linking the structure to the decoration in a way never before achieved or imagined. Pilasters, which had hitherto been purely decorative elements applied to a structural wall, he used as the supports for the ceiling, while the cross-beams above the pilasters are echoed in mosaic on the floor so that the eye is drawn along the length of the room through a perspective of diminishing oblongs. He counteracted this longitudinal emphasis by stressing the verticality of the vestibule. Here the columns are set like statues in niches so that they appear to be merely decorative, though in fact they carry the roof. Other features are no less perverse – blind window-frames of aedicules with pilasters which taper towards the base, consoles which support nothing, and a staircase which pours forbiddingly down from the library on to the entrance level (executed by AMMANATI). There is no figure sculpture, but the whole interior is treated plastically as if it were sculpture.

In 1528–9 Michelangelo was employed on the fortifications of Florence, which he designed, with characteristic perversity, for offence rather than defence. In 1534 he left Florence for Rome, where he spent the rest of his life. His first Roman commission was for the reorganization of the Capitol, to provide a suitable setting for the ancient statue of Marcus Aurelius and an imposing place for outdoor ceremonies (begun 1539). He laid out the central space as an oval – the first use of this shape in the Renaissance – and designed new fronts for Palazzo dei Conservatori and Palazzo del Senatore (neither finished before his death). His designs were strikingly original, e.g., in their use of a GIANT ORDER embracing two storeys, a device that was soon to become general. In 1546 he was commissioned to complete Antonio da SANGALLO's Palazzo Farnese. He converted the·unfinished façade into one of the most imposing in Rome, redesigned the upper floors of the *cortile*, and planned a vast garden to link it with the Villa Farnesina on the far side of the Tiber (not executed). In the conception of this grandiose vista, as in his design for the Porta Pia (1561–5) at the end of a new street from the Quirinal, he anticipated the principles of Baroque town planning.

But his most important Roman commission was, of course, for the completion of St Peter's (1546–64). Here he was faced with the task of finishing a building begun by BRAMANTE and continued by Antonio da Sangallo. He reverted to the centralized plan of the former, but made it much bolder and stronger, and demolished part of the latter's additions. His work on the interior was entirely masked in the C17; on the exterior it is visible only on the north and south arms and the drum of the dome. (The dome itself is by della PORTA and differs substantially from MICHELANGELO's model.) But although his plans were much altered the church as it stands today owes more to him than to any other single architect. In his last years he designed the Cappella Sforza, S. Maria Maggiore, Rome (*c.* 1560), on an ingenious plan rather coarsely executed after his death. He also provided plans for the conversion of the central hall of the Baths of Diocletian into S. Maria degli Angeli (1561), but here his work was completely overlaid in the C18.

The story of his architectural career is one of constant frustration. Not one of his major designs was complete at the time of his death. Yet his influence was none the less great. The Mannerists took from him decorative details which were gradually absorbed into the European grammar of ornament. But it was not until the C17 that architects were able to appreciate and began to emulate his dynamic control of mass and space. Significantly, his true heir was to be another sculptor architect, BERNINI.

MICHELOZZO DI BARTOLOMMEO (1396–1472), a sculptor and architect of extreme elegance and refinement, nevertheless lacked the genius of his great contemporaries Donatello and BRUNELLESCHI. Born in Florence, the son of Bartolommeo di Gherardo who hailed from Burgundy, he worked as assistant to Ghiberti (1417–24), then shared a studio with Donatello (1425–33). In the mid 1430s he began to turn his attention to architecture and succeeded Brunelleschi as Capomaestro at the cathedral in 1446. His first important works were for the Medici family. In about 1433 he added the graceful courtyard and loggia to their castle-cum-villa at Careggi and eleven years later began the Palazzo Medici-Riccardi in Florence, the first Renaissance palace, with massive rusticated basement and slightly smoother rusticated upper floors capped by a prominent cornice. Behind this slightly forbidding fortress-like exterior there is an arcaded *cortile* derived from Brunelleschi's Ospedale degli Innocenti. His Medicean villa at Caffagiolo (1451) is again fortress-like, in contrast with his Villa Medici at Fiesole (1458–61: but considerably altered in C18) which is exquisitely light and elegant in style.

In 1437 he began work at S. Marco, Florence, where he designed · the sacristy (1437–43), the cloisters and the light and harmonious library (1441). Between 1444 and 1455 he designed the tribune and sacristy of SS. Annunziata. The tribune (completed by ALBERTI) is centrally planned, inspired no doubt by Brunelleschi's S. Maria degli Angeli, but closer to an ancient Roman model, the temple of Minerva Medica. This was the first centralized building to be erected in the Renaissance, and it reflects both a desire to revive an antique form and a preoccupation with the circle as a symbol of the universe and eternity. At Pistoia he built the little church of S. Maria delle Grazie (1452), where he employed the Early Christian and Byzantine form of a square building with central dome and subsidiary domed chapels at the four corners. In about 1462 he was in Milan, probably working on the Medici Bank. He also built the Portinari Chapel in S. Eustorgio, Milan (c. 1462), which owes much to Brunelleschi's S. Lorenzo sacristy. With this chapel he introduced the Renaissance style to Lombardy. From 1462 to 1463 he was in Dubrovnik, where he designed the Palazzo dei Rettori.

MIES VAN DER ROHE, Ludwig (1886–1969), worked under Bruno Paul, and then from 1908 to 1911 in Peter BEHRENS's office in Berlin. His earliest independent designs are inspired by SCHINKEL and the Berlin Schinkel Revival of the early C20 (Kröller House, 1912). At the end of the First World War he was, like GROPIUS, caught up in the frenzy and enthusiasm of Expressionism, and he designed then his revolutionary glass skyscrapers (1919–21). When Germany settled down to its rational responsible style of the later twenties and the early thirties, Mies van der Rohe excelled in this as well (housing, Berlin and Stuttgart, 1925–7). His true greatness as an architect was first revealed in the German Pavilion for the Barcelona Exhibition of 1929, with its open plan and masterly spatial composition, its precious materials – marble, travertine, onyx, polished steel, bottle-green glass – a sign of a striving after the highest quality and the most immaculate finishes. The planning principles of the Barcelona Pavilion were tested for domestic purposes in the Tugendhat House at Brno (1930), a private house.

From 1930 to 1933 Mies van der Rohe was director of the BAUHAUS, first at Dessau and then when it moved to Berlin for its last harassed phase of existence. In 1938 he was made Professor of Architecture at the Armour Institute (now Illinois Institute) of Technology in Chicago. In 1939 he designed a complete new campus for the Institute, whose plan has since developed and whose buildings have grown. They are characterized by cubic simplicity – envelopes which easily adapt to the various requirements of the Institute – and a perfect precision of details, where every member makes its own unequivocal statement. These qualities pervade all Mies van der Rohe's work. 'I don't want to be interesting, I want to be good,' he said in an interview. The volume of his work, remarkably small until after the Second World War, has since grown considerably. Among private houses the Farnsworth House at Plano, Illinois (1950), must be mentioned; among blocks of flats the Promontory Apartments (1947) with a concrete frame, and Lake Shore Drive (1951) with a steel frame, both at Chicago; among office buildings, the Seagram Building in New York (1956–9), with a bronze and marble facing. They are all a final triumphant vindication of the style created in the early C20 and assimilated gradually in the thirties, and they do not participate in the neo-sculptural tendencies of the last fifteen or twenty years.

MIHRAB. A prayer-niche facing Mecca in a mosque; first appears in the early C8.

MILESIAN LAYOUT. A city plan of regular gridiron pattern with streets of uniform width and blocks of houses

of approximately uniform dimensions,
It probably originated in the Hittite,
Assyrian and Babylonian empires and
developed in Ionia in the C7 B.C. It is
named after the city of Miletus. Other
notable examples in Antiquity are
Cryne in Lydia (founded 630–24) and
Paestum (built by Greek colonists in
C6 B.C.). This type of plan was
advocated by HIPPODAMOS who is,
sometimes, incorrectly said to have
invented it.

MILLS, Robert (1781–1855), who was of
Scottish descent, was discovered by
JEFFERSON and articled to LATROBE,
with whom he stayed from 1803 to
1808. His practice started in Philadelphia in 1808 (notably Washington
Hall, perhaps influenced by LEDOUX).
He designed the former State House
at Harrisburg in 1810 with a semicircular portico and a dome over the
centre; a circular church at Charleston
as early as 1804; an octagonal and a
large circular one in Philadelphia in
1811–13 (the latter with 4,000 seats);
and then the Washington Monument
for Baltimore, an unfluted Doric
column (1814–29). His principal later
works are governmental buildings for
Washington, all Grecian and competent (Treasury, 1836–9; Patent Office,
1836–40; Post Office, 1839 etc.), but
his most famous work is the Washington Monument at Washington, won
in competition in 1836 and completed
only in 1884. It is an obelisk 555 ft high
and was originally meant to have a
Greek Doric rotunda at its foot. Mills
also did engineering jobs and a number of hospitals. The Columbia Lunatic Asylum (1822) has none of the
grimness of its predecessors. It is like a
monumental hospital (Greek Doric
portico), and has all wards to the south
and a roof garden. It is of fireproof
construction.

MINARET. A tall, usually slender tower
or turret, connected with a MOSQUE.
Minarets have one or more projecting
balconies from which the muezzin
calls the people to prayer. The first

instance of a tower being utilized for
this purpose was probably at Damascus
in the early C8 (the Great Mosque).
See figure 60.

Fig. 60. Minaret

MINBAR. The high pulpit in a MOSQUE.

MINOAN ARCHITECTURE, see CRE-
TAN AND MYCENAEAN ARCHITEC-
TURE.

MINSTER. Originally the name for any
monastic establishment or its church,
whether a monastery proper or a
house of secular canons, it came to be
applied to certain cathedral churches
in England and abroad (e.g., York,
Strassburg) and also other major
churches (Ripon, Southwell, Ulm,
Zürich).

MINUTE. In classical architecture a unit
of measurement representing one
sixtieth part of the diameter of a
column at the base of its shaft. It may
be either one sixtieth or one thirtieth
part of a MODULE.

MIQUE, Richard (1728–94). Leading
Louis XVI architect and the last of the
royal architects at Versailles. He was
trained under J.-F. BLONDEL in Paris,
then employed by ex-King Stanislas
at Nancy who ennobled him (1761).

On Stanislas's death in 1766 he returned to Paris. He built the Ursuline convent, now Lycée Hoche, at Versailles (1767–72) with quietly elegant conventual buildings and a church inspired by Palladio's Villa Rotonda, and in 1775 the Carmelite church at Saint-Denis (now Justice de la Paix) with an Ionic portico and cupola. The same year he succeeded GABRIEL as first architect to Louis XVI and in this capacity was responsible for numerous minor works at Versailles – the decoration of the Petits Appartements of Marie Antoinette in the main palace, the theatre at the Petit Trianon, the exquisite circular Temple de l'Amour, the Belvédère, and, his best known work, the picturesquely rustic Hameau with exposed beams and irregular roofs. He was finally guillotined.

MISERICORD (or MISERERE). A bracket on the underside of the seat of a hinged choir stall which, when turned up, served as a support for the occupant while standing during long services.

MIXTEC ARCHITECTURE, see MESO-AMERICAN ARCHITECTURE.

MNESICLES. A prominent architect in Periclean Athens. He designed the Propylaea, Athens (437–432 B.C., but never finished).

MODILLION. A small bracket or CONSOLE of which a series is frequently used to support the upper member of a Corinthian or Composite CORNICE, arranged in pairs with a square depression between each pair. See figure 42.

MODULE. A unit of measurement by which the proportions of a building or part of a building are regulated. 1. In classical architecture, either the diameter or half the diameter of a column at the base of its shaft, in either case divided into minutes so that the full diameter represents 60 minutes. 2. In modern architecture, any unit of measurement which facilitates prefabrication.

MODULOR. The system of proportion advanced by LE CORBUSIER in his Le Modulor (1951). It is based upon the male figure and is used to determine the proportions of building units.

MOGHUL ARCHITECTURE, see INDIAN AND PAKISTANI ARCHITECTURE.

MOLINOS, see GILLY.

MOLLER, Georg, see GILLY.

MONASTERY. Monasticism originated in Egypt, where the first men to choose a monastic life were hermits. A more organized monastic existence was conceived by St Pachomius (346): monks now still lived on their own like hermits, but so close together that they had a joint chapel and a joint refectory. Such monks are known as coenobites. This form of monasticism reached Europe by way of the South of France and from there entered Ireland (Skellig Michael). But the monastic architecture of medieval England and the Continent is that created in the C6 as the expression of the rule of the order established by St Benedict at Montecassino. Its first surviving complete expression is the plan of c. 820 made by a cleric of Cologne for St Gall in Switzerland; here we have the axial arrangement of ranges – the coenobites' layouts were haphazard – the cloister with its arcaded walks, the chapterhouse and dormitory in the east range, the refectory in the range opposite the church, the stores in the west range. Abbots or priors usually lived near the west end as well, while the infirmary was beyond the claustral parts to the east. There were also a guest house, kitchens, brewhouse, bakehouse, smithy, corn-mills, stables, cowsheds, pigsties, etc., and workshops. In terms of architectural composition the monastery is infinitely superior to the medieval castle. See figure 61.

MONOLITH. A single stone, usually in the form of a monument or column.

MONTFERRAND, August Ricard (1786–1858). French Empire architect who emigrated to Russia and became, with ROSSI and STASSOV, a leading post-Napoleonic architect in Leningrad. He was trained under PERCIER and worked at the Madeleine in Paris

Ancient Architecture (1728), *Lectures on Architecture* (1734), and the posthumous *Select Architecture* (1755) which had a wide influence, e.g., on JEFFERSON's Monticello.

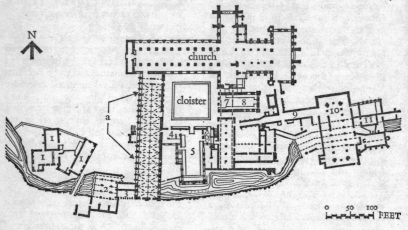

Fig. 61. Plan of Fountains Abbey

Key:
1. Guest houses
2. Lay brothers' infirmary
3. Reredorter
4. Kitchen
5. Monks' refectory
6. Warming house
7. Upstairs dormitory
    (shown by dotted lines)
8. Chapterhouse
9. Corridor
10. Infirmary hall
11. Infirmary chapel

a = storerooms

under VIGNON. His masterpiece is the vast and sumptuous St Isaac's Cathedral in Leningrad (1817–57). The dome (completed *c.* 1842) is framed in iron – an early example of the use of metal structure, preceding the dome of the Capitol in Washington by a decade. His enormous granite Alexander Column in Winter Palace Square (1829) is imposing though less original in conception than MILLS's almost contemporary Washington Monument in Washington.

MORRIS, Robert (1701–54), a relation of Roger MORRIS, was a gifted writer on architectural theory. His books include *An Essay in Defence of*

MORRIS, Roger (1695–1749). One of the most gifted and original exponents of PALLADIANISM, though of the CAMPBELL rather than the BURLINGTON school. Most of his work was done in association with the 9th Earl of Pembroke, an amateur architect whose share in his designs is difficult to assess; works include Marble Hill, Twickenham (1728), and the ornamental Palladian Bridge at Wilton (1736). Towards the end of his life he turned neo-Gothic at Inveraray Castle, Argyllshire (1746 etc.).

MORRIS, William (1834–96), was not an architect, but holds an unchallengeable place in a Dictionary of

Architecture because of his great influence on architects. This influence acted in three ways. Morris had begun by studying divinity, then for a short time turned to architecture and worked in the Oxford office of STREET, and subsequently in a desultory way learnt to paint under Rossetti. When he furnished his digs in London, and more so when, after his marriage, he wanted a house, he found that the architecture as well as the design of his day were not to his liking. So he got his friend Philip WEBB to design Red House for him, and this straightforward, red-brick, made-to-measure house had a great deal of influence. Secondly, as the result of the search for satisfactory furnishings, Morris and some friends created in 1861 the firm Morris, Marshall & Faulkner (later Morris & Co.), for which enterprise Morris himself designed wallpapers, the ornamental parts (and, rarely, the figure work) of stained glass, chintzes (i.e., printed textiles), and later also carpets, tapestries and woven furnishing materials, and in the end (1890-6) even books and their type and decoration (Kelmscott Press).

All his designs shared a stylized two-dimensional quality which contrasted with the then prevailing naturalism and its unbridled use of depth; but they also possessed a deep feeling for nature which itself contrasted with the ornamental work of a few slightly older English reformers (PUGIN; Owen Jones). These qualities impressed themselves deeply on younger architects of Norman SHAW's office and school, so much so that some of them took to design themselves. However, they might not have gone so far, if it had not been for Morris's third way of influencing architects, his lectures, which he began in 1877 and continued till his death. They were impassioned pleas not only for better, more considered design, but for abolishing the ugliness of towns and buildings and of the things made to fill buildings, and for reforming the society responsible for towns, buildings, and products. Morris was a socialist, one of the founders of organized socialism in England. That he was also a poet would not be of relevance here, if it were not for the fact that his poetry and his prose romances developed from an avowed medievalism to a strongly implied social responsibility for the present. At the same time the medievalism, displayed, for example, by the self-conscious use of obsolete language, is a reminder of the medievalism – admittedly adapted and even transmuted – of all his designs. There is, indeed, a medievalism even in Morris's theory, for his socialism is one of labour becoming once more enjoyable handicraft. And although Morris fervently believed, harking back again to the Middle Ages, that all art ought to be 'by the people for the people', he could never resolve the dilemma that production by hand costs more than by machine, and that the products of his own firm therefore (and for other reasons) were bound to be costly and not 'for the people'. It needed a further reform and a revision of this one essential tenet of Morris's to arrive at the C20 situation, where architects and artists design for industrial production and thereby serve the common man and not only the connoisseur. But Morris started the movement, and it was due to him that artists such as van de VELDE or BEHRENS turned designers, and that architects like VOYSEY did likewise. It was also due to him that the criteria of two-dimensional design rose from C19 to C20 standards. Webb's work for Morris had the same effect on furniture design.

MOSAIC. Surface decoration for walls or floors formed of small pieces or *tesserae* of glass, stone, or marble set in a mastic. The design may be either geometrical or representational. Mosaic reached its highest pitch of accomplishment in Roman and Byzantine buildings.

MOSBRUGGER or MOOSBRUGGER, Caspar (1656–1723), was born at Au in the Bregenzerwald – the headquarters of the Vorarlberg masons' guild – and was a founder of the Vorarlberg school of architects which included the BEER and THUMB families. He was apprenticed to a stone-cutter, then became a novice at the Benedictine monastery of Einsiedeln in 1682 and remained there as a lay-brother for the rest of his life. He became the greatest Swiss Baroque architect. Already in 1684 he was asked for advice at Weingarten Abbey, though building did not begin there until many years later. His masterpiece is the abbey church at Einsiedeln (begun 1719), a spatial composition of unusual complexity even for a Baroque architect. He did not live to see it completed. He also designed the parish church at Muri (1694–8). He probably played some part (even if only an advisory one) in the design of the vast Benedictine abbey church at Weingarten (1714–24) with a façade much like that at Einsiedeln, and he probably built the church at Disentis (1696–1712).

MOSLEM ARCHITECTURE, see ISLAMIC ARCHITECTURE.

MOSQUE. A Moslem temple or place of worship. The primitive mosque at Madinah, built by Mohammed in 622, was the prototype: a square enclosure, surrounded by walls of brick and stone, partly roofed. By the end of the C7 all the chief ritual requirements of a congregational mosque had been evolved.

MOTTE. A steep mound, the main feature of many C11 and C12 castles. See MOTTE-AND-BAILEY.

MOTTE-AND-BAILEY. A post-Roman and Norman defence system consisting of an earthen mound (the *motte*) topped with a wooden tower, placed within a BAILEY with enclosure ditch, palisade, and the rare addition of an internal bank.

MOUCHETTE. A curved DAGGER motif in curvilinear TRACERY, especially popular in England in the early C14. *See figure 62.*

Fig. 62. Mouchette

MOULDINGS. The contours given to projecting members. *See* Bead, Cable, Keel, Ogee, Roll, Wave moulding; Beakhead; Billet; Bowtell; Chevron; Dogtooth; Hood-mould; Nailhead.

MOZARABIC. The style evolved by Christians under Moorish influence in Spain from the late C9 to the early C11, e.g., San Miguel de Escalada near León (consecrated in 913) with its arcade of arches of horseshoe shape, Santiago de Peñalba (931–7) and Santa Maria de Lebeña (also C10). The style is Christian in inspiration but Islamic in conception and has many Islamic features such as the horseshoe arch. Mozarabic churches are usually small and stand in the open countryside. They form the largest and best preserved group of pre-Romanesque buildings in Europe.

MUDÉJAR. Spanish Christian architecture in a purely Moslem style. (Literally, the term refers to Moslems who remained in Christian Spain after the reconquest.) The style was evolved by Moslems in Spain or by Christians working within the Spanish Moslem tradition. Notable examples are Alfonso VIII's early C13 chapel at the monastery of Las Huelgas, Burgos, and the C14 Alcázar, Seville, which has Kufic inscriptions extolling Christian rulers. Mudéjar motifs persisted in Spanish Gothic architecture and may also be found in PLATERESQUE buildings of the C16.

MULLION. A vertical post or other upright dividing a window or other opening into two or more LIGHTS.

MUNGGENAST, Josef (d. 1741). Cousin and pupil of PRANDTAUER for whom he worked as foreman and whom he succeeded as architect at Melk. In collaboration with the Viennese sculptor, engineer and architect Matthias Steinl (1644–1727) he built the church for the Augustinian canons at Dürnstein, with a boldly *mouvementé* interior and outstandingly handsome tower (1721–7). His main independent work is the reconstruction of the monastery of Altenburg where he provided a richly coloured, exuberantly Baroque casing for the Gothic church and created one of the best of all Baroque libraries (1730–33).

MUNTIN. The vertical part in the framing of a door, screen, panelling, etc., butting into, or stopped by, the horizontal rails. *See figure 39.*

MUSHRABEYEH WORK. Elaborate wooden lattices used to enclose the upper windows in Islamic domestic architecture.

MUTULE. The projecting square block above the TRIGLYPH and under the CORONA of a Doric CORNICE.

MYCENAEAN ARCHITECTURE, *see* CRETAN AND MYCENAEAN ARCHITECTURE.

MYLNE, Robert (1734–1811), a contemporary and rival of Robert ADAM, descended from a long line of Scottish master masons. He was trained by his father in Edinburgh, then went to Paris (1754) and Rome (1755–8), where he had amazing success by winning First Prize at the Accademia di S. Luca in 1758. But he did not fulfil this early promise. His first work after settling in London (1759) was to be his most famous, Blackfriars' Bridge (1760–9, demolished), in which he introduced elliptical arches. Thereafter he worked extensively both as architect and engineer. His largest country house, Tusmore (1766–9, altered by W. Burn 1858), was neo-Palladian. More elegant and original is The Wick, Richmond (1775), a small suburban 'box', while his façade of the Stationers' Hall, London (1800), shows him at his most neo-classical.

N

NAILHEAD. An Early English architectural enrichment consisting of small pyramids repeated as a band. *See figure 63.*

Fig. 63. Nailhead

NAOS. The sanctuary or principal chamber of a Greek temple, containing the statue of the god. In Byzantine architecture, the core and sanctuary of a centrally planned church, i.e., the parts reserved for the performance of the liturgy.

NARTHEX. I. In a Byzantine church, the transverse vestibule either preceding nave and aisles as an inner narthex (esonarthex) or preceding the façade as an outer narthex (exonarthex). An esonarthex is separated from the nave and aisles by columns, rails or a wall. An exonarthex may also serve as the terminating transverse portico of a colonnaded ATRIUM or quadriporticus. 2. In a general medieval sense, an enclosed covered ANTECHURCH at the main entrance, especially if the direction is transverse and not east–west and several bays deep; sometimes called a GALILEE. *See figure 10.*

NASH, John (1752–1835), London's only inspired town-planner and the greatest architect of the PICTURESQUE movement. He was the exact opposite of his contemporary SOANE, being self-confident and adaptable, socially successful and artistically conservative, light-handed and slipshod in detail, but with an easy mastery of general effects on a large scale. Again, unlike Soane, he was an architect of exteriors rather than interiors. The son of a Lambeth millwright, he was

trained under TAYLOR, but quickly struck out on his own and by 1780 was building stucco-fronted houses, then a novelty in London. In 1783 he went bankrupt, retired to Wales and recovered, then joined the landscape gardener REPTON, with whom he developed a fashionable country-house practice. His output was enormous and in every conceivable style – classical (Rockingham, Ireland, 1810 (demolished)), Italian farmhouse (Cronkhill, *c.* 1802), castellated Gothic (Ravensworth Castle, 1808 (demolished); Caerhays Castle, 1808), even Indian and Chinoiserie (Brighton Pavilion, 1815). He also built thatched cottages (Blaise Hamlet, 1811). With their fancy-dress parade of styles and irregular planning and silhouettes, these buildings epitomize the Picturesque in architecture. The same picturesque combination of freedom and formality marks his greatest work, the layout of Regent's Park and Regent Street in London (1811 onwards), a brilliantly imaginative conception foreshadowing the garden city of the future. He was already sixty, but still had the enthusiasm and organizing ability to carry the whole scheme through, and he lived to see it finished. The park is sprinkled with villas and surrounded by vast terraces and crescents of private houses built palatially with grandiose stucco façades. There are also cottage terraces and make-believe villages of barge-boarded and Italianate villas. Of his Regent Street frontages nothing now remains except the eye-catcher, All Souls, Langham Place (1822–5). During the 1820s he planned Trafalgar Square, Suffolk Street, and Suffolk Place, built Clarence House and Carlton House Terrace, and began

Buckingham Palace, all in London. But he shared in his royal patron's fall from public favour, was suspected of profiteering and sharp practice, and his career came to an abrupt end when George IV died in 1830. He was dismissed from Buckingham Palace (completed by Edward Blore) and from the Board of Works of which he had been one of the Surveyors General since 1813. His reputation remained under a cloud for the next fifty years or more.

NAVE. The western limb of a church, that is, the part west of the CROSSING; more usually the middle vessel of the western limb, flanked by AISLES.

NAZZONI or NASONI, Niccolo (d. 1773), who was born near Florence, settled in Portugal (1731), where he became one of the leading Baroque architects. His main work is São Pedro dos Clérigos, Oporto (1732–50), a large and impressive church on an oval plan with a very richly decorated façade, embraced by a bold pattern of ascending staircases.

NECKING. A narrow MOULDING round the bottom of a CAPITAL between it and the shaft of the column.

NEEDLE SPIRE, see SPIRE.

NEO-CLASSICISM, see CLASSICISM.

NEO-GOTHIC, see GOTHIC REVIVAL.

NERING, Johann Arnold (1659–95). Prussian architect who, despite his early death, laid the foundations for architectural developments in C18 Berlin. He was trained as a military architect, sent to Italy and made Oberingenieur in 1680, later Oberbaudirektor. He was much employed on urban planning and built the Leipziger Tor (1683), the covered arcade with shops on the Mühlendamm in Berlin and the Friedrichstadt suburb with 300 two-storey houses, all in military order (1688 onwards). He enlarged the Burgkirche at Königsberg, on the model of the Nieuwekerk in The Hague (pre 1687), gave the Oranienburg Palace its pre-

sent appearance (1689–95), began the Charlottenburg Palace, Berlin, the Arsenal, Berlin (1695 completed by SCHLÜTER and de BODT), and the Reformed Parish Church on an interesting quatrefoil plan. His style is severe and owed much to PALLADIO by way of the Dutch Neo-Palladians.

NERVI, Pier Luigi (b. 1891), took his degree in civil engineering in 1912, but had a long wait before he was allowed to establish himself as what he undoubtedly is, the most brilliant concrete designer of the age. Nervi is as inventive and resourceful a technician as he is aesthetically sensitive an architect. He is, moreover, an entrepreneur and a university professor, a combination which would be impossible, because it is not permitted, in Britain.

The stadium in Florence was built in 1930–2; it seats 35,000, has a cantilever roof about 70 ft deep and an ingenious flying spiral staircase sweeping far out. In 1935, for a competition for airship hangars, he produced his idea of a vault of diagonally intersecting concrete beams with very massive flying-buttress-like angle supports. Such hangars were built at Orbetello from 1936 onwards (destroyed). A second type with trusses of precast concrete elements was carried out at Orbetello in 1940. 1948 is the date of Nervi's first great exhibition hall for Turin. The concrete elements this time are corrugated, an idea which went back to experiments of 1943–4. The second hall followed in 1950, again with a diagonal grid. The building of 1952 for the Italian spa of Chianciano is circular, and has a grid vault. By this time Nervi's fame was so firmly established that he was called in for the structure of the Unesco Building in Paris (1953–6). His also is the splendid structure of the Pirelli skyscraper in Milan (1955–8; see also PONTI) – two strongly tapering concrete pillars from which the floors are cantilevered. With Jean PROUVÉ as the other consultant engineer, Nervi was responsible for the enormous new exhibition hall on the Rond-point de la Défense in Paris (1958): a triangle, each side 710 ft long, with three triangular sections of warped concrete roof, rising to a height of 150 ft.

Nervi's most recent buildings are the Palazzetto dello Sport in Rome (1959), circular with V-shaped supports for the dome all round; the Palazzo dello Sport, also in Rome (1960), with a 330-ft span and seating 16,000; yet another exhibition hall for Turin (1961), a square with sides 520 ft in length, supported on sixteen enormous cross-shaped piers; and the vast audience hall for the Pope in the Vatican (1970–71).

NESFIELD, Eden, see SHAW.

NEUMANN, Johann Balthasar (1687–1753), the greatest German Rococo architect, was master of elegant and ingenious spatial composition. He could be both wantonly sensuous and intellectually complex, frivolous and devout, ceremonious and playful. His churches and palaces epitomize the mid-C18 attitude to life and religion. But despite their air of spontaneity, few works of architecture have been more carefully thought out. His designs are as complex as the fugues of Bach; and for this reason he has been called an architect's architect.

The son of a clothier, he was born in Bohemia but worked mainly in Franconia where he began in a cannon foundry and graduated to architecture by way of the Prince Bishop's artillery. He visited Vienna and Milan (1717–18) and soon after his return began the Bishop's new Residenz in Würzburg, consulting HILDE-BRANDT and von Welsch in Vienna and de COTTE and BOFFRAND in Paris about his designs. The influence of Hildebrandt is very evident in the finished palace, which was executed under a succession of five bishops over some sixty years, though it was struc-

turally complete by about 1744. Outstanding here are the Hofkirche or Bishop's Chapel (1732–41, Hildebrandt collaborating on the decoration) and the magnificent ceremonial staircase leading up to the Kaisersaal (designed 1735, ceiling decoration by Tiepolo 1752–3). This staircase is one of his most original and ingenious conceptions, second only to his superb staircase at Bruchsal (1731–2, damaged in Second World War but restored). He later designed the imposing staircase at Schloss Brühl near Cologne (1743–8). These ceremonial staircases formed the most important single element in each palace and are at the same time masterpieces of engineering ingenuity and exhilarating spatial play. At Schloss Werneck (1734–45) he again collaborated with Hildebrandt, but this time impressed his own stamp on all parts of the building. His secular work was by no means limited to palace architecture: he was engaged in town planning and laid out whole streets of town houses, e.g., the Theaterstrasse at Würzburg. The house he built for himself in the Kapuzinergasse (No. 7) at Würzburg, reveals his ability to work in a minor key.

He was much employed as a church architect, designing the parish church at Wiesentheid (1727), the pilgrimage church at Gössweinstein (1730–39), the church of St Paulinus, Trier (begun 1734), the church of Häusenstamm near Offenbach (1739–40) the Holy Cross Chapel at Etwashausen (1741) and additions to St Peter, Bruchsal (1738) and the Dominican church at Würzburg (1741). In 1743 he began his great masterpiece, the pilgrimage church of Vierzehnheiligen, where the foundations had already been built by a previous architect. His first task was to accommodate his own ideas to a somewhat inconvenient plan and this provided a spur to his genius. He worked out a remarkably complicated scheme based on the grouping of ovals, both in the vaulting and ground plan, which provides a breathtakingly exciting spatial effect, enhanced by the foaming and eddying Rococo decoration. Nowhere did the *mouvementé* quality of Rococo architecture find better expression: not only the statues but even the columns seem to be executing an elegant minuet. (The central altar, pulpit and much of the plasterwork were not completed until after Neumann's death.)

In the larger abbey church at Neresheim (begun 1747) he had a much freer hand and his plan is much simpler, though again based on ovals. By the use of very slender columns to support the large central dome he achieved an almost Gothic airiness. His last work of importance, the Marienkirche at Limbach (1747–52), is on a much smaller scale, but is unusual for him in being no less elaborately decorated on the exterior than inside.

NEUTRA, Richard (1892–1970). He was Austrian by birth and studied in Vienna. In 1912–14 he worked under LOOS, and in 1921–3 he was with MENDELSOHN in Berlin. In 1923 he emigrated to Chicago, but finally settled down at Los Angeles in 1925. He became one of the chief propagators of the new European style in America. His work is predominantly domestic, and mostly of a wealthy and lavish kind. His forte is a brilliant sense for siting houses in landscape and linking building and nature; many of his houses are indeed on a scale rarely matched in Europe: Desert House, Colorado, 1946; Kaufmann House, Palm Springs, 1947; and his own house at Silverlake, Los Angeles, 1933 and 1964. Neutra also designed some excellent schools and, towards the end of his life, some religious and commercial buildings. His style remained essentially that of his youth; it was unchanged in its direction by the anti-rational tendencies of the last ten or fifteen years.

NEW TOWNS. Those towns designed in the British Isles under the Act of 1946 – eight in the London region (Harlow, Crawley, Stevenage, etc.) and six in other parts of England, Scotland, and Wales. More are now being added. Although most of them have an existing town or village as a nucleus, they are entirely independent units, with populations of about 60,000 to 80,000. The development of these planned towns over the years has been of very great interest from sociological, architectural, and planning points of view.

NEWEL, *see* STAIR.

NIEMEYER, Oscar (b. 1907), studied in his home town Rio de Janeiro, then worked in the office of Lucio COSTA and received his diploma in 1934. In 1936 he belonged to the team of Brazilian architects working with LE CORBUSIER on the new building for the Ministry of Education at Rio. He built the Brazilian Pavilion for the New York World Fair of 1939 with Costa, but only came fully into his own with the casino, club, and church of St Francis at Pampulha outside Belo Horizonte (1942–3). Here was a completely new approach to architecture, admittedly for non-utilitarian purposes: parabolic vaults, slanting walls, a porch canopy of a completely free double-curving form – a sculptural, frankly anti-rational, highly expressive style. The style suited BRAZIL with its past of the extremest Baroque; it also became one of the elements in that general turn away from rationalism which is principally familiar in Le Corbusier's buildings after the Second World War.

Niemeyer was made architectural adviser to Nova Cap, the organization instituted to create Brasilia, the new capital, and in 1957 became its chief architect. He designed the hotel in 1958 and the exquisite president's palace in the same year. The palace has a screen of freely and extremely originally shaped supports in front of its glass façade, and Niemeyer has varied this theme in other buildings at Brasilia as well (Law Courts). The climax of the architectural composition of the capital is the Square of the Three Powers, with the Houses of Parliament – one with a dome, the other with a saucer-shaped roof – and the sheer, quite unfanciful skyscraper of the offices between. The slab blocks of the various ministries are also deliberately unfanciful. Niemeyer certainly varies his approach according to the spiritual function of buildings. Thus the cathedral of Brasilia, circular, with the excelsior of a bundle of curved concrete ribs rising to the centre, is highly expressive; the block of flats for the Interbau Exhibition in Berlin (Hansa Quarter, 1957) is rational, without, however, lacking in resourcefulness; and Niemeyer's own house outside Rio (1953) is a ravishing interplay of nature and architecture.

NOBILE, Pietro (1773–1854), a neo-classicist of a rather archaeologizing tendency, worked in Vienna (Theseus-tempel, a miniature of the Haiphesteion, Athens, built to house a statue by Canova, 1820–3; the Burgtor, 1824) and in Trieste (S. Antonio, 1826–49).

NOGGING, see TIMBER-FRAMING.

NOOK-SHAFT. A shaft set in the angle of a PIER, a RESPOND, a wall, or the JAMB of a window or doorway.

NORMAN ARCHITECTURE, see ENGLISH ARCHITECTURE.

NORWEGIAN ARCHITECTURE, see SCANDINAVIAN ARCHITECTURE.

NYMPHAEUM. Literally a 'temple of the nymphs' but generally a Roman pleasure-house, especially one containing fountains and statues.

O

OBELISK. A tall tapering shaft of stone, usually granite, monolithic, of square or rectangular section, and ending pyramidally; much used in ancient Egypt.

OCTASTYLE. Of a portico with eight frontal columns.

OCULUS. A round window.

ŒIL-DE-BŒUF WINDOW. A small circular window, similar to that in the vestibule at Versailles known as the *Salle de l'œil-de-bœuf*.

ŒILLET. In medieval architecture, a small opening in fortifications through which missiles could be discharged.

OFF-SET. The part of a wall exposed horizontally when the portion above it is reduced in thickness; often sloping, with a projecting drip mould on the lower edge to stop water running down the walls, e.g., in Gothic buttresses. Also called the *water-table*. See WEATHERING.

OGEE. A double-curved line made up of a convex and a concave part (s or inverted s).

OGEE ARCH, *see* ARCH.

OGEE MOULDING, *see* CYMA RECTA *and* CYMA REVERSA.

OGIVE. The French name for a pointed arch; hence *ogival*, a term applied to French Gothic architecture, but no longer used.

OLBRICH, Joseph Maria (1867–1908), studied at the Vienna Academy, gained the Rome prize in 1893, returned to work under Otto WAGNER, and in 1897–8 built the Secession in Vienna, the premises of a newly founded society of the young progressive artists of Austria and the work which immediately established Olbrich's reputation. The little building, with its strongly cubic walls and its delightful hemispherical openwork metal dome, is both firm in its basic shapes and fanciful in its details. It is this unusual combination of qualities which attracted Ernst Ludwig Grand Duke of Hessen to Olbrich. So in 1899 Olbrich was called to Darmstadt and there, on the Mathildenhöhe, built the studio house (Ernst Ludwig Haus) and some private houses, including one for himself. The group of houses, some of them by other members of the group of artists assembled at Darmstadt (e.g., BEHRENS), was first built and furnished and then, in 1901, presented as an exhibition, the first of the kind ever held. Later Olbrich added another exhibition building and a tower, the Hochzeitsturm (1907). His last major building was the Tietz department store at Düsseldorf, the closely set uprights of whose façade, deriving from Messel's Wertheim store in Berlin, were very influential.

Olbrich's historical role is among those who succeeded in overcoming the vegetable weakness of ART NOUVEAU by providing it with a firmer system of rectangular co-ordinates. The other leading architects working in this direction were HOFFMANN and MACKINTOSH. Both Mackintosh and Olbrich succeeded in preserving the fancifulness of Art Nouveau sinuosity within this new, more exacting framework, whereas Hoffmann, and of course Behrens to a still greater extent, moved right away from Art Nouveau.

OLMSTED, Frederick Law (1822–1903), the principal landscape architect of America after DOWNING's death and America's leading park designer, studied engineering and travelled widely in America, Europe, and even China, before being made superintendent for the Central Park to be formed in New York (1857). He

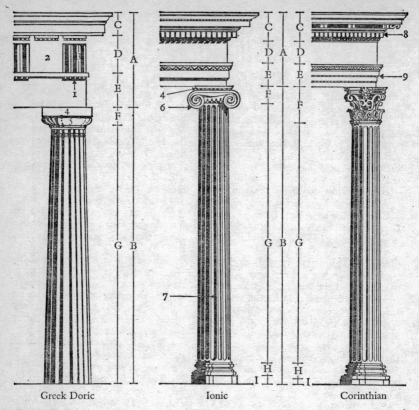

Greek Doric   Ionic   Corinthian

Fig. 64. Order

Key:

A. Entablature	D. Frieze	G. Shaft	1. Guttae	4. Abacus	7. Fluting
B. Column	E. Architrave	H. Base	2. Metope	5. Echinus	8. Dentils
C. Cornice	F. Capital	I. Plinth	3. Triglyph	6. Volute	9. Fascia

visited European parks in 1859, then for a while supervised a mining estate in California (1863–5) and at that time suggested making the Yosemite area a reserve, and finally returned to the Central Park job in 1865. Olmsted also planned the parks system of Boston, the Niagara reserve, millionaires' estates, and the campus of the newly founded Leland Stanford University at Palo Alto. Among his pupils the most important was his nephew John Charles Olmsted (1852–1920).

OPISTHODOMOS. The enclosed section at the rear of a Greek temple, sometimes used as a treasury.

OPTICAL REFINEMENTS. Subtle modifications to profiles or surfaces to correct the illusion of sagging or disproportion in a building. *See* ENTASIS.

Tuscan   Roman Doric   Composite

OPUS ALEXANDRINUM. Ornamental paving combining mosaic and OPUS SECTILE in guilloche design.

OPUS INCERTUM. Roman walling of concrete faced with irregularly shaped stones.

OPUS LISTATUM. Walling with alternating courses of brick and small blocks of stone.

OPUS QUADRATUM. Roman walling of squared stones.

OPUS RETICULATUM. Roman walling of concrete faced with squared stones arranged diagonally like the meshes of a net.

OPUS SECTILE. Ornamental paving or wall covering made from marble slabs cut in various, generally geometric, shapes.

ORANGERY. A garden building for growing oranges, with large windows on the south side, like a glazed LOGGIA.

ORATORY. A small private chapel, either in a church or in a house.

ORCAGNA (Andrea di Cione) (active 1343–68). He was primarily a painter – the most important in Florence after Giotto's death – but also a sculptor and architect. He was admitted to the Guild of Painters in 1343/4 and to the Guild of Stonemasons in 1352. By 1356 he was *capomaestro* at Orsanmichele,

Florence, and by 1358 at Orvieto Cathedral where he is frequently mentioned until 1362, though mainly in connection with the restoration of mosaics on the façade. In 1350 he became adviser on the construction of Florence Cathedral and until 1366 was active as a leading member of various commissions including that which evolved the definitive design.

ORCHARD, William (d. 1504), master mason, was probably designer of Bishop Waynflete's Magdalen College at Oxford (1468 etc.). The initials W.O. in the ingenious vault of the Divinity School, completed in the 1480s, allow this to be attributed to him, and if so, the similarity in design of the vaults of the Divinity School and the chancel of Oxford Cathedral make him a likely candidate for this even more ingenious vault. Both are characterized by the pendants which look like springers built on non-existing piers between a nave and aisles. It is a technically daring, highly original, and visually most puzzling solution.

ORDER. 1. In classical architecture, a column with base (usually), shaft, capital, and entablature, decorated and proportioned according to one of the accepted modes – Doric, Tuscan, Ionic, Corinthian, or Composite. The simplest is the Tuscan, supposedly derived from the Etruscan-type temple, but the Doric is probably earlier in origin and is subdivided into Greek Doric and Roman Doric, the former having no base, as on the Parthenon and the temples at Paestum. The Ionic order originated in Asia Minor in the mid C6 B.C. The Ionic capital probably developed out of the earlier Aeolic capital, of Semitic origin. (The Aeolic capital has an oblong top supported by two large volutes with a PALMETTE filling the space between.) The Corinthian order was an Athenian invention of C5 B.C., but was later developed by the Romans, who provided the prototype for the Renaissance form. The Composite order is a late Roman combination of elements from the Ionic and Corinthian orders. The Doric, Tuscan, Ionic, and Corinthian orders were described by VITRUVIUS, and in 1540 SERLIO published a book on the orders which established the minutiae of the proportions and decorations for Renaissance and later architects. See figure 64.

2. Of a doorway or window, a series of concentric steps receding towards the opening.

ORIEL, see BAY WINDOW.

ORIENTATION. The planning of a building in relation to the rising sun, especially of West European churches which are usually orientated east–west with the altar at the east end. But there are many exceptions, e.g., St Peter's, Rome, which is orientated west–east.

ØSTBERG, Ragnar (1866–1945). His international fame derives entirely from his Stockholm City Hall (begun 1909, completed 1923), a building transitional – like BERLAGE's and KLINT's work – between C19 historicism and the C20. The City Hall makes extremely skilful use of elements of the Swedish past, Romanesque as well as Renaissance. Its exquisite position by the water suggested to Østberg certain borrowings from the Doge's Palace as well. But these motifs are converted and combined in a highly original way, and the decorative details, rather mannered and attenuated, are typical of the Arts and Crafts of Germany, Austria, and Central Europe in general about 1920. The City Hall was very influential in England in the twenties. Østberg had studied in Stockholm (1884–91) and travelled all over Europe as well as in America (1893–9). He was professor at the Stockholm Konsthögskola in 1922–32.

OUBLIETTE. In medieval architecture, a secret prison cell reached only through a trapdoor above, and into which a prisoner could be dropped and, presumably, forgotten. -

OUD, Jacobus Johannes Pieter (1890–1963), worked for a short time under Theodor Fischer in Germany in 1911. In 1915 he met Theo van Doesburg and with him and RIETVELD he became a pillar of the group De Stijl. Architecturally this group stood for an abstract cubism in opposition to the fanciful School of Amsterdam with its Expressionist compositions (de Klerk, Piet Kramer). There exist designs by Oud in a severely cubic manner which date from as early as 1917 and 1919. In 1918 he was made Housing Architect to the City of Rotterdam, a position he retained until 1927. His most important estates are one at Hoek van Holland (1924–7) and the Kiefhoek Estate (1925–30). Later Oud mellowed, abandoned the severity of his designing, and helped to create that curiously decorative, somewhat playful Dutch style which was nicknamed locally Beton-Rococo. The paramount example is the Shell Building at The Hague (1938–42).

OVERDOOR, *see* SOPRAPORTA.

OVERHANG. A system of timber construction, popular in the C15, in which the upper storey is thrust out over the lower by weighting the overhang of the JOISTS with the upper wall and thereby strengthening them. Overhanging is also known as *oversailing* or *jutting*. An overhang on all four sides of a building needs strong cornerposts. Upon each is projected the *dragon beam* from the centre of the house, which in turn receives the shortened rafters on both sides. All the rafters are mortised into the main beams. On their outer projecting ends is placed the cill of the walling for the next storey. Sometimes curved braces are slotted into the lower framing to strengthen the rafters. *See also* ROOF.

OVERSAILING, *see* OVERHANG.

OVERSAILING COURSES. A series of stone or brick courses, each one projecting beyond the one below it.

OVOLO MOULDING. A wide convex moulding, sometimes called a quarter round.

P

PAD STONE, *see* TEMPLATE.

PAGODA. A Buddhist temple in the form of a tower, usually polygonal, with elaborately ornamented roofs projecting from each of its many storeys; common in India and China and, as CHINOISERIE, in Europe.

PAINE, James (c. 1716–89), was born and lived in London, but worked mainly as a country-house architect in the Midlands and North. Solid and conservative, he carried on the neo-Palladian tradition of BURLINGTON and KENT: he and Sir Robert TAYLOR were said to have 'nearly divided the practice of the profession between them' during the mid-century. His houses are practically planned and very well built, with dignified conventional exteriors and excellent Rococo plasterwork, e.g., Nostell Priory interior (begun c. 1733) and the Mansion House, Doncaster (1745–8). Later on he showed more originality. At Kedleston (begun 1761, but soon taken over by ADAM) he had the brilliant idea of placing in sequence the antique basilica hall and a Pantheon-like circular saloon. At Worksop Manor (begun 1763, but only a third built) he envisaged a gigantic Egyptian Hall, and at Wardour Castle (1770–6) he designed a magnificent circular staircase rising towards a Pantheon-like vault. But by this date he had been superseded in the public eye by Robert Adam, and his reputation and practice declined rapidly. As a result of some domestic trouble during his last years he retired to France, where he died. Most of his work is illustrated in his two volumes of *Plans, Elevations and Sections of Noblemen's and Gentlemen's Houses* (1767 and 1783).

PALLADIAN WINDOW, *see* SERLIANA.

PALLADIANISM. A style derived from the buildings and publications of PALLADIO. Its first exponent was Inigo JONES, who studied Roman ruins with Palladio's *Le antichità di Roma* and his buildings in and around Vicenza (1613–14), and introduced the style into England. Elsewhere in Northern Europe, especially Holland (van CAMPEN) and Germany (HOLL), Palladian elements appear in buildings – temple fronts, the SERLIANA window, etc. – but here the leading influence was SCAMOZZI rather than Palladio. The great Palladian revival began in Italy and England in the early C18: in Italy it was confined to Venetia, but affected churches as well as secular buildings; in England it was purely domestic. The English revival, led by CAMPBELL and Lord BURLINGTON, was at the same time an Inigo Jones revival. Numerous books were published under Burlington's aegis and these provided a set of rules and exemplars which remained a dominant force in English architecture until late in the C18. From England and Venetia, Palladianism spread to Germany (KNOBELSDORFF) and Russia (CAMERON and QUARENGHI). At Potsdam accurate copies of Palladio's Palazzo Valmarana and Palazzo Thiene were built in the 1750s under the influence of Frederick the Great and his courtier, the Paduan Count Algarotti. From England the style also spread to the U.S.A. in the 1760s (JEFFERSON). Outside Italy the Palladian revival was concerned mainly with the use of decorative elements. Little attention was paid to Palladio's laws of HARMONIC PROPORTIONS except in Italy, where his ideas on this subject were examined by BERTOTTI-SCAMOZZI and elaborated by a minor architect, Francesco Maria Preti (1701–84).

PALLADIO, Andrea (1508–80). The most influential and one of the greatest Italian architects (*see* PALLADIAN-ISM). Smooth, elegant, and intellectual, he crystallized various Renaissance ideas, notably the revival of Roman symmetrical planning and HARMONIC PROPORTIONS. An erudite student of ancient Roman architecture, he aimed to recapture the splendour of Antiquity. But he was also influenced by his immediate predecessors, especially BRAMANTE, MICHELANGELO, RAPHAEL, GIULIO ROMANO, SANMICHELI, and SANSOVINO, and to some extent by the Byzantine architecture of Venice. His style is tinged with MANNERISM, and it was understandably thought to be 'impure' by later neo-classical architects and theorists.

The son of Piero dalla Gondola he was born in Padua and began humbly as a stone mason, enrolled in the Vicenza guild of bricklayers and stone masons in 1524. Then, in about 1536, he was taken up by Giangiorgio Trissino, the poet, philosopher, mathematician, and amateur architect, who encouraged him to study mathematics, music, and Latin literature, especially VITRUVIUS, and nicknamed him Palladio (an allusion to the goddess of wisdom and to a character in a long epic poem he was then writing). In 1545 Trissino took him to Rome, where he studied the remains of ancient architecture for two years. On returning to Vicenza he won a competition for the remodelling of the Early Renaissance Palazzo della Ragione or Basilica and work began in 1549. He surrounded it with a two-storey screen of arches employing a motive derived from SERLIO but henceforth called Palladian. This columned screen gives to the heavy mass of the old building a grandeur wholly Roman and an airy elegance no less distinctively Palladian. It established his reputation, and from 1550 onwards he was engaged in an ever-increasing series of overlapping commissions for palaces, villas, and churches.

The first of his palaces in Vicenza was probably Palazzo Porto (begun *c.* 1550), on a symmetrical plan derived from ancient Rome, with a façade inspired by Raphael and Bramante but much enriched with sculptured ornament. Soon afterwards he began the more original Palazzo Chiericati (completed in the late C17). This was built not in a narrow street but looking on to a large square; so he visualized it as one side of a Roman forum and designed the façade as a two-storey colonnade of a light airiness unprecedented in C16 architecture. In Palazzo Thiene (begun *c.* 1550, but never completed) he used a dynamic combination of rectangular rooms with a long apsidal-ended hall and small octagons similar to those of the Roman *thermae*. For the convent of the Carità in Venice (planned 1561, but only partly executed) he produced what he and his contemporaries supposed to be a perfect reconstruction of an ancient Roman house; it also contains a flying spiral staircase, the first of its kind. But while his plans became ever more archaeological, his façades broke farther away from classical tradition towards Mannerism, probably the result of a visit to Rome in 1554. Thus the façade of Palazzo Thiene gives an impression of massive power, emphasized by the rustication of the whole wall surface. It has rusticated Ionic columns on either side of the windows – barely emerging from chunky bosses – heavy quoins and *voussoirs* which contrast with smooth Corinthian pilasters. Palazzo Valmarana (begun 1566) is a still more obviously Mannerist composition with a mass of overlapping pilasters and other elements which almost completely obscure the wall surface. The end bays are disquietingly weak, no doubt intentionally. But only in the Loggia del Capitano (1571) did he wilfully misuse elements from the orders. The Loggia is by far his richest building, with a mass of *horror vacui* relief decoration. His last building in Vicenza was the Teatro Olimpico (begun 1580 and finished by SCA-MOZZI) – an elaborate reconstruction of a Roman theatre.

His villas show no similar process of development. In the 1550s he evolved a formula for the ideal villa – a central block of ruthlessly symmetrical plan, decorated externally with a portico and continued by long wings of farm buildings, either extended horizontally or curved forwards in quadrants, as at La Badoera (*c*. 1550–60), and linking the villa with the surrounding landscape. On this theme he composed numerous variations – from the elaboration of La Rotonda (begun *c*. 1550), with its hexastyle porticos on each of its four sides, to the simplicity of La Malcontenta (1560) and Fanzolo (*c*. 1560–5), where the windows are unmarked by surrounds and the decoration is limited to a portico on the main façade, to the stark severity of Poiana, where columns are replaced by undecorated shafts. The use of temple-front porticos for houses was a novelty (Palladio incorrectly supposed that they were used on Roman houses). Sometimes they are free-standing but usually they are attached; and at Quinto (*c*. 1550) and Maser (1560s) he treated the whole central block as a temple front. The relation of the portico to the rest of the building and the sizes of the rooms inside were determined by harmonic proportions.

Temple fronts and harmonic proportions also play an important part in his churches, all of which are in Venice: the façade of S. Francesco della Vigna (1562), and the churches of S. Giorgio Maggiore (begun 1566) and Il Redentore (begun 1576). The latter two appear inside to be simple basilicas, but as one approaches the high altar the curves of the transepts opening out on either hand and the circle of the dome overhead produce a unique effect of expansion and elation. Both churches terminate in arcades screening off the choirs and adding a touch of almost Byzantine mystery to the cool classical logic of the plan.

In 1554 Palladio published *Le antichità di Roma* and *Descrizione delle chiese . . . di Roma,* of which the former remained the standard guide-book for 200 years. He illustrated Barbaro's *Vitruvius* (1556) and in 1570 published his *Quattro libri dell' architettura,* at once a statement of his theory, a glorification of his achievements, and an advertisement for his practice. (His drawings of the Roman *thermae* were not published until 1730, by Lord BURLINGTON.)

He was the first great professional architect. Unlike his most notable contemporaries, Michelangelo and Giulio Romano, he was trained to build and practised no other art. Though he was erudite in archaeology and fascinated by complex theories of proportions, his works are surprisingly unpompous and unpedantic. But the rules which he derived from a study of the ancients, and which he frequently broke in his own work, came to be accepted almost blindly as the classical canon, at any rate for domestic architecture.

PALMETTE. A fan-shaped ornament composed of narrow divisions like a palm leaf. *See figure 3.*

PANTHEON DOME. A dome similar to that of the Pantheon in Rome, though not necessarily open in the centre.

PANTILE. A roofing tile of curved S-shaped section.

PARADISE. 1. An open court or ATRIUM surrounded by porticos in front of a church (some medieval writers gave this name to the atrium of Old St Peter's). 2. The garden or cemetery of a monastery, in particular the main cloister cemetery (e.g., Chichester Cathedral, where the cloister-garth on the south side is called the 'paradise'). PARVIS seems to be a corruption of *paradisus*.

PARAPET. A low wall, sometimes battlemented, placed to protect any spot where there is a sudden drop, for example, at the edge of a bridge, quay, or house-top.

PARCLOSE. A screen enclosing a chapel or shrine and separating it from the main body of the church so as to exclude non-worshippers.

PAREKKLESION. In Byzantine architecture, a chapel, either free-standing or attached.

PARGETTING. Exterior plastering of a TIMBER-FRAMED building, usually modelled in designs, e.g., vine pattern, foliage, figures; also, in modern architecture, the mortar lining of a chimney flue.

PARKER, Barry, see UNWIN.

PARLER. The most famous family of German masons in the C14 and early C15. The name is confusing, as *Parlier* is German for the foreman, the second-in-command, in a masons' lodge and can thus occur in reference to masons not members of the family. The family worked in South Germany, chiefly Swabia, and in Bohemia, chiefly Prague. More than a dozen members are recorded. The most important ones are Heinrich I and his son Peter. Heinrich I was probably *Parlier* at Cologne, and then became master mason at Schwäbisch-Gmünd, one of the most important churches in Germany for the creation of the specifically German Late Gothic style (*Sondergotik*). It is likely that he designed the operative part, the chancel, a design on the HALL CHURCH principle which had great influence. A Heinrich of the same family, quite possibly he, also designed the chancel at Ulm (begun 1377).

Peter (d. 1399) was called to Prague in 1353, aged only twenty-three, to continue the cathedral begun by Matthias of Arras (*c.* 1340). He completed the chancel and went on to the west, working first on a synthesis of the French cathedral plan with the hall principle of Gmünd and its consequences. In the chapels farther west he developed interesting and fanciful lierne vaults, curiously similar to English ones built a generation and more earlier. He probably designed and worked also at Kutná Hora (Kuttenberg) and Kolin.

The Parlers, and especially Peter, also exercised great influence through the sculptural work of their lodges. Another member of the family, Johann, was master mason of the town of Freiburg from 1359 and perhaps designed the chancel of the minster there (1354–63). Yet another, again called Heinrich of Gmünd, was at Milan Cathedral in 1391–2 ('Enrico da Gamondia'), but left under a cloud, having been unable to win the authorities over to his ideas. The Hans of Freiburg ('Annes de Firimburg') who, also in vain, made a report to the Milan authorities earlier in 1391 may be yet another Parler.

PARQUET. Flooring of thin hardwood (about $\frac{1}{4}$ in. thick) laid in patterns on a wood subfloor and highly polished. Inlaid or plated parquet consists of a veneer of decorative hardwood glued in patterns to squares of softwood backing and then laid on a wood sub-floor.

PARVIS(E). 1. In France the term for the open space in front of and around cathedrals and churches; probably a corruption of *paradisus*, see PARADISE. 2. In England a term wrongly applied to a room over a church porch.

PASTOPHORY. A room in an Early Christian or Byzantine church serving as a DIACONICON or PROTHESIS; as a rule, flanking the apse of the church.

PATERA. A small, flat, circular or oval ornament in classical architecture, often decorated with ACANTHUS leaves or rose petals. *See figure 65.*

Fig. 65. Patera and rosette

PATIO. In Spanish or Spanish American architecture, an inner courtyard open to the sky.

PAVILION. An ornamental building, lightly constructed, often used as a pleasure-house or summerhouse in a garden, or attached to a cricket or other sports ground; also a projecting subdivision of some larger building, usually square and often domed, forming an angle feature on the main façade or terminating the wings.

PAXTON, Sir Joseph (1801–65), the son of a small farmer, became a gardener and in 1823 worked at Chiswick in the gardens of the Duke of Devonshire. The Duke discovered his exceptional ability and in 1826 made him superintendent of the gardens at Chatsworth. He became a friend of the Duke, with whom he visited Switzerland, Italy, Greece, Asia Minor, Spain, etc., and in 1854 became Liberal M.P. for Coventry. He designed greenhouses for Chatsworth, the largest being 300 ft long (1836–40), tried out a new system of glass and metal roof construction in them, laid out the estate village of Edensor (1839–41), and so, in 1850–1, moved into architecture proper by submitting, uninvited, his design for a glass-and-iron palace for the first international exhibition ever held. The Crystal Palace was truly epoch-making, not only because this was the most direct and rational solution to a particular problem but also because the detailing of this 1,800-ft-long building was designed in such a way that all its parts could be factory-made and assembled on the site – the first ever example of PREFABRICATION. Paxton was also nominally responsible for a few large country houses (Mentmore, Ferrières, for members of the Rothschild dynasty), but they were partly or largely designed by his son-in-law. He was, further, one of the founders of the *Gardener's Chronicle*, and was interested in public parks as well as private grounds (Birkenhead, 1843–7).

PEARCE, Sir Edward Lovet (*c.* 1699–1733). He was the leading exponent of PALLADIANISM in Ireland alongside CASSELS. His father was first cousin to VANBRUGH like whom he began his career in the army. Nothing is known of his architectural training – if he had any – but he became one of the most interesting and original architects of the BURLINGTON school. His masterpiece is the Parliament House (now the Bank of Ireland) in Dublin (1728–39). The octagonal House of Commons was burnt in 1792 and later demolished. He also built the S. front of Drumcondra House (1727) and Cashel Palace (*c.* 1731). He became Surveyor-General for Ireland in 1730.

PEARSON, John Loughborough (1817–97), was a pupil of Ignatius Bonomi, SALVIN, and HARDWICK. Under Hardwick he worked on the Hall of Lincoln's Inn, where one may well discover his hand in the niceness of the detailing. In 1843 he set up practice, and almost at once was commissioned to design small churches. His first important church is St Peter, Kennington Lane, Lambeth, London (1863–5), French Gothic and vaulted throughout, the ribs of stone, the webs of brick. This building displays his faith in truth in building and in a nobility to fit the religious purpose. Pearson also designed country houses – e.g., Quar Wood, Gloucestershire (1857), which is Gothic, and Westwood, Sydenham, London (1881), which is French Renaissance – but essentially he is a church architect and a Gothicist. His best churches of the 1870s and 1880s are among the finest of their day not only in England but in Europe. Their style is C13 Franco-English, their decorative detail extremely sparing, and their spatial composition quite free and unimitative. Examples are St Augustine, Kilburn Park, London (1870–80); St Michael, Croydon (1871); St John, Red Lion Square, London (1874, demolished); Truro Cathedral (1879–1910); St John, Upper Norwood, London (1880–1); Cullercoats, Northumberland (1884). He was also surveyor to Westminster Abbey.

PEBBLEDASH, *see* ROUGHCAST.

PEDESTAL. In classical architecture, the base supporting a column or colonnade; also, more loosely, the base for a statue or any superstructure. *See figure 66.*

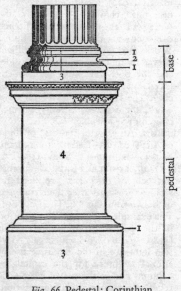

Fig. 66. Pedestal: Corinthian

Key: 1. Torus   3. Plinth
           2. Scotia   4. Die or dado

PEDIMENT. Not a Greek or Roman term but signifying in classical architecture a low-pitched GABLE above a PORTICO, formed by running the top member of the ENTABLATURE along the sides of the gable; also a similar feature

Fig. 67. Pendant

above doors, windows, etc. It may be straight-sided or curved segmentally. The terms *open pediment* and *broken pediment* are confused and have been employed to describe pediments open or broken either at the apex or base. For clarity, a pediment where the sloping sides are returned before reaching the apex should be called an *open-topped* or *broken-apex pediment*; and one with a gap in the base moulding an *open-bed* or *broken-bed pediment*.

PELE-TOWER. A term peculiar to Northern England and Scotland, signifying a small tower or house suitable for sudden defence.

PENDANT. A BOSS elongated so that it hangs down; found in Late Gothic vaulting and, decoratively, in French and English C16 and early C17 vaults and also stucco ceilings. *See figure 67.*

PENDENTIVE. A concave SPANDREL leading from the angle of two walls to the base of a circular DOME. It is one of the means by which a circular dome is supported over a square or polygonal compartment (*see also* SQUINCH), and is used in Byzantine (Hagia Sophia, Istanbul) and occasionally Romanesque architecture (Périgueux), and often in Renaissance, Baroque, and later architecture. *See figure 38.*

PENTHOUSE. A subsidiary structure with a lean-to roof (*see* ROOF); also a separately roofed structure on the roof of a high block of flats.

PERCIER, Charles (1764–1838), studied in Paris under A. F. Peyre and in Rome (1786–92) with his future partner P. F. L. FONTAINE. They worked together from 1794 until 1814, becoming the leading architects in Paris under Napoleon and creating the Empire style in decoration. For their joint works and publications, *see* FONTAINE.

PERGOLA. A covered walk in a garden usually formed by a double row of posts or pillars with JOISTS above and covered with climbing plants.

PERIPTERAL. Of a building, surrounded by a single row of columns.

PERISTYLE. A range of columns surrounding a building or open court.

PERPENDICULAR STYLE. *See* ENGLISH ARCHITECTURE.

PERRAULT, Claude (1613–88), a doctor by profession and amateur architect, was partly if not mainly responsible for the great east front of the Louvre in Paris (begun 1667), one of the supreme masterpieces of the Louis XIV style. LE VAU and the painter Lebrun were also members of the committee appointed to design this façade. It owes something to BERNINI's rejected project for the Louvre, and is notable for its great colonnade or screen of paired columns. He also designed the Observatoire, Paris (1667), and brought out an edition of VITRUVIUS (1672). In 1683 he published *Ordonnance des cinq espèces de Colonnes*. His brother Charles (1626–1703) was a theorist and Colbert's chief assistant in the Surintendance des Bâtiments.

PERRET, Auguste (1874–1954). The son of the owner of a building and contracting firm. After studies under Guadet he and two brothers joined the firm which was known from 1905 as Perret Frères. His first outstanding job was the house No. 25b rue Franklin near the Trocadéro in Paris, a block of flats on an interesting plan; it has a concrete structure with the concrete members displayed and ART NOUVEAU faience infillings. Next came a garage in the rue Ponthieu (1905), even more demonstratively expressing its concrete frame. The Théâtre des Champs Élysées (1911–14) was originally designed by van de VELDE, but in its final form it is essentially Perret's, and its distinguishing feature is again the proud display of its concrete skeleton. Details, however, are decidedly classical, even if with a minimum of traditional motifs, and Perret was subsequently to develop in that direction. Nevertheless, until the mid-twenties bold concrete experiments still prevailed: the 65-ft arches across the vast workroom of the Esders tailoring establishment (1919), and the decorative concrete grilles of the windows and the concrete excelsior of the steeple of the churches of Notre Dame du Raincy (1922–3) and of Montmagny (1926). Examples of Perret at his most classical – basically the successor to the most restrained French C18 style – are the Museum of Public Works (1937, though with a brilliant curved flying concrete staircase inside) and the post-war work for Amiens (skyscraper 1947) and Le Havre (1945 etc.). The latter includes Perret's last work, the strange centrally planned church of St Joseph.

PERRON. An exterior staircase or flight of steps usually leading to a main, first-floor entrance to a house.

PERSIAN ARCHITECTURE. The nomadic peoples of Persia produced no architecture until after their conquest of Babylon in 539 B.C. The only notable example of the succeeding period is the palace group at Persepolis (518–*c.* 460 B.C.), which reveals Assyrian influence in the extensive use of animal sculpture for the capitals of columns and in the use of large-scale relief decorations. Relief decorations in brightly coloured glazed brickwork (now in the Louvre, Paris) were also employed at Susa. The Hall of a Hundred Columns at Persepolis, so far as it can be reconstructed, shows that other elements were derived from Egypt though treated with greater lightness and elegance. Buildings erected under the Sassanian dynasty (226 B.C.–A.D. 642) were constructed of bricks and decorated with carved stucco; vaults and domes were much employed, as in the palace at Ctesiphon (A.D. 550). Other partially surviving Sassanian buildings of note are the palaces at Sarvistan (A.D. 350) and at Feruz-Abad (A.D. 223–41).

Persia made an important contribution to the development of ISLAMIC architecture, notably in the design of the cruciform mosque (in which an often very high vaulted niche is placed in each of the four walls of the court), e.g., the Friday Mosque in Isfahan (C12) and Majid-i Shah, Isfahan (1616). The Persians made great use of internal and external revetments of glazed tiles of great beauty. Also they developed the domed tomb-chamber, the most notable being the mausoleum of Uljaitu, Sultaniyeh (c. 1309–13).

PERUVIAN ARCHITECTURE. Vast and impressive remains of stone-built civil, religious, funerary, and military buildings survive in the Andes mountains. It is impossible to estimate their age with any precision; they have been dated variously between c. 13,000 B.C. and c. 3000 B.C., but are now thought to be much later, probably from towards the beginning of the Christian era. Walls were built of huge blocks of finely cut masonry fitted together without cement; doors and windows usually taper towards the top. Small and usually circular sepulchral buildings (kullpis and chullpas) were roofed with slabs of stone. The most important of the early sites is Machu Picchu. Buildings at Chanchan incorporate much carved stone and stucco relief decoration. Numerous large terraced monuments (stepped pyramids with flat tops), built of ADOBES and containing labyrinths of passages and cells, have survived – e.g., Huaca Juliana, Huaca Trujillo, and the Aramburu group, near Lima. The Inca Empire, which succeeded the more primitive cultures (1438–1532), introduced a greater air of sophistication, evident in the buildings of its capital, Cuzco.

PERUZZI, Baldassare (1481–1536). One of the best High Renaissance architects in Rome. His works are much indebted to BRAMANTE and RAPHAEL, but have an almost feminine delicacy which contrasts with the monumentality of the former and the gravity of the latter. Born in Siena, he began as a painter under Pinturicchio. In 1503 he went to Rome, where he was employed by Bramante and assisted him with his designs for St Peter's. He probably built S. Sebastiano in Valle Piatta, Siena (c. 1507), a centralized Greek cross church derived from Bramante. His first important work was the Villa Farnesina, Rome (1508–11), one of the most exquisite of all Italian houses both for its architecture and for its interior decoration (frescoes by Peruzzi himself, Raphael, GIULIO ROMANO, Sodoma, and Ugo da Carpi), which combine to make it the outstanding secular monument of the High Renaissance. The plan is unusual: a square block with an open loggia in the centre of the garden front and projecting wings. The main rooms are on ground level. The façade decoration is rich with two superimposed orders of pilasters crowned with a boldly carved frieze of putti and swags in which the attic windows are set.

On Raphael's death (1520) Peruzzi completed his S. Eligio degli Orefici, Rome, and succeeded him as architect of St Peter's. In 1527 he fled from the Sack of Rome to Siena, where he was appointed city architect, but returned soon afterwards. With Antonio da SANGALLO the younger he began the Villa Farnese, Caprarola, on an unusual pentagonal plan (c. 1530, completed by VIGNOLA). His last work, Palazzo Massimo alle Colonne, Rome (1532–6), is perhaps his most interesting, for its unorthodox design seems to echo the uneasy atmosphere of Rome in the years after the Sack. The façade is curved; there is a disturbing contrast between the ground floor with its deeply recessed loggia and the papery-thin upper part, with shallow window surrounds on the first floor and curious flat leathery frames round those on the floors above. In the *cortile* the sacrosanct orders are wilfully misused. The self-confidence of the High Renaissance has here given way to the sophisticated elegance and spiritual disquiet of Mannerism.

PEW. A fixed wooden seat in a church, in use at least by the C14. In medieval times pews were partially enclosed at the ends next to the aisles with *bench-ends*, which sometimes rise above the WAINSCOT and terminate in carved FINIALS (*see* POPPYHEAD). A *box-pew* is one with a high wooden enclosure all round and a small door; it is essentially a Georgian type.

PHAROS. A Roman lighthouse.

PIANO NOBILE. The main floor of a house, containing the reception rooms. It is usually higher than the other floors, with a basement or ground floor below and one or more shallower storeys above.

PIAZZA. 1. An open space, usually oblong, surrounded by buildings. 2. In C17 and C18 England, a long covered walk or LOGGIA with a roof supported by columns.

PICTURESQUE. Originally a landscape or building which looked as if it had come out of a picture in the style of Claude or Gaspar Poussin. In the late C18 it was defined in a long controversy between Payne KNIGHT and Uvedale PRICE as an aesthetic quality between the sublime and the beautiful, characterized in the landscape garden by wild ruggedness (chasms, dark impenetrable woods, rushing streams, etc.), and in architecture by interesting asymmetrical dispositions of forms and variety of texture – as in the COTTAGE ORNÉ and the Italianate or castellated Gothic country houses of John NASH.

PIER. 1. A solid masonry support, as distinct from a COLUMN. 2. The solid mass between doors, windows, and other openings in buildings. 3. A name often given to Romanesque and Gothic pillars varying from a square to a composite section (*see* COMPOUND PIER).

PIERMARINI, Giuseppe (1734–1808), the leading neo-classical architect in Milan, trained in Rome under VANVITELLI and settled in Milan in 1769. His most famous work is the façade of Teatro della Scala, Milan (1776–8). He also built several vast palaces, all rather severe with long façades on which ornament is reduced to a bare minimum, e.g., Palazzo Reale, Milan (1773), Palazzo Belgioioso, Milan (1779), and Villa Reale, Monza (1780).

PIERRE DE MONTEREAU (or MONTREUIL) (d. 1267) was master mason of Notre Dame, Paris, in 1265. The High Gothic work at St Denis Abbey, begun in 1231, is ascribed to him. On his tombstone he is called *doctor lathomorum*.

PIGAGE, Nicolas de (1723–96), was born at Lunéville and trained in Paris, visited Italy and probably England, and in 1749 became architect to the Elector Palatine Carl Theodor in Mannheim, for whom all his best work was executed. His masterpiece is Schloss Benrath near Düsseldorf (1755–69), a large pavilion, apparently of one storey (but in fact of three), somewhat similar to Sanssouci at Potsdam, and decorated internally in the most exquisitely refined and restrained Rococo manner that hovers on the verge of Louis XVI classicism. At Schwetzingen he laid out the Elector's garden (1766), and built a miniature theatre and various follies, including a mosque, a romantic water castle, and a bath-house with a mirror ceiling.

PILASTER. A shallow PIER or rectangular column projecting only slightly from a wall and, in classical architecture, conforming with one of the ORDERS.

PILASTER-STRIP, *see* LESENE.

PILGRAM, Anton (d. *c.* 1515), was mason and sculptor first at Brno and Heilbronn (at Heilbronn he did the high-spired tabernacle for the Holy Sacrament), and later at St Stefan in Vienna, where the organ foot (1513) and the pulpit (1514-15) are his, both very intricate in their architectural forms and both including a self-portrait of the master.

PILLAR. A free-standing upright member which, unlike a COLUMN, need not be cylindrical or conform with any of the orders.

PILLAR PISCINA, *see* PISCINA.

PILOTIS. A French term for pillars or stilts that carry a building, thereby raising it to first-floor level and leaving the ground floor open.

PINNACLE. A small turret-like termination crowning spires, buttresses, the angles of parapets, etc.; usually of steep pyramidal or conical shape and ornamented, e.g., with CROCKETS. *See figure 78.*

PIRANESI, Giovanni Battista (1720-78), who was mainly an engraver of views of Roman antiquities and an architectural theorist, exerted a profound influence on the development of the neoclassical and Romantic movements. Born in Venice, he was trained as an engineer and architect, and settled in Rome *c.* 1745. His highly dramatic views of Roman ruins and imaginative reconstructions of ancient Rome helped to inspire a new attitude to Antiquity. In *Della magnificenza ed architettura dei Romani* (1761) he championed the supremacy of Roman over Greek architecture and in *Parere sull'architettura* (1765) advocated a free and imaginative use of Roman models for the creation of a new architectural style. He put his theories into practice only once, not very successfully, at

S. Maria del Priorato, Rome (1764-6), which combines an antique flavour with allusions to the Knights of Malta, who owned the church; but it lacks the power and imagination of his engravings.

PISANO, Nicola (d. *c.* 1280), and his son Giovanni (d. shortly after 1314), the greatest Italian sculptors of their generations, are also recorded as architects. In the case of Nicola we have no documents, but tradition (VASARI) and some stylistic arguments; in the case of Giovanni we are on firmer ground. He appears as master mason of Siena Cathedral in 1290 and at Siena some years earlier, during the time when the cathedral received its Gothic façade. About 1296 he moved to Pisa and was there probably also master mason. Andrea Pisano (d. 1348-9) is not a relation of Giovanni. He is the finest Italian sculptor of the generation following Giovanni's and was also an architect. As such he is traceable in records of Florence Cathedral as master mason probably after Giotto's death in 1337, and at Orvieto Cathedral also as master mason from 1347. However, at Orvieto by that time the most important sculptural and architectural work on the façade was over, and at Florence also nothing architectural can be attributed to him with certainty.

PISCINA. A stone basin in a niche near the altar for washing the Communion or Mass vessels; provided with a drain and usually set in or against the wall south of the altar. A free-standing piscina on a pillar can be called a *pillar piscina.*

PLAISANCE. A summerhouse or pleasure-house near a mansion.

PLATERESQUE. Literally 'silversmith-like', the name is given to an ornate architectural style popular in Spain during the C16. It is characterized by a lavish use of ornamental motifs - Gothic, Renaissance, and even Moorish - unrelated to the structure of the building to which it is applied. The main practitioners, many of whom were sculptors as well as architects, included Diego de SILOE, Alonso de COVARRUBIAS, Rodrigo GIL DE HONTAÑÓN.

PLAYFAIR, William Henry (1789–1857), was the leading GREEK REVIVAL architect in Edinburgh alongside T. HAMILTON. He was the son of James Playfair (d. 1794) who designed Melville Castle (1786) and Cairness House (1791–7) the latter in an advanced neo-classical style with neo-Egyptian features inside. W. H. Playfair may have studied under SMIRKE in London but returned to Scotland in 1817 on being commissioned to complete R. ADAM's Edinburgh University. This established him professionally. He followed Adam's designs closely, but the interiors are his, notably the Library (c. 1827) which is among his finest works. In 1818 he also began the Academy at Dollar and the New Observatory on Calton Hill, Edinburgh, where he also built a Doric monument to his uncle John (1825) and another to Dugald Stewart (1831) based on the Choragic Monument to Lysicrates. His best known works are the Royal Scottish Academy (1822, enlarged and modified 1831) and the National Gallery of Scotland (1850), both Doric and rather dour. The Surgeons' Hall (begun 1829), with its elegant and crisp Ionic portico, is perhaps his masterpiece. Though essentially a Greek Revival architect Playfair worked in other styles as well, e.g., neo-Gothic at New College, Edinburgh (1846–50) and neo-Elizabethan at Donaldson's Hospital, Edinburgh (1842–51).

PLINTH. The projecting base of a wall or column pedestal, generally CHAMFERED or moulded at the top. See figures 64 and 66.

PLINTH BLOCK. A block at the base of the architrave of a door, chimneypiece, etc., against which the skirting of the wall is stopped.

PODIUM. 1. A continuous base or plinth supporting columns. 2. The platform enclosing the arena in an ancient amphitheatre.

POELZIG, Hans (1869–1936), studied at the College of Technology in Berlin, and in 1899 was appointed to a job in the Prussian Ministry of Works. In the next year, however, he became Professor of Architecture in the School of Arts and Crafts at Breslau (Wroclaw), and in 1903 its director. He stayed till 1916, then became City Architect of Dresden (till 1920), and after that Professor of Architecture in the College of Technology and the Academy of Arts in Berlin. In 1936 he accepted a chair at Ankara, but died before emigrating.

His first building of note was the water tower at Posen (Poznan), built in 1910 as an exhibition pavilion for the mining industry. It is of iron framing with brick infilling and details of exposed iron inside. Of 1911–12 are an office building at Breslau, with the motif of bands of horizontal windows curving round the corner – a motif much favoured in the 1920s and 1930s – and a factory at Luban, equally advanced in its architectural seriousness and its grouping of cubic elements. During and immediately after the First World War Poelzig was one of the most fertile inventors of Expressionist forms, chiefly of a stalagmite or organ-pipe kind. These fantastic forms characterize his House of Friendship (1916), designed for Istanbul, his designs for a town hall for Dresden (1917), and those for a Festival Theatre for Salzburg (1919–20), none of which was executed. However, he did carry out the conversion of the Grosses Schauspielhaus in Berlin (1918–19), with its stalactitic vault and its highly Expressionist corridors and foyer. Later buildings were more conventionally modern (the enormous office building of 1928 for the Dye Trust, I. G. Farben, at Frankfurt and the equally enormous building (1929) for the German Broadcasting Company in Berlin).

POINT-BLOCK HOUSING. A point-block is a high block in which the centre is reserved for staircases, lifts, etc. and the flats fan out from that centre.

POINTED ARCH, see ARCH.

POINTING. In brickwork, the strong mortar finishing given to the exterior of the joints.

POLISH ARCHITECTURE. The oldest surviving building in Poland is the small quatrefoil Chapel of St Mary on the Wawel Hill at Cracow. It is of the C10 and in this and all the rest the exact parallel to the oldest building of Bohemia, on the Prague Hradshin. The Romanesque style in Poland is part of that of Germany. Italian connections are largely explicable via Germany. The best preserved cathedral is at Plock (1144 etc.). Its rounded transept ends indicate inspiration from Cologne. The cathedral on the Wawel has its (German) crypt and parts of the W. towers. At Gniezno splendid bronze doors survive, at Strzelno some columns decorated with small figures under arches.

As in other countries the way was paved for the Gothic style by the Cistercians. Their first abbey was at Jedrzejow near Wroclaw in Silesia (1140 etc.), and there are a number of other abbeys. More determinedly Gothic are the buildings of the friars, starting with that of the Blackfriars at Sandomierz (1227 etc.). The E. part of Wroclaw (Breslau) Cathedral, of 1244–72, has the straight ambulatory of Cistercian tradition. The nave followed in the C14, the century in which Cracow Cathedral on the Wawel was also rebuilt. Gniezno Cathedral of c. 1360 etc. has an ambulatory and a ring of straight-sided radiating chapels on the pattern of Cistercian architecture.

Late Gothic Polish churches have the high proportions and the ornate figured rib vaults of Germany.

Wroclaw, Gdańsk (Danzig), Torun (Thorn), the Cistercian abbeys of Oliva and Pelplin, were of course all German. A characteristic Eastern feature however – though even this originated in Germany – is the so-called folded vaults, i.e., complicated space frames without ribs. Basilican sections are more frequent than halls. There are also a few two-naved halls. The church at Goslawice is an octagon with four cross-arms.

Of secular buildings by far the proudest is the town hall at Torun of 1259 etc. but mainly the late C14, a bold oblong with blank giant arcading, an inner courtyard and one mighty tower. The surviving early buildings of Cracow University are also among the most interesting buildings of their kind anywhere in Europe.

The Renaissance reached Poland early, and probably by way of Hungary and Czechoslovakia. The Early Renaissance parts of the Wawel (castle) of Cracow were begun as early as 1502 and the domed chapel of King Sigismond attached to Cracow Cathedral in 1517; the architects in both cases were Italians. Yet closest to the windows of the Wawel palace is the Vladislav Hall at Prague, closest to the chapel that of 1507 at Esztergom. Specially characteristic of the indigenous later C16 and early C17 style are lively top crestings instead of battlements (Cracow, Cloth Hall, 1555) and courtyards or façades with arcading at two or three levels (Poznan, i.e., Posen, Town Hall, 1550–61). The former also occurs in the other East European countries, the latter in them and Germany. Castles in the country were often square or oblong with courtyard and with or without angle towers (Niepolomice, 1550 etc., Baranów, 1579 etc., Ujazdow, 1606 etc.).

Much interesting church work went on as well, with stuccoed tunnel vaults, their decoration being either Gothic Survival or simple geometrical patterns (Pultusk, 1556–63) or strap-work. Architects continued to be Italian, and that remained so in the C17 as well. Poland has proportionately more churches of Italian inspiration in the C16 and early C17 than Germany.

The Italian church type of the Gesù in Rome was taken over before 1600 (Jesuit Church, Cracow, 1597 etc. by J. M. Bernardone and J. Trevano); and Poland contributed much to the Italianate Baroque of the later C17 (Cracow University Church, 1689 etc.). Besides longitudinal there are central churches. Klimontov, 1643 etc., is oval, Gostyn, 1677 etc., octagonal, and the church of the Perpetual Adoration in Warsaw, 1683 etc., round with four short arms. The latter is by the Dutch Tylman van Gameren (1632–1706) who became the leading Polish architect about 1700.

The plans of the C18, with their predilection for elongated central themes, show affinities with Bohemia and once more South Germany (Lwow, Dominicans, 1744 etc., Berezwecz with its curvaceous twin-tower façade, 1750 etc.). The principal country house of the first half of the C17 is Podhorce of 1635–40, still square with angle towers, and with the pedimented windows and superimposed orders of pilasters which one would find at the same time in Austria and Czechoslovakia. The full-blown Baroque came with Wilanow near Warsaw of 1681 etc. (by A. Locci). In opposition to it was van Gameren's Franco-Dutch style (Warsaw, Krasinski Palace 1689 etc.). This however did not apply to his ecclesiastical architecture throughout. St Anne at Cracow (1689 etc.) is thoroughly Italian and Baroque. The C18 saw a large activity both by the Saxon court and the native nobility. They culminated in PÖPPELMANN'S designs for the Royal Palace. Style again varies from his exuberant Baroque to the classical French restraint of others.

Neo-classicism came early, and its earliest and finest phase corresponds with the reign of King Stanislaw Augustus Poniatowski (1764–85). Earlier still is the chapel belonging to the country palace of Podhorce. This is of 1752–66, by an architect signing himself C. Romanus. It is round, with a giant portico and a dome. Round and domed also, with a Roman Doric portico and decidedly French, is the Protestant Church at Warsaw of 1777 by S. B. Zug (1733–1807). The leading court architects of Stanislaw were Giacomo Fontana (1710–73) and Domenico Merlini (1730–97). Theirs is the Ujazdow Palace of 1768 etc. and by Merlini and the younger J. K. Kamsetzer are the remodelling of the Lazienki Palace of Ujazdow (1788) and the excellent interiors of the Royal Palace (1780–85). Kamsetzer's church at Petrykosy of 1791 is wholly of the French Revolution type. At the same time the grounds of the country houses were converted in the English picturesque way (Arcadia, 1778 etc., Natolin, Warsaw Belvedere). Between c. 1780 and c. 1825 Poland produced a number of spacious country houses in the classicist style and also the two town halls of Wilno and Grodno with detached giant porticoes. But the most monumental of the giant porticoes is that of Wilno Cathedral of 1777–1801, and that is by the Polish architect W. Gucewicz (1753–98). The leading early C19 architect in Warsaw was Antonio Corazzi (1792–1877). He designed the Polish Bank (1828–30), which is very French, and the Grecian Grand Theatre (1826–33). The later C19 went through the same historicist motions as all European countries, but in the early C20 Poland had a kind of national (in this case free neo-Romanesque) romanticism which is more characteristic of Russia, Finland and Sweden than of the West. It is exemplified by the church of St James at Warsaw of 1909 etc. by Oscar Sosnowski (1880–1939).

POLISH PARAPET. A decorative device consisting of a large-scale cresting of blind arcades, pinnacles, pyramids, etc., used to crown the façades and mask the roofs of many Polish buildings, notably the Cloth Hall at Cracow (1555) and the Town Halls of Poznań (c. 1550–61) and Culm (1567–97). It also occurs in Czechoslovakia.

POLLACK, Mihály (1773–1855), the leading Hungarian classicist, was born in Vienna. His father was an architect, and his step-brother was Leopoldo POLLAK. He studied under his brother in Milan and settled in Budapest in 1798. His style is moderate, never outré, and not very personal. Occasionally he also used Gothic features (Pecs, or Fünfkirchen, Cathedral, 1805 etc.). He built large private houses and country houses, but his chefs-d'œuvre are public buildings at Warsaw, notably the Theatre and Assembly Room (completed 1832), the Military Academy (Ludoviceum, 1829–36), and the National Museum with its Corinthian portico and its splendid staircase (1836–45).

POLLAK, Leopoldo (1751–1806). He was born and trained in Vienna, settled in Milan in 1775 and became an assistant to PIERMARINI. His masterpiece is the Villa Belgioioso Reale (1793), now the Galleria d'Arte Moderna, a very large and very grand but strangely frenchified version of PALLADIO, with a rusticated basement, giant Ionic order, and lavish use of sculpture. He also built several villas near Milan and laid out their gardens in the English style, e.g., Villa Pesenti Agliardi, Sombreno (c. 1800).

POLLINI, Gino, see FIGINI.

PONTI, Gio (b. 1891), designer and architect, was also a painter and draughtsman in the twenties. His drawing reflects the style of the Vienna Secession (see OLBRICH), and his designs for porcelain of around 1925 may also be inspired by the Wiener Werkstätte. Ponti is a universal designer: his œuvre includes ships' interiors, theatrical work, light fittings, furniture, and products of light industry. Most of his best work in these fields dates from after the war, e.g., the famous very delicately detailed rush-seated chair (1951). His fame as an architect rested for a long time on three buildings: the Faculty of Mathematics in the Rome University City, dated 1934 and one of the incunabula of INTERNATIONAL MODERN architecture in Italy (though preceded by Terragni's few buildings); and then the two twin office buildings (1936 and 1951) designed for the Montecatini Company, both in Milan. The first, with its subdued modernity and its elegant detail, was a pioneer work and at the same time very personal, the second is more conventional. Ponti's finest building is the Pirelli skyscraper in Milan (1955–8), built round a hidden structural concrete core by NERVI; the building is 415 ft high, a slender slab of curtain walling with the long sides tapering to the slenderest ends.

PONZIO, Flaminio (1560–1613), official architect to Pope Paul V (Borghese), was able but rather unadventurous; he never developed far beyond the Late Mannerist style in which he was trained. His most notable work is the Cappella Paolina in S. Maria Maggiore, Rome (1605–11), very richly decorated with sculpture and panels of coloured marbles and semi-precious stones. He also built the very long façade of Palazzo Borghese, Rome (1605–13), and the handsome Acqua Paola fountain on the Janiculum (1612). Early in the C17 he rebuilt, with a new dome, RAPHAEL and PERUZZI's S. Eligio degli Orefici, Rome.

PÖPPELMANN, Matthaeus Daniel (1662–1736). He was the architect of the Zwinger at Dresden, a Rococo masterpiece. He was born at Herford in Westphalia and settled in Dresden in 1686, being appointed Kondukteur in the Landbauamt in 1691, and eventually, in 1705, succeeded Marcus

Conrad Dietze as Landbaumeister to the Elector of Saxony and King of Poland, Augustus the Strong. In 1705–15 he built the Taschenberg Palais in Dresden for the Elector's mistress. For a state visit in 1709 he built a temporary wooden amphitheatre which the Elector then decided to replace with a stone construction (the Zwinger) which would be incorporated in the great new royal palace which Pöppelmann was commissioned to design. In 1710 he was appointed Geheim Cämmeriere and sent off to study and gather ideas in Vienna and Italy. His designs for the palace show some influence from both the Viennese Baroque of HILDEBRANDT and the Roman Baroque of Carlo FONTANA. But the Zwinger itself could hardly be more original in general conception – a vast space surrounded by a single-storey gallery linking two-storey pavilions and entered through exuberant frothy gateways – the whole composition resembling a giant's Meissen table-centre. Only a section was ever built (1711–20; the Kronentor in 1713, the Wallpavillon in 1716. It was damaged in 1944 but is now rebuilt). The sculptural decoration was executed by Balthasar Permoser and the brilliance of the total effect is largely due to the successful collaboration between sculptor and architect. Pöppelmann's other buildings are far less exciting: the 'Indian' Wasserpalais at Schloss Pillnitz on the Elbe (1720–23) with Chinoiserie roofs and painted figures of Chinamen under the eaves; the Bergpalais at Schloss Pillnitz (1724); Schloss Moritzberg, begun 1723 but executed under the direction of LONGUELUNE; and, from 1727 onwards, extensions to the Japanisches Palais in Dresden, executed under the direction of de BODT. His designs for the Dreikönigskirche in Dresden Neustadt (1732–9) were executed by Georg BÄHR. From 1728 onwards Pöppelmann collaborated with Longuelune in Warsaw on the designs for a vast new Saxon Palace of which only the central section was built (c. 1730). His son Carl Friedrich (d. 1750) succeeded him in Warsaw.

POPPYHEAD. An ornamental termination to the top of a bench or stall-end, usually carved with foliage and fleur-de-lis-type flowers, animals, or figures. A poppyhead is in fact a FINIAL.

PORCH. The covered entrance to a building; called a PORTICO if columned and pedimented like a temple front.

PORTA, Giacomo della. (c. 1537–1602), a Mannerist architect of Lombard origin working in Rome, is notable mainly as a follower of MICHELANGELO, whom he succeeded as architect of the Capitol. Here he finished the Palazzo dei Conservatori to Michelangelo's design with slight alterations (1578) and also built the Palazzo del Senatore (1573–98) with rather more alterations. He followed VIGNOLA as architect of the Gesù, Rome, designing the façade (1573–84), which was destined to be copied for Jesuit churches throughout Europe. In 1573–4 he became chief architect at St Peter's, where he completed Michelangelo's exterior on the garden side and built the minor domes (1578 and 1585) and the major dome (1588–90) to his own design. The large dome is his masterpiece, though it is rather more ornate and much nearer in outline to the dome of Florence Cathedral than Michelangelo's would have been. He also built the Palazzo della Sapienza (begun c. 1575); the nave of S. Giovanni dei Fiorentini (1582–92); S. Andrea della Valle (1591, completed by MADERNO 1608–23); Palazzo Marescotti (c. 1590), and the very splendid Villa Aldobrandini, Frascati (1598–1603).

PORTCULLIS. A gate of iron or iron-inforced wooden bars made to slide up and down in vertical grooves in the JAMBS of a doorway; used for defence in castle gateways.

PORTE-COCHÈRE. A porch large enough for wheeled vehicles to pass through.

PORTICO. A roofed space, open or partly enclosed, forming the entrance and centre-piece of the façade of a temple, house, or church, often with detached or attached columns and a PEDIMENT. It is called *prostyle* or *in antis* according to whether it projects from or recedes into a building; in the latter case the columns range with the front wall. According to the number of front columns it is called *tetrastyle* (4), *hexastyle* (6), *octastyle* (8), *decastyle* (10), or *dodecastyle* (12). If there are only two columns between pilasters or antae it is called *distyle in antis*.

PORTUGUESE ARCHITECTURE. Until about 1500 Portugal participates in the development of Spanish architecture: there are Roman remains (temple at Évora); S. Frutuoso de Montélios is a c7 church on a Greek cross plan with horseshoe apses and domes, clearly inspired by Byzantium; Lourosa is MOZARABIC of 920; and the principal monuments of the Romanesque style also have their closest parallels in Spain. They are the cathedrals of Braga (begun *c.* 1100) and Coimbra (begun after 1150), inspired by Santiago de Compostela, in the style of the so-called pilgrimage churches of France: high tunnel-vaulted naves, arcades and galleries, and no clerestory lighting. On the other hand, they have no ambulatories. Individual buildings of special interest are the Templars' church of Tomar of the late c12, with a domed octagonal centre and a lower sixteen-sided ambulatory, and the Domus Municipalis of Braganza, a low irregular oblong with rows of short arched windows high up.

The Romanesque style died hard; the cathedral of Évora (begun 1186) is still pre-Gothic. The Gothic style was introduced by the Cistercians, and the outstanding Early Gothic building is Alcobaça (begun 1178) on the pattern of Clairvaux and Pontigny, i.e., with ambulatory and radiating chapels forming an unbroken semicircle. Its tall rib-vaulted interior is one of the noblest of the order in all Europe. The monastic quarters are well preserved and very beautiful too. But Alcobaça is an exception; for, generally speaking, the Gothic style does not begin in Portugal until the mid c13. Among the most important buildings are a number of friars' churches (S. Clara, Santarém) and a number of cathedral cloisters (Coimbra, Évora, Lisbon – all early c14).

But Portuguese architecture comes properly into its own only with the great enterprise of Batalha, a house of Blackfriars commemorating the battle of Aljubarrota. It was begun in 1388 with a vaulted nave of steep Spanish proportions and an east end of the type peculiar to the Italian friars. But in 1402 a new architect appeared, called Huguet or Ouguete, and he introduced a full-blown Flamboyant, i.e., a Late Gothic style, mixed with many reminiscences of the English PERPENDICULAR. The façade, the vaults of cloister and chapterhouse, and the chapel of João I are his work. He also began a large octagon with seven radiating chapels east of the old east end, but this was never completed. Here, as in the link with the old east end, the vaults are of complex English types. The climax of the Late Gothic in Portugal is the MANUELINE STYLE, named after King Manuel I (1495–1521). It is the parallel to the Spanish style of the Reyes Católicos and, like it, springs from the sudden riches pouring in from overseas. But whereas the Spanish style is essentially one of lavish surface decoration, the most significant works of the Manueline style show a transformation of structural members as well, especially a passion for twisted piers. These appear at Belem, a house of the order of the Jerónimos (1502 etc.) – together with richly figured vaults and ample surface incrustation – and also at Setúbal (1492 etc.). In addition there are the wildly over-decorated doorways and windows of Golegã and Tomar (1510 etc.). The portal to the unfinished east chapels of Batalha suggests East Indian inspiration. The leading masters were one Boytac, a Frenchman, at Setúbal and Belem, Mateus Fernandes in the portal of Batalha, and Diogo de ARRUDA in the nave and the windows of Tomar.

But Tomar also contains the most important examples in Portugal of the Italian Renaissance in its Roman Cinquecento forms. The buildings in question are the cloister and the church of the Conception (both c. 1550). But, as in Spain, the Renaissance had arrived earlier and in playful Quattrocento forms. Among cathedrals the Cinquecento style is represented by Leiria (1551 etc.), the work of Afonso Álvares. His nephew Baltasar designed the Jesuit church of Oporto (c. 1590–1610) with its typically Mannerist, high and restless twin-tower façade. Also as in Spain, the Baroque was long in coming, but when it came it was less wild than in the neighbouring country; it influenced Brazil considerably (e.g., the Seminary at Santarém, 1676). The leading Baroque architects were João Turriano (1610–79) and João Antunes (1683–1734), and the most completely Baroque town is Aveiro. Octagonal and round plans are typical of Portuguese Baroque churches. The climax of the Baroque is well within the C18. It appears in the buildings of Niccolò NASONI (d. 1773), a native of Italy – such as the palace of Freixo and several churches at Oporto – and the buildings of J. F. LUDOVICE (c. 1670–1752), a native of Germany – such as the grand abbey of Mafra (1717–70) and the chancel of Évora Cathedral (1716–46).

Opposition to the Baroque set in about the middle of the C18. There were two centres: Oporto, where the large hospital is by John CARR of York (design 1796) and the Terceiros Church has decoration inspired by Robert ADAM; and Lisbon, where rebuilding (to a plan) after the disastrous earthquake of 1755 was done on French principles. The most spectacular piece of the rebuilding is the Terreiro do Paço, the large square facing the Tejo.

POST, George Browne (1837–1913), graduated in civil engineering and then worked in HUNT's office. He conducted his own practice from 1860 and started again after the war in 1868. Post was an eclectic, without commitment to any one style in particular. He was interested in structure and planning, and late in life was partly responsible for evolving the standard American hotel plan with a bath to every room, a system which is complete in the Statler Hotel at Buffalo (1911–12). He did a number of millionaires' residences (Cornelius Vanderbilt, 1889 and 1895) and several prominent office buildings in New York, e.g., the Equitable Building of 1869 (the first with lifts), the New York Times and Pulitzer Buildings (both 1889), and the St Paul Building (1897–9) which, with its twenty-two storeys, was the tallest in New York at that time.

POST, Pieter (1608–69), began as van CAMPEN's right-hand man at the Mauritshuis and Amsterdam Town Hall. He became a leading exponent of Dutch PALLADIANISM, an unpretentious, placid, and economic form of classicism, characterized by its use of brick with stone dressings and straightforward, almost diagrammatic use of pilasters. His masterpiece was the Huis-ten-Bosch near The Hague (1645–51, exterior ruined by C18 additions: interior decoration supervised by van Campen and C. Huygens), but the small Weigh-house at Leiden (1657), with its Tuscan pilasters on a rusticated base and supporting a simple pediment, is more typical. The Town Hall of Maastricht (begun 1659) is more ambitious. His style had great influence, and was later imported into England by Hugh MAY and others.

POSTERN. A small gateway, sometimes concealed, at the back of a castle, town, or monastery.

POWELL & MOYA (A. J. Philip Powell and John Hidalgo Moya, b. 1921 and 1920) established themselves by winning the City of Westminster competition for the large housing estate in Pimlico, later named Churchill Gardens (1946). The clarity, precision, and directness of their style has been maintained in all their later work, such as the Mayfield School in Putney, London (1956), the Princess Margaret Hospital at Swindon (1957 etc.), the ingenious sets for Brasenose College, Oxford (1956 etc.), the Festival Theatre at Chichester (1962), and large additions to St John's College, Cambridge (completed 1967), and Christ Church, Oxford (completed 1968).

PRANDTAUER, Jakob (1660–1726), was the architect of Melk (1702–14), perhaps the most impressive of all Baroque abbeys. The church, with its undulating façade, many-pinnacled towers, and bold dome, is clasped between two long ranges of monastic buildings which stretch forward to form a courtyard. Prandtauer took every advantage of the unusually dramatic site above the Danube to create a picturesque group of buildings which seems to rise out of the rock. The interior of the church (completed by other architects) is rich and *mouvementé*, with an almost Gothic sense of height. Prandtauer's other works are less exciting: the church at Sonntagberg (1706–17), a smaller version of Melk; completion of CARLONE's church at Christkindl; the magnificent open stairway (1706–14) and Marmorsaal or Marble Hall (1718–24) at St Florian near Vienna;

the priory of Dürnstein (begun 1717); the little hunting-lodge of Hohenbrunn (1725–9); alterations to the Gothic cathedral at St-Pölten (1722) and town-houses in St-Pölten. He belonged to an ancient tradition of master masons and (unlike HILDEBRANDT) supervised every stage of the works entrusted to him. Close sympathy with his religious patrons is suggested by his buildings no less than by his personal piety. He was a member of a lay confraternity and contributed handsomely to the expense of building his parish church at St-Pölten (1722) and town-houses in St-Pölten.

PRATT, Sir Roger (1620–84), a gentleman amateur, learned and widely travelled, was the most gifted of JONES's followers. His few buildings were very influential, but have all been destroyed or altered. At Coleshill (1650, now destroyed), Kingston Lacy (1663–5, altered by BARRY), and Horseheath (1663–5, destroyed) he invented the type of house later erroneously called the 'Wren' type. Clarendon House, London (1664–7, destroyed), was the first great classical house in London and was widely imitated and copied, e.g., at Belton House, Lincolnshire, by Stanton (1684–6).

PRECAST CONCRETE. Concrete components cast in a factory or on the site before being placed in position.

PREFABRICATION. The manufacture of whole buildings or components in a factory or casting yard for transportation to the site. *See also* INDUSTRIALIZED BUILDING.

PRESBYTERY. The part of the church which lies east of the choir and where the high altar is placed.

PRESTRESSED CONCRETE. A development of ordinary REINFORCED CONCRETE. The reinforcing steel is replaced by wire cables in ducts, so positioned that compression can be induced in the tension area of the concrete before it is loaded. This is done by stretching or tensioning the cables before or after casting the concrete. It results in more efficient use of materials and greater economy.

PRICE, Sir Uvedale (1747–1829), landscape gardening theorist, was a friend of REPTON and R. P. KNIGHT, whom he joined in a revolt against the 'Capability' BROWN style. In reply to Knight's poem *The Landscape* he published a three-volume *Essay on the Picturesque* (1794), which defined the PICTURESQUE as an aesthetic category distinct from the Sublime and the Beautiful as defined by Burke. His approach was more practical than Knight's and laid great stress on the need for landscape gardeners to study the works of the great landscape painters.

PRIMATICCIO, Francesco (1504/5–70), was primarily a decorative painter and sculptor and, as such, head of the First School of Fontainebleau. His few buildings date from towards the end of his career, notably the Aile de la Belle Cheminée at Fontainebleau (1568) and the Chapelle des Valois at St Denis, largely built after his death by BULLANT and now destroyed.

PRINCIPAL, *see* ROOF.

PROFILE. The section of a MOULDING or, more generally, the contour or outline of a building or any part of it.

PRONAOS. The vestibule of a Greek or Roman temple, enclosed by side walls and a range of columns in front.

PROPYLAEUM. The entrance gateway to an enclosure (usually temple precincts), as on the Acropolis at Athens.

PROSCENIUM. 1. In a Greek or Roman theatre, the stage on which the action took place. 2. In a modern theatre, the space between the curtain and orchestra, sometimes including the arch and frontispiece facing the auditorium.

PROSTYLE. Having free-standing columns in a row, as often in a PORTICO.

PROTHESIS. In Byzantine architecture, the room attached to or enclosed in the church and serving for the prepara-tion and storage of the species of the Eucharist before Mass; generally used for the storage of the Eucharist after Mass.

PROUVÉ, Jean (b. 1901). Trained as a metal-craftsman and now one of the masters of light-metal construction, a fervent believer in industrialized production not only of parts but of whole buildings (housing estate of small units made of aluminium, at Meudon, 1949). He has worked as a consultant and collaborator with Baudouin, Lodz, Lopez, Zehrfuss and others, but is on his own capable of great architectural elegance (Buvette, Evian, 1957).

PSEUDO-DIPTERAL. In classical architecture, a temple planned to be DIPTERAL but lacking the inner range of columns.

PSEUDO-PERIPTERAL. In classical architecture, a temple with porticos at either end and engaged columns or pilasters along the sides.

PTEROMA. In a Greek temple, the space between the walls and colonnades.

PUGIN, Augustus Welby Northmore (1812–52). His father, Augustus Charles (1762–1832), came from France to London in 1792, became a draughtsman in the office of NASH and later a draughtsman and editor of books on Gothic architecture (*Specimens*, 1821 onwards; *Gothic Ornaments*, 1831). The son helped on these, but soon received decorative and then architectural commissions. He designed furniture for Windsor Castle and stage sets for the theatre (*Kenilworth*, 1831) before he was twenty. He found himself shipwrecked off the Firth of Forth in 1830, got married in 1831, lost his wife one year later, got married again in 1833, lost his second wife in 1844, got married once more in 1849, and lost his mind in 1851.

He had a passion for the sea, and, after his conversion to Catholicism in 1834, a greater, more fervent passion for a Catholic architecture, which had to be Gothic of the richest 'Second

Pointed', i.e., late c13 to early c14 in style. He leaped to fame and notoriety with his book *Contrasts* (1836), a plea for Catholicism illustrated by brilliant comparisons between the meanness, cruelty, and vulgarity of buildings of his own day – classicist or minimum Gothic – and the glories of the Catholic past. Later he wrote more detailed and more closely considered books (*The True Principles of Pointed or Christian Architecture*, 1841, etc.), and in them showed a deeper understanding than anyone before of the connections between Gothic style and structure and of the function of each member. From these books he even appears a founder father of FUNCTIONALISM, though this is true only with qualifications.

His buildings mostly suffer from lack of means. He was rarely allowed to show in stone and wood the sparkling lavishness he could achieve on paper. He was as interested in furnishings, altars, screens, stained glass, metalwork, as in the building itself. This is how BARRY got him to work for the Houses of Parliament, where not only the Gothic details of the façades but even such fitments as inkstands and hatstands were designed by Pugin. He was a fast and ardent draughtsman. Perhaps his best churches are Cheadle in Staffordshire (1841-6), the cathedral of Nottingham (1842-4), and St Augustine, Ramsgate (1846–51), which he paid for himself and which stands next to his own house. As against earlier neo-Gothic churches, Pugin's are usually archaeologically correct, but often have their tower asymmetrically placed, and this started the calculated asymmetry of most of the best English c19 church design.

PULPIT. An elevated stand of stone or wood for a preacher or reader, which first became general in the later Middle Ages (the AMBO was used in the early Middle Ages). Often elaborately carved, and sometimes with an acoustic canopy above the preacher called a SOUNDING BOARD or TESTER. Occasionally found against the outside wall of a church.

PULPITUM. A stone screen in a major church erected to shut off the choir from the nave. It could also be used as a backing for the return choir stalls.

PULVIN. In Byzantine architecture, a DOSSERET above the capital supporting the arch above.

PULVINATED. Convex in profile; a term usually applied to a FRIEZE.

PURBECK MARBLE. A dark conglomerate from the Isle of Purbeck capable of receiving a high polish. In fashion in England from the later c12 onwards and favoured particularly in the c13. Used for COMPOUND PIERS in churches. Purbeck shafts in conjunction with shafts of normal limestone give a striking effect of light and dark. Also used for effigies all over England.

PURLIN, see ROOF.

PYCNOSTYLE. With an arrangement of columns set $1\frac{1}{2}$ times their diameter apart. *See also* ARAEOSTYLE; DIASTYLE; EUSTYLE; SYSTYLE.

PYLON. In ancient Egyptian architecture, the rectangular, truncated, pyramidal towers flanking the gateway of a temple; also, more loosely, any high isolated structure used decoratively or to mark a boundary.

PYRAMID. In ancient Egyptian architecture, a sepulchral monument in the form of a huge stone structure with a square base and sloping sides meeting at an apex: also, more loosely, any structure of this form.

PYTHIOS (*fl.* 353–334 B.C.). Architect and theorist working in Asia Minor. With Satyros he designed and wrote an account of the most famous and elaborate sepulchral monument of antiquity, the richly sculptured Mausoleum built for the Carian satrap Mausolos at Halicarnassus and numbered among the seven wonders of the world (begun before 353 B.C. and finished after 350; sculptured fragments now in the British Museum). He was also the architect of the large temple of Athena Polias at Priene (dedicated 334; fragments now in Berlin and in British Museum) in which the Ionic order was thought to have achieved its canonical form. In a treatise on· this building (known to Vitruvius but now lost) he extolled the perfection of its proportions, criticized the Doric order and, apparently for the first time, recommended a wide training for the architect who, he said, 'should be able to do more in all the arts and sciences than those who, by their industry and exertions, bring single disciplines to the highest renown'.

Q

QUADRANGLE. A rectangular court-yard enclosed by buildings on all sides and sometimes within a large building complex. The arrangement is often found in colleges and schools.

QUADRATURA. *Trompe l'œil* architectural painting of walls and ceilings. In the C17 and C18 it was frequently executed by travelling painters who specialized in it and were known as *quadraturisti*.

QUADRIGA. A sculptured group of a chariot drawn by four horses, often used to crown a monument or façade.

QUARENGHI, Giacomo (1744–1817), a very prolific architect, was much admired and patronized by Catherine II of Russia. Born near Bergamo, he went to Rome in 1763 to study painting, but soon turned to architecture. He designed the interior of S. Scolastica, Subiaco (1771–7), in a light, elegant vein of neo-classicism. In 1776 he accepted an invitation to St Petersburg where he spent the rest of his life. His first important building is the English Palace, Peterhof (1781–9, destroyed), a sternly aloof Palladian house with no decoration apart from a vast projecting portico on one side and a recessed loggia on the other. He employed a similar formula for the State Bank (1783–90) and the Academy of Sciences (1783–9), both in Leningrad. The Hermitage Theatre, Leningrad (1783–7), is smaller and richer. His later work is more accomplished and excellent in its precision and clarity of mass, e.g., Imperial Pharmacy, Leningrad (1789–96), Alexander Palace, Tsarkoe Selo (1792–6), the Riding School (1805–7) and Smolny Institute (1806–7), both in Leningrad.

QUARRY (or QUARREL). A small, usually diamond-shaped pane, or a square one placed diagonally, with which medieval leaded windows were glazed. The term can also apply to any small quadrangular opening in the TRACERY of a window. The word probably derives from the French *carré*. Various devices and patterns were painted on quarries, particularly during the Perpendicular period.

QUATREFOIL, *see* FOIL.

QUEEN ANNE ARCHITECTURE, *see* ENGLISH ARCHITECTURE.

QUEEN-POST, *see* ROOF.

QUIBLA. The direction in which every Moslem turns when he prays: originally towards Jerusalem, but changed by Mohammed in 624 to Mecca.

QUIRK. A sharp v-shaped incision in a moulding and between mouldings.

QUOINS. The dressed stones at the corners of buildings, usually laid so that their faces are alternately large and small. From the French *coin* (corner). *See figure 68.*

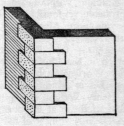

Fig. 68. Quoins

R

RABBET. A rectangular recess made along an ARRIS: any channel or groove cut along the face of a piece of stone, wood, etc., so as to receive a tongue or edge of another piece.

RABIRIUS (*fl.* 81–96 A.D.). Roman architect who, according to Martial, was employed by Domitian to build the palace on the Palatine in Rome which became the permanent residence of Roman emperors (the word palace is derived from it) and was still in use in the late c6. Enough survives to reveal the grandeur of this vast building or complex of buildings, erected on two levels of the hill and incorporating a hippodrome, libraries and courtyard gardens as well as innumerable state and private apartments. It was both a symbol of the Emperor's power and a perfect setting for the ceremony of his court (poets were quick to associate the several domes above the official rooms with the arc of the heavens). With its rich decorations and many fountains splashing in marble lined courtyards it was the epitome of luxurious opulence. He has been credited with many other buildings, without evidence, but was probably responsible for Domitian's villa near Albano, of which little survives.

RADBURN PLANNING. A planning idea conceived in the United States after the First World War by a group including Lewis Mumford, Clarence Stein, Henry Wright, and others. It was first tried out at Radburn, New Jersey. The main object of the plan is the complete segregation of traffic and pedestrians. Areas known as super-blocks are ringed by roads from which cul-de-sac service roads lead to the interior. All paths and walks linking the blocks with each other and the town centre pass over or under the roads. Examples of towns planned under some such system are Välling-by, near Stockholm, and Cumbernauld, one of the NEW TOWNS in Scotland.

RAGUZZINI, Filippo (d. 1771). The most original and spirited Rococo architect in Rome, where he built the hospital and church of S. Gallicano (1725–6) and Piazza di S. Ignazio (1727–8). The latter is a masterpiece of scenic town planning.

RAINALDI, Carlo (1611–91), was born and lived in Rome. Son of a minor architect, Girolamo Rainaldi (1570–1655), he came into his own only after his father's death. He evolved a typically Roman grand manner notable for its lively scenic qualities and for its very personal mixture of Mannerist and North Italian features with the High Baroque style of his great contemporaries, especially BERNINI. With his father he began S. Agnese in Piazza Navona, Rome, on a conservative Greek cross plan in 1652, but was dismissed in the following year when BORROMINI took over the work. His principal buildings are all in Rome – S. Maria in Campitelli (1663–7); the façade of S. Andrea della Valle (1661–5); the exterior apse of S. Maria Maggiore (1673); and the artfully symmetrical pair of churches in Piazza del Popolo, S. Maria in Monte Santo and S. Maria de' Miracoli (1662 etc.), which punctuate the beginning of the three main streets radiating into the centre of the city (Bernini replaced him as architect of the former in 1673).

RAINWATER HEAD. A box-shaped structure of metal, usually cast iron or lead, and sometimes elaborately decorated, in which water from a gutter or parapet is collected and discharged into a down-pipe.

RAMP. 1. A slope joining two different levels. 2. Part of a staircase handrail which rises at a steeper angle than normal, usually where winders (*see* STAIR) are used.

RAMPART. A stone or earth wall surrounding a castle, fortress, or fortified city for defence purposes.

RAMSEY, *see* WILLIAM OF RAMSEY.

RAPHAEL (Raffaello Sanzio, 1483–1520). The greatest exponent of High Renaissance classicism in architecture as well as in painting. His buildings are few, but they quickly took their place beside ancient Roman buildings and the late works of BRAMANTE as architectural models. Though he owed much to Bramante, his style is sweeter, softer, and simpler. Born in Urbino, he was trained as a painter under Pietro Perugino at Perugia. An early painting of *The Betrothal of the Virgin* (1504, Brera Gallery, Milan) is dominated by a domed building, which reveals an exquisite sensitivity to architecture and a particular interest in centrally planned structures. In 1508 he settled in Rome, where he was almost immediately employed by Pope Julius II to paint the Stanza della Segnatura in the Vatican, including *The School of Athens* with its wonderful architectural perspective of coffered vaults. His first building was S. Eligio degli Orefici, Rome (designed *c.* 1511–12, construction begun 1514. The dome was begun, probably under PERUZZI, in 1526 and completed in 1542: but the whole church was rebuilt, with a new dome, by Flaminio PONZIO in the early C17). He designed the Palazzo Bresciano-Costa, Rome (*c.* 1515, now demolished) and Palazzo Pandolfini, Florence (*c.* 1517, but executed by Giovanni Francesco Sangallo and, after 1530, by Aristotile Sangallo). These derive from Bramante's Palazzo Caprini with notable variations, e.g., unbroken horizontal lines of rustication on the basement,

and at Palazzo Costa alternate triangular and segmental pediments above the windows on the first floor, between clusters of three pilasters. (Palazzo Vidoni-Caffarelli, Rome, of *c.* 1525 has often been attributed to Raphael but is not by him.)

In 1515 he was appointed Superintendent of Roman Antiquities and probably proposed a scheme (also attributed to Bramante) for measuring and drawing all the Roman remains and restoring a large number of them. The most notable result of his archaeological interests was the design for Villa Madama, Rome (begun 1517, but never completed), with a circular courtyard and numerous apsed and niched rooms inspired by the Roman *thermae*. The only part completed was decorated with exquisitely subtle stucco reliefs and GROTESQUE paintings by Giovanni da Udine and GIULIO ROMANO, derived from such Imperial Roman buildings as Nero's Golden House. Here Raphael re-created the elegance of Roman interior decoration as effectively as Bramante had reproduced the solemnity and monumental grandeur of Roman architecture. He was appointed architect of St Peter's (1514) with Fra GIOCONDO and A. da SANGALLO, and drew up a basilican variant to Bramante's plan. His centrally planned Chigi Chapel in S. Maria del Popolo, Rome, of 1512–13 was completed by BERNINI.

RASTRELLI, Bartolommeo Francesco (1700–71), the leading Rococo architect in Russia, was the son of an Italian sculptor who went to St Petersburg with LE BLOND in 1716. He studied in Paris under de COTTE and his style is, with occasional Russian overtones, purely French. In 1741 he was appointed official architect to the Tsarina Elizabeth Petrovna, for whom all his main buildings were designed: Summer Palace, St Petersburg (1741–4, destroyed); Anichkov Palace on the Nevski Prospekt, St Petersburg

(1744); Peterhof (1747–52), a colossal enlargement of Le Blond's building with lavish if slightly over-ripe Rococo decoration inside; the Cathedral of St Andrew, Kiev (1747–67); and the curious Russo-Rococo Smolny Convent, St Petersburg (1748–55). His masterpieces are the Great Palace, Tsarskoe Selo, now called Pushkino (1749–56), and the Winter Palace, St Petersburg (1754–62), both with immensely long façades, and both painted turquoise-blue, with white trim. But he is seen at his best in the delicate little pavilions he designed for Tsarskoe Selo. He was an exquisite miniaturist, usually forced to work on a heroic scale.

RAVELIN. In military architecture, an outwork formed of two faces of a salient angle and constructed beyond the main ditch and in front of the CURTAIN WALL.

RAYMOND, Antonin, see WRIGHT.

RAYMOND DU TEMPLE (active c. 1360–1405). Master of the King's Works in Masonry, and also master mason of Notre Dame in Paris. The king was godfather to his son.

REAR ARCH. The arch on the inside of a wall spanning a doorway or window opening.

REAR VAULT. The small vaulted space between the glass of a window and the inner face of the wall, when the wall is thick and there is a deep SPLAY.

REBATE. A continuous rectangular notch or groove cut on an edge, so that a plank, door, etc. may be fitted into it.

REDAN. A small RAVELIN.

REDMAN, Henry (d. 1528), was the son of the master mason of Westminster Abbey, and is first found working there in 1495. He succeeded his father at the Abbey in 1516 and also worked for the king, holding the post of King's Master Mason from 1519, jointly with William VERTUE, and in the end alone. He was called in with Vertue for an opinion at King's College Chapel, Cambridge, in 1509,

and again appears with him at Eton for the design of Lupton's Tower in 1516. He was also Cardinal Wolsey's architect, and may have designed Hampton Court. At Christ Church, Oxford (Cardinal College), he was, jointly with John Lebons or Lovyns, in charge from the beginning (1525).

REEDING. Decoration consisting of parallel convex mouldings touching one another.

REGINALD OF ELY (d. 1471). First master mason, and so probably the designer, of King's College Chapel, Cambridge (begun 1446). However, his design did not include the present fan vaulting; it seems that he intended a lierne vault (see VAULT) instead. Reginald in all probability designed Queens' College too (1446 etc.), and perhaps the archway of the Old Schools (begun 1470), now at Madingley Hall.

REGULUS. The short band between the TENIA and GUTTAE on a Doric ENTABLATURE.

REINFORCED CONCRETE. Since concrete is strong in compression and weak in tension, steel rods are inserted to take the tensile stresses which, in a simple beam, occur in the lower part; the concrete is thus reinforced.

RENAISSANCE. The Italian word rinascimento (rebirth) was already used by Renaissance writers themselves to indicate the restoration of ancient Roman standards and motifs. Today the term means Italian art and architecture from c. 1420 (BRUNELLESCHI) to the mid C16. It was replaced by MANNERISM and BAROQUE, though the old mistaken custom is still occasionally found of extending Renaissance to include the Baroque. In countries other than Italy the Renaissance started with the adoption of Italian Renaissance motifs, but the resulting styles – French Renaissance, German Renaissance, etc. – have little in common with the qualities of the Italian Renaissance, which are details of ancient Roman derivation and a sense of stability and poise.

See also CLASSICISM; and BELGIAN;
CZECHOSLOVAK; DUTCH;
FRENCH; GERMAN; HUNGARIAN;
ITALIAN; POLISH; RUSSIAN;
SPANISH; SWISS architecture.

RENDERING. The plastering of an outer
wall.

RENNIE, John (1761–1821), son of a
farmer, was trained by an inventive
millwright and then at Edinburgh
University. In 1784 he was put in
charge of installing the new Boulton
& Watt steam engine at the Albion
Works in London. In 1791 he set up
in business on his own. He was first
interested in canals (Kennet and
Avon), later also in fen drainage, har-
bours and docks, lighthouses, and also
bridges. He designed the Plymouth
Breakwater (begun 1806) and Waterloo Bridge (1810), as well as other
London bridges. His sons George
(1791–1866) and Sir John (1794–1874)
were both famous engineers too.

RENWICK, James (1818–95), the son
of an English engineer who emigrated
to America and became the most
prominent man in his field in the
United States, graduated at Columbia
College, New York, and became
famous as an architect of churches
(Grace Church, Broadway, 1843 etc.,
St Patrick's Cathedral, 1853–87).
His other best-known buildings are
the sweetly picturesque neo-Norman
Smithsonian Institution in Washington (1846), and Vassar College, an
essay in a free Renaissance mixture
(1865).

REPTON, Humphry (1752–1818), the
leading English landscape gardener of
the generation after BROWN, was
a contemporary of PRICE and
KNIGHT, with whose defence of
wildness and ruggedness, however, he
did not agree. The innovation of his
layouts, an innovation which pointed
forward into the C19, is the treatment
of the garden close to the house not
naturally and picturesquely, but formally with parterres and terraces, to
which in his late work he added such

'Victorian' motifs as rose-arbours,
aviaries etc. He also was responsible
for a certain amount of architectural
work though this was mostly left to
his sons John Adey (1775–1860) and
George (1786–1858). Repton had lived
as a country gentleman until a financial setback forced him to make a
living out of his passion for gardening.
He was at once successful, and the
total of parks and gardens treated by
him is in the neighbourhood of two
hundred. He wrote *Sketches and Hints
on Landscape Gardening* in 1795, *Observations on the Theory and Practice of
Landscape Gardening* in 1803, *An In-
quiry into the Changes of Taste in Landscape Gardening* in 1806, and *Fragments
on the Theory and Practice of Landscape
Gardening* in 1816. The term 'landscape gardening' is his.

REREDOS. A wall or screen, usually of
wood or stone, rising behind an altar,
and as a rule decorated.

RESPOND. A half-PIER bonded into a
wall and carrying one end of an arch;
often at the end of an ARCADE.

RETABLE. A shelf or ledge above the
back of an altar; also an altar-piece
either painted or carved, attached to
the back of an altar.

RETAINING WALL. A wall, usually
battered, which supports or retains a
weight of earth or water; also called a
revetment.

RETICULATED, *see* TRACERY.

RETRO-CHOIR. The space behind the
high altar in a major church.

RETURN. The side or part which falls
away, usually at right angles, from the
front or direct line of a structure. Two
particular uses of the term are: *a.* that
part of a dripstone or HOOD-MOULD
which, after running downwards,
turns off horizontally; *b.* the western
row of choir stalls which runs north–
south, set against the screen at the
west end of the choir.

REVEAL. That part of a JAMB which
lies between the glass or door and the
outer wall surface. If cut diagonally,
it is called a SPLAY.

REVETMENT, *see* RETAINING WALL.

REYNS, *see* HENRY OF REYNS.

RIB. A projecting band on a ceiling or vault, usually structural but sometimes purely decorative, separating the CELLS of a groined VAULT.

RIBBON DEVELOPMENT. The construction of continuous strings of houses along main roads. This was responsible for much spoliation of the English countryside during the first quarter of this century, but was largely halted by the passing of the Ribbon Development Act of 1935.

RIBERA, Pedro de (*c.* 1683–1742), the leading Late Baroque architect in Madrid, carried the CHURRIGUER-ESQUE style to its ultimate point of elaboration. In the neo-classical period he was held up for derision by one authority, who published a complete list of his buildings as an object lesson to students, with the result that his *œuvre* is unusually well documented. Of Castilian origin, he began working for the city council of Madrid in 1719, and became its official architect in 1726. With the exception of the tower of Salamanca Cathedral (*c.* 1738) and a chapel attached to S. Antonio, Ávila (1731), all his buildings are in Madrid. His most celebrated work is the doorway to the Hospicio S. Fernando (*c.* 1722), an overpowering extravaganza of boldly and somewhat coarsely carved draperies, festoons, top-heavy *estípites*, urns, and flames rising in staccato leaps above the roofline. In 1718 he built the little church of the Virgen del Puerto, which has an exterior like a garden pavilion, with a picturesque bell-shaped spire, and an octagonal interior with a *camarín* behind the altar. Other works include the Toledo Bridge (designed 1719, built 1723–4), with elaborately carved tabernacles perched above the arches; the Montserrat Church (1720, incomplete); and S. Cayetano (1722–32, incomplete).

RICCHINO, Francesco Maria (1583–1658). The most important Lombard architect of the early Baroque. His S. Giuseppe in Milan (1607–30) broke away from the prevailing academic Mannerism as decisively as did MADERNO'S S. Susanna in Rome (1603). Both in its plan (a fusion of two centralized units) and in its aedicule façade S. Giuseppe is entirely forward-looking. Nearly all his later churches have been destroyed. Of his surviving works the best are the concave façades of the Collegio Elvetico, Milan (1627), and the Palazzo di Brera, Milan (1651–86), with its noble courtyard. His vast central cortile of the Ospedale Maggiore, Milan, was designed with G.-B. Pessina (1625–49, restored 1950s).

RICHARDSON, Henry Hobson (1838–86), studied at Harvard, and then studied architecture at the École des Beaux Arts in Paris (1859–62), where, after the Civil War, he returned to work under LABROUSTE and then HITTORF. Back at Boston he started a practice, and in 1870 won the competition for the Brattle Square Church, in 1872 that for Trinity Church. These established him as an original, and at the same time a learned, architect. His favourite style was a very massive, masculine Romanesque, inspired by architects such as VAU-DREMER. But the tower of the Brattle Square Church, with its frieze of figures right below the machicolated top, is Romanesque only in so far as it is round-arched. In 1882 he travelled in Europe, and only then saw French and North-Spanish Romanesque buildings at first hand. The Romanesque suited him as a style: it was direct and powerful, and thus capable of fulfilling American requirements Rockfaced rustication was also a favourite with him. In fact, he was always attracted by utilitarian jobs. The most monumental of these is the Marshall Field Wholesale Building in Chicago (1885). He also designed small railway stations in the eighties. Before then he had done some small libraries (North Easton, 1877; Quincy, 1880), two buildings for Harvard (Sever Hall, 1878, which is remarkably independent of any stylistic imitation; Austin Hall, 1881, which is Romanesque), and also some private houses (the shingle-faced, very original and forward-pointing Stoughton House at Cambridge, 1882–3; the Glessner House at Chicago, 1885). Richardson was a *bon vivant*, a designer of zest and conviction. His Romanesque was soon widely imitated – to its detriment – but helped greatly in liberating America from the indiscriminate imitation of European revivals. Among his pupils were MCKIM and WHITE, and he also influenced ROOT and SULLIVAN decisively.

RICKMAN, Thomas (1776–1841), moved late from medicine and business into architecture. From sketching and writing about old churches he went on to open a practice as an architect. This was in 1817, the year in which he also published some lectures under the title *An Attempt to discriminate the Styles of Architecture in England.* This little book established our terms Early English, Decorated, and Perpendicular. As a church architect Rickman could be remarkably conscientious in trying to create credible Gothic interiors. Such churches as those at Hampton Lucy (1822–6) and Oulton (1827–9) must have struck his contemporaries as archaeologically convincing. They were done in partnership with Henry Hutchinson, his former pupil (1831), who was also largely responsible for Rickman's most familiar building: New Court, St John's College, Cambridge (1826–31), with the attached so-called Bridge of Sighs. Rickman was a Quaker, but late in life turned Irvingite.

RIDGE. The horizontal line formed by the junction of two sloping surfaces of a roof. *See figure 69.*

RIDGE-RIB, *see* VAULT.

RIDINGER or RIEDINGER, Georg (1568–after 1616). Leading German Renaissance architect, a contemporary of Elias HOLL, Heinrich SCHICKHARDT and Jacob WOLFF. His masterpiece was Schloss Aschaffenburg (1605–14, destroyed but rebuilt) built for the Archbishop of Mainz, Ulrich von Gemmingen (the patron of Matthias Grünewald) and his successor Johann Schickard von Kronberg. The square ground-plan of four wings and corner towers round a central courtyard was probably derived from French château design through DU CERCEAU's engravings. Though still rather medieval and fortress-like, the elevations were articulated with strong horizontal mouldings and occasional Netherlandish ornamentation. Ridinger thought it 'heroic'. It had great and longlasting influence in Germany, e.g., on Petrini's (1624–1701) Marquardsburg of almost a hundred years later.

RIETH, Benedict (d. 1534). German mason working as Master of the King's Works in Bohemia. His *chef-d'œuvre* at Prague is the Vladislav Hall in the castle with its intricate lierne vault, including curved ribs, and its curious italizing details of windows and doorways, Quattrocento in style, but including strange Gothic twists. This work must belong to the years 1485–1502. By Rieth also may be the Royal Oratory in Prague Cathedral, fancifully Late Gothic (*c.* 1490–93). It has ribs in the form of naturalistically imitated branches. At St Barbara, Kutná Hora, Rieth altered the existing plans for the nave and aisles, and designed the vault, a vault whose ribs form a net of lozenges (1512 etc.). Equally intricate is the vault of Louny (1520 etc.).

RIETVELD, Gerrit Thomas (1888–1964), was the son of a joiner to whom he was apprenticed. He was later in the cabinet-making business. He came into contact with De Stijl in 1919. His most famous design for a building is the Schroeder House at Utrecht (1924). With the growth of rationalism in architecture he was eclipsed, but once more received work when, in the fifties, the style of the twenties began to be revived.

RINALDI, Antonio (c. 1709–94). One of the leading Late Rococo architects in Russia. His main works are the Chinese Palace, Oranienbaum (1762–8), with a pretty CHINOISERIE interior, and the Marble Palace, Leningrad (1768–72), derived from JUVARRA's Palazzo d'Ormea, but rather more austere and classical, faced with red granite and grey Siberian marble. It is of interest also as the first ever example of the use of iron beams in architecture.

RINCEAU. An ornamental motif consisting of scrolls of foliage.

RISER, see STAIR.

ROBERT DE LUZARCHES. The master mason who began Amiens Cathedral in 1220.

ROCOCO ARCHITECTURE. The Rococo is not a style in its own right, like the BAROQUE, but the last phase of the Baroque. The great breaks in European art and thought take place at the beginning of the Baroque and again at the beginning of NEO-CLASSICISM. The Rococo is chiefly represented by a type of decoration initiated in France, by lightness in colour and weight, where the Baroque had been dark and ponderous, and, in South Germany and Austria, by a great spatial complexity, which, however, is the direct continuation of the Baroque complexity of BORROMINI and GUARINI. The new decoration is often asymmetrical and abstract – the term for this is *rocaille* – with shell-like, coral-like forms and many c- and s-curves. Naturalistic flowers, branches, trees, whole rustic scenes, and also Chinese motifs are sometimes playfully introduced into *rocaille*. In French external architecture the Rococo is only noticeable by a greater elegance and delicacy. England has no Rococo, apart from occasional interiors. But the playful use of Chinese,

Indian, and also Gothic forms in garden furnishings can well be ascribed to Rococo influence.

RODRÍGUEZ, Ventura (1717–85), the leading Spanish Late Baroque architect, began under SACCHETTI at the Royal Palace, Madrid, and was employed by the Crown until 1759. His first important work was the Church of S. Marcos, Madrid (1749–53), built on an oval plan derived from BERNINI's S. Andrea al Quirinale, Rome. In 1753 he built the Transparente in Cuenca Cathedral. In 1760 he became professor at the Madrid academy and his work began to assume a more dogmatic appearance. The Royal College of Surgery, Barcelona (1761), is almost gaunt in its severe renunciation of ornament. His noblest work is the façade of Pamplona Cathedral (1783), with a great Corinthian portico flanked by square towers, archaeologically correct in detail yet still reminiscent of early C18 Rome.

ROLL MOULDING. Moulding of semicircular or more than semicircular section.

ROMAN ARCHITECTURE. Whereas GREEK ARCHITECTURE is tectonic, built up from a logical series of horizontals and verticals (the Doric temple has been called 'sublimated carpentry'), Roman architecture is plastic with much use of rounded forms (arch, vault, and dome), so that buildings tend to look as if they had been made of concrete poured into a mould. In Greek and HELLENISTIC ARCHITECTURE the column was the most important member; in Rome the column was frequently degraded to merely decorative uses, while the wall became the essential element. Hence the Roman predilection for the PSEUDO-PERIPTERAL temple (Temple of Male Fortune, Rome, mid CI B.C.; Maison Carrée, Nîmes, begun c. 19 B.C.), for the Corinthian order, and for elaborately carved ENTABLATURES and other ornamentation. It was the development of concrete used in conjunction with brick that made possible the construction of the great Roman domes and vaults. Concrete proved as economical of material as of labour, since the masons' rubble could be used for filling. Surfaces were either stuccoed or clad in marble. The earliest concrete dome in C2 B.C. (Stabian Baths, Pompeii), while the earliest large-scale concrete vault is that of the Tabularium in Rome of 78 B.C., where the half-columns are used ornamentally – the first important instance of the divorce of decoration and function. The concrete barrel vault on a large scale appears in Nero's Golden House, Rome, by the architect SEVERUS (mid CI A.D.) and in the palace buildings by RABIRIUS for Domitian on the Palatine in Rome (late CI A.D.). Later vaulted buildings of importance include the Baths of Caracalla (c. A.D. 215), Baths of Diocletian (A.D. 306), and the Basilica Nova of Maxentius (A.D. 310–13), all in Rome.

Roman architecture reached its apogee in the Pantheon, Rome (c. A.D. 100–25), with a dome 141 ft in diameter), which is both a feat of engineering and a masterpiece of simple yet highly satisfying proportions – it is based on a sphere, the height of the walls being equal to the radius of the dome. Comparison of the Pantheon with the Parthenon reveals the contrast between the tectonic and extrovert nature of Greek and the plastic, introvert nature of Roman architecture. This is equally evident in the most typically Roman of all buildings, the BASILICA, which, with its interior colonnades, is like a Greek temple turned outside in. Other typically Roman buildings are: THERMAE, with their rich decoration and complicated spatial play; AMPHITHEATRES, of which the Colosseum, Rome (A.D. 69–79) is the largest; triumphal arches, a purely decorative type of building of which the earliest

recorded examples were temporary structures of the C2 B.C. Always of the Corinthian or Composite ORDER, these arches vary from the relative severity of that at Susa near Turin to the elaboration of that at Orange in the south of France (c. 30 B.C.). City gateways were hardly less profusely decorated, e.g., Porta Nigra at Trier (late C3 or early C4 A.D.).

In domestic architecture three types were developed; the *domus* or townhouse; the *insula* or multi-storey apartment house or tenement block; and the *villa* or surburban or country house. The *domus* derived from the Greek and Hellenistic house and was usually of one storey only and inward-looking, the rooms being grouped axially and symmetrically around an atrium and one or more peristyle courts. The street façade was plain and without windows, or was let off as shops, as can still be seen at Pompeii. The *insula* had several identical but separate floors and was often vaulted throughout with concrete construction. A decree of Augustus limited their height in Rome to 75 ft. During the Neronian rebuilding of Rome after the fire of 64 A.D. new quarters of *insulae* were laid out symmetrically along arcaded streets and round public squares. The *villa* derived from the traditional farm-house and was more casual and straggling in plan than the *domus*. It was also more outward-looking, and great variety in planning and room shapes was attained in the more luxurious examples. The exteriors were enlivened with porticos and colonnades, rooms were designed to catch the view, or the sun in winter or the shade in summer, as at Pliny's villa at Laurentum.

Hadrian's fantastic sprawling villa at Tivoli (c. A.D. 123) illustrates almost the whole range of Imperial Roman architecture at its sophisticated best. Indeed it is perhaps over-sophisticated already. The last great architectural monument of the Roman Empire is Diocletian's Palace at Split in Yugoslavia (*c.* A.D. 300), built after the Pax Romana had begun to disintegrate. Yet even here the Roman genius for experimentation was still at work. Certain decorative elements, e.g., engaged columns standing on isolated corbels, anticipate the language of BYZANTINE ARCHITECTURE.

ROMANESQUE ARCHITECTURE. The style current until the advent of GOTHIC. Some experts place its origins in the C7, others in the C10: the former view includes CAROLINGIAN in Romanesque architecture, the latter places the beginning of Romanesque at the time of the rising of the Cluniac order in France and the Ottonian Empire in Germany. The first view also includes Anglo-Saxon architecture, the second identifies the Romanesque in Britain with the Norman.

The Romanesque in the Northern countries is the style of the round arch. It is also characterized by clear, easily comprehended schemes of planning and elevation, the plan with staggered apses (*en échelon*) at the east end of churches, the plan with an ambulatory and radiating chapels, plans (mainly in Germany) with square bays in nave, transepts, and chancel, and square bays in the aisles one quarter the area. The compositions of the walls also stress clearly marked compartments, e.g., in the shafts which in Norman churches run from the ground right up to the ceiling beams.

The Early Romanesque had not yet the skill to vault major spans. Experiments began about 1000, but remained rare till after 1050. Then various systems were developed which differentiate regional groups: tunnel vaults in France, often pointed (Burgundy, Provence), and also in Spain; groin vaults in Germany; domes in the South-west of France; rib vaults at Durham and in Italy. The spread of the rib vault and the pointed vault, however, is usually a sign of the approaching Gothic style. In the exteriors the two-tower façade plus a tower over the crossing is most typical of England and Normandy, whereas screen façades with no towers are characteristic of the South of France, and a multitude of towers over the west as well as the east parts is typical of Germany. *See also* ENGLISH ARCHITECTURE, GERMAN ARCHITECTURE, ITALIAN ARCHITECTURE, SPANISH ARCHITECTURE.

ROMANO, *see* GIULIO ROMANO.

ROOD. Originally the Saxon word for a cross or crucifix. In churches this was set up at the east end of the nave, flanked by figures of the Virgin and St John. It was usually wooden, and fixed to a special beam stretching from RESPOND to respond of the CHANCEL ARCH, above the ROOD LOFT. Sometimes the rood is painted on the wall above the chancel arch.

ROOD LOFT. A gallery built above the ROOD SCREEN, often to carry the ROOD or other images and candles; approached by stairs either of wood or built in the wall. Rood lofts were introduced in the C15, and many were destroyed in the Reformation.

ROOD SCREEN. A screen below the ROOD, set across the east end of the nave and shutting off the chancel.

ROOF

Elements

Braces. Diagonal subsidiary timbers inserted to strengthen the framing of a roof. They can be straight or arched (the arched brace is a refined version of the CRUCK), and connect either a tie-beam with the wall below, or a collar-beam with the rafters below.

Collar-beam. A tie-beam applied higher up the slope of the roof.

Crown-post. A post standing on a tie-beam and supporting a collar-purlin running immediately under the collar-beam of a rafter roof. Frequently four braces or struts spring from the crown-post to the collar-purlin and the collar-beam.

Hammerbeam. A horizontal bracket, usually projecting at the wall plate level, to carry arched braces and struts, and supported by braces. Hammerbeams lessen the span and thus allow shorter timbers. They also help to reduce lateral pressure.

King-post. A post standing on a tie- or collar-beam and rising to the apex of the roof where it supports a ridge-piece.

Principals. The main rafters of a roof, usually corresponding to the main bay divisions of the space below.

Purlin. A horizontal timber laid parallel with the wall plate and the ridge beam some way up the slope of the roof, resting on the principal rafters and forming an intermediate support for the common rafters.

Queen-posts. A pair of upright posts placed symmetrically on a tie-beam (or collar-beam), connecting it with the rafters above.

Rafter or *common rafter.* A roof timber sloping up from the wall plate to the RIDGE.

Strut. A timber, either upright, connecting the tie-beam with the rafter above it, or sloping, connecting a king- or queen-post to the rafter.

Tie-beam. The horizontal transverse beam in a roof, connecting the feet of the rafters, usually at the height of the wall plate, to counteract the thrust.

Wall plate. A timber laid longitudinally on the top of a wall to receive the ends of the rafters.

Wind-braces. Short, usually arched, braces connecting the purlins with the principal rafter and the wall plate, and fixed flat against the rafters. Wind-braces strengthen the roof area by increasing resistance to wind pressure. They are often made to look decorative by foiling and cusping.

See figure 69.

Types

A *Belfast* or *bowstring roof* is constructed with curved timber trusses

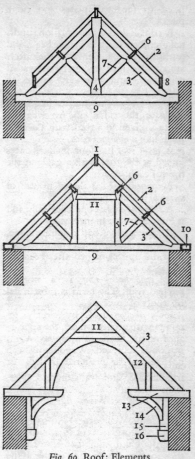

Fig. 69. Roof: Elements

Key:

1. Ridge	9. Tie-beam
2. Common rafter	10. Wall plate
3. Principal rafter	11. Collar-beam
4. King-post	12. Arched brace
5. Queen-post	13. Hammerbeam
6. Purlin	14. Brace
7. Strut	15. Wall post
8. Sole plate	16. Corbel

and horizontal tie-beams, connected by light diagonal lattices of wood.

A *coupled* roof is constructed without ties or collars, the rafters being

241

fixed to the wall plates and ridge pieces.

A roof is *double-framed* if longitudinal members (such as a ridge beam and purlins) are used. Generally the rafters are divided into stronger ones called principals and weaker subsidiary rafters.

A *gambrel roof* terminates in a small gable at the ridge; in America the name is given to a roof with a double pitch like a *mansard* roof.

A *helm roof* has four inclined faces joined at the top, with a gable at the foot of each.

A *hipped roof* has sloped instead of vertical ends.

A *lean-to roof* has one slope only and is built against a higher wall.

A *mansard roof* has a double slope, the lower being longer and steeper than the upper; named after François MANSART.

A *saddleback roof* is a normal pitched roof. The term is most usual for roofs of towers.

In a *wagon roof*, by closely set rafters with arched braces, the appearance of the inside of a canvas over a wagon is achieved. Wagon roofs can be panelled or plastered (ceiled), or left uncovered. Also called a *cradle roof*.

See HYPERBOLIC PARABOLOID ROOF *and figure 70.*

ROOT, John Wellborn (1850–91), was born in Georgia, went to school near Liverpool and studied at Oxford. He then took an engineering degree at the University of New York. In 1871 he went to live at Chicago. There he met BURNHAM and went into partnership with him, a suitable partnership to which Burnham contributed his organizational acumen and interest in planning, Root his resourcefulness and his aesthetic accomplishments, which included not only drawing but also music. On the work of the partnership *see* BURNHAM.

RÖRICZER. A family of C15 German masons, master masons of Regensburg

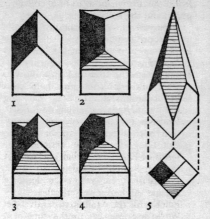

Fig. 70. Roof: types

Key:

1. Saddleback   4. Mansard
2. Hipped   5. Helm
3. Gambrel

Cathedral for three generations. Wenzel died in 1419. His style was so clearly influenced by Prague and the PARLERS that he must have been trained in their lodge. The surviving drawing of the west front of the cathedral may be his. Konrad, his son, is mentioned as master mason to the cathedral in 1456 and 1474. Concurrently, he had the same job at St Lorenz in Nuremberg (*see* HEINZELMANN) from *c.* 1455 onwards. At Regensburg he probably designed the triangular porch. He was consulted for St Stefan in Vienna in 1462, and for the Frauenkirche in Munich in 1475. He must have died *c.* 1475. His son Matthäus was Konrad's second-in-command at Nuremberg from 1462 to 1466. He wrote an important small book on how to set out Gothic finials (published 1486), was also master mason of Regensburg Cathedral, and died shortly before 1495, whereupon his brother Wolfgang was appointed his successor. Wolfgang was executed for political reasons in 1514.

ROSE WINDOW (or WHEEL WINDOW). A circular window with FOILS or patterned TRACERY arranged like the spokes of a wheel.

ROSETTE. A rose-shaped PATERA. See *figure 65.*

ROSSELLINO, Bernardo (1409–64), was primarily a sculptor. As an architect he began under ALBERTI, carrying out his designs for Palazzo Rucellai, Florence (1446–51), and his restoration and alterations to S. Stefano Rotondo, Rome. He designed the *cortile* of Palazzo Rucellai, and in 1451 was appointed architect to Pope Nicholas V, for whom he designed the east end of a completely new St Peter's (never completed). His chief works are the palace and cathedral at Pienza (1460–3), commissioned by Pope Pius II (Piccolomini). The former is a heavier and much less subtle version of Palazzo Rucellai, the latter a not unattractive cross between Alberti's Tempio Malatestiano, Rimini, and S. Maria Novella, Florence. Palazzo Venezia, Rome (1455), has sometimes been attributed to him.

ROSSI, Giovanni Antonio de' (1616–95). A prolific Roman High Baroque architect. His most important work is in the domestic field, e.g., the grandiose Palazzo Altieri, Rome (1650–4 and 1670–6), and the smaller, more elegant Palazzo Asti-Bonaparte, Rome (*c.* 1665), which set a pattern for C18 architects in Rome. In his ecclesiastical work he showed a preference for oval plans and lavish sculptural decoration. His Cappella Lancellotti in S. Giovanni in Laterano, Rome (*c.* 1680), and S. Maria in Campo Marzo, Rome (1676–86), are minor masterpieces of Roman High Baroque.

ROSSI, Karl Ivanovich (1775–1849). The leading architect in post-1815 St Petersburg where he was responsible for replacing the Greek Revival style of THOMON, VORONIKHIN and ZAKHAROV with a much juicier Rome-inspired brand of classicism. The son of an Italian ballerina, he was trained in Russia and visited Italy only in 1802. Until 1816 he worked mainly in Moscow, but his principal buildings are in Leningrad: the New Michael Palace (now the Russian Museum, 1819–28) together with the square and surrounding buildings, the huge and richly Roman General Staff Arch and the vast hemicycle of office buildings on either side; the Alexander, now Pushkin, Theatre (1827–32); and the Senate and Synod (1829–34). But he is perhaps less important for these buildings than for the town planning around them.

ROSTRAL COLUMN. See COLUMNA ROSTRATA.

ROTUNDA. A building (often surrounded by a colonnade) or room circular in plan and usually domed, e.g., the Pantheon.

ROUGHCAST. An external rendering of rough material, usually applied in two coats of cement and sand on to which gravel, crushed stone, or pebbles are thrown before the second coat is dry; also called *pebbledash.*

RUBBLE MASONRY. Rough unhewn building stones or flints, generally not laid in regular courses. *Coursed rubble* is walling with the stones or flints roughly dressed and laid in deep courses. *Speckled rubble* is walling with stones of varying sizes with small rectangular fillings or snecks between them.

RUDOLPH, Paul (b. 1918), was a pupil of GROPIUS at Harvard. In 1958 he became head of the school of architecture at Yale University, New Haven, for which he designed the new building (1961–3), but shortly after left Yale. The building for the school unmistakably belongs to the trend often termed BRUTALISM, but Rudolph – like SAARINEN and Philip JOHNSON – is one of those who do not feel compelled to adhere to one style in all their designs, even those of the same years, though this in no way impairs his sincerity. Rudolph's other principal buildings are the Sarasota

High School (1958–9), Cocoon House, Siesta Key, Florida (1960–1), and the fortress-like Endo Laboratories at Garden City, New York (1961–4).

RUNNING DOG. A classical ornament often used in a frieze, similar to the wave ornament. It is sometimes called a *Vitruvian scroll*. See figure 71.

Fig. 71. Running dog

RUSKIN, John (1819–1900), was not an architect, but the source of an influence as strong on architecture as it was on the appreciation of art. This influence made itself felt in two ways: by the principles which Ruskin tried to establish, and by the styles whose adoption he pleaded for.

As for the former, they are chiefly the principles of the *Seven Lamps of Architecture*, which came out in 1849: Sacrifice (architecture, as against mere building, takes into account the venerable and beautiful, however 'unnecessary'); Truth (no disguised supports, no sham materials, no machine work for handwork); Power (simple grand massing); Beauty (only possible by imitation of, or inspiration from, nature); Life (architecture must express a fullness of life, embrace boldness and irregularity, scorn refinement, and also be the work of men as men, i.e., handwork); Memory (the greatest glory of a building is its age, and we must therefore build for perpetuity); Obedience (a style must be universally accepted: 'We want no new style', 'the forms of architecture already known are good enough for us'). From this last point, Ruskin proceeded to list the styles of the past which are perfect enough to be chosen for universal obedience. They are the Pisan Romanesque, the Early Gothic of West Italy, the Venetian Gothic,

and the earliest English Decorated. This last, the style of the late C13 to early C14, had in fact been the choice of PUGIN, of the Cambridge Camden Movement (*see* BUTTERFIELD), and of SCOTT. But Ruskin's next book on architecture was *The Stones of Venice* (1851–3), which, being in praise of the Venetian Gothic, led admirers of Ruskin to imitate that style – J. P. Seddon, J. Prichard, early STREET, early E. Godwin. But *The Stones of Venice* also contains the celebrated chapter *On the Nature of Gothic*, which for the first time equated the beauties of medieval architecture and decoration with the pleasure taken by the workman in producing them. This was the mainspring that released the work of MORRIS as creator of workshops and as social reformer.

RUSSIAN ARCHITECTURE. Russian architecture sets out as a branch of BYZANTINE ARCHITECTURE: stone churches from the C11 to the C16 have the characteristic motifs of the inscribed cross and the five domes (Chernigov, 1017 etc.). The principal apse is flanked by subsidiary apses, and occasionally there are also subsidiary outer aisles (Novgorod, St Sophia, 1045 etc.). Occasionally also churches carry a lavish display of external relief sculpture (Vladimir, St Dimitrius, 1194). There must also have been many log-built churches, but none is preserved earlier than the C17.

The Renaissance came to Russia remarkably early. Ivan the Great (1462–1505) was married to a Byzantine princess educated in Rome. Aristotile Fioravanti, an architect of Bologna, went to Moscow from Hungary in 1474, and another Italian, Alevisio Novi, arrived shortly before the death of Ivan. Fioravanti built the Church of the Dormition in the Kremlin, Moscow, on the accepted Byzantine plan, but with modifications for the sake of greater spatial clarity. Novi, in St Michael in the Kremlin, Moscow (1505–9), went much further in Renaissance detail such as the Venetian semicircular shell-gables. But in plan and elevation – inscribed cross and five domes – the Russian tradition was retained by Novi and by others building in the C16. However, a new indigenous type, derived probably from early wooden churches, appeared at Kolomenskoe in 1532, a type with a much simpler central plan and a tall, octagonal, central tower with spire. This type was made more and more decorative in the course of the C16, and invaded the Kremlin precincts in the shape of the fabulous Church of Basil the Blessed (1555–60), which is overcrowded with motifs, just as contemporary buildings of Renaissance-Mannerism in Germany and England can be. The plan, with eight instead of four domed subsidiary spaces round the central tower, is novel too.

Mannerism like this continued throughout most of the C17 (Nativity, Moscow, 1649–52; Trinity, Ostankino, 1668), until the next foreign assault, that of the Baroque, brought final westernization. The church of the Virgin of Vladimir in Moscow (1691–4) has Baroque detail, the church of the Intercession at Fili (1693) a quatrefoil plan, the church at Dubrovitsi (1690 etc.) decoration as wild as if it were in Spain. With the former State Pharmacy (late C17), and the Menshikow Tower, both in Moscow (1704–7), more structural Baroque elements came in.

But it was Peter the Great's St Petersburg that was intended to be the wide open gate for the West to enter Russia. SCHLÜTER was called to Russia in 1713, but died in 1714. In 1713 the German Gottfried SCHÄDEL (1752) began the Menshikow Palace at Oranienbaum. The Cathedral in the Fortress (1714 etc.) is by the Italo-Swiss Domenico TREZZINI (1670–1734), the Library and Cabinet of Rarities (1718 etc.), by the German Georg Johann Mattarnovi (1719).

With the Empress Elizabeth Russian architecture finally reached above the provincial level. RASTRELLI's Summer Palace (1714 etc.), Peterhof (1747 etc.), Tsarskoe Selo (1749 etc.) and Winter Palace (1754 etc.) and also his Smolny Cathedral (1748 etc.) are in a grand and glorious Rococo. Yet the plan of the cathedral is unmistakably Russian. The interiors of the palaces are decorated with almost overdone luxury.

The turn to the neo-classical style came no later than in most other countries, with the Academy and the Marble Palace at Leningrad, the former (1765 etc.) by the Frenchman Vallin de la Mothe (1729–1800), the latter (1768 etc.) by the Italian RINALDI. Only a little later Russian architects began to replace foreigners, and STAROV's round tower at Nikolskoe (1774–6) is as severely neo-classical in the new Parisian sense as anything of the same date in the West. Starov had, in fact, studied in Paris and Italy.

Concurrently QUARENGHI began to build in the style of PALLADIO and CAMERON in that of Robert ADAM. Grecian in design, again influenced by France, are the Exchange of 1804 by Thomas de THOMON (1754–1813), ZACHAROV's Admiralty (1806), and VORONIKHIN's Mining Academy (1811). Altogether, Leningrad can be considered of all cities the one with the most consistent and the most sweeping classicist character. Meanwhile, churches remained less exactingly classical, and the Cathedrals of the Virgin of Kazan (by Voronikhin, 1801 etc.) and of St Isaac (1817 etc. by August Ricard MONTFERRAND, 1786–1858), both at Leningrad, carry their domes as a token of classicism as well as of the Russian tradition. The Picturesque in garden furnishings (ruins, etc.) hit Russia in the late C18 (QUARENGHI and especially V. I. Bazhenov, 1737–99) and produced the historicism of the C19, as in other countries. What is peculiar to Russia is an Ancient Russian Revival starting, it seems, in the 1830s and culminating in the Moscow Historical Museum of 1874 etc. by V. O. Sherwood (1832–97).

Events of the C20 are the short-lived adherence of Russia to the most advanced architectural concepts of the early 1920s (LISSITZKY, TATLIN, VESNIN, Leonidov, Ladovski), and then (after 1932) the enforced return to a grandiloquent classicism (Red Army Theatre, Moscow; University, Moscow; Moscow Underground). Recently this classicism has been disavowed, and large-scale housing programmes with prefabricated elements show Russia at one with Western interests and viewpoints.

RUSTICATED COLUMN. A column whose SHAFT is interrupted by plain or rusticated square blocks. *See figure 72.*

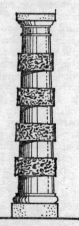

Fig. 72. Rusticated column

RUSTICATION. Masonry cut in massive blocks separated from each other by deep joints, employed to give a rich and bold texture to an exterior wall and normally reserved for the lower part of it. Various types have been used: *banded* with only the horizontal joints emphasized; *chamfered* with smooth stones separated by V joints, as in *smooth* rustication described below; *cyclopean* (or *rock-faced*), with very large rough-hewn blocks straight from the quarry (or artfully carved to look as if they were); *diamond-pointed*, with each stone cut in the form of a low pyramid; *frosted* with the surface of the stones carved to simulate icicles; *smooth*, with blocks, neatly finished to present a flat face, and chamfered edges to emphasize the joints; *vermiculated*, with the blocks carved with shallow curly channels like worm tracks. Sometimes it is simulated in stucco or other compositions, e.g., by PALLADIO. *See figure 73.*

smooth   cylopean

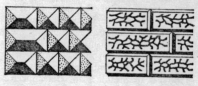

diamond-pointed   vermiculated

Fig. 73. Rustication

RY, Paul du (1640–1714). He came of a family of French architects and was the grandson of Charles (*fl.* 1611–36), the son of Mathurin (*fl.* 1639) and nephew of de BROSSE. A Huguenot, he left France after the revocation of the Edict of Nantes in 1685 and settled in Kassel where he built the Oberneustadt to house other Huguenot refugees. This trim piece of urban lay-out included the simple, centrally-planned Karlskirche (1698–1710), badly damaged but restored. In his post of Oberbaumeister in Kassel he was succeeded by his son, Charles-Louis (1692–1757) who built the

Mint and Militarkasino (both destroyed). Simon-Louis (1726–99), the son of Charles-Louis, was an architect of greater importance. He began under his father, then studied under the Swedish court architect Carl Harleman in Stockholm (1746–8) and Jacques-François BLONDEL in Paris before beginning a tour of Italy from which he returned in 1756. His first work was at Schloss Wilhelmstal near Kassel where he was involved in completing the building begun according to designs of CUVILLIÉS and added the two severely simple little lodges (1756–8). In Kassel he was responsible for laying out the spacious rectangular Friedrichsplatz with the austerely Palladian Fredericianum (1768–79) which is important as the first ever museum-library building designed as such. At Wilhelmshöhe, outside Kassel, he built the S. and N. wings of the vast and imposingly classical Schloss (1786–90), completed later by H. C. JUSSOW, and probably some of the follies in the Park (e.g., Der Mulang, a Chinese village and the 'Felseneck'). He was also responsible for numerous buildings in Kassel most of which were destroyed in 1945.

S

SAARINEN, Eero (1910–61), the son of Eliel SAARINEN, went with his father to the United States, but spent part of his study years in Paris (1929–30). In 1931–4 he was at Yale, in 1935–6 back in Finland. His important works are all of the post-war years, and taken together they are admirable for their variety and their sense of visual and structural experiment. The General Motors' Technical Centre at Warren, Michigan (1948–56), has severely rectangular buildings in the style of MIES VAN DER ROHE, plus a circular auditorium with a shallow aluminium-roofed dome, and a highly original water-tower 132 ft high as a vertical accent. The Kresge Auditorium of the Massachusetts Institute of Technology at Cambridge (1953–5) has a warped roof on three supports, and the chapel there has undulating inner brick walls and a central opening in a dome whose top is of an abstract sculptural form. The chapel of Concordia Senior College (1953–8) has a steeply pointed, decidedly Expressionist roof, while the Yale University Hockey Rink (1953–9) has a central arch of double curve spanning the length, not the width of the building. The Trans-World Airline's Kennedy Terminal, New York (1956–62), with its two dramatically outward-swinging arches, is consciously symbolic of flight and has elements inside of almost GAUDÍ-like heavy curving. After that the T. J. Watson Research Centre at Yorktown, New York (1957–61), is, with its 1000-ft curved shape, perfectly crisp and unemotional; but the Ezra Stiles and Morse Colleges at Yale (1958–62), a unified composition, have the stepping-forward-backward-and-upward movement so characteristic of Louis KAHN's Medical Research

Building in Philadelphia, begun one year earlier. Saarinen's last fling was the Dulles Airport for Washington (1958–63), with a long down-curving roof ridge on lines of closely set, heavy and outward-leaning concrete supports. Saarinen also designed the United States Embassies in London (1955–61) and Oslo (1959 etc.).

SAARINEN, Eliel (1873–1950). His most famous building is the railway station at Helsinki, which was built in 1905–14 after a competition he won in 1904. The style is inspired by the Vienna Secession (see OLBRICH), but in a highly original version, and the building takes its place in the series of outstanding Central European railway stations characteristic of the years from the end of the C19 to the First World War (Hamburg begun 1903; Leipzig, 1905; Karlsruhe, 1908; Stuttgart, 1911). Saarinen took part in the Chicago Tribune competition of 1922, and his design, though placed second, was much admired. As a result he left Finland and emigrated to the United States, where his best-known buildings are Cranbrook School (1925 etc., 1929 etc.) and Christ Church, Minneapolis (1949).

SACCHETTI, Giovanni Battista (1700–64). A pupil of JUVARRA, whom he followed to Spain and whose designs he executed for the garden façade of the palace La Granja at S. Ildefonso (1736–42). His main work is the Royal Palace, Madrid (begun 1738), where he greatly enlarged Juvarra's scheme by reference to BERNINI's Louvre project: the result is imposing, almost overpowering and rather top-heavy. He also laid out the area of the city surrounding the palace.

SACCONI, Count Giuseppe (1853–1905). His *magnum opus* is the National

Monument to Victor Emmanuel II in the centre of Rome, won in competition in 1884. Among other works the Assicurazioni Generali in Piazza Venezia, Rome (1902–7) might be mentioned.

SADDLE BARS. In CASEMENT glazing, the small iron bars to which the lead panels are tied.

SADDLE STONE, see APEX STONE.

SADDLEBACK ROOF, see ROOF.

SAKAKURA, Junzo, see TANGE.

SALLY-PORT. A POSTERN gate or passage underground from the inner to the outer works of a fortification.

SALOMÓNICA. The Spanish word for barley-sugar column, a feature much used in Spanish Baroque architecture.

SALVI, Nicola (1697–1751), designed the Trevi Fountain in Rome (1732–62), a Late Baroque masterpiece. It consists of a classical palace-façade, based on a Roman triumphal arch; this is set on an enormous artificial outcrop of rock out of which fountains gush into a lake-size basin at the bottom. Marble tritons and Neptune in a shell preside over the whole fantastic composition.

SALVIN, Anthony (1799–1881), came of an old North Country family and was the son of a general. A pupil of NASH, he became an authority on the restoration and improvement of castles, and his work in that field includes the Tower of London, Windsor, Caernarvon, Durham, Warwick, Alnwick, and Rockingham. But he by no means devoted himself exclusively to castles, though he was emphatically a domestic rather than an ecclesiastical architect. The range of styles used by him includes the sober Tudor of Mamhead in Devon (1828, a remarkably early use of the Tudor style), the lush Italian Renaissance interiors of Alnwick (1854 etc., not designed but approved by him), and the elaborate Jacobean of Thoresby, Nottinghamshire (1864–75). But his most stunning building is quite an early one: Harlax-

ton in Lincolnshire (1834 etc.), which is in an elaborate, indeed grossly exuberant, Elizabethan. The building was carried on by W. Burn.

SAMBIN, Hugues (1515/20–1601/2). French Mannerist architect, sculptor and furniture designer. He worked in Burgundy where he led a school of gifted provincial architects who indulged in rich surface effects with elaborately cut rustication (e.g., Petit Château at Tanlay, c. 1568) or with high relief sculpture (e.g., Maison Milsand, Dijon, c. 1561). Sambin also built the Palais de Justice at Besançon and his style had considerable influence, even in Paris, e.g., Hôtel de Sully. He published Termes dont on use en architecture (1572).

SANCTUARY. Area around the main altar of a church (see PRESBYTERY).

SANFELICE, Ferdinando (1675–1750), a leading Neapolitan architect of his day, was spirited, light-hearted, and unorthodox. He is notable especially for his ingenious scenographic staircases, e.g., Palazzo Sanfelice, Palazzo Serra Cassano.

SANGALLO, Antonio da (Antonio Giamberti), the elder (1455–1534), was born in Florence. His only notable building is one of the great masterpieces of Renaissance architecture, S. Biagio, Montepulciano (c. 1519–26). It was inspired by BRAMANTE's plan for St Peter's, i.e., a Greek cross with central dome and four towers (only one of which was built) between the arms.

SANGALLO, Antonio da (Antonio Giamberti), the younger (1485–1546), who was born in Florence, was the most notable member of the Sangallo family: nephew of Antonio the elder and Giuliano. He became the leading High Renaissance architect in Rome for two decades after RAPHAEL's death. He began as an architectural draughtsman, employed first by BRAMANTE then by PERUZZI. In 1520 he became Raphael's assistant as architect at St Peter's, and was employed there to strengthen Bramante's work. His masterpiece is Palazzo Farnese, Rome (begun 1534, completed after 1546 by MICHELANGELO), the most monumental of Renaissance palaces. The façade is astylar and the walls are smooth except for string courses dividing the storeys and bold quoins, which combine to give a horizontal emphasis stressing the gravity of the composition. It is at once sober, elegant, and restful. Several other palaces have been attributed to him, notably Palazzo Sacchetti, Rome (begun 1542). In 1539 he became chief architect of St Peter's, and supplied designs for the alteration of Bramante's plan (not executed). He designed the interior of the Capella Paolina in the Vatican (1540). For many years he was employed as a military engineer on the fortifications around Rome. On his death he was succeeded as architect of St Peter's by Michelangelo, whose dynamic style makes a striking contrast to Sangallo's suave, self-confident classicism.

SANGALLO, Giuliano da (Giuliano Giamberti, 1445–1516), military engineer and sculptor as well as architect, was born in Florence. The brother of Antonio da Sangallo the elder, he was one of the best followers of BRUNELLESCHI, and maintained the Early Renaissance style into the age of BRAMANTE and RAPHAEL. Most of his buildings are in and around Florence: Villa del Poggio a Caiano (1480–5, later altered internally); S. Maria delle Carceri, Prato (1485), the first Renaissance church on a Greek cross plan, with a marble-clad exterior and Brunelleschian interior; probably Palazzo Corsi, Florence (now the Museo Horne); and Palazzo Gondi, Florence (1490–4), with a rusticated façade deriving from Palazzo Medici-Riccardi and a monumental staircase rising from the interior courtyard. He also worked in Rome, where he built S. Maria dell'Anima (1514) and provided a project for St Peter's (c. 1514).

SANMICHELI, Michele (c. 1484–1559), the leading Mannerist architect in Verona, was famous as a military engineer; most of his works have a rather fortress-like appearance, and the façade he designed for S. Maria in Organo, Verona (1547), might almost be mistaken for one of the fortified gateways to the city. He is often compared with PALLADIO, who was indebted to him and succeeded him as the leading architect in the Veneto, but there is a striking contrast between the massive muscularity of Sanmicheli's works and the far more intellectual and polished buildings of Palladio.

Born in Verona, the son of an architect, he went to Rome c. 1500. He supervised work on the Gothic façade of Orvieto Cathedral (1510–24), where he also designed the altar of the Magi (1515). In 1526 he was employed by the Pope on the fortifications of Parma and Piacenza, and in the following year he settled in Verona. He was much in demand as a military architect, fortifying Legnago (1529), in charge of the fortifications at Verona (from 1530) and Venice (from 1535), and also in Corfu and Crete. The buildings he designed in this capacity are among his best – boldly rusticated gateways and whole fortresses with robust Doric columns and a few strongly effective ornaments such as coats of arms and giant heads frowning out of keystones, e.g., Porta Nuova, Verona (1539–50), Forte di S. Andrea a Lido, Venice (1535–49), Porta S. Zeno, Verona (1542), and most forceful of all, the Porta Palio, Verona (1557).

His palaces begin in the tradition of BRAMANTE and RAPHAEL with Palazzo Pompei, Verona (c. 1529), but he soon developed a more individual style, making much play with strong contrasts of light and shade. Palazzo Canossa, Verona (c. 1530), has a very high rusticated base and simplified Serlian windows on the first floor; Palazzo Bevilacqua, Verona (c. 1530), is richer, with an elaborate pattern of windows, spiral columns, and a rather oppressive use of sculpture. Here he adopted a device which later became very popular, projecting the triglyphs of the order to form consoles for a balcony. In his later palaces he strove towards the elimination of the wall surface, and at Palazzo Grimani, Venice (begun 1556, later altered), he almost entirely filled the spaces between the pilasters and columns with windows. He was little employed for churches, but the Cappella Pellegrini which he added to S. Bernardino, Verona (c. 1528), and Madonna di Campagna, Verona (1559), are of interest for their peculiar domes, rather squat, on high drums decorated with alternating groups of two blank arches and three windows.

SANSOVINO, Jacopo (1486–1570), who was primarily a sculptor, introduced the High Renaissance style of architecture to Venice. Born in Florence, the son of Antonio Tatti, he was trained under Andrea Sansovino, whose name he took. From 1505 he worked mainly in Rome as a sculptor and restorer of antique statues. In 1517 he quarrelled with MICHELANGELO, and became even more classical in style as a result. At the Sack of Rome (1527) he fled to Venice, intending to go to France, but he was commissioned to repair the main dome of S. Marco, appointed Protomagister of S. Marco in 1529, and then stayed on in Venice for the rest of his life. Friendship with Titian and Aretino introduced him into the Venetian 'establishment', and he soon became the leading architect, a position he maintained until the arrival of PALLADIO, who owed much to him.

His main buildings are all in Venice: the Library and Mint (1537–54) facing the Doge's Palace, and the nearby Loggietta (1537–40) at the base of the Campanile. They show a happier combination of architecture and figure sculpture than had previously been achieved in Venice. Palladio called the Library the richest building erected since classical times. Sansovino built several churches, notably S. Francesco della Vigna (1534, completed by Palladio) and the façade of S. Giuliano (1553–5). In Palazzo Corner on the Grand Canal he adapted a Roman-type palace to Venetian requirements (before 1561). On the mainland he built Villa Garzoni, Pontecasale (c. 1530), a somewhat severe structure surrounding a wide courtyard, where he came nearer to the feeling of an antique villa than any other C16 architect.

SANT'ELIA, Antonio (1888–1916), the architect of Italian Futurism. He was killed in the war, too early to have had a chance to do any actual building. However, his drawings, chiefly of 1913–14, are a vision of the industrial and commercial metropolis of the future, with stepped-back skyscrapers, traffic lanes at different levels, factories with boldly curved fronts. The forms are influenced by the Vienna Secession (see OLBRICH), but are also curiously similar to those of MENDELSOHN's sketches of the same years. The metropolitan content, however, is Futurist.

SANTINI, see AICHEL.

SARACENIC ARCHITECTURE, see ISLAMIC ARCHITECTURE.

SASH WINDOW. A window formed with sashes, i.e., sliding glazed frames running in vertical grooves; imported from Holland into England in the late C17.

SATELLITE TOWN. A self-contained town which is nevertheless dependent upon a larger centre for certain facilities, such as higher education.

SCAGLIOLA. Material composed of cement or plaster and marble chips or colouring matter to imitate marble; known in Antiquity but especially popular in the C17 and C18.

SCALLOP. An ornament carved or moulded in the form of a shell.

SCAMOZZI, Vincenzo (1552–1616), the most important of PALLADIO's immediate followers, was a conservative and rather pedantic formalist who maintained the principles of the c16 Mannerist style in the age of the Baroque. But he designed a handful of buildings of outstanding merit. Born in Vicenza, he was the son of a carpenter-cum-architect, from whom he received his training. Before 1576 he built his masterpiece, the Rocca Pisana at Lonigo, a villa perched on a hilltop and commanding spectacular views which the windows were designed to frame in an unprecedented manner. The villa is a simplified version of Palladio's Rotonda with an inset portico on the main façade and Venetian windows on the others. (Lord BURLINGTON took elements from both villas for Chiswick House.) His later houses, e.g., Villa Molin alla Mandria near Padua (1597), tended to be enlargements and elaborations of Palladian themes. From 1578 to 1580 he travelled in South Italy, visiting Naples and Rome, where he gathered material for his *Discorsi sopra le antichità di Roma* (1582). After Palladio's death he took over several of his unfinished works, notably S. Giorgio Maggiore, Venice. At the Teatro Olimpico, Vicenza, he added the elaborate permanent stage set (1585). In 1588 he designed a similar theatre at Sabbioneta. In 1582 he began the somewhat overweighted church of S. Gaetano, Padua. The same year he won the competition for the Procuratie Nuove in Piazza S. Marco, Venice, with a design based on Sansovino's Library – much elongated and heightened by a third storey. Also in Venice, in 1595, he began S. Nicola da Tolentino, a derivation from Palladio's Redentore. In 1599 he went to Prague, then across Germany to Paris, returning to Venice in 1600; four years later he visited Salzburg, where he made designs for the cathedral (not executed), a cross between the Redentore and S. Giorgio Maggiore. The fruits of these travels were incorporated in his *L'idea dell'architettura universale*

(1615), the last and most academic of the theoretical works of the Renaissance and the first to mention medieval as well as classical and Renaissance buildings. It also provided the final codification of the ORDERS and thus exercized a wide and lasting influence especially in N. Europe.

SCANDINAVIAN ARCHITECTURE. The beginnings are auspicious: the ship-shaped houses of c. 1000 near Trelleborg in Denmark, sixteen of them, each nearly a hundred feet long, and with an outer veranda all round, arranged in four squares of four, all in one round enclosure, and the superb and frightening decoration of the Oseberg ship, cart and sledges, all superb Viking work of c. 800. The Vikings were heathens and intrepid explorers. They conquered parts of England, settled down in Normandy, and reached Iceland, Greenland and America. At the same time the Swedes conquered Russia and reached the Dnieper. The christianization of Denmark and Sweden took place from North Germany in the c9 and c10, of Norway only at the end of the c10. The style of the intricate Viking ornamentation continued in the next outstanding contribution of Norway, the stave churches of the c12 (Urnes, Borglund, Lom) with their timber arcading structurally as ingenious as it is visually fascinating. Apart from stave churches there were also straightforward log churches of the type of Greensted in Essex. The best examples are Hedared and St Mary Minor at Lund in Sweden of c. 1020. But the most impressive Swedish contribution to timber architecture is her detached bell-towers of unboarded skeletal construction. Where stone was used, the northern countries looked primarily to Germany for guidance, (cf. for an early example the c11 WESTWORK of Husaby). Another source, though less pronounced, is Anglo-Saxon England (e.g. Sigtuna, St Peter). The principal c12 cathedrals were Lund (in Sweden) which became an archbishop's see in 1104, Viborg (in Finland) and Ribe (in Denmark). Their twin W. towers, their projecting transepts, their hall crypts and their details all derive from Germany. Lund is the most interesting. Its origin is Speier in Germany and *via* Speier, Lombardy. A master Donatus working at Lund may well have been Italian himself. At Ribe the dome over the crossing seems S.W. French in origin, but the mid-C13 sexpartite rib vaults of the nave are Early French Gothic. Brick may have reached Denmark from Lombardy and was at once adopted (Ringsted, 1160 etc., the Cistercian Sorø, 1161 etc.). The most interesting Danish building of the Middle Ages is of brick: the church of Kalundborg, a centrally planned late C12 building with a centre on the Byzantine (Russian?) inscribed-cross plan, but with four arms of equal length, projecting and crowned by four towers, which with the broader and higher central tower creates a splendid skyline.

Of brick also is Roskilde Cathedral much changed by picturesque later additions. Its ambulatory is French Romanesque, but other elements mark the transition to the Gothic style. The two most important Norwegian cathedrals point unmistakably to England. Stavanger has a nave of c. 1130 etc. with typically English short round piers and a Gothic chancel of 1272 etc., equally English. Trondheim has a singular E. end in which the straight-ended chancel is continued by an octagon to house the shrine of St Olav. The corona of St Thomas at Canterbury, evidently the source for the centrally planned E. shrine, had been completed in 1185. Trondheim must have been begun just about then. The details of octagon and choir are derived from Lincoln, begun in 1192. The screen between chancel and octagon is of c. 1330 and has its parallels also in England. The W. front, left incomplete, is entirely English too, of

the screen type with late C13 sculpture and two W. towers set outside the aisle fronts. The finest secular building of the Middle Ages in Scandinavia is King Haakon's Hall at Bergen, completed in 1261. The largest Scandinavian cathedral is that of Uppsala, begun c. 1270 and with a French Gothic ambulatory and radiating chapels and continued from 1287 by Étienne de Bonneuil. Linköping Cathedral, also C13, has a nave of hall type more probably derived from English hall choirs such as those of Salisbury and the Temple Church than from Germany. But German HALL CHURCHES, more and more the favourite church type in that country, also had an impact on the North, and an increasing impact (Malmö St Peter, Aarhus Cathedral). The friars, settling from the 1230s onwards, preferred halls. One of the earliest friars' churches is that of the Dominicans at Sigtuna (c. 1240), one of the finest is that of the Carmelites at Elsinore (Helsingborg) of the late C15. Both have brickwork in the decoratively enriched patterns so dear to the North German builders. Altogether the churches of the Late Gothic period depend on North Germany and especially Westphalia. Examples are the cathedrals of Strängnäs and Västerås in Sweden with their figured rib vaults. Swedish parish churches are notable for the survival of a large number of Late Gothic wall paintings.

The Renaissance made itself felt late and slowly. A house like Hesselagergård in Denmark of c. 1550 has semicircular gables on the Venetian pattern, but otherwise shows little of a true understanding of the Renaissance. The two great castles or country palaces of the Danish kings, Frederick II's Kronborg and Christian IV's Frederiksborg, date from 1574–85 and c. 1602–20 respectively. In style they derive from the Netherlands, and Antonis van Opbergen and Hans Steenwinckel Sen., working at Kronborg, and Hans and Laurens Steenwinckel, the architects of Frederiksborg, were in fact Dutchmen. Rosenborg in Copenhagen, a summer palace, dates from 1606–17, the delightful Exchange in Copenhagen by the Steenwinckels, from 1619–25. Its spire, which is in the form of three entwined dragons' tails, is a landmark of the city. The style of all these buildings is close to that of the Netherlanders who built at Danzig or Emden, and not too distant from that of Jacobean England. The same style in ecclesiastical architecture appears in Holy Trinity, Kristiansstad in Sweden of 1618 etc., probably by the Steenwinckels. The church is a hall church with very slim piers and still has the shaped gables of the Netherlandish style. The burial chapel of Christian IV attached to Roskilde Cathedral was begun even a few years earlier (1614) and has Netherlandish gables of a slightly more advanced type and in addition Gothic windows, a case of Revival rather than Survival.

Kristiansstad was founded by Christian IV and is laid out regularly with a grid of streets and oblong blocks. The king laid out other towns as well. One of them is Oslo (1624), but the most regular is Kristiansand in Norway (1641). In Sweden shortly after 1625 the present-day centre of Stockholm was laid out as a grid. Kalmar was built on a grid plan after 1647. Karlskrona, also a planned town, was founded in 1679. In 1662 the area of Copenhagen east of Kongens Nytorv and towards the new Citadel was laid out with a grid of straight streets, and in the course of the late c17 and the c18 this area filled up with private palaces and houses as stately as those of the best quarters of Paris during the same period. Their style throughout is the classical style which by then had begun to dominate Denmark and Scandinavia.

The classical style also reached the Northern countries from the Netherlands. Justus VINGBOONS visited Sweden in 1653–7. But already before then the style of van CAMPEN and POST had been developed. The de Geer House in Stockholm of 1646 is a perfect example of it. The initiator may have been Simon de LA VALLÉE who had arrived in 1637 and died in 1643 or his son Jean de la Vallée. Their work (and Vingboons') is the Riddarhus in Stockholm of 1652–65. Jean at the same time provided in the Oxenstjerna Palace of 1650 an example of the Roman palazzo façade. In Denmark the former Vordingsborg of 1671 by Lambert van Haven is entirely Dutch. The Charlottenborg Palace, also in Copenhagen (1672–83), and forming part of the new area already referred to, is essentially Dutch too. The former Sophie-Amalienborg in Copenhagen of 1667–73 on the other hand is an attempt at the Italian villa in Denmark.

Churches are of course all Protestant and hence all variations on Dutch types. There are a remarkable number of them, starting with St Katharine in Stockholm by the younger LA VALLÉE, begun in 1656. It is a Greek cross with a dome and four corner turrets. Kalmar Cathedral by Nicodemus TESSIN the Elder of 1660 etc. is also basically a Greek cross with corner turrets, but the W. and E. arms are lengthened and apsed. Our Saviour at Copenhagen by Lambert van Haven is again a Greek cross, but has a W. tower and a centre with an inscribed cross. To the churches must be added the Kagg Mausoleum at Floda in Sweden of 1661, again a Greek cross, and the grand Carolean Mausoleum attached to the Riddarholm Church at Stockholm by the elder Tessin with its splendid columnar exterior. This was designed in 1671.

Openness to influences from several countries remained characteristic of Scandinavia in the c18, or rather of Denmark and Sweden; for Norway had been left behind ever since the

Middle Ages. Much Norwegian domestic architecture was still of wood even in the C18. (The largest wooden building is Stiftsgården at Trondheim of 1774–8, nineteen windows wide, the finest is Danisgård at Bergen of the 1770s too, with its Rococo details.)

The most monumental building of Scandinavia, the Royal Palace in Stockholm by the younger TESSIN, begun in 1697, reflects more powerfully than any other palace in Europe the impact made by BERNINI's plans for the Louvre in Paris. In 1693 Tessin had made for the King of Denmark a similar design. Tessin knew both Rome and Paris. His country house Steninge of 1694–8 has an entirely French plan, derived from Vaux-le-Vicomte. His father's Drottningholm of the 1660s and Eriksberg had been French throughout.

About and after 1700 Frederiksborg (1699 etc.) and Fredensborg (1719 etc.), both in Denmark and both much altered, were Italian in inspiration; Christiansborg, the former Royal Palace of Copenhagen, of 1733 etc. (by E. D. Häusser; 1687–1745) is South German. So is the charming Hermitage in the Deer Park north of Copenhagen of 1734–6 (by Laurids Thura; 1706–59). Svartsjö in Sweden on the other hand of 1735–9 (by Carl Hårleman) is a French *maison de plaisance*. The East India Company Warehouse at Göteborg of *c.* 1740 (by the same architect) is a paramount example of early commercial architecture, nineteen windows wide and four storeys high. About the middle of the C18 the Picturesque movement made its mark in Scandinavia too, inspired by England which had been visited by F. M. Piper (1746–1824) before he designed the landscape park of Haga, and followed an English *jardinier* in dealing with the landscape park of Drottningholm. The finest mid-C18 work in the Northern countries is Amalienborg in Copenhagen, built by Nils EIGTVED

in 1750–54 as an octagon with four palaces in the diagonals and four streets branching off in the main directions. The style is French, the quality of the highest. Eigtved also designed the Frederiks-Church, magnificent, with a dominating dome on a high drum. But this was not carried out; Laurits Thura made another, more classical, design, and Nicolas-Henri Jardin, called in from France, a third, in its details even more classical, with a giant portico of detached columns and columns round the drum.

The Classical Revival or neo-classicism indeed began remarkably early in Denmark, and C. H. Harsdorff's Moltke Chapel at Karise of 1761–6 and his Chapel of Frederik V in Roskilde Cathedral (final design 1774) are among the purest works of their date anywhere on the Continent. The paramount neo-classical buildings in Sweden are the theatre of Gripsholm Castle (1782) by Erik Palmstädt (1741–1803) and the works of Jean-Louis Desprez (1743–1804), who had belonged to the most advanced Parisian circle and settled down in Sweden in 1784. Between that year and the tragic death of Gustavus III in 1792 he was the centre of the strictest Scandinavian classicism. However, such was the mood of the later C18 that he also designed in the Chinese style for the park of Haga.

The neo-Greek leaders are C. F. HANSEN (1756–1845) in Denmark and the Danish F. Linstow and C. H. Grosch in Norway. The principal works are the Law Courts on the Nytorv of 1803–16 and the Church of Our Lady of 1810–26, both in Copenhagen, and in Oslo the Royal Palace of 1824–48 (Norway in 1814 had at last broken free of Denmark and become linked by common monarchs with Sweden) and the University of 1840 etc., the former by Linstow, the latter by Grosch. All on his own is Gottlieb Bindesbøll (1800–1856) whose Thorwaldsen Museum in

Copenhagen of 1839–47 is as original within the Greek Revival as the work of Greek THOMSON in Glasgow.

For 'Victorian' historicism the best examples are the castellated and turreted Oskarshall outside Oslo of 1848 and then the Copenhagen University Library (1855–61) by J. D. Herholdt (1818–1902) in the 'Rundbogenstil', but with elegant exposed iron members inside, the Royal Theatre at Copenhagen (1872–4) by V. Dahlerup in the Italian Renaissance, the University at Uppsala (1879–87) by H. T. Holmgren in a grander Renaissance, the Magasins du Nord (1893 etc.) at Copenhagen by A. Jensen with French pavilion roofs, the Nordisk Museum (1890–1907), Stockholm, by I. G. Clason in the Northern Renaissance and the finally completed Frederik Church (1876–94) at Copenhagen by F. Meldahl in a surprisingly early grand French Baroque following the style of the original design of Jardin's.

From the 1890s onwards, however, some Danish architects joined the vanguard of those who endeavoured to get away from Victorian obtrusiveness and from historicism. The Copenhagen Town Hall by Martin Nyrop (1849–1921) was begun in 1893 and is as important as BERLAGE's Exchange in Amsterdam as an example of the imaginative treatment of elements from various styles of the past to achieve an original whole. ØSTBERG's City Hall (1911–23) in Stockholm belongs to the same category; so does L. I. Wahlman's Engelbrecht Church (1906–14) in Stockholm, externally a homely Renaissance, internally with parabolic arches. KLINT's Grundvig Church, begun finally only in 1919, straddles the gap between latest traditionalism and the Expressionism after the First World War. But the Grundvig Church is an exception in Denmark. The way to C20 liberty was as a rule not via a free Gothic but via Classicism. The paramount examples

are the Fåborg Museum of 1912–15 by Carl Petersen (1874–1923) and the Copenhagen Police Headquarters of 1918 etc. by Hack Kampmann (1856–1920) and the brilliant Aage Rafn (1890–1953). From then Denmark entered its moderate, sensitive C20 style, illustrated at its most Danish in Aarhus University by Kay Fisker (1893–1965), C. F. Møller and P. Stegmann (1932 etc.), at its most international by the impeccable work of Arne JACOBSEN and others such as H. Gunnløgsson (Kastrup Town Hall 1961) and Jørgen Bo & V. Wohlert (Louisiana Museum 1957–8). Only Jørn Utzon (b. 1918) has broken the perfect Danish restraint with his rhapsodic design for the Sydney Opera House (1956 etc.).

Denmark reached the INTERNATIONAL MODERN later than Sweden. Sweden had been inspired to classicism by Denmark, and Tengbom, Sigurd Lewerentz and ASPLUND belonged to it. But Asplund in the buildings for the Stockholm Exhibition of 1930 broke away from it and introduced a brand of the International Modern, more delicate, with thinner steel and more glass than heretofore. Examples of the International Modern of the thirties at its best are the schools by P. Hedqvist and by N. Ahrbom and H. Zimdahl, the Göteborg Concert Hall by N. E. Erikson (1931–5), the point-block housing by e.g. S. Backstrøm and L. Reinius (c. 1945 etc.), Eskil Sundahl's factory and housing among the trees on an island near Stockholm, and Vällingby, an outer suburb of Stockholm, not a satellite town. The excellent plan by MARKELIUS was drawn up in 1949. Building began in 1953. Compared with the freshness of all this Swedish and Danish architecture, the Oslo Town Hall of 1933–50 by A. Arneberg and M. Poulsson is heavy and uncouth.

SCARP or escarp. In military architecture, the bank or wall immediately in front of and below the rampart. It is often the inner side of the ditch or fosse.

SCHÄDEL, Gottfried (d. 1752). A German working in St Petersburg, where his masterpiece was the vast, exuberantly Baroque palace for Prince Menshikov at Oranienbaum (1713–25), the first large Western-style palace to be built in Russia. Its scale was immense, a central block with long curving wings which terminated in domed pavilions, built on an escarpment faced with decorative niches to give the appearance of two storeys below the ground floor.

SCHAROUN, Hans (b. 1893), presents us with the curious case of an architect who, because of his style, stood in the forefront when he was thirty, who through a shift in style among others fell into oblivion, and who, with a return to something approaching the style which had been his in his youth and which he had never felt compelled to change, found himself in the forefront once again at the age of sixty-five to seventy. Scharoun belongs among the Expressionists and fantasts of post-1918 Germany; like them he freely penned his dreams. In the later twenties he built some houses and flats, but major jobs were offered him only in the post-Second-World-War mood, in which sympathy with the twenties plays such an important part; then the *Wirtschaftswunder* made it possible to build what had remained on paper forty years earlier. His chief recent jobs are an estate at Charlottenburg-North, Berlin (1955–61); Romeo and Juliet, a twin scheme of flats at Stuttgart (1955–9); and the Berlin Philharmonie (1956–63).

SCHICKHARDT, Heinrich (1558–1634). One of the first German Renaissance architects, less well known than Elias HOLL because none of his buildings survives, but of great historical importance. He was trained by Georg Beer (d. 1600) whom he helped to design the Neues Lusthaus at Stuttgart (1584–93, demolished). In 1590 he became official architect to the Duke of Württemberg with whom he visited Italy (1598–1600). His newly acquired knowledge of Italian Renaissance architecture was manifested in the new wing he added to the Schloss at Stuttgart on his return (1600–1609, destroyed 1777) – a symmetrical building with some sixty Tuscan columns in the ground floor stables. He also designed and laid out the small town of Freudenstadt around a large central arcaded square with church, town hall, market hall and hospital at the corners (destroyed in the Second World War but rebuilt) – an unusually progressive example of North European town planning. The church is L-shaped, with altar and pulpit in the corner.

SCHINDLER, Rudolf M. (1887–1953). Born and trained in Vienna. In 1913 he emigrated to America, where in 1918 he began to work under Frank Lloyd WRIGHT. In 1921 he started practising on his own in Los Angeles. About 1925 he had developed his personal style inspired by Wright and the INTERNATIONAL MODERN, especially of OUD. Cubism also must have inspired him. From 1925 onwards, for a few years, he worked in partnership with NEUTRA. Like Neutra, Schindler specialized in expensive private houses. His *magnum opus* is Beach House (Lowell House) at Newport Beach (1925–6).

SCHINKEL, Karl Friedrich (1781–1841), the greatest German architect of the C19, was Prussian and worked almost exclusively in Prussia. He was the son of an archdeacon, went to school in Berlin, and received his architectural training there too, under GILLY, in whose father's house he boarded, and at the newly founded Academy. He was powerfully influenced by the original and francophile style of Gilly. He stayed in Italy and in Paris in 1803–5, then worked as a painter of panoramas and dioramas, and a little later (chiefly *c.* 1810–15) did independent paintings too, in an elevated Romantic style (landscapes and Gothic cathedrals). This led on to theatrical work, and Schinkel designed for the stage from 1816 right into the thirties (forty-two plays, including *The Magic Flute*, *Undine*, *Käthchen von Heilbronn*). Meanwhile, however, he had begun to submit architectural designs, hoping to attract attention to himself. The first was for a mausoleum for the much beloved Prussian Queen Luise. This was eminently romantic in the Gothic style, with coloured glass in the windows and life-size white angels by the head of the sarcophagus. It was followed by church designs, e.g., a cathedral in the trees, centrally planned with a steep Gothic dome. In 1810 Schinkel had secured a job in the administration of Prussian buildings, with the help of Wilhelm von Humboldt. In 1815 he was made Geheimer Oberbaurat in the newly created Public Works Department, a high title for so young a man, and in 1830 he became the head of the department.

All his principal buildings were designed between 1816 and 1830. The earliest are pure Grecian, yet always serviceable, functionally planned, and with the motifs of the façade, in the spirit of Gilly, modified with originality to ensure that the stylistic apparatus does not interfere with the use of the building. The Neue Wache or New Guard House in Unter den Linden, Berlin, came first (1816; Greek Doric portico, transformed internally 1966), then the Theatre (1818–21), large, with a raised Ionic portico and excellent interiors (badly damaged 1945 but being restored), and after that the Old Museum (1823–30, interior partly destroyed 1945), with its unbroken row of slender Ionic columns along the façade, its Pantheon-like centre rotunda, taken obviously from DURAND, and its staircase open to the portico and picturesquely introducing a degree of interpenetration of spaces not to be expected from outside. This is the first sign of hidden resources in Schinkel, making it impossible to label him a Grecian and leave it at that. Side by side with these major buildings, Schinkel designed the War Memorial on the Kreuzberg (1818), Gothic and of cast iron, Tegel, Humboldt's country house (1822–4), in a characteristic domestic Grecian, and the Werdersche Kirche (1821–31). The design for this last was submitted in a classical and a Gothic version, both vaulted; the Gothic version won, evidently inspired by the English type of Late Gothic Royal Chapels with their four angle turrets.

Schinkel was, indeed, keenly interested in England and in 1826 travelled through the country, after staying for a while in Paris. It was not his first major journey since Italy: in 1816 he had been to the Rhine, where he developed an interest in the preservation of monuments, and in 1824 he went again to Italy. In England he was more interested in industrial developments than in architecture proper, the promotion of crafts and industry being part of his official responsibilities.

His principal late works show a remarkable change of style and widening of possibilities. They include unexecuted designs for an exchange or merchants' hall with warehouse (1827?) and for a library (1830s), both utilitarian without any period trimmings. Among executed works, the Nikolaikirche at Potsdam (1830–7, badly damaged 1945 but being restored) is classical, whereas the building for the Academy of Architecture is only vestigially period (North Italian Quattrocento), but essentially also unenriched functional. A widening in another direction led to projects for centrally and longitudinally planned churches in arcuated styles, vaguely Early Christian or Italian Romanesque (the so-called *Rundbogenstil* of Lombardy; *see* GÄRTNER), while a broadening of yet another kind is represented by two small buildings in the park of Potsdam – Charlottenhof and the Roman Bath (1826 and 1833) – and the costly projects for a palace on the Acropolis (1834) and in the Crimea (1838), in all of which Grecian motifs are applied to picturesquely irregular compositions where architecture and nature collaborate.

SCHLAUN, Johann Conrad (1695–1773). A Westphalian Baroque architect who began with small and simple churches for Capuchin friars, e.g., Brakel (1715–18). He then studied under NEUMANN at Würzburg (1720–21), travelled to Rome and returned to Münster by way of France and Munich (1724). In 1725 he was appointed architect to Clemens August, Elector of Cologne, for whom he began Schloss Brühl (later altered by CUVILLIÉS) and the very elegant little cruciform hunting-lodge Clemenswerth, near Sögel (c. 1736–50). For the Elector's minister, Graf von Plettenberg, he erected various buildings in the park at Nordkirchen, notably the Oranienburg (from 1725). Still clinging to the Baroque style, by then rather démodé, he built the Clemenskirche, cleverly inserted into a corner of the House of the Brethren of Mercy at Münster (1745–53), the Borrominesque church of St Johann Nepomuk at Rietberg (1744–8), the Erbdrostenhof in Münster (1754–7) and the Schloss at Münster (1767–73). The two houses he built for himself are remarkably original: the Rüschhaus outside Münster (1745–8) in the Westphalian rustic tradition with a few sophisticated Baroque flourishes, and a town-house in Münster (1753–5) stylistically similar.

SCHLÜTER, Andreas (c. 1662/9–1714). He was equally distinguished as sculptor and architect. As an architect he ranks slightly below his great contemporaries HILDEBRANDT and FISCHER VON ERLACH. He was trained in Danzig (and was probably born there) but is first heard of in Warsaw in 1689–93 as the sculptor of pediments on the Krasiński Palace. He does not seem to have worked as an architect in Poland. In 1694 he was called to Berlin by the Elector Friedrich III who sent him to France and Italy to study. On his return in 1699 he was commissioned to carve the very elaborate sculptural keystones for windows and doors on the Berlin Arsenal designed by NERING. He succeeded Nering as architect at the Arsenal in 1698. In the same year he was put in charge of the building of the Royal Palace in Berlin, and in 1698 became its Surveyor General. The Royal Palace (bombed 1945, demolished 1950) was his masterpiece. Some of his sculptural decoration on the Lustgarten façade, on the great staircase and Baronial Hall, was fortunately removed before demolition in 1950. The influence of BERNINI and LE PAUTRE is evident in the design, as well as that of Fischer von Erlach and Nicodemus TESSIN both of whom were in Berlin while it was being built. In 1701–4 he also built the Old Post Office in Berlin (demolished 1889), but he fell into disgrace shortly afterwards as a result of the collapse of the Munzturm water-tower at the north-west corner of the Royal Palace. He was dismissed from his appointments in 1707. In 1711–12 he built the Villa Kamecke in Dorotheenstadt, Berlin (destroyed 1945, but fragments preserved in the Bode Museum, E. Berlin). After the king's death he left Berlin and settled in St Petersburg in 1714, dying there the same year.

SCHOCH, Johannes or Hans (c. 1550–1631). His masterpiece is the Friedrichsbau in Heidelberg Castle (1601–7) in which the architectural elements are closely knit and vigorously moulded though still somewhat heavy-handed as compared with later and more accomplished German Renaissance buildings, e.g., Jacob WOLFF's Pellerhaus in Nuremberg of the same years. Schoch may have worked with Speckle (1536–89) on the Neuer Bau at Strassburg (1582–5) and perhaps also on the Grosse Metzig in Strassburg (1586). The Fleischhalle at Heilbronn (*c.* 1600) and the S. wing of the Arsenal at Amberg (1604) may derive from designs by Schoch.

SCONCE. In military architecture, a small fort or earthwork, usually built as a counter-fort or to defend a pass, castle gate, etc.

SCOTIA. A concave moulding which casts a strong shadow, as on the base of a column between the two TORUS mouldings. *See figures 66 and 74.*

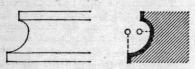

Fig. 74. Scotia

SCOTT, Sir George Gilbert (1811–78), the son of a clergyman and himself an evangelical, regarded himself as an architect of the multitude, not of the chosen few, and his sturdy stand on the *juste milieu* secured him an unparalleled multitude of buildings. He started with workhouses – a speciality of Sampson Kempthorne, the architect under whom he had worked – and he did them in partnership with W. B. Moffatt. The Royal Wanstead School at Wanstead, Essex, formerly an Orphan Asylum, is their first important work; it is Jacobean in style. But one year later they built St Giles, Camberwell, London, and here Scott found his feet. This is a Gothic church which was substantial, no longer papery as the earlier neo-Gothic churches had been, and which was, moreover, both knowledgeable and, with its properly developed chancel, ritualistically acceptable to the Cambridge Camden group. In the same year Scott began to restore Chesterfield church, and so started on his career as a busy, undaunted restorer. In the next year, 1844, he won the competition for St Nicholas at Hamburg with a competent German Gothic design which established him internationally. He restored more cathedrals and parish churches than can be remembered, was made surveyor of Westminster Abbey in 1849, and built – to name but a few – the grand Doncaster parish church (1854 onwards), the chapels of Exeter College, Oxford (1856), and St John's College, Cambridge (1863–9), and the parish church of Kensington, London (1869–72). His style is mixed Anglo-French High Gothic (late C13 to early C14).

He was also active as a secular architect. Examples are Kelham Hall, Nottinghamshire (1857 etc.), the St Pancras Station and Hotel in London (1865, etc.), the Albert Memorial (1864, etc.), and the group of houses in Broad Sanctuary, just west of Westminster Abbey (1854). Scott even wrote a persuasive book to prove that the Gothic style was as suited to secular as to clerical C19 tasks (*Remarks on Secular and Domestic Architecture*, 1858), and was deeply hurt when he found himself forced by Lord Palmerston to do the new Government offices in Whitehall in the Renaissance style (final design 1861). Scott was ambitious and fully convinced he was as good an architect as any; this comes out clearly in his *Personal and Professional Recollections* (1879). He was, in fact, a highly competent architect, but he lacked genius. As a restorer he believed in careful preservation, but was ruthless in action. In spite of this he was quite a medieval scholar, as is demonstrated by his *Gleanings from Westminster Abbey* (1862).

His sons George Gilbert (1839–97) and John Oldrid (1842–1913) were both Gothicists too, competent and careful like their father, but they had in addition a sensitivity which belongs to the Late as against the High Victorian milieu. George Gilbert's *chef d'œuvre* was St Agnes, Kennington,

London (1877), remarkably bare and grand; John Oldrid, following his brother, did the grand Catholic church of Norwich (1884–1910).

SCOTT, Sir Giles Gilbert (1880–1960), rose to sudden and very early fame with his design for Liverpool Cathedral, won in competition in 1904 and very evidently inspired by BODLEY. This means that it is still Gothicist in the C19 manner. However, it has an originality of plan and a verve of verticals which promised much. Scott's early ecclesiastical buildings, such as St Joseph, Lower Sheringham, Norfolk (1910–36), and the Charterhouse School Chapel (1922–7), are indeed both original and bold, and in addition much less dependent on a style from the past. Scott exploited a surprising variety of possibilities. The results included Battersea Power Station in London (1932–4), which became the pattern for post-war brick-built power stations all over England, and the new Waterloo Bridge (1939–45), with the fine sweep of its shallow arches. However, his official representational architecture lost the early tensions and turned commonplace: Cambridge University Library (1931–4), the new building for the Bodleian Library, Oxford (1936–46), Guildhall Building, London (1954–8).

SCREENS PASSAGE. The space at the service end of a medieval hall between the screen and the buttery, kitchen, and pantry entrances.

SCROLL. 1. An ornament in the form of a scroll of paper partly rolled. 2. In classical architecture, the VOLUTE of an Ionic or Corinthian CAPITAL. 3. In Early English and Decorated Gothic architecture, a moulding in such a form. See figure 75.

SEDILIA. Seats for the clergy, generally three (for priest, deacon, and subdeacon), and of masonry, in the wall on the south side of the CHANCEL.

SEGMENT. Part of a circle smaller than a semicircle.

Fig. 75. Scroll

SELVA, Antonio (1751–1819), a leading neo-classical architect in Venice, trained under TEMANZA, then visited Rome, Paris, and London (1779–83). His early works are in a simplified neo-Palladian style, e.g., Teatro La Fenice, Venice (1788–92, burnt down but rebuilt to his design). But he developed a much stronger neo-classical manner later on, e.g., Duomo, Cologna Veneta (1806–17), with its vastly imposing octastyle Corinthian portico.

SEMPER, Gottfried (1803–79), the most important German architect of the Early and High Victorian decades, was born at Hamburg and studied at Göttingen, and then in Munich (under GÄRTNER). In 1826, after fighting a duel, he fled to Paris, where he worked under GAU and HITTORF. The years 1830–33 were spent in Italy and Greece, and after that journey Semper published a pamphlet on polychromy in Greek architecture, immediately influenced by Hittorf. In 1834 he was appointed to a chair at the Dresden Academy and there built his finest buildings. The Opera came first (1838–41). It was, in its original form, neo-Cinquecento, with subdued ornamentation and an exterior that expressed clearly its interior spaces. The semicircular front was inspired by Moller's theatre at Mainz (see GILLY). After that followed the synagogue, a mixture of Lombard, Byzantine, Moorish, and Romanesque elements (1839–40); the Quattrocento Villa Rose (1839); and the Cinquecento Oppenheim Palace (1845). Then came the Picture Gallery, closing with its large arcuated façade the Baroque Zwinger at the time left open to the

north (1847–54), and the Albrechts-
burg, a grand terraced Cinquecento
villa above the river Elbe (1850–5),
symmetrical, yet the German equivalent of, say, Osborne. After the revolution of 1848 Semper fled Germany and
went first to Paris (1849–51) – an un-
successful time, which made him contemplate emigration to America – and
then to London (1851–5), where he
did certain sections of the 1851 Exhibition and advised Prince Albert on the
tasks for the museum which is now the
Victoria and Albert.

Semper was, in fact, keenly interested in art applied to industry, and
his *Der Stil* (1861–3, only two
volumes published) is the most interesting application of materialist
principles to craft and design, an attempt at proving the origin of ornament in certain techniques peculiar to
the various materials used. In architecture Semper believed in the expression
of the function of a building in its
plan and exterior, including any decorative elements.

In 1855 Semper went to the Zürich
Polytechnic and taught there till 1871.
During that time he made designs for
the Wagner National Theatre (1864–
6) which considerably influenced the
building as it was erected at Bayreuth
(by O. Brückwald, 1841–1904; opened
1876). Semper's last years were spent
in Vienna. His style then, as is clearly
seen in the Dresden Opera (re-
designed 1871 after a fire), was more
Baroque, less disciplined, and looser.
This is also evident in the two large
identical museum buildings for Vienna, forming a forum with the Neue
Hofburg (1872 etc., and 1881 etc.),
and in the Burgtheater (1873). These
last buildings were executed by
Karl von Hasenauer (1833–94), but
the well-thought-out, clearly articulated plans are Semper's.

SENS, *see* WILLIAM OF SENS.

SERLIANA (or SERLIAN MOTIF). An
archway or window with three openings, the central one arched and wider

than the others: so called because it
was first illustrated in SERLIO's
Architettura (1537), though it probably
derived from BRAMANTE. It was
much used by PALLADIO, and became
one of the hallmarks of PALLADIAN-
ISM, especially in C17–18 England. It is
more commonly known as Venetian
or Palladian window. *See figure 76.*

Fig. 76. Serliana

SERLIO, Sebastiano (1475–1554), painter
and architect, was more important as
the author of *L'Architettura*, which
appeared in six parts between 1537
and 1551 (augmented from his
drawings 1575). This was the first book
on architecture whose aim was practical rather than theoretical, and the
first to codify the five ORDERS: it
diffused the style of BRAMANTE and
RAPHAEL throughout Europe, and
provided builders with a vast repertory of motifs. Born and trained in
Bologna, he went to Rome *c.* 1514,
and remained there until the sack of
1527 as a pupil of PERUZZI, who be-
queathed him plans and drawings used
extensively in his book. He then went
to Venice until 1540, when he was
called to France, and advised on building operations at Fontainebleau. Here
he built a house for the Cardinal of
Ferrara, known as the Grand Ferrare

(1544-6, destroyed except for the entrance door) and the *château* at Ancy-le-Franc, near Tonnerre (begun 1546) which survives. The *Grand Ferrare* established the standard form for the HÔTEL or town-house in France for more than a century. The fantastic designs, especially for rusticated portals, in the later parts of his books, which were published in France, were much imitated by French Mannerist architects.

SERT, José Luis (b. 1902). He comes from Barcelona, worked from 1929 to 1932 for LE CORBUSIER and emigrated to America in 1939. He became GROPIUS's successor at Harvard. He designed Students' Halls of Residence for Harvard in 1962 – a restless design. Other works of his are the U.S. Embassy at Baghdad and the Fondation Naeght at St Paul near Nice.

SERVANDONI, Giovanni Niccolò (1695-1766), born in Florence and trained as a painter under Pannini, began as a stage designer in France in 1726, but soon turned to architecture. In 1732 he won the competition for the west façade of St Sulpice, Paris. Though not executed until 1737, and revised meanwhile, this is among the earliest manifestations of a reaction against the Rococo. He later worked in England, designing the gallery of R. MORRIS's Brandenburg House, Hammersmith (1750, demolished 1822).

SEVERUS (*fl.* 64 A.D.). Roman architect employed by Nero to build the Domus Aurea on the Esquiline after the disastrous fire of A.D. 64. Tacitus and Suetonius testify to the grandeur of the whole concept, the spacious gardens with which the buildings were integrated, the size, number and richness of the rooms decorated with gold, gems, mother of pearl and ivory, the baths of sea water and sulphur water, the dining-rooms fitted with devices for sprinkling the guests with scent from the ceiling. Nero is reported to have remarked that he was 'beginning to be housed like a human being'. The parts which survive reveal the architect's genius in designing a large series of rooms of contrasting forms and creating ingenious systems of indirect lighting. He was assisted by the engineer Celer in this work and also in a project to build a canal from Lake Avernus to the Tiber. It is probable that he was also in charge of the rebuilding of Rome after the fire and the author of the new city building code.

SEVERY. A compartment or bay of a vault.

SEXPARTITE VAULT, *see* VAULT.

SGRAFFITO. Decoration on plaster of incised patterns, the top coat being cut through to show a differently coloured coat beneath.

SHAFT. The trunk of a column between the base and CAPITAL. *See figure 64.* Also, in medieval architecture, one of several slender columns attached (in a cluster) to a pillar or pier, door jamb or window surround. *See* COMPOUND PIER *and figure 30.*

SHAFT-RING (or ANNULET). A motif of the C12 and C13 consisting of a ring round a SHAFT.

SHARAWADGI. Artful irregularity in garden design and, more recently, in town planning. The word, probably derived from the Japanese, was first used in 1685 to describe the irregularity of Chinese gardens: it was taken up again and popularized in mid-C18 England and, in connection with town planning, some thirty years ago.

SHAW, Richard Norman (1831-1912), was a pupil of William Burn (1789-1870), a very successful, competent, and resourceful architect of country houses, and won the Academy Gold Medal in 1854, after having travelled in Italy, France, and Germany. He published a hundred of the travel sketches in 1858 and in the same year went as chief draughtsman to STREET, following WEBB in this job. He started in practice with a friend from Burn's office, Eden Nesfield

(1835–88), but they mostly worked separately. Shaw began in the Gothic style, and did a number of churches, some of them remarkably powerful (Bingley, Yorkshire, 1864–8; Batchcott, Shropshire, 1891–2), and one at least partaking of his happily mixed, mature style (Bedford Park, West London, 1880). But this style was not reached by Shaw and Nesfield at once. A few years intervened of highly picturesque, still somewhat boisterous country mansions, timber-framed as well as of stone (Leys Wood, Sussex, 1868; Cragside, Northumberland, 1870 etc.). At the same time, however, a change took place to a more intimate style, simpler details, and local materials (Glen Andred, Sussex, 1868). This both architects have entirely in common.

Shaw and Nesfield's mature style is much more subdued, and its period sources are mid-C17 brick houses under Dutch influence and the William and Mary style, rather than Gothic and Tudor. Decoration is more refined than was usual, and interior decoration was here and there left to MORRIS's firm. Which of the two architects really started this style is not certain. Nesfield is the more likely – see his Dutch C17 Lodge at Kew Gardens (1866) and his William-and-Mary-cum-Louis-XIII, Kinmel Park (c. 1866–8) – but Shaw made an international success of it. That some inspiration from Webb stands at the beginning is indubitable. The key buildings were New Zealand Chambers in the City of London (1872), Lowther Lodge, Kensington (1873, now Royal Geographical Society), Shaw's own house in Ellerdale Road, Hampstead (1875), and the exquisite Swan House, Chelsea Embankment (1876). At the same time Shaw designed Bedford Park, Turnham Green, London, as the earliest garden suburb ever. About 1890 (Bryanston, Dorset) Shaw turned away from the dainty elegance of this style towards a grand classicism with giant columns and Baroque details (Chesters, Northumberland, 1891; Piccadilly Hotel, 1905); this also was very influential.

SHELL. A thin, self-supporting membrane on the eggshell principle; used for roofing in timber or concrete.

SHEPPARD, Richard (b. 1910). The most interesting buildings by R. Sheppard, Robson & Partners to date are Churchill College, Cambridge (1959 etc.), with a number of small and medium-sized courts grouped loosely round the towering concrete-vaulted hall; hostels for Imperial College, London (1961–3); the School of Navigation of Southampton University (1959–61); Digby Hall, Leicester University (1958–62); and the West Midland Training College at Walsall (1960–3).

SHINGLE STYLE. The American term for the Domestic Revival of the 1870s and 1880s, influenced initially by Norman SHAW, but replacing his tile-hanging by shingle-hanging. The pioneer building is the Sherman House at Newport, Rhode Island, by H. H. RICHARDSON (1874). McKIM, Mead & WHITE also participated. The masterpiece is Richardson's Stoughton House at Cambridge, Massachusetts (1882). The shingle style is almost exclusively a style of the medium-sized private house, and its most interesting and most American feature, not implied in the name, is open internal planning.

SHINGLES. Wooden tiles for covering roofs and spires.

SHOULDERED ARCH, see ARCH.

SHUTE, John (d. 1563), the author of the first English architectural book, *The First and Chief Groundes of Architecture* (1563), described himself as a painter and architect, and was a member of the household of the Duke of Northumberland who sent him to Italy about 1550. His book included illustrations of the five orders, derived mainly from SERLIO. It went into four editions before 1587 and must have been widely used.

SHUTTERING, see FORMWORK.

SILL. The lower horizontal part of a window-frame.

SILOE, Diego de (c. 1495–1563) was a sculptor as well as an architect, and one of the main practitioners of the PLATERESQUE style. Born in Burgos, he studied in Italy (Florence and possibly Rome), where he acquired a Michelangelesque style of sculpture and picked up the vocabulary of Renaissance architecture. His finest work as both sculptor and architect is the Escalera Dorada in Burgos Cathedral (1519–23) – a very imposing interior staircase rising in five flights and derived from that designed by BRAMANTE to link the terraces of the Belvedere Court. To decorate it *putti*, portraits in roundels, winged angel heads, and other Renaissance motifs are used with a still Gothic profusion. In 1528 Siloe began his masterpiece, Granada Cathedral, where his main innovation was a vast domed chancel very skilfully attached to the wide nave. Here he adopted a purer and more severe manner which was to have wide influence in Spain. His other buildings include the tower of S. Maria del Campo, near Burgos (1527); the Salvador Church, Ubeda (1536); Guadix Cathedral (1549); and S. Gabriel, Loja (1552–68), with its unusual trefoil *chevet*.

SIMA RECTA, see CYMA RECTA.

SIMA REVERSA, see CYMA REVERSA.

SIMÓN DE COLONIA (d. c. 1511). Son of Juan de Colonia (d. 1481), and father of Francisco de Colonia (d. 1542). Juan no doubt came from Cologne, and, indeed, the spires of Burgos Cathedral (1442–58) look German Late Gothic. Juan was also the designer of the Charterhouse of Miraflores outside Burgos (1441 etc.). Simón, sculptor as well as architect, followed his father at Burgos Cathedral and Miraflores and designed, in a typically Spanish wild Late Gothic, the Chapel of the Constable of the cathedral (1486 etc.) and the façade of S. Pablo at Valladolid (1486–99). He became master mason of Seville Cathedral in 1497. Francisco, who probably completed the façade of S. Pablo, is responsible (with Juan de Vallejo) for the crossing tower of Burgos Cathedral (1540 etc.), still essentially Gothic, though Francisco had done the Puerta de la Pellejería of the cathedral in the new Early Renaissance in 1516. Francisco was made joint master mason with JUAN DE ÁLAVA at Plasencia Cathedral in 1513, but they quarrelled over the job and also over Álava's work at Salamanca Cathedral. Álava commented on Francisco's '*poco saber*'.

SINAN (1489–1578 or 1588), the greatest Turkish architect, was supposedly of Greek origin. He worked for Suleiman I 'The Magnificent' throughout the Ottoman Empire, from Budapest to Damascus, and, according to himself, built no less than 334 mosques, schools, hospitals, public baths, bridges, palaces, etc. His mosques developed from Hagia Sophia, the most famous being the enormous Suleimaniyeh in Istanbul (1550–6), though he himself considered his masterpiece to be the Selimiye at Edirne (Adrianople) (1570–4).

SITTE, Camillo (1843–1903), Austrian town-planner and architect, was director of the Trades' School of Salzburg (1875–93), and then of Vienna (1893 onwards). His fame rests entirely on his book *Der Städtebau* (1889), which is a brilliant essay in visual urban planning. Sitte, with the help of a large number of diagrammatic plans, analyses open spaces in towns and the many ways in which irregularities of plan can cause attractive effects. His subject is really 'townscape', in the sense in which this term is now used by the *Architectural Review* and such critics as Gordon Cullen.

SKELETON CONSTRUCTION. A method of construction consisting of a framework (*see* FRAMED BUILDING) and an outer covering which takes no load (*see* CLADDING). The skeleton may be visible from the outside.

SKEWBACK. That portion of the ABUTMENT which supports an arch.

SKIDMORE, OWINGS & MERRILL (Louis Skidmore, 1897–1962; N. A. Owings, b. 1903; and J. O. Merrill, b. 1896). One of the largest and at the same time best architectural firms in the United States. They have branches in New York, Chicago, and other centres, each with its own head of design. Gordon Bunshaft (b. 1909), a partner in 1945, is an especially distinguished designer. Outstanding among the works of the firm are the following: Lever House, New York (completed 1952), which started the international vogue for curtain-walled skyscrapers rising on a podium of only a few storeys, and which has, moreover, a garden-court in the middle of the podium; the Hilton Hotel at Istanbul (begun 1952); the United States Air Force Academy at Colorado Springs (begun 1955). Other important buildings are the Manufacturers' Trust Bank in New York (1952–4), memorably low in a city of high buildings and (although a bank and in need of security) largely glazed to the outside, and the Connecticut General Life Insurance at Hartford (1953–7), beautifully landscaped and detailed. Skidmore's style is developed from that of MIES VAN DER ROHE and, until recently, rarely departed from its crispness and precision. For some years now the firm has gone in for concrete used in pre-cast members. In this field their Banque Lambert in Brussels of 1959 has proved as influential as Lever House less than a decade before. In some others of their recent buildings a playfulness – even though a structural playfulness – has appeared which is less convincing.

SKIRTING. The edging, usually of wood, fixed to the base of an internal wall.

SKYSCRAPER. A multi-storey building constructed on a steel skeleton, provided with high-speed electric elevators and combining extraordinary height with ordinary room-spaces such as would be used in low buildings. The term originated in the United States in the late 1880s, about ten or twelve years after office buildings in New York had reached the height of ten or twelve storeys or *c.* 250 ft. To go much beyond this was impossible with traditional building materials, and further development was based on the introduction of metal framing. This took place at Chicago in 1883 (*see* JENNEY). Steel skeleton construction for skyscrapers was first established by HOLABIRD & ROCHE's Tacoma Building in Chicago (1890–94) which had twenty-two storeys and a complete steel skeleton. The highest skyscraper before the First World War was C. Gilbert's Woolworth building in New York (792 ft.); the highest to date is the Empire State Building of 1930–32 (1,250 ft).

SLATEHANGING. A wall covering of overlapping rows of slates on a timber substructure.

SLEEPER WALL. An underground wall either supporting SLEEPERS, or built between two PIERS, two walls, or a pier and a wall, to prevent them from shifting. The foundation walls of an ARCADE between nave and aisle would thus be sleeper walls.

SLEEPERS. In a building, strong horizontal beams on which the JOISTS rest. The term can apply to: *a.* beams laid lengthwise on the walls under the ground floor, supporting the floor joists; *b.* in buildings of more than one storey, the beams between the principal posts, marking the divisions and carrying the joists and any other similar cross-beams. With a span of more than 15 ft or so, transverse sleepers are inserted to carry longitudinal joists. The modern term comes from the medieval *dormant*, so called because lesser timbers 'slept' on them.

SLYPE. A covered way or passage, especially in a cathedral or monastic church, leading east from the cloisters between transept and chapterhouse.

SMIRKE, Sir Robert (1780–1867), the leading GREEK REVIVAL architect in England, nevertheless lacked the genius of his almost exact contemporary in Germany, SCHINKEL, by whom he may have been influenced. The son of a painter and Academician, he was articled to SOANE, but quarrelled after a few months. From 1801 to 1805 he travelled in Italy, Sicily, and Greece, sketched most of the ancient buildings in the Morea, and on his return to London published the first and only volume of his projected *Specimens of Continental Architecture* (1806). His first buildings were medieval in style – Lowther Castle (1806–11) and Eastnor Castle (c. 1810–15). He made his name with Covent Garden Theatre (1808, destroyed), the first Greek Doric building in London and as such very influential. It showed with what simple means gravity and grandeur might be achieved. His cool businesslike efficiency quickly brought him fame and fortune, and in 1813 he reached the head of his profession when he joined Soane and NASH as Architect to the Board of Works. His masterpieces came in the next decade, first the British Museum (1823–47), then the General Post Office (1824–9, demolished), both large in scale and massively Grecian in style. Though less uncompromising and less impressive than Schinkel's Altes Museum in Berlin (1825) the British Museum with its tremendous Ionic colonnade has a noble dignity and illustrates his admirable directness and scholarly detailing at their best. Knighted in 1832, he retired in 1845.

SMITHSON, Peter and Alison (b. 1923 and 1928). Their school at Hunstanton

in Norfolk (1954) was one of the most controversial buildings of the time; it is not informal but a symmetrical group, and in its details is inspired by MIES VAN DER ROHE. The Smithsons then turned in the direction of BRUTALISM, but their biggest and most mature building, for the *Economist* in London (1962–4), has none of the quirks of that trend. It is a convincingly grouped scheme of various heights, with a façade to St James's Street that succeeds in establishing a *modus vivendi* with the C18 clubs around, and with two high blocks of different heights behind.

SMYTHSON, Robert (c. 1536–1614), the only Elizabethan architect of note, perfected the spectacular if rather outlandish country-house style developed by the courtiers and magnates of the period. First heard of at Longleat, where he worked as principal freemason (1568–75), he built his masterpiece, Wollaton Hall, during the next decade (1580–8). This was a revolutionary building – a single pile with corner towers and a central hall, planned symmetrically on both axes. The plan probably derives from SERLIO and the whimsical Flemish carved ornamentation of banded shafts, strapwork, etc., from de VRIES, but the fantastic and romantic sham-castle silhouette is his own invention and wholly English. He settled near Wollaton, acquiring property there and the style of a 'gentleman'. But he almost certainly had a hand in the design of three later houses of note, Worksop Manor (c. 1585, now destroyed), Hardwick Hall (1590–7) and Burton Agnes (1601–10). His son John (d. 1634) designed Bolsover Castle (1612 etc.), perhaps the most romantic of all the sham castles.

SOANE, Sir John (1753–1837). The most original English architect after VANBRUGH. His extremely personal style is superficially neo-classical but, in fact, romantic or 'picturesque' in its complicated and unexpected spatial interplay. Intense, severe, and sometimes rather affectedly odd, his buildings reflect his tricky character. He was always slightly uncertain of himself and, despite his genius, never achieved complete confidence and authority even in his own style. The son of a Berkshire builder, he trained under DANCE and HOLLAND, then studied for three years in Italy, where he probably knew PIRANESI; but French influence, especially that of Peyre and LEDOUX, was more profound. He returned to London in 1780, but his career only really began with his appointment as Surveyor to the Bank of England in 1788. His work at the Bank, now destroyed, was among the most advanced in Europe. The Stock Office (begun 1792) and Rotunda (begun 1796) must have seemed shockingly austere, with their shallow domes and general emphasis on utility and structural simplicity, not to mention his reduction of classical ornamentation to rudimentary grooved strips and diagrammatic mouldings. The romantic or picturesque element in his work is felt increasingly after 1800, notably in Pitzhanger Manor (1800–1803; Ealing Public Library) and in the Dulwich College Art Gallery (1811–14, restored 1953), a 'primitivist' construction in brick with each element curiously detached by some slight break or recession, and, above all, in his own house, No. 13 Lincoln's Inn Fields, London (1812–13), now Sir John Soane's Museum. This is highly eccentric and personal to the point of perversity, especially inside, with its congested, claustrophobic planning, complicated floor-levels, ingenious top-lighting, hundreds of mirrors to suggest receding planes and blur divisions, and hanging, Gothic-inspired arches to detach ceilings from walls. The exterior perfectly illustrates his linear stylization and emphasis on planes rather than masses. His last buildings of note are the astylar utili-

tarian stables of Chelsea Hospital (1814–17), St Peter's, Walworth (1822), and Pell Wall (1822–8) a villa-type gate-lodge with curious features reminiscent of VANBRUGH. He was made Professor of Architecture at the Royal Academy in 1806 and knighted in 1831. He published *Designs in Architecture* (London, 1778, re-issued 1790).

SOCLE. A base or pedestal.

SOFFIT. The underside of any architectural element, e.g., an INTRADOS.

SOFFIT CUSPS. Cusps springing from the flat soffit (*see* INTRADOS) of an arched head, and not from its chamfered sides or edges.

SOLAR. An upper living-room in a medieval house; from the Latin *solarium* (a sunny spot or a sun-roof).

SOLARI, Guiniforte (1429–81), a Milanese 'last-ditch' Gothic conservative, completed FILARETE's Renaissance Ospedale Maggiore in the Gothic style, built the simplified Gothic nave of S. Maria delle Grazie, Milan (1465–90, completed by BRAMANTE), and worked on the Gothic Milan Cathedral.

SOLARI, Santino (1576–1646), one of the first Italian architects to work extensively in Germany and Austria, came of a large family of artists from Como. His main work is Salzburg Cathedral (1614–28), an entirely Italian basilican church with dome and with twin towers flanking the west façade. For the Bishop of Salzburg he built the Italianate *Lustschloss* at Hellbrunn, outside Salzburg (1613–19). He also designed (c. 1620) the solemn little shrine of the black-faced Virgin at Einsiedeln, Switzerland, later surrounded by MOOSBRUGGER's fantastic Baroque abbey church.

SOLARIUM. A sun terrace or LOGGIA.

SOLEA. In an Early Christian or Byzantine church, a raised pathway projecting from the BEMA to the AMBO.

SOLOMONIC COLUMN. A barley-sugar or twisted column, so called from its supposed use in Solomon's temple. *See also* SALOMÓNICA.

SOMMARUGA, Giuseppe (1867–1917), a native of Milan, was a pupil of the Brera Academy and of Boito and Beltrami, but turned to ART NOUVEAU and became, side by side with Raimondo d'Aronco (1857–1932; buildings for the Turin Exhibition, 1902), its most important representative in Italy. His principal works are the Palazzo Castiglioni on the Corso Venezia, Milan (1901) and the Hotel Tre Croci at Campo dei Fiori, near Varese (1909–12).

SOPRAPORTA. A painting above the door of a room, usually framed in harmony with the doorcase to form a decorative unit.

SOUFFLOT, Jacques Germain (1713–80), the greatest French neo-classical architect, was the son of a provincial lawyer against whose wishes he went off to Rome to study architecture in 1731. He stayed seven years, settling on his return in Lyon, where he was commissioned to build the enormous Hôtel Dieu (1741 etc.). This made his reputation, and in 1749 he was chosen by Mme de Pompadour to accompany her brother, M. de Marigny, to Italy, where he was to spend two years preparing himself for his appointment as Surintendant des Bâtiments. The tour was very successful and may be regarded as marking the beginning of NEO-CLASSICISM in France, of which the great masterpiece was to be Soufflot's Ste Geneviève (called the Panthéon since the Revolution) in Paris (begun 1757). This was a revolutionary building for France and was hailed by the leading neo-classical critic and theorist, LAUGIER, as 'the first example of perfect architecture'. It perfectly expresses a new, more serious, not to say solemn attitude towards Antiquity, and combines Roman regularity and monumentality with a structural lightness derived from Gothic architecture. Soufflot himself said (1762) that one should combine the Greek orders with the lightness one admired in Gothic buildings. He continued working on his masterpiece to the end of his life, but did not live to see it finished. His other buildings are of much less interest, e.g., École de Droit, Paris (designed 1763, built 1771 onwards) and various follies in the park of the Château de Menars (1767 etc.) including a rotunda, nymphaeum, and orangery, all in an elegant but rather dry neo-classical style.

SOUNDING BOARD, see PULPIT.

SPACE-FRAME. A three-dimensional framework for enclosing spaces, in which all members are interconnected and act as a single entity, resisting loads applied in any direction. Systems can be designed to cover very large spaces, uninterrupted by support from the ground, and the surface covering can be integrated to play its part in the structural whole. Some types have the appearance of egg-boxes (pyramidal in their elements), others are based on hexagonal or other geometric figures. The chief exponents to date are Z. Makowski (*space-grid*), Le Ricolais, Konrad Wachsmann, and Buckminster FULLER, whose dome, designed for the Union Tank Car Co., Baton Rouge, U.S.A. (1958), has a diameter of 384 ft. *See figure 77.*

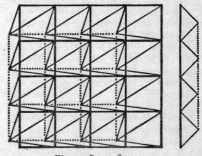

Fig. 77. Space-frame

SPANDREL. The triangular space between the side of an arch, the horizontal drawn from the level of its apex, and the vertical of its springing; also applied to the surface between two arches in an arcade, and the surface

of a vault between adjacent ribs.
SPANISH ARCHITECTURE. After the
Roman aqueducts, etc., the first noteworthy monuments in Spain are a few
relics of the Visigothic age, notably
S. Juan de Baños (661), originally with
a very odd plan with a square chancel
and square chapels of the same size
attached to the long narrow transepts.
The plan of S. Miguel at Tarrasa
(c9 or earlier) – Tarrasa being one of
the rare surviving examples of a
'church family' – is of the Early Christian and Byzantine inscribed-cross
plan, that of S. Pedro de Nave (c7)
a composition of square or oblong
compartments like the English *porticus*.
This latter scheme became that of the
eminently interesting Asturian churches of the c9 such as Sta Cristina de
Lena and S. Miguel de Lino. One of
them, now a church, was originally a
royal hall (Sta Maria de Naranco).

Meanwhile the Mohammedans had
captured most of Spain (711 etc.), and
the Mosque of Cordoba had been begun in 786. It grew to be in the end a
vast rectangle of *c*. 550 × 420 ft, filled
with a forest of columns so as to form
nineteen parallel naves. The most
ornate parts date from *c*. 970. The
vaults of these parts with their intersected ribs must have inspired certain
Gothic and certain Baroque vaults.
However, Islam's architecture also
immediately inspired Spanish Christian architecture. The term MOZARA-
BIC means such mixtures of Mohammedan and Christian elements as are
exemplified by S. Miguel de Escalada
(consecrated in 913), with its arcade
arches of horseshoe shape, Santiago de
Peñalba (931–7) and Santa Maria de
Lebeña (also c10). The term MUDÉJAR
refers to Christian architecture in a
purely Moslem style, and this remained
characteristic of secular architecture in
Spain nearly to the end of the Middle
Ages. No wonder, considering the
glories and luxurious comforts of the
Alhambra of Granada which – in the
one remaining Moslem part of the

peninsula – was built as late as the
c14. Among the Christians such
Mudéjar towers of the c13 as those of
Teruel look back at the splendour of
the Giralda at Seville of *c*. 1185–90,
and palaces of Christian rulers established Mohammedan forms of
decoration, of plan and of life. The
palace of Tordesillas is of the 1340s,
the Alcázar at Seville of the years
of Pedro the Cruel (1349–68), and at
Seville the so-called House of Pilate
carried Mudéjar right into the c16,
even if the last-built parts of the house
(which was completed in 1553) take
full note of Gothic as well as developed
Renaissance motifs.

But this anticipates the story by
several centuries. The Romanesque
style had started in the early c11 in
Catalonia in a version similar to that
of Lombardy (Ripoll, 1010–32, desperately restored; Cardona, consecrated 1040). The c11 in Spain is particularly important for decorative
sculpture. It seems that ever since S.
Pedro de Nave in the c10 the Spanish
were ahead of the French in this field.
There is certainly nothing in France to
compare with the capitals of Jaca. The
French Romanesque of the great
pilgrimage churches has an outstanding
representative in the far north-west
corner of Spain in the celebrated
church of Santiago de Compostela
(begun *c*. 1075 and completed with the
splendidly sculptured Pórtico de la
Gloria in 1188). Other Romanesque
churches are S. Martin de Frómista of
c. 1060 etc., S. Isidoro at León with
its antechurch known as the Panteón
de los Reyes also of *c*. 1060, and Lugo
Cathedral, a direct descendant of
Santiago, and S. Vicente at Ávila, both
of the c12. The Late Romanesque of
Spain is best represented by the Old
Cathedral of Salamanca and the Cathedral of Zamora, both with curious
domes of West and South-West
French affinities, but essentially original.

To determine the date when the

Gothic style arrived is as difficult for Spain as for England. The Old Cathedral of Salamanca for instance has pointed arches almost entirely. But pointed arches are not necessarily Gothic. The Cistercians who came directly or indirectly from Burgundy brought the pointed arch as a Burgundian Romanesque motif. The Cistercians arrived in Spain in 1131, and soon large buildings were erected by them in many places: Moreruela, Meira, La Oliva, Huerta, Veruela, Poblet, Santas Creus have the standard French plan with chancel and transeptal east chapels. But while these are mostly straight-ended it is also usual in Spain to have the chancel apsed (Oliva, Huerta, Meira) or even an ambulatory and apsed radiating chapels (Moreruela, Poblet, Veruela). Whereas in many of these churches one can be in doubt as to what to regard as Romanesque, what as Gothic, La Oliva must clearly be considered Gothic, and the date of the beginning is 1164.

With the C13 the North French cathedral style entered Spain. The most French cathedrals of the C13 are those of Burgos (1221 etc.), Toledo (1226 etc.), and León, but the most original version of the Spanish Gothic is Catalan (Barcelona Cathedral, 1298 etc.; Sta María del Mar, Barcelona, 1329 etc.; Palma Cathedral, Majorca), with very wide and high naves and very high aisles or with aisles replaced by chapels between internal buttresses (Sta Catalina, Barcelona, 1223 etc.; Sta María del Pino, Barcelona, c. 1320 and Gerona Cathedral whose nave with a span of 74 ft is the widest in Europe). The Late Gothic style was much influenced by Germany and the Netherlands, as is shown by such works as the towers of Burgos Cathedral by Juan de Colonia (*see* SIMÓN DE COLONIA) (begun 1442). Late Gothic vaults with their lierne rib patterns also have German origins. Spatially, however, Spain was entirely Spanish: the vast rectangles of her cathedrals hark back to the mosques of Islam, but their height and the height of the aisles are her own. Seville Cathedral was begun in 1402 and is 430 ft long and 250 ft wide, with a nave 130 ft high and aisles 85 ft high. Spain continued to embark on new cathedrals on this scale right up to the time of the Reformation. Salamanca was started in 1512, Segovia in 1525. In Spain those were the years of greatest wealth, resulting in the many funerary monuments and the excessively lavish decoration of such buildings as the Constable's Chapel at Burgos Cathedral (1482 etc.) and S. Juan de los Reyes, Toledo (1476 etc.), or of such façades as those of S. Pablo (1486 etc.) and S. Gregorio (c. 1492), both at Valladolid. No square inch must remain without its complicated and lacy carving. The spirit of Islam re-asserted itself in this, and the desire to over-decorate surfaces was carried on with Renaissance details in the C16 (PLATERESQUE style) and with Baroque details in the C18 (CHURRIGUERESQUE style).

Spain is the country of the most spectacular castles. For the C12 the most magnificent display is the walls of Ávila, for the C13 the castle of Alcalá de Guadaira, for the C13 Bellver on Majorca (1309–14) which is round and has a round courtyard, for the C15 Coca, vast and all of brick.

The Italian Renaissance had actually reached Spain early, and such monuments as the courtyard of the castle of La Calahorra (1509–12) or the staircase of the Hospital of Toledo (1504 etc.) are pure and perfectly at ease. But almost at once the crowding of motifs started again, and the façade of the University of Salamanca (c. 1515 etc.) is no more than a furnishing of the Late Gothic façade, with new motifs. Soon, however, the pure Italian High Renaissance also entered Spain. The first and for a while the only example is Charles V's unfinished palace on the Alhambra (1526 by MACHUCA), with its circular courtyard and its motifs reminiscent of RAPHAEL and GIULIO ROMANO. The severest and vastest palace in the Italian style is Philip II's Escorial (1563 etc. by Juan Bautista de TOLEDO and HERRERA). Ecclesiastical architecture in the C16 reached its climax in the east end of Granada Cathedral by SILOE (1528 etc.), and the parts of 1585 etc. of Valladolid Cathedral by Herrera. But such austerity remained rare, and Spain came once again into her own when, in the late C17, she developed that style of excessive Baroque surface decoration which culminated in such buildings as the façade of Santiago de Compostela (1738 etc.), the sacristy of the Charterhouse of Granada (1727 etc.), the Transparente in Toledo Cathedral (1721–32), the portal of the Hospital of S. Ferdinand in Madrid (1722) and that of the Dos Aguas Palace at Valencia (1740–44). Greater sobriety in an Italian and French sense characterizes the circular Sanctuary of St Ignatius of Loyola, begun in 1689 and designed by Carlo FONTANA, the Royal Palace in Madrid by G. B. SACCHETTI begun in 1738, the Royal Palace of La Granja, partly by Filippo JUVARRA (1719 etc.), and the Royal Palace of Aranjuez, by another Italian, Bonavia (1748 etc.). Among the Spanish academics Ventura RODRÍGUEZ was the most conspicuous figure; his giant portico for Pamplona Cathedral was built in 1783. Of 1787 is the even more neo-classical design for the Prado in Madrid by Juan de VILLANUEVA.

To the C19 and C20 Spain has not made any essential contributions except for the fabulous work of GAUDÍ at Barcelona which is the international climax of ART NOUVEAU in architecture.

SPENCE, Sir Basil (b. 1907), before the war designed mostly large country houses in Scotland; after the war he made his name in England as well by exhibition work (Sea and Ships,

Festival of Britain, 1951). In 1951 he won the competition for Coventry Cathedral, and the building was consecrated in 1962. It is outstanding in the use made of the steeple of the old Perpendicular cathedral as its one vertical accent; in the use of the shell of the old nave and chancel as a landscaped atrium; in the saw-tooth side walls treated so that only those sides have windows which face towards the altar; and in the ample opportunities given to artists and craftsmen (Graham Sutherland, John Piper, Geoffrey Clarke). Since 1954 Sir Basil Spence and his firm have done much university work (Edinburgh, Southampton, Nottingham, Liverpool, Sussex) and most recently and spectacularly the Barracks in Knightsbridge and the Chancellery of the British Embassy in Rome (completed 1971).

SPERE-TRUSS. A wooden arch with PIERS – the latter attached with trusses to the side walls – which stood, at least at wall-plate height, at the kitchen end of a medieval timber-framed hall, marking the division between the hall proper and the SCREENS PASSAGE; so-called from the screen or *spere* which separated the hall from the kitchen.

SPIRE. A tall pyramidal, polygonal, or conical structure rising from a tower, turret, or roof (usually of a church) and terminating in a point. It can be of stone, or of timber covered with SHINGLES, or lead. A *broach* spire is usually octagonal in plan, placed on a square tower and rising without an intermediate parapet. Each of the four angles of the tower not covered by the base of the spire is filled with an inclined mass of masonry or broach built into the oblique sides of the spire, carried up to a point, and covering a SQUINCH. A broach spire is thus the interpenetration of a lower-pitch pyramid with a much steeper octagon. A *needle* spire is a thin spire rising from the centre of a tower roof, well inside a parapet protecting a pathway upon which scaffolding could be erected for repairs. *See figure 78.*

SPIRELET, *see* FLÈCHE.

SPLAY. A sloping, chamfered surface cut into the walls. The term usually

SPUR. An ornament, usually of foliage, on the corner of a square plinth surmounted by a circular PIER; also called a *griffe*.

SPUR STONE. A stone projecting from

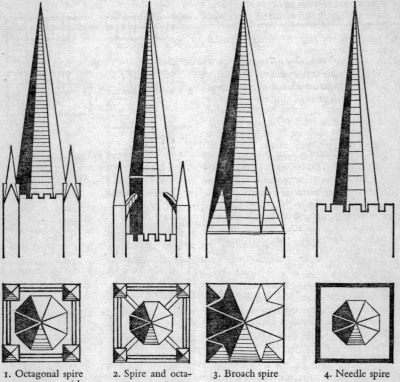

1. Octagonal spire over tower with pinnacles

2. Spire and octagon over tower with flying buttresses

3. Broach spire

4. Needle spire

Fig. 78. Spire

refers to the widening of doorways, windows, or other wall-openings by slanting the sides. *See also* REVEAL.

SPRINGING LINE. The level at which an arch springs from its supports. The bottom stone of the arch resting on the IMPOST each side can thus be called a *springer. See also* SKEWBACK *and figure 4.*

the angle of a corner or arch to prevent damage by passing traffic: it is usually circular in section.

SQUINCH. An arch or system of concentrically wider and gradually projecting arches, placed diagonally at the internal angles of towers to fit a polygonal or round superstructure on to a square plan. *See figure 38.*

SQUINT. An obliquely cut opening in a wall or through a PIER to allow a view of the main altar of a church from places whence it could not otherwise be seen; also called a *hagioscope*.

STADDLE STONES. Mushroom-shaped stones used as bases to support timber-built granaries or hay barns, especially in Sussex.

STAIR, STAIRCASE. There are special names for the various parts of a stair: the *tread* is the horizontal surface of a step; the *riser* is the vertical surface; a *winder* is a tread wider at one end than the other. A *newel staircase* is a circular or winding staircase with a solid central post in which the narrow ends of the steps are supported. The *newel* is also the principal post at the end of a flight of stairs; it carries the *handrails* and the *strings* which support the steps. A *dog-leg staircase* consists of two flights at right angles, with a half landing. *See figure 79.* A *geometrical staircase* is composed of stone steps each of which is built into the wall at one end and rests on the step below; generally built on a circular or elliptical plan.

Staircases seem to have existed as long as monumental architecture: a staircase of *c.* 6000 B.C. has been discovered in the excavations of Jericho. Monumental staircases also existed at Knossos in Crete and Persepolis in Iran. The Greeks and the Romans were not apparently much interested in making an architectural feature of the staircase, and medieval staircases were also utilitarian as a rule. In the Middle Ages the accepted form was the newel staircase, which could assume a monumental scale (Vis du Louvre, Paris, late C14), but only did so to any extent after 1500 (Blois). The standard form of the Italian Renaissance is two flights, the upper at an angle of 180° to the lower, and both running up between solid walls. However, a few architects, notably FRANCESCO DI GIORGIO and LEONARDO DA VINCI, worked out on paper a number of other, more interesting types, and these seem to have been translated into reality in the C16, mostly in Spain. There is the staircase which starts in one flight and returns in two, the whole rising in one well; the staircase

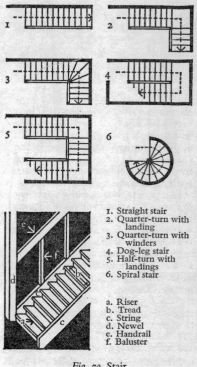

1. Straight stair
2. Quarter-turn with landing
3. Quarter-turn with winders
4. Dog-leg stair
5. Half-turn with landings
6. Spiral stair

a. Riser
b. Tread
c. String
d. Newel
e. Handrail
f. Baluster

Fig. 79. Stair

which starts in one and turns at right angles into two (BRAMANTE's Belvedere Court in the Vatican; Escalera Dorada, Burgos); and, the most frequent type, the staircase which runs up in three flights at right angles round an open well, i.e., a squared spiral stair with intermediate landings. But Bramante in the Vatican still built a normal spiral stair, though also with an open well, and BERNINI (Palazzo Barberini) made this oval, a characceristically Baroque turn. PALLADIO invented the geometrical or flying staircase (Academy, Venice), a spiral staircase without any support other than the bonding of the steps into the outer wall.

The Baroque is the great age of monumental and inventive staircases. The finest of all are in Germany (Würzburg, Brühl, and especially Bruchsal, all by NEUMANN), but there are excellent ones also in France (MANSART at Blois) and in Italy (Naples).

In C20 architecture the staircase has assumed a new significance as the element in a building which is most expressive of spatial flow. The earliest staircase in a glass cage is GROPIUS's at the Cologne Werkbund exhibition (1914). Since then much has been made of flying staircases, staircases without risers, and similar effects.

STALACTITE WORK. Ceiling ornament in ISLAMIC ARCHITECTURE formed by corbelled SQUINCHES made of several layers of brick scalloped out to resemble natural stalactites.

STALL. A carved seat of wood or stone in a row of similar seats; if hinged, often carved on the underside (see MISERICORD).

STANCHION. A vertical supporting member, nowadays mainly of steel.

STARLING. A pointed projection on the PIER of a bridge to break the force of the water. See CUTWATER.

STAROV, Ivan Yegorovich (1743–1808), the first Russian-born architect to work successfully in the West European manner, was born in Moscow and trained at the St Petersburg Academy of Fine Arts. He then went to Paris, where he was trained under DE WAILLY (1762–8). His works are neo-classical and rather solid, e.g., church and columned rotunda belfry at Nikolskoe (1774–6, destroyed 1941), Cathedral of the Trinity, Leningrad (1776). His masterpiece is the vast Tauride Palace, Leningrad (1783–8), built for Potemkin and very rich in

columns inside and out but later re-modelled by Luigi Rusca.

STASSOV, Vasili Petrovich (1769–1848). The best-known Russian architect of the later neo-classical period in Leningrad, i.e., after the great period of THOMON, VORONIKHIN and ZAKHAROV. His bell-tower of the village church in Gruzino (1815) is geometric almost in the LEDOUX manner. His masterpiece is the Triumphal Gate in Leningrad (1833–8), a trabeated Greek Doric propylaeon entirely constructed in cast iron. His earlier Church of the Transfiguration (1826–8) and Trinity Cathedral (1828–35), both in Leningrad, have Greek cross plans and five domes.

STAVE CHURCH. A timber-framed and timber-walled church; the walls are of upright planks with corner-post columns. The term is applied exclusively to Scandinavian churches built from the early or mid C11 onwards. Later stave churches usually have inner rows of posts or piers, sometimes an external covered arcade, and roofs arranged in tiers. A third system was also used from c. 1200, incorporating a central column from the floor to the roof.

STEEPLE. The tower and spire of a church taken together.

STEREOBATE. A solid mass of masonry serving as a base, usually for a wall or a row of columns.

STETHAIMER, Hans (d. 1432), worked at Landshut in Bavaria. He came from Burghausen, is usually called Hans von Burghausen and may not have been called Stethaimer. He began St Martin's, the chief parish church of Landshut, in 1387. On his funerary monument other works of his are mentioned: they include the chancel of the Franciscan Church at Salzburg (begun 1408). He was one of the best of the German Late Gothic architects, believed in the 'HALL CHURCH', in brick as a material, where he could use it, and in a minimum of decoration. At Salzburg the most fascinating motif is that of the long slender piers of the chancel with one of them placed axially, due east, so that the eye faces not an interstice but a pier with the light from the east playing round it. Stethaimer's monument may indicate that he was also concerned with sculpture. His source is the style of the PARLER family.

STIFF-LEAF. A late C12 and early C13 type of sculptured foliage, found chiefly on CAPITALS and BOSSES, a development from the CROCKETS of crocket capitals; almost entirely confined to Britain. *See figure 24.*

STILE LIBERTY. The Italian term for ART NOUVEAU.

STILTED ARCH, *see* ARCH.

STIRLING & GOWAN (James Stirling and James Gowan, b. 1926 and 1924). Their small housing estate at Ham, near London (1958), established their sympathy with the trend influenced by LE CORBUSIER and often called BRUTALISM. Their Department of Engineering, Leicester University (1959–63), is their most complete statement. After James Stirling had separated from James Gowan, he designed the building for the History Faculty for Cambridge (1965–8), and a new building for the Queen's College, Oxford (1968–70). They have a ruthlessness which militates against their achieving a more than passing success.

STOA. In Greek architecture, a detached colonnade. In Byzantine architecture, a covered hall, its roof supported by one or more rows of columns parallel to the rear wall; in Latin, porticus.

STOEP. The Dutch term for veranda.

STONE, Edward (b. 1903). Successful American architect who likes to clothe his façades with an ornamental veil, usually including arched elements. He designed his own house, 7 East 67th Street in New York, in 1956. Other buildings of his are the U.S. Embassy at New Delhi (1954–8), the U.S. Pavilion at the Brussels International Exhibition (1958) and the Huntington Hartford Museum in Columbus Circle in New York (1958–9).

STOP-CHAMFER. An ornamental termination to a CHAMFER, common in the Early English period and very much favoured by Victorian architects bringing the edge of the pared-off stone or beam back to a right angle; also called a *broach-stop*. *See figure 80.*

Fig. 80. Stop-chamfer

STOPS. Projecting stones at the ends of HOOD-MOULDS, STRING COURSES, etc., against which the mouldings finish; often carved. *See also* LABEL-STOP.

STOREY (or STORY). The space between any two floors or between the floor and roof of a building. In England the ground-level storey is usually called the ground floor, in America the first floor, in France the *rez-de-chaussée*.

STOREY-POSTS. The principal posts of a timber-framed wall.

STOUP. A vessel to contain holy water, placed near the entrance of a church; usually in the form of a shallow dish set against a wall or pier or in a niche.

STRAINER ARCH, *see* ARCH.

STRAPWORK. Decoration originating in the Netherlands *c.* 1540, also common in Elizabethan England, consisting of interlaced bands and forms similar to fretwork or cut leather; generally used in ceilings, screens, and funerary monuments. *See figure 81.*

STREET, George Edmund (1824–81), a pupil of George Gilbert SCOTT, was in practice in 1849, after having

Fig. 81. Strapwork

already designed some churches in Cornwall. In 1850–1 he travelled in France and Germany, in 1853 in North Italy (resulting in a book on the marble and brick buildings of North Italy which came out in 1855), in 1854 in Germany again, in 1861–3 three times in Spain (his important book on Spanish Gothic architecture was published in 1865). In 1852 Street started a practice at Oxford, and among his first assistants were WEBB and MORRIS. The first important building is the Cuddesdon Theological College. Street was a High Church man much appreciated by the Cambridge Camden group (*see* BUTTERFIELD), a tremendous worker and a fertile draughtsman who liked to design all details himself. His first large church was St Peter, Bournemouth (1853 etc.).

The practice was moved to London in 1855, and there Street's most characteristic early church is St James the Less, off Vauxhall Bridge Road (1860–1), a very strong design encouraged no doubt by Butterfield but not in imitation of him, and inspired by RUSKIN. The Gothic is Continental rather than English. Among Street's most notable churches are Oakengates, Shropshire (1855); Boyne Hill, Berkshire (1859); St Philip and St James, Oxford (1860–2); All Saints, Clifton, Bristol (1863–8); St John, Torquay (1861–71); St Mary Magdalen, Paddington, London (1868–78); and Holmbury St Mary, built at his own expense (1879). Street is always unconventional and inventive, yet hardly ever as aggressive as Butterfield. His principal secular work is the Law Courts, won in competition in 1866.

It is a high-minded essay in C13 Gothic, yet picturesque in grouping. The Great Hall inside is particularly impressive.

STRESSED-SKIN CONSTRUCTION. A form of construction in which the outer skin acts with the frame members to contribute to the flexural strength of the unit as a whole.

STRETCHER, *see* BRICKWORK.

STRICKLAND, William (1788–1854), a pupil of LATROBE in Philadelphia, rose to fame with the Bank of the United States, Philadelphia, now the Custom House. This had first been designed by Latrobe, but was then built to a modified design by Strickland (1818–24). It is Grecian in style, whereas Strickland's earlier Masonic Temple (1810) had been Gothic. His finest building is the Philadelphia Merchants' Exchange (1834 etc.), with its elegant corner motif crowned by a copy of the Lysicrates Monument. He also built the United States Mint, Washington (1829–33), in a style similar to MILLS's, and the United States Naval Asylum (1827) with an Ionic portico and tiers of long balconies left and right. Strickland was a very versatile man: in his early days he painted and did stage design, and he was also throughout his later life engaged in major engineering enterprises (canals, railways, the Delaware Breakwater).

STRING COURSE. A continuous projecting horizontal band set in the surface of an exterior wall and usually moulded.

STRINGS. The two sloping members which carry the ends of the treads and risers of a STAIRCASE. *See figure 79.*

STRUT, *see* ROOF.

STUART, James 'Athenian' (1713–88), a minor architect, is nevertheless important in the history of GREEK REVIVAL architecture for his temple at Hagley (1758), the earliest Doric Revival building in Europe. He and Revett went to Greece in 1751–5 and in 1762 published the *Antiquities of Athens* (2nd vol. 1789), which had little immediate influence except on interior decoration. Indolence and un-reliability lost him many commissions, and he built very little. He designed several first floor rooms at Spencer House, London (1760 onwards). His No. 15 St James's Square, London (1763–6) was later altered internally by James WYATT (c. 1791). The Triumphal Arch, Tower of the Winds, and Lysicrates Monument in the park at Shugborough are his best surviving works. They date from between 1764 and 1770. His chapel at Greenwich Hospital (1779–88) seems to have been designed largely by his assistant William Newton.

STUART ARCHITECTURE, see ENGLISH ARCHITECTURE.

STUCCO. Plasterwork.

STUDS. Upright timbers in TIMBER-FRAMED houses. See figure 83.

STUPA. A Buddhist sepulchral monument, usually domed or beehive-shaped.

STYLOBATE. The substructure on which a colonnade stands; more correctly, the top step of the structure forming the CREPIDOMA.

SUGER, Abbot (1081–1151), was not an architect; neither does he seem to have been responsible, even as an amateur, for any architectural work. But as he was abbot of St Denis, outside Paris, when the abbey church was partly rebuilt (c. 1135–44), and as this was the building where the Gothic style was to all intents and purposes invented, or where it finally evolved out of the scattered elements already existing in many places, his name must be recorded here. He wrote two books on the abbey in which the new building is commented on, but nowhere refers to the designer or indeed explicitly to the innovations incorporated in the building.

SULLIVAN, Louis Henry (1856–1924), was of mixed Irish, Swiss, and German descent. He was born in Boston, studied architecture briefly at the Massachusetts Institute of Technology,

and moved to Chicago in 1873. He worked there under JENNEY, then, after a year in Paris in VAUDREMER's atelier, returned to Chicago. In 1879 he joined the office of Dankmar Adler, and the firm became Adler & Sullivan in 1881. Their first major building, and no doubt the most spectacular in Chicago up to that time, was the Auditorium (1886–90), which was strongly influenced by RICHARDSON. The auditorium itself is capable of seating more than 4,000. Sullivan's interior decoration is exceedingly interesting, of a feathery vegetable character, derived perhaps from the Renaissance but at the same time pointing forward into the licence of ART NOUVEAU. His two most familiar skyscrapers, the Wainwright Building, St Louis (1890), and the Guaranty Building, Buffalo (1894), have not the exclusively functional directness of HOLABIRD & ROCHE's Marquette Building of 1894, but they do express externally the SKELETON structure and the cellular interior arrangements. However, Sullivan, though pleading in his Kindergarten Chats (1901) for a temporary embargo on all decoration, was himself as fascinated by ornament as by functional expression, and this appears even in the entrance motifs of his major building, the Carson, Pirie & Scott Store (1899–1904), which is most characteristic of the 'Chicago School'. For the Chicago Exhibition of 1893 Sullivan designed the Transportation Building, with its impressively sheer giant entrance arch. He recognized the setback which the classicism otherwise prevailing at the exhibition would mean to the immediate future of American architecture.

Adler died in 1900, and after that time Sullivan's work grew less until it dried up almost entirely. He was a difficult man, uncompromising and erratic, but his brilliance is undeniable – see the passages which his pupil WRIGHT has devoted to his Lieber Meister.

SUMERIAN ARCHITECTURE, see AS-SYRIAN AND SUMERIAN ARCHITEC-TURE.

SUSTRIS, Friedrich (1524–99 or 91?). Netherlandish Mannerist painter and architect working in Munich at the same time as Peter CANDID and the Mannerist sculptor Hubert Gerhard. He studied in Italy where he acquired a sophisticated Mannerist style derived from VASARI. His main work in architecture is the chancel and transept of St Michael's Church in Munich (1592, built after the collapse of a tower in that year). He probably designed the Grotto Court (c. 1581) in the Residenz, very Florentine Mannerist in style. In 1584 he remodelled the parish church of Dachau. His design for the interior decoration of Schloss Landshut survives (1577) and the Akademie der Wissenschaften (formerly the Jesuit College) in Munich is attributed to him.

SWAG. A FESTOON in the form of a piece of cloth draped over two supports.

SWAN-NECK. An OGEE-shaped member, e.g., the curve in a staircase handrail where it rises to join the newel post.

SWEDISH ARCHITECTURE, see SCAN-DINAVIAN ARCHITECTURE.

SWISS ARCHITECTURE. Switzerland has all the architectural advantages and disadvantages of a position between three larger countries (Germany, France and Italy): the advantage of variety of styles, the disadvantage of little visual identity.

The country is uncommonly rich (given its small size) in early buildings. At Romainmôtier a small, aisleless C5 church with two transeptal porticos (in the English sense of the word) has been excavated, and a larger church consecrated in 753 and still of the same archaic plan. Chur has the C8 E. end of St Lucius with a ring-crypt and above it three parallel apses on Italian Early Christian precedent. The same E. end is at St Martin at Chur, Müstair and Disentis.

The earliest Romanesque churches are inspired by Burgundy and especially the second church of Cluny. They are the third building of Romain-môtier with a typically Burgundian antechurch, and Payerne. Both are C11. Schaffhausen on the other hand of the late C11 and early C12 looks to Germany and the chief German Cluniac centre Hirsau. The Romanesque style culminates in the cathedral of Basel, connected closely with Alsace. It contains a little of the early C11, but dates mostly from c. 1180 and later.

At that same time the cathedral of Lausanne had already been begun, and this as well as Geneva Cathedral are again orientated towards France and now a Gothic France. Lausanne Cathedral in particular actually belongs to the Burgundian school of the C13. The principal Late Gothic churches on the other hand are an outlier of South Germany: Berne Minster (1421 etc.), St Oswald at Zug (1478 etc.) and St Leonard at Basel (1489 etc.).

It is understandable that the Renaissance appears first in the cantons bordering on Italy. The portal of St Salvator at Lugano of 1517 is close to Como in style. Of later C16 buildings it is enough to refer to the three-storeyed courtyard arcades of the Ritter House at Lucerne (1556–61) and to the Geltenzunft (1578) and Spiesshof (late C16) at Basel, both more classical than such buildings usually are in Germany. The Spiesshof in particular with its SERLIANA windows is indeed closely dependent on SERLIO.

The C17 gives a mixed impression. There is the fascinating Gothicism of the church of the Visitandes at Fribourg, a quatrefoil in plan but with the most intricate rib vaults (1653–6), there is the Zürich Town Hall, still Renaissance rather than Baroque, though as late as 1694–8, and there are the beginnings of a German Baroque in such a church as that of Muri, designed by MOOSBRUGGER and begun in 1694. Its centre is a spacious octagon. Moosbrugger then designed the spatially complex Einsiedeln (1703).

The C18 in Switzerland stands under the sign of the contrast between the dazzling and melodramatic South German Baroque (St Gall 1755–69) and the cool restrained French Dix-huitième (private houses, Geneva). There is in this of course also a contrast between Catholic and Protestant. Typically Protestant churches of un-usual interior are the entirely French Temple at Geneva (1707–10 by Vennes), and Holy Ghost, Berne (1726–9 by Schildknecht). The church at Berne is oblong and has four entries in the middles of the four sides and as its only asymmetrical accents a (German) W. tower and the pulpit inside close to the E. end. The cathe-dral of Solothurn of 1762 etc. (by G. M. Pisoni) is mildly classicist, the noble W. portico of Geneva Cathe-dral of 1752–6 (by Count ALFIERI) much more radically so. But the most exactingly neo-classicist building of the late C18 in Switzerland is the town hall of Neufchâtel of 1782–90 (by P. A. Pâris).

For the C19 the most interesting series of buildings are the *hôtels*, but they have not yet been sufficiently studied. For the C20 Switzerland con-tributed good architecture in the pre-first-war years (Badischer Bahnhof, Basel, by Curjel & Moser, 1912–13), outstanding Expressionism of the same and the immediate post-first-war years (Goetheanum Dornach by Rudolf Steiner 1913 and again after a disas-trous fire 1923–8) and much good and early work in the International Mod-ern of the twenties and thirties. Some of the churches were highly influential abroad (e.g., St Anthony, Basel, by Moser 1925–31). LE CORBUSIER who was born at La Chaux-de-Fonds con-tributed one block of flats at Geneva (1931–2). The standard of architecture in Switzerland has remained high, and even the newest buildings keep away from extremism and irrationalism – a Swiss trait no doubt.

SYNTHRONON. In Early Christian and Byzantine churches, the bench or benches reserved for the clergy in the semicircle of the apse or in rows on either side of the BEMA.

SYSTYLE. With an arrangement of columns spaced two diameters apart. *See also* ARAEOSTYLE; DIASTYLE; EUSTYLE; PYCNOSTYLE.

T

TABERNACLE. 1. An ornamented recess or receptacle to contain the Holy Sacrament or relics. 2. A free-standing canopy.

TABLINUM. In Roman architecture, a room with one side open to the ATRIUM or central courtyard.

TAENIA, see TENIA.

TALMAN, William (1650–1719), WREN's most distinguished contemporary, was the leading country-house architect until eclipsed by VANBRUGH. Little is known about him personally, though he seems to have been difficult and quarrelsome. His country houses are by far the largest and most lavish of their period in England, and display a mixed French and Italian Baroque character. They were very influential, e.g., in the use of giant pilasters with architrave and frieze to frame a façade, the cornice alone continuing across. Thoresby (1683–5, destroyed), the east front of Chatsworth (1687–96), Dyrham Park (1698–1700), Dorchester House, Surrey (c. 1700), and the new front at Drayton (c. 1701) were his main works, all country houses. He designed the state apartments at Burghley House, Northants (1658, destroyed). He succeeded Hugh MAY as Comptroller of the Office of Works in 1689, serving under Wren, whose design for Hampton Court he probably revised and altered in execution.

TAMBOUR. 1. The core of a Corinthian or Composite CAPITAL. 2. The circular wall carrying a DOME or CUPOLA (see DRUM).

TANGE, Kenzo (b. 1913), studied at Tokyo University 1935–8 and 1942–5, then joined the office of Kunio Maekawa (see JAPANESE ARCHITECTURE). His mature buildings are all dramatically plastic: the Kagawa prefectural offices at Takamatsu (1958), with a ruthlessly expressed post-and-beam structure; the waterfront Dentsu offices at Osaka (1960); the Atami Gardens Hotel at Atami (1961), meticulously furnished by Isamu Kenmochi; the challenging, somewhat sombre City Hall at Kurashiki (1960), standing four-square and quakeproof; St Mary's Roman Catholic Cathedral, Tokyo (1965), a cruciform arrangement of paraboloids; and the joyful Golf Club at Totsuka (1962), in which an upswept traditional roof is typically contrasted with aluminium curtain walls. With Yoshokatsu Tsuboi as engineer, Tange designed the magnificent tensile catenary roof spanning the 15,000 seat National Gymnasium, ready for the Tokyo Olympic Games in 1964. Tange's leadership of the younger generation principally results from his research work into town planning at Tokyo University, the absence of which has reduced Japan's expanding industrial cities to a critical state of congestion. Tange's plan for Tokyo (1960) shows a logical hierarchy of rapid transit roads within connecting ring roads, enclosing environmental areas of high density housing; his idea was to extend the city in this way on piles over Tokyo Bay. He won the international competition for replanning Skopje in Yugoslavia (1965), with a system of multi-purpose blocks. He has designed prototypes of these for the Dentsu building and Tsukiji area, Tokyo (1965), with flying bridges clad in criss-cross concrete grilles (an alternative, much reduced design will be carried out), and for the Yamanashi broadcasting centre, Kofu (built 1966–7), which is held together by sixteen cylindrical towers of lifts and services. Tsuboi was engineer for Dentsu, and Fugaku Yokoyama for the astonishing Yamanashi project. In 1967 Tange was also appointed (with Uzo Nikiyama) master planner of the international exhibition of 1970 at Osaka.

TARSIA, *see* INTARSIA.

TAS-DE-CHARGE. The lowest courses of a vault or arch, laid horizontally and bonded into the wall.

TATLIN, Vladimir (1885–1953). Tatlin was a painter with special interest in certain crafts, especially ceramics. He also did theatrical work. In 1913 he visited Paris. After the Revolution he turned to the same kind of abstract, Constructivist architectural fantasies as did Gabo occasionally. The Memorial to the Third International, a skew spiral composition, made in 1919–20, is his one and only famous design. It was meant to be 1300 ft high, i.e. higher than the Eiffel Tower.

TAUT, Bruno (1880–1938), a pupil of Theodor Fischer in Munich, settled in Berlin in 1908. He was professor at the College of Technology, Berlin, in 1931, and at Ankara in 1936; between these posts he visited Russia in 1932 and Japan in 1933. Taut was first noticed for his highly original glass pavilion at the Werkbund Exhibition of 1914 in Cologne (*see* GROPIUS, van de VELDE), a polygonal building with walls of thick glass panels, a metal staircase inside, and a glass dome, the elements set in lozenge framing (a SPACE-FRAME). In the years of the wildest Expressionism in Germany, Taut wrote his frantic *Die Stadtkrone* (1919) and designed fantastic buildings for imprecisely formulated purposes.

TAYLOR, Sir Robert (1714–88), son of a mason-contractor, trained as a sculptor under Cheere and visited Rome *c*. 1743. Though sufficiently successful to be commissioned by Parliament to design and carve the monument to Captain Cornewall in Westminster Abbey (1744), he soon abandoned sculpture for architecture and by assiduity and businesslike methods quickly built up a large practice. He and PAINE were said to have 'nearly divided the practice of the profession between them' during the mid-century. He was conservative and uninspired but highly competent, and worthily carried on the neo-Palladian tradition of BURLINGTON and KENT. Most of his work has been destroyed, notably that in the Bank of England which included his last and by far his most original work, the Reduced Annuities Office, a top-lit hall with circular clerestory carried on segmental arches. It anticipated SOANE. Asgill House, Richmond (1758–67), and Stone Building, Lincoln's Inn, London (begun 1775), are the best of his surviving buildings. He was knighted when sheriff of London, 1782–3, and left the bulk of his large fortune to found the Taylorian Institute in Oxford for the teaching of modern languages.

TEBAM. A dais or rostrum for the reader in a synagogue. Adjoining it to the east is the Chief Rabbi's seat.

TECTON. A team established by Berthold Lubetkin (b. 1901) to which among others Denys LASDUN belonged. The team did the Highpoint Flats I and II at Highgate, London, in 1936 and 1938, the Finsbury Health Centre in 1938–9, and the blocks of flats in Rosebery Avenue in 1946–9. Their most popular work was for the London Zoo (1934–8). The details here of freely moulded concrete are prophetic of the 1950s.

TELAMONES, *see* ATLANTES.

TELFORD, Thomas (1757–1834), son of a Scottish shepherd, trained as a mason, worked in Edinburgh, then in London, and by 1784 had been made supervisor of works on Portsmouth Dockyard. In 1788 he became surveyor to the county of Shropshire. He built several churches in the county, notably Bridgnorth (1792), and several bridges, notably the brilliant Buildwas Bridge (1795–8), which was of iron (the Coalbrookdale Bridge had been built in iron in 1777) and had a 130 ft span. In 1793 work started on the Ellesmere Canal, and Telford was put in charge. He built the Chirk Aqueduct at Ceiriog, 700 ft long and 70 ft high (1796 etc.), and the Pont Cysylltau Aqueduct, 1000 ft long and 120 ft high (1795 etc.). In 1800 he suggested the rebuilding of London Bridge with a single span of 600 ft. Telford was responsible for other canals (Caledonian, 1804 etc.; Göta, 1808 etc.), for the St Katherine's Docks (1825; see HARDWICK), for fen drainage, for roads, and for further bridges, including the beautiful Dean Bridge, Edinburgh, of stone (1831), the Menai Straits Suspension Bridge, of iron, with a 530 ft span (1819 etc.), and the Conway Suspension Bridge, also of iron (1826).

TEMANZA, Tommaso (1705–89). The most sensitive of Venetian neo-Palladians. His masterpiece is the little church of the Maddalena, Venice (c. 1760), with its interior freely derived from PALLADIO's chapel at Maser. He wrote Le vite dei più celebri architetti e scultori veneziani (1778).

TEMPLATE. The block of stone set at the top of a brick or rubble wall to carry the weight of the JOISTS or roof-trusses; also called a pad stone.

TENIA. The small moulding or fillet along the top of the ARCHITRAVE in the Doric ORDER.

TERM. A pedestal tapering towards the base and usually supporting a bust; also a pedestal merging at the top into a sculptured human, animal, or mythical figure: also called terminal figures or termini. See figure 82.

TERRACE. 1. A level promenade in front of a building. 2. A row of attached houses designed as a unit.

TERRACOTTA. Fired but unglazed clay, used mainly for wall covering and

ornamentation as it can be fired in moulds.

TERRAZZO. A flooring finish of marble chips mixed with cement mortar and laid in situ; the surface is then ground and polished.

TESSERAE. The small cubes of glass, stone, or marble used in MOSAIC.

Fig. 82. Term

TESSELLATED. A cement floor or wall covering in which TESSERAE are embedded.

TESSIN, Nicodemus, the elder (1615–81), a leading Baroque architect in Sweden, was born at Stralsund and began by working under Simon LA VALLÉE. In 1651–2 he made a tour of Europe and in 1661 was appointed city architect of Stockholm. His main work is Drottningholm Palace (begun 1662), built in an individual Baroque style derived from Holland, France, and Italy. His other works include Kalmar Cathedral

(1660), Göteborg Town Hall (1670), the Carolean Mausoleum attached to the Riddarholm Church, Stockholm (designed 1671), and numerous small houses in Stockholm. His son Nicodemus the younger (1654–1728) succeeded him as the leading Swedish architect. Trained under his father, he travelled in England, France, and Italy (1673–80), and completed his father's work at Drottningholm. His main building is the vast royal palace in Stockholm (begun 1697), where he adopted a Baroque style reminiscent of, and probably influenced by, BERNINI's Louvre project.

TESTER. A canopy suspended from the ceiling or supported from the wall above a bed, throne, pulpit, etc.

TETRASTYLE. Of a PORTICO with four frontal columns.

THATCH. A roof covering of straw or reeds, Norfolk reeds being the best in England.

THERMAE. In Roman architecture public baths, usually of great size and splendour and containing libraries and other amenities as well as every provision for bathing. Their remains in Rome were closely studied by architects from PALLADIO onwards and had great influence on planning.

THERMAL WINDOW. A semicircular window divided into three lights by two vertical mullions, also known as a Diocletian window because of its use in the Thermae of Diocletian, Rome. Its use was revived in the C16 especially by PALLADIO and is a feature of PALLADIANISM.

THOLOS. The dome of a circular building or the building itself, e.g., a domed Mycenaean tomb.

THOMON, Thomas de (1754–1813). Leading NEO-CLASSICAL architect in Russia. He was born in Nancy, probably studied under LEDOUX in Paris and completed his training in Rome c. 1785. In 1789 he followed the Comte d'Artois into exile to Vienna where he found a patron in Prince Esterhazy. From there he went to Russia. His

designs for the Kazan Cathedral were rejected (1799) but in 1802 he became architect to the court of Alexander I in St Petersburg and immediately obtained important commissions – the Grand Theatre (1802–5, demolished) and the Bourse (designed 1801–4, built 1805–16), a Tuscan Doric temple with blank pediments, great segmental lunettes and flanking *columna rostrata*. The Bourse is his masterpiece and a major neo-classical building of the most severe and radical kind, more advanced than anything in Paris at that date. In 1806–10 he built a Doric mausoleum to Paul I in the park at Pavlovsk. He published *Recueil de plans et façades des principaux monuments construits à St Petersburg* (1808, republished in Paris 1819 with an amended title).

THOMSON, Alexander (1817–75), lived and worked at Glasgow, and was in practice from about 1847. He was known as 'Greek' Thomson, and rightly so, for to be a convinced Grecian was a very remarkable thing for a man belonging to the generation of PUGIN, SCOTT, and RUSKIN. The formative influence on his style was SCHINKEL rather than English Grecians. This comes out most clearly in such monumental terraces as Moray Place (1859), where the purity of proportion and the scarcity of enrichment suggest a date some thirty years earlier. His churches, on the other hand, though essentially Grecian, are far from pure: they exhibit an admixture of the Egyptian, even the Hindu, as well as a boldness in the use of iron, which combine to produce results of fearsome originality. The three churches – all United Presbyterian – are the Caledonian Road Church (1856), the Vincent Street Church (1859), and the Queen's Park Church (1867). All three are among the most forceful churches of their date anywhere in Europe. Equally interesting are Thomson's warehouses, especially the Egyptian Halls.

THORNTON, William (1759–1828), was an English physician who emigrated from the West Indies to the U.S. and became an American citizen in 1788. He designed the Philadelphia Library Company building in 1789 and in 1793 won the competition for the Capitol, Washington, though his runner-up, Stephen Hallet, was put in charge of the execution of his designs. The foundation stone was laid by George Washington in the same year. Hallet modified Thornton's designs and was replaced in 1795 by James HOBAN who proposed further alterations and was dismissed in 1798. But by 1800 the N. wing containing the Senate had been completed substantially to Thornton's designs. In 1803 LATROBE took charge and completed the S. wing by 1807. He also supervised the rebuilding after the Capitol had been sacked and burnt by British troops in 1814. Latrobe followed Thornton's designs for the exterior though not for the interior. In 1827 BULFINCH connected the two wings, again following the original design. (The dome and further extensions were added by T. U. WALTER, 1857–63.) Thornton also designed the Octagon House, Washington (1800) and Tudor Place, Washington (1815).

THORPE, John (c. 1565–1655), an unimportant clerk in the Office of Works and later a successful land surveyor, was not, as is sometimes thought, the architect of Longleat, Kirby, Wollaton, Audley End, and other great Elizabethan and Jacobean houses. Plans and a few elevations of these and many other Elizabethan buildings are in a volume of drawings by him in the Sir John Soane Museum, London.

THUMB, Michael (d. 1690). He was born at Bezau in the Bregenzerwald and was a founder of the Vorarlberger school of architects which included, besides the Thumb family, the MOSBRUGGER family and the BEER family. The latter intermarried with the Thumb family. The long series of buildings of this school, mostly for Benedictine monasteries in S.W. Germany and Switzerland, was eventually to mark the triumph of German over Italian elements in S. German Baroque architecture (i.e., over the domination of such Italians as ZUCCALLI and VISCARDI from the Grisons). Michael Thumb's pilgrimage church of Schönenberg near Ellwangen (begun 1682) is a prototype of the *Vorarlberger Münsterschema* – a pillared HALL CHURCH, the internal buttresses being faced with pilasters and projecting so deep as to form chapels, usually connected above by a gallery. He continued the type at the Premonstratensian abbey church of Obermarchtal (1686–92). Both churches are notable for their plain-spoken dignity. His son Peter (1681–1766) worked as a foreman for Franz BEER from 1704 and married his daughter. He later occupied an influential position at Constance. As an architect he developed a much more sophisticated manner than his father and achieved a wonderfully light and sparkling Rococo unity of effect in his best interiors. In 1738 he built the library of the monastery of St Peter in the Black Forest, successfully adapting the Vorarlberger Münsterschema of internal buttresses with columns and a balcony swirling round them. His masterpiece is the pilgrimage church of Birnau on Lake Constance (1746–58) where he had the collaboration of Feuchtmayer on the decoration. At the great Benedictine abbey of St Gallen he worked for eleven years (1748–58) but the extent of his contribution to the abbey church is uncertain. He was probably mainly responsible for the great central rotunda and he probably influenced the design of the two-towered E. façade, built by Johann Michael BEER in 1771–8. For the library in the monastery at St Gallen (1758–67) he employed the same system as at St Peter in the Black Forest.

Christian Thumb (1683–1726) worked with Michael Thumb at Schönenberg and at Obermarchtal, where he continued after Michael's death in 1690. His masterpiece is the Schlosskirche at Friedrichshafen (1695–1701). He probably collaborated with Andreas Schreck at the abbey church at Weingarten (1716–24).

TIE-BEAM, *see* ROOF.

TIERCERON, *see* VAULT.

TILEHANGING. A wall covering of overlapping rows of tiles on a timber structure.

TIMBER-FRAMING. A method of construction (also called *half-timbering* or *half-timber construction*) where walls are built of timber framework with the spaces filled in by plaster or brickwork (known as nogging). Sometimes the timber is covered with plaster or boarding laid horizontally (*see* WEATHERBOARDING). *See figure 83.*

TOLEDO, Juan Bautista de (d. 1567), philosopher and mathematician as well as architect, spent many years in Italy and for some time before 1559 was architect to the Spanish Viceroy in Naples. In 1562 he was appointed architect of the Escorial, drew up the entire ground plan, but built only the two-storeyed Court of the Evangelists, modelled on SANGALLO's Palazzo Farnese, Rome, and the vast severe south façade.

TOLTEC ARCHITECTURE, *see* MESO-AMERICAN ARCHITECTURE.

TOMB-CHEST. A chest-shaped stone coffin, the most usual medieval form of funerary monument. *See also* ALTAR-TOMB.

TOMÉ, Narciso (active 1715–42), began as a sculptor with his father and brothers on the façade of Valladolid University (1715). His famous Transparente in Toledo Cathedral (1721–32) is the most stupefying of all Baroque extravaganzas in spatial illusionism. It goes farther than anything invented by Italian Baroque architects and is exceptional even for Spain.

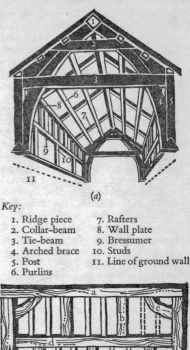

(a)

Key:

1. Ridge piece	7. Rafters
2. Collar-beam	8. Wall plate
3. Tie-beam	9. Bressumer
4. Arched brace	10. Studs
5. Post	11. Line of ground wall
6. Purlins	

(b)

Key:

a. Wall plate	d. Bressumer
b. Stud	e. Bracing
c. Post	f. Ground wall

Fig. 83. Timber-framing

TORRALVA, Diogo de (1500–66), the leading Portuguese Renaissance architect, was the son-in-law of ARRUDA but abandoned his rich MANUELINE style for one much simpler, sterner, and more Italianate. His main work is the cloister of the Cristo Monastery, Tomar (1557), with the SERLIAN MOTIF used as an open arcade on the upper floor. He designed the apse for the Jeronimite Church at Belem (1540–51). Several other buildings have been attributed to him, notably the octagonal church of the Dominican Nuns at Elvas (1543–57).

TORROJA, Eduardo (1899–1961). Concrete engineer and architect in Spain. His principal works are the grandstand of the Zarzuela racecourse near Madrid (1935), and the Algeciras market hall (1933).

TORUS. A large convex moulding of semicircular profile, e.g., at the base of a column. *See also* ASTRAGAL *and figure 66*.

TOUCH. A soft black marble quarried near Tournai, used chiefly for monuments.

TOURELLE. A turret CORBELLED out from the wall.

TOWN, Ithiel, *see* DAVIS.

TRABEATED. The adjective describing a building constructed on the post-and-lintel principle, as in Greek architecture, in contrast to an ARCUATED building.

TRACERY. The ornamental intersecting work in the upper part of a window, screen, or panel, or used decoratively in blank arches and vaults. The earliest use of the term so far traced is in Sir Christopher WREN, the medieval word being *form-pieces* or *forms*.

In windows of more than one light in Early Gothic churches the SPANDREL above the lights is often pierced by a circle, a quatrefoil, or some such simple form. This is known as *plate tracery*. Later, and first at Reims (1211 etc.), the circle is no longer pierced through a solid spandrel; instead the two lights are separated by a moulded MULLION and the mouldings of this are continued at the head forming bars of circular, quatrefoil, etc., forms and leaving the rest of the spandrels open. This is called *bar tracery*, and throughout the later Middle Ages it was one of the principal decorative elements of churches. The patterns made by the bars were

first the simple geometrical forms already indicated (*geometrical tracery*), later fantastical forms including double curves (*flowing tracery*), and later still – at least in England – plain, vertical, arched panels repeated more or less exactly (*panel tracery*). In Germany, France, and Spain forms similar to the English flowing tracery became the rule in the late Middle Ages. With the end of the Middle Ages tracery generally disappeared.

Bar tracery, introduced at Reims and brought to England *c.* 1240, consists of intersecting ribwork made up of slender shafts continuing the lines of the mullions up to a decorative mesh in the window-head.

Flowing tracery is made up of compound or OGEE curves, with an uninterrupted flow from curve to curve; also called *curvilinear* or *undulating tracery*. It was used from the beginning of the C14 in England, and throughout the C15 in France, where it rapidly became fully developed and FLAMBOYANT, with no survival of the geometrical elements of the early flowing tracery of England.

Geometrical tracery is characteristic of *c.* 1250–1300 and consists chiefly of circles or foiled circles.

In *intersecting tracery* each mullion of a window branches into curved bars which are continuous with the mullions. The outer arch of the window being of two equal curves (*see* ARCH), all subdivisions of the window-head produced by these tracery bars following the curves of the outer arch must of necessity be equilateral also. The bars and the arch are all drawn from the same centre with a different radius. Such a window can be of two, or usually more, lights, with the result that every two, three, or four lights together form a pointed arch. Additional enrichment, e.g., circles, CUSPING, is always of a secondary character. The form is typical of *c.* 1300.

Kentish tracery is FOILED tracery in a circle with barbs between the foils.

Panel tracery is Perpendicular tracery formed of upright, straight-sided panels above the lights of a window, also called *rectilinear*.

Plate tracery is a late C12 and early C13 form where decoratively shaped openings are cut through the solid stone infilling in a window-head.

Reticulated tracery, a form used much in the early to mid C14, is made up entirely of circles drawn at top and bottom into OGEE shapes resulting in a net-like appearance.

In *Y-tracery* a mullion branches into two forming a Y shape; typical of *c.* 1300.

See *figure 84*.

TRACHELION. The neck of a Greek Doric column, between the SHAFT-RING and HYPOTRACHELION.

TRANSENNA. An openwork screen or lattice, usually of marble, in an Early Christian church.

TRANSEPT. The transverse arms of a cross-shaped church, usually between NAVE and CHANCEL, but also occasionally at the west end of the nave as well, and also doubled, with the eastern arms farther east than the junction of nave and chancel. The latter form is usual in English Gothic cathedrals.

TRANSITIONAL ARCHITECTURE. A term usually referring to the period of transition from the ROMANESQUE to the GOTHIC, or in Britain from the NORMAN to the EARLY ENGLISH style. Sometimes details of the later styles are used on the general forms of the earlier.

TRANSOM. A horizontal bar of stone or wood across the opening of a window or across a panel.

TRANSVERSE ARCH, *see* VAULT.

TREAD, *see* STAIR.

TREFOIL, *see* FOIL.

TREZZINI, Domenico (Andrei Petrovich Trezini, 1670–1734), the first of the Western European architects employed by Peter the Great of Russia, was of Italo-Swiss origin. He is first recorded in 1700 working on the

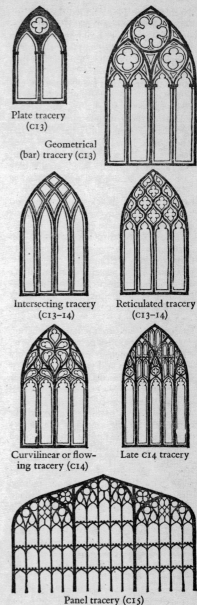

Plate tracery (C13)

Geometrical (bar) tracery (C13)

Intersecting tracery (C13–14)

Reticulated tracery (C13–14)

Curvilinear or flowing tracery (C14)

Late C14 tracery

Panel tracery (C15)
Fig. 84. Tracery

palace of Frederick IV in Copenhagen. In 1703 he was invited to become architect of the new city of St Petersburg. He was employed mainly to design small wooden houses, also the Summer Palace (1711–14 superseded by RASTRELLI's Summer Palace of 1741–4, also destroyed) in a predominantly Dutch style and the rather gawky Dutch Baroque Cathedral of St Peter and St Paul, St Petersburg (1714–25). His main work was the terrace of twelve pavilion-like buildings to house the government ministries, each with a colossal order of pilasters and a high hipped roof (1722–32, later altered).

TRIBUNE. 1. The APSE of a BASILICA or basilican church. 2. A raised platform or rostrum. 3. The GALLERY in a church.

TRICLINIUM. The dining-room in an ancient Roman house.

TRIFORIUM. An arcaded wall-passage facing on to the NAVE, at a level above the arcade and below the CLERESTORY windows (if there are any). The term is often wrongly applied to a TRIBUNE or GALLERY.

TRIGLYPHS. Blocks separating the METOPES in a Doric FRIEZE. Each one has two vertical grooves or glyphs in the centre and half grooves at the edges. If the half grooves are omitted (as occasionally in post-Renaissance architecture) the block is called a diglyph. *See figure 64.*

TRILITHON. A prehistoric monument consisting of a horizontal stone resting on two upright ones, as at Stonehenge.

TRIM. The framing or edging of openings and other features on a façade or indoors. It is usually of a colour and material (wood, stucco, or stone) different from that of the adjacent wall surface.

TRIUMPHAL ARCH, *see* ROMAN ARCHITECTURE.

TROPHY. A sculptured group of arms or armour used as a memorial to victory, sometimes with floreated

motifs intermingled to form a FESTOON.

TRUMEAU. The stone MULLION supporting the middle of a TYMPANUM of a doorway.

TRUSS. A number of timbers framed together to bridge a space or form a BRACKET, to be self-supporting, and to carry other timbers. The trusses of a roof are usually named after the particular feature in their construction, e.g., king-post, queen-post, etc. *See* ROOF.

TUDOR FLOWER. An upright ornamental motif, rather like a formalized ivy leaf, often used in English Late Gothic and Tudor architecture, especially for BRATTISHING.

TUFA. The commonest Roman building stone, formed from volcanic dust; it is porous and grey.

TURKISH ARCHITECTURE. In the Seljuq period (C11–13) religious architecture was derived from Persia, though stone was employed instead of brick. With the advent of the Ottomans (c. 1400) and their capture of Constantinople in 1453 the BYZANTINE style was adopted with modifications. As in other countries under Islamic rule, the Moslems began by adapting existing buildings: thus Hagia Sophia and other Christian churches were converted into MOSQUES. The influence of Byzantium persisted in later buildings, e.g., the Suleimaniyeh, Istanbul, by SINAN (1550–6), and the Ahmediyeh or Mosque of Ahmed I, Istanbul (1608–14). A new type of minaret was developed – a very tall and slender circular tower capped by an attenuated cone like a candle-snuffer. Glazed tiles were much used for decoration. Domestic buildings, of which the KIOSK is the most typical, were constructed mainly of wood and are notable for the elaborate carved wood MUSHRABEYEH lattices.

TURRET. A very small and slender tower.

TUSCAN ORDER, *see* ORDER.

TYLMAN VAN GAMEREN (before 1630–1706). Dutch architect chiefly responsible for introducing the Baroque style into Poland where he settled in 1665. His three centralized churches in Warsaw – Holy Sacrament (1688), St Casimir (1688–9) and St Boniface (1690–92) – reveal him as a somewhat stolid, classicizing master of the Baroque. St Anne, Cracow (1689–1705) is livelier, but this may be due to collaboration with Baldassare Fontana. He rebuilt the palace of Prince Sanguszko, Warsaw (enlarged in c18), designed Castle Nieborów (1680–83) and completed the Krasiński Palace, Warsaw (1682–94).

TYMPANUM. The area between the LINTEL of a doorway and the arch above it; also the triangular or segmental space enclosed by the mouldings of a PEDIMENT.

U

UNDERCROFT. A vaulted room, sometimes underground, below an upper room such as a church or chapel.

UNITED STATES ARCHITECTURE. The incunabula of New England's domestic architecture, dating from the C17, are of no more than strictly local interest, first Dutch in inspiration, then English. A monumental scale was only rarely achieved (William and Mary College, Williamsburg, 1695, much restored as is the whole of Williamsburg). Churches are entirely Georgian in the C18, often influenced in their spires by GIBBS. Houses are equally Georgian, in the country as well as the towns. But in both houses and churches timber plays a prominent part alongside, or instead of, brick. Among the best churches are Christ Church, Philadelphia (1727 and 1754); Christ Church, Cambridge (1761); St Michael, Charleston (1761); and the Baptist Church at Providence (1775). The finest Early Georgian house is Westover, Virginia (1726). From the mid C18 notable examples are Mount Airy, Virginia, Mount Pleasant, Philadelphia, and Whitehall, Maryland, with its giant Corinthian portico. Later porticos tend to have attenuated columns (Homewood, Baltimore). As town *ensembles* Salem and Nantucket (Mass.) and Charleston (South Carolina) may be singled out. The United States has still quite a few C18 public buildings: Old State House, Boston (1710); Independence Hall, Philadelphia (1732); Faneuil Hall, Boston (1742); and so to the Capitol in its original form (1792) and the Boston State House by BULFINCH (1793–1800). The earliest university buildings are also Georgian: at Harvard (1720, 1764 etc.); at Yale (1750–2); and then Thomas

JEFFERSON's University of Virginia at Charlottesville (1817–26), the first American campus, i.e., with buildings composed round a spacious lawn. Jefferson's own house, Monticello, is of 1770–1809.

The Greek Revival starts with LATROBE's Doric Bank of Pennsylvania of 1798. From 1803 he did much in a Grecian taste inside the Capitol in Washington. His finest work, comparable with that of SOANE in elegance and originality, is Baltimore Cathedral (begun 1805). But for this building he also submitted a Gothic design; a country house of his (Sedgeley, Philadelphia) was Gothic too. However, except in church design, Gothic made slow progress, and the most thoroughly Grecian years are the 1820s and 1830s, with the big government buildings in Washington by MILLS and several state capitols by TOWN & DAVIS. Davis experimented in many styles, including the Egyptian and the Old-English cottage. The most prominent Gothic churches are RENWICK's Grace Church, New York (1846), and UPJOHN's Trinity Church, New York, of the same years. Henry Austin deserves a special mention; if ever there was rogue architecture, his New Haven railway station (1848–9) is it. Its style cannot be derived from any clear direction.

Already in the second quarter of the century certain American specialities began to appear. One is hotels, especially of the size and type that became standard in Europe later (Tremont House, Boston, by Isaiah Rogers, 1828–9); another is such technical equipment as bathrooms and lifts.

The United States moved from a marginal to a central position with the work of H. H. RICHARDSON, both in the field of the massive uncompromising commercial building for which his style was a French-inspired Romanesque (Marshall Field Wholesale Warehouse, Chicago, 1885-7) and in the field of the informal, comfortable, moderately dimensioned private house (Sherman House, Newport, 1874-6). Even more independent are some of the houses designed in their early years by McKIM, Mead & WHITE, notably one at Bristol, Rhode Island (1887). Otherwise that firm is principally remembered for their Italian Renaissance Revival (Villard Houses, New York, 1885; Boston Public Library, 1887), Colonial Revival, and also Palladian Revival, the latter on a grand scale (Pennsylvania Station, New York, 1906-10).

Meanwhile, however, Chicago had established a style of commercial architecture all her own and vigorously pointing forward into the C20 (Chicago School). It started from the introduction of the principle of steel framing (*see* SKYSCRAPER) about 1884 and reached its climax in such buildings as the Tacoma (1887-9) by HOLABIRD & ROCHE, the Marquette (1894) by the same firm, and, most personal, the Wainwright at St Louis (1890) by SULLIVAN. With Sullivan's Carson, Pirie & Scott Store, Chicago (1899 etc.), a totally unhistoricist style of unrelieved verticals and horizontals was reached, though Sullivan was perhaps at his most original in his feathery, decidedly ART NOUVEAU ornament.

Sullivan's principal pupil was Frank Lloyd WRIGHT, whose work, chiefly in the domestic field, bridges the whole period from *c.* 1890 to nearly 1960. But his brilliant style of sweeping horizontals and of intercommunication between spaces inside a house and between inside and outside spaces found little recognition in his own country. In fact, the C20 style on a major scale had to be imported from Europe: the pioneer building was the Philadelphia Savings Fund Building by HOWE & Lescaze (1930-32 – a relatively late date in European terms), but the spectacular development of C20 architecture in the United States belongs entirely to the years after the Second World War. The flowering was fostered by such distinguished immigrants as GROPIUS, MIES VAN DER ROHE, NEUTRA, and BREUER. The first stage belongs to the rational, cubic, crisp so-called INTERNATIONAL MODERN and culminates in Mies van der Rohe's houses and blocks of flats of *c.* 1950 onwards and most of the work of SKIDMORE, OWINGS & MERRILL. The second stage is that of the neo-sculptural, anti-rational, highly expressive style current in many countries while this dictionary is being produced. The United States is richer than any other part of the world in such buildings, from a love of novelty as well as from a prosperity that encourages display. Trends within this trend cannot here be separated: they run from the powerful concrete curves of Eero SAARINEN to the dainty eclecticism of Edward STONE (Huntingdon Hartford Museum, New York, 1958-9), and include such mercurial and controversial figures as Philip JOHNSON, Minoru YAMASAKI (b. 1912, St Louis Airport), and Paul RUDOLPH. *See also* FULLER and KAHN.

UNWIN, Sir Raymond (1863-1940). The leading English town-planner of his day and the man who – in partnership from 1896 to 1914 with Barry Parker (1867-1941) – translated into reality the garden city scheme conceived by Ebenezer HOWARD. The 'First Garden City', as the company for its realization was actually called, was Letchworth in Hertfordshire (begun 1903). However, while the growth of Letchworth did not progress as rapidly or as smoothly as had been anticipated, two garden suburbs did extremely well, the Hampstead

Garden Suburb outside London (begun 1907), and Wythenshawe outside Manchester (begun 1927). The Hampstead Garden Suburb in particular must be regarded as the *beau idéal* of the garden city principles of domestic and public planning, with its formal centre – the two churches and the institute designed by LUTYENS – its pattern of straight main and curving minor vehicular roads and its occasional pedestrian paths, its trees carefully preserved and its architectural style controlled in no more than the most general terms of a free neo-Tudor. Unwin also showed his sense of subtle visual planning effects in his *Town Planning in Practice*, first published in 1909, and a textbook to this day.

UPJOHN, Richard (1802–78), was born at Shaftesbury, where he was later in business as a cabinet-maker. He emigrated to America in 1829 and opened a practice as an architect at Boston in 1834. His speciality was Gothic churches: the first came in 1837, and the principal ones are Trinity Church, New York (1841–6), an effort in a rich Anglo-Gothic, and Trinity Chapel, W. 25th Street (1853), also Anglo-Gothic. He built in other styles as well (Trinity Building, New York, 1852, is Italianate). Upjohn was the first president of the American Institute of Architects.

URBAN RENEWAL. The replanning of existing towns or centres to bring them up to date and to improve amenities and traffic circulation.

V

VACCARINI, Giovan Battista (1702–68), was born in Palermo. He studied under Carlo FONTANA in Rome and settled in Catania (1730), where his exuberant Sicilian Rococo style is seen in the façade of the cathedral (begun 1730), Palazzo Municipale (1732), Collegio Cutelli (1754), and S. Agata (begun 1735).

VALADIER, Giuseppe (1762–1839), archaeologist, town-planner, and a prolific though rather reactionary architect. His main buildings are neo-Palladian rather than neo-classical, e.g., interior of Spoleto Cathedral (1784), interior of Urbino Cathedral (1789), and façade of S. Rocco, Rome (1833), though the boldly simple S. Pantaleo, Rome (1806), is more in tune with his times. His masterpiece is the reorganization of Piazza del Popolo, Rome, for which he published a design in 1794 and which he began in 1813, executed 1816–20.

VANBRUGH, Sir John (1664–1726), soldier, adventurer, playwright, and herald, was also the outstanding English Baroque architect. His father was a Flemish refugee who became a rich sugar-baker and married the daughter of Sir Dudley Carleton. He was brought up as a gentleman and commissioned in the Earl of Huntingdon's regiment in 1686. In 1690 he was arrested in Calais for spying and imprisoned for two years, part of the time in the Bastille. After his release he took London by storm with his witty and improper comedies *The Relapse* and *The Provok'd Wife*. Then he switched his talents to architecture – 'without thought or lecture', said Swift – having been invited by the Earl of Carlisle to try his hand at designing Castle Howard (1699). Lord Carlisle also had him appointed Comptroller at the Office of Works (1702), and thus he became, without any training or qualifications, WREN's principal colleague. But he turned out to be an architect of genius. The Tories later deprived him of his Comptrollership, but he was reinstated after the death of Queen Anne and knighted (1714). Witty and convivial, a friend of Tonson and Congreve and a member of the Kit Cat Club, he lived on terms of easy familiarity with the great men who became his clients.

His style derives from Wren at his grandest – e.g., Greenwich Hospital – and probably owes much to HAWKSMOOR, his assistant from 1699 onwards. But every building he designed is stamped with his own unique personality – expansive, virile, and ostentatious, more Flemish than English and often rather coarse and theatrical. Castle Howard (1699–1726) is an amazing trial of strength by a young undisciplined genius. His great opportunity came in 1705 at Blenheim Palace, the nation's gift to Marlborough in honour of his victories. Here he had almost unlimited funds at his disposal and the whole megalomaniac conception suited his temperament perfectly. He was always at his best on the largest possible scale, and his genius for the dramatic and heroic, for bold groupings of masses and for picturesque recessions and projections and varied skylines had full play.

His style reached sudden maturity at Blenheim – indeed, English Baroque architecture culminates there – and it changed little afterwards. The best of his surviving houses are Kimbolton (1707–9), King's Weston (1711–14), Seaton Delaval (*c.* 1720–8), Lumley Castle (entrance front and interior alterations, *c.* 1722), and Grimsthorpe (north range only, *c.* 1723–4). He said he wanted his architecture to be 'masculine' and to have 'something of the Castle Air', and nowhere does his peculiar version of the Baroque come closer to the massiveness of a medieval fortress than at Seaton Delaval. Sombre and cyclopean, this extra-ordinary house is unlike any other building in England or anywhere else. His strong sense of the picturesque led him to further and more explicit medievalisms elsewhere, notably at his own house at Greenwich (after 1717), which is castellated and has a fortified-looking round tower. He seems here to have foreshadowed the romantic spirit of later Gothic revivals.

VANVITELLI, Luigi (1700–73), was born in Naples, the son of the painter Gaspar van Wittel, studied painting under his father in Rome, and emerged as an architect only in the 1730s. He worked at Pesaro, Macerata, Perugia, Loreto, Siena, Ancona, and Rome (monastery of S. Agostino and remodelling of S. Maria degli Angeli) before he was summoned to Naples by Carlo III in 1751 to build the enormous 1,200-room palace at Caserta. This is the last great Italian Baroque building. Its immense internal vistas, ceremonial staircase, and central octagonal vestibule rival the most extravagant stage-set in scenographic fantasy, though the exterior already veers towards neo-classical restraint. Almost equally impressive are his Chiesa dell'Annunziata (1761–82), Piazza Dante (1757–63), and twenty-five mile long Acquedotto Carolino (1752–64).

VARDY, John (d. 1765). Friend and close associate of KENT, whose designs for the Horse Guards, London, he carried out (with W. Robinson, 1750–8). His most important surviving work is Spencer House, London (1750–65), an excellent example of PALLADIANISM freely interpreted.

VASARI, Giorgio (1511–74). A painter and author of the famous *Vite de' più eccellenti architetti, pittori e scultori italiani* (1550, revised 1568), which by its eulogistic account of MICHELANGELO exerted an important influence on architectural taste. As an architect he had a hand, with VIGNOLA and AMMANATI, in designing the Villa di Papa Giulio, Rome (1551–5). His only important independent work is the Uffizi, Florence (begun 1560), with a long narrow courtyard stretching down towards the river and closed by a range with two superimposed Serlian arcades – an adaptation of Michelangelo's Laurentian Library to external architecture.

VAUBAN, Sébastien le Prestre de (1633–1707). Architect, town-planner and the most famous of all military engineers. According to Voltaire he constructed or repaired the fortifications of 150 'places de guerre' and he was said to have directed some 53 sieges. A close friend of Louvois (minister of war 1666–91) and of Colbert, he became *Commissaire Général des Fortifications* in 1677. In 1703 he was made a *Maréchal de France*. His genius as a military engineer lay in the resourcefulness with which he used and adapted traditional means rather than in the invention of new ones. His ingenuity is well displayed at difficult sites, e.g., Mont-Louis in the Pyrenees and Mont-Dauphin and Château Queyras on the Savoy frontier. But his most famous fortifications are those of Lille (1668–74), Maubeuge (1683–5) and Neuf-Brisach (1697–1708). Some of his fortresses were in effective military use up to the 1914–18 war, notably Langwy (built 1678). He laid out the new towns he brought into being, such as Neuf-Brisach, and occasionally designed individual buildings, e.g., the governor's house, church and arsenal at Lille and churches at Givet and Briançon. He restored the châteaux of Auney and Ussé. But his merit as an architect is best appreciated in the massive simplicity of such ramparts as those of Oléron, Gravelines and Bayonne and in his monumental gateways which range from the Baroque splendour of the Porte de Paris at Lille, enriched with columns, entablatures, trophies and sculptured panels, to the simple grandeur of the Mons Gate at Maubeuge. In these Vauban approached the noble severity and grandeur achieved by his contemporaries Libéral BRUANT and François BLONDEL. His memoirs, *Plusieurs maximes bonnes à observer pour tous ceux qui font bâtir* contain a complete treatise on building.

VAUDOYER, Léon (1803–72). French architect. His *chef d'œuvre* is Marseilles Cathedral (begun in 1852) which combines convincingly a Romanesque plan with a Byzantine elevation and the polychrome horizontal striping of e.g. Siena Cathedral.

VAUDREMER, Joseph - Auguste - E. (1829–1914), after a training under the sober utilitarian architects Blouet and Gilbert, started with the large Santé Prison, Paris (1862 etc.), in the same spirit. However, in 1864 he was commissioned to build the church of St Pierre de Montrouge in Paris (1864–70), and here his very sobriety and directness made him choose the Romanesque rather than the Gothic style. The building must have impressed H. H. RICHARDSON. Romanesque also, but internally with much grander stone vaults is Notre Dame, rue d'Auteuil, Paris (1876 etc.). The much larger and more famous Sacré Cœur on Montmartre is by Paul Abadie (1812–84) and was started in 1876. It is inspired by St Front at Périgueux, which Abadie disastrously restored.

VAULT. An arched ceiling or roof of stone or brick, sometimes imitated in wood or plaster.

Barrel vault, *see* tunnel vault.

Cloister vault, *see* domical vault.

Cross vault, *see* groin vault.

Domical vault. A dome rising direct on a square or polygonal base, the curved surfaces separated by GROINS. In America called a *cloister vault*. *See figure 38*.

A *fan vault* consists of solid concave-sided semi-cones, meeting or nearly meeting at the apex of the vault. The areas between are flat and, if the cones meet, form concave-sided lozenges. The cones and centres are decorated with panelling so as to give the appearance of a highly decorated rib vault. *See figure 85*.

A *groin vault* is produced by the intersection at right angles of two tunnel vaults of identical shape. *See figure 85*.

Lierne. A tertiary rib, that is, one which does not spring either from one of the main springers or from the central BOSS. *See figure 85*. A *lierne vault* is a ribbed vault with liernes.

For *Net vault* see definition under RIETH.

A *ploughshare vault* or *stilted vault* has the wall ribs sprung from a higher level than the diagonal ribs, in order to increase the light from a clerestory window.

In a *quadripartite vault* one bay is divided into four quarters or CELLS.

A *rib vault* is a framework of diagonal arched ribs carrying the cells which cover in the spaces between them. *See figure 85*.

Ridge-rib. The rib along the longitudinal or transverse ridge of a vault, at an angle of approximately 45° to the main diagonal ribs. *See figure 85*.

In a *sexpartite vault* one bay of quadripartite vaulting is divided transversely into two parts so that each bay has six compartments.

A *stellar vault* is one with the ribs, liernes and tiercerons arranged in a star-shaped pattern.

Tierceron. A secondary rib, which springs from one of the main springers, or the central boss, and leads to a place on the ridge-rib. *See figure 85*.

A *transverse arch* separates one bay

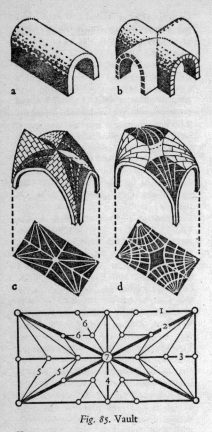

Fig. 85. Vault

Key:

a. Tunnel vault   c. Rib vault
b. Groin vault   d. Fan vault

1. Transverse rib;   5. Tiercerons;
2. Diagonal rib;   6. Liernes;
3. Transverse ridge-rib; 7. Boss
4. Longitudinal ridge-rib;

of a vault from the next. It can be either plain in section or moulded.

Tunnel vault (also called *barrel vault* and *wagon vault*). The simplest form of a vault, consisting of a continuous vault of semicircular or pointed sections, unbroken in its length by cross vaults. BUTTRESSING is needed to ground the thrust, which is dispersed all along the wall beneath. Tunnel vaults can be subdivided into bays by transverse arches. *See figure 85.*

Wagon vault, see tunnel vault.

VAULTING SHAFT. The vertical member leading to the springer of a vault.

VAUX, Calvert, *see* DOWNING.

VÁZQUEZ, Lorenzo, to whom the earliest works of the Renaissance in Spain are now attributed, was master mason to Cardinal Mendoza, and for the Cardinal the Colegio de Santa Cruz at Valladolid, begun in 1486, was transformed in 1491 by Vázquez, with its Quattrocento frontispiece medallion. The next buildings in order of date were also commissioned by members of the Mendoza family: the palace at Cogolludo (probably 1492–5), with windows still floridly Late Gothic; the palace at Guadalajara (before 1507); and the castle of La Calahorra (1509–12). In the latter case, however, it is known that Michele Carlone of Genoa was called in to take charge. For other early major Renaissance designs in Spain *see* EGAS.

VELDE, Henri van de (1863–1957). He was born at Antwerp of a well-to-do family and was first a painter influenced aesthetically by the Neo-Impressionists (Pointillists), socially by the ideals which at the time also inspired van Gogh. About 1890, under the impact of RUSKIN and MORRIS, he turned from painting to design and in 1892 produced the first works that are entirely his own and at the same time are entirely representative of ART NOUVEAU, the anti-historical movement just then emerging. They are works of typography and book decoration, with long flexible curves, and an appliqué panel called *The Angels Watch*. Their stylistic source seems to be the Gauguin of Pont Aven and his circle, especially Émile Bernard.

In 1895 van de Velde designed a house and furnishings at Uccle near Brussels for his own young family.

It was his first achievement in architecture and interior design, and both now became his principal concerns. He was commissioned to design interiors for Bing's newly established shop L'Art Nouveau in Paris (1895) and then showed most of this work at an exhibition in Dresden (1897). In both centres its impact was great, but whereas reactions were largely hostile in France, they were enthusiastic in Germany, and so van de Velde decided to leave Brussels and settle in Berlin. In the next years he did much furnishing work for the wealthy and the refined, including the shop of the imperial barber (Haby, 1901). In 1901 he was called to Weimar as a consultant on the coordination of crafts, trades, and good design. He furnished the Nietzsche-Archive there (1903), and rebuilt the Art School and the School of Arts and Crafts (1904, 1907), of which latter he became director. He also did the interior of the Folkwang Museum at Hagen (1901-2) and the Abbe Monument at Jena (1908).

His style is characterized by the long daring curves of Art Nouveau, endowed by him with a peculiar resilience, and in architecture also by the use of the curve rather than the angle – e.g., for roofs. For the Werkbund Exhibition at Cologne in 1914 (*see* GROPIUS; TAUT) he did the theatre, also with curved corners and a curved roof.

Being Belgian he left his job in Germany during the war, lived through restless years of émigré life and only in 1925 settled down again, now back in Brussels. However, the years of his great successes and his European significance were over. His late style is less personal, close to that of the School of Amsterdam (*see* OUD): its finest example is the Kröller-Müller Museum at Otterlo in Holland, beautifully coordinated with the heath scenery around (1937-54).

VENETIAN DOOR. An adaptation of the SERLIANA to a doorway, i.e., with the central opening arched and flanked by tall narrow square-topped windows.

VENETIAN WINDOW, *see* SERLIANA.

VERANDA. An open gallery or balcony with a roof supported by light, usually metal, supports.

VERMICULATION. Decoration of masonry blocks with irregular shallow channels like worm tracks. *See figure 72.*

VERTUE, Robert (d. 1506) and William (d. 1527), were brothers and both masons. Robert, the elder, appears at Westminster Abbey from 1475. About 1501 both brothers were master masons for Bath Abbey, begun at that time by Bishop King. This grandly Perpendicular building has a fan VAULT which, so they told the bishop, would be such that 'there shall be none so goodly neither in England nor in France'; and as at that moment neither the vault of King's College Chapel, Cambridge, nor that of Henry VII Chapel in Westminster Abbey, or that of St George's Chapel, Windsor, existed (though the latter was building), the claim was just. The Vertues' precise connection with these three works cannot be proved, but as they were jointly the King's Master Masons, with Robert Janyns and John Lebons (*see* REDMAN), it is likely that a connection existed. William, in any case, signed a contract with another (John Aylmer) to vault the chancel at Windsor, and visited King's College Chapel once in 1507, once (with Redman) in 1509, and once (with WASTELL) in 1512, if not more often.

In 1516 Vertue appeared at Eton (with Redman), where he made a design (the design?) for Lupton's Tower. From 1515 he was joint King's Mason with Redman. In 1526 he probably designed the fan-vaulted cloister chapel in the Palace of Westminster.

VESICA. An upright almond shape; found chiefly in medieval art to enclose a figure of Christ enthroned.

VESNIN, Alexander (1883–1959). Vesnin took an engineering degree in 1913. He did important theatrical work, but also the setting for the May-Day celebrations in the Red Square in 1918 (with his brother) and the Karl Marx Memorial, also in Moscow, in 1920.

VIADUCT. A long series of arches carrying a road or railway.

VICE. A winding or spiral staircase.

VICENTE DE OLIVEIRA, Mateus (1710–86), the leading Portuguese Rococo architect, began under LUDOVICE but forsook his grandiose manner for one more delicate and intimate. His masterpiece is the Palace of Queluz (1747–52, interior destroyed), where a large building is disguised behind an exquisitely frivolous façade swagged with garlands of carved flowers. He also designed the very large Estrêla Church in Lisbon (1778).

VIGNOLA, Giacomo Barozzi da (1507–73), the leading architect in Rome after the death of MICHELANGELO, was born at Vignola, near Modena, and studied painting and architecture at Bologna. In 1530 he settled in Rome. His first important work was the completion of Palazzo Farnese, Caprarola (1550), begun on a pentagonal plan by PERUZZI: he designed the rather stern façades, the very elegant circular courtyard in the centre, and probably the garden. He seems to have played the leading part in designing the Villa di Papa Giulio, Rome (1551–5) in collaboration with AMMANATI and VASARI. It is a masterpiece of Mannerist architecture and garden design, with much play with vistas from one courtyard to another, hemicycles echoing each other, a curious rhythmical use of the orders, and very shallow relief decorations applied to the surfaces.

In 1564 he took over the building of Palazzo Farnese in Piacenza. He may also have designed the Villa Lante, Bagnaia (begun 1566), with its wonderful hillside water gardens. In about 1550 he built the little Tempietto di S. Andrea, Rome, for Pope Julius III, using for the first time in church architecture an oval plan which he was to repeat on a larger scale in his design for S. Anna dei Palafrenieri, Rome (begun 1573), and which was to be used extensively by Baroque architects. His most influential building was the Gesù, Rome (begun 1568); it has probably had a wider influence than any church built in the last 400 years. The plan, which owes something to ALBERTI's S. Andrea, Mantua, combines the central scheme of the Renaissance with the longitudinal scheme of the Middle Ages. The aisles are replaced by a series of chapels opening off the nave, and various devices – e.g., lighting and the placing of the nave pilasters – direct attention to the higher altar. (The interior was redecorated in High Baroque style in 1668–73.)

Vignola was architect to St Peter's (1567–73) and continued Michelangelo's work there faithfully. In 1562 he published Regole delle cinque ordini, a simple MODULAR interpretation of the architectural ORDERS which, on account of its straight-forward approach, enjoyed immense popularity. It became the architect's alphabet, and one of the most important textbooks ever written.

VIGNON, Pierre (1762–1828). French Empire architect famous for the Madeleine in Paris (1806–43), his one important building. He was trained under J.-D. Leroy and LEDOUX and in 1793 became Inspecteur général des bâtiments de la République. His Madeleine is an enormous peripteral Corinthian temple on a high podium, as imposingly and imperially Roman in scale as in its slightly vulgar ostentation. It superseded a building designed by Pierre Contant d'Ivry in 1764, revised by G. M. Couture c. 1777. This had hardly begun to be built when Napoleon called in Vignon in 1806, having decided that it should be a *Temple de la Gloire* and not a church. But he reversed this decision in 1813 after the Battle of Leipzig and the loss of Spain. Vignon did not live to see his masterpiece completed and it was finished by J.-J.-M. Huvé (1783–1852).

VILLA. In Roman architecture, the landowner's residence or farmstead on his country estate; in Renaissance architecture, a country house; in C19 England, a detached house 'for opulent persons', usually on the outskirts of a town; in modern architecture, a small detached house. The basic type developed with the growth of urbanization: it is of five bays, on a simple corridor plan with rooms opening off a central passage. The next stage is the addition of wings. The courtyard villa fills a square plan with subsidiary buildings and an enclosure wall with a gate facing the main corridor block.

VILLANUEVA, Juan de (1739–1811), the leading Spanish neo-classical architect, was the son of a sculptor under whom he trained. He began in the CHURRIGUERESQUE tradition, then became a draughtsman to SACCHETTI in Madrid and adopted an Italianate Baroque style. He was sent by the Royal Academy to Rome (1759–65), and on his return his brother Diego (1715–74) published his *Colección de papeles críticos sobre la arquitectura* (1766), the first neo-classical attack on the Churrigueresque and Rococo to appear in Spain. Rather tentatively he began to put these ideas into practice in the Palafox Chapel in Burgo de Osma Cathedral (1770), Casita de Arriba at the Escorial (1773), and Casita del Príncipe at El Pardo (1784). His outstanding work is the Prado Museum, Madrid, designed (1787) as a museum of natural history but later adapted to house the royal collection of pictures. With its sturdy Tuscan portico in the centre and its boldly articulated wings with Ionic colonnades at first-floor level, it is an effective and undoctrinaire essay in neo-classicism.

VILLARD DE HONNECOURT, a French architect who was active around 1225–35 in the North-West of France and was probably master mason of Cambrai Cathedral, which no longer exists. Villard is known to us by the book of drawings with short texts which he compiled for the learners in his lodge, the masons' workshop and office. The book is in the Bibliothèque Nationale in Paris and contains plans of buildings (both copied and invented), elevational details, figure sculpture, figures drawn *al vif*, foliage ornament, a lectern, a stall end, a *perpetuum mobile*, and in addition many small technical drawings, more of an engineering kind, which were added to the book by two successors of Villard. From the text and the examples illustrated it is certain that Villard knew Reims, Laon, Chartres, Lausanne, and that he travelled as far as Hungary. The sculptural style of his figures connects him with work of about 1230 at Reims. Villard's book gives us the clearest insight we can obtain into the work of a distinguished master mason and the atmosphere of a lodge.

VINGBOONS or VINCKEBOONS, Philips (1614–78), was the leading exponent of van CAMPEN's Dutch classicism for middle-class domestic architecture in Amsterdam. He worked for the prosperous merchants while Pieter POST was patronized by the upper class. Being Roman Catholic he obtained no commissions for public buildings or churches. He created a new type of town-house, sober, unpretentious and eminently practical, with strictly symmetrical planning and severely simple elevations. His designs, published as *Œuvres d'Architecture* in two volumes (1648 and 1674), were very influential especially in England. His brother Justus (*fl.* 1650–70) designed the façades of LA VALLÉE's Riddarhus in Stockholm (1653–6) and built the imposing Trippenhuis in Amsterdam (1662).

VIOLLET-LE-DUC, Eugène-Emanuel (1814–79), was born into a wealthy, cultured, and progressive family. His opposition to the 'establishment' began early: he helped to build barricades in 1830 and refused to go to the École des Beaux Arts for his training. In 1836–7 he was in Italy studying buildings with industry and intelligence. His future was determined by his meeting with Prosper Mérimée (1803–70), author of *Carmen* and Inspector in the newly founded Commission des Monuments Historiques. Viollet-le-Duc, inspired by Victor Hugo's enthusiasm on the one hand and by Arcisse de Caumont's scholarship on the other, now turned resolutely to the French Middle Ages and soon established himself both as a scholar and as a restorer. His first job was Vézelay (1840). He then did the Sainte Chapelle in Paris with Duban, and Notre Dame with Lassus. The number of his later restorations is legion.

As a scholar he developed new and highly influential ideas on the Gothic style, which to him is socially the outcome of a lay civilization succeeding the sinister religious domination of the earlier Middle Ages. The Gothic style to Viollet-le-Duc is also a style of rational construction based on the system of rib vault, flying buttress, and buttress. The ribs are a skeleton, like a C19 iron skeleton; the webs or cells are no more than light infilling. All thrusts are conducted from the ribs to the flying buttresses and buttresses, and thin walls can be replaced by large openings. These ideas were laid down and made universal property by Viollet-le-Duc's *Dictionnaire raisonné de l'architecture française* (published 1854–68). A comparison between Gothic skeleton and C19 iron skeleton building was drawn, or rather implied, in Viollet-le-Duc's *Entretiens* (2 vols., published 1863 and 1872), and especially in the second volume. Here Viollet-le-Duc appears as a passionate defender of his own age, of engineering, and of new materials and techniques, especially iron for supports, for framework, and for ribs. The plates to the *Entretiens* are extremely original, but aesthetically they are none too attractive. As an architect Viollet-le-Duc had in fact little merit. Time and again one is struck by the discrepancy between the consistency and daring of his thought and the looseness and commonplace detailing of his original buildings, e.g., Saint-Denys-de-l'Estrée, St Denis (1864–7).

VISCARDI, Giovanni Antonio (1647–1713). He was born in the Grisons and went, like his compatriot and bitter rival ZUCCALLI, to work in Munich where he became master mason to the Court in 1678 and chief architect in 1685. Zuccalli helped to oust him from this post in 1689 but he was in charge of enlarging Nymphenburg palace from 1702 onwards (he began the saloon and added pavilions etc.) and he was reinstated as chief architect 1706–13. His most important building is the Mariahilfkirche at Freystadt (1700–1708) with a very high central dome, on a plan that was to have widespread influence even beyond Bavaria (BÄHR used it as a model for the Frauenkirche in Dresden). He also designed the Cistercian church of Fürstenfeld (1701–47). His last works were the Jesuit assembly hall or Bürgersaal, Munich (1709–10) and the church of the Holy Trinity in Munich (1711–14).

VITRUVIAN OPENING. A doorway or window of which the sides incline slightly inwards towards the top, giving it a heavy, Egyptian look. It was described by Vitruvius.

VITRUVIAN SCROLL, see RUNNING DOG.

VITRUVIUS POLLIO, Marcus (active 46–30 B.C.), a Roman architect and theorist of slight importance in his own time but of enormous influence from the Early Renaissance onwards, served under Julius Caesar in the African War (46 B.C.), built the basilica at Fano (destroyed), and in old age composed a treatise on architecture in ten books *De architectura*, written in a somewhat obscure style and dedicated to Augustus. This is the only complete treatise on architecture to survive from Antiquity. Several manuscript copies were known and used in the Middle Ages. In 1414 Poggio Bracciolini drew attention to a copy at St Gall, and the treatise soon came to be regarded as a vade-mecum for all progressive architects. Both ALBERTI and FRANCESCO DI GIORGIO derived much from it for their writings and buildings. The first printed text was published in Rome *c.* 1486 and the first illustrated edition by Fra GIOCONDO in 1511; an Italian translation was prepared under RAPHAEL's direction *c.* 1520, and another translation was printed in 1521 with an extensive commentary by Cesare Cesariano and numerous illustrations. A vast number of subsequent editions and translations in nearly all European languages appeared. The obscurity of the text, which made a strong appeal to the Renaissance intellect, enabled architects to interpret its gnomic statements in a variety of ways.

VITTONE, Bernardo (1704/5–1770), a little-known architect of real if rather freakish genius, worked exclusively in Piedmont where he was born. He studied in Rome and edited GUARINI's posthumous *Architettura civile* (1737). His secular buildings are dull; not so his numerous churches, mostly small and scattered in remote villages, in which the unlikely fusion of Guarini and JUVARRA had surprising and original results in a gay Rococo vein. Of his structural inventions the pendentive-squinch (e.g., S. Maria di Piazza, Turin, 1751–4) and fantastic three-vaulted dome are the most successful. His churches at Vallinotto (1738–9), Brà (1742), and Chieri (1740–4) show his structural ingenuity

at its prettiest. Later churches – Borgo d'Ale, Rivarolo Canavese, Grignasco – are larger, less frivolous, but suavely calm and sinuous. He had several followers and disciples in Piedmont, but no influence whatever farther afield.

VOLUTE. A spiral scroll on an Ionic CAPITAL; smaller versions appear on Composite and Corinthian capitals. *See figure 64.*

VORONIKHIN, Andrei Nikiforovich (1760–1814), one of the leading figures in the neo-classical transformation of St Petersburg, was born a serf on the estates of Count Stroganov, who sent him to study in Moscow, then on a European tour (1784–90), and finally employed him to design the state apartments in his palace. His main works are in Leningrad, e.g., Cathedral of the Virgin of Kazan (1801–11), the most Catholic and Roman church in Russia, and the Academy of Mines (1806–11) with a dodecastyle Paestum portico.

VOUSSOIR. A brick or wedge-shaped stone forming one of the units of an arch. *See figure 4.*

VOYSEY, Charles F. Annesley (1857–1941), worked first under Seddon, then with Devey, and set up in practice in 1882. He was at once as interested in design as in architecture, under the general influence of MORRIS and of MACKMURDO in particular. The earliest designs for wallpapers and textiles are of 1883 and are indeed very reminiscent of Mackmurdo. His first commissions for houses date from 1888–9, and from then until the First World War he built a large number of country houses and hardly anything else. They are never extremely large, never grand, never representational; instead they are placed in intimate relation to nature – perhaps an old tree preserved in the courtyard – and developed informally. They spread with ease and, having lowish comfortable rooms, are often on the cosy side. The exteriors are usually rendered with pebbledash and have horizontal windows. They are no longer period imitations at all – in fact, more independent of the past than most architects ventured to be before 1900 – but they never lack the admission of a sympathy for the rural Tudor and Stuart traditions. Voysey designed the furniture and all the details, such as fireplaces, metalwork, etc., himself, and the furniture is again inspired by Mackmurdo's (and in its turn inspired MACKINTOSH's). It is reasonable, friendly, and in the decoration not without a sweet sentimentality; the same is true of textiles and wallpapers.

Among his houses which had a tremendous influence at home (right down to the caricatures produced between the wars by speculative builders) and abroad, the following may be listed: Perrycroft, Colwall, 1893; Annesley Lodge, Hampstead, London, 1895; Merlshanger (Grey Friars), Hog's Back, 1896; Norney, Shackleford, 1897; Broadleys and Moor Crag, both Gill Head, Windermere, 1898; The Orchard, Chorley Wood, 1899. After the war Voysey was rarely called upon to do any architectural work.

VRIES, Hans Vredeman de (1527–1606), began as a painter, settled in Antwerp, and published fantastic ornamental pattern-books – *Architectura* (1565), *Compertimenta* (1566), *Variae Architecturae Formae* (1601) – which had enormous influence on architecture all over Northern Europe including England (e.g., SMYTHSON's Wollaton). His style lacks FLORIS's grace and wit but well represents the Flemish and Dutch contribution to MANNERISM and expresses the northern feeling for flat pattern in strapwork or carved decoration of interlaced bands and forms similar to fretwork or cut leather.

VYSE. A spiral staircase or a staircase winding round a central column.

W

WAGNER, Otto (1841–1918), became professor at the Academy in Vienna in 1894, and delivered an inaugural address pleading for a new approach to architecture, for independence of the past, and for rationalism ('Nothing that is not practical can be beautiful'). Before that time he had himself designed in the neo-Renaissance style. His most familiar achievement is some stations for the Vienna Stadtbahn (1894–7), ART NOUVEAU with much exposed iron, though more restrained than Hector GUIMARD's contemporary ones for the Paris Métro. But his most amazingly modern and c20-looking job is the Post Office Savings Bank, Vienna (1904–6), the exterior faced with marble slabs held in place by aluminium bolts and the interior featuring a glass barrel vault realized with a clarity and economy hardly matched by anyone else at so early a date. Wagner had a decisive influence on the best younger architects of Vienna (see HOFFMANN, LOOS, OLBRICH). His most monumental building, closer to the style of the Secession, is the church of the Steinhof Asylum, outside Vienna, with its powerful dome (1906).

WAGON ROOF, see ROOF.

WAGON VAULT, see VAULT.

WAINSCOT. The timber lining to walls. The term is also applied to the wooden panelling of PEWS.

WALL PLATE, see ROOF.

WALL RIB, see FORMERET.

WALTER, Thomas U. (1804–87), was of German descent, and was born in Philadelphia where his father was a mason. He studied under STRICKLAND and started on his own in 1830. As early as 1833 he was commissioned to design Girard College, an ambitious, wholly peripteral (and thus functionally dubious) white marble building. In 1851 he began the completion of the Capitol in Washington: he added the wings, and the dominant dome on a cast-iron framing is his. He also completed MILLS's Treasury. Like nearly all the leading American architects, Walter was also capable of major engineering works – see a breakwater he built in Venezuela (1843–5).

WARD. The courtyard of a castle; also called a *bailey*.

WARE, Isaac (d. 1766). A protégé of Lord BURLINGTON and a strict Palladian. His buildings are competent but uninspired, e.g., Chesterfield House, London (1749, destroyed), and Wrotham Park (c. 1754). However, his *Complete Body of Architecture* (1756) was very influential and became a standard textbook.

WASTELL, John (d. c. 1515), lived at Bury St Edmunds and, though evidently highly appreciated, was not in the King's Works. He had probably started under and with Simon CLERK, and followed him both at the abbey of Bury and at King's College Chapel, Cambridge, where he appears from 1486 and was master mason throughout the years when the glorious fan VAULT was built and the chapel completed. The vault can therefore with some probability be considered his design, though the King's Masons, William VERTUE and Henry REDMAN, visited the building in 1507, 1509, and 1512. Wastell was also Cardinal Morton's mason and then the master mason of Canterbury Cathedral, where he was presumably the designer for Bell Harry, the crossing tower of the cathedral (built 1494–7). Other buildings have been attributed to him on stylistic grounds.

WATERHOUSE, Alfred (1830–1905), started in practice at Manchester in 1856 and moved to London in 1865. In Manchester he won the competitions for the Assize Courts (1859) and Town Hall (1869–77), both excellently planned and externally in a free, picturesque Gothic which yet does not depart too far from symmetry. Soon after, his style hardened and assumed that odd character of sharp forms and harsh imperishable materials (terracotta, best red brick) which one connects with him. He remained a planner of great clarity and resourcefulness and used ironwork freely for structural purposes. But he was a historicist all the same, happiest in a rigid matter-of-fact Gothic, but also going in for a kind of Romanesque (Natural History Museum, London, 1868 etc.) and for French Renaissance (Caius College, Cambridge, 1868 etc.). Of his many buildings the following may be mentioned: some very interestingly planned Congregational churches (Lyndhurst Road, Hampstead, 1883; King's Weigh House Chapel, 1889–91); the headquarters of the Prudential Assurance in Holborn (1876 etc.); the City and Guilds Institute in Kensington (1881); St Paul's School (1881 etc.; (demolished)); the National Liberal Club (1884); and a number of country mansions (Hutton Hall, Yorkshire, 1865; enlargement of Eaton Hall, Cheshire, 1870 etc.).

WATER-LEAF. A leaf shape used in later C12 CAPITALS. The water-leaf is broad, unribbed, and tapering, curving out towards the angle of the ABACUS and turned in at the top. See figure 24.

WATER-TABLE, see OFF-SET.

WATTLE AND DAUB. A method of wall construction consisting of branches or thin laths (wattles) roughly plastered over with mud or clay (daub), sometimes used as a filling between the vertical members of TIMBER-FRAMED houses.

WAVE MOULDING. A compound moulding formed by a convex curve between two concave curves; typical of the Decorated style.

WEALDEN HOUSE. A timber-framed house peculiar to England. It has a hall in the centre and wings projecting only slightly and only on the jutting upper floor. The roof, however, runs through without a break between wings and hall, and the eaves of the hall part are therefore exceptionally deep. They are supported by diagonal, usually curved, braces starting from the short inner sides of the overhanging wings and rising parallel with the front wall of the hall towards the centre of the eaves.

WEATHERBOARDING. Overlapping horizontal boards covering a TIMBER-FRAMED wall; the boards are wedge-shaped in section, the upper edge being the thinner.

WEATHERING. A sloping horizontal surface on sills, tops of buttresses, etc., to throw off water. See OFF-SET.

WEB, see CELL.

WEBB, Sir Aston (1849–1930). Perhaps the most successful of the providers of large public buildings in suitable styles around 1900. His favourite style, especially earlier in his career, was a free François I. Later there are also buildings in the Imperial-Palladian of the years of Edward VII. Chief buildings: Law Courts, Birmingham (with Ingress Bell, 1886–91); Metropolitan Life Assurance, Moorgate (with Bell, 1890–3), one of his best; Victoria and Albert Museum (1891 etc.); Christ's Hospital, Horsham (with Bell, 1894–1904); Royal Naval College, Dartmouth (1899–1904); Royal College of Science (1900–6); University, Birmingham (1906–9), Byzantino-Italian; Imperial College, Kensington (1911); Admiralty Arch (1911); façade of Buckingham Palace (1913).

WEBB, John (1611–72). A pupil and nephew by marriage of Inigo JONES, whose right-hand man he appears to have been from the 1630s onwards, e.g., at Wilton. He acquired technical skill and scholarship from Jones, but lacked imagination and originality. His independent work dates from after his master's death and much of it has been destroyed. Lamport Hall (1654–7), the portico and some interiors at The Vyne (1654–57), and the King Charles Building at Greenwich Hospital (1662–9) are the best that survive.

WEBB, Philip (1831–1915), hardly ever designed anything but houses. Among the architects of the great English Domestic Revival, he and Norman SHAW stand supreme: Shaw much more favoured, more inventive, more voluble, more widely influential; Webb harder, more of a thinker, totally deficient in any architectural bedside manner, and perhaps more deeply influential, even on Shaw himself. Webb chose his clients and never agreed to having a stable of assistants. His style is strangely ruthless: from the first he mixed elements from the Gothic and the C18, not for the fun or devilry of it, but because one should use the most suitable motifs regardless of their original contexts. He also liked to expose materials and show the workings of parts of a building.

His first job was Red House (1859) for William MORRIS, whose closest friend he remained throughout. For Morris's firm he designed furniture of a rustic Stuart kind, and also table glass and metalwork. He also joined in the stained glass work. His principal town houses are No. 1 Palace Green (1868) and No. 19 Lincoln's Inn Fields (1868–9). Of his country houses Joldwyns, Surrey (1873), Smeaton Manor, Yorkshire (1878), and Conyhurst, Surrey (1885) come nearest to Shaw in character – gabled, cheerful, with weatherboarding, tilehanging, and white window trim. Standen (1891–4) is best preserved. Clouds (1876) is the largest and least easy to take, strong no doubt, but very astringent indeed, designed, as it were, in a take-it-or-leave-it mood. Webb's

interiors from the later seventies onwards often have white panelling and exhibit a marked sympathy with the C18 vernacular. In 1901 he retired to a country cottage and ceased practising.

WEINBRENNER, Friedrich (1766–1826), was born at Karlsruhe and visited Berlin (1790) and Rome (1792). His major achievement is the transformation of Karlsruhe into a neo-classical city, rather like a miniature version of Leningrad. The Marktplatz (1804–24), with balancing but not identical buildings and a pyramid in the centre, and the circular Rondellplatz (1805–13), with the Markgräfliches Palais are masterpieces of neo-classical town planning. He also built a handsome circular Catholic church (1808–17).

WELLS, Joseph Merrill, see McKIM.

WESTWORK. The west end of a Carolingian or Romanesque church, consisting of a low entrance hall and above it a room open to the nave and usually flanked or surrounded by aisles and upper galleries. The whole is crowned by one broad tower, and there are occasionally stair turrets as well. In the main upper room stood an altar as a rule.

WHEEL WINDOW, see ROSE WINDOW.

WHITE, Stanford (1853–1906), was of old New England stock and was brought up in a cultured house. He was a pupil of RICHARDSON and from 1879 a partner of McKIM and Mead. White was a rich *bon vivant*, a man who entertained sumptuously, and exuberant in other ways as well. He was a brilliant and effortless designer, his range stretching from magazine covers to a railway carriage, including Gordon Bennett's yacht, and houses more original than any by anyone anywhere at the time. The temerity of the Low House at Bristol, Rhode Island (1887, recently demolished), with its enormous spreading pitched roof, is almost beyond belief. For other buildings see McKIM. White was shot dead during a theatre rehearsal in 1906.

WILKINS, William (1778-1839), son of a Norwich architect, was educated at Caius College, Cambridge, where he was elected Fellow in 1802. He travelled in Greece, Asia Minor, and Italy (1801-4) and published *Antiquities of Magna Graecia* on his return. He pioneered the GREEK REVIVAL in England with his designs for Downing College, Cambridge (begun 1806), Haileybury College (1806-9), and the temple-style country house Grange Park (1809) with its Theseum peristyle and other rather pedantically Athenian references. In fact, he was rather priggish and doctrinaire, and his rival SMIRKE had little difficulty in overtaking his lead in the movement. But Downing College is important historically as the first of all university campuses – separate buildings round a park-like expanse of lawn – preceding JEFFERSON's Charlottesville. His other university buildings in Cambridge were neo-Gothic, e.g., New Court, Trinity (1821-3), and the screen and hall-range at King's (1824-8). He had greater opportunities in London to develop his neo-Greek style but muffed them – University College (1827-8), St George's Hospital (1828-9), and finally the National Gallery (1834-8), which ruined his reputation. Only the main block of University College is his, and though the portico itself is very imposing he seems to have been unable to unite it satisfactorily with the rest of the composition. This inability to subordinate the parts to the whole resulted at the National Gallery in a patchy façade unworthy of its important site.

WILLIAM OF RAMSEY (d. 1349). A member of a family of masons who worked in Norwich and London from about 1300 onwards, William appears first in 1325 as a mason working on St Stephen's Chapel in the Palace of Westminster (*see* MICHAEL OF CANTERBURY). In 1332 he became master mason of the new work at St Paul's Cathedral, which meant the chapter-house and its cloister. In 1336 he was appointed Master Mason to the King's Castles south of Trent, which included the Palace of Westminster and St Stephen's Chapel. William was also commissioned in 1337 to give his *sanum consilium* on Lichfield Cathedral. In the early thirties he may have been master mason to Norwich Cathedral also: the cloister there was taken over by one William of Ramsey from John of Ramsey, probably his father, who was already master mason to the cathedral in 1304. William was evidently an important man, and what we know from an old illustration and surviving fragments of the chapter-house of St Paul's indicates that the creation of the Perpendicular style was due to him, or at least that he made a style out of elements evolved in London and especially at St Stephen's Chapel in the decade preceding 1330.

WILLIAM OF SENS (d. *c.* 1180). Designer and master mason of the chancel of Canterbury Cathedral, rebuilt after a fire had destroyed it in 1174. He was a Frenchman (or else his successor would not have been known as William the Englishman) and came from Sens Cathedral, which was begun *c.* 1140 and which contained features repeated at Canterbury (also in the Englishman's work, no doubt on the strength of drawings left in the lodge by William of Sens). He was, however, also familiar with more recent French work, notably Notre Dame in Paris (begun 1163), St Rémi at Reims, Soissons, and buildings in the north-west such as Valenciennes. William, as the true master mason of the Gothic Age (*see also* VILLARD DE HONNECOURT), was familiar with wood as well as stone and with devices to load stone on to ships. He had been chosen at Canterbury from a number of English and French masons assembled for consultation on action to be taken after the fire.

WILLIAM OF WYNFORD (d. *c.* 1405-10), was made master mason of Wells

Cathedral in 1365, after having worked at Windsor Castle, where William of Wykeham was then clerk of the works. Wynford remained in the royal service and in 1372 received a pension for life. He also remained William of Wykeham's protégé, and worked for him at Winchester College and from 1394 at Winchester Cathedral, where he probably designed the new nave and west front. New College, Oxford, has also been attributed to him. He was obviously a much appreciated man; he dined with William of Wykeham, at the high table of Winchester College, and at the prior's table at the cathedral, and received a furred robe once a year from the cathedral. On several occasions he appeared, no doubt for consultations, together with YEVELE.

WIND-BRACE, see ROOF.

WINDE, William (d. 1722), was born in Holland, the son of a Royalist exile. He took up architecture in middle age about 1680, and became, with PRATT and MAY, a leader of the Anglo-Dutch school. His Buckingham House, London (1705, destroyed), with its unpedimented attic storey, fore-buildings, and quadrant colonnades, was very influential. None of his buildings survives.

WINDER, see STAIR.

WOLFF, Jacob the elder (c. 1546–1612). Master mason to the city of Nuremberg. His most notable work was the *überherrliche* (super-magnificent) house which he and Peter Carl built for Martin Peller in Nuremberg (1602–7, destroyed in the Second World War but partially rebuilt). Martin Peller had been a consul in Venice and the Pellerhaus is a curious compromise between Venetian and German taste, its three heavily rusticated storeys being crowned with a rich three-storey German gable. On the Marienberg, above Würzburg, he connected the wings of the existing castle to make a vast elongated rectangular court (1600–1607) very sparingly

decorated. His son Jacob Wolff the younger (1571–1620) travelled and studied in Italy and brought back a more highly developed Italian Renaissance style which he used in a striking manner in his additions to the Nuremberg Town Hall (1616–22, destroyed in the Second World War but rebuilt).

WOMERSLEY, J. L. (b. 1910). City Architect of Sheffield 1953–64 and a pioneer in England of large-scale housing in high and ingeniously interlocked ranges of flats (Parkhill Housing, 1955–60).

WOOD, John, the elder (1704–54), a competent exponent of PALLADIANISM (e.g., Prior Park near Bath, 1735–48), revolutionized town planning with his scheme for Bath (1727 etc.), unfortunately only partly executed. He began with Queen Square (1729–36), treating the north side as a palace front with a rusticated ground floor and attached central pediment. (This had recently been attempted in Grosvenor Square, London, c. 1730, by Edward Shepheard, but only partially realized.) Entirely original was the Circus (1754 etc.), a circular space with three streets radiating out of it; the elevations have superimposed orders so that it looks like the Colosseum turned outside in. He intended to follow the Circus with a Forum, of which North and South Parades are fragments, and an enormous Gymnasium (unexecuted), and thus make Bath once more into a Roman city. He died soon after placing the first stone of the Circus, but his work was carried on by his son John Wood the younger (1728–81), who took it a step further towards open planning with his Royal Crescent (1761–5), the first of its kind and an artistic conception of great originality and magnificence. It has been widely copied ever since. His other buildings - e.g., the Assembly Rooms (1769–71) and Hot Baths (1773–8) - are excellent late examples of Palladianism.

WREN, Sir Christopher (1632–1723). The greatest English architect. His father was Dean of Windsor and his uncle Bishop of Ely, both pillars of the High Church. He was educated at Westminster School and at fifteen became a demonstrator in anatomy at the College of Surgeons; then he went up to Oxford. Experimental science was just then coming to the fore, and he found himself in company with a group of brilliant young men who were later to found the Royal Society. He was entirely engrossed in scientific studies. Evelyn called him 'that miracle of a youth' and Newton thought him one of the best geometricians of the day. In 1657 he was made Professor of Astronomy in London, in 1661 in Oxford; but two years later his career took a different turn with his appointment to the commission for the restoration of St Paul's. After the Great Fire of London he was appointed one of the Surveyors under the Rebuilding Act (1667) and in 1669 became Surveyor General of the King's Works. Then here signed his Oxford professorship and was knighted (1673). He was twice M.P. (1685–7 and 1701–2) and, despite his Tory connections, survived the Whig revolution of 1688, but on the accession of George I in 1714 he lost his office. He was twice married, first to a daughter of Sir John Coghill, and secondly to a daughter of Lord Fitzwilliam of Lifford. He died aged ninety-one having, as he wrote, 'worn out (by God's Mercy) a long life in the Royal Service and having made some figure in the world'.

If Wren had died at thirty he would have been remembered only as a figure in the history of English science. His first buildings, the Sheldonian Theatre, Oxford (1663), and Pembroke College Chapel, Cambridge (1663), are the work of a brilliant amateur, though the trussed roof of the Sheldonian already displays his structural ingenuity. In 1665–6 he spent eight or nine months studying French architecture, mainly in Paris, and may well have visited Flanders and Holland as well. He met BERNINI in Paris, but learnt more from MANSART and LE VAU, whom he probably knew and whose works he certainly studied. French and Dutch architecture were to provide the main influences on his own style. The Fire of London in 1666 gave him his great opportunity. Though his utopian city plan was rejected, every facet of his empirical genius found scope for expression in the rebuilding of St Paul's and the fifty-one city churches. The latter especially revealed his freshness of mind, his bounding invention, and his adventurous empiricism. There were, of course, no precedents in England for classical churches except in the work of Inigo JONES. Wren's city churches were built between 1670 and 1686, nearly thirty being under construction in the peak year of 1677. Plans are extremely varied and often daringly original, e.g., St Stephen, Walbrook (1672–87), which foreshadows St Paul's, and St Peter's, Cornhill (1677–81), in which his two-storeyed gallery church with vaulted nave and aisles was first adumbrated. This type was later perfected at St Clement Danes (begun 1680) and St James's, Piccadilly (begun 1683). But his originality and fertility of invention are best seen in the steeples, which range from the neo-Gothic of St Dunstan in the East to the Borrominesque fantasy of St Vedast and St Bride.

More scholarly and refined in detail than his sometimes rather hastily conceived and crudely executed city churches is his masterpiece, St Paul's Cathedral. Nothing like it had ever before been seen in England. It was a triumph of intellectual self-reliance, and the dome is one of the most majestic and reposeful in the world, purely classical in style. Baroque influences are evident elsewhere in the building, notably in the towers, the main façade, and such illusionist features as the sham-perspective window niches and the false upper storey in the side elevations to conceal the nave buttresses. The interior is ostensibly classical, but contains many Baroque gestures. It was begun in 1675, and Wren lived to see it finished in 1709.

His secular buildings range from the austere Doric barracks at Chelsea Hospital (1682–92) to the grandest and most Baroque of all his works, Greenwich Hospital (1694 etc.), where the Painted Hall (1698) is the finest room of its kind in England. Of his vast and elaborate additions and alterations to Whitehall Palace, Winchester Palace, and Hampton Court only a fragment of the latter survives (and this was probably revised and altered by his assistant William TALMAN). Like nearly all his work, these great schemes were carried out for the Office of Works. Of his few independent commissions the best are Trinity College Library, Cambridge (1676–84), and Tom Tower, Christ Church, Oxford (1681–2). Apart from Marlborough House, London (1709–10, now much altered), no town or country house can be certainly attributed to him, though his name has been optimistically given to many. HAWKSMOOR was his only pupil of note, but he had a wide and profound influence through his long reign at the Office of Works.

WRIGHT, Frank Lloyd (1869–1959). The greatest American architect to date. His *œuvre* ranges over more than sixty years and is never repetitive, routine, or derivative. He first worked with SULLIVAN, whom he never ceased to admire, and was responsible for much of his master's domestic work. The first type of building he developed as an independent architect is what he called the prairie house – low, spreading, with rooms running into each other, terraces merging with the gardens, and roofs far projecting.

Houses of this type are located in the outer suburbs of Chicago (Oak Park, Riverside, etc.). The development was extremely consistent, ending up with designs more daringly novel than any other architect's in the same field. The series was heralded by houses before 1900 and was complete by about 1905; its climax is the Robie House, Chicago (1908). Concurrently he had done one church, Unity Temple, Oak Park (1905–6), and one office building, Larkin Building, Buffalo (1904) – both with the same stylistic elements and the same freshness of approach as the private houses. The Larkin Building might well be called the most original office building of its date anywhere.

Some bigger jobs came along about the time of the First World War: Midway Gardens, Chicago (1913), a lavish and short-lived entertainment establishment, and the no longer surviving Imperial Hotel at Tokyo (1916–20). His assistant here, Antonin Raymond (1888–1976), then settled in Japan. Both these buildings were very heavily decorated, and the elements of this decoration, polygonal and sharp-angled forms, are entirely Wright's, favoured by him from the very beginning, but less in evidence in the prairie houses, at least externally. The houses of the twenties introduced a new technique which allowed Wright to use surface decoration on the outside as well: precast concrete blocks.

In fact, from then onwards, Wright went more and more his own way, and it is very rare for his work to run parallel to international developments and conventions. One exception is Falling Water, Bear Run, Pennsylvania (1937–9), which is closer to the so-called INTERNATIONAL MODERN of Europe (and by then of America) than anything else Wright designed. His own work which, about 1914–17, influenced GROPIUS as well as the Dutch De Stijl Group (*see* OUD) is not represented in Europe at all, as his harmless little Memorial Hostel for Venice was prevented from being executed. In his autobiography Wright tells of many such calamities, but as a writer he was biased and monotonously convinced that he was always right and blameless. This attitude seems to have distinguished his Taliesin community in Wisconsin from the fraternity ideals of RUSKIN: it was more of a master-and-disciples than a guild relationship. Wright built at Taliesin three times (1911, 1914, and 1925 etc.), and then added a Taliesin Winter Camp in Arizona (1927 etc.), eminently fantastical and very exciting.

World-wide recognition came late to Wright, and only in his last twenty years or so, that is from the time when he was nearly seventy, did large commissions come his way fairly evenly. The first was the Johnson Wax Factory at Racine, Wisconsin (1936–9). Here he built an office block with walls of brick and glass tubes, and an interior with reinforced concrete mushroom columns (see MAILLART). The laboratory tower was added in 1949. The chapel of Florida Southern College dates from 1940, the Unitarian Church at Madison from 1947, the design for the Guggenheim Museum in New York from 1942 (completed 1960), and the office skyscraper at Bartlesville, Oklahoma, was completed in 1955. The museum, designed as a spiral ramp on a circular plan, is functionally indefensible but formally certainly startling. The skyscraper and the two ecclesiastical buildings display Wright's inborn passion for sharp angles more radically than any of his earlier buildings, and it is interesting to observe that the recent turn of architecture towards aggressive sharp angles (see BREUER, SAARINEN) has given this pre-1900 passion of Wright's a new topicality. He lived through three phases of free decorative play in international architecture: the Arts and Crafts, Expressionism, and the most recent anti-rationalism.

WYATT, James (1747–1813), the most successful architect of his day, rivalled the ADAM brothers and even overshadowed CHAMBERS, whom he succeeded as Surveyor-General in 1796. But his brilliance was superficial, and his reputation now rests mainly on his neo-Gothic extravaganzas, though the best of these have been destroyed. The son of a Staffordshire timber-merchant and builder, he went to Venice for six years in 1762, studying there under the painter–architect Visentini. He leapt to fame on his return to London with the Pantheon in Regent Street (1770, now destroyed), an astonishing neo-classical version of Hagia Sophia in Constantinople. He was inundated with commissions from then onwards, despite his outrageously bad manners to clients and his general unreliability. His classical houses, very smooth and elegant, include Heaton House (1772), Heveningham (1788–99), Castle Coole in Northern Ireland (1790–7), and Dodington (1798–1808), the latter very solemn and severe, owing much to the Greek Revival. His neo-Gothic work ranges from the exquisite miniature Lee Priory (1782, destroyed, but one room survives in the Victoria and Albert Museum) to the fabulous Fonthill Abbey (1796–1807, destroyed) for William Beckford and the almost equally extravagant Ashridge (1806–13). His numerous and ruthless restorations and 'improvements' to Gothic buildings include work at Salisbury, Durham, and Hereford Cathedrals, and earned him the name of 'Wyatt the Destroyer'.

WYATT, Thomas Henry (1807–80), and his brother Sir Matthew Digby (1820–77), are not related to James WYATT. Thomas Henry's chef-d'œuvre is Wilton Church, Wiltshire (1842–3), in an Early-Christian-Italian-Romanesque manner; it is perhaps the finest example of that style of the 1840s, rarer in England than in Germany. He also designed many Gothic churches (for a time in partnership with David Brandon). Sir Matthew Digby belonged to the circle of Henry Cole and Owen Jones, who were responsible for much of the work on the Exhibition of 1851; Wyatt himself was Secretary of the Executive Committee. He was a poor architect (*see* the architectural parts of Paddington Station, 1854–5), but an extremely intelligent and far-seeing architectural journalist, a believer in the new materials of his century and the possibilities of machine production.

WYATVILLE, Sir Jeffrey (1766–1840). He was the nephew of James WYATT under whom he trained and whose work at Ashridge he completed in 1817 (adding the N. entrance, E. wing and stables). Although a competent classical architect (e.g., his entrance hall and stable court at Longleat 1801–11), he specialized in neo-Gothic and 'Tudor collegiate' mansions. His masterpiece is Windsor Castle which he remodelled for George IV between 1824 and 1837, giving it a picturesque silhouette by raising the Round Tower 33 ft to make it a dominant feature around which to group his newly battlemented and machicolated towers. He added the George IV Gateway and Lancaster Tower and rebuilt the Chester and Brunswick Towers. His Waterloo Gallery and new royal apartments are still in use. He changed his name to Wyatville when he began work at the Castle and was knighted in 1828.

WYNFORD, *see* WILLIAM OF WYNFORD.

X

XYSTUS. An AMBULATORY. In Greek architecture, a long portico used for athletic contests; in Roman architecture, a long covered or open walk bordered by colonnades or trees.

Y

YAMASAKI, Minoru (b. 1912). His most important building is St Louis Airport (1953–5), designed with Hellmut and Leinweber. Its crossing concrete vaults are eminently impressive. Later buildings tend to be playful and weak: American Concrete Institute, Detroit, 1958; Reynolds Metals Building, Detroit, 1959; Conference Center and Education Building, Wayne State University, Detroit, 1958 and 1961; Michigan Consolidated Gas Company, Detroit, 1962; School of Music, Oberlin College, 1964.

YEVELE, Henry (d. 1400), was admitted a citizen of London in 1353, became mason to the Black Prince about 1357, to the King (for Westminster, the Tower, and other palaces and castles) from 1360, and to Westminster Abbey from 1388 at the latest. It is probable that he had designed the nave of the abbey (as begun c. 1375), and the nave of Canterbury Cathedral, built in the 1390s, has also been attributed to him. He designed Westminster Hall in 1394. He was a wealthy man with property in many places, and he engaged in business both in connection with and apart from his duties as the King's Master Mason.

YORKE, F. R. S. (1906–62), one of the pioneers in England of the INTERNATIONAL MODERN style of the twenties and thirties, started with a number of white cubic private houses in 1934. He was in partnership with Marcel BREUER 1935–7, and later the name of the firm became Yorke, Rosenberg & Mardall; it has been responsible for flats, housing, hospitals, schools (e.g., Stevenage, 1947–9) and for Gatwick Airport (1957 etc.).

YORKSHIRE LIGHTS. In a mullioned window, a pair of lights, one fixed and the other sliding horizontally.

Z

ZAKHAROV, Adrian Dmitrievich (1761–1811), the leading Russian neo-classicist and perhaps the greatest Russian architect, was trained at the St Petersburg Academy of Arts, then in Paris under CHALGRIN (1782–6), and travelled in Italy. His masterpiece is the Admiralty, Leningrad (1806–15), vast, bold, and solid, with a façade a quarter of a mile long, a huge columned tower supporting a needle-like spire over the central gate, and dodecastyle Tuscan porticos at the ends. To give expression to such an immense frontage without breaking its unity was a major achievement. But the end blocks are still more successful, the nearest approach to BOULLÉE's architecture of geometrical shapes on a grand scale: each is in the form of a cubic pavilion capped by a low cylindrical drum, pierced by a vast semicircular portal, and flanked by colonnades. Another of his notable works is the church of St Andrew in Kronstadt.

ZAPOTEC ARCHITECTURE, see MESO-AMERICAN ARCHITECTURE.

ZIGGURAT (or ZIKKURAT). An Assyrian or Babylonian temple-tower in the form of a truncated pyramid built in diminishing stages, each stage being reached by ramps. See figure 86.

ZIMBALO, Giuseppe (active 1659–86). The chief exponent of the wildly exuberant and rather coarse Baroque style developed at Lecce, e.g., Prefettura (1659–95), Cathedral (1659–82), S. Agostino (1663), and Chiesa del Rosario (1691). His pupil Giuseppe Cino carried his style on into the C18.

ZIMMERMANN, Dominikus (1685–1766), one of the greatest South German Rococo architects, but a craftsman before he was an architect,

retained to the last his peasant vitality, spontaneity, and unquestioning piety. Perhaps it is significant that his masterpiece, die Wies, was built neither for a great prince nor for the abbot of a rich monastery but for a simple rustic community. Born at Wessobrunn, he

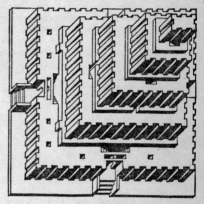

Fig. 86. Ziggurat

began there as a stucco worker, then settled at Füssen (1698), and finally at Landsberg (1716), where he eventually became mayor. He continued to work as a stuccoist after becoming an architect and frequently collaborated with his brother Johann Baptist (1680–1758), who was a painter. His earliest building is the convent church at Mödingen (1716–18), but his mature style first becomes apparent in the pilgrimage church of Steinhausen (1728–31), which is also the first wholly Rococo church in Bavaria. It broke away decisively from its Baroque predecessors, the mystical indirect lighting and rich velvety colour of ASAM giving place to flat even lighting and a predominantly white colour scheme – bright, brittle, and porcellaneous. The colours used are all symbolical, as are the motifs in both painted and carved decoration. At the Frauenkirche, Günzburg (1736–41), he adopted an oblong plan, and at die Wies (1745–54) he combined an oval with an oblong, using the former for the nave with its wide ambulatory (necessary for a pilgrimage church), and the latter for the rather long chancel, which is treated with an intensified, predominantly pink colour scheme. Here stucco work, white-painted wooden statues, and frescoes combine with architecture to delight and instruct the pilgrim, be he never so humble or so sophisticated. In more ways than one it is the meeting-place of the courtly Rococo style and an ancient tradition of craftsmanship which stretches back to the Middle Ages.

ZOOPHORUS. A frieze with animal reliefs, as on the Theseum in Athens.

ZUCCALLI, Enrico (1642–1724). Baroque architect, born in the Grisons, who settled in Munich where he and his rival VISCARDI dominated the architectural scene for several years. He succeeded BARELLI as architect to the Elector in 1672. In Munich he completed Barelli's Theatine church of St Cajetan, reducing the size of the dome. He supervised the decoration of the Residenz (Imperial suite 1680–1701; Alexander and Summer Suite 1680–85) and built the Porcia Palace (1694). Outside Munich, at Schleissheim, he built the Lustheim or Banqueting House (1684–9) and began the main palace (1701, completed by EFFNER). In 1695 he began rebuilding the palace at Bonn but this was completed after 1702 by de COTTE. He also rebuilt the abbey church of Ettal (1709–26, partly burnt and rebuilt 1742). His kinsman Gaspare (active 1685) built two Italianate churches at Salzburg: St Erhard (1685–9) and St Cajetan (1685–1700).

MORE ABOUT PENGUINS
AND PELICANS

Penguinews, which appears every month, contains details of all the new books issued by Penguins as they are published. From time to time it is supplemented by *Penguins in Print*, which is our complete list of almost 5,000 titles.

A specimen copy of *Penguinews* will be sent to you free on request. Please write to Dept EP, Penguin Books Ltd, Harmondsworth, Middlesex, for your copy.

In the U.S.A.: For a complete list of books available from Penguins in the United States write to Dept CS, Penguin Books, 625 Madison Avenue, New York, New York 10022.

In Canada: For a complete list of books available from Penguins in Canada write to Penguin Books Canada Ltd, 2801 John Street, Markham, Ontario, L3R 1B4.

AN OUTLINE OF EUROPEAN
ARCHITECTURE

Nikolaus Pevsner

This seventh revised edition of Nikolaus Pevsner's classic
history is presented in an entirely new and attractive style.
The format has been enlarged and the illustrations appear next
to the passages to which they refer. Their numbers have
swelled to nearly 300, including drawings, plans, and photographs. The final chapter of the Penguin Jubilee edition
(published in 1960 and still available) has been incorporated,
carrying the story from 1914 to the present day, and there are
substantial additions on the sixteenth to eighteenth centuries
in France as well as many minor revisions. The book tells the
story of architecture by concentrating on outstanding buildings, and reads exceedingly well in its concentration and its
combination of warmth and scholarship.

Also published

PIONEERS OF MODERN DESIGN

VASARI

LIVES OF THE ARTISTS

Translated by George Bull

Vasari's *Lives of the Artists* stretches from Cimabue and Giotto down to the golden epoch of Leonardo, Raphael, and Michelangelo. Vasari (1511–74) was himself a painter, but his fame rests on these biographies in which he gathered together all the current knowledge of the Florentine artistic heritage and triumphantly fused it with contemporary Italian theories of art. As a critic Vasari is impressive, and time has added immense historical importance to the great popular success his work achieved from the start.

STYLE AND CIVILIZATION

This series aims to interpret the important styles in European art in the broadest context of the civilization and thought of their times.

PRE-CLASSICAL *John Boardman*

From the surviving art and artefacts of the Bronze Age palaces of Crete and Mycenae and the world of Archaic Greece this study portrays the beginnings of the Western tradition.

GOTHIC *George Henderson*

Notre Dame or Westminster, exquisite illumination, stern sculpture or the stained glass of Chartres – the rich and complex nature of Gothic art has always fascinated us. Every age has held its own vision of the Gothic world – a world of barbarism, or of chivalry, or of piety. Here is an attempt to reach a deeper understanding of the Gothic style by examining its many forms in the context of contemporary religious or philosophical attitudes, and against the background of the social and political order of the Middle Ages.

EARLY RENAISSANCE *Michael Levey*

At this time new techniques, discovery of visual perspective, fresh interest in the antique past, all combined to make art a fully rational activity, incorporating truths of human nature and the universe.
This book was awarded the Hawthornden Prize in 1968 – the first paperback book to receive such an award.

also published

MANNERISM *John Shearman*
NEO-CLASSICISM *Hugh Honour*
REALISM *Linda Nochlin*

5?

PICADOR USA ✻ NEW YORK

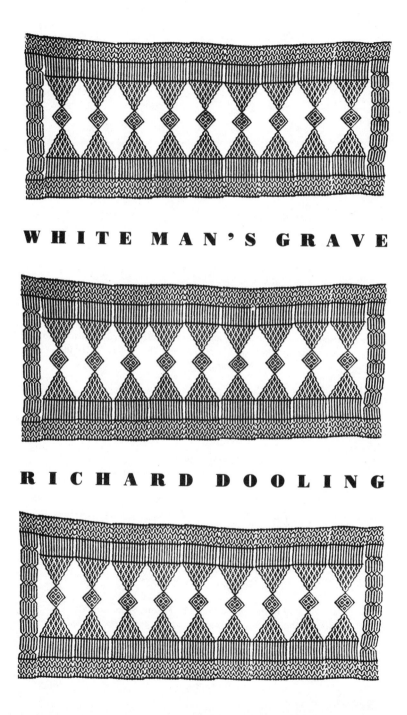

WHITE MAN'S GRAVE

RICHARD DOOLING

Picador® is a U.S. registered trademark and is used by St. Martin's Press under license from Pan Books Limited.

Library of Congress Cataloging-in-Publication Data

Dooling, Richard.
White man's grave / Richard Dooling.
p.   cm.
ISBN 0-312-13214-X
1. Americans—Travel—Africa, West—Fiction.   2. Missing persons—
Africa, West—Fiction.   3. Peace Corps (U.S.)—Sierra Leone—
Fiction.   4. Sierra Leone—Fiction.   5. Africa, West—Fiction.
I. Title.
[PS3554.0583W45   1995]
813'.54—dc20   95-4279   CIP

First published in the United States by Farrar, Straus and Giroux.
Published simultaneously in Canada by HarperCollinsCanadaLtd.

First Picador USA Edition: June 1995
10 9 8 7 6 5 4 3 2 1

For my mom,

for my big brother, Lahai Hindowa,

and in memory of Pa Moussa Gbembo

The fiend in his own shape is

less hideous than when he rages

in the breast of man.

—NATHANIEL HAWTHORNE

Young Goodman Brown

WHITE MAN'S GRAVE

(1)

Randall Killigan was a senior partner in the biggest law firm in Indianapolis, chairman of its bankruptcy department, and commanding officer when his firm did battle in federal bankruptcy court. Being the best bankruptcy lawyer in Indianapolis kept him happy for a month or two, but then he wanted to be the best bankruptcy lawyer in the Seventh Circuit, which in the federal court system comprises the states of Indiana, Illinois, and Wisconsin. Illinois contained Chicago and the biggest obstacle to his fame, because it was swarming with excellent bankruptcy lawyers operating out of huge law offices that serviced national and international clients whose bankruptcies made the front page of *The Wall Street Journal*. It would be a few years before Randall could scorch the earth in enough Chicago bankruptcy courts to make his name synonymous with commercial savagery in the Seventh Circuit, but he was working on it. He was building a national bankruptcy practice from a home base in an unremarkable midwestern city, working out of Sterling & Sterling, a partnership and professional corporation consisting of only 240 lawyers, most of whom were beholden to Killigan for the work he sent them.

He had the thin but shapeless body of a middle-aged desk jockey and courtroom general who burned most of his calories exercising his adrenal glands. Randall learned early in life that the best-paying jobs were often the most stressful ones, so he taught himself not only to endure stress but to enjoy it. Before long, he developed a craving for it, the way other people craved caffeine or nicotine. But then (at least according to his wife) he went too far and became a stress junkie—living a life that was devoid of meaning or excitement unless he was mainlining stress, arguing on behalf of a client who had paid him and his firm millions in fees to confirm a Chapter 11 plan of reorganization. Randall lived and breathed the Bankruptcy Code, and intimidated anybody who crossed him by quoting it chapter, section, and verse. The famous biologist James Watson lived and breathed the problem of DNA until the structure of the double helix was revealed to him in a dream. Descartes nodded off and discovered the order of all the sciences in a dream. The nineteenth-century chemist Friedrich August Kekulé von Stradonitz dreamed of a serpent swallowing its tail, and woke up to discover the closed carbon ring structure of the benzene molecule. When Randall Killigan slept, he dreamed sections of the U.S. Bankruptcy Code, and woke up to discover money—lots of it—eagerly paid by clients who had insatiable appetites for his special insights into the Code.

He tilted back in his leather recliner and spun around for a corner-office view of downtown Indianapolis, revealing a banner of computer paper Scotch-taped to the back of his chair, where emblazoned in four-inch bold type were the words KING OF THE BEASTS. Randall's protégé, the young Mack Saplinger, had hung the beast banner as a joke, after one of Randall's more notable victories; Randall had left it there. His desk and three enormous worktables were scattered with trophies from proceedings gone by: logos and tokens from companies he had reorganized under Chapter 11, gifts from especially grateful bank officers in the form of paperweights engraved with his name and maybe the date of a dispositive hearing.

Immediately to his right, the head of a huge stuffed black bear was mounted on the lid of a metal wastebasket. Randall had killed the bear in Alaska on a bankruptcy retreat with the boys and the lone female associate, Liza Spontoon. The bear's eyes stared up at the ceiling, the jaws were open, the white fangs gleamed, and, best of all, the thing ate paper.

Randall hated paper, which was why he glowered when Mack appeared and discreetly placed a hard copy of the lift-stay motion in the Beach Cove case somewhere on the back forty acres of Randall's partner-sized desk, so it would be handy if Randall needed it during his conference call.

"Get that out of here," Randall said, pointing first at the document, then at the computer screen, where the same document was already displayed in white letters on a blue field.

As a rule, paper contained either worthless information or valuable information that was effectively useless and unretrievable until it was stored on a computer's hard disk. His associates all knew that memos to Randall were sent by E-mail. Randall had an E-mail macro that, every hour on the hour, intercepted any memo to his terminal exceeding 6,000 bytes, or about the length of one single-spaced typewritten page. The macro automatically opened such memos, then time- and date-stamped them with the following message:

Your memo to this terminal was returned unread because it was excessively verbose. Save your prolixity for our opponents in federal district court. In the future, check your E-mail menu screen and be sure that your memo contains fewer than 6,000 bytes of information before sending it to this terminal.

RSK

Before the conference call, Randall was due to meet with the creditors in the WestCo Manufacturing case, who were waiting for him down the hall in one of the Sterling conference rooms.

"Do you want the memo on debtor-in-possession financing for the WestCo meeting?" asked Mack.

Randall shook his head in exasperation and pointed at his notebook computer. The kid was loyal and hardworking, he thought, but needed reminding.

"I'll fetch the battery packs, master," Mack said with a grin, and slipped back out.

Mack filled a place in Randall's solar system that belonged to his only son, Michael Killigan, who, instead of going to law school after college, ran off and joined the Peace Corps, and was now stationed in a country whose name Randall could never remember: Sierra Liberia, or Sierra Coast, some blighted range of snake-infested hills in West Africa, full of nothing but swamps and bush villages and naked Africans living in mud huts with no running water or electricity. For some reason, Michael Killigan chose to live there too. Trying to be his own man, Randall figured, rebelling in the shadow of a giant, looking around for footsteps that were closer together than the mighty strides of his old man. He let the kid go, hoping that a couple months of sweltering in a shack, together with the attentions of a few colonies of intestinal parasites, would have his son back at home and eager to take the law school admissions test before the year was out.

Eighteen months later, Michael had sent home a photograph of an African village girl in a headwrap, and the youthful insurrection threatened to become a permanent revolution. The camera shot was of her head and bare shoulders, with a piece of bone or horn or a large fang on a leather string around her neck, and a big toothy smile for the camera. When Michael had come home on medical leave with a case of meningitis, Randall reasoned with him, then begged, threatened, bribed, even ordered him to stay, all of which did nothing but afflict his son with the selective deafness so often seen in the offspring of desperate parents. Michael had returned to Africa as soon as he could walk.

Randall had dictated a long letter to his son. Choosing his words with a lawyer's caution, he warned him that, while two years in the Peace Corps could be viewed as a character-building experience, *three* years might cause résumé problems: a flag indicating a possible lack of ambition, the appearance of shirking responsibilities, a professional demeanor that might be rough around the edges because of lingering reverse culture shock, a concern that reentry may have been incomplete. When he read his words on paper, Randall concluded that mailing the letter would probably obliterate any chance that his son would screw his head on straight and come home; it was still in his correspondence drawer.

So, instead of having his son at his right hand, Randall made do with the eager young Saplinger, an associate who distinguished himself by sleeping on the floor of the document room for two weeks running during the plan confirmation hearings of the Marauder Corporation case.

Expecting Mack to appear with the computer battery packs he needed for the meeting, Randall was annoyed when, instead, one of the firm's messengers walked into his office bearing a package of some kind.

"What the fuck is that?" Randall asked, grabbing and tilting a cardboard box held together with frizzy twine and addressed in black marker to "Master Rondoll Killigan."

"UPS," the messenger said, unruffled and apparently accustomed to Randall's spontaneous profanity. The messenger read from the receipt, "Freetown, Sierra Leone. Some place in Africa."

Randall tore the twine off, opened the box, removed several wads of newspaper packing, and found a black bundle of tightly wrapped rags the size of a small football, with a two-inch hollow red tube made out of some kind of porous stone or mineral sticking out of the apex.

"What is this shit? An African fuck bump?" Randall looked up and found his office empty, and was quite annoyed that the messenger had left before he could give the box back to him or yell at him for bringing it into his office in the first place. No note. Nothing. Just a black bundle from Africa.

Randall had less and less time for nonbankruptcy irritations and intrusions into his professional life. His first thought was that he must have an employee somewhere to whom he could hand this object, with instructions to figure out what it was, where it came from, who sent it, and what he was supposed to do with it, but nobody came to mind.

Distinctly sinister, it looked like a dark, petrified egg, laid by some huge, extinct bird of prey. He fingered the blood-colored spout and found it was mounted or sewn securely into the parcel's interior. He dropped the thing into the box of wadded newspaper and dusted his fingers over it. A foul smell emanated from it, and he was afraid to unravel the rags, which were held together with some kind of pitch or glue. He uncrumpled one of the newspaper wads and found it was a page of the *Sierra Leone Sentinel*, published in Freetown.

He considered feeding the whole mess to his bear, then reconsidered, set it on the floor under his desk, and resolved to call his wife at the first opportunity to see if Michael had said anything about sending back any African artifacts. Maybe it was just another rattle or drum for his collection. But *Master Rondoll*? That did not fit.

Mack appeared with the batteries. Killigan grabbed his custom-made notebook computer and slipped a CD-ROM disk containing the entire annotated Bankruptcy Code into one slot, fed the battery into another slot, and headed out the door and down the hall.

The attorneys representing all the major creditors in the WestCo Manufacturing case had arrayed themselves around a conference table, with their associates sitting demurely behind them, notepads and pens at the ready. The table was studded with notebook computers, briefcases, pitchers of ice water, notepads, cellular phones, and glasses fogging in the sunlight pouring in from the bay windows. Randall took his place at the head of the table and prepared to divide the spoils of WestCo Manufacturing among the lawyers for the various classes of creditors.

In primitive societies, the dominant male of the tribe apportioned the kill according to the skill and valor of the members of the hunting party. As far as Killigan was concerned, nothing much had changed for twentieth-century man, except that the weapons had become rules—complex and abstract rules—and the warriors were now lawyers. The kill was relatively bloodless (except for the occasional unhinged, atavistic client who showed up now and again on the six o'clock news dragging a lawyer around in a noose of piano wire attached to a shotgun). In Randall's hands, the U.S. Bankruptcy Code was a weapon, anything from a blazing scimitar to a neutron bomb, depending upon how much destruction he was being paid to inflict on his client's adversaries. International corporate behemoths—like WestCo—were weakened strays bleeding money, suffocated by debt, and falling behind the pack, where they could be picked off, dropped in the crosshairs of Randall's scope rifle, and plundered like carcasses rotting in the sun.

But bankruptcy law went far beyond the hunt, for the kill was always followed by brutal, expensive combat among the contending classes of creditors. Sure, passions ran high at Troy when Agamemnon took Achilles' beautiful sex slave for himself, but a bondholder who's being asked to take out-of-the-money warrants instead of principal plus interest at 14 percent is something else. Blood and gore. Section 1129 of the Code coyly referred to it as "plan confirmation," but when things went awry every bankruptcy lawyer in the country called the process "cram down," and for a good reason. After months or years of acrimonious, adversarial proceedings, one supreme warrior eventually emerged with a plan of reorganization, which he crammed down the throats of the vanquished creditors, so the spoils could be distributed to the victorious.

As far as Randall was concerned, he might as well have stood at the head of the table smeared with the grime of warfare, reeking of smoke, streaked with blood, and blackened with powder burns. For months, he had stood in crowded courtrooms with other lawyers who were just waiting for him to look the other way so they could blindside him with a nightstick. If he dropped his guard for a moment, if he took one case too many, if he failed to take every precaution, mistakenly trusted an associate with a crucial issue that turned out all wrong, forgot to have an associate check the computer services for the newest controlling case, missed a filing deadline, made only one important mistake . . . he could look up from counsel's table just in time to catch a poleax in the solar plexus. Some ruthless mercenary who had been studying Randall's techniques for years would step on his throat and show him the face of victory—all fangs and war paint, screaming with laughter. If he stumbled once or twice, he could always recover and retake the high ground. But if he ever actually *fell* . . . Too terrible to think about. They would be on him like hyenas, ripping him apart and drinking his blood before he could draw another breath.

The meeting went well enough. Only the bondholders were in a position to make trouble for him, and they were represented by a lawyer in a toupee who was afraid of Randall. Randall made sure everyone agreed on the deal points, flashed his teeth at the attorney for the bondholders, then headed down the hallway and back to his office, pausing when his administrative assistant stuck her hand out of an inner office and fanned a stack of pink messages commemorating calls that had come in during his meeting. He paused and flipped through them, crumpled one and threw it in the wastebasket, and handed the rest back to the hand, which was still patiently supine.

"Did Bilksteen call for the Beach Cove conference call yet?"

"No," she said.

"Put him through when he does. And enter the rest of these in the to-do with a four-thirty time," he said.

"You've got Mr. Haley and the DropCo unsecured creditors calling at four-thirty," she said, scrolling through his afternoon on the screen.

"N-A-T," he said, walking away from her.

"That's tomorrow," she called after him. "The next available time is tomorrow."

"Fine," he said, drifting back into his office. "Call them all and tell them it will be tomorrow."

At his desk, he switched on his notebook computer, which had been custom-made to his specifications. He had a Pentium chip; the other lawyers had only 386s. He had a CD-ROM drive installed containing the entire, annotated Bankruptcy Code, as well as the Bankruptcy Rules and the Federal Rules of Civil Procedure; nobody else had a CD-ROM drive in their notebook computers, because there was no such animal on the market; Randall had paid a technician to build one for him. Battery life? Six hours plus. Let the other wanna-bes struggle with their extension cords and their extra battery packs. Hard disk, 340 megabytes, which his paralegal had loaded with every relevant document in each of his cases, including a complete set of the pleadings for each proceeding, which had been scanned by an optical character reader and stored in his computer. He had discovered early in his career that if he worked harder than everyone else and knew more about the Code, the facts, and the case law than anyone else in the courtroom, he would win. And each victory made him that much stronger, because he could then afford more staff and better equipment, state-of-the-art litigation support software, and MIS personnel who knew how to make it sing with evidence and case law when Killigan needed them.

Mack appeared.

"Beach Cove," said Randall, and they both laughed.

"Should we send Bilksteen to a taxidermist and get him stuffed?" asked Randall. "You could fix his head up as a cover for your wastebasket, like I did with old Benjy here."

Mack noted Randall's annoyed glance at his watch. "I'll tell Whitlow and Spontoon to get in here," he said, referring to the other two associates who were scheduled to participate in the eleven o'clock conference call from opposing counsel in the Beach Cove bankruptcy proceedings.

The speakerphone buzzed, his conference call was ready, and Mack appeared with the other two Sterling associates in tow.

"Go ahead, Tom," Randall said into his speakerphone, adjusting the volume so the other lawyers in attendance could hear, while Tom Bilksteen yammered over the speaker, his voice sounding like the Minotaur calling on a cellular phone from the bowels of the Cretan labyrinth.

"Wait a second!" barked Randall. "Who's in there with you?"

"What do you mean?" said Bilksteen. "Nobody's with me. I'm in my office alone and the door is shut."

"Then pick up, you piece of shit," yelled Randall, his belligerence belied by the grin he showed his associates. "You're not putting me on speaker just because you're too damn lazy to lift the receiver. Pick up, goddamnit!"

Mack sat in the preferred chair at Randall's right hand, wrote a message on his legal pad, and held it up, showing Randall a scrawl that said: "Should we tell him?"

Randall shook his head, slowly and definitely, another grin spreading the width of his face. He tore off the page and fed it to his bear.

"Touchy, touchy," said Bilksteen, picking up his phone, his voice surfacing from the nether regions.

One associate was never enough for any matter entrusted to Randall Killigan, and the two associates who took seats in the hard-back chairs in front of Randall's desk neatly personified his mixed feelings about female attorneys. Liza Spontoon was single, brilliant, and homely, all of which in Randall's book would earn her a ride on the bus, if she had the fare. But she was also a succinct and combative legal writer and turned in billable hours that made the firm accountants whistle softly into their computer screens. She was in Randall's office because she was the best legal draftsman in the firm and had authored a memorandum in support of a lift-stay motion that was going to end the career of the lawyer at the other end of the line.

The other female attorney was Marissa Whitlow Carbuncle—an initially appealing, highly intelligent redhead with a nervous, unhappy smile, whose good looks were promptly ruined for Randall when he learned she was a feminist. Her husband was a thoracic surgeon, and she had two small children, meaning she had taken three months of maternity leave at full pay, not once, but *twice*. She was in Randall's office because he had sent for her, so he could try once more to make her life so miserable she would quit the firm before she became eligible for partnership consideration.

In Randall's book, both women should be voted down for partner because neither one of them had ever brought in a single new piece of business. If Randall had his way, he would give Spontoon a 20 percent pay raise and make her a permanent associate, and he would send Whitlow home to raise her kids, or off to California, where she could join one of those politically correct, multicultural law firms with enlightened attitudes about working for a living. The people on the compensation and partnership committees annually and shrilly accused Killigan of chauvinism and sex discrimination.

"I'm not a chauvinist," he had objected. "All I want is for everyone to be treated equally. I'll stay home for three months and look after my family if you guys send me the same draw I make billing sixty hours a week down here."

Randall had struggled with his conscience. He wanted to understand. "Let me get this straight," he had pleaded with the management committee. "We are supposed to pay Whitlow good money for *not* working, right? You and I, we'll stay down here on Saturday afternoons billing time, and Whitlow will be home knitting booties, right? Three months at full salary for no work, is that it? Why stop there? Let's make her a fucking dairy farmer so we can pay her for not producing milk too!"

Randall made no secret of his opinion of Ms. Whitlow's chances for partnership and his avid search for the most mundane, time-consuming work he could possibly find to assign her, via E-mail, on Friday evenings at six o'clock. She in turn made no secret of her sudden interest in the law of sex discrimination and sexual harassment in the workplace, specifically a 1989 U.S. Supreme Court case called *Price Waterhouse* v. *Hopkins*, in which a female accountant sued and won after being denied partnership in an international accounting firm. Whitlow also told Randall that she believed his use of foul and obscene language in the workplace constituted a hostile environment within the meaning of Title VII. Randall marveled at the way she drew him a map, with diagrams and a big red arrow, and a legend that said: *This is my hot button. Push it if you want to make me absolutely miserable.*

Threatening Randall with litigation was like sending him two free tickets to a Chicago Bulls game at the Hoosier Dome, center court and six rows up. Just the rumor of a sex discrimination suit had Randall salivating and humming to himself: visions of Whitlow on the witness stand with a bloody nose; Whitlow thrown out on her ass by a directed verdict after her own evidence showed she had the lowest billable hours in the entire firm; Whitlow trying to explain how she had to stay home for three months and earn twenty thousand dollars plus benefits to a jury of slack-jawed minimum-wagers who could not believe they were listening to a woman who made eighty thousand dollars a year complain about hearing a bankruptcy lawyer use the F-word. *Please sue me,* Randall pleaded in his daydreams, *and don't forget, I like it hard and fast.*

All three associates were avidly taking notes of the attorney's voice coming over the speakerphone (all probably taking the same notes, Randall guessed), not that the voice was saying anything of consequence. Note taking was something Randall noticed most associates did, because they were being billed out at over $125 an hour and wanted to justify the expense by looking busy. In time, they would be nourished along their career paths and weaned of their legal pads, given Dictaphones and speakerphones, until they achieved the serene self-confidence of senior partners, who never touched writing utensils, and charged over $200 an hour just for *thinking* about legal problems.

The voice on the speakerphone—still yammering—belonged to Tom Bilksteen, the attorney for a limited partnership that owned a hundred-unit condominium complex called Beach Cove. Randall's client, Comco Banks, had lent the Beach Cove partners fifteen million dollars in secured loans to build a suburban paradise around a man-made lake, which was to be advertised as "only twenty-five minutes from downtown Indianapolis." Then the bond issue to build the spur connecting Beach Cove to Interstate 70 was voted down, leaving ninety empty Beach Cove condominium units and ten gullible souls who sat in traffic listening to drive-time talk shows, behind cars waiting to make left turns off of congested two-lane suburban thoroughfares, and then made it downtown in a little over an hour, on Sunday mornings.

The Beach Cove partners defaulted on their loan; Randall and Comco moved in to foreclose; and Bilksteen put Beach Cove into Chapter 11. Now Bilksteen was taunting Randall over the speakerphone, safe in the knowledge that the U.S. Bankruptcy Code explicitly provided for something called an "automatic stay" of all creditor attempts to collect from the debtor or seize the debtor's property, which meant that Randall and Comco could not foreclose on Beach Cove or get any of the bank's money back out of the project for at least a year, probably longer. Although Randall and his people had filed a motion to lift the automatic stay, Bilksteen and every other bankruptcy lawyer knew that lift-stay motions—though almost always filed—were almost always denied.

Bilksteen was savoring this minor triumph, jerking Randall's chain, telling him that Comco would be lucky to get ten cents on the dollar for the fifteen million it had lent to the Beach Cove partners and that if Randall did not cooperate with him, he would keep the property tied up in bankruptcy court for three years.

"Three years with all that money earning no interest," Bilksteen said. "I don't know, Randall. I'd be wanting to deal if I were Comco." What Bilksteen did *not* know was that Randall's protégé, Mack, had played softball just last night with U.S. bankruptcy judge Richard Foote's law clerk, a classmate of Mack's at Northwestern. After a few cold frosties, the clerk had let slip that Judge Foote, Randall's favorite bankruptcy judge, was going to grant Randall's motion to lift the stay on the Beach Cove properties and allow Randall's client Comco to foreclose on the complex immediately. A lift-stay order from Judge Foote would mortally wound Beach Cove, would legally annihilate the Beach Cove partners, and would publicly humiliate Bilksteen, who would be the laughingstock of the bankruptcy bar as soon as the word got out that he could not even protect his clients by filing a simple single-asset bankruptcy.

By Randall's reckoning, Judge Foote would probably issue the lift-stay order after he got back from lunch, meaning that in another hour or so the court clerk would be calling Bilksteen with the news, and Bilksteen would be turning a bluish gray, rummaging through his desk drawers looking for his nitroglycerin tablets.

"You know, Killigan," said Bilksteen, "sooner or later you and the other creditors are going to have to come to the table and give the condo people a deal they can live with."

Randall decided it was time to use the mute button on the speakerphone. When pressed, the button cut off voice transmission from Killigan's end of the line without affecting reception, allowing those in attendance to both listen to the caller and carry on private conversations, while the party at the other end of the line remained oblivious that Killigan and his crew were doing anything but listening attentively.

Bilksteen blustered over the speakerphone about how Randall and Comco would be forced to accept an unfavorable plan of reorganization, how moths would eat the bound pleadings in the case before Comco saw a penny of its money. Killigan grinned at Whitlow, then fetched a Halloween broadsword he used for a letter opener and kept in a plastic scabbard at the console. He grasped the hilt dagger-style and stabbed the speakerphone, depressing the mute button with the plastic point of the toy sword.

"You pathetic village idiot," Killigan said over Bilksteen's legal patter. "You can use your goddamned plan of reorganization as insulation in your shithouse, boy. I am going to cut your fucking head off and mount it on a pike in the middle of your front lawn, understand?"

Mack smirked. Spontoon covered her mouth and giggled. Whitlow's face flushed and then drained, leaving a livid mask dotted with freckles. She thought about leaving, until Bilksteen said something about exchanging discovery, which was her responsibility, according to the E-mail message Randall had issued when he summoned her to his royal chambers.

Killigan released the mute button. "Sure," said Killigan, wagging slightly in his recliner and cleaning a thumbnail with the point of the broadsword. "Sure, Tom, we'll get you that discovery this afternoon, right after we get Judge Foote's order on the lift-stay motion." Killigan again poked the mute button with the toy sword. "And after I cut your head off, I'm going to pull your guts out and feed them to the family dog."

"Yeah," said Bilksteen. "I can't believe you guys bill your clients for those ridiculous lift-stay motions. I mean, when was the last time a bankruptcy judge granted one?"

Mack all but swallowed his tongue in stifling a belly laugh.

"Gee," Randall said without a wrinkle. "You know, you've got me there, Tom. It's been a while since Judge Foote granted a lift-stay motion in a case as big as this one. You know, I've always admired your horse sense about these things. You didn't go to Michigan like I did, and you're not sitting on top of the biggest firm in town like I am, but you are one smart lawyer, Mr. Bilksteen." The sword stabbed the mute button. "You pig's ass. Get yourself all hog-dressed and go waddle into Judge Foote's court, because you are going to come out a six-foot fucking sausage!"

"Shucks," Bilksteen said, "I just try and do my job."

Killigan released the mute button.

"You won't tell Comco how we've been wasting their money on a lift-stay motion, will you?" Randall asked, sliding Mack a look that said: *What do other people do for fun?*

"Your secret's safe with me," Bilksteen said with a benevolent chuckle. "Long as you give me a break on down the ways."

"You bet," Randall said, then stabbed the mute button. "Break your neck for you in an act of mercy maybe. At least I'll put your clients out of their misery."

"So you'll be sending somebody over with discovery this afternoon?"

"That's right," Randall said. "Right after we get the order from Judge Foote on the lift-stay motion. I'll talk at you then."

Randall was having the time of his life, but he had phone calls to make. And he saw a message from his stockbroker flash in white letters across the sea-blue screen of his desktop computer: "Merck up 4½ on big volume. You are a very wealthy man."

Let the mass of men lead lives of quiet desperation; Randall was busy leading one of riotous exaltation. Let timid, cowardly investors follow the prevailing wisdom of the balanced portfolio; Randall dumped all the money he could get his hands on into Merck, a year ago, when it was trading down around sixty bucks a share. These days it was bouncing up from a new floor of 160, while the rest of the market was comatose.

"OK, Whitlow," said Randall after he hung up the phone. "You heard the man. Mr. Bilksteen needs his discovery this afternoon."

"I thought Judge Foote was issuing a lift-stay order?" Whitlow said, glancing at her watch with a look that said lunch plans. "If we get a lift-stay order, the discovery on the condominium properties will be moot."

"Do we have a lift-stay order?" asked Randall.

"No," said Whitlow, "but . . ."

"Well? Until we do, we will comply with the rules of the court and prepare to provide our adversary with the discovery he has requested. If you have our responses to the interrogatories and the requests for production of documents as well as the documents themselves on my desk by two o'clock, I can look them over before my two-thirty conference call from New York."

He dismissed the associates with a backhanded flip of the broadsword and looked once more at the black egg in its nest of newspapers. *Maybe there's a shrunken head inside,* he thought. Maybe he should have someone call his wife and ask her if Michael had said anything about sending a package from West Africa. This would take time and might lead to a conversation with his wife, which would take even more time because her conversations typically wandered all over the map of pointless and irrelevant topics, none of them having a thing to do with bankruptcy or advancing his career.

She was one of those innocents who thought she could call one of the most powerful bankruptcy attorneys in the Seventh Circuit—who was billed out at over $300 an hour, a third higher than any other partner in the firm—and just kind of meander along in aimless conversation.

Other people do not live this way, he often realized. They could never handle the incessant pressure, the competition, the dizzying heights, the long way down if there was just one slipup. To the rabble, self-discipline meant trying to watch less TV or lose weight. They could never live in mortal combat for months on end, litigating eight hours a day, then going back to the office and spending another eight hours preparing for the next day's campaign. He could say it, couldn't he? They were his inferiors. What were all those postal employees and factory workers doing while he was in law school reading law books twelve hours a day? They were putting in their six-and-a-half-hour shifts with two fifteen-minute breaks and an hour for lunch. Then they went home and sat on the couch with a bag of chips, a liter of diet soda, and *The Brady Bunch.* And how did society reward *him*? By taxing him.

"What are you doing now?" Mack asked his boss, watching Randall rummage through a red jacket pouch from the DropCo case.

"What am I doing now?" Randall repeated, opening several spreadsheets, which described the assets of DropCo Steel Inc. "I'm sitting here hoping a Democrat gets elected President."

"But you're a Republican," Mack said.

"I am a Republican."

"Then why are you hoping for a Democratic President?"

"Because," said Randall, "if a Democrat gets elected they'll raise my taxes. I make five hundred thousand dollars a year, and right now I only pay two hundred thousand in taxes. The Democrats will be wanting to make me pay at least three hundred thousand dollars a year in taxes."

"You're hoping for that?"

"I'm hoping for instant retirement," Randall said, "which is what will happen as soon as some fucking politician raises my taxes. My father told me never, *never* work more than two days a week for the government. I'll quit first. And do you know what will happen then?"

"What?"

"Twenty lawyers, ten paralegals, fifteen secretaries, and five ancillary personnel will lose their jobs. Poof! Is it *jobs* these shopping-mall sheep are bleating about every day on the front page of the paper? I *create* jobs, but only if I'm working, and like I said, I ain't gonna work more than two days a week for the government. Go ahead," he hollered, brandishing the toy broadsword. "Tax me! Fifty employees and their families will lose their salary, their health, life, and dental insurance, their self-esteem, and the money they pay to their cable TV companies and the IRS. If you know any of those people who are thinking about voting for people who will raise my taxes, you might mention to them that it will cost them their jobs! Go ahead! Tax me just once more, and I'll show them exactly how it works! I'll put a full-page open letter in the fucking newspaper explaining why I shut down!"

His computer beeped, a purple window opened at the top, and white letters streamed onto the screen: "Wife. Line two. Urgent!!!!"

Randall waved Mack away with the broadsword and punched line two.

"Marjorie?"

"You'd better come home, Randy."

His wife's voice was calm, almost formal, which told him something was terribly wrong, and she didn't want to tell him on the phone, because she was afraid he would lean out of the clouds on Olympus and throw lightning bolts at her.

"You wrecked the car," he said, knowing it was worse than that, because in his twenty-five years of practice she had never called him at work and told him to come home.

"They can't find Michael, Randy. He's missing from his village," she said in the same strange controlled tone. "They just phoned me from Washington."

Randall's stomach tightened, and nausea crawled up the back of his throat, but he remained calm and organized his thinking—if nothing else, he had been trained to think clearly in the face of the worst possible tragedies.

"Is this by way of the State Department or the Peace Corps?" he asked.

"Both," she said.

"It's probably nothing," he said tersely, searching his memory for other instances in which the ineptitude of the United States government had manifested itself in a false alarm of this magnitude.

"No," she said. "It's *something*. He's been missing for almost two weeks. They can't *find* him!"

The furniture and equipment in his office were suddenly drained of mass and significance. The accustomed feel of his chair, the pale blood color of his carpeting, the prints hanging on his walls, all of them became the sensations and possessions of some other, formerly powerful bankruptcy attorney. His heart skipped one beat, then raced to catch up.

"Maybe he left early to go traveling with the Westfall kid," said Randall. "They were supposed to meet in Paris, weren't they?"

"Yes, they were supposed to meet in Paris," she said quietly. "But neither the Peace Corps nor the American Embassy has any record of Michael leaving Sierra Leone. There are forms and customs, immigration people he would have to see . . . He's just gone. And the Peace Corps Director says there's some kind of political unrest, a rebellion, going on over there."

"He's off on some lark in the bush," Randall said with a catch in his voice, as his eyes landed on the black bundle of rags and the red spout in the box on the floor.

"There are guerrillas crossing the borders from Liberia into Sierra Leone," she said. "It's even on the news."

Randall had trouble breathing, unwilling to grasp the dimensions of the anxiety that was descending on him like nightfall in a black-out: never knowing if his son was dying, already dead, held in a compound somewhere by fanatics or rebels with no respect for human life. *My only son!* he screamed inside. But he carefully controlled his voice, because he knew he had to be strong for his wife.

"I actually considered not telling you about it," she said, "because . . . Your heart . . . You won't be able to sleep. I know what this is going to do to you, Randy."

He let her go on whistling in the dark and pretending that she was the strong one. She had her strengths, but an appreciation of his intellectual prowess was not one of them. She failed to realize that his fits of anxiety and his intense physical complaints were just the idiosyncrasies of an exceptionally gifted attorney, a high-strung racehorse with special physical needs.

"Where's the Westfall kid?" he snapped. "Has anybody talked to him?"

"He's in Paris and can't be reached by phone. I'm sending him a letter by two-day air to the American Express office in Paris. His mother said he gets mail there every other day or so."

"Let me make some calls," he said, steadying his voice, "and I'll come right home, hear me?"

"I'll call your mother," she said quietly. "Please don't wreck the car again," she added.

This was typical. She would now indulge in absolutely useless behaviors which had nothing to do with the problem at hand. What possible good could come from calling his mom? And the car thing? Why bring that up at a time like this? It was typical of her total inability to prioritize problems.

As soon as she hung up, blood surged into Randall's face and he pushed a button on his intercom. "Cancel everything and don't let anybody in here," he said. He pushed a speed-dial button on his phone and gritted his teeth through four rings.

"Good afternoon. Senator Swanson's office. This is Amanda, may I help you?" a voice said.

"I need to talk to him *right away*," Randall said.

"May I ask who's calling?" the voice said diffidently.

"Yeah," Randall said. "Tell him it's Mr. PAC and it's extremely important."

"Mr. *Pac*," the woman repeated. "Forgive me, but could you spell that for me?"

"Political Action Committee," Randall shouted. "Dollar signs. Money. Checks. Big ones. Tell him it's Randall Killigan on the line with a problem that needs his attention right now!"

The Senator could not be reached on his car phone, so Randall was shunted to an administrative assistant, who was hiding under her desk by the time Randall finished screaming into the phone.

He hung up and paced the floor of his office, biting his thumb and feeling pretrial heart arrhythmias erupting in his chest.

After an eternity spanning less than twenty minutes, the intercom beeped, and his secretary announced: "Mr. Warren Holmes, State Department, calling at the request of Senator Swanson."

"Mr. Killigan, I spoke with your wife earlier today, and I got off the phone with Senator Swanson just a few minutes ago . . ."

"Are you in touch with people in Africa?" asked Randall. "Are

.these embassy people, or what? I want to know what's happened to my son."

"I have been on the phone all afternoon with Ambassador Walsh and his political officer in Freetown," said Holmes succinctly. "Let me tell you what we have. Liberia and Sierra Leone are both unstable at this time. In fact, almost all of West Africa is unstable. We have three reports, two of them anonymous, which confirm the fact that your son has disappeared. The particulars differ. Normally, I would not even pass these along, because they range from unreliable to simply reliable. Nothing confirmed, you understand. But Senator Swanson said this was VIP priority and that I should pass information straight on to you . . ."

"What are the reports?" interrupted Randall.

"The accounts from all three sources agree that there was an attack of some kind on your son's village, and after it was over, no one could find him. One witness claims she heard the attackers speaking Liberian Krio, which could mean that Michael has been abducted by Liberian rebels controlled by the infamous Charles Taylor, who essentially has started his own country in the middle of Liberia. Another villager swears the attackers spoke Sierra Leonean Krio, meaning Michael might still be in-country and held by Sierra Leonean rebels, loose allies of Taylor's men across the border."

"What was the third report?" said Randall.

"The third report is . . . ah . . . probably not reliable. It's from a boy, an adolescent, a villager. Very unreliable."

"Who said what?" Randall asked.

"I don't know how much you know about indigenous Africans, Mr. Killigan," said Holmes. "Let me just say that, once you get outside the capital cities, the belief in the supernatural is pretty well entrenched in the culture."

"What did he say?" Randall said.

"This was a Krio boy who apparently reported to one of the Red Cross stations in Pujehun. The boy said he was in Michael Killigan's village attending a funeral at the time of the raid. The Red Cross people say the boy's account of the conflict was so fraught with superstitious hallucinations that they couldn't get much hard information out of him. But they did ask him if Michael Killigan was safe."

"Are you a lawyer?" asked Randall. "I said, what the fuck did the kid say?" He kicked a button on the floor operating the electromagnetic device that held his door open, and it swung quietly closed.

"He said . . ." Holmes paused to the sound of flipping pages. "I'll read it to you straight from the advisory: 'Michael Killigan now roams the paths at night in the shape of a bush devil hungry for the souls of the witchmen who killed him.'"

(2)

Three weeks before Randall received his bundle from Africa, Boone Westfall had left his home in Indianapolis, Indiana, with a backpack containing one change of winter clothes, one change of summer clothes, one extra T-shirt, a raincoat, a sleeping bag, toiletries, vitamins, and antimalarial medicine. Around his waist and inside his pants, he wore a nylon money belt into which he had zippered his passport and $5,000 in traveler's checks. He had a yellow International Certificate of Vaccinations, showing he had been vaccinated against cholera, typhoid, and yellow fever, and he had visas to India, China, Greece, and three African countries. He had no idea where in the world he would end up; he knew only that it would not be Indiana. Tired of life in the Land of the TV and the Home of the Airwaves, he was ready to try anything once—illness, rapture, misfortune, romance—as long as it was not in video. He was scheduled to meet his best friend, Michael Killigan, in Paris in three weeks; after that, life would be an open book with blank pages.

Graduation from Indiana University with a degree in fine arts had earned him a job sifting papers and making phone calls from a cubicle in his father's insurance office. He had rented a studio apartment and had acquired a bookful of car payment tickets. The single women whose apartments he had haunted all looked and sounded the same; only their majors, the names of their exboyfriends, and their hair colors varied. His work as an insurance claims adjuster had taught him what it must be like to wake up each day to a terminal illness: not yet unbearably painful, but insidiously debilitating. The cardinal virtues necessary for the job were punctuality, good grooming, and a mind-set that never looked beyond the task at hand.

In college, he had dedicated himself to art and literature. Then he graduated with everything he needed to be an artist, a painter, a sculptor, and a poet ... but where to apply? His father, a prominent insurance executive, and his three older brothers (all of whom had gone straight into the family business) had started calling Boone the "artiste," hissing the *ee* invectively through clenched teeth. His father also asked him pointedly about the nature of his degree and where he was planning to live and work, now that he was a college graduate. As an undergraduate, Boone had always shunned business, accounting, finance, marketing, and all the other members of the barbiturate class of drugs, so he was unqualified for even entry-level corporate positions. He had managed to devour four years of liberal arts without learning a single useful skill, which seemed all right to him at the time, for he had no wish to be used. His thoughts turned to income, too late.

As nonchalantly as possible, Boone had moved his stuff out of the dorm and into the basement of his family's house, where he had planned to furnish a temporary studio and struggle with the great questions of twentieth-century postmodern visual forms. Within a year or two, he had hoped, he could perfect his technique and then play the major art galleries off against each other when they called, begging for permission to display his work.

His father had interrupted him during the construction of the basement studio.

"Have you ever heard of the saying 'You can't go home again'?" the old man had asked.

"As a matter of fact, I have," Boone had admitted. "It's a figurative expression, isn't it? Thomas Wolfe, right?"

"I wouldn't know," his dad had said. "I like literal expressions. Figurative expressions are too vague and abstract. You could stay up all night arguing about whether somebody can or cannot go home in a metaphorical sense. That's why I like the version I used on your older brothers better. Have you ever heard the expression 'You may not go home again'? It's much simpler and more concrete. If rent is a problem, you may apply for a job at the company."

"But I'm an artist," Boone had protested.

"I hate art," his dad had said, for the twentieth time in four years. "And even if you were Mike Angelo, my name ain't Lorenzo de'

Medici or Cosimo d'Arrivederci, or whatever his name was, and I'd
rather patronize the National Rifle Association."

Shortly thereafter, Boone's big brother, Pete, oriented the artist
to his new job as an insurance claims processor.

Pete escorted him into a huge room partitioned into dozens of
work stations by four-foot-square interlocking beige panels, with
one patch of fabric on the interior of each panel, where the employees could tack up snapshots of their families, or their own special
wacky cartoons and slogans, something to really set their space off
from the otherwise monotonous assemblage of beige cubicles, something like a heavily photocopied "You don't have to be crazy to work
here but it helps" sign—very distinctive, probably found in less than
30 percent of the cubicles.

His brother paused at an empty cube and showed Boone into a
nine-foot-square ergonomically designed work station with a phone,
a computer terminal, and a keyboard.

"These are claims," his older brother explained, grabbing a stack
of paper-clipped and clamped wads of papers and forms from a bin
outside the cubicle marked IN. "Your job is to deny them."

"I see," Boone had said. "You mean, I sort through the claims
and deny all the fraudulent ones, right?"

His brother implored heaven for patience with a roll of his eyes,
then sighed a gust of wintry disgust. "The fraudulent claims were
picked out downstairs by high school graduates and denied three
months ago. Anybody can deny a fraudulent claim. You're a college
graduate. Your job is to find a way to deny legitimate claims."

"But . . ."

"Look," said Pete, "I know how you feel about coming to work
here. I used to be a Nietzsche scholar myself, and from there I was
on my way to Wittgenstein. But you can't pay the rent with that
kind of behavior."

"I'm familiar with your views," said Boone. "You once told me
that my salary would be society's report card."

"I said that?" asked Pete. "I better start writing this stuff down."

He handed Boone the wad of claims.

"As I said, these are claims. Claims are filed by greedy people
who do not understand how the insurance business works. People
who file claims believe that money will make them happy and will
somehow compensate them for their losses. This idea—that money
makes misfortune easier to bear—is an illusion that can only be

enjoyed by those who have *not* suffered an actual loss. Is this making any sense?"

"Not yet," said Boone, "but keep talking."

"The most terrifying thing about life is knowing that, at any moment, a freak accident, violence, mayhem, a psychotic break, an addiction, a heart attack, a sexually transmitted disease, cancer, an earthquake, or some other act of God, or worse can take all of your happiness away from you in the time it takes you to pick up the phone and get the news. That's why people buy insurance, because they think it will protect them from catastrophes."

"OK," said Boone uncertainly.

"But we are in the insurance business," said Pete. "We *know* there is no protection from catastrophes. No matter what you do, there's always a chance that a catastrophe will come along, tear your heart out of your chest, and rub it in your face."

"Uh, uh," said Boone, still frowning.

"When you're crawling on the bathroom floor sick with grief," said Pete, "wondering why God failed to give you the courage to kill yourself, a big check from the insurance company looks like a swatch of wallpaper. You're in a place money can't reach."

"So . . . ," said Boone.

"So, insurance only works if catastrophe does *not* strike," he earnestly explained. "We don't sell protection. We sell peace of mind. For a premium, we agree to give the consumer the illusion that money will protect him from every possible foreseeable catastrophe. Once the premium is paid and before catastrophe strikes, the consumer is free to wallow in the illusion that if something terrible happens money will take the sting out of it. When a catastrophe actually occurs, the illusion is shattered and there's nothing to be done but drag yourself out of bed every morning and get on with your life."

"But if what you say is true," asked Boone, "then you are charging people thousands of dollars for . . . an illusion."

"Exactly," said Pete. "Peace of mind. The money is irrelevant. You probably subscribe to the notion that insurance is a way to pool risk and share liability. You think premiums should be based upon risk. Nothing could be more wrong. Premiums should be based upon line thirty-one of your federal tax return, adjusted gross income. Our objective is to charge the insured just enough to make it hurt. We are looking for the financial pain threshold, because only when it hurts does the insured really believe he is obtaining something of value, and, as I've shown, he is indeed obtaining peace of mind for nothing more than money."

"But . . ."

"So, the first order of business is for you to understand that paying claims is not what insurance is about. Insurance is about paying *premiums*. Premiums buy peace of mind. Do you realize that there are parts of the world—whole countries!—where you can't buy peace of mind? Only in America is this really possible."

"But what about *paying claims?*" Boone asked, holding the stack of papers out to his brother.

"Here," said Pete, "I'll help you get started."

His brother unbanded the bundles of claim forms and took the first wad. "OK, here's a claim for fire damage. Looks like the guy's house burned to the ground. OK, do we pay for fire damage?"

"Yes," said Boone. "We do, I think. Don't we?"

"That's right," said his brother. "We do, sometimes. Your job is to think about what we *don't* pay for. We don't pay for wear and tear, contamination, loss by animals, structural movement, escaping water, freezing water, surface water, groundwater, neglect, intentional acts, negligent planning, construction, maintenance, earthquake, earth movement, acts of war, or nuclear or radiation hazard."

"That's a lot of stuff we don't pay for," said Boone.

"Damn straight," said his brother, clapping him on the back. "Now, start off with something easy. For instance, do we have any evidence of neglect?"

"I don't know," said Boone. "Let me see the file."

"What do you need the file for?" his brother yelled. "Here's a guy who stood back and let his fucking house burn down, and you want to see the file before you can say whether he neglected it? Well-maintained homes don't burn down. And if this yahoo wants us to pay him any money, he's going to have to *prove* that his house was not neglected or negligently maintained. Issue him a notice advising him that the claim is denied pending submission of proof by the insured in the form of a home inspection that the dwelling was well maintained at the time of the property damage."

"Wait a second," Boone had protested. "You said the house *burned down*. There's nothing to inspect."

"Exactly," said his brother. "You'll move up fast, once you learn not to belabor the obvious. Look at this," he said, riffling a few pages of the same bundle in Boone's face. "We do not cover loss by animals, which means we do not cover any loss caused by birds, vermin, insects, rodents, or domestic animals. There's not a shred of evidence in this file showing that the house fire was not caused by rodents. What if a rodent chewed through a gas line, or knocked over a jar of paintbrushes that were soaking in turpentine over the gas water heater? Have you ever seen what happens if a rodent gets its teeth into a box of those strike-anywhere matches? Poof! This is one of the flimsiest claims I've ever seen."

"It is?" Boone had said.

"Next claim."

Boone selected a sheaf from the pile and perused the cover sheet. "Looks like some kind of health insurance claim, for medical costs."

"Medical?" Pete had said. "If it's reasonable, go ahead and pay it."

"Looks like it's a bone marrow transplant for a cancer victim."

"That's totally unreasonable. A hundred grand, easy. Hugely unreasonable. Deny it."

"Deny it?" Boone had swallowed hard. "How can you deny a cancer victim's medical claims after taking his premiums for ten years?!"

"Easy," his brother said. "It's either experimental treatment or treatment for a preexisting condition. I am so sick of these ridiculous medical claims we're always getting from dying people who try to tell me that their cancer and their heart disease were not preexisting conditions. *Everything* is a preexisting condition, except maybe injuries from automobile accidents. But don't take my word for it! Who said, 'We carry the seeds of our own destruction with us from birth'? Socrates, or somebody, I don't know. And who said, 'Everyone has within him, from the first moment of his life, the cause of his death'? Voltaire, that's who. But what do they know? OK, let's say the three-toed sloths who file these claims don't know Voltaire from Fred Astaire, and let's say they think Socrates is a free safety for the Seattle Seahawks. They've heard of genetic predisposition, haven't they? They've seen it talked about on TV, haven't they? Who are they kidding? Three out of four natural grandparents and both natural parents croak from cancer, and now the insured has the face to tell me that his cancer was not a preexisting condition? Try that bone on another dog! Get him out of here! Drag him out of town with a meat hook! Send him to hell and wake him up for meals! This is the nineties! Can these people read newspapers? The savings and loan crisis is a ripple on a farm pond compared to the tidal wave of the coming insurance crisis. What are we supposed to do, give away money and make it worse?"

"You actually deny cancer patients the money to pay their medical bills?" Boone had asked in shocked disbelief.

"Master the fundamentals," said his brother, "but don't dwell on them. Don't say things like 'Gee, you mean we get to keep whatever we don't pay out' to the other employees. People will think you're the mailman's son."

Boone had hated the job from day one, and told his father as much. Complaining had gotten him nowhere.

"Why do you think they call it *work*?" his father had fairly shouted. "I send you to college, and you come out thinking you're supposed to *enjoy* working for a living? But hey! Don't listen to your dear old dad. I guess work is for capitalist pigs like me, who want to slaughter cash cows and wallow in blood money. Work is for venal philistines and grasping boors who want to send their kids to college and put food on the table. I wouldn't want a refined sensibility like yours sullying its precious self with work. Don't squander your rare talents manning a galley oar in this corporate slave ship. I think you should just quit! Far nobler pursuits are waiting for the likes of you. Resign! See what it's like sleeping in a shipping crate on the streets and eating out of garbage cans. Maybe that'll suit your artistic temperament better than earning a living in the insurance business!"

Boone realized that if he did not drink excessively, did not overeat, lived in the right parts of town, used his salad fork at the proper time, committed no physical violence against others, refrained from stealing, moved his bowels only in private, and was a coward in money matters, he would eventually succeed. His peers and progenitors would clap him warmly on the back. *"Well done, Boone. You're making money at a point and a half above prime. You should be proud."* Life would pass at a measured pace, with moments of happiness scheduled to occur during hard-won vacations. Unforeseen tragedies could be accommodated by taking sick pay or funeral leaves.

He had seen it all coming. In bed one night, in an apartment complex named after the meadow that had been paved to provide its parking lots and tennis courts, he had suddenly realized he would make money, receive a promotion, get married, spend money, bear children, receive another promotion, make more money, get sick, spend more money, and die. He would never see the ruins at Luxor, Egypt. He would buy a new car every three years, laugh along with television audiences, wait in line, watch his weight, renew his driver's license every four years, and grow too old to travel to Nepal or the heights of Machu Picchu. Danger would mean running a yellow light, or maybe cheating on his taxes. Ecstasy would consist in knowing one was well insured, or maybe the thrill of a free oil change with a tune-up, or the euphoria of a fat-free frozen dessert that tasted just like ice cream, with only half the calories.

Instead of hanging around Indiana and waiting for his first coronary bypass operation, his second wife, his third child, his fourth incremental pay raise, and his fifth of single-malt scotch, he decided to do something drastic. Something Gauguin or Henry Miller might do, something impulsive and irrational, financially irresponsible, and dangerous. He knew where to find guidance in such matters: his best friend, Michael Killigan.

What makes a best friend? Horatio had no revenue except his good spirits, but his blood and judgment were so well commeddled that Hamlet wore him in his heart of hearts. The best friends of Greek legend, Damon and Pythias, loved each other so much that when the tyrant Dionysius condemned Pythias to death and would not allow him to go home and arrange his affairs unless someone agreed to take his place and be executed if Pythias failed to return, Damon bound himself over. When Pythias was delayed, Damon was led off to be put to death, but Pythias arrived just in time, ready to take his place, save his best friend, and be executed. Dionysius was so impressed he pardoned both of them. These would be nothing but sentimental poetry and purple yarns if Boone had not grown up with Michael Killigan and met a friend for whom he would bind himself over.

Like Boone, most of their college classmates had graduated and stepped into the harnesses of house payments, car payments, and insurance premiums. Not Killigan. He had no intention of growing a belly and settling into the couch for a life of channel surfing and television commercials, listening to the Orwellian hog calls of the advertisers rattling their sticks in swill buckets. He had wanted none of it. Killigan had joined up with the Peace Corps and had gone away to Sierra Leone, West Africa, to live in a village, where there were no televisions, no electricity, no running water, and no over-weight white people talking about their cholesterol. Then, Killigan sent Africa back to Boone in letters, sometimes three or four in a week.

In the beginning, the letters were effusive celebrations of African village life, precise descriptions of the ceremonies that attended birth, death, marriage, sharing a meal, and the other universals of human existence. They evidenced a mind enchanted by the people and customs of West Africa. Later came descriptions of magic, div-ination, the clairvoyance and cultic powers of twins, the men's and the women's secret societies and their elaborate initiation rites, cer-emonial dancing devils who wore masks carved by magician black-smiths. Still later, descriptions of witchmen, juju, the various protective charms and "medicines," potions or pouches containing scorpions, the heads of snakes, even the charred remains of powerful men; the mechanics of "putting" or "pulling" a swear or curse, the abilities of "shape-shifters," people who could transform themselves into snakes, bats, or predatory animals, and the even more secret Leopard and Baboon Societies, outlawed since the British tried and hanged Leopard Men and Baboon Men from the gallows at Freetown in 1905, for dressing themselves in animal skins and performing ritual cannibalism.

It must have been a beautiful place, for Killigan had extended his two-year stint to three, and then to four, and the letters veered from enchantment with Africa into disenchantment with America —called, as Killigan had pointed out in one of his letters, "that fat, adolescent, and delinquent millionaire" by the Nigerian novelist Chinua Achebe. Killigan came to believe that Africa's misery was not an accident, not caused by primitive ignorance or the harsh equatorial climate, or disease vectors, but was, instead, a direct consequence of America's comparative wealth and the cunning of white "big men." Boone never quite decided whether he was un-convinced or unconcerned.

When Killigan had come home on medical leave with meningitis, he was cynically antisocial and used his illness as an excuse not to receive friends and visitors long after the fevers and the headaches were gone. His six-foot frame went from an already thin 160 to a flesh-fallen 140. He wanted only rice topped with various pepper sauces to eat, and he would not take alcohol. He seemed happy enough to see his parents and to see Boone, whom he called "me American brothah with yella hair," but he talked about Americans as if they were foreigners, and not very pleasant ones.

Before Killigan went back to Africa, Boone told him of his restlessness, and they made a vow to meet one year later in Paris, with enough money for a year's travel on the cheap. After Paris, they would wander in the general direction of Greece, resisting itineraries, so they could accommodate the whims of beautiful women they would meet along the way. Before Killigan got on the plane to go back to Sierra Leone, he handed Boone an envelope. Inside was a folded piece of paper that said: Paris, November 1.

In addition to his claims adjusting, Boone took a job as a night radio dispatcher for a trucking company. Making money in two jobs kept him tired for a year, but he kept telling himself that he would sleep it off in a hammock on a beach in Sri Lanka. The year passed quickly in a blur of mindless menial labor, and before he knew it, he was shopping for gear.

"One backpack," Killigan had warned him in a letter. "Everything must fit into one backpack, including the sleeping bag." But Killigan had radical ideas picked up from his time abroad. "Underwear simply collects sweat instead of letting it run off the body," he had written in one of his letters. "Leave it at home."

August had found Boone restless and ready to bag both jobs and head out. As near as he could gather from Killigan's correspondence, Killigan could not leave Sierra Leone during the rainy season—which lasted from May through October—because the dirt roads leading from his village to the paved highways were impassable; thus the plan was to meet in Paris as soon as the West African climate would permit travel. Boone was to await word by mail to the Paris American Express office of Killigan's departure from Africa and of his arrival in Paris, on or after November 1.

Boone had hit the five-grand mark in late September, and could no longer stand being a cipher crushed between two occupations. He left for Paris in early October, hoping to find the room where Henry Miller squashed bedbugs on the wall, the loft where Picasso painted Gertrude Stein's portrait, the son of the garage mechanic who told Hemingway and his expatriate pals that they were all a lost generation, the bowels of the restaurant where George Orwell peeled onions and potatoes.

Boone was unable to find Alice B. Toklas and obtain an introduction at 27 rue de Fleurus; instead he made sleeping arrangements among the dead in Montmartre Cemetery, where his squirming blue sleeping bag looked like a huge nylon maggot—royal blue against gray headstones and bone-white crypts—burrowing into sleep and the wormwood earth.

·

October predawn. Montmartre Cemetery in Paris contained several thousand unremarkable decomposing bodies resting eternally, another fifty or so famous decomposing bodies, also resting eternally, and one slumbering American vagrant resting temporally in a sleeping bag, with a sweater rolled around a pair of sneakers for his pillow. An empty bottle of table wine rested against a headstone. A screech owl waited on a branch, mistrusting the stench of the sleeping carcass, wondering if the thing could smell that bad and still have fight left in it. The resident cats nervously patrolled their territories, crouching behind tombstones every time the thing snored, wondering why the body had been left out in the night air.

Boone Westfall felt a ghoul's graveclothes brush his cheek and woke with a start to find a black cat batting the laces of the sneakers into his face.

"Scat!" he snarled, backhanding the wicked thing into a somersault and onto the grave of Hector Berlioz, a famous decomposing French composer.

Boone stretched and reached under his head, making sure he still owned both sneakers, then felt for the nylon money belt at his waist, which contained his passport and $4,200 in traveler's checks. He yawned, pulled the shoes and sweater into a steeper prop, and watched moisture from his lungs condense in the October air.

Would he one day wake up in heaven, relieved at having escaped the dreamy life of an American vagrant in Paris, the same way he was now waking up in Paris, congratulating himself on escaping the tedium of the life he had left behind in suburban Indiana?

"Yes," the cat said with a grin, and walked off in a stiff-legged huff.

The faint purples and grays of morning seeped into the clouds above him. He scratched himself and yawned again. A wind came up, and it occurred to him that perhaps God had yawned also. Paris stirred in the distance, its engines and factories rumbling faintly in the earth beneath his shoulder blades. A car passed over the rue

Caulaincourt, which straddled the cemetery on iron bridgework that clanked under the weight of the passing vehicle. The blurred silhouettes of crypts, crosses, and burial vaults slowly emerged from the misty darkness, like shrouded mourners bearing crucifixes out of the skyless fog.

He hoped this was the end of his search for decent outdoor accommodations in Paris. He had passed a restful night in the cemetery, free of the prostitutes and transvestites who had plagued his dreams in the Bois de Boulogne; safe from the prowling thieves who had snooped over him on the quays along the banks of the Seine; hidden from the gendarmes who had nudged him awake with billy clubs in the moonlit groves of the Luxembourg Gardens.

Very nice, he thought, turning his head for another look at the profile of Berlioz cameoed on a huge medallion and mounted on a new marble headstone.

The light of dawn confirmed that the image was a cameo of an older, respectable Berlioz, not the twenty-six-year-old wild man who wrote music with a headful of paregoric, a racing pulse, and a bonfire of lust for a soul.

That ain't the guy who wrote the Symphonie Fantastique, Boone thought. *That's the profile of a middle-aged music teacher.*

Potted plants surrounded the slab athwart the grave, and someone or some organization had recently thrown a bouquet. Probably the same civic-minded bunch that had uprooted the original tombstone and installed a monument.

Nothing good ever lasts, he thought. *Except maybe eternity. If it's good, and if it lasts.*

When the light permitted, he packed his sleeping bag into its stuff sack, broke camp, and wandered around looking for an exit. Once on his feet, he saw that cats had the run of the place. An emaciated gray one guarded the staircase to Zola's grave. A calico slithered through the bars of a windowed mausoleum (presumably in search of mice). A tortoiseshell tom slunk along a balustrade and pounced into a wrought-iron flower cachepot. Boone wondered if a hooded Druid might appear from behind one of the columns and light a pyre beneath the sacrificial animal.

The cold wind blew him up and down dead-end paths, and he got lost in a low-lying hodgepodge of tilted headstones, crumbling limestone vaults, and unkempt concave graves. Chains spalling rust and flaked with verdigris formed cordons around tombs, where replicas of dead dignitaries slept on biers, with their hands clasped on their stone bosoms. Railings sagged with the gravity of centuries around memorials with inscriptions and dates in faint Roman numerals. Some common graves had caved in beneath their tablets, leaving slots, where Boone could peer down into the washed-out earth and see wine bottles, cat droppings, and rubble. Others had sunk, shifting the gravestones and their ornamental sculptures askew.

The famous corpses had their renovated plots, but the rest of the deceased aristocracy were housed in crowded vaults and mausoleum row houses—slurbs of miniature stone mansions huddling together and blocking each other's entrances with toppled crosses and slabs of fallen architraves.

A dust devil danced down the sidewalk twirling a skirt of dead leaves. A piece of tin flashing rattled across a slate roof. Another gust of wind groaned in stone passages.

A wrong turn down an overgrown path took him into a clearing strung with vines and dead tree limbs. He stumbled on a Celtic cross, half submerged in topsoil, then tripped over a statueless pedestal studded with a pair of stone feet broken off at the ankles and followed his sleeping bag into a bramble, where he landed on top of the footless statue. He rolled onto his back and momentarily thrashed around like an upended turtle, until he got hold of a stone bench, realizing as he struggled to his feet that he had discovered the cemetery's junkyard. Headstones, doors from mausoleums, crosses, tablets, statues, and the rubble of desecrated memorials were stacked and scattered around him like dolmens or cairns left by an ancient civilization of Mad Hatters. The shafts of beheaded Ionic columns formed a dead man's colonnade around him, their collapsed entablatures turning to boulders in the grass, the stone foliage of their acanthus capitals clotted with moss and moldering in the weeds.

He wandered further into the maze of building materials from the city of the dead, then gasped and stood motionless, straining to hear again what he swore was a groan, a sob, some human sound, Anubis reading from *The Egyptian Book of the Dead*, Benedictine monks chanting the Day of Wrath. He suddenly realized he would follow this path around one of these sepulchers and into a clearing, where old Hector would be conducting the fifth movement, the witches' Sabbath and the Walpurgis Night, sylphs and sprites dreamily stroking violins, chubby trolls hunkering down around cellos and basses, a hunchback tolling the bell, ghouls and goblins squatting obscenely in a frenzied *danse infernale* around a bier supporting a toppled replica of the Apollo Belvedere, laid out in cold white marble, staring eyeless at the pagan sky.

Boone slashed his way back out through the overgrowth until the dirt path intersected with pavement. He took a shortcut between two headstones, smelled fresh earth and humus, and looked down just in time to keep from walking into an open grave. He peered over the lip of turf and into the dark, bottomless rectangle, feeling his heart beat with the exertion of flight. Next to a heap of clay was a pallet and a newly etched headstone of polished marble. He was afraid to look at the gilded name. Looking up, he saw a whole field of fresh, open graves, with shadows falling on the scarred walls of clay.

While zigzagging carefully through the field of fresh graves, he had a sudden fear that he had died a long time ago, in another country. Yes, he had died, and one of his relatives must have shipped his remains to Montmartre Cemetery. And now his body and soul had been resurrected on Judgment Day, and he was wandering around in a field of graves that had been opened at dawn and had given up their dead. The dead had all known where to go to be judged, but Boone was confused, still dawdling in the material world, out of touch, frightened and lost, until he heard the damned souls congregating in the distance, and knew he belonged with them. As if Judgment Day or eternity was a plane he was about to miss, if he did not hurry.

A stairwell built into a wall under the bridge led him up to a street and back to the land of the living.

He found a patisserie with an espresso machine and warmed himself over coffee and croissants, savoring butter and jam, filling his stomach, and killing hunger pains, glad that he was not interred in Montmartre Cemetery . . . yet. Glad that he had found his room at the Hotel Berlioz and could finish his tour of Paris while awaiting Killigan's arrival.

At 11 a.m., he retrieved his backpack, took the Métro to Opéra, and went to the American Express office for mail. He passed a large outdoor café and cast a casual glance at the patrons. The people at the tables erupted in laughter, staring at him and pointing. Boone blushed and looked behind him, finding a professional mime with an imaginary backpack slung over his shoulder, perfectly mimicking the gait of a corn-fed galoot from Indiana hauling thirty pounds on his shoulder.

The mime hollered a silent "Howdy" and waved, hitching up a pair of imaginary chaps and rolling along, like a bowlegged cowboy fresh from the range.

The crowd roared with laughter and threw coins. Boone dared not speak a word of French or English, lest they laugh even harder.

At the steps to the office, the prospect of mail lifted his spirits. So far, he had received nothing but letters from his girlfriend.

She had written him two letters: one emphatically stating that she would never speak to him or write to him again for any reason, under any circumstances; and another one, two days later, modifying her original decree to allow for periodic communications updating him on her insights into his utter self-indulgence, his beastliness, his fear of women, his terror of growing up, his infantile preoccupation with himself, his sloth, drunkenness, depravity, addiction to drugs, and sexual perversions.

The letter handed to him by the American Express clerk was not one of the tissue-thin blue aerogrammes he was accustomed to getting from Killigan. It was not one of Celinda's blood-red stationery envelopes either. It was a thick white business envelope from America, from Mrs. Marjorie Killigan. Killigan's mom? Boone found three letters inside, the first in a loopy feminine hand:

Dear Boone:

I hope this reaches you. Your mother said you were intending to remain in Paris until you heard from Michael and that you would be picking up mail at this address. She did not have a hotel telephone for you, so I am forced to write you with sad news. Michael is missing from his village in Sierra Leone. I had hoped this was all a terrible mistake, and that perhaps Michael simply had left to meet you in Paris, but as you can see from the copies of these letters, something is very wrong.

Randall called Senator Swanson and says he will fly to Africa himself if he has to. We are all distraught and not sleeping at all. Please, please call us collect if you have absolutely any idea what has happened, or if Michael had mentioned anything at all to you about traveling overland, etc. We are desperate!

Sincerely,
Marjorie Killigan

The second was a photocopy of a typed letter on letterhead, with a logo referencing the U.S. Peace Corps, Sierra Leone Office:

Dear Mrs. Killigan:

This will confirm my overseas telephone conversation with you of this past week. I regret to inform you that, at this time, we are still unable to locate your son, Michael Killigan, anywhere in Sierra Leone. As I described to you in our conversation, he was last seen in his village on October 15 of this year. The circumstances of his disappearance are still under investigation by the Sierra Leonean authorities and the chargé d'affaires of the American Embassy.

I can assure you that everything possible is being done at every level in both governments to locate your son. We are pressing urgently through our contacts with the various Paramount Chiefs and Mende tribal leaders, and we have dispatched couriers to all of our contacts in the Pujehun district where your son was stationed.

Unfortunately, Pujehun is politically unstable at the present time, because of bitterly contested elections for the Paramount Chieftaincy and for several national parliamentary seats. In addition, the fighting in Liberia has spilled across the southern border of Sierra Leone and displaced thousands of civilians. Elections are never a good time in Sierra Leone, but this season is one of the worst in memory. Rioting and looting have broken out in certain areas and some Volunteers were advised to leave the district. It is still unclear whether your son's disappearance is connected in any way with the unrest attending the elections, or whether he had any contact with the dominant political factions.

As I explained to you by phone, we are almost certain that your son is still in-country, as he would not be allowed to leave without obtaining an exit visa and paying the customary fees. The Sierra Leonean Ministry of Immigration has no record of his departure by air or sea from Freetown. Mr. Nathan French, a political officer with our embassy, and a Deputy Minister of Information for Sierra Leone have also traveled to the major border crossings and found no record of an exit visa issued for Michael Killigan. The only other way out of the country would be by bush paths—all but impassable during the rainy season, which has just ended here.

I will notify you immediately of any news concerning your son's whereabouts.

Please know that our thoughts and prayers are with you and your family.

Sincerely,

Paul Stevens
U.S. Peace Corps
Country Director/Sierra Leone

The third document was a copy of a letter written by a person who seemed unable to decide whether to print or write in longhand. The letters were small and poorly formed:

Dear Mrs. Killigan:
I full sorry to disturb you introducting myself for first time with bad news on Mr. Michael who pays school fees for me because I, Moussa Kamara, am servant for him. We do not find Mr. Michael and I cannot see him now for two weeks.

Trouble beaucoup is here for us because bush devils, witchmen, and baboon men have put bad hale medicine and carried bofima into our village and we are all too much afraid. Mr. Michael tried for stopping this business, but he was not able. When he was away, witchmen and bush devils been come and searched Mr. Michael's house looking for pictures snapped with him camera. We were running too fast from them. After, I cannot go back to my village and I cannot find Mr. Michael. They don't find pictures because Mr. Michael done send the picture film for development to a place the name I cannot write if because this letter go to wrong hands. Maybe if I can see what pictures Mr. Michael snapped I can learn the trouble that has found him.

Mr. Michael sometime say I write you if trouble come or sickness come. I look every day for Mr. Michael, until another day I find him.

I think of having good greetings for you and health for you and family health also.

Respect,
Moussa Steven Kamara

A drumroll jolted Boone out of his distressful reading. Two boys in red uniforms stood before him, announcing the arrival of a candy-red hut on a trailer platform drawn by a donkey. A fat man in a red, vaguely martial uniform with tinsel epaulets dismounted the cart and drew a bullwhip out its socket.

Two louvered doors at the rear of the hut opened and disgorged a well-dressed goat onto the sidewalk. A cluster of pedestrians stopped and applauded, laughing at the goat's wardrobe, which consisted of a frilled shirt, a pair of red silk suspenders, a buff Eton jacket, and white silk hose with red garters trussed up just under the goat's hindquarters. Its horns poked through a small black top hat with a silk band and a carnation. The goat climbed atop a small pedestal and bowed.

A juggler threw bowling pins into the air. A boy with a painted face and a leather jerkin lit a sword and swallowed it, sending a plume of black smoke into the air.

The doors of the hut banged open again, and a fat woman in red tights and a buckskin jacket trundled forth. She jutted her chin, displaying a silver goatee, then plopped a ten-gallon hat on her head and hollered "Hee-haw!" with a Texas twang. She walked over to the goat and took a bow. She groomed the goat's beard with a red comb, then groomed hers to match. The crowd roared with approval. The uniformed fat man cracked his bullwhip. The goat reared back onto its hind legs and rubbed goatees with the woman. People laughed hysterically and threw coins into buckets held by the drummer boys.

Boone looked away from the goat and watched the faces of the spectators, as they bared their teeth in snarls of laughter. Their eyes suddenly reminded him of Picasso, who once asked, "Why not put sexual organs in the place of eyes and eyes between the legs?"

He left the crowd and took back streets through twisting alleys of uneven bricks and cobblestones. He crossed bridges, descended into tunnels, rode the Métro, lost himself in the capillaries of transportation networks. The streets were jammed with strangers of all shapes, sizes, and ages: a cripple with a lifeless arm in tow, a man violently scratching his head, as if he had been bitten by something, a woman in love with her shopwindow reflection, children tormenting a dog, lovers on a stone bench groping obliviously.

There was a mange on the skin of the streets, a membrane coating the bricks and stones at pedestrian level. The foundations of buildings were slick with oils from human palms, the masonry seasoned with lungfuls of cigarette smoke and exhaust from the engines of cars and factories. The pores of the very stones were sweetened with spittle, sweaty paw prints, tobacco, scuff marks, shoe polish, and molting human skins. The curbs, benches, and pillars of the sidewalk arcades looked almost as if they had been worn filthy smooth by millions of eyes passing over them.

He found a grimy café with a *Menu Complet* sign, where he crouched over a twenty-franc meal and watched the habitués of the place as they watched him eat.

After the meal, he went out wandering again.

He had left his Indiana apartment looking for adventure, hoping something, anything would happen to him. Before he left, his mother had sat him down in the kitchen where she had nourished him in his youth. She begged him not to go. She had an irrational fear of travel, especially travel to uncivilized countries where the per capita crime rate was a tenth of America's murder rate.

"What if something happens to you?" she asked.

"But, Mom," he had said, "that's why I'm going. I want something to happen to me."

The dragon's teeth sown during his Indiana daydreams were now sprouting nightmares. Was Killigan dead? Was he sick? Kidnapped? Being tortured somewhere by rebels in military fatigues? Cooked over an open fire in a jungle clearing? Bitten by snakes, strangled by boa constrictors?

He took the Métro to Odéon, found a travel agency, and bought a one-way ticket to Freetown, Sierra Leone, on KLM Royal Dutch Airlines. Six hundred dollars. An outrage! He had held himself to one hundred dollars a week since his arrival. Now he was forced to cough up six weeks in Paris for a plane ticket to Sierra Leone, West Africa.

He scoured the bookstores on the Boulevard St.-Michel for African travel books written in English. He found books aplenty on traveling in East Africa, but nothing on West Africa or Sierra Leone. Tourists, it seemed, preferred lions and the Serengeti Plain to poverty and the Sahel.

Even books purporting to be guides on travel in Africa at large barely mentioned Sierra Leone. After devoting a separate chapter to the splendors of Kenya, which sounded like a sort of open-air zoo for Westerners, the authors of *Fielding's Literary Africa* dropped a single page on West Africa in its entirety, and barely a paragraph on Sierra Leone, warning their readers:

Sierra Leone, of the countries we've seen, is undoubtedly the worst. Garbage is piled, without exaggeration, two stories high on the corners of Freetown's streets, when it could be thrown in the ocean only a stone's throw away. . . . West Africans are, from our observations, more emotional, have a lower boiling point, are more aggressive and less disciplined. They do not understand the meaning of the word queue, or line, or turn taking. . . . We found a great animosity toward whites.

"All in all," the authors concluded, "traveling in West Africa is not a 'fun experience.' "

The authors of *Fielding's Literary Africa* moved on without mentioning that Graham Greene wrote *The Heart of the Matter* at the City Hotel in Freetown, or that the trip described in Greene's *Journey Without Maps* began in Sierra Leone. No word either about Syl Cheney-Coker, or any of Sierra Leone's own authors, or its rich oral tradition of story performances.

The passage told him nothing about Sierra Leone and everything about the authors. They were clearly well-bred, "fun"-seeking English people who had long ago mastered the arts of polluting the ocean and waiting patiently in line. They would patiently stand in line all day (so they thought) even if they were starving to death in 100-degree heat and 90 percent humidity, especially if breaking line would somehow draw attention to themselves. They were refined types catering to fun-seeking Americans with the money to spend on travel books. They unwittingly subscribed to the adage that most people can only feel at ease in a foreign country when they are disparaging the inhabitants. The animosity they harvested probably had less to do with the color of their skins than with their insistence that the inhabitants of all foreign countries should behave themselves and act British.

An excellent book by a fellow named Rick Berg, *Travelling Cheaply*, mentioned West Africa only to illustrate a passage on dysentery, observing that a solid shit once a month is a pretty good average for a stay in West Africa. Another guidebook advised him that ten of the world's thirty-six poorest countries could be found in West Africa. Still another warned him that, diamonds aside, disease was Sierra Leone's biggest export.

He finally hit pay dirt in the shadow of Notre Dame at Shakespeare and Company. On a dusty shelf on the second floor, the proprietor dislodged a used copy of a book in English entitled *The Mende of Sierra Leone,* by Kenneth Little. Boone instantly recognized the name of the tribe referenced in the Peace Corps Director's letter and bought the book on the spot.

His last night in Paris, Boone climbed into his sleeping bag under a half-moon and propped himself against Hector's marble monument. He tucked his flashlight under his chin. On one raised knee he placed the letters from Mrs. Killigan, on the other he propped *The Mende of Sierra Leone.*

He reread the letters, circling words as he went: "Pujehun," "witchmen," "hale," "bofima," "bush devils." He read the servant's letter twice and circled the middle paragraph:

> Trouble beaucoup is here for us because bush devils, witchmen, and baboon men have put bad hale medicine and carried bofima into our village and we are all too much afraid. Mr. Michael tried for stopping this business, but he was not able. When he was away, witchmen and bush devils been come and searched Mr. Michael's house looking for pictures snapped with him camera. We were running too fast from them. After, I cannot go back to my village and I cannot find Mr. Michael. They don't find pictures because Mr. Michael done send the picture film for development to a place the name I cannot write if because this letter go to wrong hands. Maybe if I can see what pictures Mr. Michael snapped I can learn the trouble that has found him.

The index in the back of *The Mende of Sierra Leone* had no entry for "Pujehun," "bush," or "devil." "Hale" and "bofima" referred him to "medicine," where he found copious subheadings. He selected " 'bad' medicine men and witchcraft" and flipped to the relevant pages.

The cold marble of Hector's memorial sent shudders through him as he read the passage:

> A particularly clear example of the illicit operation of *hale* is provided in the case of *ndilei* medicine. This is a medicine which can be transformed into a boa constrictor by the witch (person) owning it. It is a mineral substance whose Mende name is *tingoi,* and it is hollow inside. It can be bought from its existing owner, if the latter wishes to rid himself of it.

Disposing of it, however, carries a very grave risk, including death, because the medicine becomes an integral part of its temporary owner. This is because the latter becomes virtually the slave of the medicine in return for the work which it does for him, and is slavishly subject to its will. . . .

In terms, then, of the work done, the owner of the *ndilei* and the medicine itself may be regarded as one; since the owner becomes a witch through association with it. He may have acquired it for the purpose of avenging himself on someone who has wronged him. But once under the medicine's power, he is committed to the life of cannibalism which witches lead.

This witch-cum-boa constrictor (*ndile*) works always by night and feeds on the blood of his victims by sucking it vampirelike out of their throats. Usually, his attentions are fatal, and he has the power, also, of causing infantile paralysis in children. The *ndilemoi's* first step is to secure some article which has any kind of association with his intended victim. This may range from a piece of clothing to anything picked up from the latter's farm. Without it, the witch has no means of attacking the artery. The medicine itself is then buried close to the victim's home—outside in the bush or even at the doorway of his house, in any place from which his house can be seen. From there, it is transformed at the appointed hour into the boa constrictor.

Several pages later, he found *bofima* discussed, and almost de- cided to cash in his plane ticket and take the 25 percent penalty:

A further very powerful and antisocial medicine of the same kind is the *bofima*. This is made out of the skin from the palm of the human hand and the sole of the foot and the forehead. There are also parts of certain organs, such as the genitals and the liver, as well as a cloth taken from a men- struating woman, and some dust from the ground where a large number of people are accustomed to meet. It also contains some rope taken from a trap from which an animal has escaped; the point of a needle; and a piece of a fowl's coop. . . .

The *bofima* requires periodic "reinvigoration," otherwise it will turn on its owner and destroy him. Some *bofima* medicines have to be renewed annually; others more often. The success and power of this medicine de- pends on the parts of the body mentioned above. The oil, which is prepared from the fat of the intestines, is used to anoint the *bofima* itself, and is also used as a rubbing medicine to bring good luck and to give the person so treated a fearsome and dignified appearance.

He put his flashlight away and drew the darkness around him with his sleeping bag. The October moon shone on a field of tombstones, where Boone saw witches, fearsome and dignified in appearance, glistening with human fat, wandering among the graves, looking for fresh American body parts in a sleeping bag.

(3)

The plane dipped, settling into a rolling tundra of bright clouds, followed by white-out at Boone's window, and then flashes of blue as the wings tore the underside of the cloud bank into swirling white shreds. He watched veils of mist ghost over the wings of the airliner and drift away into seamless sea and sky. Out the window and far below the shoulder of the plane's wing, the sea crawled toward beaches shining like scimitars in the sun. The marinas and wharves gave way to tessellated roofs and buildings, then low-lying bush creeping up into the forested hills, where palms sprouted and roads twisted off into what looked like an empire of solid broccoli tops stretching inland to the horizon.

Boone's travel books advised him that for six months of the year Sierra Leone was drenched with tropical storms, which provided one of the highest annual rainfalls of any country in Africa. The other six months of the year, the streams turned to dust beds, the wells dried up, and the harmattan, a dry wind from the African interior, glazed the rain forests with dust from the Sahara. In recent years, the gross national product, per capita, was $240 in U.S. currency. The average life expectancy was thirty-nine years, with 166 of every 1,000 infants dying each year before they reached their first birthday.

He felt a bump and looked out the window at the drab, single-story terminal of Lungi airport, Sierra Leone, West Africa.

Once in the terminal, he fought off the usual assortment of "guides" and charlatans who wait in airports, train stations, and docks all over the Third World, praying to God in forty languages to please send them a common boob from Indiana. Several smiling broad-shouldered lads in dark blue polyester safari suits—intended to look like some kind of official uniform—asked for his passport and attempted to take his backpack from his shoulder. "We are special travel assistants," they explained in thick accents. "We will help you get through customs and immigration."

Boone refused their services, politely at first, and then rabidly, until the last of the special travel assistants left in search of other prey.

He changed forty dollars into 4,000 leones at a guichet outside the customs office, then rebuffed a squadron of officious baggage handlers who on closer examination turned out to be the same assortment of broad-shouldered special travel assistants, now arrayed in porter's caps and jerkins, instead of blue safari suits.

The group of porter-assistants followed him outside and earnestly warned him that he would be swindled by the taxi drivers unless he let them negotiate his fare into Freetown.

"Drivahs go tief you," said one.

"White man dae pay too much foh taxi," said another.

"Sometime drivah go tief luggage," said another, waving a cautionary finger across his face. "We go able hep you. We go show you oos-kind drivah go take you na Freetown. You put something small-small foh us," he said pointing at the palm of his hand, "and we go able save you money, beaucoup. Notoso?" he asked his fellows, who rendered a chorus of confirmation.

Boone refused in English ("No, thank you"), French ("Non, merci"), and American ("Fuck you!"), until the porters and travel assistants slunk away in groups of twos and threes, glaring at him and loudly recollecting the dire misfortunes of the last seven or eight white men who insisted on arranging their own transportation into Freetown. A few minutes later, he found the taxi stand at the other end of the terminal, where a string of drivers were stashing special travel assistant safari suits, porter's caps, and jerkins into the trunks of their cabs and donning chauffeur's hats.

After ten minutes of tenacious dickering with the drivers, who were snapping their fingers and hissing at him, he closed a deal with one of them for 3,000 leones—down from 7,000—just before a policeman intervened to advise him that the fare into Freetown was set by a municipal ordinance at 2,000 leones.

Once in the car, the driver blithely advised Boone that the ordinance had nothing to do with the going rate for a taxi into Freetown, that the "policeman" was a shill paid by the driver's competitors, and that the deal they had struck for 3,000 leones did not include the cost of the ferry they were about to board. Boone muttered something noncommittal, postponed settling up with the driver until his destination, and craned his head out the window to see what Africa at eight degrees north of the equator looked like.

Hills festooned with palm trees rose over Freetown. His guidebooks told him that Portuguese sailors named the place Sierra Leone, or Lion Mountains, in 1462, either because they thought they heard lions roaring in the hills around the bay or because they saw the rump of a lion in the shape of the same hills. Lions live in East Africa, explained the guidebooks, where they can still be seen from inside the confines of an air-conditioned tour bus. In West Africa, there are no lions or air-conditioned tour buses, and the Portuguese sailors probably heard the roar of surf crashing on the bay shores.

Before the Portuguese named the country in 1462, the last historical reference to the area came from Hanno, the Carthaginian explorer, who in 500 B.C. surveyed the area from a galley ship and recorded his observations without bothering to name the hills. During the 2,000-year interlude, generations of black Africans dreamed and made love in primitive dwellings, spirits roamed the bush paths, rain soaked the earth in the wet season, and the sun boiled it all away in the dry season, trees fell in the forests of Sierra Leone, and if any white men saw these things, they left no papers with black marks describing them. There are no books about what happened before white men came to trade slaves. The great deeds and tragedies of the African ancestors were told by the old ones with dimming memories who performed stories by firelight in the village baffas.

Boone took a seat on the ferry's deck and tried to look inconspicuous. *Just act naturally*, he thought. *Like any other white person from Indiana packed onto a ferry with five hundred Africans.* Trouble was, he had no role model. There were no other white people on board from anywhere, much less from Indiana. He wondered how the Colts were doing this season.

After disembarking from the ferry, the taxi took him through the outskirts of Freetown, a sprawling shanty town of some 470,000 inhabitants, the center of what once was a British colony, founded in 1787, when, with the generosity characteristic of civilized white people everywhere, the representatives of the British Empire bought the twenty square miles that make up the heart of Freetown from King Tombo, chief of the Temne tribe, for rum, muskets, and an embroidered waistcoat. English philanthropists talked their governments into starting a Province of Freedom for liberated British slaves. The first boatload of 411 freed British slaves and a hundred whites arrived in 1787. Three years later, 48 settlers were alive to recount the ravages of disease and hostilities with the natives. Another 1,700 ex-slaves from Jamaica and Nova Scotia arrived in 1792. Several decades later, the Americans had the same idea, when a colony of freed slaves had been started in Liberia to the south.

The British ruled Sierra Leone until 1961, when they were defeated by the climate and the backward chaos of botched colonialism, and then left. According to the Krio proverbs, the only weapon used in Sierra Leone's war of liberation from Britain was the mosquito. The headstones of the battle casualties can still be found in the white cemeteries in the hills around Freetown.

Two centuries after Britain founded Freetown and thirty years after she left, Boone Westfall arrived, feeling whiter than milk from an Indiana dairy cow and looking out from his taxi onto a street jammed with bodies so black they seemed to soak up the sunset. The streets of Freetown accommodated two-way traffic only because most of the taxis did not have side mirrors, which allowed them to pass within an inch of one another. Boone's taxi sat motionless while swarms of citizens came and went as they pleased, only begrudging cars when the alternative was imminent physical injury. Old men in skullcaps and threadbare safari shirts smoked clay pipes and laughed at the helpless cars; shirtless teenage boys in rope-belted britches chased each other through stalled traffic; women wrapped in tie-dyed cloths swayed under headloads that would stagger a pack mule; cripples dottered on gnarled crutches; toothless beggars slumped up against storefronts with baskets of coins in their laps, laughing and showing their stained gums; girls in pigtails and blue school smocks chased goats into pens; a policeman in a red beret and sunglasses arbitrated a dispute over a damaged cart.

Everywhere, the pandemonium of human beings in reckless concourse, of parents berating children, of shopkeepers shooing chickens out of their stalls, of police whistles, singing schoolgirls, nattering wives, backfiring taxis, bawling infants, blaring tape players, and barking dogs.

On both sides of the taxi, corrugated-zinc-pan roofs streaked with rust sloped to the streets from one- and two-story buildings, forming dark arcades where hordes of black bodies surged and slithered under ridgepoles strung with charred utensils, stewpots, dead chickens, tobacco leaves, dried fish, and pan scales. Under the zinc-pan eaves, citizens swashed in and out of shops and verandas and open-air markets, haggling across makeshift tables of boards and barrels stacked with secondhand goods, tobacco, peppers, kerosene, rice, matches, paste jewelry, and warm soft drinks. A crowd of young men stopped traffic by dancing in the street outside a music store. The proprietor had turned two speakers streetward to provide free samples of reggae music to passersby; a placard over the shop door proclaimed AFRICA SOUNDS in ornate cursive. Eventually, the crowded streets and ramshackle hovels opened onto a larger avenue called Siaka Stevens Street, named after the former President of Sierra Leone and lined with plumed palms.

"De cotton tree dae yonder," said the driver, indicating the biggest tree Boone had ever seen, in the middle of a roundabout walled in whitewashed concrete. Far up in the limbs of the crown, he could see shapes fluttering in the branches like pieces of night confetti. Kites cut from the cloth of night.

"Witch birds dae," said the driver.

"What kind of birds?" asked Boone.

"Witch birds," the driver repeated. "Beaucoup dae. De tree done dae five hundred year. I no lie."

The massive tree was bigger than the multistoried buildings in the center of town, with a trunk the thickness of a good-sized house. Its branches formed a dense bower, shading the entire traffic circle, the perimeter sidewalks, and the buildings that cowered under its limbs.

"If you get four eye, you go able see witch capes hanging from every limb," said the driver earnestly.

"Four eyes?" asked Boone.

"I tell you!" the driver said. "If you get two eyes only, den you no go able see ahm. But four eyes go able see ahm."

Boone shrugged his shoulders and mumbled, "Four eyes."

The driver pointed at the cotton tree, unwilling to let the white man shrug him off. "Look yonder," the driver said. "Do you see witch capes hanging in that tree?"

Boone saw only the largest assemblage of massive limbs he had seen anywhere and a swarm of huge fluttering birds. "No," he said. "Den you only get two eye. No more," the driver said. "Witch no dae inside your belly. If a witch be dae, you get four eye and you go see beaucoup witch capes hanging from those limbs. If you pick one, it go bring you magical powers. But if you show it to anyone else, even to another witch, it go kill you."

The driver's formidable store of information on witchcraft and magic seemed to have obliterated his powers of math, for he kept adding a taxi fare of 3,000 leones to a ferry charge of 1,200 leones and coming up with 5,400, excluding special travel assistant fees, portage and baggage fees, taxi negotiation fees, fees for tourist information, and fees he allegedly had paid to expedite their ferry passage, all of which were recounted at great length and liberally waived because the driver was a very generous man with a family of nine starving children and a special place in his heart for white men.

After a bitter quarrel, during which Boone heard about every misfortune that had ever befallen the driver or anyone in his extended family, the driver took 3,500 leones for the taxi fare, including the ferry, and dumped Boone before a storefront with a second-story sign that said "United States Peace Corps." The sidewalk to the only entrance was blocked by a blind man in black glasses, wearing a white skullcap and a Muslim burnoose. The man promptly held out his cup and said, "White man. Peace Koh. Do ya, help me small-small."

"The taxi driver took all my money," Boone said. "Besides, if you're blind, how is it you know I'm white?"

"Africa man no take taxi to Peace Corps house," the blind man said with a laugh. "I sabby dat. You sabby dat? You sabby talk Krio? You no sabby talk Krio? Den I talk to you in English. You no get Salone money? Now American money fine past Salone money. Ih fine-O! Now, I tell you. Do ya, paddy, help me small-small. Let me have some fine-fine American money."

Boone put a spindled American dollar into the cup.

"I tell God tank ya," the blind man said, nimbly fingering the bill. "Your wives will bear you many peekins. And those peekins will bear you many more peekins. You will die with a smile on your face, rocked in the arms of your grandchildren. They will sing you to sleep with songs of your great deeds. Because you have helped me, God will watch over you forever. God made me blind, but he gave me the power to foretell the future, so know that all I have said to you is true. I tell you these things in God's name, and may God pull out my liver and set my hair on fire with lightning if everything I have said is not true."

Boone savored the sheer grandiloquence of the blind man's blessing and followed signs along a sidewalk between two storefronts to a rear entrance of a slanted frame building. After negotiating a set of metal stairs that switchbacked up the rear of the structure, Boone opened a busted screen door and entered a big room aswirl with ceiling fans and partitioned by file cabinets.

He introduced himself to a fortyish woman whose desk was positioned to field requests for information. Boone explained himself and his purpose to her.

"You came all the way from Indiana?" the woman asked.

"I was in Paris when I found out about this," Boone explained. "Michael Killigan's mother wrote to me there."

The woman dolefully shook her head. "We talked to her over the weekend," she said. "I know how concerned you must be about Michael," she added, "but I don't think there's any good you can do in Sierra Leone. The Peace Corps, the American Embassy, the people from USAID, the Canadian, Dutch, and German development agencies, everyone is looking for Michael Killigan. These people know the country. They know the Mende tribe. They know Michael Killigan, his friends, and his haunts. Nobody is more concerned about him than this office and the people at the embassy. If he can be found, they will find him."

The woman pouted and handed him a three-by-five-inch photo of Michael Killigan—skinnier than Boone remembered him—wearing an embroidered African smock and sitting on the veranda of a mud hut surrounded by twenty or thirty villagers of all ages. The Africans were solemn, as if they knew this moment would be preserved on film forever. Killigan's expression was a draw between a smirk and a grimace.

"May I ask where you got that photo?"

"You too, huh?" she said. "Suddenly everyone wants to know about photographs. Last Friday, one of Killigan's servants, Moussa somebody, went to the Peace Corps office in Bo town asking to see the Peace Corps Director. He was told that the Director stays in Freetown. The kid said he had photos he wanted to show the Director. Said he wouldn't turn them over to anybody else. The officer in Bo was finally able to talk him out of one photo by telling him it might help them find Killigan. This week, we got word from the embassy that they're looking for the servant and the photos, and they are mad at us because we let the kid go.

"It's a mess," she said, still peering sadly into the photo. "In years gone by, we have lost Volunteers to illness or snakebite, but this kind of thing has never happened before. Volunteers do not vanish from their villages."

"I have a three-month visa," Boone said. "If nothing else, I can serve as another set of roaming eyes. I can go to Bo or Killigan's village and help look for him and his servant."

The woman shook her head ruefully. "Tromp into the bush by yourself and you'll get frustrated in a hurry," she said. "After that, you'll get sick. The Peace Corps cannot give you medicine or medical care, because you aren't a Volunteer. That leaves native medicine, which is worse than no medicine."

"I've got a three-month supply of chloroquine," Boone said. "I've already had shots for yellow fever, cholera, and typhoid."

"Good for you," the woman said. "Now go downstairs to Dr. Kallon's office and ask him to show you his chart of two hundred and forty other tropical diseases that can blind you, kill you, or put you in bed for three months with lasting kidney, liver, or heart damage. Ask him about schistosomiasis, river blindness, yaws, sleeping sickness, giardiasis, blackwater fever, hepatitis, leprosy, and elephantiasis. As for your malaria medicine, eighty-five percent of the malarial parasites in equatorial Africa are now immune to chloroquine, including *falciparum*, which can give you cerebral malaria and kill you. Nowadays we tell our Volunteers they *will* get malaria if they spend any time in the bush; it's only a matter of how often and what kind."

She put two manila folders into an accordion filer and smiled sadly. "I don't mean to be negative. It's just that, even with the proper training and medical care, living in the bush is unhealthy and dangerous. Elections are coming up, which usually means civil unrest, with a capital U. Refugees are coming across the border from Liberia, and some of the rebels have crossed into Sierra Leone in pursuit. It's not a good time to go out wandering."

"How long have you been here?" Boone asked.

"Three years," the woman said.

"And you're none the worse for wear," he said, hoping she would

discern a compliment and give him the information he was about
to ask of her.

"I live in Freetown," she said, "not in the bush. When I get sick,
I see a doctor who graduated from an American medical school."

"If I get sick," Boone said, "I'll buy a plane ticket home."

The woman grinned and pulled out a nail file. "I can see you
know all about the bush," she said. "In the bush, you will be at
least ten hours by bush taxi, or *podah-podah*, from Freetown. A
podah-podah is a Toyota pickup truck with forty Africans and two
tons of freight stuffed into it. Killigan's village is twelve hours by
podah-podah, half of it over roads that would be declared impassable
in Indiana. A ride in a *podah-podah* takes stamina; if you were sick,
the trip would kill you, and the American Embassy would be sending
you back to Indiana in the cargo hold."

"How do Volunteers get to Freetown when they're sick?" Boone
wondered out loud.

"Well, it's usually at least two days before we find out about them,
and another day or so before we get to them. Then we pick them
up in air-conditioned Land-Rovers and bring them back here," she
said. "Again, a luxury that would not be provided to you, because
you are not a Volunteer."

"What do I have to do to become a Volunteer?" he asked.

"Go back to America and fill out the paperwork," she said. "The
Peace Corps does not accept applications from within the host
country."

"It can't be that bad," Boone said. "People have been living here
for thousands of years."

"Living and dying," she said. "The average life span in the bush
is thirty-nine years. The infant mortality rate is fifteen percent in
the first year of life. After the British took over, they used to greet
one another in the mornings at Freetown by asking, 'How many
died last night?' They called Sierra Leone 'the White Man's Grave.'
Catholic Missionary Services lost a hundred and nine missionaries
in the first twenty-five years of operations. One time, six Catholic
fathers were sent in January. By June they were all dead. My advice
to you is to stay in Freetown and don't charge into the bush looking
for Michael Killigan."

"I'm here," Boone said. "I'll leave after I find him. I'll stay in
Freetown long enough to find out where I should start looking, and

if it's the bush, I'll go there. Just tell me how to get to Killigan's village, where he was last seen, and maybe who he hung around with," Boone begged.

"I can tell you those things," a voice behind him said.

Boone turned and saw a huge torso in a tie-dyed native shirt filling the doorway to the office. Shaggy hair and a dense beard covered the man's head and face, leaving two brown eyes under an overhanging brow.

"Sam Lewis," the man said, extending a hand of thick fingers, a wrist with a bronze bracelet, and an arm of thick bones with no fat on them. "Agriculture. I'm stationed just outside Pujehun."

"Boone Westfall," said Boone, feeling his palm snag on the welts and calluses of Lewis's hand, and getting a closer look at the imposing bracelet, which consisted of two bronze lizards with adjoining snouts crawling past one another in the hairy scrub of Lewis's forearm, holding themselves in place with prehensile bronze tails.

"It keeps fever away," Lewis said with a grin, noticing Boone's study of his bracelet. "I no get febah since I been wear dis medicine," he said, lapsing into the musical Krio Boone had heard from the taxi driver.

The woman at the desk took a phone call.

"Killigan talked about you," he continued. "You were planning a travel, weren't you?"

"We were," Boone chuckled grimly, "until Killigan disappeared."

"These people can't help you," Lewis said, talking over the woman's telephone conversation, and dismissing the entire office with a backhanded wave. "They know nothing about the bush. They all live in Freetown. On top of that, they're very culturally sensitive, which means they know everything about how things should be and nothing about how they are."

"I need directions to Killigan's village," Boone said.

Lewis motioned for the woman's attention and said, "I'll take him," and pushed Boone toward the door.

"I'm going for my monthly protein fix," he explained. "Why don't you come and eat some *poo-mui* food with me."

"What kind of food?" Boone asked.

"*Poo-mui*," Lewis said. "*Poo* is Mende for 'white' or 'European'; *mui* means 'man' or 'person.' If you go out to the bush in Mendeland, peekins will shout *poo-mui* at you from dawn to dusk, and you'll get plenty sick of it. There's a restaurant in Freetown that serves fried chicken and french fries. There's another one that serves cow beef."

"Cow beef?" Boone repeated.

"Once you get outside Freetown," Lewis explained, " 'beef' means the meat from any animal, usually from bush deer, or from big guinea pigs called 'cutting grass.' They taste kinda like squirrels. Ever eat a squirrel?"

Boone made a face.

"If you want to make sure about what you're eating, ask if it's cow beef."

"Cow beef, got it," said Boone.

"Then they'll lie in your face and tell you it's the sweetest cow beef you've ever had."

Back out on the sidewalk, they found a white female Volunteer waylaid by the same blind beggar.

"I tell God tank ya," the blind man said, shaking coins in his basket. "Your husband will own a huge farm and you will bear many peekins. And those peekins will bear you many more peekins. You will die with a smile on your face, rocked in the arms of your grandchildren. They will sing you to sleep with songs about their favorite grandmother. Because you have helped me, God will watch over you forever. God made me blind, but he gave me the power to foretell the future, so know that all I have said to you is true. I tell you these things in God's name, and may God pull out my spleen and may my enemies walk on my grave if everything I have said is not true."

"Morning-O, pa," Lewis said to the beggar.

"Morning-O, mastah," the beggar replied. "How de body?"

"I tell God tank ya foh it," Lewis said. "How youself?"

"I well," the beggar replied. "How de day go?"

"I fall down, I get up," Lewis said.

"Now meself-self same," said the beggar. "We go see by and by. Next time, you keep something for me, hear me?"

"We go see back," said Lewis.

"That was your first Krio lesson," Lewis said. "When the British dumped boatloads of freed slaves over here in the eighteenth century, the settlers had no common language. They were Africans from different tribes, Jamaicans, slaves who had drifted into London after slavery was declared illegal there in 1772, American slaves who had escaped to Nova Scotia during the Revolutionary War. They were forced to develop a common language out of remembered English, Portuguese, Spanish, Yoruba, bits of French, and whatever else would serve to call a spade a fucking shovel. Blessings and greetings are extremely important. Learn them and do not attempt to transact business without first greeting people. Ask about their families, ask about their health, ask how the day is going, then proceed. The American habit of getting straight down to business is considered very rude."

The restaurant was a dark wooden place lit only by a jukebox playing American music that was twenty-five years out of date: the Kinks, the Beatles, the Velvet Underground, the Moody Blues. Lewis ordered four beers and two platters of food. He swooned and smacked his lips over a meal of soggy fries and tough chicken armored in thick, deep-fried batter. Boone rated the meal far below the fast food he had been eating out of the stalls along the rue de la Huchette in Paris, and picked at the batter in between sips of beer.

"Eat up," Lewis said, washing down a mouthful of fries with half a beer. "You'll get nothing but rice and sauce out in the bush. Rice chop. No cold beer either, because there's no electricity and no refrigerators. Nothing but warm Guinness stout."

Boone forced a few more fries down and wondered what rice chop would taste like if people came all the way to Freetown for deep-fried gristle, batter, and chicken bones. In the course of the meal, he learned that Lewis was on the last leg of a two-year stint in the Peace Corps; that in two years he had had the clap three times, hepatitis twice, and a hot shower once.

"It's my kind of country," Lewis said. "It runs on bribes ('mas-mas,' in Krio, the 'sweet' of office), graft, thievery, witchcraft, and juju. In 1981, the exchange rate was one leone to the dollar. Now it's a hundred leones to the dollar. You can make a fortune trading in three currencies in the black markets at the border. When I came here, two years ago, a cold Star beer was fifty leones. Now it's two hundred leones for a warm one. I used to be able to get a woman outside the casinos at Lumley Beach for the cost of breakfast and a fifty-cent cab fare. Now they've all got diseases, and they want dinner, two hundred leones for the night, breakfast, and cab fare in the morning. The brewery shuts down once a month, and the power goes out in Freetown at least once a night. 'Better no dae,' as they say in Krio," Lewis said. "Better is not there, or nothing good is there."

"You sound like Killigan's letters," Boone said. "But he said the people made the difference. He said the poverty and despair only made them more bighearted. He said he reenlisted because of the people."

Lewis wrinkled his upper lip and snapped his fingers at the waitress.

"That's where your friend and I parted company," he said, giving Boone a hard look. "He spent too much time in his village and not enough time with *poo-muis*. He forgot about civilization, and started thinking these people were noble savages or some goddamn thing."

"What do you mean?" Boone asked, alarmed at the disgust creeping into Lewis's voice.

Lewis banged his beer bottle. "As soon as a Volunteer tells me there might be something to native medicine, or that the bush is really a fucking Garden of Eden, that's when I know they've gotten down on all fours and crossed over to the animal kingdom."

Boone nervously took the restaurant in at a glance and satisfied himself that nobody had heard Lewis over the jukebox.

"Don't get me wrong," Lewis said, in a bland tone that suggested he was unconcerned about being misunderstood. "I like to get down on all fours as much as the next guy, but come morning, I send her home, get up on my hind legs, go back to speaking English, and eat with a knife, fork, and spoon. And it's not a racial thing. It doesn't have a thing to do with skin color. It's not genetics or breeding or Darwinism. It's much simpler than that. Animals live in the bush. When people live in the bush, they turn into animals. Animals with the power of speech."

Boone peeled the label off his Star beer and wondered if Lewis's bitterness ever ripened into outright rage.

"It's a great country," he said, with a tilt of his Star. "Where else can you find beggars, lepers, whores, cripples, and children starving to death in the middle of such exotic beauty and abundant mineral wealth? I've been here almost two years, and I can say with certainty that at least once a day a hungry person has asked me for money. After careful research, I have concluded that starvation builds character. In the beginning, I gave away half my hundred-and-fifty-dollars-a-month salary to starving people, or people who were dying because they couldn't afford antibiotics or rehydration salts. Pretty soon, ten, twenty, thirty people a day were coming to me with their hands out. Their children want foh die, their bellies are empty, they get bad fever, money no dae for medicine, or 'mehricine,' as they say in Krio. I developed a system for rapid appraisal of potential beneficiaries. Adult beggars missing more than seven digits to leprosy automatically qualified for alms from this tender white man, as did blind lepers or blind polio victims with children, limbless people, or mothers with blood-tinged sputum.

"Once I had the citizens in the major-medical adult category, I eyeballed them and decided whether they had ten cents' worth of deformities, or maybe a dollar's worth. I used this system during banking hours, after that I shut the coffers down for the day and refused to give anybody a dime, unless they started dying in a bag of bones at my feet, whereupon I usually concluded that they were already almost dead and my money would be much better spent on the living.

"Star beer!" Lewis hollered, grabbing a bouquet of empty bottles and clanging them at the waitress.

"Every so often, somebody came up to me with a story about how their father 'want foh die' out in some godforsaken village eighty miles out in the bush. How they had to get there before dawn with some *poo-mui* medicine, or the old pa would croak of snakebite, or blackwater fever, or river blindness, or pneumonia. Sometimes they would get down on their hands and knees, touch my foot, dribble tears in the dust, and beg me for lorry fare and money to buy the medicine. Maybe six, seven bucks. A day's wages anyway. At least half the time, I told them to take a hike for yams and bananas. Next day, somebody would tell me that their story was true, and that the old fart had died during the night. Or else I'd give some consumptive, rachitic, old poltroon twenty bucks, only to find out that, instead of a case of tuberculosis or rickets, he'd spent the money on a case of Guinness stout and was hung over in a hammock. After a few months of that, I had to use some of their own wisdom on them. 'How foh do?' I asked, using Krio just like an old pa. 'How for do?' Better translated as 'What can you do?' Indeed. If I bought medicine for every old geezer croaking of snakebite in West Africa, I'd have to fly home tomorrow, and the clinic would be closed for good!

"Make we get Star beer!" Lewis hollered again, this time waving two clanking bouquets of empty bottles.

"And the climate," he said, returning to his conversation. "You drown in a twenty-four-hour waterfall of rain from July to September. The shit comes down in torrents. It carries away children and livestock. By January, you can't find drinking water. You have to pay people a quarter to walk five miles and fetch you a bucket of swamp water. When I lived in Bo, I had a water tower behind my compound that was filled weekly by the German development people. The villagers used to come and sit underneath the tank with little pails, collecting trickles of water that leaked out at the seams. I was pretty nice about the whole thing, and I didn't chase them away. I didn't throw rocks at them, until they started climbing up the stilts and dipping their buckets into the water supply. That truly pissed me off, because half the time the buckets had just been sitting in a heap of warm goat shit. Early on in the dry season, I'd nail them with a few good-sized rocks, and that usually did the trick. But toward the end of the season, when the nearest water was a good five miles off, and swamp water at that, a pail of cold, clean water looked so good to them that they got to thinking it was worth a few lumps on the noggin. So I had to break out the stick I kept behind the door and drive them off like livestock.

"You can't tell them a fucking thing about hygiene or drinking water. It's all hocus-pocus to them. If the water goes bad, it's because some witch in menopause put a hex on the well while everybody was asleep. To them, dirty buckets had about as much to do with it as the fall of the Roman Empire. Health care is more or less left to nature and witchcraft. Deformed children are 'devil spirits' trying to invade the village, so the Sande matrons simply kill them and throw them on the fire. At the other end of life, the old ones get sick, take to their pallets, and die within a week or so. It's a great country."

"You were saying that Killigan spent too much time in his village," interrupted Boone, who was tired of listening to invective.

"Live with animals in the bush, pretty soon you're down on all fours and can't get up again," he said, glowering at his bottle of beer, almost as if he had forgotten Boone was with him.

The waitress, a Krio girl in a headwrap, walked by them once more.

"Say, pa!" Lewis hollered to the proprietor behind the bar. "You no get waitress with better training?"

The waitress sucked her teeth.

"Training dae beaucoup," she said. "You humbug me foh whatin?"

"I no humbug you," Lewis sneered. "I want one Star beer."

"You want beaucoup Star beer," she said. "I no able foh fetch dem so."

"You suck teeth at me? You no respect me better?"

"Na, so you say," she snapped.

"Na, so I know," said Lewis. "For whatin you vex?"

"Something brings something," she said.

"Ah," he said, "the African way. Let's talk proverbs."

"Like brings like," she said.

"If you throw ashes," said Lewis, "ashes will follow you."

"Usai den tie cow, na dae he go eat grass," she countered. "Usai white mahn sit down, na dae he go drink Star beer."

"Pa, do ya, I can get one waitress with better training?"

The bartender came out and shooed the girl off, serving Lewis and Boone another round of Stars.

Lewis glowered after her. "You see what I mean? A simple concept like service is totally foreign to them. Instead, it's something to argue about.

"Anyway, I was saying . . . Oh yeah, one day, your friend, Lamin Kaikai—he preferred his African name. One day, Killigan told me he paid a medicine man to put thunder medicine on his house. Next thing I knew, he was hanging out with Aruna Sisay."

"Who's Haruna Sisay?" Boone interrupted.

"Aruna Sisay," Lewis repeated. "I'm taking you to see him tomorrow. We'll see if he can explain what happened to your buddy. If he doesn't know, he can sure find out. And if you kiss his ass long and hard enough, and pretend he's some kind of superior being because he turned himself into a Mende man, he might tell you where you can start looking."

"Does he speak English?" Boone asked.

"He's American," Lewis said. "Well, he used to be American. He's white, but he's African. He's got three African wives and he speaks fluent Mende. He even speaks deep Mende, or ancient talk, which only the old pas know. Out in the bush, they call him the white Mende man. He came here a long time ago on a grant to do anthropology fieldwork and never went back. He doesn't talk to white people anymore, unless they speak Mende to him and approach him in the African way, with gifts and gestures of respect. That's why Sisay liked your buddy so much, because Killigan took the trouble to learn Mende. If he finds out you're a friend of Killigan's, maybe he'll speak English to you, but don't count on it."

"So the Mendes speak something besides Krio?" asked Boone.

"Krio is the language spoken in Freetown," Lewis explained. "And it's the language used in the market when two people from different tribes are haggling over the price of a cup of rice. You've got eighteen tribes and eighteen different languages in a country a little smaller than South Carolina. When they want to talk to each other, they speak Krio. The Europeans drew the maps, and they didn't give a damn whether the tribes within the borders were speaking the same language or killing each other. The two biggest tribes are the Temne in the north and the Mende in the south and southeast. Where you're going, the people speak Mende. But you'll get along fine if you pick up a little Krio."

"So you think this Aruna Sisay might know something about what happened to Killigan?"

"Maybe," Lewis said. "But like I said, he's African, which means he's not to be trusted. Get information from him if you can, but don't give him any. That's how you survive in this part of the world. Ask questions, listen, but don't talk. Like the rest of these guys, he's into secret society business, and if it serves his purpose, he'll lie to you, and turn your information over to the Poro boys. Lying is a form of polite conversation over here. Lying is considered perfectly OK if you are protecting a secret, and everything's a secret. Witchcraft, bad medicine, putting swears, pulling swears, sex, politics, the Poro Society. It's all secret. If you try to find out about any of it, all you'll get will be lies."

"What's the Poro Society?" asked Boone.

"The men's secret society," Lewis explained. "It's kind of a cross between the Boy Scouts and the Freemasons. It's how young men are initiated into manhood and trained to be warriors, even though, these days, they grow up to be farmers or miners or government clerks. Once a year, the Poro devil comes into the village wearing a mask of palm raffia, with bits of mirrors and amulets attached to it. The devil blows a cow's horn with a lizard skin stretched over the opening. The women and children scatter and bury their faces inside their huts. If a woman sees her reflection in one of the mirrors on the devil's mask, she will become sterile. The devil rounds up all the initiates, and takes them out into the bush for about a month, where the elders give them new names and tribal markings. The markings on their backs are supposedly caused by the Poro spirit, which swallows them like a boa constrictor and separates them from their families. The markings on their temples supposedly appear when they see the Poro spirit. Later, the spirit delivers them back to the village as men with new names. It's a spirit with a mouth, a stomach, and a vagina. It eats children, then gives birth to men.

"Nobody will tell you what happens in the Poro bush, because it's intensely secret. Fowls are sacrificed during the ceremonies, and as the knife is severing the fowl's neck the initiates are warned that the same will happen to them if they ever tell any Poro secrets. During other ceremonies, the initiates are given rice and cautioned that this rice will choke them to death if they ever reveal Poro secrets. If you want to know something about Poro, you can only ask people who have *not* been initiated. And what you get are rumors and the anecdotes collected by anthropologists and missionaries."

Lewis finished his beer.

"It must be pretty rough," he continued, "because every so often, one of the young men doesn't come back. An elder comes to the mother's house and breaks a pot on the ground in front of her, saying, 'You asked us to build pots, we are sorry to say that yours was broken.' Nothing more is ever said about the initiate. No mourning, no grief. He simply disappears."

Lewis rocked back in his chair and went to work on a dish of soft-serve ice cream. "As I said," he added with a mirthless laugh, "animals with speech."

Boone found Lewis's opinions more reprehensible than the described rituals, but he did not risk alienating his only bush guide.

"I should warn you that you'll be going into Moiwo's territory," said Lewis, "and, as you know, it's election time."

"Moiwo?" asked Boone.

"Moiwo's the section chief," Lewis said. "He went to school in England and America, then returned to Sierra Leone with an agenda. His father was the Minister of Finance under the last regime. He lines his pockets with relief money and spends it on limos and women. There's an old Krio saying, 'Monkey works, baboon eats.' Moiwo's the baboon. His monkeys work for him all day, and he sits around and eats. An African big man. Crooked as a dog's hind leg. Now he wants to be Paramount Chief, and it's election time, so he's getting into bad medicine and secret societies. He's definitely way up on top in the Poro business."

"If no one talks about Poro, how come you know so much about it?" asked Boone.

"Most of what I know about Poro, I learned from Michael Killigan," Lewis said. "He met a missionary up around Kenema who knew a lot about Poro. And Killigan used to come back with stories about devil dancers cutting their tongues out, passing them around on plates, then putting them back into their mouths. Or shirts made of magic cloth that could stop bullets. It was great campfire stuff, until he started believing it. After he went through it himself, you couldn't get a word out of him."

"Out of whom?" Boone asked. "After who went through it? The missionary?"

"Killigan," Lewis said, smiling, then wiping it away with the back of his hand. "After Killigan was initiated, he clammed up just like the rest of them. I saw his markings one day. He took off his shirt when we were building a bridge outside of Sumbuya. Never had seen it on a white man. The scars looked kinda purple. Later on, in Bo, I asked him about it. He got up and left me at the saloon. Just the way a dog would leave another dog drinking out of a drain spout. After that, it was common knowledge: Say the word Poro in a bar, in a rest house, at a table in a restaurant, and Killigan would get up and leave."

(4)

Randall took the black bundle home from work and opened the box on the kitchen table in front of his wife. Together, they skimmed Michael's last three letters and found no mention of any forthcoming package of artifacts.

"Do you think it means something?" he asked her, pointing at the bundle and wrinkling his nose. "Do you think it's from someone who knows what's happened to Michael? Is it some kind of message? Something evil? Do you suppose it's meant to harm us? Or used to harm Michael?"

Marjorie wearily shook her head, not because she had an opinion about the black egg, but because she recognized her husband's methods. He was a creature of anxiety. Anxiety made him a successful perfectionist at work, and an unbearable pest at home. His favorite technique for acquiring peace of mind in a crisis was to bait her, siccing his fears on her like crazed hounds; her job was to soothe them one by one and send them back tamed, sleeping dogs. He was like a child who could imagine only terrible kingdoms and wicked rulers in the realms of possibility, which she pooh-poohed away, assuring him they would never come to pass.

"It could be poisonous. What if it's some kind of supernatural weapon? A witch doctor's hand grenade? Should we unwrap it and make sure there's not a spider or a snake inside?"

She was preoccupied with her own unspeakable fears and wanted only to hire a domestic to talk to her husband about life's ups and downs.

"You must be worried," he said. "Otherwise you would be telling me not to worry. You think I should be worried, don't you?"

He concluded that his wife's tight-lipped composure was a cover for internal hysteria. The last real tragedy in their lives had been a miscarriage, almost fifteen years ago, a bit of trauma clearly in the female domain. She had handled the whole thing gracefully, and had not allowed her emotional upheaval to interfere with his flawless execution of plan confirmation in what was then the largest single reorganization under Chapter 11 in the southern district of Indiana. But Michael's disappearance was a major tragedy by comparison, and something only Randall could resolve using his contacts in Washington and New York.

"You're very worried, aren't you?" he asked. "You know, the law recognizes something called estoppel by silence," he added, half playfully. "I don't want to get into it in detail, but in certain situations, I would be entitled to conclude from your silence that you agree with me, and later you would be estopped from denying that you agreed with me. You're beyond worried, aren't you? And you think I should be worried too, don't you?"

"Why don't you put this somewhere," she said, pushing the box at him.

Randall took the thing upstairs and stowed it in his closet, up on his gun shelf. Before he put it away, he unwrapped it again and studied it by the closet light. It seemed to reverberate slightly. Its textured surfaces and the patterns on the strips of cloth seemed to swarm under his inspection. The spout looked as if it had been soaked in blood, then baked in a kiln. If the thing was an omen of some kind, he reasoned, then he should hang on to it until he encountered someone who could divine its message.

When he got up the next day, he had two full-time jobs: one, as the best bankruptcy lawyer in the Seventh Circuit, and two, as a desperate parent turned tenacious international private investigator. He worked all morning putting out the usual fires in his bankruptcy practice, cramming a day's work in before lunch, so he could spend the afternoon on the phone to Washington. By day three, he was using Mack as well, to find information about the Peace Corps, Sierra Leone, the embassy there, and the names of people in the State Department who could make things happen in Freetown. By week's end, he had telephoned every relevant official in the State Department and the Peace Corps who would still take his calls.

The sympathetic administrative assistants to senators, congressional staffers, ambassadors, junior ambassadors, and state department bureaucrats offered him only earnest reassurances and extravagant descriptions of everything that was being done, and studiously avoided remarking on how little was being turned up. The telephone calls had given him the illusion that by explaining his tragedy over and over to voices at the other end of telephone lines, eventually he would project his terror and his anxiety somewhere outside himself, where it would then assume manageable proportions, take on the dimensions of just another serious problem that could be solved by doing lots of hard work. He was networking into new circles of power, using his legal contacts and political connections, looking for a capable person who could solve his problems on the promise of a cashier's check or an international money order.

At last, Swanson hooked him up with the American Ambassador in Freetown, who in turn put him on conference call with some kind of chief named Idrissa Moiwo, an African who had been educated in England and America and spoke English. According to the Ambassador, Moiwo was an up-and-comer, about to win an election for something called Paramount Chief. He was the man in charge of Pujehun district, and he personally assured Randall that he would not rest until Michael Killigan was found. When Randall faxed the servant's letter to the American Embassy in Freetown, Chief Moiwo promptly expanded the manhunt to include a search for Michael's servant and the mysterious photographs.

"These photographs may explain everything," Moiwo had said, "if we can get our hands on them."

"There's something else you should know, Mr. Killigan," said the Ambassador. "Apparently, this isn't the first time your son has disappeared."

"It's the first time I've known about," said Randall defensively.

"Turns out that about six months ago or so, your boy joined one of these secret tribal societies," said the Ambassador. "Did he tell you anything about that?"

"He *joined* the tribe?" Randall said. "You're telling me now he thinks he's an African, or some damn thing?"

"He joined the men's secret society of the Mende tribe," said the Ambassador. "It's called the Poro Society. The initiation rites last more than a month. After the rumor came in, we checked around with the Peace Corps people responsible for him, and we found out he 'couldn't be found in his village,' as the local people say, for a month or so, because he was out in the bush getting initiated. The Peace Corps considers Poro and its supernatural politics off-limits. When the field supervisor finally caught up with him, your boy had tribal markings. Poro markings from the sounds of it, but who knows? The villagers don't like telling white people about it."

"Markings?"

"Incisions, small scars around the eyes on the temples. Then there's a pattern of dots on the back."

"Great," said Randall, imagining how his son might look in a power tie and a Hart, Schaffner & Marx suit, presiding over an unsecured creditors committee meeting on the eve of a plan confirmation hearing . . . with *tribal scars* around his eyes.

"These photos," Randall said, abruptly changing the subject away from his son's contributory negligence. "You say these photos may have something to do with his disappearance."

"Cameras can cause trouble in this part of the world," the chief added. "Africans love them and beg to be 'snapped,' but only if they get to keep the photo. Otherwise, they fear a piece of their soul may fall into the wrong hands. Some of the old ones say allowing yourself to be photographed shortens your life."

By way of illustration, the Ambassador faxed Randall the embassy's official warning to tourists not to take photographs:

Local Customs

It is traditional that on festive occasions costumed "devil dance" groups are formed. Usually the devil dance groups will be in the main streets or sections of the city. There are "good" devils and "bad" devils. A "bad" devil can sometimes turn violent and can also incite others in the group to violence. If you see a devil dance group in the street take an alternate street if possible. When driving, if you can't avoid the group, lock your doors, roll up your windows and drive slowly through the group.
DO NOT TAKE PHOTOGRAPHS.

But the chief seemed confident that the servant boy and the photos could be found. Here, at last, was a person who spoke Randall's language, for Moiwo bluntly suggested that money would help, because it would enable him to purchase another vehicle to conduct the search, and would also allow him to show Randall Killigan's generosity to the villagers, and perhaps even provide a reward for valuable information.

Randall sent the money by wire and took the Ambassador's advice that, given the election unrest and the armed revolution in Liberia, no possible good could come of a trip to Freetown. The Ambassador promised to call with any news whatsoever, and would be the first to let Randall know if his presence in Africa would help in the least. After three days of insistent phone missions to Washington, Randall slumped back into his chair, alone, and stared. All these overseas phone calls and hours on hold to Washington politicos had not produced a single clue to his son's whereabouts.

At home, news of the initiation and tribal markings didn't faze Marjorie in the least, which Randall interpreted as a symptom of her mental deterioration under the strain of the crisis. In bed and unable to sleep, they argued about whether he should fly to Sierra Leone and talk to the Ambassador in person. Marjorie dropped off first, and left Randall in bed at midnight, grinding his teeth over the tribal markings and the secret tribal societies.

He took a warm bath with the latest issue of *Forbes*. Afterward, he found his wife's sleeping medication and poured two of the little blue capsules into the palm of his hand and stared at them. *Why am I taking sleeping medication?* he wondered, almost watching himself take pills he had never taken before. The anxiety was almost choking him. If he could force himself to sleep, maybe that would clear his head for the work that needed to be done tomorrow.

Back in bed, he finally fell into a trance, twitching awake when his heart skipped a beat, or when he remembered the words of the State Department report, and had dreams about his son roaming the bush paths hungry for the souls of witchmen.

Sometime later, he heard a loud, disorienting sound and woke up in a night sweat. His heart boomed in his chest, and the digital clock burned a red 3:34 a.m. into the blackness at his bedside table. He looked up from his bed toward the light of the bay windows, searching for the source of the sound, and saw . . . what could have been just a side effect of the pills.

He saw or dreamed that he saw a bat in his own bedroom. A huge bat. He saw it by the muddy glow from the night light in the corner, just enough visibility to make him wonder if he was of sound mind and vision. At first, he concluded that he was hallucinating, because the thing was so big, with a three- or four-foot wingspan, big enough to darken the bedroom bay windows. He almost felt his ear cup itself and grow toward the fluttering image, straining to hear the whisper of leather wings.

Then it almost deafened him with a loud *thwock!* that sounded like a piece of wood hitting a sounding board. Then *thwock!* again—terrifyingly close to him and so loud he could feel sound rushing around his face like a current.

Randall crawled across the floor to his closet and got a tennis racket (which someone had told him was the best weapon for killing a bat). He crawled over to the bedroom door, snaked his arm up the wall, and turned on the lights, exposing the thing in the sudden garish light of four sixty-watt bulbs in the ceiling fixture.

The bat shot directly overhead, so close he could see the massive span of its fingered wings, its furry torso, its shrieking face, which he glimpsed in one vivid instant, before blinking in terror. It had the head of a dog, or even a small horse, with a hideous, swollen snout, and lips bristling with warts or tumors. The eyes were large, innocent pools of blackness, staring in wonder, almost as if the creature did not quite believe in Randall either.

Randall ducked and blinked, the image of the grotesque head still shining in his memory. Again he heard the faintest rustle of wings, ridiculously delicate when compared to the swooping drama of its flight and the deafening *thwock!* filling his bedroom.

He covered the top of his head with his arms so the beast wouldn't get caught in his hair. When he looked up again, it was gone.

In retrospect, he probably should have awakened Marjorie first, and warned her that there was a bat in the room, and that he was going to turn on the light and kill it. Instead, she woke up terrified and irritated with him. She never even saw the bat. She saw only her husband, standing in his underwear with a tennis racket in his hand, yelling and looking as if he had seen a three-headed dog guarding the gates of hell.

The neighbors heard his yelling, the *thwock!* of the bat, or both, and called the police. The police couldn't find the bat either. They listened patiently while Randall emphatically told them how big it was, that it had a wingspan of at least three feet and a hideous horse's face. He may have caught them winking at each other once, but they were otherwise respectful and polite. They consoled him by telling him that bats always look bigger than they really are. They agreed with him that nothing was uglier than a bat's face. They said that single sightings of birds, bats, squirrels, and other rodents in dwellings were quite common, but if the creatures got into the house, they usually found their way back out again. He was probably rid of the thing and shouldn't worry, they said.

But worry he did. He got back in bed and waited, almost hoping the thing would reappear, because he wanted to know if he had actually seen it. Could an otherwise normal, highly intelligent, well-disciplined, successful attorney wake up in the middle of the night and *imagine* he had seen a winged creature in sumptuous, hideous detail? True, he had been asleep. True, he had taken two of Marjorie's sleeping pills—something he had never done! Maybe it had gotten in somehow and simply *appeared* to be five times bigger because of some trick of refracted light or a short circuit in Randall's racing imagination.

He had no idea where it came from, or where it went. Mental illness was out of the question . . . or was it? Could some metabolic disorder, or an imbalance in brain chemistry, an electrical disturbance, or a freak seizure erupt in one sudden, vivid hallucination, then disappear without a trace? Well, there were traces. Things were . . . shinier, a little brighter. The world looked almost wet, and the surfaces of things seemed overly smooth and bursting with color.

The next day, he settled into a permanent lethargy, punctuated only by catnaps and fits of anxiety. Was his son being held by rebels? Interrogated? Was he already dead? Was he in pain? Was he— Randall—now suffering from mental illness? Shock? Was this bat sighting the first symptom of a serious medical disorder?

His pretrial heart rhythm galloped into a day-of-trial frenzy, even though he had only minor hearings on the horizon. If an intelligent force governed the universe, it had a malicious sense of humor, for it had outfitted Randall, the bankruptcy warlord, with the heart of a neurasthenic invalid. He hated his heart. He wanted to trade it in for the heart of a warrior—one that would not distract him with arrhythmias on the eve of battle. He wanted the heart of the *Challenger* astronaut he had seen on TV, whose pulse was 64 fifteen seconds before takeoff. Instead he was stuck with an erratic ticker that skipped beats, then raced ahead in a string of pounding beats, as if to make up for lost blood. Sometimes it even woke him up at night. During a trial—whether it lasted a week or two months—he could finger his pulse at the artery in his wrist, day or night, and wait less than a minute to feel the world stand still during the skipped beat.

According to his high school buddy, Howard Bean, a prominent neurosurgeon, Randall's skipped heartbeats were harmless arrhythmias. Over the last few years, Randall had seen Bean at the Indiana University Hospital about his heart, and about a host of other physical annoyances, which seemed to have popped up just as Randall was really hitting his stride on his Seventh Circuit campaign. Bean had sent Randall to a cardiologist, who had sent him to a pulmonary function specialist for cardiac testing. . . . It was caused by stress, they said. It did not require medication, but Randall should watch himself.

Randall had told the doctors to go try their quackery on some other helpless duck. He wasn't buying. The episode had confirmed his suspicion that, like everyone else, doctors have an almost irresistible tendency to find what they are looking for. Saying that stress suddenly started causing his heart to skip beats made about as much sense as him showing up with cancer and having them tell him it was because he had entirely too much water in his diet. Stress was the air he had been breathing since day one of law school. Stress separated warriors from boys and girls. Stress was what happened when the dean addressed Randall's entering law school class of two hundred or so young, bright, anal-compulsive, overachieving college graduates and told them in so many words that if they wanted a good job and a lot of money when they got out of law school, they should take infinite pains to be absolutely certain that they were *all* in the top 10 percent of their class. Stress was the gleam in their eyes and the dawning revelation that, though they were unarmed and confined in classrooms and libraries with nothing but paper and books and perhaps writing utensils, they had to eliminate 90 percent of their peers without leaving any marks on the bodies. Under these extreme conditions, Randall the warrior quickly discovered that his intellect was a perfectly serviceable weapon.

And law school was stress kindergarten, because after that, all the really bright, completely anal-compulsive, outrageously overachieving law school graduates who actually *did* wind up in the top 10 percent of their class went on to earn big salaries in huge firms. Once there, the senior partners told these elite intellectual combatants that if they wanted to make partner in less than ten years and swim in sunken tubs full of money, they should take infinite pains to be absolutely certain that they were *all* in the top 10 percent of their associate class by the time they came up for partner. That was stress.

He had to laugh: *Doctors* presuming to lecture *him* about stress? All they had to do was get into med school, and residencies were waiting for them four years later. And what kind of pressure did they work under? If they fucked up on the job, one retired bus driver might croak on the table before he could run up higher hospital bills. You call that stress? If Randall fucked up on the job, entire financial empires could collapse in the space of a two-hour hearing. Institutional investors could shun stocks and kill his client on the basis of a single rumor or a single mistake in a prepackaged Chapter 11 plan. That's stress! And thank God for it, because otherwise, how do you separate really excellent lawyers from simply good ones?

Because Randall hated most doctors, he frequently took his illnesses first to his buddy Bean, who also arranged for any tests to be done on Sundays, typically the only free day in Randall's schedule. The regular doctors were not so accommodating. His family doctor, his cardiologist, his gastroenterologist, and his orthopedic surgeon all thought Randall was a raving hypochondriac, which of course he was not. His doctors were accustomed to treating patients who paid no attention to their health. Their patients were working-class drudges who *liked* being sick, because it meant they could stay home from work. Randall, on the other hand, was obliged to keep a weather eye on his health, because his exceptional career left precious little time for distractions. Even the suspicion of a serious illness could impair his performance in bankruptcy court, so he found it best to eliminate suspicions as they arose. Like the department he ran, his body had to be lean, profitable, and productive, with no slack in the lines for slackers or sickness. Internal organs, like employees, had to be responsive and dependable. Symptoms and performance deficiencies had to be promptly investigated, addressed, and rectified.

•

Dr. Howard Bean was the Chief of Neurosurgery at the Indiana University Hospital. He had square steel-rimmed eyeglasses, a runner's trim physique, and the unflappable mien of a scientist who was amused when the rest of the human race based most of its decisions on phobias and other assumptions that were unsupported by reliable data. Bean specialized in the study of magnetic fields in the brain and their applications for brain surgery. He was flush with lucrative grants from the National Institutes of Health, and was eager to try out the department's new superconducting quantum interference device—a SQUID scan. Because he had set the day aside for research, he wore blue jeans and a white lab coat, and had no plans to see any patients. He had just prepared a volunteer for scanning and had summoned several fellows to help him, when he received word from his secretary that his friend Randall Killigan was in the clinic waiting to see him.

Howard was quite accustomed to Randall airing his medical anxieties—it was a running semi-comic routine—but these sessions usually took the form of late-night phone calls, which Bean patiently fielded as a trusted companion. Until today, Randall's visits to his office had been confined to Sunday afternoons.

Randall was a good friend and highly amusing. A classic example of an exceedingly high intelligence devoted almost exclusively to irrational pursuits and nearly overwhelmed by his own eccentricities, fetishes, and ritualistic behaviors. But in Bean's mind this was a common failing of intelligent laypeople; their woefully inadequate training in math and the hard sciences allowed them to believe in things like the lottery, oat bran, or animal rights. Most of what Bean knew about the legal profession he had learned from Randall. As far as Bean could tell, the law consisted mostly of incantations and time-honored spells which had to be found in something called "precedent" and then recited or set down in documents for judges, who then either took up the chorus of magic words or called forth their own conjurations to dispel those put forth by the attorneys.

But the ironic kettle of contradictions that made Randall the lawyer an amusing friend also made him an abusing patient. Patient Randall had an insane fear of X rays, radiation from CAT scans, any sort of microwave or electromagnetic field. A common superstition, easy enough to deal with under most circumstances, except that patient Randall had an even more insane fear of cancer, so much so that he was truly at peace only after being scanned and shown images that conclusively proved he did not have cancer. Once the scan or the X rays were a month or two behind him, patient Randall came back, afraid that the scan itself may have caused a cell to mutate, and convinced that only another scan or a different, safer diagnostic test could persuade him that he was free of cancer.

Bean found Randall in his waiting room, shouting expletives into the telephone receiver at an operator who had bungled the administration of a four-way conference call. By the time they made it into an examination room, the patient had regained his composure, at least enough for Bean to notice that the arteries of the head and neck no longer stood out and only the major veins were still visible.

"Let me be straightforward about this," Randall said tersely. "Last night, I may have had a serious symptom of some kind."

"Aw, c'mon, Randall," said Bean, taking a seat and kicking his feet up onto a gurney. "Not your heart again. We're putting you on the treadmill twice a year! I have to pay those people time and a half to come in here on Sunday afternoons."

"Fuck you," said Randall. "Who gets you and your partners' taxes done for next to nothing? Who drew up your partnership agreements? Who drafted you a prenuptial agreement so you could get that first marriage out of the way for nothing?"

Bean threw up his hands. "I can't keep running these tests on you every time you get heartburn, Randy. The insurance company's giving me hell and for a good reason: THERE'S NOTHING WRONG WITH YOU! Go back to your office and sue people. No, wait. Take a vacation. Find a hobby that doesn't involve weapons or the martial arts or cussing at people on the phone."

"What about fucking computer games?" said Randall. "What about Tank Commander? That's a hobby. I love Tank Commander."

"More stress," said Bean. "Commanding tank platoons is not relaxing. I've seen you. You look like you're killing snakes with that joystick."

"Look, Howard. I'm not kidding this time. I think something happened to me."

"What? Your back again? I told you the bone scans, the X rays, the lumbar series, everything is negative. I know you read somewhere that cancer frequently presents with lower back pain. But you have been scanned to shreds and there's nothing in there, except spinelessness."

"It's not my back. It's not my heart."

"Your stomach again? Upper GI, lower GI, barium enema, ERCP.

You're clean! The ulcers aren't there yet. Give them a year or two more of this kind of behavior. They'll show up! Maybe you can *will* them into existence if you concentrate on it hard enough."

"It's not my stomach," said Randall.

"Your teeth? Did you quit wearing your bite block to bed? That's a perfect example of how you operate. First it was jaw pain. You swore it was metastatic CA of the mandible. We scanned you. Nothing. The jaw pain didn't go away. We sent you to a dentist, who sent you to an orthodontist. Remember why? Remember what the orthodontist said? 'The worst case of nocturnal grinding of the teeth that I have seen in my thirty-seven years of orthodontic practice.' His initial clinical impression was that you had gone over your molars with a double-cut machine file."

"My teeth are OK," Randall yelled. "I wear the goddamn bite block every night, OK?"

Bean dropped his feet to the floor and scooted himself foursquare in front of his friend.

"Randy, just once, listen to me. You are under tremendous stress. You work too hard. All day long, you cuss at people on the phone. Every time I call down there, you're swearing at someone on another line. Have you ever listened to yourself? Leave your Dictaphone on sometime. Studies have shown that subjects who cuss on the phone all day secrete excess bile, which makes them bilious, and distempered. Do you want to borrow my copy of *The Anatomy of Melancholy*? You've heard of the four humours? Get at least one. Get a sense of humor and go back to work. All this cussing of yours, all this swearing causes people to dislike you. It makes you splenetic, liverish, phlegmatic, choleric, and some would say just plain full of shit! This in turn causes more stress, and pretty soon stress hens are laying stress eggs everywhere and hatching more stress. Find something relaxing. I know you hate television. So go fishing!"

Planning fishing trips was a standing joke between two guys who didn't have time to order a rod out of a mail-order catalogue, much less squander a whole day boating in some mudhole with their cellular phones, pretending a twelve-pack of beer had relaxed them.

"I'm sure it's a symptom," said Randall. "Nothing like this has ever happened to me before."

"OK," said Howard, grabbing a notepad. "Are we going to do this? I guess we are. Where is the pain?"

"I wish it was pain," said Randall. "I don't have any pain. I saw something. I think it was some kind of hallucination. I'm almost positive I was awake when I saw it."

"Almost positive?" said Howard with a scowl. "Did this happen at night, and were you lying in bed grinding your teeth, with your eyes closed, cussing at people in your dreams?"

"I was awake," said Randall. "I think I woke up because I heard a loud sound. Then I saw a huge bat flying around the light fixture in my bedroom. Nobody else saw it, and we couldn't find the thing afterward."

"You don't need a doctor," said Howard. "You need an exterminator."

"We called one the next day," said Randall. "No bat. No evidence of bats in the attic. No evidence of entry."

Howard sighed mightily. "Randall, bats sometimes get into houses. We had a bat in our bedroom when we first moved into the house."

"How big was your bat?" asked Randall.

"How *big*? It was a bat. You know, like a mouse with wings."

Randall held his head in his hands. "See what I mean? The one I saw was like a *dog* with wings. Big. Huge!"

"You have a ceiling fan in that bedroom, don't you? That's it. You saw the blades of that fan, and the moonlight or maybe a night light made them look like bat wings."

Randall stared into his friend's eyes and swallowed. "Howard, I stood underneath four sixty-watt bulbs and stared this thing in the face," he said levelly. "This wasn't a shadow. This was vivid, you understand? It was as real as you and me. It was hideous, like something out of Africa."

Randall rubbed his face in his hands. "I'm almost afraid to go on about it, because what if it wasn't real? What if I *imagined* something that ugly? It had swollen lips with growths or tumors of some kind all over them. It had fingers in its wings. It had huge, black, wet eyes. I think I even saw my own reflection in them."

Howard's mouth opened.

"Can somebody imagine something so completely out of nothing?" pleaded Randall. "Is there such a thing as one sudden, vivid hallucination? For no reason, out of nowhere? Followed by a return to normal perception?"

"You've had no other visual disturbances?" asked Howard.

"No," said Randall quickly. "Well, I've only seen the one bat. But since that night," he said, his voice trailing off as he looked over Bean's head, "things have a certain shiny quality. Everything seems too . . . bright. Does that make sense? Things are more . . . colorful, or even . . . more beautiful," he said, staring off, briefly sampling and reporting on his perceptions. "Almost like I'm *seeing* more. Can the pupil of your eye get stuck open and admit too much light? So that things look brighter?"

Howard peered into his old friend's face.

"Listen, Howie, I need to forget about this thing. All I want is an explanation, and then I'll be able to put it behind me. Have you ever heard of anything like this before?"

"Perhaps," said Howard gravely. "Usually there is a history of mental illness, especially in your case," he added with a smile. "I'm ruling out schizophrenia and any psychotic episodes. It would be very unusual for someone to experience sudden, vivid hallucinations. Very unusual, but not unheard of."

"So you've heard of something like this happening to a normal person before!?" Randall cried.

"It's very rare," said Howard.

"What is it?" begged Randall. "What causes it?"

Howard shook his head, as if suddenly changing his mind. "Let's go with a wait-and-see plan here. It could be metabolic, it could be psychological. Let's just see if it happens again."

"No," said Randall. "Tell me what you were thinking."

Howard pulled out his appointment book. "Look, this is no different than anything else we've ever done, OK? I always send you to somebody else who actually does the testing, right? But this may, *may* be a neurological problem, so I'm sending you to one of our neurologists. Understand? I'm going to have you see Carolyn Gillis about this and let her decide how to handle it."

Randall was on his feet. "No way. Not in a million years. You think it's something neurological. You are going to tell me what it could be right now, and then we are doing the test before I leave."

Howard closed his appointment book.

"OK," he said, walking away from Randall and toward the door. "You're going to radiology for an MRI scan. Now."

Randall turned white and stared.

"Wait a minute," said Randall. "Why are we getting a scan?"

"What do you mean?" said Howard. "Why do we scan you twice a year? So we can tell you nothing's there. That's why."

"But you always tell me I don't *need* a scan," said Randall suspiciously. "You always emphatically tell me that I do not need a scan. You always say you'll give me your house if there is something there."

"There's nothing there," said Howard. "I just want to be able to *say* there's nothing there and have a scan back me up on it."

.

Forty-five minutes later, two technicians in white lab coats slid Randall's body into a long, smooth tube. Randall told himself it was harmless magnetic resonance imaging, but he suspected that these rays were relatives of carcinogenic electromagnetic fields from power lines, and he could feel deep tumors swelling in the glow of the radiation, like tulip bulbs sprouting in the sun's warmth.

Inside the tube, he felt like Ramses II, slid into his coffin prematurely. Then he heard a whirring sound and had the impression that he was an axle in a wheel, or a cylinder in an orrery or armillary sphere, and some great omniscient device was spinning around him like a turbine, seeing deep inside of him where nothing human had ever ventured, where light had never been, shaving him into cellophane planes to be studied on color computer monitors by scientists.

Back upstairs, he paced the examination room while trying to read an article about computer memory management. Bean came in with a pained expression on his face.

"What?" asked Randall.

"It's inconclusive," said Howard, looking away.

"That's a new one," said Randall with a catch in his voice. "What's inconclusive?"

"There's something there," Bean said, and stopped himself. "Let's be precise. There *may* be something there, but *if* it's there, we don't know what it is."

Gravity sat Randall back in his chair. He felt one skip in his chest, and then the pounding sent heat waves into his face.

"There is no reason to be alarmed," Bean said evenly, looking hard at Randall, "unless we do a different kind of scan and some more tests and actually identify something."

"But what did they see?" said Randall, aghast.

"The people in radiology call them UBOs. An unidentified bright object. The pictures of your MRI scan showed a bright intensity in the deep white matter. But it's nonspecific. They don't know what it is. It could be any number of things, so we will eliminate the possibilities, one by one, by doing specific tests."

"What kind of tests?"

"A CAT scan, an angiogram, a spinal tap, myelography, maybe a positron emission tomography scan . . . But those have to wait until tomorrow."

"Oh, great!" yelled Randall. "Now I can go home with a bright object in my head and lie in bed all night. What do they *think* it is? What do these things usually turn out to be? And how would this bright object make me see a bat?"

"If you were a patient," said Howard, "I wouldn't tell you any of this until I had all my data. The location of the anomaly could, *could* suggest peduncular hallucinosis."

"Which is?" asked Randall without breathing.

"Rare," said Howard. "Very rare. Isn't everything? But knowing how rare something is affords scant comfort once you have it. But you probably don't have it, OK?"

"What is it? What causes it? Is it a virus, or what?"

"The cardinal symptom of peduncular hallucinosis is spontaneous, brilliant hallucinations which present themselves in excruciating detail. It's caused by strokes or injury to the cerebral peduncles or the midbrain near the brain stem, which is where the radiologist saw the bright object in the deep white matter, the UBO."

"Stroke!" Randall said, a skipped beat followed by the trademark pounding. "I haven't had a stroke."

"I hope not," said Howard with a smile that fell just shy of consoling him.

"And I haven't been injured. Nothing's happened to me. No recent trauma."

"Injury is a broad medical term," Howard said. "Any midbrain dysfunction: encephalitis, lesions, craniopharyngioma . . . Injury means anything from an infarct to a blow to the head, to any lesion or . . . neoplasm."

"What?" said Randall. "What's that?"

"Infarct?"

"Neoplasm, you shithead," Randall shouted. "What's a fucking neoplasm? And that thing you said that had 'oma' on the end of it."

"A neoplasm is any new . . . growth," said Howard. "Look, don't let yourself run away with this thing. It's pure speculation until we get data . . ."

"New growth," said Randall, using the wind knocked out of his lungs. "You think I don't know what you're saying! Say it to me, you fuck!"

"Most new growths are benign," said Howard. "OK, not most. *Many* new growths are benign. Well, OK, in the brain, *some* new growths are benign."

Randall suddenly remembered something and started up, causing Howard to lean back in his chair.

"It was a joke you told. We were at a Christmas party," Randall said, staring over Howard's head as if memory were a mountain range spread out across the wall.

"Somebody was saying that their father had something wrong with his heart, and they were complaining because it was a heart attack but the cardiologist wouldn't use those words; he kept telling the family it was a coronary event. And they were like, what's a coronary event? And you defended the cardiologist. You told them how important it is to keep a cardiac patient calm. And afterward, we were riding home in your car, and you said, 'Can you believe those morons? They want their cardiologist to call a heart attack a heart attack. You can just see the patient,' you said. You were clutching your chest, and we were laughing. You said, 'Hey, Doc, what's happening to me?' And then you said, 'You? That's easy. I've seen it a thousand times. You're having a heart attack! But do stay calm.'

"That's what you're doing to me now, isn't it? It's a neospasm or whatever, not a tumor. It's pediculosis or something; it's not a stroke. What the fuck do you think it is? Talk to me!"

"You're panicking over the very small chance that you have a malignancy or a structural defect," said Bean. "I still think it's a fluke, one-time freak of the imagination caused by emotional stress. And the UBO is a false positive. That's what I think."

"*Please* don't say it's stress," said Randall, gritting his teeth and lunging at the neurologist. "Stress makes me high, do you understand? Stress makes me secrete testosterone and endorphins. It's brain candy, OK? I like to make myself sick on the stuff every day, understand?"

"I've known you since you were sixteen," said Howard. "I don't need your history. I'm just telling you that when you start getting older, as we all do, stress can do funny things to you."

"Sure," Randall sneered. "Very funny things. I guess that's why I'm laughing most of the day. It's a big conspiracy with you guys. You never really come clean with the patient. I know. I lie to my clients every day. The truth would kill them!"

"I told you exactly what the radiologist told me," said Bean.

"Sure," Randall said. "I'd love to hear what the radiologist said. 'Looks like a tumor, but the patient is a lawyer, so we better be damn sure before we use the C-word.' "

"He did not say that," argued Bean. "I told you what he said. I explained it using the same terms the people in radar use. It's an unidentified bright object on your MRI scan, and we won't know anything more until we do more tests."

"Right," said Randall with a roll of his eyeballs.

"OK," Howard said suddenly. "I can solve this. I'm calling my radiologist. You'll like him because he cusses a lot, and he has a string of bleeding ulcers to prove it. I'll see that you get unadulterated information from a real expert, the Randall Killigan of Radiology."

Howard pressed a button on one of the phones, raising an announcement of "Switchboard" from the speaker.

"Radar," said Howard.

A ringing tone was followed by another voice. "Radiology," it said.

"This is Bean. Is Ray still on?"

"One moment, please."

"Dr. Rheingold," said a voice.

"Ray, it's Bean. Patient name Killigan. The MRI you did for me this afternoon, what did you find?"

"Bean? I just talked to you half an hour ago. Go away. I told you, I'm dying down here. I'm supposed to be at my kid's birthday party. I already gave you the results."

"Tell them to me again," Howard said with a silent chuckle. "I lost my notes."

A heavy sigh filled the speaker with static. "Bean, I think you should do some research into an aberrant phenomenon you find in everybody except neurosurgeons. It's called *memory*. I read you the guy's MRI not forty-five minutes ago. It's a UBO. A hyperdense signal intensity on the T2-weighted phase in the deep white matter, right midbrain tegmentum and cerebral peduncle. OK? I dictated it. It's being typed up now. It'll be up there in an hour, so you can read it in case you forget it again. UBO, remember? An unidentified bright object. A bright intensity in the deep white matter, to be exact. And this is the Indiana University Medical Center. My staff and I are here to serve you. It was a pleasure working with you and your staff, and I thank you once again, as the referral of your case was most insurance, I mean, most interesting. I have to go, Bean, but I hope my staff and I have the opportunity to assist you in the future."

"One more thing," said Howard with a look at Randall. "Do you think it's a malignancy?"

"Do I what? Did I *say* malignancy? I said a bright intensity in the deep white matter. A UBO, an unidentified bright object, but maybe in your case it's an unidentified hopelessly dull and obtunded object: your brain, Bean."

"But *could it be* a malignancy?" asked Bean.

Silence filled the speaker.

"Bean, I suspect you are up there sitting in a room filled with sunlight, maybe looking out the window at some trees rustling in an autumn breeze. I've been down here in a dark room in the basement looking at ghosts of people's insides since five-thirty this morning. Is it the cocktail hour up there or what? The operative initial in the acronym UBO is U, for unidentified. Unidentified is a complex, obscure medical term that means we don't know what it is. It could be nothing. It could be an arteriovenous malformation, it could be an infarct, it could be a malignant tumor, it could be a benign meningioma, it could be a cyst, it could be a piece of shrapnel from a hand grenade thrown at My Lai, it could be a new computer chip from Intel which was implanted so the guy could use cellular technology without the inconvenience of lugging a phone around. I DON'T KNOW WHAT IT IS. Do you know why I don't know? BECAUSE IT'S UNIDENTIFIED, THAT'S WHY. It could be a napkin ring. It could be Caesar's remains, for all I know. No, wait, it's Brutus's remains, yeah, that's it. No, hold on, it's a bone fragment from the attending neurosurgeon's skull, dating back to a cerebral vascular accident that scattered good Dr. Bean's brains all over the examination room. Further tests may show that it's the Holy Grail. A skull series could detect a piece of the copper astrolabe of Shiraz for all I fucking know, OK?

"But let me take this opportunity to thank you once again for sending us this most interesting referral, and please be aware that our department has recently added a new positron emission tomography scan which will assist us in serving you with the latest technology. Please call me or my staff with more insurance, I mean, with more interesting cases like this one. Let me say thank you once again."

Howard turned off the speakerphone and looked at his friend.

"Dr. Rheingold's bedside manner is really quite professional," said Bean, "but I figured you wouldn't trust that. You heard him. There may be something there, but we don't know what it is. We have to do more tests."

(5)

Outside the restaurant, children took Boone and his drunken escort by their pockets and pulled them toward stalls and mats spread with wares along the sidewalks, where their mothers and sisters, dressed in headwraps and frocks, sold brochettes and pineapple slices, jewelry and flip-flops, groundnuts and fried plantain. White men smelling of alcohol had a way of spreading money around. Boone sensed the excitement in the children, who knew that if they could just strike the proper chord with these white big men, they would be showered in wealth. Sometimes these lugs would give three or four months' pay for a carving that wasn't worth a sick fowl.

Even after his gargantuan repast in the bar, Lewis grazed out of the food stalls, haggling with the ten-year-old girls over the price of their snacks.

"Ten-ten leone? Ih too dear, I tell you. You no go less me small?"

"Na all day long I been sell dem so, mastah. I no go less you small."

"Less me five-five leone," he said. "Let me have the sweet one dae foh five leone."

"Put two leone on top, krabbit man. You too dry eye."

After more unceremonious gorging, they staggered out to the roundabout in search of taxis. Buses, crammed full of black bodies hanging out of glassless windows, streamed out of the roundabouts, blaring African and reggae music; each bus had a young boy with one foot on the running board and a handhold on the luggage rack, calling out the destination of the transport: "Wilbahfoss! Wilbahfoss! Wilbahfoss!"

In the last century, explained Lewis, the mountain villages had two names, one English, one African, and when the villages became suburbs of Freetown, it was the English names that survived: Wilberforce, Leicester, Regent, Gloucester, Leopold, Charlotte, Bathurst, York.

They took a taxi to the Peace Corps rest house, high up in the foothills forested in palms and mahogany, with long, looping roads cut into steep grades, where the British had originally settled to escape the mosquitoes breeding in the low-lying marshes and the poverty breeding in the slums of East Street and Kroo town. When the British left, the European mining company officials, wealthy Lebanese merchants, Sierra Leonean government ministers, and American Embassy or USAID employees moved into the old British neighborhoods and built more whitewashed compounds, gated and fenced, manned by old Krio pas snoozing in their watchmen's hammocks, guarding the Audis and Mercedeses. As Lewis told it, these compounds were staffed with squadrons of servants tending the grounds, keeping house, and minding the children of people with money.

"Labor," he said, "is the cheapest commodity in the country. Cheaper than palm oil, cocoa, coffee, or any of the cash crops. You can hire adults who are willing to work twelve hours a day for the cost of their children's school fees. For a hundred bucks a month, a whole retinue of servants will follow you around, cooking your food, washing your clothes, raising your kids, guarding the house. If you start a company, you can pay good men with strong backs three dollars a day to hack out the tree stumps on your farm with a cutlass or sift through snake-infested swamp mud for diamonds. When the snakes and disease vectors wipe out the workforce, you go back to the villages and hire a new crew."

As they talked, the driver turned off the taxi's ignition and coasted down a sloping stretch of road, swerving to avoid pedestrians and stopped cars. At the bottom of the hill, he restarted the engine for the ascent up the other side.

"Saves gas," Lewis observed, "but it's hell on the brakes, even though brakes are only used as an absolute last resort. Once fuel is burned to get going, nobody wants to squander it all by applying brakes. Most taxis don't have brake pads. You take your life in your hands."

"White man no take life in hand," the driver suddenly said. "White man take drivah's life in hand, notoso?"

After a fifteen-minute journey up into the hills the taxi coasted into the driveway of the Peace Corps rest house. The driver must have been the brother of the one that had brought Boone in from the airport, for they both drove bargains better than they drove their cabs. The haggling started out with the driver at the equivalent of about $1.75 and Lewis at 40 cents. After five minutes of strenuous dickering, the fare was fluctuating between 90 cents and a $1.10, depending upon whether it was customary to charge more for an extra passenger, a bitterly contested sticking point. Finally, the parties insulted one another and broke off negotiations at 100 leones, or one American dollar. Boone resisted the temptation to ask about the going rate for a taxi from the airport.

"All that bickering for sixty cents?" Boone asked.

"It's the principle, not the money," Lewis said. "If you're white they try to stiff you every time."

The rest house sat atop a terrace crudely landscaped with stones, shrubbery, and rock gardens strewn under the trunks of splendid palms. The smell of salt arrived on a faint breeze that stirred the fronded shrubbery and opened winking blue peepholes to the sea. Gecko lizards crept in and out of crevices, their skins the texture of sandpaper and the color of stained glass, their heads atilt with an anxious curiosity, watching the white men with first one eye, then the other, before they disappeared in a blaze of changing colors that seemed to steam off of them and hang in the air like rainbows in a mist.

It was resort weather outside, but the interiors of the rest house offered nothing resembling resort accommodations. The walls were whitewashed concrete stained with rust from window grillworks and slashed screens. A ceiling fan wobbled along on ball bearings that rattled in their races. Upside-down geckos clung to the rafters, motionless, except for their tiny, panting lungs; their black eyes bulging and staring, as if they were interior domesticated gargoyles charged with scaring away intruders.

An old pa, fresh from a nap, greeted them and showed first Lewis, then Boone, to their rooms. Boone's featured a rancid mattress with no frame or box springs, draped in a torn mosquito net. Shredded curtains hung motionless over the window grilles. The fetor of the mattress hung in the air, suspended by humidity so dense it verged on condensation. *Nothing half as nice as the Hotel Berlioz,* he thought, longing for the crisp October mornings he had spent idling among the slumbering corpses.

During the night, he heard taps on the door and girlish voices. "Peace Koh, you want friend? Oo, Peace Koh, you want friend?"

Lewis must have let them in. A skinny girl in a grimy rayon dress appeared at Boone's bedside.

"Peace Koh," she said. "You want friend?"

Her eyes shone in the crooked hollows of her face. Her hair was ratted into tufts clipped with plastic red barrettes.

"No," he said, watching her sit on the side of his bed.

"Whay you wife?" the woman asked.

"I don't have a wife."

"You no get wife? Me, I no get man. I go want make you me friend."

Her left cheekbone must have been broken at one time, along with her nose. On one side of her throat was a raised scar the size and color of a leech. He glanced from her shining eyes to the neckline of the dress, where he could see empty breasts folded and drooping under her hollow clavicle.

"I don't want a friend," said Boone.

She looked down where his eyes had been and touched her scar. "Dirty water self can out fire," she said.

"What?" said Boone, embarrassed that she had so easily seen him appraising her.

"Dirty water self can out fire," she repeated.

He turned his head away from her on the pillow. "I don't know what that means," he said. "I have no money."

He heard giggling from the other room, then hollering from Lewis and laughter from Lewis's consort.

"It's a Krio proverb," Lewis yelled. "Dirty water itself can put out a fire. Make do with what you have. Something is better than nothing. You can't always get what you want. You na gentry man," he said, lapsing into Krio and giggling with his companion. "You get plenty money, now share am, and sex dat sweeteye gal. Keep your raincoat on, though, boy, there's no telling what they got."

She lifted the mosquito net and curled up next to him.

He could still hear Lewis chortling through the wall. "Gentry man say he no get money. Na lie! Botobata!"

"Botobata," Lewis's companion repeated with a snicker.

"What's botobata?" Boone asked wearily.

"Nonsense!" yelled Lewis. "Bullshit! Hogwash! Horsefeathers! Bibble-babble! Twiddle-twaddle! Gibble-gabble! Skimble-skamble! Botobata!"

More laughter.

"Gentry man no get money," Lewis's companion said, sucking her teeth and giggling. "Ay, bo, I no believe ahm. Botobata!"

"Malarkey!" said Lewis. "Pishposh! Bunkum! Piffle! Humbug! Hokum! Hooey! Bosh! Moonshine! Bushwa! Flapdoodle! Fiddle-deedee!"

A breathless pause came through the wall. "Botobata!" they both hollered, pealing laughter and thumping the mattress.

Five minutes later, Boone hazarded a peek over his shoulder and found his partner sleeping. After a while, he heard Lewis grunting through the wall.

"Yeah," he said. "That's fine-O. I like dat too much. Beaucoup bread and jam dae foh you na morning."

At dawn, Boone watched an old pa in ragged shorts and a safari jacket set out a tray of bread, a bowl of margarine, some jelly, and a pot of coffee. Upon closer inspection, the bread was stale and rimed with mold, the margarine was lard dyed yellow, the jelly was see-through pink pectin, and the coffee was a pot of boiled water with a couple measures of coffee grounds stirred into it. The geckos were winding up a night of devouring insects, killing off a few strays before retiring again to the eaves. Boone left the sleeping woman and went out to a table in the common area, where he dipped stale bread into hot brown water.

After a few minutes, she appeared at his elbow, looking even skinnier by day.

"You keep something for me?" she said, putting out her hand. "I no get money."

Boone gave her two hundred leones. She put one piece of bread in her pocket and another in her mouth and left.

In the shower, the hot and cold taps both delivered freezing cold water. He clenched his teeth and got out before he had finished washing.

After Boone emerged, Lewis went in, and spent fifteen minutes under the arctic spray contentedly singing "Roland the Headless Thompson Gunner," by Warren Zevon.

After breakfast, a taxi took them back into Freetown and dropped them at the massive cotton tree. Lewis advised that in this part of the world the cotton tree was a landmark, that it had been a land-mark since the Portuguese had landed, and that slaves had been traded in the shade of its limbs. Then he gave his charge a sly look, and asked, "What do you think of all the capes hanging from the limbs? Aren't they beautiful?"

"Right," said Boone. "Capes."

"Well den," Lewis said with a laugh, "you no get four eye."

They went to a lorry park next to an open-air market, where they were promptly set upon by hordes of children trying to sell them everything from cakes and chewing gum to jewelry, fingernail clippers, and key rings.

"Do you have a wallet?" Lewis asked.

"Money belt," said Boone.

"Congratulations. Experienced travelers use money belts; tourists with wallets get tiefed by the Tiefmahn," said Lewis, exaggerating his Krio. "The best pickpockets in the world live in Sierra Leone. I had a billfold stolen out of a pair of button-down Army pants. Women Volunteers have had money taken from their bras in the middle of the market. If you sleep in a room with bars on the windows, they'll steal your shirt with a fishing pole and a hook. Thieves are celeb-rities, famous for their daring and cunning, as long as they don't get caught. God help them if they get caught."

"What happens to them if they get caught?"

"It ain't pretty," said Lewis. "It makes Shirley Jackson's 'The Lottery' look like high tea."

The *podah-podah* for Pujehun was a small Japanese pickup, with a sheet-metal canopy and a luggage rack over a truck bed fitted out with wooden benches. Bob Marley's portrait was daubed on each door, and painted on the flap of the canopy overhead were the words LIVELY UP YOUSELF. The tires were as smooth as the dirt road, and Boone saw no hope for friction between the two surfaces.

Lewis got into a rhubarb with the driver, who had tried to charge them double. Lewis maintained it was because they were white; the driver pleaded that he had just made an innocent mistake. The driver gave a signal, and the loading process began. Boone followed several Africans onto the sheltered truck bed and took a seat on a wooden bench worn as smooth as a bone.

He discovered a latent claustrophobia as the driver escorted ten or twelve more adults—with as many children, goats, and chickens—into the lorry and onto the benches. The women wore tie-dyed gara cloths and headwraps. The children wore nothing, except small leather pouches of "medicine" tied to their arms and waists with strings. Some of them had huge umbilical hernias, which sprouted from their navels like bananas.

After the humans were loaded, in came bundles of hairy cassava roots, baskets of kola nuts, burlap bags, a woven cage containing two chickens ("fowl," the woman said, as she passed them to Boone, who relayed them on into the truck bed), another goat (this one had busted horns, was afflicted with mange, and had a sightless white eye bulging out of its socket), a basket of dried fish ("bonga"), a jug of petrol, a gallon of orange palm oil, a rack of Guinness stout bottles filled with kerosene and stoppered with waxed paper, several fifty-pound bags of rice, a case of motor oil, a roll of steel screen, stewpots filled with more dried fish, a bolt of country cloth, another jug of palm oil, a fardel of unknown shrubbery, a box of tools, a bald spare tire worn through to the fabric on one rim, more peekins passed from hand to hand until claimed by relatives, four fence posts, a spool of baling wire, a bag of cement, a rusted coffeepot stuffed with twine, a satchel of plastic thongs, and three dead chickens ("dead fowl") bound to a stick by their feet.

No sooner had all the bodies and goods been packed into the back of the lorry than in came a stream of soft bundles and bags, which the occupants wedged into every available crevice, until the lorry was packed as tightly as a golf ball. If everyone took a deep breath simultaneously, Boone thought, the ribs of the canopy would buckle like tin.

Meanwhile, the luggage rack on top was stacked eight feet high with bags of rice and peanuts, baskets of cocoa beans, more bolts of country cloth, and bundles of clothing and palm raffia. Young boys—"bobos," Lewis called them—ranging in age from ten to sixteen, helped load the lorry in exchange for reduced fare and a perch high atop the mounded luggage racks. Boone wondered if it might be safer on top, for he could then at least jump off if the thing tipped over.

The passengers bore the prolonged loading process with patience. An older woman engaged Lewis in an exchange which included a nod of her head in Boone's direction. Boone could make out the words *"poo-mui,"* "belly," "run," and "peekin," after which the passenger compartment—Lewis included—erupted in laughter.

"What happened?" Boone asked, feeling his rib cage displace several parcels when he drew a speaking breath.

"She says she hopes you aren't another *poo-mui* with dysentery whose belly runs like a small peekin's, or else we'll be stopping and unloading all morning. Apparently the last *poo-mui* she rode with had to get out every five miles to trot into the bush and let his belly run."

Boone imagined the ordeal of unpacking the entire rear of the lorry and shifting the other passengers enough to create an opening large enough for an adult to exit; he shuddered at the magnitude of the task and the logistics of packing and repacking the three-dimensional jigsaw puzzle of cargo pieces.

"She says white men have the bellies of children, and that they are constantly sick with fever, runny belly, or headache. She wants to know if white people lie in bed sick all day in the land of *Poo*, and how they manage to stay so sick when they have so many powerful medicines and magical machines."

Once on the road, the passengers fell into a stupor induced by the concurrent forces of heat, overcrowding, bone shock, sweat, noise, and the odors of humans and animals. Every hill was a laborious fifteen-mile-per-hour ascent, during which the two-liter aluminum engine surged and groaned with no result other than a redoubling of the oily smoke wafting back into the ascending lorry. The ensuing descent was punctuated by the shrill whinny of padless brakes, the thud of ruts in the truck bed, and the creaking of welded joints in the canopy overhead. Each time the lorry bobbed and swayed up onto two wheels, the bobos atop the mountain of parcels screamed with terror and delight.

By midday, the inside of the *podah-podah* was a hothouse of sweating flesh. The humans and animals instinctively realized that the environment was unbearable and responded by lapsing into artificial comas. Everyone apparently had mastered the art of self-hypnosis, even Boone's Peace Corps escort. Boone tried it in spurts, but came to each time a child screamed or an animal defecated on the truck bed.

Sweat streamed into his lap, evaporated, and clung to him. The ruts in the laterite road were transmitted without interruption to the bones of his pelvis, as if the lorry's bench had been bolted directly to the axle. His shins suddenly broke out in a ferocious itch: the impulse to gouge them was so powerful that his fingernails would have produced an immediate bloodletting, except that he was pinioned on either side by sweating Africans.

The goat with the mooneye wormed his head up between the cage of fowls and a burlap bag and brayed at Boone, studying the white man with its blank eye.

The eye—white as milk, but swirling with the colors of a pearl—mesmerized him. The goat blinked, and a pale blue lid slid over the mooneye. As Boone stared through his misery, the eye acquired a wicked gleam, and the goat's braying became urgent and expressive, almost as phatic as human speech. In a trance of heat exhaustion and misery, Boone stared into the swollen, chatoyant eyeball and listened to the brays of the goat, as if the eye, or the goat, or an evil spirit within the goat was speaking to him in tongues, telling him in an ancient, arcane language: *You're an animal just like me*, the goat said. *You used to eat off vinyl countertops in an air-conditioned kitchen. Not anymore. Welcome to Wild Kingdom, white boy. Stick around. Maybe we can fix you up with an eye that looks just like mine.*

The goat brayed satanically, then took to butting children in an effort to vent misery with its head. A boy squatting in the center of the lorry bed scolded the goat, then casually upended it and tied its hooves together with cords. The child scowled, then parted a forest of human legs and shoved the goat under a bench.

Through the ribs of the lorry's canopy, Boone saw another planet consisting of a laterite road dropped like a thread in a sea of chlorophyll. Every half hour or so, the driver and the three bobos riding up front yelled, "Beef! Beef!" and swerved violently on the rutted highway, as knee-high animals scurried from under the wheels of the *podah-podah* and into the bush. These were bush deer the size of cocker spaniels, called duikers, or the fat rodents called cutting grass. Boone thought the driver was swerving to avoid the animals. Until one time the cry of "Beef!" went up and the axle welded to Boone's pelvis registered a soft thump. The driver pulled over, ran back along the highway, and came back swinging the carcass of a bush deer aloft and shouting jubilantly, "Beef!" One of the bobos dismounted, bound the hind legs, and handed the carcass aloft.

At the roadside villages, Boone saw black skin and brown dirt, structures made out of mud and dead vegetable matter, hemmed in on all sides by impenetrable green. The bodies had risen up out of the earth, cleared some of the green away, and built huts with zinc-pan roofs to live in. Other than the ubiquitous green of the bush, color appeared only in clothing. Gara cloths, robes, headwraps, and the lappas used to bind children to the backs of women provided a tie-dyed riot of colors and patterns.

After nine hours, Boone's joints locked up and blood no longer made it below his waist. Just before sunset, Lewis hollered ahead through the windowless cab and the lorry slowed.

"Get out at the junction," Lewis said. "Walk up the dirt path about a mile. You'll see people coming in from the farms. When you see them, say, 'Cusheo, paddy.' Hello, friend."

Boone stifled the urge to panic. "I thought you were coming with me."

"If you show up with me," Lewis advised, "Sisay might tell us both to get lost. If you show up alone and helpless and tell him you're a friend of Michael Killigan, he will never turn you out. Don't mention my name," he added. "You'll have an easier time of it."

"Cusheo, paddy," Boone repeated.

"Cusheo!" the passengers sang out with a laugh. "How de body?"

"Good," said Lewis. "After that, say, 'I no sabby talk Krio. I want make you show me usai dat white Mende man, Aruna Sisay, dae.' "

Boone repeated the words and jumbled them. The lorry riders laughed uproariously.

"How about just 'Usai Aruna Sisay,' " Lewis said. " 'Usai' means 'which side' or 'where.' If you need a place to stay, come back to this junction in the morning and wait for a *podah-podah* going south. Tell the driver you want to go to Pujehun."

Lewis spoke briefly to one of the women.

"You just bought that speckled fowl in the wicker cage to your right," Lewis said. "You also bought three kola nuts. When you get out, give her four hundred leones and take the fowl and the kola nuts to Aruna Sisay as gifts. Don't ever go to an African's house without bringing a present with you."

At the junction, the bobos opened a hole in the passenger compartment big enough to disgorge the *poo-mui*. His legs barely functioned, but he managed to pay the woman, and was handed the caged fowl and three smooth, pinkish, kidney-shaped kola nuts the size of throwing rocks. The bobos handed down his backpack. The vulture-eyed goat crawked a goodbye from under the bench, and the passengers cried, "Cusheo, paddy!"

As the *podah-podah* pulled away, Lewis hollered out, "Stay in the village and don't go in the bush!"

Boone stooped to gather his backpack and gifts and jumped when he heard the sound of a human voice.

"Meestah West fall," the voice said, splitting Boone's name in two.

A small boy stood no more than fifteen feet from him. Either Boone had missed seeing the boy's approach, which was unlikely given the distance from the road to the bush path, or the boy had appeared like a hallucination.

He looked just shy of ten years. The fly of his dusty shorts had been sewn shut, and the waist puckered on each side where his belt loops had been tied together to take in the slack. One bare foot, gray with dust, stood on the other, and one skinny arm flopped over the top of his head dangling fingers that lazily scratched an ear. He twisted from side to side without moving his stacked feet. As soon as Boone looked into his big eyes, he looked away.

"Meestah West fall," the boy said again.

Boone was dumbfounded.

"Meestah Aruna say come," the boy said.

Before Boone could respond, the boy folded his legs into a squat, crawled under the backpack, and stood up with it balancing on his head.

"I'll carry that," Boone protested. "It's too big for you." But the boy was already walking away from him, his upper body perfectly steady under the pack, while his skinny legs crept up a rutted ascending path into the bush.

In short order, the path became a tunnel through a bower fronded with palm trees and strung with hairy vines the thickness of suspension cables. The humidity absorbed all ambient sound, as in a carpeted room with heavy drapes, leaving only the sough of their lungs and the thud of their feet on the earth. The screech and chatter of birds and animals seemed always just ahead of them, until Boone realized that the creatures were everywhere, and they simply fell silent in the bow wave and wake of the passing human disturbance. Every so often, he heard delicate rustling behind the curtain of bush, but he followed the lead of his diminutive guide and ignored it.

After a steady fifteen-minute walk, they met women and children straggling in from the farms on intersecting footpaths. Boone acquired an entourage of peekins carrying platters and buckets on their heads, crying, "*Poo-mui! Poo-mui!*" in high-pitched voices. When he lifted his arm to wave hello to them, they sagged behind the skirts of women and giggled in terror. When he dropped his arm and resumed walking, he could hear them creeping up behind him, daring one another to touch him.

At last the tunnel opened into a wide clearing surrounded by towering palms. Mud huts with thatched roofs and small houses of whitewashed concrete huddled in groups around dusty, interlocking common areas.

The boy bobbed gracefully up and down under the backpack and led Boone into a series of dirt courtyards. A woman wrapped in a lappa pounded rice in a mortar carved from a stump. Goats and chickens scattered before them, and children gathered to watch the parade pass.

As Boone entered the first courtyard, rock music greeted his ears, but he was unable to localize the source in the scramble of huts. Before he could name the tune, an orange Frisbee sailed over a cluster of thatched roofs, and a teenager in a University of Wisconsin T-shirt emerged from an adjoining courtyard in pursuit. The kid outran the Frisbee and caught it six inches off the ground, then executed a brilliant backhand return toss over the thatched roofs.

Boone caught glimpses of the adjoining courtyards through the passageways between huts. The music grew louder as he followed his guide between two wattle-and-daub compounds and emerged into a another sunny courtyard, where a huge boom box was mounted on a stump. In the middle of the village of Nymuhun, Sierra Leone, twenty miles southeast of Bo, in equatorial West Africa, Boone heard the Grateful Dead slip into the refrain to "Cumberland Blues."

He had trouble integrating Jerry Garcia's banjo licks with the scene in the courtyard, where he nearly fell over a naked child wearing leather amulets and chasing chickens off a patch of cement where cocoa beans were drying in the sun. Toothless old mas in headties stared out at him from the shadows of mud verandas. A mother suckled an infant on a stoop, while another child screamed in the dust at her feet.

His guide walked past the boom box and onto the veranda of an L-shaped house on the far side of the courtyard. One whitewashed wall of the L had been frescoed with an exact replica of the skeleton crowned with roses from the Grateful Dead's *Skull & Roses* album, another contained an equally precise rendering of the wreath of roses from *American Beauty*. Over a red door was a net with a piece of bamboo cane, and under it, in bold black letters: "Deadheads Unite."

The red door opened and a hairy blond man in a University of Wisconsin T-shirt, madras Bermuda shorts, and running shoes strolled out onto the veranda with his hands in his pockets. His clothes wafted on a gaunt frame, which would have seemed almost unhealthy but for the light in his eyes, the color in his cheeks, and the musculature evident in his torso. A formidable necklace of cowrie shells, animal teeth, and bones depended from his neck, along with a leather pouch, tightly lashed with a thong. On the skin of each of his temples were fan arrangements of short incisions, tribal markings opening outward in the direction of vision.

"Excuse me," Boone said, "I'm looking for the University of Wisconsin."

"We are no longer affiliated with that institution," the man said with a smile and a twinkle of blue eyes behind rimless granny glasses.

"Boone Westfall," said Boone, taking the man's hand.

"Aruna Sisay," said the man. "We will, however, proudly display any logo or message on one hundred percent cotton T-shirts, as long as the T-shirts are provided free of charge," he added, glancing down at his shirt.

"These are for you," Boone said, holding out the caged fowl and the kola nuts.

"Right hand only," Sisay said, making an unpleasant face and looking at the kola nuts in Boone's left hand.

"What?" asked Boone, setting the cage down and transferring the nuts to his right hand.

"Gift giving is important, but the first thing to remember is that it's done with the right hand. In this part of the world, your left hand is used for one thing, cleaning yourself after using the latrine. Do not touch people with your left hand. Do not touch your mouth, face, or any utensils with your left hand."

Boone presented first the fowl, then the kola nuts, thinking that he didn't mind going through this hand ritual once because it was kind of cute, but it wasn't something he intended to make a point of remembering for the duration of his stay.

"If you shake hands with an elder or an important person, you may grasp your right wrist with your left hand," he added. "It's a gesture of respect, kind of like a double handshake."

Clusters of children were forming in the perimeters of the courtyard, and whispers of *poo-mui* were rising to a chant.

"Let's hide inside until dusk," said Sisay, motioning Boone toward the compound. "First, your room," he said, opening a door into a separate room with one wall common to the compound, "at least for tonight."

Inside was a dark rectangle with a roof over low rafters. A square, screenless window with hooked shutters opened onto the courtyard. A tick mattress ran the length of the end wall, and a table with a hurricane lamp occupied most of the common wall, leaving just enough space for the two of them to turn around and exit.

A separate door led from the veranda to the main living area—behind the skull and roses wall—where he found clean, modest quarters fitted out as a study or a library, but with a bed and cane chairs included and a shelf with eating utensils.

"I have wives and children," said Sisay, "but they stay in another compound."

Boone politely ignored the uxorial plural and toured the premises instead. "Books," he said, peering around a corner and into a darkened room fitted out with long, crowded shelves. "Lots of them." As his eyes grew accustomed to the shadows, he could make out the moldering bindings of dead volumes. The spines of the hardbacks were blighted with mildew, and the paperbacks were clumps of stained pulp with rounded edges.

"My books have all rotted, or been eaten by rats and cockroaches," Sisay said. "I can't say I miss them. You'll find the rest of them in the latrine, and feel free to use them. I do. When I want a good story, I go out to the baffa at night and watch the storytellers perform. They tell better stories than the ones you find embalmed in print. Even the same story is different every time, because it's told by a different person, or the crowd is in a different mood. The audience, you see, assists in the telling of the tale."

"Lots of anthropology," Boone said, still looking over the shelves and making out a few of the titles.

"I was a graduate student," Sisay said. "I came here to study the Mende tribe of Sierra Leone." He gestured toward one of the cane chairs for Boone, then took a seat for himself in the lotus position on the earthen floor. "I gave up on anthropology quite a while ago. As you'll soon discover, it is impossible for a white man to study the Mende people, because they are constantly absorbed in studying him. Someday I may return to America and study the savage, violent, unspeakably greedy people who live there, but first I have to work up the courage."

Boone could not tell where Sisay's self-mockery ended and his bemusement with the rest of the world began.

Sisay fingered the pouch around his neck. "I turned my Claude Lévi-Strauss books over to the villagers some years ago. Portions of *Structural Anthropology* turned up as far away as Sulima beach, which borders on Liberia, where the pages are still being used and reused to wrap five-cent orders of peanuts, or "groundnuts," as they are called in Salone. A mori man—a kind of textual medicine man—up in Kenema folds individual pages from Lévi-Strauss's *Totemism* into compact squares, sews them into leather pouches, and attaches them around the waists, wrists, and ankles of peekins to protect them from witches who transform themselves into fruit bats, owls, and boa constrictors at night and swallow the limbs of infants, causing paralysis. You probably thought polio was caused by a virus," he said with an arid smile.

"The Fula man out on the highway wraps kola nuts in pages from *A View from Afar. Nothing* is thrown away. There's no garbage problem, because there is no garbage. Nothing is wasted here, except people. Only *poo-muis* throw things away. And if a *poo-mui* throws a page of a book away after eating his groundnuts, I can promise you that a villager will be two steps behind him to retrieve the precious paper to wrap something else in."

Boone's impatience surfaced, and he decided to at least begin the task of bringing this oddball's attention to the problem at hand. "I'm really here to . . ." Boone began.

"I know why you're here," Sisay said. "You're looking for Lamin Kaikai. You went to the American Embassy or the Peace Corps. They probably told you that the entire country is a mess, and the development agencies and embassies know even less than usual about what's going on out in the bush. They told you the gangsters from Liberia are making incursions into the south of Sierra Leone, and the country is swarming with refugees and mercenaries. They told you what elections mean in this country. They may even have told you about our section chief, Idrissa Moiwo, his electioneering methods, and his bitter struggle to wrest the Paramount Chieftaincy from Chief Kabba Lundo, who has held the office for fifty years. Then somebody told you about me. But it had to be somebody who lives in the bush, because all the white people in Freetown who have heard about me think I'm some kind of deviant or lunatic. That leaves Volunteers, and it had to be a Volunteer who's been here long enough to know that the Western relief organizations and government agencies don't know anything about the bush. Probably somebody whose tour is almost up. Probably somebody from Bo District or Pujehun District, where they'd hear about me. I'm gonna guess Sam Lewis out of Pujehun, or Kent Garrison out of Bo. No, not Garrison, he'd have sent you to his buddy who's the Speaker for the Paramount Chief in the district. It was Lewis, and he didn't come with you because he knew I wouldn't let him stay here for more than five minutes. He told you I knew your friend and that I spoke Mende."

"The white Mende man," Boone said. "He said you might have information that the Peace Corps and the government can't get. Native information."

"Information is a white word," Sisay said. "You can get information at the U.S. Embassy from overfed white guys wearing suits and sitting in front of computer screens. An African would correctly conclude that the *poo-muis* in the embassy know about only one thing: computer screens. If you can get past the few proud galoots with shaved heads who stand in the bulletproof booths and operate the buzz-bolt locks, you'll be seen by someone with information."

Boone watched Sisay sneering in the dim light and realized he was in the keeping of another misanthrope. Lewis hated Africans. This guy hated Americans, which didn't strike him as a characteristic that would be useful in finding his buddy.

"You don't need information. You need to *know*. You need *vision*. You don't come into that kind of knowledge by dropping in for a week and asking a few questions. When you need to know something in this part of Africa, you hire a looking-around man," he said, pronouncing it in Krio with a hard "g" as "looking-ground mahn." "A diviner," he continued, "one part priest, one part psychiatrist, and one part fortune teller. How do you think I knew you were coming?" he asked with a grin.

"A crystal ball, I suppose," said Boone.

Sisay shook his head. "Stones. The looking-around man threw stones, and the stones said you were coming."

"I'll bite," said Boone. "Where does one find a looking-around man?" He decided to humor this character, privately concluding that Sisay had eaten acid one time too many back in his Grateful Dead days.

"You pay money," said Sisay. "You have to try them out until you find one who's not a charlatan and who knows what he's doing. One simple test is to hide one of your belongings in a secret place where it will be difficult to find. Then tell the looking-around man to find it for you. Some of them can tell you where it is without even leaving the room, but they are expensive. It also takes time, because you have to bring the good ones in from up-country, which means you have to send a messenger and wait for a reply, and then wait for your appointment. It's called West African Internal Time, also known by its acronym: WAIT. Over here, you don't kill time, it kills you. Especially if you're a *poo-mui*."

"A white person," Boone said.

Sisay went over to a covered pail and removed the lid. He ladled water into two cups and handed one to Boone.

"That's one translation," said Sisay. "But then you would be hard put to explain why the Mende call African-American Volunteers *poo-muis* and are uncharacteristically aloof toward them. When the tours of African-Americans come over here wearing their kente cloths and clutching a copy of *Roots*, they are warmly received as long-lost brothers and sisters, as long as they stay in Freetown and meet with Sierra Leoneans from the Ministry of Culture. If they come out here to the villages, they will be coolly received as *poo-muis* in black skins. The loneliest people you will meet in Sierra Leone are African-American Volunteers stationed in villages.

"*Poo* means 'white' or 'modern' or 'European,' but it's more of a personality trait than a color. *Mui* means 'person.' But some say that in old or 'deep' Mende, *pu* means 'to add' or 'to acquire,' which is what Americans and Europeans do best. So some would translate *poo-mui* as 'greedy person' or maybe 'selfish person.' To the Mende, you and I are *poo-muis*. We constantly and effortlessly *acquire* new and better possessions, presumably because we have access to powerful medicines."

Here was a guy who left his calling back in the States, thought

Boone. *How many of these lectures did he have and what good could possibly come from them?*

"My guess is that you have more money in traveler's checks right now than most of these people will earn and spend in their entire lives."

Great, thought Boone. *Now he's going to ask me how much money I have.*

"You must imagine how far your eyes would bug out of your head if someone came to visit you in America and pulled more cash out of his billfold than you make in three years."

It might not be much money at all depending on how many years I have to listen to speeches about the desperate poverty of the Mende people.

"That's how these people feel when they hear about white people buying plane tickets for seven hundred dollars. It's inconceivable. Three years' salary for a plane ticket! Even the diamond diggers average only the equivalent of about three or four hundred dollars a year, and they are wealthy indeed."

Sisay drank from his cup; Boone stared down at his.

"Is the water . . . safe?" asked Boone.

"No," said Sisay, "but there's nothing you can do about it. Use caution for the first couple of weeks. You'll get sick four or five times, you'll have runny belly for a month or two, and then you and the parasites will settle down in a happy symbiosis."

"Months? I don't plan on being here for months," Boone said, thinking that he would be lucky to live a month if he had to stay in a place like this.

"Just WAIT and see," said Sisay with a grin. "You may stay at my place for one or two nights, but if you plan to stay any longer, arrangements will have to be made."

Boone quickly protested that he did not wish to inconvenience Sisay in any way.

Sisay dismissed him with a wave of his hand. "I'm not talking about convenience," he said. "If you decide to stay here for any length of time you will need a grandfather and a name."

"A grandfather?" Boone asked.

"And an African name," Sisay said. "As you'll soon discover, you are now part of a community. You'll spend very little time alone, and the rest of the time, everyone in the village will be in your business, and you will be in theirs."

Joining a family and whiling the days away in enforced conviviality with smiling natives did not quite fit in with what he wanted to accomplish during his stay, but Boone wondered if joining a family would permit him to enlist more help from his "relatives."

"Without a name and a grandfather, you don't really have a social identity. The villagers have no frame of reference for you. Whose son are you? Who is responsible for you? To whom should they address their compliments or complaints about you? Without a family, you are just an unsettling enigma, rolling around like a stray white chess piece in a game of checkers. It will take you at least two months to find your friend," he said, "unless he shows up of his own accord. I'll set up the naming ceremony."

No need to make any decisions in these parts, thought Boone. *This mother hen will do it for me, if I let him.*

"What makes you think it will take so long?" asked Boone. "Do you have some idea of what happened?"

"I'm not sure what happened," Sisay said, "but in this country it's a safe bet that it's either witchcraft or politics, or, more likely, it's both. Not only is there trouble in the south with the Liberian rebels making incursions into the country, it's also election time. During elections, the entire country erupts in anxiety, and sometimes violence, at the prospect of power changing hands. Certain secret societies take measures to obtain *power*, a sort of palpable essence, which can be accumulated and wielded by medicine men. Members of these secret and illegal societies—the Baboon Society or the Leopard Society—supposedly transform themselves into animals—Baboon Men or Leopard Men—then go in search of victims for sacrifice. Powerful charms and fetishes are made from the flesh of human victims. But the *medicine* needs to be 'replenished,' or 'fed,' or it loses its potency. It's been going on since the last century, and probably even before that. The British cleaned house every ten years or so by holding Leopard and Baboon trials in Freetown and hanging all the society members from public gallows. On top of that, during elections, the practice of witchcraft rises to a fever pitch, because everyone is putting swears on each other to obtain an advantage over their political enemies. Once a swear is let loose and its intended victim hears about it, a counter-swear must be effected as protection, and so on."

LSD, thought Boone. *Lots of LSD followed by lots of malarial delusions. After that, he probably fell in love with a woman who believes in all this voodoo. Somebody or something had damaged the guy's psyche.*

Boone finally blinked, opened his mouth, and produced a question. "People . . . *believe* in this stuff?"

"Of course," Sisay said.

"And people openly practice witchcraft?"

"Witchcraft is prevalent," said Sisay, "but it is technically illegal. People do, however, openly protect themselves from witches, which is legal . . . and prudent."

He pointed toward the rafters over the door to the veranda, where Boone saw a small red net spread neatly above the lintel with a strip of bamboo cane suspended in the webbing.

"The net is called *kondo-bomei*, witch net; it will catch any witch that tries to enter the house. The bamboo is called *kondo-gbandei*, witch gun; it will shoot the witch and kill it."

"You believe in that?" Boone asked with a half laugh.

"I don't believe in anything," said Sisay with absolute conviction. "I'm only interested in results. You don't have to worry about *kondo-gbandei*," he said, pointing at the red net and giving Boone a chilly smile, "unless you are a witch."

"Right," said Boone, "I'm a witch," feeling Sisay's eyes on him and not liking it, "and you're Merlin, I suppose."

"White people usually want to know if witchcraft is *true*," he said. "Whatever that means. They think science is somehow *true*. They forget that the West puts all of its faith in science, not because it is true, but because it *works*. Who cares if science is true, so long as it makes your car go and heats your house? Who cares if witchcraft is true, so long as it destroys your enemies and protects your crops? I assure you that in this country witchcraft works."

"So Killigan's been abducted by politicians or witches, is that it?"

"I said witchcraft, politics, or both," said Sisay. "And you're not drinking your water."

Boone stared into his cup. "No matter how long it takes to find Killigan, I think I'll stay with my water tablets," he said.

"You'll have a problem there," said Sisay. "I don't care what you do in my house, but you are going to be traveling about. You will be staying with others. It would be the height of bad manners to refuse water from your hosts. A Mende man simply will not understand. If you insist on purifying your water in another village, you will be implying that you believe their water has been tainted by witchcraft, which, as we all know, is the most common cause of waterborne diseases. Imagine how you would feel if you invited people over to your house in America for dinner, and they asked you if they could purify your food before eating it."

"Well, what do you expect me to do?" asked Boone. "Get sick on purpose?"

Sisay's eyes traveled the length of Boone's frame. "You have plenty of money. You should have no trouble feeding yourself and a colony of parasites, if they should move in. You could stand to lose a little weight anyway. If you're going to travel through parts of the world where people are starving to death, don't you think it's a bit unseemly to be overweight? I mean, how does it feel walking around in this country where starvation gnaws on everyone's elbow, knowing that you come from a country full of fat people trying to lose weight? I can think of even better reasons to lose weight. Over there in Liberia, after the rebel factions took power, they shot all the fat people on the assumption that anybody fat must have been working for the government. Probably a safe assumption in this part of the world."

Boone examined his stomach. "I had my insurance updated before I left America. I was exactly normal for my height."

"Normal back there is overfed over here," he said dismissively. "As for Killigan's whereabouts, there's another possibility we haven't discussed. I know you came here to find Michael Killigan, but have you wondered whether he wants to be found?"

"Meaning?" said Boone. "He would be hiding?"

"If he really wanted to disappear, there are plenty of places you can only get to by bush path, parts of the country where people still scream and run away when they see a white man."

"From whom would he be hiding?"

"Real or imagined enemies," said Sisay. "I was getting worried about him. He was becoming . . . marginal, I guess you would say. Too African," he added with a smile, "which is what they still say about me. The more he mediated disputes among the village people, the development agencies, and the Peace Corps, the more he became involved in local politics, and the more he disliked white people. He was getting squeezed. The Peace Corps explicitly forbids political activity, but the development agencies and government ministries funded by the development agencies kept giving him more and more power because he was a rare creature, a white man who spoke fluent Mende. He moved easily among the village, the bush, and the world of the white development agencies, where there is money, lots of money, and lots of corruption. Being too African probably isn't dangerous, but being too honest is. If the Dutch send a hundred bags of cement from Bo to Makeni to build a bridge, you can bet that only sixty or seventy will arrive, and that the official in Makeni will simply sign off on the receipt, and the missing cement goes . . . to certain powerful people.

"When Killigan started working on those projects, he had his own men at the work site counting, and if a hundred bags of cement did not arrive, he raised hell until he found the person responsible and fired him. Meanwhile, each time he successfully planned and completed a project, he was held in higher esteem by the villagers. His reputation was spreading. But the certain powerful people were missing their bags of cement."

"It's a nice theory," said Boone, "but I have information that there was some kind of raid on his village by witches or Baboon Men or something."

"There was a funeral in his village," said Sisay. "The raid could have been election business, terrorism directed at Kabba Lundo, the Paramount Chief, who also lives in Ndevehun, or the chaos could have erupted because a *Ndogbojusui* was sighted."

"A what?" asked Boone.

"Dog-bo-joo-shwee," Sisay enunciated slowly, "a bush devil. Tomorrow, I will take you to see Pa Gigba, who was in Ndevehun when all of this happened. I don't know how much he will tell us, but I know he was there. And yes, Baboon Men have been sighted, and not just in Killigan's village. Like I said, it's election time."

"Witches, Baboon Men, and now bush devils," sighed Boone. "Any other creatures you haven't told me about?"

"Americans," said Sisay, without laughing. "Lebanese. British. Germans. The diamond miners. The murderers who own the mining companies. They are the most fearsome creatures in the bush. A bush devil is nothing compared to them."

"OK," said Boone, "I get the message. I'm not here to reform Western civilization; I'm looking for my best friend. What is a bush devil?"

"What is a regular devil?" asked Sisay, mocking him with a quick grin. "A *Ndogbojusui* is a spirit who lives on top of a mountain by day, and at night roams the bush paths looking for straggling hunters or other wanderers who are foolish enough to travel alone in the bush at dusk. Like most genies and devils, *Ndogbojusui* are white," Sisay added, with an almost imperceptible pause. "A bush devil usually has white hair and a long white beard, but he can change his shape at will. He attempts to trick travelers by asking them questions and by charming them into going with him into the bush, where those who follow him are lost forever. Some anthropologists speculate that the original bush devils were the Portuguese who 'tricked' hunters and travelers into following them, and then sold them as slaves at the docks in Freetown."

"This mythology stuff is interesting, and if I was here on vacation I'd listen to it by the hour," Boone said, "but it doesn't tell me how to find Michael Killigan."

"No," Sisay said, "but it might keep you from getting lost. You seem far too impatient to learn anything about the bush, so I'll keep it simple: Do not go into the bush at night. Ever. For any reason. Plan your journeys so that you end up in a village well before dark. Even in daylight, you must be careful in the bush. Anyone traveling alone in the bush is not to be trusted. If you meet a lone hunter or a solitary traveler, be polite, but keep your distance, do not engage the person in conversation or follow them. Don't eat anything they may offer you. If you meet a beautiful woman, do not touch her or accept any gifts from her. Understand? It's not like the woods or the wilderness back home. It's not just a place . . ."

"I suppose *Ndogbojusui* is how the natives explain missing persons over here," Boone said, convinced that Lewis had steered him into the keeping of a psychotic Deadhead. "Again, it's interesting, but I need to know if Michael Killigan is lost, or if somebody kidnapped him, or . . . injured him, or what? I have a letter from one of his servants," Boone said, suddenly recalling Lewis's advice from the restaurant in Freetown: *Don't trust him. Ask questions, listen, but don't talk. That's how you survive in this part of the world.* "I should say I *saw* a letter from one of his servants. Killigan's mother showed it to me in Paris. It talked about bad medicine and witchmen coming to the village while Killigan wasn't there," he ventured, deciding for the moment to keep the mention of photographs to himself. "It was a letter from his servant. Moussa . . ."

"Moussa Kamara," Sisay interrupted. "Pa Gigba is Moussa Kamara's uncle, and as I said, Gigba was in Killigan's village when this disturbance occurred."

"Well, great. We can talk to Gigba first," Boone said, "but then I plan to go to Killigan's village and talk to this Moussa guy, and take it from there."

"You can go to Ndevehun if you like," said Sisay, "but you won't be able to talk to Moussa Kamara."

"I suppose that's forbidden," said Boone sarcastically, "or I suppose he's a witch or a bush devil."

"According to the section chief, who sent word to our village chief," said Sisay, "Moussa Kamara is dead. They found him a week ago outside Ndevehun hanging from a cotton tree. Somebody slit his belly open and stuffed him with hot peppers. They found a live gecko sewn inside his mouth."

(6)

The Origin of White People

Long ago, there lived a man with two wives. One year, his big wife told him that she could no longer bear working with the new wife on the same farm. The big wife wanted her own farm. To keep peace among his wives, the man went to find more bush for his wives to farm. He went all the way to England looking for more bush. There he bought a vast farm of *poo-mui* bush, wrapped it in newspaper, set it on his head, and carried it home to his wives.

The man divided the bush into two farms: one for his big wife and one for the new wife. Though he tried not to show it, the man favored the new wife over his big wife. The new wife was young, and her breasts were round and full of milk. Everyone in the village knew that the new wife was a "love wife," because the man had gotten almost nothing from her parents. The man spent much more time brushing the new wife's farm with his cutlass, and only brushed his big wife's farm when it was too overgrown to manage.

The big wife became jealous. When the husband gave his wives the seed rice to plow, the big wife told the younger one that the rice should be boiled and dried in the sun before planting it. Despite this trick, the new wife's parboiled rice somehow grew into thick pods. The big wife gnashed her teeth with jealousy. She hired a coven of witches to put a curse on the new wife's farm. She and the other witches turned themselves into the large rodents known in Mendeland as "cutting grasses" and ate the young wife's rice. Each night, the big wife and the witches went to the farm, took off their human skins, put them in a lake at the edge of the farm, dressed themselves in cutting grass skins, and ate the girl's rice.

"Human skin go off," the witches chanted. "Cutting grass skin come on."

Morning after morning, the new wife found her rice crop ravaged, until finally she went to consult a looking-around man to find out who was destroying her rice crop. The looking-around man cast stones and told her that the big wife and her coven of witches were changing themselves into cutting grasses every night and eating the rice on the young wife's farm.

"To stop her," the looking-around man advised, "buy twenty bags of pepper, take them down to the lake at the edge of your farm, grind the pepper up, and pour it into the lake." The girl did as she had been instructed.

That night, the big wife led her coven of cutting grasses to the young wife's farm. They put their human skins in the peppered lake, put on their cutting grass skins, and gorged themselves all through the night on rice. At first light, they went back to the lake, took their human skins from the peppered water, and put them on their bodies.

"Cutting grass skin go off," they chanted. "Human skin come on."

Soon the pepper started to burn. As her human skin caught fire, the big wife and head of the cutting grasses began to cry, "Human skin go off! Human skin go off!"

In the morning, when the new wife and others from the village came to the farm, they found the big wife and her coven of witches standing by the lake at the end of the farm, with their bellies full of rice and their skins removed, leaving only a plump whiteness.

These skinless witches were the first white people. All white people came from them.

Jenisa waded into the stream and spread her family's clothes on a flat washing rock. Her co-wives, Amida and Mariamu, stood next to her, knee-deep in the tug of the stream's current and the spume of suds from palm-oil soap. Their conversation was punctuated by soft grunts of effort and the thud and squish of soapy garments pounding heavy stones. The sun had settled below the palm trees, and Jenisa could hear the shouts and songs of people returning from the bush farms. The long shadows of mango and pearwood trees fell across the water on either side of the rock where the women brooked their clothes. The drone of huge, carnivorous flies and the chatter of birds echoed in the tunnel of bush overhanging the stream. Muddy water rushed over the washing rock in twisted rivulets and tore itself into white tassels of soapsuds and foam.

Amida and Mariamu were complaining about how the day's work

had been assigned by Yotta, the big wife of their common husband, the powerful section chief, Idrissa Moiwo. They made fun of her fat behind, called "waist" in Krio, and the smell of her genitals, called "private."

"Ai O!" said Amida. "Dat big wife Yotta, ihn business strangah. Look ihn waist spread like bush cow yone."

"To God," said Mariamu. "And ihn private dae smell like rotten fish bonga. You no know whatin dat woman dae do na night. She dae wash ihn waist wit sansan and sapo. Still it get dat rank scent."

"Imagine," added Jenisa, "she dae expect us foh brook ihn drawers. I no able. Dat fish bonga scent dae go 'pon person tae it no dae come out. I no know whatin make dat wife man take ahm."

"Den say she been fine-fine befoh traday, O. Ihn body been fresh, ihn face fine. But usai she done wowo tae dat ugly dancing devil, Kongoli, self dae 'fraid ahm. Ihn nose flat like benni cake."

"I been hear dat. She been get one boyfriend wi ihnself no de wash. Una been sabby dat yella pa wi been dae sell den haf-haf ting dem na ya?"

"Pa Mustapha?"

"Na ihm."

"Lawd have massi. Dat pa dae, he been dirty like whatin. All dem peekin dem been mock ihm foh dat. Ihn dirty one."

"Well, Yotta done meet up ihn matches. Mastah and Missus Rank!"

They all laughed bitterly and pretended they were beating Yotta with their washing stones, until Mariamu warned of the approach of Fati, Yotta's daughter and spy.

Jenisa, Amida, and Mariamu all hated Yotta, and so did Fati. But whenever it suited her schemes, Fati told Yotta everything her mates said about the big wife. Then Yotta would retaliate by spreading stories about the men her mates were sleeping with, and why their children either died or received poor training, whereas hers were models of Mende rectitude who respected their mother and served their father. Yotta's stories would then filter back to the young wives, who would point out Yotta's infidelities and speculate about her real motives for spreading lies about her mates. And the gossip went in and out of the *mawes*, up and down the banks of the stream where clothes were brooked, out along the lines of women bearing head-loads in from the outlying farms, and back into the markets.

In Krio, the word for this kind of vicious, backbiting gossip is *congosa;* it is rumormongering designed to poison hearts and trigger palavers. When the men gossiped, it was called village planning, or "hanging heads," though, except for a pronounced emphasis on the profit angle, the content of the conversations was the same.

Jenisa moved to the other side of the washing rock, so that her lengthening shadow would not fall on the deeper parts of the stream. A turtle or, worse, a crocodile could swallow her shadow if she was not careful. Just a short time ago, Amida, her mate and close friend, had seen a *Njaloi*, a genie with a brilliant gem set in his forehead, swimming deep in this stream. The light from the *Njaloi*'s stone had blinded Amida, and the genie called to her to come under the water, and promised he would take her to a cave filled with a vast treasure. The whole village talked excitedly about the sighting for days, and, at night, in the baffa, by the light of a single hurricane lamp, Amida's aunt again told the story of how, when she was a small girl bathing with her mother in the stream, a water genie, a *tingowei*, appeared to her as a long golden chain lying on a rock. While she was admiring the golden chain, the *tingowei* stole her shadow. The aunt said that without her shadow she became instantly dizzy and fell into the water. The genie dragged her down and took her to a cave filled with treasure and showed her an evil white spirit, a thing so horrible she could not now describe it, for if she was successful in her description, anyone who heard it would be unable to forget the terrible image. It promised to give her towns filled with treasures if she would agree to do things that were so terrible, a person hearing of them would never again trust anyone wearing a human shape. Only a powerful medicine finally allowed her to put the hideous thing out of her mind.

The stream was a dangerous place, frequented by mermaids, genies, and capricious spirits that liked nothing better than making people insane or saddling them with curses and misfortunes. The stream was visited only in groups, and then only to bathe or to brook clothes.

When Fati joined them at the washing rock, she brought news of the arrival of a white stranger, word of which was spreading through the community of huts and *mawes* like vibrations traveling along a delicate spider's web, touched at one point by the intruder.

"White strangah been come," said Fati.

Fati was Yotta the big wife's daughter, but because Amida and Jenisa were nearly the same age as Fati, they all behaved as sisters to one another and as daughters of Yotta. Only Mariamu was older, being the second wife of their husband, the section chief.

"Usai dat white man come out?" Jenisa asked.

"I think say he American man. He been come out na Freetown," Fati replied. "I no see ahm. I been dae brook me clothes, when I hear he been come, jus now."

"Whatin he been come na hya foh do?" Amida asked, winking at Jenisa.

"Den say he come foh find dat Peace Koh man. Den say dat Peace Koh man done go wakka-wakka. Dey no see ahm. He done go alackey. Trouble dae, beaucoup. Water roof. Better no dae."

"Peace no dae inside the country. Dese rebels been come out Liberia with bloody hands and put bad medicine na Salone."

News of the white man's arrival made Jenisa's heart beat faster, and she shared her excitement by returning Amida's knowing glance. As Jenisa's confidante, Amida knew that a looking-around man had told Jenisa that a white stranger would come to the village and give her a gift that would change her life. This gave Jenisa hope that her hard life of sorrow and despair might soon change for the better. She was twenty years old, and still she had no children of her own. Her charmed life as the young, beautiful, new wife of Section Chief Moiwo had become a Mende woman's nightmare—she had lost two children in childbirth, and *Ngewo*, the Mende god, was taking his time in sending her more.

All her life had been spent in preparation for bearing and raising children, and now she had none. When Jenisa was still a child, her mother took her aside and told her that her father was so proud of her, he had decided to give her as a wife to Section Chief Moiwo, a man whose farms were so vast he could feed the entire village. She would also go to school, because Moiwo had been to school in England and America and wanted a clever, educated, new wife. So, while she was still very young, she went to live in Section Chief Moiwo's compound under the care and training of his big wife, Yotta. She obeyed Yotta, even though Yotta was cruel and jealous of the pretty girl who would one day be a new wife for her husband. She entered the Sande Society, the woman's secret society, full of joy and eager to become a woman. In the Sande bush, a special sequestered place near her village, she was trained by the woman whose name she now bore. She went into the Sande bush with her sisters and her cousins, and left her childish ways and her childhood name behind. All trace of man was removed from her private, and she was born Jenisa, the most beautiful and best-trained woman to emerge in all her finery from the Sande bush. Her skin glistened with scented oils. The entire village gave her gifts, and she proudly danced and sang for her admiring elders.

Before they cut the man part out of her, the matrons had showed her the eyeball of a fish. And her Sande mother said to her, over and over, "Enter this fish and swim far below your pain." The drums beat and blood pounded in her head, and her grandmothers removed the small stick of maleness from her. The pain happened somewhere far above her. She bore it easily, and proudly, according to her training, and gloried in the greatest moment of her life. She was now one with her sisters, a pure woman, ready for marriage and childbirth. Even before she left the Sande bush, the matrons had let it be known all over the village that she was first in her class, daughter of a big man, and already given as wife to a section chief.

In the Sande bush, she had learned how to serve her husband. She had learned the arts of loving a man, of bearing children, of weaving, of dancing, and music making. She learned that her love for the wife man must always be complete, but not unconditional. For, the matrons had told her, the wife man, too, must love his wives completely and treat them with respect. If this was not the case and her husband ever mistreated her, then the Sande matrons had ways of bringing these misbehaving husbands into line, first by complaining to the big men in Poro, the men's secret society, and second, if necessary, by afflicting bad husbands with genital atrocities. For instance, no man may see what happens in the Sande bush. Those intrepid men who dare spy on Sande proceedings suddenly develop hideous deformities of the private: hydrocele, elephantiasis, hernias, and swollen testicles.

Soon after her wife man took her as his new wife, she heard delicious rumors that she was a "love wife," meaning, even though the marriage had obvious practical benefits for both her father and the section chief, the women of the village said that Moiwo would have taken her even if her parents had had nothing, because she was young and clever and very beautiful. Yotta's jealousy grew by the day, but Jenisa managed to be both modest and tactful. She learned early that most women were jealous of her, because she was clever and beautiful; Yotta's jealousy was sharper only because

Yotta wanted to be the big wife, as well as the best-loved wife of her husband. Jenisa gave Yotta her due as the big wife, but was not slow to exploit the wife man's infatuation with her as the new young wife.

She took no sexual pleasure from Moiwo's climbing on her to make children, but she enjoyed influencing the way things were run in the compound just by whispering things in his ear. If Yotta made some ridiculous rule, and enforced it only to make the lives of the young wives miserable, Jenisa found that it could be changed with a whisper. If she wanted some special treat or a new dress, a whisper brought it to her. More than anything, she wanted to give the section chief a child, for this would make her father big with pride and her wife man even happier. But after the first year, during which it seemed that Moiwo was always wanting her when it was her turn to stay with him, he stopped sending for her, or if he sent for her, he did not love with her, but only spoke of work to be done around the compound, of relations to be cared for, and crops to be looked after. This was normal, the Sande matrons told her. Her Sande mother told her that a man's love is like a big splash in the river, but a woman's is a strong and steady current. She kept herself busy and flirted with young men to pass the time. If she fancied one of the young village men, she knew she could make him love her, but she was waiting for the right one.

She pounded more clothes on the washing rock and realized her thoughts were racing away from her, like the soap in the stream.

Her co-wives laughed, beat the clothes, complained of Yotta's insufferable ways, and worked.

All of her co-wives had love men because their wife man had five wives in two villages, and he was always gone to another village, to Freetown, or even to America, and it was clear that he wanted as many sons and daughters as possible, the first as laborers for his farms, the second as a means of acquiring ownership interests in more farms through marriage. It also seemed that he did not care *how* these children came about, as long as any woman damage fines were paid in money or servitude to him.

But Jenisa decided that if she was going to take a love man, she wanted a very special one. Not the misfits her co-wives had taken up with. Yotta's love man, Pa Mustapha, "Mastah Rank," was the laughingstock of the village, because he never washed himself.

Mariamu had a love man who could barely see because of river blindness. Amida had two love men, both young soccer players who were always fighting and drinking palm wine.

She bided her time, until she met a white Peace Corps man—Mistah Michael—whose Mende name was Lamin Kaikai, and who came to the village one day to see Mistah Aruna Sisay on business. Here was a love man! She quickly learned that even though this *poo-mui* had money spilling out of his pockets, he had no wives or children! He didn't need wives or children to work his farms. He didn't need farms, because he had bank accounts full of money all over the world! This Lamin Kaikai's skin shone like the sun, and he had a fine and beautiful body. He was a "sportsmahn" and wore magic shoes that made him run like the wind. But even when the village boys made him take off the magic shoes before racing him, he always won, probably because of some other hidden medicine. His pockets were full of medicines that were capable of protecting from every evil and bestowing every comfort on him and on those he loved.

And even though he was a *poo-mui*, he spoke her language and loved her people, and her people loved him. She knew when she first met him that she could have him, because he openly admired her training and she felt his eyes on her skin. He teased her, and she teased him back. He mocked her with a Mende proverb, and she promptly bested him with a better one in front of a crowd on her veranda.

He came again and again to see Mistah Sisay, until one time she had found Lamin sitting alone on the veranda. She wanted to touch the beautiful yellow hair on his arms. She had asked him why African women always want to touch the hair on the arms of *poo-mui* men.

"Because it makes them pregnant," Lamin had said with a laugh and a funny face.

"Pregnant with whatin?" she had said, besting him again. "A white bush pig?"

They both had laughed and she smoothed the hair on his arm.

"I would like to see what this yellow hair looks like in the moonlight," she had said, and that night she did.

Six weeks later, she was the happiest Mende woman in Sierra Leone, for she knew she would be having the *poo-mui*'s child, and what a child that would be! She would be the envy of every woman in the village; even her husband would probably be delighted, so she had thought, because she had grown up in his house, watching his co-wives love with whomever they pleased. The village men did not ask too many questions about their wives' suspicious pregnancies, only because as far as anyone knew they came from the wife man's loins and no other. She learned too late that this pretense would be impossible if she delivered a mulatto child. For whatever reason, her wife man went into a rage when he learned that his young love wife lost a child because of unconfessed adultery.

One child had been born dead. A second child lived for only two days, when it was killed in its sleep by a witch. When the first peekin died in childbirth, Jenisa took a splinter and placed it under the little finger of the stillborn's left hand, so that if her second child was born with a scar under the same finger, she would know that it was a witch child trying to come back into the world. When she had difficult labor with the second child, the Sande matrons, the leaders of the women's secret society, told her the child probably was not coming out because of unconfessed adultery. If not adultery, then a witch was holding the child inside. They dragged Jenisa about the birthing hut and beat on her belly with sticks, chastising the witch and calling it names. Finally, they concluded that no witch could hold up under such blows, and that either Jenisa had committed adultery and had not confessed it to her husband, or a bad medicine man or jujuman, called a *hale-nyamubla* in Mende, had taken an egg from a sitting hen and had buried it in an anthill to put a swear on her. This would place her in "stocks," and she would be unable to deliver the child, and would, instead, die. Her only hope, the Sande matrons told her, was to confess and hope that adultery was the cause of her problems.

Jenisa dared not reveal her love man. Her wife man had many powerful, illegal medicines and used them freely to destroy his adversaries. So instead of confessing to loving with Lamin, she told the Sande matrons that she had been loving with Vande, Pa Gigba's son, which was true, in the sense that she had once loved with him before she was married.

Minutes after this confession, the child was born. She was afraid its color would give her away, but no whiteness appeared in its skin, though she knew it was Lamin's child. It died before its naming day, before Jenisa could take it out into the morning sun on the third day, spit on its forehead, and pronounce, "Resemble me in all my ways and deeds, being named after me."

She wrapped the tiny body in leaves, sat on a mound of earth that had been dug away from under a banana tree, and pushed the child backward into the grave, to avoid any witch spirit that may have killed it. She did not cry, because her grandmother had told her that a mother's tears for her dead infant would scald its skin. God gives; God takes away. The infant was not meant to be a person.

The Sande matrons said that the witch must have come in the night and eaten the baby from the inside out. They shook their heads, clucked their tongues, and wondered how, after all that good Sande Society training, a young wife could be stupid enough to try childbirth without first confessing adultery to her husband.

On the evening of the third day after the child's death, the town crier walked around the village and announced, "Everybody listen! Everybody listen! The man who is loving with the young wife of Section Chief Moiwo had better come forward or he will be sworn. Should he not show himself before tomorrow, a powerful medicine will search him out and take revenge on him. His testicles will shrivel like cocoa pods in the sun! His liver will turn to dust! If he tries to sleep, his heart will stop! If he tries to go by water, spirits will overturn his boat and drown him! If he reaches for his wife, he will embrace a corpse! If he goes into the bush, snakes will bite him and the boa constrictor will strangle him! If he tries to think or speak, his mind will be crazed until he is insane! Such are the swears that will be put on the man who is loving Section Chief Moiwo's young wife if he does not come forward and admit woman damage."

This announcement brought forth both of Amida's boyfriends, and later a protesting Vande, who swore he had not touched Jenisa since before her marrying day and was bewildered by the accusations of the looking-around man, who claimed to have knowledge of Vande's woman damage. Late into the night and on into the early morning, the court *barri* was filled with men from all the families, drunk on palm wine, and swept up in a classic West African palaver over the appropriate fines to be assessed against the three offenders for woman damage. All three young men ended up having to work for many months on Moiwo's farms to pay off large fines. But Vande escaped his debt by leaving for Freetown. One of Amida's lovers stayed, and told Amida in their secret meeting place that he would work forever on Section Chief Moiwo's farm if it meant he could hold her each night in his arms.

Jenisa was afraid she would lose another child to witchcraft or bad medicine, because her secret lover did not reveal himself and the swear had been let loose. What if the swear found him or her and bestowed some new calamity on them? Then she had learned that her love man had chased a *Ndogbojusui* into the bush outside his village of Ndevehun and had disappeared. The rumors were that he had gone crazy, as white men sometimes do, but she did not believe them.

Why was there so much evil in the world? If her ancestors were watching over her, why did they let these terrible things happen? Had she done something to offend them? Had someone in her family failed to perform the proper sacrifices and offerings, or otherwise shown disrespect? Perhaps her ancestors were hungry, and she had not given them enough food? Adultery explained nothing. Other women had three, four, five, or more healthy children with no troubles. They too had lovers, because they were the third and fourth wives of old men, but they had only strong boys and beautiful daughters to show their husbands.

The ancestors were supposed to intervene on her behalf and ask *Ngewo*, the father of all the Mende, to help her bear strong, healthy children, and to bless her with food to feed them. Instead, *Ngewo* allowed witches to take her children from her and fill her heart with bitter sorrow. Already, Amida had overheard Yotta, the big wife, asking other wives in the village if they thought Jenisa herself was a witch because two of her children had been taken. The loss of a third would be almost conclusive evidence of witchcraft, and Jenisa would be the first suspect. For everyone knows that a witch must supply her coven with fresh infants to eat, sometimes even her own.

To discover the source of her troubles, Jenisa had saved money for months, skimming pennies from her sales of palm oil in the market and saving them in the pouch under her bed. Then she had paid the money to a very powerful looking-around man, who moved stones on a board and cast cowrie shells. The looking-around man told her that a woman in the village—a widow who had not re-married and had not observed the rituals of purification after her husband's death—had put a swear on her. Jenisa knew at once the identity of her enemy.

The woman's name was Luba and her husband had fallen out of a palm tree during the last rainy season and had died. A spitting cobra, waiting for him in the palm tree, had blinded him with its venom and bit his face, and the men in the village said that as he fell from the tree, he screamed "Luba!," his big wife's name, and died when he struck the ground.

As a Mende woman, and as one of the man's three wives, Luba had to be washed of him before she could take another husband or love with another man. The water that was used to wash the soles of the dead man's feet was saved. Luba and the other bereaved wives were kept apart from the rest of the village and did not see or speak to anyone. Three days after her husband's death, an old woman poured the water on the ground in front of his house. The old woman then made mud with a pestle from the wet earth. Luba and her mates were summoned. The old woman took each wife by the hair and dragged her through the house. Another old woman followed, driving each widow ahead of her, in turn. When they arrived again at the front door of the house, each wife put her face close to the mud and shouted to her husband, "Husband of mine, I am in trouble!" Then the mud was smeared on the bodies of the grieving widows and baskets were hung by strings from their heads. Sympathizers filled the baskets with gifts, and the brothers of the dead man who were interested in taking a particular wife gave that one a big gift. But the widow Luba received only tokens, and no brother gave her a big gift. Everyone knew that none of the dead man's brothers wanted her.

Luba and the other wives accompanied the old woman into the bush, where each wife rested her head on a plantain tree. The old woman knocked down the tree with a pestling log and made a dish of boiled plantain, which they ate that evening for their food. Luba and her mates were smeared with mud again and dressed in rags, so that their husband's spirit would no longer desire them. Other women stayed with the widows to prevent them from sleeping that night, for if they slept, their husband might slip back in to stay with them.

The next day, Luba and her mates went to the river and washed away the last thing that belonged to their husband: the dust from the soles of his feet. She and the other widows were then to have remained in the dead man's compound for forty days, during which time their hair was shaved off and the sisters of the dead husband cursed them and told their dead brother that he would be a fool to linger in this world for such vile, ugly women.

But before ten days had passed, there were rumors that Luba was sneaking out of the compound at night and was loving with Sherrif, one of the dead man's brothers, out in the bush. Then there was talk that she had also slept with another brother, Alimami, also in the bush. With her hair shorn and wearing muddy rags, she sexed the brothers of her dead husband on land their fathers had farmed. She disgraced herself and then bewitched her husband's brothers into desecrating the family farm and their dead brother's wife. Crops no longer grew on the farm. But Luba did not care. Her only pleasure was in knowing she had defiled those who thought they were her betters: *You did not want me enough to put a big gift in my funeral basket, but you sexed me in the bush when your brother was barely ten days dead. You spilled your human seed on the land that feeds your families.*

And if her infernal sexing kept her husband from crossing the river to the village of white sands, Luba did not care. Her utter depravity was more powerful than any wandering spirit.

Now Luba lived alone in a shed. She still wore rags and kept her head shaved. The village children said that they had seen Luba change herself into a leopard and hide in the bush behind the latrines. On moonless nights, they could see Luba's orange eyes floating in the darkness. Their grandmothers told them that if they followed those orange eyes into the bush, they would be lost forever. Always, they would see the orange eyes just ahead of them, until they found themselves lost in trackless, eternal bush, and then a bush devil would trick them, or a witch wearing the shape of an animal would fall on them, paralyze them, suck blood from their throats, and eat them from the inside out.

As soon as the looking-around man told Jenisa about the swear that Luba had let loose on her, the chaos and tragedy of her life made perfect, terrible sense. A swear! The Sande matrons were right; Jenisa had committed adultery, but it was her enemy's swear that had killed her children and brought trouble, sorrow, and death into her life.

It was useless to ask why Luba had put her in stocks and had turned a swear loose on her. One might as well ask why driver ants bite people. A woman who would sex her dead husband's brothers in the bush during her mourning time would do anything. Luba's vile behavior had probably sent her husband to the evil place of everlasting hunger, where the dead till barren soil with their elbows and gnaw their own knees in savage hunger. If so, Luba would laugh out loud. Such a woman probably put swears on people just so she could shriek with delight while watching them suffer.

Jenisa needed protection. She needed a powerful medicine to kill her enemy. She borrowed large sums of money and consulted the looking-around man again and again. There were so many questions. Was Luba a witch? Some said yes. Some said her husband had screamed her name as he fell from the tree because he had recognized her in the shape of the spitting cobra. What kind of swear had Luba let loose on her? Simple protection was probably not enough; Jenisa needed to attack and kill her enemy with a more powerful swear. If Jenisa could kill Luba with a powerful medicine, would it also "pull" Luba's swear? This kind of bad medicine was illegal. How was it done without others finding out about it? Should she tell her wife man about Luba and what the looking-around man had told her? But her wife man, the chief, had been to school in England and America. He got very angry when his wives spent money on looking-around men and medicine men. He believed in white medicine, which was very powerful in curing afflictions that came from God, but was useless in protecting one from witchcraft and swears.

She had heard stories of powerful witch-hunting cults from the north who had bound a confessed witch and carried her into the bush. The witch hunters dug a shallow grave and buried the witch alive, throwing stones and garbage in on top of her until she died. But the witch's shade came back to haunt the village. Confined to its human shape, the witch was far less dangerous than its shade. The living, human shape was the shade's roost or cage. When the human shape was killed, the shade escaped and could no longer be trapped or harmed, except by witchfinders. Once free, the shade took its revenge by flying about the village and settling its weight on the faces of sleeping people. The witch hunters were called back again; this time a powerful witchfinder captured the witch's shade in the shape of a lizard and tied it safely inside a leather bag. Though the cults were very effective, they cost more money than she had ever seen.

The looking-around man told Jenisa that to remove Luba's swear, Jenisa had to cook a meal and serve it to a white stranger, who would then give her a gift. The looking-around man told her to bring the white stranger's gift back to him, and he would make a very powerful and dangerous medicine from it that would kill her enemy.

Jenisa rested her stone on the washing rock and fingered the horn of a bush deer, which she wore on a leather string around her neck, and prayed. She remembered the story her father had told her when he had given her the horn filled with medicine and told her never to eat the meat of *mbende*, the bush deer. His great-grandfather— now one of the fathers who are remembered, called *kekeni* when prayers and sacrifices are offered—was bathing in this stream, when an alligator seized him in its jaws and carried him to a cave underneath the bank of the stream. Her ancestor had no way out of the cave, because a wall of water rushed past the opening and would drown any man who tried to swim through it. The alligator left the ancestor in the cave and went to tell its family about the sweet human beef he would be serving them for dinner that night. But on the bank above the cave, a bush deer was about to give birth. The pains of her labor were so great that she stamped and stamped her hooves on the bank, until she stamped so hard that one of her hooves broke through to the cave below. The ancestor clawed at the hole until it was big enough, then climbed out of the cave to safety. After he was free, he summoned his family to the bank of the stream and announced, "Look, alligators almost ate me, but I was saved by the bush deer. These bush deer are now our brothers and sisters, and we must return their favor by never eating them again."

The next morning, she went with her family to the praying place at the foot of the cotton tree. The praying man arrived and spoke to the ancestors on the family's behalf. Jenisa's father brought forth a cooked fowl and a pot of rice.

"Oh, fathers and grandfathers, see the big pot we have brought you to eat. Watch over us. Keep safe our wives and our children. Keep our chiefs safe. Take care of us. Too many infants have died before their mothers could hold them in their arms. Our little bobos are being bitten by snakes. People have drowned in the rivers. We beg you to keep us safe from these misfortunes. Please keep us safe. See the big pot of sweet food we have brought for you."

The praying man poured water on the ground. "Fathers and grandfathers, here is some water for you to wash your hands. Now you may eat the rice."

The praying man mixed portions of the food with red palm oil on a banana leaf and placed it on a sacred stone.

Oh, fathers and grandfathers, Jenisa prayed, turning the horn of medicine over in her fingers, *let my thoughts reach you. Keep my love man safe. Keep my wife man safe. Protect me from my enemy and give me healthy children.*

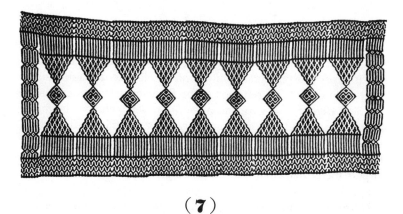

(7)

Randall spent a sleepless night pondering the unidentified bright object in his deep white matter. The terminology sounded almost astrophysical, except it described inner space. His. Testing was scheduled to resume at 8 a.m. Meanwhile, he was supposed to go home, forget about the bright object in his brain, and sleep. Right. While Bean and Rheingold and the other doctors were at home dreaming about tax-sheltered annuities, Randall stared at the ceiling, grinding his teeth, certain that his brain tumor was seeding his bloodstream with metastatic satellites. He had an almost irresistible urge to do a total backup of all his software and data files onto a mini data cartridge capable of holding 400 megabytes of compressed data. He could carry it in his breast pocket, just in case he could take it with him.

He waited for the bat to show again, almost hoping it would, so he could get a better look at it. But then, what for? Either way he was in trouble. If there was a bright object in his deep white matter causing him to hallucinate, it was probably a brain tumor that would kill him in six months. If the bright object was a false positive, and there was nothing organically wrong with him, then he was a stranger to his own imagination. He would spend the rest of his life waiting around for newer, weirder, and more private hallucinations to move in with him and crowd out the rest of the world. At night, he would stare into the darkness and watch giant, repulsive bats appear out of thin air.

At four in the morning, he called Mack's extension at Sterling and left a voice mail: "The CEO of Nimrod Products just called me from some place in California. He's a friend and a client. His wife has come down with something called peduncular hallucinosis. The family gets their estate planning done upstairs. Get on the computers and find me some medical dope on peduncular hallucinosis. Bill it to my personal matters file, and I'll allocate the time later."

At eight o'clock, he returned to the Radiology Department at the Medical Center and gave his name to a clerk who sat behind a sliding glass panel. She gave him a big paper cup filled with contrast solution and pointed at a vinyl bench in the hallway. Randall held his nose and drank it, certain that the stuff would probably set off airport metal detectors and make Geiger counters natter at high frequency.

Normally, technicians conducted the scan, then provided the doctors with films to read. But this meant that Randall often had to wait for the results to be read by a radiologist and reported to his doctor, who would then report them to Bean. This time, Randall insisted that Bean be *at* the scan with a radiologist, so that when it was over, the doctors could walk right out of the booth and tell him what they had seen.

Scan time came and went, and still Bean failed to show. Randall waited, feeling a huge tumor swelling inside his skull, causing increased cranial pressure, wrath at Bean and the technicians, and desperate fear. Finally, a technician came out and told him that Dr. Bean was stuck inside someone else's brain with a surgical team and a lot of complications. Bean's message was for Randall to go ahead and be scanned, then wait for the results like everyone else.

Two technicians fetched Randall from the vinyl bench. If they already knew about the UBO, their manner didn't show it. They helped him onto a table that had an eight-foot doughnut at the head of it, with a hole for him and the table to slide through. First, they injected radioactive dye into his arm.

"More dye, for contrast," they told him with a smile.

"It's harmless," they said, wearing goggles, lead aprons, and black rubber gloves.

"Nothing to be afraid of," they told him, via microphone from a booth with three-foot-thick lead walls.

"You get more radiation from a sunburn," a bromide they presumably could not offer their skin cancer patients.

Randall usually argued with them about how much contrast fluid he had to drink and how much radioactive glop they were injecting into his arm. But this time, he was passive and agreeable. They positioned his head in the doughnut and then ran back to their booth. A small red light flashed, the tray moved in increments, slowly and precisely feeding him through the doughnut. Again the whirring sounds of some huge hydraulic engine spinning around him, punctuated by soft clicks whenever radiation was released. He could ⸍ see one of the monitors in the booth, a colorful representation of a vertical slice of torso—probably his—with heads on white lab coats staring into it.

After twenty minutes, the technicians came out of the booth.

"You guys watched it on those monitors while the scan was being done, didn't you?" asked Randall.

"Yes," they said. "We did."

"Well," he stammered. "Did you see anything?"

Their faces instantly froze in precisely neutral expressions.

"We are not permitted to disclose test results," said one.

"Your doctor will provide you with the results," said the other. "We are not physicians. We are not permitted to evaluate or interpret results. We just obtain the scan and send it on videotape to the radiologist, who . . ."

"*I know that,*" Randall said, clenching his teeth. "But you know damn well if it was positive for anything, or negative, or whatever," he said, flashing them a humble smile, which failed to alter their precisely neutral expressions.

"Sorry," they said in a precisely neutral tone of voice.

"Very sorry, I'll bet," growled Randall.

Although their expressions did not change, Randall was suddenly convinced that they had just seen a huge brain tumor in living color on his scan, and now they were hiding it from him. Sure. At least once a week for years, these guys had seen tumors light up like alien warships all over their monitors. They had practiced this routine hundreds of times. Just walk out of the booth, keep your face straight, and try not to think about how you are talking to a guy who doesn't know he is going to be dead in six months.

When he left the room and closed the door, Randall felt them shake their heads behind him. As he walked down the hall, he imagined them going back into their booth for a second look. *Did you see the size of that thing?* they were probably saying. *Way past graveyard ugly!*

Next, he was due up in Bean's office for a spinal tap. In the hallways, he passed people whose fortunes had already been told.

A young couple beaming over an ultrasound photo of their unborn child. A stone-faced mother and father grimly towing a bald little girl. A stroke victim fidgeting in a wheelchair.

Two nurses prepared him for the spinal tap, something he'd never had before. He was at once grateful for another source of information about his condition and apprehensive about potentially dangerous side effects, like severing his spinal cord on a misguided syringe. The sting started at the base of his spine and spread up to the back of his neck. Afterward he seemed able to walk, but his toes tingled, probably a nerve or something they sliced in there. Or maybe all these dyes they were shooting into his blood were pickling him like a frog in fixative.

Back in Howard's office, the secretary told him that Howard had been in an emergency aneurysm repair since six that morning. A very complicated case. Could take hours.

"Is there any way you can call down and get me the results of that scan?" asked Randall, feeling like he was going to cry, or throw up blood, or discharge electricity, or give off radiation, erupt in some new way, because he had never been so afraid.

"I'm sorry," she said. "Only physicians are allowed to disclose test results to the patients. A pretty hard-and-fast rule around here. No exceptions."

"But my doctor is in surgery," said Randall, swallowing his nausea. "He could be in surgery all day, and I'm not going to be able to get . . . I want to know everything is OK, so I can go back to work."

"Sorry," she said, with a look that said she wasn't the least bit sorry. "Rules. You'll have to be a big boy and follow them."

Randall chewed on his fingernails for forty-five minutes until Bean showed up and hustled him into a consultation room.

"Where were you!?" Randall yelled.

"Do you really want to know?" asked Bean. "It's called standstill. We put a fifty-two-year-old aneurysm repair into hypothermic arrest, disconnected his heart, hooked him to a bypass pump, refrigerated his blood, and took his brain down to sixty degrees so we could go in and repair the aneurysm without him bleeding to death. Cold brains use less oxygen and blood than warm ones, so we just disconnected everything for ten or twenty minutes. After we clamped off the aneurysm, we hooked his heart back up to his major vessels, jump-started him, and prayed like mad that the thing would take a charge. Pretty standard stuff, really, but before you get pissed off, may I suggest that this patient, for a short time, needed me more than you did."

"OK, OK. I'm selfish. So what'd the scan show?"

"Angiography negative," said Bean. "It is not an arterio-venous malformation."

"Forget arterio-veno!" shouted Randall. "Is it a fucking brain tumor?"

"I don't know," said Howard softly. "Too deep for a CAT scan. We'll repeat the MRI, but nine times out of ten, you just get another UBO and nothing new."

"What about the spinal fluid?"

Bean sighed. "Elevated protein," he said.

"Which means," said Randall.

"It's nonspecific," said Bean, shifting in his chair and jittering his leg. "It could be an infection . . . Could be a . . . lesion . . ."

"Could be a brain tumor the size of an asteroid," said Randall. "You don't know shit from toilet paper, do you?" he shouted, leaping out of his chair and marching up and down, glaring at his friend. "Now what? More tests, I suppose?"

"Probably not," said Bean levelly. "Look, you *made* me your attending physician," he said. "I'm trying to be objective and do what I would do if you were any other patient. If you don't like my treatment, go see Carolyn!"

"I'm not any other patient," Randall yelled, marching some more. "What am I supposed to do? Go home and forget about it? Think about garbage or something?"

"We usually have to just wait and see," pleaded Howard. "Keep a close eye out for any symptoms and if something happens we'll be all over it. An infection usually gets better and goes away."

"And a tumor?" Randall croaked.

"Usually grows until we can see it," said Bean, "or until it begins causing other symptoms."

"Like a blinding headache, right?" said Randall. "Double vision, and the stone-cold comfort that you won't have to put up with it for long, right?"

"Look," said Bean. "Think about it. You're working ninety hours a week. OK, that's normal. Then your kid disappears in Africa. You can't sleep. You take some sleeping pills and wake up two hours later and see something that at first looks very weird, then it's gone.

Sounds like a one-time, hypnagogic hallucination. At worst, a freak occipital lobe seizure. It probably won't happen again. If I were you, I'd think real hard about whether you saw *something* that just looked different under the circumstances. And I'm talking to you as your friend, not your neurosurgeon."

Randall held his head in his hands.

"Go to work," said Bean. "Think about what I said tonight. Talk it over with Marjorie. If you want to talk some more, call me, no matter how late it is, OK?"

.

Randall breezed through the Sterling lobby as he always did, without saying hello to anyone, unless they were on the compensation committee. He switched on his computer and answered the blinking message from his secretary, who had a list of bankruptcy people to call, and one message from Senator Swanson, who had left the name and telephone number of Warren Holmes, the same bureaucrat who had called Randall on the first day of his son's disappearance.

He stabbed the button on his phone that connected him to Mack.

"Sir," Mack said, with a supercilious chuckle.

"Call that expert witness service we use," said Randall. "I need an expert on bats."

"Bats," said Mack. "Baseball bats?"

"Winged, nocturnal mammals," said Randall. "And I'm not talking about the sonar stuff. I'm interested in the different kinds of bats. If they ever make noises that people can hear. Where they live. How big they can get. What's the biggest kind, and so on."

"Morphology," said Mack. "I'll bet there's such a thing as a bat morphologist."

"Whatever. Tell him I've got a case I might need to use him on. Get him on the line, and then hook me up with him," said Randall. "Today."

"Mr. Bilksteen on four. Beach Cove," said his secretary over the intercom.

Randall normally would not have even returned a call from the likes of Bilksteen, but he had a sudden, sentimental craving for the familiar pleasures of kicking opposing counsel's ass around the bankruptcy court.

"Bilksteen," Randall said, jabbing the speakerphone button with his broadsword and settling back into his swivel chair.

"Pick up, you piece of shit," said Bilksteen bitterly.

"Are you still alive?" asked Randall. "Somebody said they saw you in hell having whiskey and cracked ice with the devil. I figured you for dead. I don't mean to have you on speaker, but my hands are full. I'm editing a bill we're sending to Comco Banks for one of those ridiculous lift-stay motions we were talking about just the other day. Hold on a second," said Randall.

An office courier came into Randall's office and placed a firm newsletter in his hands; Randall fed it to Benjy, and pushed it on through the bear's alimentary canal with his broadsword.

"Wait a second," said Randall. "Now that I get a closer look at this statement of services. This bill is for the Beach Cove case! That's your case, isn't it, Bilk?"

"If you believe in anything," pleaded Bilksteen. "If you believe in anything that would ever allow you to help another human being in trouble, I'm asking you . . . please, give me a deal, give me *any* deal I can take to the limited partners. Even if they won't take it in a million years, just give me something. I could at least go back with something . . . and a little of my self-respect."

"You mean, do you a favor?" asked Randall. "Please, no begging. It gives me heart trouble. Doing you a favor would be inconsistent with my client's interest. Comco writes my checks, not Beach Cove, and I hope you are not offering to write me checks," said Randall.

"You're the one who belongs in hell," said Bilksteen.

"Are you threatening me with punishment in the afterlife?" asked Randall. "This is bankruptcy. Pull yourself together. And once you get yourself together, if you're still ashamed to show your face in bankruptcy court, then try implementing some of those new Japanese management techniques that are supposed to be so good for firm culture and whatnot. You could start by publicly disemboweling yourself in front of the courthouse, to atone for your abysmal incompetence as a bankruptcy lawyer."

"I mean it," pleaded Bilksteen. "Any deal. Any deal at all."

"I'm adding this phone call to the bill," said Randall, "and we are approaching the second increment of billable time."

"If you don't care about me," said Bilksteen, "think about the limited partners. Some of them put their kids' college money into this thing."

Randall disconnected Bilksteen and punched the number of Mr. Warren Holmes, some kind of cultural relations officer with the State Department according to the voice mail messages. He beeped his way through the usual automated answering obstacle course, cursing himself for not telling his secretary to get the guy on the line.

Finally he reached Holmes, who reminded him of their first conversation and reintroduced himself—a good friend of Senator Swanson, eager to help in any way he could, particularly if Randall had questions about native matters, which apparently Mrs. Killigan had been calling Senator Swanson about. Randall listened with half an ear, while Holmes tried to impress him with his qualifications.

"My training was in the hard sciences," said Holmes, "but then I went into anthropology, and from there to foreign service. I was stationed at various embassies in Africa for almost ten years. Senator Swanson said you had some witchcraft questions."

"My wife tells me there's some suspicion of witchcraft, some kind of juju, or gris-gris, or whatever they call it," Randall said. "We have certain letters from my son's servant that said something about witchmen and bush devils. What do you know about this kind of supernatural stuff?"

"Well, Mr. Killigan," said Holmes with a polite sigh, "it takes some doing to answer that kind of a question. It's not a simple thing. Before you can explain things like witchcraft, you have to understand the African mind."

"If understanding the African mind will help me find my son," said Randall, "I'm listening."

"I used to be with the embassy in Ouagadougou, in what was then Upper Volta," Holmes continued. "Now it's called Burkina Faso, or some damn thing. I studied these people for years. They're primitives. They don't understand things the way we do. When something out of the ordinary occurs, they have to invent explanations to account for it."

"Because they are superstitious," Randall inserted helpfully.

"Exactly," said Holmes. "I stayed in a village for a couple of weeks over there. And while I was there, one of the men went crazy. He started seeing things at night, screaming, he stopped eating, he didn't make any sense when he talked. All the other villagers tried to tell me that the man had a witch in his belly, and that the witch was gradually taking over his soul."

Holmes laughed derisively into the phone. "They actually believe that some kind of being or force could enter a person and assume control of his personality. They don't realize that the universe obeys perfectly rational laws of science. Instead, they make the whole thing up as they go along."

"Christ," said Randall, secretly wondering just what it was the man had seen at night that had made him scream.

"They don't realize that the crazy person is probably just afflicted with a garden-variety acute hebephrenia with a lithium-resistant bipolar component, most likely caused by synaptic dysfunction in the pineal body, resulting in elevated serotonin levels and proportionately increased stimulation of neuroreceptors in the hippocampus and the amygdala. Know what I mean?"

Randall was still imagining what a person might act like if a force or a being was taking over his personality. Would the person be aware of the force?

"Of course I know what you mean," snapped Randall. "Psychiatry. Or neurology, or whatever."

"Now. Why don't Africans know what makes people go crazy? Because they know nothing about brain chemistry and metabolic disorders. Because they don't have positron emission tomography, or superconducting quantum interference devices, or single-photon emission computerized tomography. Does that sound like witchcraft? Hell no. That's science. And you can take it to the bank."

Randall was hearing every other word. How, he wondered, would such a being or force present itself?

"What else do you have for me?" he asked irritably.

"That's not the half of it," Holmes said. "They think the entire world is full of invisible spirits, and these spirits live right there with them on the land, appearing to them in dreams and influencing everything that happens in the village. They think they live and dream in some kind of force field, inhabited by demons, witches, devils, genies, sorcerers, and disgruntled ancestors. Any strange or significant place, or any huge or odd object or being—animals, trees, waterfalls, places of ritual—can have a spirit, or a witch. Can you believe it? They're so ignorant and superstitious, they don't realize that everything is actually made up of molecules, consisting of electrons, muons, and neutrinos in orbit around atomic nuclei, together with protons, neutrons, pi mesons, mesons, baryons, kaons, and hadrons, all held together by gluons and made up of quarks of all 'colors' and 'flavors': up quarks, down quarks, top quarks, bottom quarks, anti-quarks, strange quarks, mirror-image quarks, and charmed quarks. Know what I mean?"

"Physics," said Randall, "of course."

"Of course, no one's ever 'seen' these elementary particles in any pedestrian sense of the word, but we 'know' they are there, because we've bombarded them with other elementary particles and observed certain indirect behaviors . . . and, just as you might suspect, all of these particles conform to perfectly rational laws of physics. Does that sound like witchcraft? No, praise God. That's quantum mechanics, and solid enough to build a house on. So let these African villagers go ahead and think spirits run everything, we know better, right?"

"Right," said Randall.

"See, the difference between us and them is that when something out of the ordinary happens over there, they have to invent an explanation, stories, myths, tales of old. Over here, we know that nothing is out of the ordinary, because someone, somewhere, has a perfectly rational scientific explanation for what happened, so we don't have to invent any stories. And frankly, I sleep better because of it."

"Me too," said Randall.

"They think a Great Spirit named *Ngewo*, who lived in a cave, made the world and made all the men and women and animals in the world. Over here, we have scientific evidence. We *know* that the universe really came from a single infinitely dense point of matter, which exploded in the big bang a hundred or so billion years ago. Now, if I had to choose between a story about a spirit in a cave and another one about a single infinitely dense point of matter exploding billions of years ago, I don't have to tell you which one I'd put my faith in."

"Yeah," said Randall.

Mack's intercom light lit up.

"Thanks for the information," said Randall. "I'd like to have my secretary or my wife fax you a copy of that servant's letter, so you can take a look at the description he has of these witchmen coming into the village."

"That would be fine," said Holmes.

Randall turned Holmes over to his secretary, with instructions to get Holmes's fax number, call his wife, and have her fax a copy of the servant's letter. Then he stabbed Mack's intercom light.

"Yeah," said Randall.

"Bat man on line three," said Mack Saplinger over the intercom. "University of California at San Diego. His name is Dr. Veldkamp, Ph.D. in zoology, with a heavy emphasis on you know what. He doesn't speak much English. It's mostly Latin, until he hears the word 'money.' I told him we might need an expert witness on bats, and that you were a lawyer with some bat questions. He said he'd talk to you if he could charge the same hourly rate you do."

"Put him through."

Mack confirmed the connection and hung up.

"Professor Veldkamp," said Randall breezily, "I trust my associate gave you some idea of what we're after. It's really quite a peculiar case, but I guess in my twenty-some years of lawyering, I've used every other kind of expert witness, so why not a bat expert?"

"I hope I can help," said the professor. "Mr. Saplinger gave me your address, so you'll be receiving my résumé and monographs of my journal articles. I'm also the author of two books: *The Ecology of the Dwarf Epauletted Fruit Bat* and *Bat Morphology*. I received my training at the University of Chicago, under Dr. Blanford."

"Right. That's exactly what we need. See, we have a guy who's trying to give away a lot of money. A *lot* of money. I'll stay away from legal terminology, if you stay away from bat terminology. The rich guy—let's call him Midas—has hired us to set up a series of big, complex trusts for him. But one of his would-be heirs—let's call him Harry—is trying to stop Midas and us from giving away the money, because Harry says Midas is incompetent. Nuts. And one of the reasons Harry says Midas is nuts is because Midas claims that one night he saw a big bat. A *huge* bat. I mean, Midas claims this thing had at least a four- or five-foot wingspan. Big! Now, I've got plenty of brainsick clients who tell me all kinds of daffy stories about money, but I've never had one with a bat story, so I'll ask you: Do bats come with wingspans the width of Volkswagens?"

"Of course," said Veldkamp. "Bats have wingspans ranging from five centimeters, about the size of a butterfly, to just under two meters, almost the armspread of a human being. They weigh anywhere from two grams to twelve hundred grams, or three pounds. But where did, uh, Midas see this bat?"

"In his bedroom," said Randall, "in the middle of the night. But he got a pretty good look at it, because he turned on the lights and tried to kill it with a tennis racket."

"I meant, what part of the world? What country?"

"Does that make a difference?"

"No," demurred the professor. "Maybe it doesn't make any difference. Maybe bats are the same everywhere, just like laws. It doesn't matter whether you live in Madagascar or Marin County, the bats and the parking ordinances are the same, right?" He chuckled. "The largest bat in North America is the mastiff bat, *Molossidae eumops*, with a wingspan of about a foot and a half. If Midas was vacationing in Papua New Guinea with some cannibals, he could have seen a flying fox, *Pteropus*, which is more around the size you're talking about, wingspans of one and a half to two meters."

"Let's see," Randall said, "two meters . . ."

"About six feet," said Veldkamp. "Once you get over two feet, you're almost certainly talking Old World. And you're almost certainly dealing with *Megachiroptera*, as opposed to *Microchiroptera*."

"You can't use Latin on the witness stand," said Randall. "Jurors hate it."

"Old World fruit bats. They live in Eurasia, Australia, and Africa. Big, fruit-eating bats," said Veldkamp, "as opposed to other bats, including New World fruit bats, which are much smaller, and different in other ways. Many zoologists speculate that the big Old World fruit bats have an entirely different ancestry than regular bats, because the large fruit bats for the most part do not echolocate."

"Echo . . ." said Randall.

"Echolocate," the professor repeated. "They don't use sonar to hunt and navigate. The big fruit bats see with large, animal-like eyes; most of them don't emit the ultrasonic sounds you've probably heard so much about."

"Fruit bats don't make noise, then?" Randall said. "Because . . ."

"I didn't say that," the professor interrupted. "Bats make some noises, including squeaks and chirps audible to the human ear, but echolocation is almost always ultrasonic, which means humans can't hear it. It's how bats *see*."

"I know that," said Randall. "But this bat made a loud, almost percussive sound . . . definitely audible to the human ear . . . or so Midas said. Like really loud castanets or something. Kind of like a loud *thwock*, Midas says. See, that's another reason Harry says

Midas is nuts, because Harry claims that bats make only noises that humans can't hear, which of course would mean that if Midas *heard* a bat making loud *thwock* noises, then he must be too nuts to handle his money. Belfry syndrome, I guess you might call it."

"Some fruit bats make loud, low-frequency sounds audible to the human ear," said Veldkamp. "The loud *thwock*, that's definitely a fruit bat, and a very special kind of fruit bat. Probably *Hypsignathus monstrosus*, from what you've described to me, since it's known for its distinctively loud voice. Very interesting creatures. They are quite large frugivores, with wingspans well over three feet. They are the so-called hammer-headed or horse-faced bat."

"Yeah!" said Randall, almost too enthusiastically. "It looked like a horse, or a dog's head, with wings!"

"It has a grotesque, swollen muzzle and its lips are covered with wartlike growths."

"That's it!" said Randall. "That's the bat . . . I mean, the one Midas described."

"It has a large, well-developed larynx—almost a sounding board really—for making those distinctive *thwock* sounds."

"That's it! Then he's not crazy," Randall said. "He just found a *hypsig*-whatever in his house."

"If he found a fruit bat with a wingspan of more than two feet, he lives in Asia, Australia, or Africa," said Veldkamp. "If he found *Hypsignathus*, or the horse-faced bat, in his house, then he lives in Africa. Central Africa or West Africa."

Randall swallowed. "He lives in Indianapolis."

Professor Veldkamp chuckled into Randall's ear. "I would love to be an expert witness for you, Mr. Killigan, but I am afraid that there is no way I could convince a jury that a sane person could find an Old World fruit bat with a wingspan of five feet in his bedroom in Indianapolis, unless he put it there himself."

"I see," Randall said, staring into the sea blue of his computer screen. "Maybe I'll call Midas and check on some of those measurements and . . . some of the other stuff. Maybe he's taking medication or something."

"Maybe," said Veldkamp. "If he wants to say he saw it in Indiana, get him down to about a foot, foot and a half tops. And, more important, get rid of the loud *thwock* sound, OK? Otherwise, he was traveling in West Africa when he saw it."

"I'll be back in touch," said Randall.

A ring-again call came through as soon as his line opened.

"I've got that Nimrod medical stuff you wanted," said Mack over the speaker.

"Nimrod?" said Randall blankly.

"The CEO's wife," Mack said. "I've got it right here. My guess is that she's seeing things and she can't sleep at night."

"Get on with it," said Randall.

"*Annals of Neurology*," said Mack. "May 1990. 'Peduncular Hallucinosis Associated with Isolated Infarction of the Substantia Nigra Pars Reticulata.' " He paused and chuckled. "Already I can tell you she won't like the bill. In law as in medicine, mouthfuls of Latin mean the bill is going up."

"Talk," barked Randall.

"Here's another one. *Neurology*. October 1983. 'Peduncular Hallucinations Caused by Brain-Stem Compression.' Peduncular hallucinations are vivid, colored visual images of people, animals, plants, scenes, or geometric patterns, usually associated with brainstem lesions of vascular and infectious etiology.

"The *Annals* article gives a history of the disease. They used to think it was a dissociated state of sleep in which the visual hallucinations were dreams occurring in a state of relative wakefulness. Another guy, Van Bogaert or some such, says peduncular hallucinosis is a state of ego dissolution with loss of the ability to distinguish external reality from imagination.

"Hello?" said Mack.

"I'm here," said Randall, feeling his ego dissolve and seep through his imagination into external reality.

"So, if she has peduncular hallucinosis, it would seem that she has a vascular lesion, an infectious lesion, or a craniopharyngioma, which is a tumor of the . . ."

"What kind of tests do they run on people to find out what's causing it?" asked Randall, not wanting to hear about tumors just now.

"CAT scans and MRIs mostly," said Mack. "But before those were invented, they usually had to wait for an autopsy. As near as I can tell, nobody really knows how or why midbrain lesions disturb sleep or give rise to visual hallucinations. Sleep is disturbed, intense visual hallucinations occur, the guy dies about six months later, and when they open his head and scoop it out, they find midbrain lesions."

Modem lights blinked, and messages flashed across the top of his computer screen. He recognized his stockbroker's logo graphic followed by a streamer of bright white letters: "Get happy! Merck up 6½ on steady volume."

(8)

Boone woke from a sleep as deep and dank as death, shrouded in the bone-white cloud of his mosquito net, steeped in his sweaty sleeping bag, and raw from the prickles of the tick mattress. Had he heard a man shouting, or had he dreamed it?

"ALLAH AKBAR! ALLAH AKBAR! ALLAH AKBAR!"

In the foredawn silence, a voice bawled the vowels out in the full-throated sonority of a town crier, punctuated by the thud of a drum. Someone stirred on Sisay's side of the wall.

"Sisay," Boone said, in a voice he hoped would make it up the cement wall, over the din from outside, under the zinc-pan roof, and into Sisay's quarters. "Someone is shouting outside. It may be an emergency or something. I can't tell. Is something wrong?"

"Only with you," Sisay said. "It's morning and you're still in bed."

"But the yelling," Boone said. "What is he saying? What time is it?"

"I can see you're a real world traveler," said Sisay derisively. "Half the planet has been hearing 'Allah akbar' five times a day for the last thirteen hundred years, and you've never even heard it once."

"I'm from Indiana," Boone protested. "You know, one of those American high school graduates who can't find Africa on a map of the world."

"The village muezzin is filling his lungs with the mighty breath of Allah and is calling the men to morning prayers. He is telling you, in Arabic, that God is great. That's one translation. God is most mighty is another. When I was new to the country, I asked a wise old pa to translate 'Allah akbar' for me. He told me it means God is very, very big."

"What time is it?"

"Morning time."

"ALLAH AKBAR! ALLAH AKBAR! ALLAH AKBAR!"

This time the bellowing was so loud it reverberated in Boone's open, empty aluminum canteen, setting up a dissonant, antiphonal moan.

"Consider yourself blessed," Sisay advised. "In many villages, they use battery-powered bullhorns to tell people just how big God is."

Boone heard sandaled feet scuffling across woven mats in the next room.

"I'll be back in half an hour," he said, banging the screen door behind him.

Boone turned over and listened to Sisay greeting other villagers on their way to prayers.

"Morning-O, Mistah Aruna. How de body?"

"I tell God tank ya," Sisay replied.

"Na de *poo-mui* stranger, he no come foh morning prayers?" a voice asked.

"Na America he been come out," Sisay explained. "America man, he no pray." Then in a loud voice Boone felt was directed at his window, Sisay said, "In America they pray to television sets and video display terminals."

"Vee-dee-oh dees-play tah-me-nahls," a voice repeated.

"Whatin tele-vish-ee-ohn?" asked another voice.

"Na foh make you stupid," said Sisay. "Foh make you eyes big, and you brain small. Foh make you greedy too much. Foh make you one greedy big eye. Naim dat."

"ALLAH AKBAR! ALLAH AKBAR! ALLAH AKBAR!"

As soon as the muezzin left off, Boone drifted back into a doze populated by hooded figures calling from minarets. Then he heard what sounded like a soul shrieking in the seventh rung of Dante's Hell, where the violent and the bestial gnaw their flesh in a river of boiling blood. *What now?* he wondered. He had already been awakened during the night by a "palaver," which, according to Sisay, had arisen out of a woman damage case. Some of the young men in the village had slept with two young wives of the section chief, which gave the chief the right to seek healthy fines for woman damage. The actual offense had occurred some time ago, but last night Moiwo's representative and the young men and their extended families stayed up half the night in the neighboring *barri* arguing about the amount of labor required to discharge the fines.

Geckos had also kept him up most of the night. The geckos he had seen in Freetown were apparently an urban, domesticated variety; these village geckos were far more aggressive. They rattled the underside of the zinc-pan roof through the night—saurian warriors marauding and devouring their weight in insects. And now in the first light of dawn, he could see them wearing green and orange war paint, streaking across the ceiling like iridescent lightning bolts, preying godlessly on the orders of the insects, their mouths crusty with the guts of night killings.

Again he heard wraiths of hell braying in terror and agony. *Roosters*, he suddenly concluded. *Cocks crowing*. Not just any cocks, though. Not the Old MacDonald cock-a-doodle-doo American barnyard domestics. These shrieking voices were as old as time and crowing with the terror of the first and last dawn. In the blender of his hypnopompic imagination, the cocks grew human voices and began a horrid chorus in strophe and antistrophe: "The world ends today!" squawked one forlorn soul, with a rasping wail from a throat that would be slit before sundown. "The world ends today!" cried another in the same anguished squall that passioned the night when Peter denied Christ. "Never heard of the guy!" another repeated thrice, with the squawk of a doomed parakeet in a collapsed mine shaft. "Who's he?" crowed one in rut, mounting a hen from behind and drawing blood from her neck with its beak. It was the cry of Nature taking God's name in vain and devouring itself in a rage of famine.

After the cocks left off, a dozen infants with dry bellies took over, sending up a rondo of bloodcurdling squalls for milk from the breasts of mothers who were in no apparent hurry to feed them. Boone listened to the jabber of women and children in neighboring dwellings, their voices twining like strands in a communal fabric, with distinctive aural patches forming at various dwellings within earshot. A husband and wife quarreled to the left of him. Several women argued over a howling infant to his right. A small boy sang songs to his brothers and sisters behind. The infant's howling changed to choking, accompanied by the excited chatter of the women in attendance.

In the courtyard outside his window, small children had gathered with trays, calling out the virtues of their wares:

"I got de sweet benny seed cake."

"I got de fine-fine kola nut."

"De sweet orange ih dae foh you. Three foh five cent. No moh."

He heard sandals scuffling across the veranda, followed by the squeak and clatter of a falling pot handle.

"Kong, kong," said a female voice at the door to Sisay's quarters.

Boone opened his door and found a young woman bearing a pot, a platter of cakes, and two canteen cups.

"Is that coffee?" he asked hopefully.

"Ih dae," she said, setting the coffee and cups on the concrete knee wall of the veranda. "Fine-fine cakes dae," she added, lowering a platter of fried dough and sesame seed cakes. She was plump, but still shapely and graceful. He watched her pour coffee into cups.

"Whay you name?" she asked with a grin, looking over her shoulder and catching him in the act of admiring her.

"Boone," he said. "Boone Westfall."

"Usai you come out so?"

"What?" said Boone.

She smiled apologetically and covered her mouth. Then she straightened, assumed the posture of a child reciting her school lessons, and said in careful, exaggerated English, "Where you come from?"

"America," said Boone.

"A name, Jenisa," she said. "A yam young wife to Section Chief Moiwo. He say me send you dis food foh welcahm you na Salone."

"Tell him thank you very much," said Boone. "I'd like very much to meet him. Does he live here, in this village?"

"He is a big man," she said. "He has many houses. Sometime he stay na hya. Sometime he stay na Ndevehun. Sometime he stay Freetown. Sometime he stay Bo. Na elections dae come. He go wakka-wakka, talking for elections. He go wan make ihnself Paramount Chief. He no hya foh sometime. Naim dat."

Her eyes went from Boone to his backpack.

"Whay you wife?"

"I don't have a wife," he said.

"Na lie you dae lie," she said. "You get beaucoup wife na America."

"I don't have a wife. I've never been married."

"You think me stupid? You wan wash me face foh me? You get beaucoup wife dae na America. Whatin na you come na hya foh do?"

"I am looking for my friend. Michael Killigan. He is a Peace Corps Volunteer."

"Peace Koh," she repeated. "I sabby ihm. Den say he been come out Ndevehun."

"What do they say happened to him?"

"I no know. Dey no see ahm," she said. "Den say he been go alackey."

"Alackey?" Boone asked.

"He craze. He done run off. Den say he come out Ndevehun. Dey no go able foh see ahm. Better no dae inside Ndevehun."

"What can you tell me about something called *hale* medicine?" Boone asked.

"*Hale*?" she said, pouring brown water into one of the cups. "Na medicine. Which kind *hale*?"

"How about the kind of *hale* that witchmen or bush devils use?" he said.

She averted her eyes. "I no know," she said, setting the pot back onto the tray with a clatter. "I no know."

Her eyes fell on the table with the hurricane lamp and personal items he had strewn there.

"What ees thees?" she said, picking up a stick applicator of mosquito repellent.

"It's mosquito repellent," he said, again admiring the look of her. "It keeps mosquitoes away." Then, noting the fascination shining in her eyes: "Would you like to have it?"

"I can have it?" she asked eagerly.

"Sure," said Boone. "And maybe you can do something for me?"

"Whatin?" she asked.

"Some people say that witchmen or bush devils came to my friend's village and did something to him with *hale*, or took him away into the bush. Have you ever heard about anything like that happening before?"

"I no understand," she said. "I no know." She slipped the repellent into her lappa and wiped her hands. "Better no dae," she said, becoming distressed. "I dae go." She put her hand on the door latch and showed him her round, black Mende face. Her nostrils flared slightly with emotion, and one tear beaded in the corner of her eye.

"Could you ask around for me," said Boone, "and see if that sort of thing ever happens to white men? And maybe where these witches and devils hide out or meet?"

"I no understand," she said, her eyes widening. "I no get word for talk. I dae go."

She rounded the corner of the veranda and disappeared into the adjoining courtyard.

Apparently, all over Sierra Leone, coffee was brewed by dumping grounds in a pot of water and boiling it. It fell to the coffee drinker to sip the hot water out of the cup and leave the sediment behind. Boone fingered a cake, and found a small, sealed white envelope under the cakes. Neatly printed with a fountain pen on watermarked bond was the following message:

We can help you find your brother, if you will feed the medicine.
Don't speak about this with *anyone* until we meet. I will reach you.

Idrissa Moiwo
Section Chief

Boone heard the sounds of men returning from prayers. He stuffed the paper into his pocket and ate another cake. He heard Sisay's voice briefly, before it was drowned out by the braying of domestic animals, the clatter of utensils on stones, and the continued choking and howling of the neighboring infants. He was relieved to see his host.

"The babies," Boone said with a wince, "are they sick or what?"

"Noisy, aren't they?" said Sisay. "And you want to know why? Well, for simplicity's sake, let's say we're hearing six kids scream their lungs out. According to the field studies, one is bawling because he will die of dysentery or malnutrition before his first birthday, another has the same afflictions but will make it past his first birthday, only to die of something else before his fifth, the other four are howling because they are enraged at the prospect of spending their infancy sucking on dry dugs, sweltering in mud huts, and listening to the death rattles of their cousins."

Sisay cocked his head and listened to more wailing and choking. "However, just now, I think we are hearing young Fatmata and her sister Nyanda choking her little Borboh with cassava pap. A Mende mother is taught to force-feed her infant until its stomach is 'hard,' whatever that means. It's a senseless custom, but the women swear by it. The first year I was here, an infant 'stopped breathing' shortly after one of these feeding sessions. No connection between that and the cassava packing, of course."

The sputtering and gagging continued, punctuated with screams of anguish when the infant managed a breath.

"And you just let it happen?" Boone asked, not bothering to conceal his exasperation.

"No," said Sisay. "I tried to tell them that it was a poor nutritional regimen. I told them the babies could choke to death from being force-fed. I said I knew of no possible benefit to be gained from cramming food down an infant's throat."

"And?"

"They ignored me. What would a white man know about raising a Mende peekin in the bush?"

The infant hacked and spat, coughed, choked, gagged, and let out a shriek, followed by the nattering of women, presumably telling each other the best technique for force-feeding an infant.

"I can't stand it," Boone said. "I have to do something."

"That makes me nervous," said Sisay. "That's when white people are most dangerous. When they try to make things 'better' for Africans. When white people are trying to enslave Africans or rob them, the Africans usually know just what to do. They've dealt with slave traders, invaders, and plunderers for centuries. They usually quench the world's thirst for slaves by capturing some of their enemies and selling them to the slave traders. But when white people come in with a lot of money or 'know-how' and try to make things 'better,' that's when things really go to hell. Why can't white people just visit? Why must they always meddle? It's as if you were invited to dinner at someone's house and during your brief visit you insisted on rearranging all the furniture in the house to suit your tastes."

The infant gagged violently and choked.

"But you can't just sit here and let a helpless infant choke to death, can you?"

"I can," Sisay said. "Maybe you can't. Maybe you should go see what you can do. Some of the women Volunteers down south tried to do something about it. Like most white people, they fancied themselves as some kind of cultural police. They were quite upset with the way the Sande matrons trained young women: the mandatory clitoridectomies during the initiation rituals, the force-feeding of infants, the polygamy, the brutal manual labor for women, while the men drink palm wine and gamble. The Volunteers held clinics for the village women and tried to convince them that the Sande matrons were part of an ageless male conspiracy to devalue and enslave women. The Volunteers announced that the Sande Society initiation, which young girls are taught to anticipate with great joy and excitement, was nothing but genital mutilation and brainwashing, designed to turn women into chattel kept by men.

"The Mende women said, in essence, 'Thanks for your opinion, but we've been doing things this way for thousands of years, and we don't need you to come in and tell us what to do with our bodies,' an argument which one would think might appeal to these *poo-mui* feminists. But no such luck. They stepped up their cultural chauvinism and did everything they could to rearrange the furniture during their visit.

"A few of the Volunteers were actually making progress, and by that I mean some of the more educated women at least started listening to them . . . until the word got out."

"The word?"

"Somebody made the mistake of telling one of the village women about abortion rights, and it was over. The next time the women organized their clinic, one of the Sande matrons took the floor and said, in essence, 'These *poo-mui* women are trying to tell you that initiation is harmful and bad, that we should tell our husbands they can have only one wife, and that we should not force-feed our peekins. Guess what? In America, they let medicine men cut healthy peekins out of their mothers' bellies, then they throw the peekins into latrines. How's that for savagery?'

"So much for the clinic. The Volunteers had to be reassigned, because the village women thought the *poo-mui* women were witches trying to trick them out of their children so they could take them into the bush and eat them."

More sputtering, coughing, hacking.

"Nothing is simple when it comes to mixing cultures," Sisay said. "That's why many people argue that Africa would be better off if you and your countrymen just . . . left, and took your money and your 'good' intentions with you."

"Kong, kong," came from the wooden door, this time male voices.

Two men appeared wearing Muslim burnooses and skullcaps. Sisay introduced them, and each of them bestowed a kola nut on Boone, which he learned was to bring him good luck during his stay in Sierra Leone. After exchanging greetings for a good half an hour, the men went on their way, and Boone bit into one of the kola nuts, finding the texture of a damp macadamia nut and a taste so violently bitter it seemed to absorb every trace of moisture in his mouth.

"What the hell is it?" asked Boone with puckered lips and a screwed-up face.

"Caffeine, nicotine, and aspirin all found in the same nut. It's given as a gift of greeting or farewell, as medicine, or primarily as a stimulant to keep hungry people working when there is nothing to eat, or to keep devil dancers going all night and into the next day. You took too big of a bite. You'll get quite a buzz off even a nibble or two."

"It tastes like a macadamia nut pickled in turpentine."

Sisay sat on the floor and took a bite.

"More trouble in the village," he said. "Mama Saso miscarried a set of twins last night, which will make things very touchy around here for a while. The birth of these twins had been foretold in a dream, but now they are dead. Twins have special cultic powers. They can foretell the future and protect the family from witches. But now, of course, the villagers are saying that the witches ate these twins before they could be born."

"What isn't caused by witches?" asked Boone.

"The Mende will stoically accept almost any hardship," said Sisay. "But when an abnormally high number of infants start to die, it's usually because of witchcraft."

He went to the water pail and served up two cups of water.

The most annoying thing about his host, Boone thought, was the way he pointedly omitted expressing disapproval of anything native, especially witchcraft, or this barbaric stuffing of infant bellies. He also had displayed a respect for native medicines, even though, according to Lewis, the native cures for such things as snakebite were not nearly as effective as the antivenin found in the clinics.

Boone was suddenly tired—perhaps because the kola-nut buzz had worn off—and was thinking about retiring to his room for a nap before lunch.

"I have arranged the naming ceremony," Sisay said, interrupting his inclinations to rest alone for a while. "Bring a gift for your father. Do you have any cigarettes, another T-shirt, or anything else in your immense American backpack that you could bestow upon your father as a gift?"

"No cigarettes," Boone said. "But I have several tobacco pipes."

"The perfect gift," said Sisay, "and not by chance. Your ancestors are looking out for you."

Boone rummaged and grumbled, deciding that this relentless gifting of authority figures who suddenly wanted to be related to him would get old fast, unless he put his foot down, preferably in his host's mouth during one of his speeches. The entire cultural history of the village was being played out for him, while hours, days—two days!—were almost gone. In America, a missing person was an emergency. Here, there were more important things to do, like pretend you are related to somebody you never saw before.

Boone selected the most battered of his three briar pipes and took along a small pouch of terrible French tobacco.

He followed his host through the meandering courtyards of the village, where the workday was under way. Women in groups of three or four, some with children strapped to them, pestled rice by lifting eight-foot logs and dropping them into mortars carved from tree stumps. Steady and rhythmic as human derricks, they sang to the thud of wood on rice on wood. Others winnowed the husks from the kernels by tossing the pulverized rice with fans, allowing the shredded hulls to flutter off like insect wings in the morning breeze. A small peekin with a goatee of bluish breast milk bounced in his mother's lap, slinging her sagging breasts about by the dugs like a drunkard with the nozzles of two tapped kegs in hand. A naked boy zealously guarded a patch of poured cement, where cocoa beans were drying in the sun, pelting marauding chickens with stones. Boone later learned the peekin's zeal was inspired by the prospect of a meal if he did his job, and nothing for supper if his mother found roosters in the cocoa beans.

Boone wandered over to a group of women hulling rice and greeted a scrawny grandma who looked as if the effort of hoisting the huge pestle would kill her before lunch.

She laughed and smiled, until he put his hands on the pole and offered to hull a little while for her.

A look of horror broke out on her face and she called her relatives to come share her apparent indignation.

Boone hulled a few times to show them what he had in mind.

Their mouths fell open. They shouted. They stared, their eyes bloodshot with shock and disbelief. The old woman screamed with a vile look. She was insulted and enraged. She looked like she was getting ready to spit in his face, as if he had just asked her to go to bed with him, or to watch him go to the bathroom.

The women quickly decided, *poo-mui* guest or no, they would take matters into their own hands. Two of them took the pestle from him and the rest of them pushed him away angrily, shouting at him and calling for Sisay to please take control of his stranger.

"What the fuck are you doing?" Sisay yelled, pulling him away from them.

"I was trying to help," said Boone, shrugging him off. "She looked tired and sweaty and too old for the job."

Behind him the women were now in a circle pointing at him and calling their neighbors out of their houses to hear about the *poo-mui*'s outrageous behavior.

"Hulling rice is women's work," said Sisay. "Now they think you are mentally ill. And you touched the thing with your left hand!"

"I was trying to help," said Boone.

"You failed," said Sisay. "A man doing women's work is about as acceptable as cross-dressing over here. You would have made a better first impression if you'd come out of your room wearing a negligee. Now they are saying you grabbed the pestle because you don't have a penis."

His host seemed truly upset, but Boone cared less and less. He was on the verge of leaving the village to find this Moiwo fellow and see what "feeding the medicine" was all about. For now, he followed his host through the courtyards, around wells, and under shaded baffas, waving at the citizenry and hoping the naming ceremony would be a short one. Emaciated, ancient women sat in shaded verandas, batting flies away from their faces, while peekins braided their grandmothers' hair and listened to the ancestral songs. An old pa wobbled one of his last teeth out of its socket and held the bloody enamel gem in his fingertips, considering it philosophically. One woman was so decrepit, she sat alone in a dark, shaded corner, her arms wrapped around the folded bones of her legs. She coughed softly into her kneecaps. When she called to the white men in Mende, Boone saw bare gums stained orange by kola nuts. She gestured at them with a fingerless hand, a stump with smooth, rounded knobs where the digits belonged.

Sisay greeted her, then shrugged his shoulders, gestured at Boone, and spoke Mende, continuing on his way.

"What did she want?" Boone asked.

"Medicine," he said. "The old ones all think you have medicine and snuff because you are white. Every once in a while, one will follow you all day, like a stray, asking everybody you visit with if you gave them any snuff. The old grandmas love snuff. The British used to hand it out like candy."

"What happened to her? Where did she find a piece of machinery that could do that to her hand?"

"Hands plural," Sisay said. "Leprosy. There are no machines around here. No gas or electricity. Plenty of diseases, though."

Until Lewis had mentioned lepers in Freetown, Boone thought leprosy had gone out with chariot races and the fall of the Roman Empire, but he was afraid to show his ignorance.

"I know what you're thinking," said Sisay. "It's still quite common in the Third World, but you don't hear about it much anymore, because white people don't get it. You need dark, overcrowded, unsanitary conditions. Nine people sleeping in one room with chickens, goats, and a few peekins. We also still have lots of polio, measles, whooping cough, and a dozen other diseases that have been eradicated where you come from. You probably won't get any of those, but don't worry, you will get malaria, whether you take the chloroquine or not. You can bet on that. It's the common cold of West Africa."

"How bad is it?" asked Boone.

"I don't know whether it's the high fevers or the chloroquine you take to get rid of it," said Sisay, "but you'll see things . . . like the inside of your soul. The first time is the worst. You'll be so hot, they'll be frying eggs on you."

"I'm taking the prophylactic," said Boone. "That should protect me for a week or two."

"It might brighten up your fever delusions a little bit," said Sisay with a threatening laugh, "but it won't protect you."

They arrived at a compound several courtyards distant, and Sisay tapped on the door.

"Kong, kong," he said. "Mistah Aruna done come foh name ihn strangah."

A man in a clean safari-style shirt, matching pants, and sandals greeted them and introduced himself as a schoolteacher. He showed them into a single large room, darkened by drawn shutters, with a cooking fire in one corner and ten or twelve tick mattresses arranged around the perimeters. Small curtains or stacks of chests and boxes separated some of the berths into private cubicles. Bundles and bags hung from the tie beams, along with cutlasses and rusted farm implements. On one wall hung a calendar from 1957 showing the snow-capped Grand Tetons; on another was a stained and tattered poster of Ronald Reagan, the actor, circa 1940, gift-wrapping a carton of Chesterfield cigarettes and smoking a fag. Ron was advising, "I send cartons of Chesterfields to all my friends . . . What better Christmas gift?" Hard by Ron's poster was a glossy of an African couple romantically sharing a glass of Guinness stout. The look on the woman's face was calculated to separate a male of any race, color, or creed from a day's pay for two bottles of Guinness stout.

The three men took seats on a hardened mud floor. After introductions the teacher interviewed Boone briefly on the particulars of his visit, then poured what looked like dirty dishwater out of a brown jug into four cups. A woman in a headwrap and a lappa emerged from the shadows and ladled rice and sauce onto plates. Then the teacher took the pot and ladled food onto a plate-sized leaf, setting that portion aside, together with a bowl of water. He closed his eyes, and spoke Mende, while pouring one of the cups of dirty dishwater slowly onto the dirt floor.

"What's he doing?" asked Boone.

"The ancestors are gathering to celebrate your naming day," said Sisay.

Boone looked askance into the shadows. "Their ancestors or my ancestors?"

"Your American ancestors live in Indiana," Sisay said, "and they probably stopped having anything to do with you long ago, because you do not honor them, or feed them. Today, your African ancestors are gathering to baptize you as a new member of their family and to share in this meal."

"These gathering ancestors," Boone said, again scouting the interior of the hut. "I'm assuming they are dead, right? So they don't actually eat or drink, do they? I mean, it's symbolic or something, right?"

The teacher laughed. "If the ancestors did not eat or drink, I am quite sure we would not be wasting real food and good palm wine on them."

Sisay and the teacher shook their heads and commiserated with one another on the incongruous stupidity of white people.

"The teacher is preparing food and pouring libation for them. The rice has been cooked in red palm oil with no pepper. The dead hate pepper. The teacher is telling the ancestors that, if they will intervene for you and ask Our Father, *Ngewo*, to keep you safe and to help you find your brother, you will return and offer them a big pot of sweet upland rice and a cooked fowl."

The teacher offered Boone a cup of the dirty dishwater and handed another to Sisay. Sisay and the teacher drank. Boone stared into his cup.

The teacher is handing me hemlock, thought Boone, mentally mocking the monotonous piety of Sisay's tone.

"Palm wine," Sisay said.

"Is it . . . ?"

"Why don't you put some of your water tablets in it before you drink it," he said acidly, then added, "And if you do that, you can pack and take the next *podah-podah* to Pujehun and stay with Sam Lewis."

Boone thought that sounded like a fine idea. He pretended to take a swallow, smiling broadly, though he discovered that the stuff not only looked like dirty dishwater, it tasted like it too.

Sisay set his cup aside and rose. "You, and you alone, must be the first person to hear your name. I'll wait outside."

Once Sisay had gone, the teacher handed Boone another cup of palm wine. "Your name is Gutawa Sisay," he said solemnly. "You are Pa Ansumana Sisay's grandson and the brother of Mistah Aruna Sisay. *Hota gama hota ta mamaloi mia.* A stranger's stranger is the grandchild of the host. I have asked that our prayers and our offerings reach *Ngewo*. I have asked that they reach *Kenei* Amadu and *Kenei* Nduawo and all our forefathers who have crossed the waters and stay in the bosom of *Ngewo*. From this day forward, you will never be alone. Whether you are traveling in this world or in the village of white sands across the waters, your ancestors will be with you. They will be watching you. When you are sleeping, your ancestors will appear to you in dreams. When you suffer, they will hear your prayers. When you need *Ngewo*'s help because you are in trouble, they will take your part and speak to Him on your behalf. When you are hungry, they will see that your farm gives you crops and that fish swim into your nets. When you are in pain, they will make you strong and teach you to bear it. When you are afraid, they will give you courage. And when you are alone on your deathbed and remembering your sweet life of dancing and feasting, they will be with you. They will greet you when you cross the waters and go to the village of white sands, where you will live with them forever in the bosom of *Ngewo*."

The teacher filled the cups with more palm wine, then called out, "Mistah Aruna! Come, look you brothah, Gutawa Sisay, done come."

Sisay reappeared in the doorway and spoke Mende to the teacher, who promptly rose to his feet. Then, turning to Boone, Sisay said, "Get up. Your grandfather is coming."

Sisay stepped back from the door and motioned to Boone, reminding him to grasp his right wrist with his left hand as a gesture of respect.

A backlit silhouette in a short-sleeved tunic barely filled the doorway that both Boone and Sisay had stooped to enter. Pa Ansumana Sisay entered the quarters with the gait of an aged man who was still used to having things his way. He greeted the teacher and the white men in quiet musical Mende, acknowledging Boone's two-handed handshake with a hoot of merriment and a nod of approval to Sisay. A threadbare skullcap sat lightly on his baldness, and a clay pipe was held in place by ragged molars. In the firelight, his face was a graven image, cratered by the elements and undiagnosed skin disorders—the eyes set in small, dark caverns over a bluff Mende nose that was as broad as the snout of an ox.

The face belonged on a statue peering down from a pedestal or from the second story of a cathedral, the features masterfully exaggerated by a sculptor. Words were unnecessary. Let young mortals use words. Pa Ansumana had only to lift his stately head, as black and weathered as a crag of obsidian. It said: I have survived seven decades of witchcraft, politics, cholera, floods, droughts, military coups, famine, tribal wars, failed crops, court cases, fines, squabbling with relatives, dysentery, falls from palm trees, riots, taxes, tainted water, corrupt Paramount Chiefs, poverty, thieves, deadly swears, driver ants, secret societies, yellow fever, government men, leopards, white mining speculators, intestinal parasites, the British, snakebite, chronic malaria, and bush devils . . . What have you done?

His age put everyone on notice that they were dealing with a force of nature and a powerful human being who had surpassed insurmountable odds in a land where most people died before their fortieth birthday. His enemies were all dead, and their debts to him had been paid by their survivors. He was well into his second set of wives—six of them—with as many farms, tended by legions of children, grandchildren, and boyfriends to his junior wives, all owing ultimate fealty to Pa Ansumana. Swears bounced off him like rubber bullets from toy guns. He knew more about witchcraft than witches, more about secret societies than the headmen, and more about the bush than bush devils. When the well was tainted by witchcraft or poor sanitary techniques, whole compounds took to their pallets with fever and dysentery, infants died, robust diamond miners were laid low in latrines for days on end, but Pa Ansumana belched, rubbed his tummy, picked up his cutlass, and went out to brush his farms.

"This is your grandfather," Sisay said. "He is your grandfather because he is my father and you are my stranger. Therefore, you are now my little brother. Michael Killigan is a good man and a good friend. His friend is my brother. But I must warn you," he said. "You must never do anything to shame me or to shame my father. Understand?"

Boone nodded and wondered what would happen to him if he inadvertently shamed Sisay or Pa Ansumana.

Pa Ansumana looked upon his new grandson with twinkling eyes and said, "*Nyandengo!*"

Boone presented the pipe and tobacco, and his grandfather's eyes gleamed with appreciation.

"*Nyandengo!*" This was followed by more Mende spoken to Sisay.

Then Pa Ansumana turned and lifted his arms, placing his hands over Boone's head. Boone looked up and saw gnarled muscles spangled with veins, swaddled in creased black skin, scaly as a tortoise's. He felt compelled to kneel or bow, as Pa Ansumana summoned the Mende God, *Ngewo*, with the familiarity of an Old Testament prophet entreating Yahweh, and bestowed Mende blessings on his new grandson.

> "*Ngewo i bi mahugbe.*
> *Ngewo i bi lamagbate panda.*
> *Ngewo i bi yama gole.*
> *Ngewo i bi go a ndileli nya hangoi hu.*
> *Ngewo i bi go a ndevu hu guha.*
> *Ngewo i bi go a ndenga*
> *Ngewo i bi go a gbotoa.*"

"God take care of you," translated Sisay. "God walk you well (safe journey). God keep you in a good way. God give you a clean face (good fortune). God give you peace after I am dead. God give you long life. God give you children. God give you many blessings."

Boone suddenly felt charmed, convinced that this man had the power to bless him and approach God on his behalf.

"He says you are a good grandson, and that I have trained you very well, that this is a very fine gift that would make any grandfather's heart big with pride. He is very happy you are here and happy you will be his grandson."

"Tell him I am happy and honored to be his grandson," said Boone.

News of Boone's African name spread quickly, and his neighbors were anxious to try it out on him. Everywhere he went, citizens sang out from the verandas, "Afternoon-O, Mistah Gutawa. How de body?"

When he answered in Krio and allowed how he told God thank you for it, they laughed and slapped their thighs.

A troop of adolescents arrived at Sisay's compound and called him "Mastah Gutawa," which rubbed his American civil rights sensibilities the wrong way. They wanted to sweep his room, brook his clothes, fetch water for bathing and drinking, and cook his food. Among them, he recognized the woman named Jenisa, who had brought him his morning coffee and cakes.

He proudly told them that he would not be needing help with these activities, as he was quite capable of looking after them himself. He was not the sort of white man who wanted African people to do menial labor for him, and he had no intention of hiring them as servants. One of the youngsters comprehended the gist of Boone's message and explained it to his companions, causing their faces to contort in distress and disappointment.

"Mastah? You no go hire us foh work?"

"I am not your master," Boone said. "Do you understand? I'm just a person, like you. Not a master."

They looked at each other in dismay.

"Mastah, we no understand whatin you dae talk."

"I am not your master," he repeated. "Do you understand?"

"Yes, mastah," they said disconsolately.

"You don't understand," he said, becoming equally distressed. "I am not your master. Do not call me master."

"Yes, mastah," they said in unison.

He threw up his hands. They hung their heads and walked away grumbling.

Sisay watched the entire exchange from the veranda, shaking his head, the usual derisive twist adorning the corners of his mouth.

"Congratulations," he said. "You just told six kids whose pas make about two hundred bucks a year that they can't have any of your money, even though it's all but spilling out of your pockets."

"But they wanted to be my servants!" Boone protested. "They were calling me their master."

"You can't live here without spreading some of that money around. You're a millionaire. Enjoy yourself. Share the wealth. For twenty-five cents, someone will clean your room. During the dry season, for a dime, someone else will walk two miles for you to get a bucket of water for you to bathe in. For fifty cents, someone will cook you a meal and serve it to you. Nobody here is going to admire you for not hiring servants. You'll just be thought of as unbelievably stingy, a krabbit man, as they say in Krio."

"But I don't want servants," he complained. "I don't like to be waited on."

"Think of yourself as a major corporation," said Sisay, rising from the hammock. "You can't come into town and not hire anyone. It just won't work. You can think about it, Mistah Gutawa Sisay, on your way to meet your neighbors and ask after your friend."

Sisay picked up the chicken and a sack of onions and handed them to Boone. "Fowl," he said, handing him the chicken. "Yabbas," he added, passing him the sack of onions. "Pa Gigba is in from the fields. He was in Killigan's village for a funeral on the day Michael Killigan disappeared. Follow me with your sambas."

Dusk was upon the village. The boom box was cranked up again, this time putting out "Sugar Magnolia." Sisay led Boone across a neighboring courtyard, past a well and a thatched gazebo, and into another courtyard, where they approached a hut with a flap of canvas for a door.

Sisay called through the flap in Mende and voices came from within. Several peekins banged open the flap and stared at Boone. "Poo-mui! Poo-mui!"

Sisay spoke more Mende, and a male voice inside the hut responded. A stream of chattering women and children emerged. Sisay held the flap back and waved Boone into the hut.

Inside was a mud-walled den of chaos, lit by a kerosene lantern and filled with squawking chickens, more naked children, a dog, dirty plates in a bucket, and bundles of bedding. The rafters were strung with belongings and implements. The lantern scattered swollen shadows of people and objects.

An old pa in a white stocking cap and a Bart Simpson T-shirt rose out of the shadows and half stood under the low ceiling to take Boone's hand. The man spoke Mende to Boone. Boone nodded and smiled.

Geckos chased cockroaches in the bevels of the smooth earthen floor; chickens chased the geckos; an old ma chased the chickens; and the food chain came full circle when a cockroach clambered onto an untended dish of rice.

"Give him the sambas," said Sisay, smiling at Pa Gigba.

Boone presented the fowl, careful to use his right hand, and followed with the onions.

"*Nyandengo!*" Pa Gigba cried, showing crooked teeth set in gray gums. "Sweet yabbas!"

"Pa Gigba traveled to Ndevehun, the village where Lamin Kaikai, Michael Killigan, lives," said Sisay. "He attended the funeral of his niece there some weeks ago, and saw Michael Killigan before he disappeared."

Pa Gigba spoke Mende and motioned at a patch of earthen floor. He kicked a trough of bananas aside and removed a small child from the area. He said something in Mende to the child, and the child bowed its head and shuffled off.

Sisay promptly squatted, and Boone gingerly lowered himself onto the ground, not sure that he wanted to assume a cross-legged squat in such a place, afraid a chicken or a peekin might flounder into his lap.

Sisay and Gigba exchanged pleasantries and asked after one another's families for a good half an hour. Boone sighed loudly and studied the interior of the place, wondering if it would be impolite for him to pull out his Swiss Army knife and cut his fingernails.

Finally, Boone heard the words "Mistah Lamin" and "Ndevehun."

"*Sabu gbiina,*" the man said anxiously. "Kaikai no dae. Better no dae."

"What?" Boone asked curtly. "Kaikai is Killigan's African name, right?"

"Oh," said Sisay sarcastically, "I thought you were interrupting to ask Pa Gigba how his family is doing. I thought you were about to ask if his wives, sons, and daughters are healthy, and how the harvest is going for him this year. I should have known better."

"My best friend is missing and probably in some kind of trouble," Boone said with a clenched smile. "I'm here to find him. Does this guy know anything, or not?"

Sisay took a deep breath and fixed a baleful eye on his companion.

"Maybe I should just tell all the villagers to drop everything they are doing. Leave their cutlasses on the farms, let the sick children die in the huts, forget the harvest, and assemble for a meeting in the *barri*, so we can all devote ourselves to the only task that is really important to the welfare of the village," he said, "*finding the poo-mui's friend!*"

Pa Gigba picked a toenail, as if he was embarrassed to be witnessing anger between *poo-muis*.

"If we find Michael Killigan, the first thing I have to talk to him about is training *you!* 'Sabu gbiina' is Mende," Sisay explained. " 'Better no dae' is Krio. They mean the same thing. Better—good —is not there, or nothing good is there. Yes, Kaikai is Killigan's African name." Sisay looked at the Mende man again. "He says Killigan is not there, nothing good is there. Only bad news. Only evil."

"What kind of evil?" Boone asked.

Sisay spoke again.

"*Ndogbojusui*," the man said. "*Hale nyamubla, honei, ndile-mui. Koliblah.*"

Sisay waited for elaboration, but none was forthcoming. The old pa quietly stared at his feet, peeking once at Sisay, hoping the white men were satisfied and the conversation was over.

Sisay pronounced the words slowly for Boone's benefit. "As I've already told you, 'Dog-bo-joo-shwee,' is 'bush devil.' 'Ha-lay,' is 'medicine,' " he said. " 'Nya-moo-blah' is 'bad' or 'evil,' so 'evil medicine.' 'Ho-nay' is 'witch spirit,' and 'ndee-lay-mui' is a witch who takes on the form of a person or animal. 'Koliblah' are Leopard people, or Baboon people, people who take on the shape of animals."

Sisay again spoke to the man, repeating each of the Mende words.

The old pa responded by offering Sisay and Boone a plastic Esso oil jug smeared with grime and dirt. Sisay accepted two cups from Pa Gigba and poured what looked like more dirty dishwater from the jug into the cups, handing one to Boone, and filling a third cup for the old pa. Without thinking, Boone examined the palm wine, because he thought he had seen a foreign object flow out of the jug and into his cup. Then he smelled something sour and sniffed the cup, wrinkling his nose at the odor.

"Make another face like that," Sisay said without a trace of humor in his voice, "and you are on your own."

His glare of intense indignation startled Boone. "Pa Gigba risked his life climbing a palm tree so he could make this palm wine and offer it to his guests. Once he climbs a hundred feet up into the palm, it's not uncommon to find a mamba snake waiting for him. It's palm wine. Drink it and like it, or you will be insulting this man, and shaming me."

Boone was suddenly damn sick of being told how to eat and drink, whom to hire, how to shake hands, what time to get up in the morning, and what gifts to give and to whom. He resolved to take the next *podah-podah* to Killigan's village and do his own investigating. And if he was not welcome there, he would go stay with Sam Lewis in Pujehun. Meanwhile, he was all but certain that Pa Gigba knew something about Killigan's disappearance, so he drank the thing to the dregs and held his cup out for more.

"Does all this evil business have anything to do with Killigan disappearing?" Boone asked, gritting his teeth, while toasting Pa Gigba with another swig.

Pa Gigba shrugged his shoulders, drank, and held out his cup.

"He knows nothing about bad medicine or witches," Sisay said.

The man interrupted Sisay and again shrugged with a palms-up gesture of helplessness.

"He knows absolutely nothing about such things," Sisay continued. "Furthermore, he doesn't know of anyone who *does* know about such things. He can tell us nothing about what happened in the village, except that nothing good is there."

Boone kept his eyes on the old pa, but, at least on the subjects of bad medicine and witches, the man clearly did not want their eyes to meet.

"Can't he just tell us whether all of this witch business has anything to do with Killigan's disappearance?"

Sisay spoke Mende; the man shook his head and stared at the floor.

"He knows nothing," Sisay said.

"Bullshit," Boone said. "He looks like a kid with a joint who's just been told to empty his pockets."

"You're acting very *poo-mui*," Sisay said sharply, the curl of his lip indicating that this was no compliment. "There's a lesson in this for you, if you can step out of your two-hundred-dollar hiking boots and go barefoot for just a day or two."

Pa Gigba poured more palm wine into Sisay's cup.

"I have an African proverb for you," Sisay said, still suppressing a sneer. "The Krios call them *paluibles*. If television hasn't already obliterated your story sense, you might learn something."

Sisay straightened his back and settled his hams into the dirt floor:

"A hunter was out chasing game through the bush, when he stubbed his toe on a human skull, half sunk into the earth. 'What is this?' exclaimed the hunter. 'How did you get here?'

" 'Talking got me here,' the skull replied mysteriously.

"The hunter was astounded and ran back to his village, telling everyone he met about the talking skull. After a time, the chief heard about the talking skull and ordered the hunter to take him to see it. The hunter took the chief into the bush, found the skull, and asked it, 'How did you get here?'

"The skull said nothing. The hunter stubbed his toe on the skull, and said, 'What is this? How did you get here?' repeating exactly his previous words to the skull. The skull said nothing. The chief became very angry, accused the hunter of lying, and ordered his men to chop off the hunter's head on the spot.

"After the bloody work was done and the chief had gone, the skull spoke again. 'How did you get here?' it asked the hunter's head.

" 'Talking got me here,' the hunter replied."

Sisay set his cup on the ground in front of his legs.

"Talking about witchcraft has a way of getting you accused of witchcraft. That goes for *poo-muis* too," he said, impassively delivering a chilling look. Boone had a sudden intuition that Sisay would do little to intervene if a white boy from Indiana was mistakenly accused of witchcraft.

"This man has lost children to witchcraft. Witches sent army ants swarming through his house for two years. He dug a moat around the house and filled it with kerosene and poison at a cost of about two years' salary. But nothing could stop the ants. They simply built bridges out of their dead and kept on coming. Someone worked a medicine called *tilei* against his wife, and it ate away her nose. *Ngelegba*—'thunder medicine'—destroyed his father's house, because his father supported the wrong candidate for Paramount Chief. Now you come in here and demand to know about witchcraft?

"If you want to find out what happened to Michael Killigan, you've got a long sit-down ahead of you. These people have many secrets, most of which I do not know after living here for fourteen years. Don't expect to storm in here and spend a week investigating a culture that has kept its secrets for thousands of years. You will go home with nothing."

"May I ask one thing," Boone said impatiently. "Are we talking about witches or bush devils, and does it make a difference?"

Sisay translated, then turned to speak to Boone. The old pa interrupted them, speaking Mende.

"When he was a young man," Sisay said, "he was hunting in the bush with his father. It was twilight and they got lost while pursuing a wounded bush deer. A *Ndogbojusui*, an old man with yellow hair and white skin, just like yours, appeared in the path before him. At first, they thought it was the spirit of a dead ancestor, but then it spoke to them and asked, 'Usai you come out so?' or 'Where do you come from?' Then they knew it was a *Ndogbojusui* because of its white skin, and because it began, not by greeting them in the Mende fashion, but by asking them questions, which is how a *Ndogbojusui* discovers the thoughts of its victims. His father had told him many times how to deal with the questions of the *Ndogbojusui*. One must never reveal what one is thinking, one must instead be stubborn, contrary, and best the *Ndogbojusui* at its own game. If the *Ndogbojusui* gets the upper hand in the exchange, even for a moment, then it will trick its victim into following it deep into the bush, where the poor soul will be lost forever. 'Usai you come out so?' the *Ndogbojusui* repeated. 'Na the moon I come out, jus now,' his father replied. 'How do you fetch water from the well?' asked *Ndogbojusui*. 'With a fishing net,' his father said. 'How you go sex woman?' asked *Ndogbojusui*. 'With a blade of grass,' said his father. And with that, the *Ndogbojusui* stamped his foot and disappeared."

"So at least we know he knows something about bush devils," Boone said with a glance at his translator, getting the sickening feeling that his questions seemed only to provide the occasion for lengthy stories having almost nothing to do with the topic under discussion.

The old pa looked from Boone to Sisay and back again. Sisay

leaned forward and fingered the pouch around his neck, speaking quiet, urgent Mende.

The old pa rose slowly, went to the flap over the door, and looked out into the courtyard. He spoke Mende and left.

"He is inspecting his house," said Sisay, "checking for witches in the form of fruit bats hiding in the rafters and eavesdropping."

So far, Boone thought, it was the mental hygiene of the occupants that needed inspecting. He could not decide whether to humor them along or leave.

The old pa returned and took his seat, speaking Mende in a hushed voice.

During pauses in the old pa's speech, Sisay translated for Boone.

"What he is going to tell us was told to him by others who saw what has been happening. Other than what he has heard, he knows nothing about what has happened."

The old pa rose again and peeked through a crack between the flap and the mud doorframe. Then he returned to his seat and spoke Mende in a low, urgent voice, while Sisay translated.

"Two children died suddenly in the village, and the blacksmith and a mori man suspected witchcraft. Several days later, while the families were mourning, a witch was seen in the village. It came into the village in the shape of a young girl who said she had come from Pujehun for the funeral rites. Later in the day, a villager saw the woman take an article of clothing belonging to someone in the village, presumably to get control over its owner. The villager watched the young woman hide the clothing and other articles in a bush. The villager promptly told the chief of the woman's suspicious behavior. When the chief and two elders looked into the bush, they found a snake swimming in a bucket of blood and, next to it, a pile of stones equal in number to the huts in the village."

Sisay paused and the man looked from Boone to Sisay again. Sisay nodded and said something in Mende.

"The villagers set up a cry and chased the woman. But on the path out of the village, she turned abruptly and looked back at her pursuers and the village. People saw the sun burning in her eyes. Two huts burst into flames, and the woman escaped into the bush. When the fires were controlled, the villagers followed the path taken by the witch and found the fresh skin of a huge boa constrictor lying in the path just outside the village."

The man continued, slipping back and forth from Krio to Mende, Sisay roughly translating in the wake stirred up by the man's distressed words.

"The villager who told the chief about the girl became paralyzed soon after and died. It was widely believed that someone foolishly killed the witch. As everyone knows, a dead witch is far more dangerous than a live one, because the spirit of a dead witch can roam free without worrying about returning to its human form. According to the villager's neighbors, the shade of the dead witch settled on the man's face while he was sleeping. He woke up paralyzed and screamed, helplessly watching as the witch smothered him to death.

"The villager's family gave the *ngua-mui*—the probing man— permission to examine the intestines of the informer. The spleen was removed from the corpse and dropped into a bucket of water mixed with herbs. The spleen sank to the bottom, proving that the spirit of a witch had entered the man and killed him. The villager was buried under a mound of stones. A stake was driven through the grave to prevent the witch spirit from wandering and harming other people, but as is often the case, the shade of the dead witch returned again and again to terrorize the village."

"But what about Killigan?" said Boone, again having the sickening feeling that these people were incapable of linear discourse, and that every conversation was a walk in the bush.

"Killigan was not in the village at the time, but his house was ransacked or looted. Pa does not know who went through the house. Other dwellings were also looted, so it is hard to say if Killigan's was targeted."

Pa Gigba again rose. This time he left his hut, and Boone could hear him walking softly around it. Then he returned, took his seat, and whispered to Sisay in Mende.

"His nephew, Moussa Kamara, has photos, pictures snapped by Michael Killigan. Bad men want these photos."

The old man touched Sisay's arm and placed a finger over his lips. He turned toward Boone and implored him desperately for something.

"What's he saying?" Boone urged.

"He's"—Sisay paused—"talking about the photos, I think. I'm not sure."

"Photos of whom?" asked Boone. "What are they?"

Pa Gigba grimaced, then moaned and covered his ears.

"He doesn't know," said Sisay. "He can't say."

The old pa looked earnestly into Boone's eyes and spoke at length, nodding, as if he was assuring Boone that he could help him and that everything would be fine.

"What about that?" asked Boone. "What was that?"

"He says he doesn't know where your brother is," Sisay repeated. "He can't say."

Boone thought the translation was far shorter than the original conversation and didn't match the look on Pa Gigba's face. But Sisay, who seemed to take umbrage at the slightest breach of manners, would almost certainly throw him out of the village if Boone challenged his understanding of Mende.

"Ask him if he has any idea at all where my brother is or what happened to him."

Sisay rendered what sounded like a statement instead of a question.

The old pa resolutely shook his head, as if he now regretted even letting them into his house.

"The conversation is finished," said Sisay.

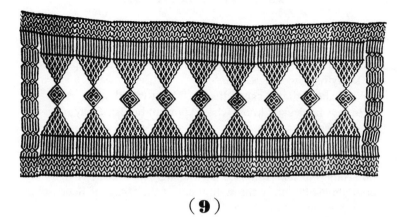

(9)

Boone's trip to Killigan's village was postponed by a storm system that moved through his bowels with the ferocity of a tropical cloudburst. His fourth day in Africa was spent deep in the interior of a remote, unmapped equatorial latrine exploring the dark incontinent.

It was a wattle-and-daub shed with a door of unpainted planks and no window—one of a long row of pan-roofed outhouses that backed up into the bush about twenty yards from the edge of the village. Each family compound—or *mawe*—had its own latrine, built according to Peace Corps specifications. Inside was an earthen floor and a wooden platform with a ragged, dark hole in the middle. Sisay had shown him the facilities, and stressed the importance of replacing the lid—a wooden disk with a handle—to keep the flies from carrying human excrement around the village. On either side of the hole, smooth, shiny impressions of human feet had been worn into the wood. Sunlight shafted in through chinks in the mud walls and illuminated motes of dust—or maybe they were protozoa—buffeted about by powerful odors and adrift in the soup of West African humidity.

The first time Boone squatted and peered into the hole, he realized his psychology professors had been right in asserting that there is some inexorable, subliminal association between shit and death. The interior of the latrine had a sense of place as powerful as any grave or altar. Something other than an intense odor emanated from the dark hole. Was it a sound? A subaudible vibration? The thrumming of cryptozoa assiduously turning shit back into dirt? Or was he hearing only movements in the symphony of the bowel?

On one corner of the wooden platform was a stack of past issues of *The Guardian*, an international newspaper of tissue-thin pages offering selections from *Le Monde* and *The Washington Post*. There were also several stacks of semi-bound volumes from Sisay's decomposing library; they were spineless, and whole sections had been torn from their bindings and mixed in with others. He found pages of Rilke crosshatched with a tour guide to Mali, Hemingway jammed in with a collection of essays on International Development, Kierkegaard, a manual on installing hand pumps for wells, Thomas Pynchon, Frazer's *Golden Bough*, Kurt Vonnegut, a Peace Corps health manual, Gaston Bachelard—all reduced to toilet paper—some of it better than others. The acid-free paper tended to make for a sturdy but abrasive product; the moldering paperbacks had a softer, more absorbent texture—apparently also the consensus of the other members of Sisay's compound, as the paperbacks were ravaged, whereas some of the bound volumes were left almost wholly intact.

But *The Guardian* was clearly the favored product, and after experimenting, Boone found out why. It provided low abrasion, absorbency, and a fascinating perspective on ten-year-old world events. While Boone's bowels evacuated quarts of precious fluid from his system, he read about Britain's successes in the Falklands or the Contras' valiant maneuvers against the women and children of Nicaragua. While waiting for another knot to form in his abdomen, he read all about Jimmy Carter's moral equivalent of war, the release of hostages in Teheran, and the promises of supply-side economics. Ultimately, history followed dysentery into the hole, and Boone stood, took one step toward the door, and felt another knot form in his lower abdomen. He wearily settled back into a squat over the black hole and fingered another *Guardian*, cursing softly between cramps and peristaltic convulsions, listening to the schloop and plip-plop of shit landing in the chthonic darkness below.

If shit and death had something in common, it was somewhere down that dark hole—an invisible node where scatology intersected with eschatology, where saprophytes gorged on sap, where man met manure, where the human became humus, where brain, bone, and heart were swallowed by the earth and moldered back into minerals and elements.

He tried a page of Bachelard. Too stiff. The poetics of shit. Maybe human beings are simply composters, biological garbage disposals designed to accelerate the transformation of plants and animals back into soil, the same way leaves turn to mulch faster if they are ground up first.

He had the Western compulsion to name the bug. Was it giardiasis? Common amoebic dysentery? Some other unnamed, unclassified microbe? Maybe it was cholera, in which case he wouldn't have to worry about anything much longer.

After the eighth trip in the space of an afternoon, he complained to Sisay about the difficulty of defecating into an open hole with no toilet seat to rest his hams upon. According to Sisay, who showed no compassion whatsoever for his plight, it was time for Boone to pay the fiddler for having lived his life in antiseptic American kitchens and bathrooms. Eating sterilized food and drinking chlorinated water had rendered his intestines utterly helpless against even the most harmless Third World bacteria. There was nothing for it but to acquire resistance the old-fashioned way. Even sickness, it seemed, was Boone's fault, America's fault, and the African climate was blameless.

"I take it this doesn't happen to you anymore," said Boone. "You're immune, or you've adapted, or whatever."

"I was sick on and off for the first year or so," he admitted. "Now I get sick only when I go back to America. After five years here, I went back for about a week. I was standing in somebody's kitchen in Rochester, New York. My American friends were shoveling platefuls of leftover food into the garbage disposal. I threw up all over the counter. I had forgotten what perfectly good food looked like going down the drain to the sewer. It was like watching a disgustingly drunk billionaire burn hundred-dollar bills in front of beggars.

"Next day, I resolved to sit on my mother's front porch and soak up some American village life, to remind myself of what I had left behind. It was Saturday. My mother's next-door neighbor, a well-groomed, weight-gifted, vertically challenged accountant named Dave, brought out a leaf blower, a lawn mower, a leaf grinder, a mulcher, an edger, and a weed trimmer. He worked all day, making a terrific racket, chopping, trimming, and spraying toxins on a small patch of ground, which produced absolutely no food, only grass. The rest of the world spent the day standing in swamp water trying to grow a few mouthfuls of rice, while Dave sat on his porch with a cold beer admiring his chemical lawn. Sickening? You bet. It was time to go back to Africa."

Sisay offered only a change in technique. He squatted on his calves for Boone, and gave him a "look, no hands" gesture. "It's really quite comfortable after a couple weeks of practice. But until then, you're going to be too weak to develop new muscles, so try this instead."

He picked up one of his straight-back chairs and removed the seat, leaving a bare wooden frame. "I think you should just move in up there for a day or two. Why keep trudging back and forth? Spend a day or two and really get to know yourself."

He poured a foil packet of UNICEF rehydration salts into a plastic jug of water and handed it to Boone, along with the seatless chair. "Don't stay out past dark, though," he said. "There's a witch who hangs out behind the latrines in the shape of a leopard. You don't want to be mixing it up with her."

Boone noticed another disturbing phenomenon in the form of ulcers that appeared on his arms and legs. He showed them to Sisay, who shook his head and remarked, "Tropical sores. You've been scratching your mosquito bites."

"Doesn't everybody?" Boone rejoindered.

He had discovered (too late) a number of gaping holes in his mosquito net—holes so large they had created a kind of mosquito trap, allowing mosquitoes in, but not out, so they could suck his blood all night and inject him with who knows what kind of diseases. By the time he found them in the morning, they were as fat as ticks, and were taking after-dinner naps in the gossamer folds of his mosquito net. When he killed them, they left gouts of his own blood in the netting. Then he had unconsciously scratched the bites, the way he had learned to do in the land of his birth, and had turned the itching welts into small wounds. In America, when the skin broke, a scab formed, and the lesion healed in a matter of days. All well and good in the U.S.A., where the environment is so sterile, you can eat off any given floor, or perform open-heart surgery in the bathroom, because the surfaces have all been sterilized by cleansers and disinfectants, until nothing remains but a refreshing medicinal odor. The worst thing wounds are exposed to in America are photons from a TV set.

The regimen backfired in West Africa. There, scratching a mosquito bite opened a hole in the protective envelope of the skin, exposing the interiors of his body to the contagion called air; for air in equatorial Africa is nine-tenths humidity, teeming with airborne microbes in suspension, just waiting to sink their cell walls into an enfeebled white organism. In three days' time, the tiny pinpricks became suppurating, festering, gaping holes the size of fifty-cent pieces. Dolor, tumor, rubor, thermor galore!

"Protein is very scarce in these parts," Sisay said. "You shouldn't waste fuel mending unnecessary bullet holes."

Sisay advised him that the only way to halt the cratering process was to boil water twice a day, wash the sores, douse them with hydrogen peroxide, then daub them with antiseptics. This required a trip to the village Fula man, who operated a pharmacy, convenience store, kerosene filling station, and hardware store all out of a shack the size of a toll booth. After obtaining the antiseptics, Sisay took him on a brief tour of the surrounding farms.

Boone followed, the muscles in his legs twitching and heat flashes reverberating painfully in his open sores.

They came almost at once on an old pa wearing nothing but rags and leggings and a stocking cap, beating a small stone dwarf with a leather scourge. The pa cursed and swore in a language Sisay claimed no one understood or had ever heard before. Every now and again, the pa hauled off and kicked the thing with all his might, then danced around the farm holding his toe and howling in agony, glowering at the stone dwarf, as if it had maliciously smote him with a stone limb.

"That's Pa Usman and his *nomoloi*," said Sisay. "Mende farmers have been digging up prehistoric soapstone statues of dwarves on their farms for as long as anyone can remember. They are depictions of the *tumbusia*, the spirits of dwarves who farmed this land before the Mende people came. Because these dwarves were the original owners of the land, they are jealous of the current Mende owners, and they sometimes take revenge by preventing crops from growing. Then the farmer must threaten or cajole the peevish *nomoloi* to enlist its cooperation. Sometimes the *nomoloi* accepts the sacrifices offered to it and will zealously watch over the crops and prevent vermin, thieves, and witches from traversing upon the land; other times the *nomoloi* stubbornly refuses all gifts and thwarts the farmer's every effort to grow food on the land. That's when it must be whipped, which is what Pa Usman is doing as we speak."

As they drew near, Pa Usman kicked the dwarf once more, then howled and hopped around the field, glaring over his shoulder at the dwarf and shouting harsh syllables at it. He had a tatterdemalion stocking cap, which looked as though he threw it up in the morning and stepped under it. The cap appeared to have two layers, with gaping holes in each layer that somehow never intersected, so that his head remained covered. The ornamental fuzzball which adorns the peak of such hats had long ago severed all its moorings, except for one tenuous thread that provided enough slack for the fuzzball to bobble about somewhere above Pa Usman's ear.

"Afternoon-O, Pa," said Sisay.

Pa Usman made harsh guttural sounds and pointed at the dwarf, showing Sisay and Boone a look of unmitigated contempt. He ended his diatribe by spitting a thick wad of kola-nut paste onto the dwarf and kicking it ferociously. His face contorted in pain and disbelief, as if he was shocked to discover that he had again stubbed his toe, and that somehow the blow must have been administered by the stone dwarf.

His shirt was made of mosquito netting, with holes slashed in the back of it. For leggings he had an oversized pair of walking shorts with the crotch ripped out so that it hung free like a loincloth or a short zippered skirt. A rope held it closely at the waist.

He picked up the leather scourge and showed it to the dwarf, making menacing guttural sounds.

"Pa Usman is . . . different," said Sisay, as they watched the old pa violently flog the dwarf. "I think he's gone a little overboard in his relationship with this *nomoloi*. He carries it with him in a box and feeds it at meals, disciplines it as if it were a willful child, and prays to it at night. He's had particularly good success recently by serving it Coca-Cola just before bedtime, which you can get—warm, of course—at the Fula shack."

Pa Usman threw the scourge aside, pointed to the dwarf, sweat coursing down his gnarled arm and dribbling off the tip of his finger.

"He lives alone in a shack made entirely out of zinc pan," said Sisay. "All the other villagers think the shack has baked his brains and made him crazy. But they still feed him when his crops won't grow."

As Sisay spoke, Usman pointed again at the dwarf and nodded smugly at the white men, as if he had finally taught the thing a lesson. Then he hauled off for one last good kick, and stared in amazed disbelief, as he grabbed his foot and danced around the *nomoloi*.

"What is he saying?" asked Boone, wishing he could tie the old pa's feet together and spare him the loss of his toes.

"No one knows," said Sisay. "He's a Mende man. Always was and always will be. But some time ago, after fever took his wife, he started speaking in a language that no one understands. It's not Mende, not Temne, not Koranko, not deep Mende . . . No one knows what he's saying. Except maybe his *nomoloi*."

Sisay took Boone back to the village and taught him how to treat tropical sores. First, the technique of the bucket bath, or how to take a shower in one bucket of water, which was the way white men bathed. Boone was shown to a small outdoor stall at the fringe of the compound, where he was given one bucket of water, one cup, and soap. His instructions were, first, to wet in preparation for washing: one cup for the head, two cups for the torso, one front, one back, one cup for each arm, one cup for the "private," one cup for each leg. Next, lather generously with soap, and rinse using the same number of cups. Sixteen cups in all, or one gallon of well water.

Africans bathed in the streams and rivers, where they picked up schistosomiasis, a parasite that incubates in freshwater snails, until it gets the opportunity to burrow into a human host, where it takes up residence with colonies of hookworms, whipworms, giant intestinal roundworms, tapeworms, threadworms, amoebas, flukes, trichina, spirochetes, plasmodia, mycobacteria, and a host of other parasites which inhabit humans living in warm moist climates, turning them into savage planets teeming with colonies of organisms. The parasites are astute ecologists, though; they usually do not quite kill the bodies they inhabit, carefully leaving just enough blood and nutrients to allow their lethargic hosts to find food and sleep in a hammock, while they go carousing in the bloodstream and intestines, dining out on the proceeds. In America, humans usually are not food for worms until they die; in Africa, the worms move in early and stake their claims in advance of the big day.

On his way back out to the latrine—one arm crooked in the seatless chair, the other cradling the jug of rehydration salts—he had to walk by several families huddled around cooking fires. The villagers tried out his new name a few times, and he replied, using the few stock Mende greetings that Sisay had taught him.

Every common Mende expression had its Krio equivalent, and Sisay had painstakingly translated both versions of the most likely greetings, blessings, and requests for assistance. The most common greeting, the Mende equivalent of "How are you?" is expressed in

Krio as "How de body?" or "How is the body?" The Krio response, "I tell God tank ya," is heard thousands of times an hour all over Sierra Leone. The Mende equivalent of "How de body?" is *"Bo bi gahun,"* and the response is *"Kaye ii Ngewo ma,"* or "There is no fault on God," literally: "There is no rust on God," also heard and used by every Mende citizen dozens of times a day, and commonly understood to mean that God is keeping me healthy, or I am living proof of God's goodness.

Boone got plenty of mileage out of *"Kaye ii Ngewo ma,"* pronounced something like "Kiyangowoma." No matter what anyone said to him, Boone replied, *"Kaye ii Ngewo ma."* The reaction from the clusters of Mende spectators was invariably jocular disbelief, followed by an exclamation, such as "Ai O!" and a slapping of knees and thighs. *Too funny. Another white man trying to talk Mende.*

But when the villagers saw him staggering latrineward with the chair and the jug, they knew he had runny belly, so they did not ask how his body was (for no one wanted to hear that there was in fact at least some rust on God). Instead, they said, "Oh sha," a Krio expression of condolence, which seemed to communicate a compassion for the sick that stopped short of pity.

"Oh sha," the children called softly from their mothers' laps when they heard about the *poo-mui*'s gastrointestinal misfortunes.

"Oh sha," said the mothers and young wives. "Mistah Gutawa's belly dae run. Mehrisine no dae foh mend ahm. He no feel better."

"Oh sha," said the toothless grandmas. "Poor Mistah Gutawa's belly dae run like small peekin. Sickness been come 'pon him tae he no able for eat."

"Oh sha, Mistah Gutawa. Leh God mend you, yaaa!"

By the time evening settled over the village, the latrine felt a lot like a second home to him. There was his room attached to Sisay's place, the veranda where he visited briefly with other villagers, played with children, ate bananas, listened to infants screaming; then there was his shit bungalow, where he spent the better part of the day, sitting in his seatless chair, shaking with the rigors of dysentery.

He was intimately acquainted with the wattle-and-daub walls of the latrine: the wasp's nest under the eave, the shadows of the stick rafters, the well-worn bevel between the boards where the cockroaches came and went, the slightly larger cranny where a huge but well-behaved spider hung out. The subtle changes in earth tones in different parts of the wall, where clay of a different place or a different season must have been used—all nuances of place, a place he came to know in the same way a victim learns the moods and quirks of his tormentor's personality, or an invalid learns the patterns of the cracks in the ceiling he stares at all day.

He passed the time feeding the spider driver ants and wounded cockroaches, fascinated by the creature's ruthless efficiency in pithing its prey, injecting venom that liquefied the innards of the victim, then siphoning out the guts. He sipped from the rubber jug of rehydration fluids and lit a candle to keep him company and serve as a reading light during his shit vigil.

He had plenty of time to think about just how he had arrived at this pass. He had nothing but the noblest of motives, but maybe he had erred in selecting his method. What good could he do for Killigan, or anyone else for that matter, when he was stranded in a latrine, waiting to be killed by equatorial parasites? Maybe he could have done more good by staying in Freetown, or even by staying in America. Why was he letting an ex-Deadhead tell him what to do? Did he really have to use African methods? Based on what he had seen so far, they were nothing more than superstitions of the most disorganized kind, consisting of swears, charms, curses, and taboos having no organized application or function. What could he possibly learn by consulting a looking-around man, or by staying in this village taking orders from a radical expatriate with three wives and a chip on his shoulder for his own kind?

Each knot in the lower abdomen, each tremor of nausea, each aimless blast of fecalia took fluids, nutrients, strength, and hope from him. He tore a page out of a book called *Paths Toward a Clearing*, by Michael Jackson, and read it by candlelight:

Traditional African thought tends to construe the unconscious as a force-field *exterior* to a person's immediate awareness. It is not so much a region of the mind as a region in space, the inscrutable realm of night and of the wilderness, filled with bush spirits, witches, sorcerers, and enemies.

He was getting weaker. He could feel his pulse beating in the swollen craters surrounding his tropical sores. His hamstrings twitched (probably from dehydration), his scalp oozed sweat, and his asshole caught fire in its cradle over the black hole. This was not a part of the world where he wanted to be dependent on others. He had seen enough to know that in this country people had a habit of shrugging their shoulders at the thought of death or disease taking their neighbors. Already, he had heard the expression "Ihn want foh die" more than once, in reference to a sick villager or an elder approaching death. It was a passing observation, delivered in the same tone of voice one might use in America to say, "He wants to go shopping at the mall."

Death was as random as the placement of the mud huts, as common as a stray stool, as insignificant as a mosquito bite. It was as quick as a mamba snake, as slow as tuberculosis tubercles sprouting in the lung.

Boone imagined himself dying on a tick mattress with a bunch of old pas standing around scratching their heads, while Sisay told him to wait another hour or two, until the witch doctor answered his beeper. Before long, he would be praying again, another sign of just how bad things were. *God is very big*, he thought. *Very, very big*, he hoped. *Big enough to absorb all of this and more. Big enough to protect his best friend from rebels or juju men or the corrupt bureaucrats missing bags of cement.*

When not in his room or in his latrine bungalow, Boone was with villagers, or they were with him. Each morning, he stepped out of his semi-private room and waded into a stream, a swamp, a forest of humanity, and for the rest of the day, he was never alone. If he went into his room, happy faces appeared in a row at his window, "*Poo-mui! Poo-mui!*" If he dozed off in the hammock, he woke up in a bird's nest of small African heads chirping, "*Poo-mui! Poo-mui!*" If he left anything out of his backpack, it was promptly seized and passed around for examination, comment, and above all questions.

"What is this?"

"How is it made?"

"What does it do?"

"How much does it cost?"

He was alone only when moving his bowels or sleeping; the rest of life was lived constantly and relentlessly in the company of others, and the others had no concept of or respect for solitude. Sisay was never alone either, but he welcomed company and spent the day singing, telling proverbs, and laughing. When Sisay spoke to villagers, the sour world-weariness disappeared from his voice; his face came to life and his eyes lit up. Whether he was addressing a toddler or a senile adult, he gave total attention to that person. A conversation was something people had in England. A discussion was something you had with white people. What Sisay had with his extended Mende family was raillery, jokes, stories, spoofs, insults, wild conceits, extrapolations from proverbs, and Krio parables. The Mendes howled and shook one another and laughed insanely. No matter how many times they had seen it, they still could not believe a white man could do such things with their language. With the notable exception of several renowned missionaries, a white man had never thought enough of the Mende, their language, and their way of life to actually stay and live among them.

Whether he was besting witty elders or being bested by a twelve-year-old diamond digger, he never dropped the ball, he constantly redoubled the joke, turned it back on itself, turned it back on himself if need be, anything to keep the ironic farce in motion. If Sisay tried to leave the village, it always took him a good hour or two just to make it to the path leading out, because he had to stop and jaw with each conclave on each veranda—mainly joking back and forth in Mende. Most conversations consisted of jokes, blessings, or proverbs:

If you have a big cock, tell the tailor before he sews your pants.

Don't put your finger in someone's mouth and then hit them on top of the head.

Love is like the lard in soup: it is only sweet when it is hot.

A hen with chicks does not jump over a fire.

Love is like an egg—if you want to fully enjoy it, you should not hold it too hard or too lightly.

One finger cannot catch lice.

Nothing went further than a good spoof, pun, bluff, witticism—it was the national pastime. And in the evening, the favorite entertainment seemed to consist of verbal jousting. Two clever comedians began by insulting each other, then matched wits before an audience, who rated the performance of the contestants by laughing or shouting after each verbal thrust, parry, and riposte. The contest ended when one of the wags managed such a scintillating display of repartee that his opponent was speechless in the face of the crowd's roar of approval.

Boone laughed along with the audience, even though he did not understand enough Krio to comprehend all of what was said. It was enough to watch what appeared to be an argument erupt into laughter and thigh slapping from a steadily growing knot of spectators. Altogether, he felt like the most aloof, unsociable, and unaffectionate person in the world. An emotional runt. They laughed and kissed one another, blessed one another back and forth, teased each other. And Boone sat watching, or rose wearily and went to his shithouse.

Hunger is the best sauce, according to the Krio proverb, and despite his disorders of the belly, Boone always had plenty of hunger sauce by day's end. Each evening, they ate one large meal of rice and sauce served on a large communal platter, from which Boone, Sisay, Sisay's three wives, his five peekins, and guests all ate using their right hands. The first night, Boone had noticed everyone freely picking their teeth while digesting their food and savoring the after-dinner conversation, so he had absentmindedly reached up and picked a piece of gristle out of his teeth with his left thumbnail, causing everyone present to turn their heads aside and retch.

"That's your bathroom hand," Sisay had reminded him, while holding his nose in mock disgust. "Remember?"

Every evening, the smell of food or the sight of a steaming pot of chop being carried to the *poo-muis'* quarters also brought out the beggars, the blind, widows, widowers, and other social strays, who showed up coincidentally just as dinner was served, and were promptly welcomed, seated, and fed by Sisay and his family. Even at meals in other *mawes* in the village, Boone noticed that no matter how poor his host, or how ill he could afford feeding an extra mouth, the sudden appearance of a remote relative, who just happened to be visiting a friend, always prompted an invitation to dinner, and the invitation was always accepted. Sisay had told him that, although a Mende man will almost always scowl at the burden of feeding yet another relative, the food will be served. He will complain about it to his relatives; he will grouse about it to his wife, the chief, the beggar's other remote relatives who steered the hungry person in his direction, but the food will not be denied. Or as Lewis had remarked in Freetown, "Asking a Mende man to stop being generous with his food is like asking him to stop lying—an impossible request."

The head male of each *mawe* apportioned the meat, favoring the *poo-muis* with large portions, followed by progressively smaller portions to other males, smaller still for women, and none at all for the children. Once weaned from mothers and the force feedings, Sisay had explained, peekins had to fend for themselves at mealtimes, for they received almost nothing in the way of a serving, and instead subsisted on whatever fell on the floor, was left on the plates or in the pots, or whatever they could cadge from doting adults, who were disinclined to waste food on unproductive family members.

The head male then gave a signal and the scrimmage was on for food, which usually disappeared just as Boone was reaching for his second mouthful. He had a terrible habit of chewing his food slowly, searching carefully with his teeth for bits of bone, gravel, or gristle. Eventually, they realized he was as helpless as a peekin with no training, so they took mercy on him and set aside a small section of the platter at the beginning of each meal for him; then they gorged on the rest of the platter, finished it, and stared irritably at the reserved portion, while Boone worked his way slowly through it.

The secret, Sisay had advised, was to swallow without chewing, and without stopping to breathe, until you had packed in as much as possible during the crucial first three minutes. After the initial frenzy, rough territorial partitions of the rice usually had been tacitly agreed upon, and one could slack off for a few breaths.

After dinner, Boone visited his latrine. At dusk, he staggered back to Sisay's compound and curled up on the floor in his sleeping bag, feverish and trembling.

"Oh sha," said Sisay.

"Fuck you," said Boone. "I figure it's either the water or the palm wine."

"It's neither," said Sisay. "It's your delicate digestive tract. You didn't have to join the human race. You could have stayed in America, where five percent of the world's population consumes seventy-five percent of the world's resources."

They were interrupted by visitors, including Pa Ansumana, who had a couple of grandsons in tow, Dowda and Alfa. The grandsons expressed their condolences, and Boone watched them explain his condition to Pa Ansumana. His father indicated his understanding with a grunt, then showed Boone his flexed arm and a fist, as if to say, "Be strong, or you are no son of mine."

Boone decided to sit up.

The two grandsons pulled a pile of *National Geographics* out of the study and began examining the pages. Apparently, this was a nightly ritual in Sisay's compound. The young men of the village stopped by after their farming or diamond digging and went through old issues, selecting photographs, showing them to Sisay, who would then explain them in Mende or Krio.

The men lit pipes. Sisay provided a clay ashtray, which contained several of Boone's used pipe cleaners.

"What ees thees foh?" asked one of the grandsons, fingering a used pipe cleaner that was well gaumed with resin and carbon.

"It is for cleaning the pipe," Boone said, making pipe-reaming motions.

Dowda examined the pipe cleaner intently. "I see," he said. "And then how do you clean this"—holding the pipe cleaner up—"after it has cleaned the pipe?" he asked, rolling the pipe cleaner between his fingers and the ball of his thumb, showing Boone how the tar and resin made his fingers stick together.

Boone smiled indulgently and explained that pipe cleaners were meant to be used only once and then discarded.

After this was translated, the grandson and Pa Ansumana both huddled over the pipe cleaner, studying it even harder, and occasionally wiping their fingers on his sleeping bag. They spoke Mende together on the matter, the young miner going through the motions of reaming out the pipe and holding it in the direction of the fire. Finally Pa Ansumana seemed to grasp the idea of a pipe cleaner that was to be used once and discarded. A smile glimmered in his eyes, a kind of delight in the absurdity, the extravagant pointlessness of having such a well-constructed wire tool meticulously fitted out with absorbent fibers and plastic bristles, all created by a machine several oceans away for the fleeting, profligate purpose of cleaning one pipe, one time, and then thrown away.

After a couple more headshakings and muttered exchanges between grandfather and grandson, both men turned toward Boone, and the grandson, with purposeful seriousness, asked, "Why?"

Boone wanted to be honest, but he could tell that the Africans were on the verge of concluding that a man who could afford the luxury of squandering meticulously machine-crafted pipe cleaners probably had whole kingdoms at his disposal, as well as twelve wives, three farms, armies of servants, and a backpack full of extremely powerful medicines.

"Well," Boone said, "it's too difficult to clean a dirty pipe cleaner, and they are made very cheaply by a machine. They are *meant* to be thrown away."

"How much?" Dowda asked.

"How much for what?" Boone rejoindered.

"How much one pipe cleaner?"

"They don't sell them one by one," said Boone, doing a mime of a shopkeeper distributing single pipe cleaners to a queue of eager customers. "They sell them in packets . . . bundles." He showed them a packet by way of illustration.

"How much packet?" asked the young man.

Boone quickly converted $1.69 into leones and gave Dowda the figure.

Dowda entered into another excited exchange with the old pa.

"What now?" Boone asked.

Sisay produced a sigh. "He's telling his grandfather that a day's pay will buy two bundles of pipe cleaners, and from there they are trying to figure out the cost of one pipe cleaner. It's kind of like those sportswriters who figure out how much Michael Jordan gets paid per free throw or per minute of play."

Pa Ansumana chuckled, shook his head, and spoke Mende.

"What did he say?" asked Boone.

"He said, if you live long enough, you will see everything."

"What ees thees?" asked one of the young men, showing Sisay a photograph of a man in a suit holding a fan-shaped aluminum reflector under his chin and soaking up rays with his face. The caption below the photo said: "Manhattan Commuters Sunbathe on the Run While Waiting for a Bus."

The explanation, all in Krio, took the better part of twenty minutes, because the reflector and its purpose had to be explained, as well as the concept of a white man wanting to darken his skin by exposing it to the sun. This took some doing, for if, as they knew, a white man would be crazy to turn himself black, then he must be half crazy if he wanted to turn himself brown.

As Sisay spoke, they were interrupted by a racket that was even worse than the woman damage palaver of his first night in the village. Sisay froze and for a split second his usual smirk tightened into a grimace that told Boone this was no ordinary village palaver. He and his guests rose from the floor to meet the commotion before it reached his door. Boone heard the crowd calling Sisay's name, the wailing of women, and the shouts of angry men.

Sisay opened the door onto a moonless night, with the courtyard lit only by the guttering flames of swinging hurricane lamps. A crowd of villagers swept up to the steps to the veranda, shouting and quarreling in Mende and Krio. Children hid behind the knee walls of the courtyard and the lappas of their mothers. Old pas shouted at one another over the din, losing their dignity to panic.

Boone searched the crowd for a focal point and found none, until the mass of black bodies parted, and three men appeared bearing a limp body, and behind them a man pinioned and escorted by two strong men. The captive was bandoliered in ammunition and charms. Amulets, the teeth and bones of animals, pouches, and cartridge belts hung from his neck and shoulders.

The man was arrayed before Sisay, as if to give testimony, and the apparently dead body was placed at his feet, the head propped up by a stone. When the bearers of the body stepped back from their cargo, the crowd gasped at the face of death.

Pa Gigba! The wailing of women rent the night air, and the men resumed quarreling, some of them appeared to be accusing the captive man and some defending him.

A shiver swept up his spine and pringled the hair at the back of his neck when Boone recognized the face of old Pa Gigba, the bloodied Bart Simpson T-shirt now up around his neck—the old pa who had been in Ndevehun the day Killigan had vanished. Just off-center in Gigba's forehead was a powder-burned hole plugged with coagulated blood. Where his right ear belonged there was an excavation in the flesh and clumps of gouted blood, still oozing with serous fluid and new blood.

It was the first fresh dead body Boone had ever seen.

"Death is come!" a woman shrieked. "Death is come! Death is come!" cried the women and children, some collapsing on the ground and hiding their faces in terror and anguish.

"You killed this man with this gun, notoso?" a man cried showing the hunter a gun.

"I killed a leopard," the hunter retorted with the ferocity of a man defending his life. "Section Chief Moiwo hire me foh hunting. He say, 'Lahai, do ya, kill me some sweet beef this day.' I say, 'Yes, Chief Moiwo, God willing, I find you the sweet one this day.' Chief Moiwo been give me two cartridge, like usual, and I been go bush. Dae, I been see one leopard. Ihn come at me just when evening been come. Ihn come at me strong, foh eat me!"

"Na lie!" a man said, accosting the hunter. "Lie! You dae lie!"

The hunter tore his right arm free of his escort and opened his bloody, clenched fist in the light of the hurricane lamps. "I no lie! Look dae! Look dae and see! I no lie!" He held his palm up and showed the crowd the furry, vesseled, triangular ear of a jungle cat. "I cut-cut de ear befoh de man change back. I killed a witch! Dees man was traveling trew de bush in leopard shape. I kill ihm, and ihm change back. I been see dis ting!" the man shouted, pointing at his eyes. "My eyes no get fault! As I cut de ear, the man been change back to ihn human shape."

The crowd disintegrated into dark fringes of wailing women, clusters of children covering their eyes and shrieking at the night sky, and factions of men hanging heads, shambling slowly away from the body, muttering forebodings of witch business in the village.

Pa Ansumana descended the steps of the veranda and faced the hunter over the lifeless body of Pa Gigba. He put out his hand and spoke Mende to the hunter. The hunter placed the leopard's ear— a crumpled flap of fur and skin, scabbed in black where the ear had been severed—in Pa Ansumana's palm. The old man stooped to one knee and fitted the animal ear to the wound in the side of Pa Gigba's head, where a dark gout of clotted blood still seeped trickles of bright red.

He returned the bush cat's ear to the hunter, and took a lamp from one of the men, holding it out and above to inspect the corpse.

Boone too inspected the body, and shook with fear or the early tremors of a greater illness, gathering like a storm in his foreconscious. The night air passed through him in a frigid tinge of fever and raised gooseflesh on him. He must have stood up too quickly when the alarm had sounded, then went swimming in the crowd's hysteria. Blood pounding in his eyeballs made his field of vision vibrate, as he stared at the torchlight and shadows dartling on the dead man's features—a mask of skin sagging into the skull—almost shriveling into the snout of an animal.

He put an arm out and staggered, pinpoints of light teeming like maggots in the furry black collar constricting his field of vision. He remembered men speaking Mende and hoisting him by the armpits, before his head fell back into blackness.

He woke up in his sleeping bag on Sisay's floor.

"If you are well enough to travel tomorrow," Sisay said urgently, "you should. This is bad. The village is in total upheaval. First Mama Saso's twins, now this! There will be an investigation. Pa Gigba will be examined for signs of witchcraft. The *ngua-mui*, the washing and probing man, will open his abdomen, remove the spleen, and place it in a bucket of water mixed with special herbs. If it floats, Pa Gigba is not a witch, and the hunter will not be believed. He will be tried for murder before the Paramount Chief. If the spleen sinks, Gigba is a witch, the hunter is telling the truth, and you and I are in serious trouble," he said, meeting Boone's eyes and holding them.

"Witches are even more powerful after they are dead," he said. "But, more likely, the spleen will neither sink nor float, but will settle somewhere in the middle of the bucket, meaning malign influences were present but were not in total control of him."

Boone's eyes widened and his head shook in total exasperation.

"The old pas will hang heads in the court *barri* for days before deciding what to do. Assuming he's not a witch, there will be a funeral. All of this is going to be complicated by the presence of a white stranger, which is why, if you're able, you should travel."

"I will," said Boone, hoisting himself onto an elbow.

"Tomorrow is the last Friday of the month, which is payday for Peace Corps Volunteers," he explained. "Every Volunteer left in the southern district will ride their motorcycle into Bo tomorrow and get their check. They'll all be at the Thirsty Soul Saloon in Bo, which is where white people get drunk on the weekends. It's less than an hour by bush taxi. I suggest you spend the weekend there, and see if the Peace Corps has been able to learn anything new. I doubt it, but you may stumble onto something. When you return, I'll have a looking-around man here for you. A good one. His name is Sam-King Kebbie. He is a blacksmith from Kenema. He's not a charlatan. He knows what he's doing."

"Where can I find this Section Chief Moiwo?" asked Boone.

Sisay looked at him suddenly.

"What do you want with him?" he asked.

"Nothing," Boone said. "I'd just like to meet him. If he's the section chief, maybe he can help us."

"He's running for election," said Sisay darkly. "He won't help you, unless you happen to have a lot of money, in which case he'll offer to help and take the money. He's probably in Bo too. But I wouldn't go looking for him. People get . . . funny when they are running for election."

"If I run into him," Boone said, "I'll just introduce myself and see what happens."

"My advice would be to not run into him," said Sisay, cocking his head and listening to another argument somewhere out in the courtyard.

.

That night, the toothless, fingerless old grandma who had asked Boone for medicine sat on her veranda with her grandchildren, who were crying and still terrified by the sight of Pa Gigba's corpse. Grandma Dembe told them why children cry themselves to sleep at night and the story of how the ugly toad of Death came into the world.

"Every night we die," she said, "and every morning we rise from the dead. Every night infants cry because they feel night coming on, they feel death coming on. They writhe like snakes in their anguish. Some are more clever than others, and it is the clever ones who scream the loudest, for they fear sleep the most. They are afraid that if they die and go to sleep, they will never wake up again. They do not know that they will wake up in the morning feeling better.

"It is the same when people know they must die. They live a long life, and then they cry and beg and writhe like snakes in their anguish when the time comes to die. They are afraid they will die and go to sleep forever, instead of waking up the next day, across the river, in the village with white sands.

"And that is why infants cry themselves to sleep at night," said Grandma Dembe.

"How did the ugly toad of Death come into the world?" asked one of the children.

"*Ngewo* made a man and a woman," Grandma Dembe said. "*Ngewo* gave the man and the woman all they wanted. But every time he gave them something, they wanted more: first food, then fire, then animals, then tools, then medicines.

"At that time, the ugly toad of Death did not haunt men. Instead, God sent his servants to collect living people when their time was spent. But one day, a proud man refused to go with God's servants, though he was politely asked several times. God sent Mr. Sickness to get hold of the proud man and shake him with fevers.

" 'Mr. Sickness has caught me, but I can't see him,' the man cried, and he could not move.

" 'You have lived long enough,' said Mr. Sickness. 'It is time for you to go.' But the man refused.

"The next day, God sent the ugly toad of Death to bring the man caught by Mr. Sickness. The man died and was buried.

"Mr. Sickness and the ugly toad of Death stayed in the world to catch and bring those who will not come when they are called."

(**10**)

Mack wheeled a stack of documents in on a cart.

"Here's DropCo Steel," he said with a proud flourish, indicating several foot-high stacks of crosshatched documents. "Petition, proposed cash collateral orders, schedule of affairs, creditor matrix, list of twenty largest creditors, and memoranda in support. After you sign them, I'll box them and cab them over."

Randall selected a document from the top of the heap and flipped through it.

"You have a floater for a secretary, today," he said, studying the signature page.

"I do," said Mack. "Sally's sick. How did you know?"

"No secretary in this department would print a document for my signature on 25 percent cotton bond paper. Tell her to redo it on 100 percent bond."

"Redo the whole set?" Mack asked.

"We can't file them like this," Randall said, "can we? Tell her to print them again. And tell her I want four blank lines between the body and the signature line. She's only got three here," he complained, pointing at the signature block.

Mack left with his cart and his tail between his legs.

A single trill from the phone announced an in-house call.

"Killigan," said a voice over the intercom, "Stone. I'm down here in the War Room working on the Swintex case. I'm deep into section 507. Seems like I remember a partnership retreat. I think we were both shitfaced at the time," Stone continued, "but I remember you telling me that Thomas Aquinas would have to come back as a bankruptcy lawyer before anybody could really understand all the

things you could do to a creditor using 507. You were doing Mag-
netron or Metalink at the time. I think you were in front of Judge
Baxter in the southern district."

"Magnalink," said Randall with a sentimental chuckle. "They
were holding their ankles and begging for mercy."

Stone laughed. "You said you found a way to skin an unsecured
creditor, leaving nothing but vital organs and a nervous system
behind." He giggled. "They were still alive, you said. They were still
conscious, but they were absolutely powerless to do anything but
scream themselves to death."

"Magnalink," said Randall. "Talk about fun."

"I need to know how you did it," said Stone. "I've got a guy on
the other side who's asking for it. I want to crush his skull, but I
need him left alive so we can use him to deal with the other creditors
in his class."

"Go into the Magnalink directory. I think it's on the F drive of
the token ring server," said Randall. "Look at the plan confirmation
documents. In the meantime, think about it this way. Section 1129
is the sun. Section 507 is the moon. If you align them just so, it's
like an eclipse. There's a penumbra. That's where you want to be.
Read it first, and then I'll come up and explain it to you. We'll have
this guy breathing through a hole in his neck before he knows what
hit him."

"Thanks, boss," said Stone.

"Mention it," said Randall. "Preferably to the Swintex CEO.
They've got a sister corporation in Chicago on the verge of going
under. We could use that work. Tell him we saved him a bundle
in fees by hitching him a ride on the Magnalink documents."

Randall hung up the phone and wistfully wondered why all of
life couldn't be as simple and as immediately rewarding as a thriving
bankruptcy practice unfettered by administrative meddling. But
such vocational glows were becoming increasingly short-lived and
infrequent. The department was straining at the seams of the usual
managed chaos. The tumor scare, the time out for the tests, the
phone calls to Washington, all of it was showing up in his concentration and his performance. His career-building cases were at least
temporarily in the hands of junior partners and associates. Actually
trusting them could only lead to trouble. If a minion turned on him,
mistakes could be made (using the political passive), it could be let
known that Randall wasn't quite riding herd on his cases the way

he usually did, and other lawyers were doing most of the work. Actually confiding in the other partners was out of the question. He had learned early never to reveal his true thoughts or let them get the upper hand in any exchange. Instead, when confronted, he was stubborn, contrary, and quick to beat them at their own game.

The management committee had received a report that Randall was becoming too volatile. That at least one big client had suggested they might look around for the same bankruptcy expertise in another lawyer with more stability of mood and manner. This, he knew, was a false report, intentionally leaked, probably by somebody drawing a bead on him from behind. The substance of the rumor was the kind of bullshit a bull shits when it has eaten bullshit. Somebody was fucking with him and getting ready to suggest he was being distracted by events in his personal life. This was Firm Code used to identify weakness and an inability to swear allegiance body and soul to the partnership. He decided it was time again to plant the rumor that he was leaving with a tribe of Sterling warriors unless the committees got off his back and let him get on with the business of commercial warfare.

Meanwhile, Africa was an expanding continent taking up more and more of his day, swelling the wrong columns in his performance profile with hours of nonbillable time. He had kept in close contact with the American Ambassador in Freetown, who in turn was in touch, from time to time, with the section chief, to whom Randall was writing checks. This Moiwo fellow seemed quite confident that Michael was alive and off in the bush being initiated into some magic cult of sorcerers or diviners, some mystical gig, the description of which fit his kid like a glove. There was abundant hope that he would turn up in one piece, which was not to say that he was out of danger. Dabbling in this sort of magic always carried risk, said the embassy people, especially at election time.

At home, things were even worse than at work. Marjorie took the pronouncements of the section chief regarding Michael's possible safety as an answer to the prayers she had been buying from a convent of cloistered nuns. Her belief in the power of prayer was so strong that she commissioned custom-designed prayers fashioned by experts, in this case monastic nuns, insiders who spent their lives in transports of devotion to God. These women left the material world at age eighteen and never looked back. Randall remembered them from his Catholic youth. They were sanctified and full of grace and gave undivided attention to God. In their presence, even Randall, the indifferent Catholic, momentarily suspended his belief that money was the only thing you could count on in a crisis. Here were very different creatures indeed, for they passionately believed in something not described anywhere in the Uniform Commercial Code. They were a highly specialized breed. If the cause was a worthy one, these cloistered nuns could touch God's sleeve and whisper into his bended ear.

He saw the prayer money when his monthly bank statement came over the modem, passed across his screen, and into the predefined categories of his personal financial software. When he pressed Marjorie for details, he learned that the prayers were for Michael, and not a word of prayer to protect him from a potential brain tumor. Why? Because she didn't believe he had a brain tumor, she explained. She went so far as to frankly admit that she thought he was a hypochondriac.

Very low. Age was giving her fangs and claws, and he was discovering a host of mental blemishes. He had put up with her irritating complaints about how he supposedly had been almost intolerable lately, that he ranted and raved and raced from one worry to the other, that he was allegedly panicking, "heartsick," she said, about his scans and Michael's disappearance. He reasoned with his loudest, best voice, explaining his special medical needs to her one by one. But after he finished, she walked him over to the desk where she kept track of the family health insurance and asked him in a nice way if he would go with her to see a psychiatrist, a doctor recommended by a family friend of hers. Randall decided to pacify her and go along. He thought of it as a way of helping her confront her own need for professional counseling.

Once he got there, he found out the guy was not a doctor at all, but a Ph.D. in psychology who called himself a doctor. Randall looked at his watch and realized that he was going to be stuck in a small room with his wife and a patronizing dweeb in a sport coat and turtleneck for an hour. The good doctor kept throwing out phrases like "marital dynamics" and "dysfunctional codependency," which Randall instantly recognized as *billing* words, or words that one charged by the hour to explain. What did this overeducated Dutch uncle who made his living by nodding his head think Randall did all day? Randall could tell that Dr. Dweeb was anxious to find marital troubles, which would mean referral to a marriage counselor and a cut of the fee.

After forty-five minutes of pussyfooting around, the untenured academic made his move and pulled a shiv out of his sock.

"Marjorie is very concerned about your health and your happiness," he said. "I think that's one of the reasons she wanted you to come here with her today."

Dweeb smiled so hard his dental work showed. He bowed his head, and looked up at Randall. The good doctor's benevolence and selflessness threatened Randall's airway. A platter might come in handy if all that genuine concern started dripping off his face. Randall kept his hand on his wallet.

"Some of the events I've heard you and Marjorie discuss here today sound like you're having an understandably difficult and stressful time coping with your son's disappearance," he said. "No one blames you for your feelings of loss and anxiety. Indeed, it would be unnatural if you did not find this a stressful and trying time. Sometimes anxiety and stress manifest themselves in unpredictable ways, sometimes the fear takes on a life of its own, and the stress-afflicted person exhibits an anxious flight of ideas, a symptom that can be quite trying for a spouse. Do you use alcohol to relieve stress?"

Marjorie avoided Randall's sudden black stare.

This was an assassination attempt, with the dweeb as the hit man, and she was using Randall's money to pay for the job.

"Out of concern for you," continued Dweeb, "Marjorie also has advised me that lately you've had more than the usual number of physical complaints, and that you had a brief episode of nocturnal disorientation."

This brought Randall up short on the lip of a cliff overlooking the abyss of outright betrayal. *So that's the game*, he realized, always amazed when people had even worse motives than he, the cynosure of cynicism, could imagine. *Your wife tells me you're nuts, and she's hired me to help you*, which in essence was this amateur's pitch. The guy was hiring himself out as a private investigator of Randall's private life. Here was a "doctor" who needed to be sued. Wasn't this a solicitation of some kind, reeking of a professional conflict of interest? He had a sudden urge to see this man's children on the street lamenting the day that their dad had stepped into the shadow of Randall Killigan.

He nearly exploded, thinking about how some clerk in the outer office was probably taking an imprint of his insurance card even as he sat there. He had a few things to say, but he was smart enough to keep his mouth shut. A sudden premonition of divorce court swam before his eyes, with the dweeb taking the stand, dressed in a suit and tie for the occasion. Ambush! He could see the raiding party coming into formation on the high ground around him, scavengers looking for ammunition, which, if he didn't watch himself, would fall out of his mouth and into their laps.

The internal effort nearly killed him, but he kept his counsel.

As a parting volley, Dweeb smoothly weaved in another reference to the "flight of ideas," which he solemnly proclaimed could be alleviated by the proper administration of certain medications.

Randall bit his tongue and mentally drafted a letter he would send after he was safely out of enemy artillery range:

Dear Camp Counselor Dweeb:
Regarding our one and only meeting and your pitiful attempt to extort money from me using that pataphysical, pseudoscientific drivel you bill out as psychological counseling.

I have three relevant observations:
(1) You make 35 grand a year.
(2) I make 500 grand a year.
(3) One of us has a mental problem.

Yours very truly,
Randall Killigan, Esq.

This flight business was a new one on Randall, or so he thought, until he asked the doctor exactly what it was. Dweeb described the flight of ideas as a "rambling from subject to subject in a wearisome harangue, with nothing but superficial associative connections holding the topics of conversation together."

Randall looked at his wife and waited patiently for elaboration.

"That's it?" he had asked. "A rambling harangue held together by superficial associations?" He looked again at his wife. "Let me ask you something, Doctor. Are you married? And if so, have you ever tried to read the paper while your wife's on the phone? You want to hear a rambling harangue held together by superficial associations?"

Randall went home shaking his head, once again amazed at the kind of blather people lined up to pay for by the hour. Did he need to lose an afternoon at the office and pay some transactional analyst to tell him about the flight of ideas? He had half a mind to hire his own trigger man to look into Marjorie's mental health. Her ideas had been flapping around loose like kites in a storm since the first day he had met her! So it's *flighty ideas* they're worried about? Well, if they meant to get a handle on the notions gusting around inside Marjorie's skull, they had better round up the varsity falconry squad and bring on the toils and meshes! If he asked her a simple question, her ideas scattered, spooking themselves like birds without a single feather in common, a symptom the good doctor would have to agree was especially trying for her spouse.

He could not even imagine living inside such a mental state. His ideas were orderly and rectilinear.

That night, he lay his head on his pillow, closed his eyes, and listened to her piloting her ideas madly through the airspace surrounding his head. In his mind's eye, he could see each garish, flaffing idea winging aloft: a coot, a booby, a loon, a cuckoo, a cockatoo, a barnacle goose, a fool duck, a crow, a dodo, a goatsucker, a buzzard, a grouse, a gull, a jackdaw, a kite, a laughing jackass, a mockingbird . . . Scattershot flocks spreading out against the sky, unfurling in swirling skeins, disintegrating helixes, always breaking formations and converging again—a soaring, panicking, unstructured stimulus. Sparrows bolting in innocent terror. Dithering woodcocks, turkeys galloping just off the runway, peacocks riffling their awesome fanfares of color . . . The flur of pigeons wheeling around steeples, alighting on the beveled edges of bells, setting up whispering tintinnabulations in the belfries, where slumbering bats hung from the traceries, grinning like gargoyles, waiting for night, to riot and swoop and snag their bony, winged claws in the hair of madmen, screeching in high-decibel, eldritch sonars tracking insects . . . so shrilly that only the insane can hear them. Bats sleeping in cracks, fissures, sulci, fossi, sulculi . . . Bats in the oculi of domes. Bats shitting guano all over the spandrels, the stained glass and flying buttresses, the five classical orders, and even the noble statues!

Randall yawned and pumped his pillow. *At least I'm not crazy,* he thought. *At least one of us is not flying ideas around like dodo birds. You'd have to be daffier than old Daffy himself to get caught*

up in something like the flight of ideas. But the bat was never far
from his thoughts. It had now almost become a part of his personality. He could no longer stand up before the chief bankruptcy judge
in the southern district of Indiana as a simon-pure and single-
minded warrior, because a voice in the back of his head was saying,
"Your honor, I stand before you, not as a devoted officer of the court,
an instrument of commercial litigation, and a warlord of the Code,
but as a man who saw a West African bat with a four-foot wingspan
in his bedroom." It subtly undermined his self-confidence, in the
same manner that he imagined illegal drugs or secret sex crimes
compromised the performance of otherwise competent profession-
als, because these people knew they were living lies, they had a
Jekyll personality they showed to their clients, but Hyde was always
giggling over their shoulder.

Analysis of the problem did not help any. He turned it over in his
mind, at night, after his wife had gone to sleep. Would thinking
about it somehow bring the thing back? He knew no ordinary,
rational explanation could account for the bat's appearance, so
he explored—dabbled, really—in extraordinary, irrational explanations. Either his mind, his universe, or both had produced a hideous
aberration: Had it come from within, or from without? Had he
hallucinated the thing into being? Was it some confluence of nightmare and sleeping medication? Had the rational universe ruptured
and issued some inexplicable freak?

He flirted with believing in the supernatural, but the supernatural
was even more frightening than brain tumors. If there were supernatural events, they were probably populated by supernatural
beings who operated somewhere outside the jurisdiction of the
bankruptcy court. It could mean afterlife, maybe even . . . all the
things he had forgotten about after leaving his position as head altar
boy at St. Dymphna's Cathedral some forty years ago. Once out of
grade school, he had wisely and heavily invested in science, reason,
and money. But if he could admit at least the possibility of miracles
or occult phenomena, it might allow him to blame the bat on something outside himself. As it was, reason and science relentlessly
turned his suspicions inward. He could not reorder the material
universe to account for a West African bat in his Indiana bedroom:
The only remaining variable in the equation was Randall Killigan.

And if Randall Killigan had a brain tumor, the investing could
become even more intense and conflicted. His odds would be very

bad, and odds that low bring out the gambler in everyone. He recalled the spirit, if not the letter, of Pascal's Wager, which he conformed to his own reduced circumstances: Even a 5 percent chance that God exists starts looking better than a 3 percent chance of living five years. Which made him think about rearranging his portfolio.

After Marjorie fell asleep, he reached over to his nightstand and grabbed his Bankruptcy Code. Whenever he had a big case coming up, a confirmation hearing, a hearing on a lift-stay motion, or any other dispositive proceeding, instead of girding his loins and painting his face, he prepared himself, late at night, by studying the Code. After the clamor and the smoke of the daily battles had cleared, after everyone else had gone to bed, after his opponents had gone home to weaken themselves with alcohol or distract themselves with women or children, after it was absolutely quiet, Randall sat up absorbed in the Code, the source of all his power.

In any bankruptcy proceeding, no matter how big or how much money was involved, the parties usually ended up arguing over the meaning of a mere six or seven sections of the Code that were crucial to the disposition of assets in that particular case. Randall already knew most of those sections by heart, but early in his career he discovered that if, on the eve of battle, he read those crucial provisions, over and over, ten or twenty times, late into the night, and on into the morning, he often discovered some new relationship between them, some new bit of legislative history, or an obscure but creative judicial gloss on one of the clauses, which in turn affected the provision and its relationship to the other provisions in that section, and ultimately the relationship of the section to the other sections and to the Code itself, which in turn led to another theory of the case, and before he knew it—almost as if by magic— he discovered an entirely new method for destroying his client's adversaries and recapturing the assets that had wrongfully been taken on a fraudulent promise to repay.

Randall was Magister Ludi, the Code was his glass-bead game. Everyone knew the sections and the provisions in the sections, but it was the *relationships* between them that only the masters understood. When an eager young associate bounded into his office, all wild-eyed about some new interpretation of a provision that appeared to mean that vast sums of money would soon flow out of the bankruptcy court and onto their clients' ledgers, Randall loved to kick back in his chair and laugh. "That's pretty good, boy," he would say, "but take a look at section 507. It directly contradicts your theory, and there is no such thing as a contradiction in the Code. It's already been picked over by thousands of lawyers and legislators who had big money at stake and who have judicially interpreted it and legislatively modified it until it is a thing of perfect symmetry. Go read 507, and then we'll talk."

Armed with his late-night Code revelations, Randall destroyed the lives of devious debtors. Of course, he would take all the property he could get his hands on and see that it was returned to his client, the bank. Of course, he would sue them so hard they landed in the emergency room clutching their chests. The common folk who spent their lives in front of TV sets thought Randall was greedy or wicked or both. They did not understand that if debtors were allowed to break their promises and defraud banks of money, pretty soon the banks would have no money to lend! No one would be able to get a loan! They didn't understand how things worked, because they had been bewitched by television, and were too lazy to understand the fundamental truths of commercial litigation.

When Randall was on his feet in the bankruptcy court, the world was simple and Manichaean. Creditors were businesslike, law-abiding institutions that lent money to borrowers on a promise to repay at a set rate of interest. The borrower freely assented to the terms of repayment and had signed notes, contracts, and personal guarantees to that effect. Then, one day, the borrower said, "I changed my mind. I'm breaking my promise. I am not going to pay the money back."

People once trusted each other. There was a thing called honor. There was no money and no laws, only a man's word. People said things like "You have my word on it," or "He is as good as his word." But then society got bigger, and all the innocent, well-meaning citizens couldn't know absolutely everyone they were dealing with, so they developed an anonymous warrant, a symbol of their good intentions. Instead of favors and promises, people relied on money. If money took the place of favors and promises, then what are debtors? They are people who selfishly subvert the symbols of good faith and promises. They *owe*, usually because they were able to defraud others. They come to the bank and gladly take our money, our good intentions, our good faith, and squander it on selfish and unprofitable ventures. Are they filled with remorse, now that they have defiled our good faith? Do they keep their promise to repay? No, they repay our good faith, our promises, our good intentions by lying, cheating, deceiving, fabricating records, writing bad checks, debasing and undermining the entire system of good faith. And who pays for them?

Needless to say, the speech was altered slightly when he agreed to represent the debtor.

As he was turning these things over in his mind he noticed the closet door was open. The closet light operated off a door switch and so was on, throwing a yellow nimbus on the pale interior crowded with his empty clothes. Who would wear those clothes if his bright object turned out to be a brain tumor? As he stared at the wall and thought of Marjorie crying only for herself at his funeral, he saw one shadow pass like a film across the white wall. Had he imagined it? He heard one faint tap, a drop of liquid striking the wood floor, then another, forming a single pit-a-pat. For no reason at all, he suddenly heard bat professor Veldkamp's words chuckling in his ear: *I am afraid that there is no way I could convince a jury that a sane person could find an Old World fruit bat with a wingspan of five feet in his bedroom in Indianapolis, unless he put it there himself.*

Randall moved swiftly, but took care not to awaken the enemy sleeping next to him. His heart lurched and throttled into overdrive as he went to the closet and flung it open, ready to duck if anything flew out. Nothing did. He stepped into the closet with his back to the closet light and pulled the box down into his own shadow. He set in on a low bench, reached in, and took the bundle in his hands.

Instead of screaming, he took a single gasp for air when his fingers stuck in viscous ooze. He dropped the box and held the bundle up into the light, watching fresh blood stream in rivulets over his hands, down his forearms, and onto the floor, where he had heard the drops fall. He hyperventilated through his teeth and stared at the bloody bundle. More than blood, he feared that if a scream escaped from him, his wife would find him standing in the closet holding a dry bundle of rags with his head stuck in some private hallucination. *Then what?*

He set the sticky bundle back in the box and cleaned up the puddle of blood with a stack of paper tissues. He flushed them down the toilet and washed his trembling hands in the sink, watching pink-tinged water pool in the flutes of the sink and course to the drain's black hole.

Not even Bean was going to hear about this. Visual bat hallucinations, maybe. But tactile? Auditory? Even olfactory hallucinations? Because a suffocating stench came off the thing in waves, smelling like death, rotten blood, and musty dollar bills. He instinctively realized that, real or unreal, showing this poultice from hell to his wife or Bean or anyone else would be a confession of mental illness. If it was real, they would think he had made it himself. If it was not real, then it was another hideous specter that only he could see.

He needed proof that this was not another freak of his rupturing imagination. He needed objective verification of this thing's constituent elements before he would proceed. Laboratory analysis, that was the solution. He needed disinterested scientists to examine the thing and tell him what it was. Mack would know where to send it. The firm had running accounts with labs for testing in product liability cases.

And what if the lab said it was an old bundle of rags from Africa? What if Bean's lab said he was seeing and feeling a private nightmare, a hallucinatory solipsism created by his own neurological disorders? Maybe it was the aura before a seizure.

Something real was happening, but only to him. Maybe it was his bright object growing fingers into the soil of his brain.

(11)

Bo—which means "the potter's clay"—is the capital of Mendeland and is situated in the lower midsection of Sierra Leone almost equidistant from Freetown on the west coast and Sierra Leone's border with Liberia to the east. Bo grew from nothing around an ill-fated railroad that once joined the hinterlands to Freetown and hence the world. Since the mid-1960s, when a former President decided the country did not need a railroad, the rusting, overgrown tracks have stood as a monument to failed human endeavor in a country and a continent jinxed by colonialism, witchcraft, political disasters, and corruption.

With a population of 40,000, Bo remained—even without the railroad—the third-largest city in Sierra Leone, consisting primarily of dusty roads lined with shacks, where tailors pedaled at their sewing machines, Fula men and other petty traders sold matches, cigarettes, and aspirin, matrons of chophouses served platefuls of rice and sauce, and bartenders sold tepid beer out of kerosene-powered refrigerators. The roads wound into roundabouts with small markets or lorry parks, then spun out again into a sprawl of ramshackle buildings and pan-roofed arcades. Taxis roamed the roads, coasting down hills with their engines switched off whenever possible. In dusty trails on each side of the roads, strings of women and children bore headloads and buckets, led goats, and shouted "*Poo-mui!*" at the passing white man.

As it turned out, what Sisay had called a "bush taxi" was nothing more than the first car or truck to come along with room for a passenger and a driver willing to negotiate a fare. Boone simply stood at the side of the road with a cupped supine palm, which in

Sierra Leone means: *How about a lift? I'm willing to pay.* Within half an hour, he had a ride from a Sierra Leonean government employee who spoke Krio so quickly and used so many proverbs and slang expressions that conversation was impossible. The man was not Mende, so Boone's prolific *Kaye ii Ngewo ma*'s were politely ignored. They rode in silence, except for an occasional burst of Krio from the driver, and an awkward shrug from Boone, followed by irritation at each other's inability to understand plain English. Still, compared to the *podah-podah*, the bush taxi was luxurious. He was dropped off at the intersection of Damballa Road and Fenton Road, across from a prosperous Lebanese market, at the doorstep of an institution Peace Corps Volunteers have been patronizing since President Kennedy sent them to Sierra Leone in the 1960s.

The Thirsty Soul Saloon began as a counter facing out into a roofed concrete veranda, open on three sides, where tables of planks and barrels were flanked by long benches. The clientele consisted of white people—Peace Corps Volunteers, USAID workers, European development workers, British, Dutch, and Canadian Volunteers, and the occasional diamond prospectors, though their tastes ran more to the casinos, discos, and resort hotels along the beaches in Freetown. Now and again, a black African came in—a government clerk or a low-level administrator from one of the development companies—ready to piss a week's pay away on a drunk with white people, who drank twice as much on less than half a day's pay.

The place had previously been as accessible as an open-air beer market, where white people came to water their livers and to maunder over their *poo-mui* concerns—things like cold sodas, potable water, air conditioning, antimalarial medications, decent tobacco, cow beef, soap, and toilet paper. But the accessibility of the saloon led to a phenomenon known among the *poo-mui* as "beggar creep." Of an evening, when the *poo-muis* gathered and fell into lubricated conversation, hungry children and beggars surrounded the establishment, standing haggard and shiftless in the open archways, sometimes calling softly, sometimes hissing in the Arabic fashion, trying to attract the attention of the white people without annoying them.

"Do ya, paddy, let we have ten cents."

"White mahn, look me empty belly. I no get notting foh eat."

They raised their eyebrows imploringly, or indicated paralyzed limbs or missing fingers, coughed demonstratively into bloody rags, or showed the patrons empty bottles of medicine that would not be refilled without a contribution. As the afternoon wore on into evening and the drinking and conversation grew more riotous, the beggars, of necessity, crept closer, lest they be shut out by the din and the failing light and the ever duller sensibilities of the clientele. Soon mendicants were touching the patrons' bended elbows and falling down on the ground in desperate supplication, where they blocked the passage of waitresses and generally obstructed the flow of Star beer and commerce.

The proprietor, a Krio with a Mende mother, from whom he had inherited his warrior's temper, could spend only so much time kicking beggars across the floor and driving them ahead of him with an old golf club, given to him by a white man for just this purpose. Ultimately, he sealed off the open arches with heavy steel mesh, keeping the riffraff at bay, allowing the white people to drink in peace, and leaving a single entrance to the Thirsty Soul, which could be monitored from the bar. But the caged arcades still filled with beggars, their britches hitched up with rope belts, zippered flies torn asunder, T-shirts stained and caps torn. Their mouths looked like talking wounds sown with broken teeth. They crawled up and down the mesh, pantomiming their needs through the rusty iron webwork, pleading for leones over the songs and laughter of the white people.

Every now and again, the proprietor came out and doused them with a bucket of water.

Boone made his way down a row of Honda dirt bikes parked outside and into the bar area, which was populated by young whites in tie-dyed native shirts, drinking in clusters, calling out to one another across the plank-and-barrel tables. He was amazed to find Sam Lewis sitting at a table with a writing pad and a plate of food fenced in by empty bottles of Star beer.

Lewis waved at him nonchalantly, and seemed not the least surprised to see him.

"Ain't it funny how white people run into each other in this country," he said, dropping a chicken bone back into a bed of rice and palm oil. "Sit and drink," he said, pointing at the bench across from him. "Or have some chop, if you want," he added, giving the plate a nudge.

Boone's bowels were still rumbling with the effluvia of his latrine vigils, and the thought of food caused his intestines to buckle and knot with vapor lock. He guessed that during the rest of his stay in Sierra Leone, he would always be acutely aware of the distance to the nearest latrine.

"What's that?" he asked, indicating Lewis's paperwork.

"I'm getting out soon," said Lewis, still writing. "And I think I've got a job lined up with a couple of Lebanese smug—I mean, diamond miners. The Shahadi brothers out east in Koidu, Kono District. But I'm covering all the bases. I understand the employment situation is grim back in the States, and many of the Volunteers are jobless for months upon return. So I'm writing ahead to potential employers there, just in case my mining job falls through. This particular letter will also be published in our local newsletter for Bo Province Volunteers and will serve as a model résumé and job query letter for departing Volunteers who are in search of employment.

"Here," said Lewis, lifting freshly scribbled pieces of notebook paper dribbled with sweat and beer and handing them to Boone. "Tell me what you think."

> Mr. Samuel B. Lewis
> United States Peace Corps
> Pujehun
> Sierra Leone, West Africa

Mr. U. R. Grasping
President and Chief Executive Officer
Crapulent Manufacturing Corp.
1212 Mammon Drive
Porcine, Wisconsin

Re: Application for Employment with Crapulent Manufacturing

Dear Mr. Grasping:
As my résumé indicates, I majored in behavioral psychology, graduated with a bachelor of arts, and then went straight into the Peace Corps, where I have been an Agriculture Volunteer for almost two years. You may be tempted to conclude that the only practical skill I have acquired is how to grow rice in bush swamps. It's true, I have no experience in the American business world and no knowledge of widgets or any of the other products manufactured by Crapulent. However, I do have an extensive background in dealing with greedy, ruthless people who are as dumb as pig iron and who don't care about anybody but themselves, all of which I feel make me uniquely suited

for a position with your company. After all, for the last two years, I have been living quite prosperously in one of the poorest countries in the world. If I can extract food, sexual favors, precious stones and minerals, illegal drugs, and money from these people, who have an average annual income of around $240, just think what I will do to your customers. I have a nimble sense of humor, I am pleasant when approached, I am prompt, courteous, hold my liquor, and work very well with others, especially attractive young women.

In the course of my travels, I have become something of a fanatic about the reproductive rites of women. I have made myself a skilled lingualist in subtropical female languages and can speak fluently to the better-looking ladies of many different cultures and countries. I realize this last skill may not have immediate on-the-job application, but it is one of those intangibles that will contribute to corporate goodwill and the company's persona, once I get at all the girls whose husbands don't speak the same language to them at home, if you take my meaning. Even if you don't take it, suffice it to say that I'm talking about quality of life, corporate culture, and boosting morale in the workplace.

I am a veritable human turbine when it comes to willpower and self-discipline, as evidenced by my having frequently and repeatedly used every recreational drug known to man, without once having a problem with addiction or dependency. I follow a daily spartan regimen of exercise and diet, I quit drinking every night at midnight, and I'm up next day at the whack of dong.

Although I work very hard, I am also a family man, with dozens of children in many different African countries and several different states, not to mention a set of twins in Thailand, issuing from a 48-hour layover in Bangkok. Nothing was more important to me than the mothers of these children. So, although I will work myself to the bone for the good of the company, rest assured that I will always find time to be active in the community and to continue being a father to unborn children.

I look forward to putting my formidable talents to work for you at Crapulent, and I eagerly await your reply.

Yours very truly,
Samuel B. Lewis

"Don't worry about the handwriting," Lewis said. "I'll have one of the girls in the Bo office type it up for me. Do you think it's too strong?" he asked, taking another pull on a Star, concern furrowing his brow. "I can't be bashful about my strengths, but I don't want to seem immodest either."

"I think it's you," said Boone.

"Here," Lewis said, shoving a plate of bones, skin, and grease at Boone, "have a piece of chicken."

Boone surveyed the plate for a limb that had not already been gnawed on and settled on a drumstick half concealed by rice and palm oil.

"I have to warn you, though," Lewis said. "It's an experimental undertaking. My cook brought me the thing this morning after it was killed by a snake. Don't ask me what kind, she couldn't say. All we know is that a snake bit the chicken and it died. I brought it here, and they cooked it up for me out back. Now, you tell me: Is it OK to eat a chicken that has been killed by a poisonous snake?"

"I don't know," Boone confessed.

"I don't either," said Lewis, "but we'll find out pretty soon, won't we? Because I just ate the whole thing."

"Why didn't you ask one of the villagers?"

"Ask a villager?" Lewis said. "Are you kidding? I'd ask a villager if I should be in long bonds or tax-free munis before I'd ask them about what's safe to eat."

Boone gently returned the drumstick to its position on the plate. "I'll pass," he demurred.

"It sure tastes good," said Lewis, stripping the last bone of meat in two bites and pouring half a bottle of beer in behind it.

Suddenly, Lewis sat bolt upright and clutched his throat. His eyes bulged and he showed Boone a mouthful of shredded chicken. Volunteers at the surrounding tables turned and stared.

"It's the snake venom!" Lewis hollered. "It's taking effect! Quick, before I die, I want to make one last woman . . . I mean wish."

The patrons burst out laughing and shot bottle caps at Lewis.

"Well, say, gang," Lewis crowed, "what say we get all fucked up and talk about our feelings? Star beer!"

Boone decided to test the depths of his irritable bowels with a cold Star. Lewis fell into a bottle cap shooting contest with two other Volunteers, wagering that they could hit an empty kerosene can at forty paces. Bets were placed and money came out on the table.

Dark fingers appeared in the grillwork, followed by heavy breathing at the sight of so much money in plain view and about to be won or lost on the flick of a bottle cap.

"Mastah, I beg. Let we have ten cents. Do ya, I beg."

"White man, I no get notting foh eat. Febah been make me wife want foh die. I no get food foh me peekins. I pray God, let we have five leone, no moh."

Lewis shot a bottle cap, missed the kerosene can, drank half a Star, and shoved the money at his opponent. He surveyed the gallery of mendicants hanging on the grille.

"Is it only male beggars today? Where are all the women beggars? Let we get some women beggars, do ya. How about some sweet-eye gal beggars, pa, you can do that for me?"

This earned Lewis a round of censure from the other Volunteers and facefuls of unmitigated disgust from the women among them.

"Never mind about the female beggars, pa," Lewis said, beaming at the women Volunteers. "These *poo-mui* gals look like dey like me too much. Look, see ahm! Dey go want make me be dae boyfriend."

Over another round, he introduced Boone to ten or twelve other white people, American Volunteers warming up for something they called *Poo-mui* Night, which, if the tales of *Poo-mui* Nights gone by were any indication, sounded like a cross between Saturnalia and hog-killing time.

Boone met Joe from Duluth, Bill from Phoenix, Mary from Tacoma, Helen and Frank from Billings, who came over as a husband-and-wife Peace Corps team and were divorced within six months of their stay, Harry from Minneapolis, Pete from some place in New Jersey . . . a blur of young white people in embroidered African shirts, American shorts, and plastic thongs. They hailed each other by their African names and mixed Valley girl and post-surf-punk slang with Mende and Krio sayings. "Totally awesome" came out hard by "Better no dae" or "Peace no dae inside de country."

Everyone knew about Killigan's disappearance, but no one had so much as a rumor of what had happened to him, nor did they offer Boone any advice on how to find him. After introducing them, Lewis gave Boone the lowdown on the person as he or she walked away to rejoin the revelry in progress.

"That's Frank Nation," he said, "formerly of Frank and Helen fame." He indicated an emaciated balding Volunteer, who appeared stooped with age and saddened by a lifetime of sorrow at the age of no more than thirty.

"He used to be married to Helen, the skank yonder in the denim skirt," said Lewis, indicating a not unattractive, somewhat thick-boned brunette. "The one with the sturdy, homegrown set of briskets flopping around loose inside the tie-dyed T-shirt.

"She divorced Frank, and you'll get a high-decibel account of just why if you ever get within her considerable broadcasting area. When they first got to their village, she must have tied old Frank down out there, then done brain surgery on him with her voice-activated trepanning device. The guy looked like he'd had a lobotomy by the time he got away from her."

Three planks away, Helen filled the ear of a British Volunteer, her voice shrilling easily over the beer-hall ruckus and the imprecations of the beggars. One sample and Boone knew that Helen was what Schopenhauer had in mind when he said that the amount of noise which anyone can bear undisturbed stands in inverse proportion to his mental capacity.

"She's nice to look at, but she won't do nothing for you, no matter how hard you breathe on her. She's here for the Third World experience. She's busy discovering a village that never existed until she arrived to experience it and give it deep meaning. She's into multiculturalism and hates dead white males, because they have been enslaving and debasing women for centuries. The history of Western civilization began right around the day she was born. All the art, history, music, literature, and philosophy before her time are really just spoors left by an ageless conspiracy of white male animals who roamed the earth with the dinosaurs of old and kept themselves busy making war, getting drunk, and enslaving and debasing women. She'd rather listen to some spasm band out in the bush banging on rusty saws than to Mozart or Elvis Costello. If it weren't for white males conspiring against the truth and beauty of the Third World, and enslaving and debasing women, she believes, we would be teaching our children about Bob Marley and Gloria Steinem instead of Beethoven and Kant. Just look ahead a couple hundred years; all the longhaired musicians will be tuning up the cellos and violins at the Vienna Philharmonic, chalking up and getting ready to tear into a version of 'No Woman, No Cry,' and instead of reading what Plato had to say about the soul, we'll be memorizing Gloria's immortal insights on self-esteem.

"Helen wanted to start Western civilization over with the heretofore missing radical-feminist component. She kicked things off by marrying Frank, so she could use him as Exhibit A whenever she got into an argument about the natural superiority of women. Anything men can do, she can do better. Take, for instance, enslaving and debasing her husband. Did someone say pathetic? Just look at the guy! Do I need to say any more about men? What a pitiful creature of his own fears and inadequacies! Do you want to hit him, or just watch Helen do it for you?

"She's got vision," Lewis said. "I've never seen such a clear-sighted creature in my life. She understands the central truth: That men are animals, and women are reptiles. I agree with everything she says, and I have been begging her every Friday night for months and months to please go with me over to the rest house after the saloon closes, so she can enslave and debase me, but she won't hear of it."

Lewis and Boone tipped their Stars and had another gander at Helen.

"After Helen," Lewis continued, "Frank lost all sense of judgment. First he went bush with a vengeance, then he made the mistake of falling for a village girl and married her in a tribal ceremony. Then he tried to take her home to America. This girl had never even been to Freetown before, for the love of Christ, and this fool wanted to take her to see his parents in Manhattan . . . that's New York, not Kansas. After that, he figured they would go settle down in Iowa or Missouri or Kansas, I guess, someplace quiet and not too fast for her. He really thought he could do this. As I said, his brain had been damaged by prolonged exposure to certain frequencies.

"The noise and disorder of Freetown nearly killed his new bride. Just getting her out to Lungi airport was like dragging a damned soul by its hair through the gates of hell. She thought the buildings were on fire because the sun was glaring in the plate-glass windows. She thought the people swarming in the streets were at war with each other and would soon turn on her. At the airport, Frank fed her tranquilizers for the plane flight, so she slept through most of that. But then she woke up at La Guardia and went into shock.

"Forty-eight hours later, Frank and his African bride were back in her village," said Lewis. "Now old Frank's got the look of somebody who bites himself and likes a good head banging now and then in the privacy of his own mud hut. He's living out in some half acre of hell, with four dozen African relatives feasting off him like leeches, while he slowly goes insane. Wait until you hear about his 'research,' " Lewis said, making quote marks with his fingers, his tone a mix of scorn and pity. "Poor bastard's gone off his feed. He don't even drink beer anymore. You'd think he'd at least go back to the States and get his head shrunk."

"Maybe he likes it here," said Boone, watching Frank stare glumly into a plate of rice chop.

"Right," said Lewis, "that's why he has that incandescent smile."

A scuffle occurred at the entrance to the saloon as clutches of vendors vied for admission. The proprietor allowed in two groundnut girls, a woman with a platter of cakes, and a crippled beggar who got about on a square of three-quarter-inch plywood fitted out with casters.

"OK," continued Lewis. "At the other table, the tall skinny guy with the red beard is Bill Sutter from Phoenix. He's an anthropologist studying famine. A real disaster groupie. He goes to places where there are droughts and famines, and records data on the physiological processes that accompany starvation. All the villagers know him; he's always bending over people collecting blood samples and vital signs before they die. He also collects blood samples from dying tribes so that their genetic codes can be preserved and studied by future genealogists. He reminds me of those missionaries who used to baptize people who were dying of thirst. He's well funded too, but he spends all the money on instruments to assist him in the collection and analysis of data on the patterns and processes of starvation.

"Sitting with him is Otto," said Lewis, indicating a stout, blowsy man in khakis surrounded by an arc of empty Stars. "He's with the German development company. He's going back down to the Sewa River to see about rebuilding a bridge that's been torn down twice already. About three years ago, he found the villagers using a ropeway ferry to pull themselves and their produce back and forth across the river and decided a bridge would make their lives a lot easier. Of course, he didn't speak any Mende and barely any Krio at all, but from what little he could make out, the inhabitants seemed to agree that, indeed, a bridge would make their lives a lot easier. So Otto put in for the money to build the bridge, and his request was approved because, coincidentally, the bridge would also make it easier for the rutile, bauxite, diamond, and timber companies to get equipment to the work sites.

"What the villagers didn't tell him was that, although a bridge would make their lives a lot easier and they were quite capable of building one themselves, they did not do so because a bridge would also make it a lot easier for a particularly notorious bush devil to cross the river at night and terrorize the villages on the east bank of the Sewa. As it was, the ferry did not run after dusk, and the bush devil had no way of crossing the river after dark . . . until Otto built his bridge.

"The villagers were much too polite and deferential to the wisdom of *poo-muis* to disagree with him or stand in the way of his project. They simply let him finish his important work, then tore it down the day after he left. A year later he went back, this time to *educate* the people first, then build the bridge. And after weeks of head bobbing as an interpreter described the social and economic advantages of a bridge over the Sewa, and more head bobbing as the interpreter explained how bush devils were make-believe creatures who could not be allowed to obstruct progress and prosperity, everyone agreed that a bridge made all the sense in the world.

"Three months later Otto had another bridge up. Two days after he left, the villagers had it down again. When pressed, the villagers confessed that they agreed with everything the *poo-mui* had said. Furthermore, he seemed so sincere and devoted that they had let him build his bridge, because they could see how much the project meant to him and could not find it in their hearts to keep him from his dream. What harm could there be in letting him build the bridge? Chances were, he'd go back to the land of *Poo* and would never know if the bridge had been torn down. Hadn't they done the same for the *poo-mui* who so desperately wanted to dig a well in the middle of an unmarked graveyard? Wasn't it easier just to let him dig the well and then not use it?"

More Volunteers streamed into the Thirsty Soul and more beggars adorned the mesh. The conversation at the tables was buoyed up by the steady flow of Star beer, allowing all the Volunteers to float their concerns about "the Killigan thing." The favored method for dealing with the anxiety it created was to suggest that this kind of thing had never happened before, and that the best explanation was that he had crossed into the realm of politics, which, together with drugs, was absolutely forbidden by the Peace Corps. Drug abuse is a bit easier to define than political activity, and though several Volunteers got tossed out each year for buying or selling Nigerian marijuana, nobody in recent memory had ever been expelled for political activity, and the Volunteers were unsure about the elements of the crime. Political activity was one of those things the Peace Corps Director of Sierra Leone would instantly recognize without having to define it, the way certain Supreme Court Justices were unwilling or unable to define pornography, preferring instead to remark, "I know it when I see it."

There was speculation about raids by Liberian rebels. Fifty years after the British first repatriated freed slaves by sending them to Sierra Leone, freed American slaves tried the same idea to the south and founded Liberia in 1822. The capital, Monrovia, was named after James Monroe, and America managed to keep its hand in things, until Liberia became an American outpost, communications station, and Voice of America broadcasting center for all of Africa. Even the currency—U.S. dollars—was American, and the country was dominated by large U.S. rubber, timber, and mining companies, with Firestone the largest employer and landowner. Most recently, the Reagan administration bribed Liberia's former President, Samuel K. Doe, a member of the Krahn tribe, with the usual foreign aid, but Doe loved blood and tribal warfare more than money. Heavily into witchcraft and bad medicine, Doe once gave the CIA Director, William Webster, a pouch of magic dust. (There was no word about what Webster had done with the stuff, but some said he intended to use it in a run for the presidency in 1996.)

When an army commander from the Gio tribe tried to overthrow him, Doe had the rebel publicly disemboweled. Then he dispatched his Krahn soldiers to Gio villages, where they randomly machine-gunned and bayoneted civilians in retribution. The massacre ignited the tribal war still raging all over Liberia. It also allowed the infamous Charles Taylor to start his own country in the middle of Liberia, with his own army of teenagers toting automatic weapons, his own currency, and the power to sell protection and access to the mines to U.S. and European corporations.

Harry from Minnesota had recently crossed over from Liberia and had seen the rebels at their checkpoints, fifteen-year-old bobos with automatic weapons. Body parts were strewn in ditches at the side of the road. Krahn civilians were being interrogated, then executed, in huts on either side of the checkpoints.

Killigan's village was farther north than the rebels had ever ventured, but they were becoming more aggressive by the week. Killigan had administered at least one program that had distributed aid to Krahn refugees. So the fear was that a raid to capture Krahn refugees may have also netted one of their benefactors.

The thought of his buddy being interrogated by teenage rebels gave Boone a case of nausea and anxiety, which he promptly treated with more Star beer. He was on the verge of concluding that he had blundered into the upper circles of hell, and there was nothing for it but to drink from the river Lethe and turn himself into a barnacle on the Stygian wharves of West Africa.

Some Volunteers felt the Liberian scenario was entirely too far-fetched and instead suspected that any intrigue had originated in-country, and that Killigan must have blundered into one of many exploits and disputes that erupted all over the countryside during elections. There was speculation that he had somehow interfered with diamond smuggling, the most lucrative trade in the country, run by networks of criminals and corrupt politicians—Ministers of the Interior who extended an open palm and looked the other way when they received enough foreign currency. If the diamonds mined in the deep mines of the Kono District were exported through official channels, the country would be one of the wealthiest in Africa. Instead, the diamonds were smuggled across porous borders, leaving bribes in the pockets of a handful of venal government officials and nothing in the national treasury.

Lewis, whom Boone had learned to respect as having an almost infallible eye for the despicable motive in any confrontation, subscribed to the latter theory, but he left to water the ground out back before he finished his exposition.

Frank Nation drifted over to keep Boone company and (Boone later concluded) to glom on to an unwitting victim. The haggard, stoop-shouldered youth took a seat across from Boone and stared into his cola.

"Sam says you're living in a village up north," said Boone, deciding conversation was probably the best policy.

Frank slowly lifted a pair of eyes that seemed to be set in the sockets of a flesh-toned skull.

"I used to be in the Peace Corps, but then I sort of had to stay in-country," he said. "So I found work with some graduate students in international development who wanted me to do fieldwork and research for them."

"What kind of research?" asked Boone, doing all he could to keep Frank from returning like a genie to his cola bottle.

"The causes and origins of poverty in the Third World."

"Interesting," Boone said, again losing Frank's gaze to the fizz of warm soda. "Was this for a thesis or a dissertation of some kind?"

"A thesis on what?" Frank said, looking up suddenly, as if Boone had just asked him the most ridiculous question in the history of Western civilization.

"I don't know," Boone said. "I just . . . thought . . ."

"What's there to write about?" he asked Boone, demanding an answer. "What's there to say? I can summarize all of my research and conclusions in one sentence."

Boone looked away in search of something to notice in the crowd of *poo-mui* revelers, because the tone of Frank's voice and the deranged look in his eyes convinced him that the less he knew about Frank's research, the better.

"The people in the First World are eating the children of the Third World every night for dinner," he said, staring at Boone, as if he expected this statement to elicit a critique from his listener.

"That's . . . unusual," said Boone. "But I don't know what it means."

"Cannibalism," said Frank. "You are what you eat; but they aren't, because we eat it all; therefore we are eating them."

"But . . ." Boone began.

"Ever hear of the pineal body?"

"The what?" Boone asked, staring hard at two eyes lit up with conviction.

"The pineal body," Frank repeated. "It's a small conical body arising from the third ventricle in the human brain. In the Middle Ages, scientists said it was the seat of the soul. A little later, they said it was a vestigial third eye. Then they said it was an endocrine gland. Before long, they'll conclude that it's really all three."

A certain giddiness came over Boone, as if Frank's dementia was catching, or the Star beer was doing its work. He looked for Lewis and wondered how much more unhinged discourse old Frank had in him.

"Seeing used to be an active sense," Frank explained. "The pineal body used to emit its own internal ray, which together with the sun's light made all of creation shimmer like a tapestry illuminated by light from the seat of the soul. Then they invented television, and the preponderance of artificial light caused the pineal body to atrophy, and we lost our ability to see nature by the light of our own internal ray. That's why only so-called primitive people can see the spirit world, because they still have active pineal bodies."

"I see," said Boone.

"Ever been out in the bush at night?" asked Frank, as if this was a prerequisite to understanding his theories.

"I have," Frank said, without waiting for an answer. "But it's nothing you can tell anybody about. You wouldn't believe me anyway."

"Try me," said Boone.

"Go out to the bush late at night. If you don't have a soul, you won't be able to see. The moon won't help you. You can only see by the light of your own internal ray. It's one way to find out if your pineal body still works."

"What's your medication . . . I mean, what's your motivation for continuing this research?"

Boone saw Lewis at the bar gathering a bouquet of Star bottlenecks with his knuckles and coming to the rescue.

"Boys," he said, "you're probably trying to solve the problems of the First, Second, Third, and Fourth Worlds. And I have a Star beer for each one of them. Be careful, though," he said to Boone. "You shouldn't overindulge in this part of the world. Back home, if you have a few too many, you can step into a nice, clean, air-conditioned bathroom and talk to Ralph on the big white telephone. Over here, you have to get down on your knees and hang your head over a hole in the ground and hope you don't lose your balance."

Lewis distributed Stars and tipped one toward the ceiling. Frank crept off in search of other prey. Boone watched the beggars crawling the steel mesh.

"What did Sisay say you should do?" Lewis said as soon as he had Boone alone at the table.

"I'm to consult with a looking-around man when I return. Some witch doctor from Kenema who is going to help me find Michael Killigan."

"A fortune teller," Lewis said, taking a deliberative swig on his Star. "These diviners and looking-around men are small-time astrologists compared to the medicine old Sisay uses when he's in trouble. What's he doing? Starting you out slow? Ask him about thunder medicine. If you had one of those thunder boys show up in Killigan's village and announce that thunder medicine was going to be turned loose on whoever knows anything about Killigan but ain't saying, my guess is they'd come out of the bush on their hands and knees. I can't believe he's pissing around with a diviner. Ask him about real medicine. The bad stuff. For starters, ask him what's in that bag around his neck. Ask him why he lives in the bush instead of going back to America."

"As near as I can tell," Boone said, "he likes living in the village. He's happy."

"You bet he's happy. He's pinching himself every morning he's so happy," Lewis said, wrinkling his lips in disgust.

"What's wrong with him being happy in the bush?" asked Boone.

"Let me help you out," Lewis said. "You said he's happy, right? You and I are citizens of the world? We understand each other, don't we? I don't care how long he's lived here, he's still basically an American male, right? If he's an American male and he's happy, what does that tell you? He ain't watching the Super Bowl or the NBA playoffs, is he? OK. That means he's either getting laid or making money, right?"

Boone shrugged his shoulders and said, "Not necessarily."

"Whaddaya mean, not necessarily?" said Lewis. "He ain't into drugs, is he?"

"Not that I know of," Boone confessed. "I think he's just very happy here."

"If he's *very* happy, he's got to be getting laid *and* making money, which might explain why he would want to live in a snake-infested hothouse of a country full of parasites and terrible food. OK, he's *very* happy. Why does he like it? Power, that's why. He's running half the country. He's into that Poro shit up to his eyebrows. Did you see his markings? Did you see that pouch around his neck? Probably full of snake heads and body parts. He's a killer shark in a little pond. I'll tell you why he likes it. He's got three wives and a lot of land. He's got armies of people working for him on his farms. All he has to do is go for a walk every once in a while and wave to all the pickaninnies out slaving in his fields. He puts on a big front, like he's sworn off American greed and embraced the life of a simple bush farmer. Botobata. The guy is a power broker. Talk about big men. He's up there. He's connected.

"Put yourself in his position. Let's say you decided to go bush and settle down here. Let's do a little simple math. You probably got at least a couple grand in traveler's checks. OK, you can rent a four-room house and compound for about a hundred twenty dollars a year. You can't buy land. Nobody can, because the dead ancestors own it all, but you can rent all the land you can farm for five bucks an acre. OK, you can get a wife for thirty-three dollars. You can get a *good* wife for about fifty bucks. And you can get the cream of the crop—big teats, no diseases, a young tight one with good training —for under a hundred. And good training over here means she does what she's told, you understand? OK, you pay her family a hundred bucks, and that means she has to serve you for the rest of your life. She can't divorce you unless you beat her too much in public. You can beat her senseless in the privacy of your own home, but not in front of her own family. It's some kind of honor thing I don't remember.

"OK, that's only the beginning! Because, guess what? You can buy as many as you want! Let's say you got four wives: Fatmata, Adima, Sallay, and Fatu. OK, let's say you want Fatmata to salute the flag on Friday nights, and on Saturdays you want Adima to get down on her hands and knees and bark like a dog. You got it! Sunday, Sallay plays the flute while humming 'The Star-Spangled Banner,' and Monday Fatu takes it from behind with a smile on her face. You got it! Next week, if you're in the mood, you can dip them all in palm oil and pretend like you're an axle with eight nippled ball bearings. Am I making sense?"

"You are disgusting," said Boone, unable to suppress a grimace of revulsion.

"I know," said Lewis. "And you selflessly spend time with me because you want to show me how to be a better person. OK, while you're in the compound purging fluids from your tubes, you got droves of big Africans out working your farms for you and sifting mud in the swamps looking for diamonds. Why? You're white and you got money! Are you getting the picture yet? This ain't suburban Indiana, pal. Women are chattel, got it? Livestock. Beasts of the field. These people are starving, illiterate stiffs who would praise God for the chance to earn five cents washing your feet. You na mastah, OK? Understand? You're a master and there's nothing you can do about it. And if you try and pretend like you're not a master, these beggars are not flattered or impressed, or enlightened. No, they are shocked and annoyed at your bizarre behavior, not to mention pissed off because you won't give them any of your money."

"You're worse than disgusting," said Boone.

"I know," he said again. "And the thought that I might be leading a virtuous person like you astray causes me almost unbearable personal anguish."

"So if we all acted like you, nothing would ever change here. These people would remain in bondage."

"Who's holding them in bondage? Go home if their way of life offends your Western notions of human dignity. I guess in America they'd all be free, right? Free to squat in some East St. Louis tenement watching Oprah on a rent-to-own TV, only thirty-nine dollars and ninety-nine cents for sixty months.

"You're operating under the assumption that, one, you could change things, and, two, that what you have to offer is better. Sure, it's better for you, it's what you grew up on. It's like asking a fish if he'd like to grow legs and walk on land. You can't teach these people anything about your way of life. You can't set up an American outpost over here and expect them to start building shopping malls, delivering pizzas, and suing each other just because you think it works for you and yours. Look at the bright side. Once you get outside of Freetown, there's no television over here. None. Talk about progress! These people have never wasted so much as a single hour staring at dots of light on a square screen. No books either. Let the rest of the world sit around staring at black marks on paper. There's work to be done here. People are too busy farming and getting laid for that."

"I think you're both nuts," Boone said. "He tells me about bush devils and witches. You tell me about thunder and bags of medicine. As usual, nobody can tell me what all of these superstitions have to do with Killigan's disappearance."

"I can help you there," Lewis said. "But you ain't gonna like it."

He hollered at the proprietor for two more Stars. Boone had the sickening feeling that Lewis was prepping him with a tranquilizer before administering the bad news.

"Moiwo," said Lewis. "I did a little asking around."

"The name keeps coming up," Boone said, remembering the girl who brought him his coffee, and the note.

"Monkey works, baboon eats, didn't I tell you? Now, it's election time, he's getting into body parts, if you know what I mean. Ritual cannibalism. And the leftovers are used to make the most powerful medicines in the country. Some say he's been to see the Baboon Men."

"Oh, great," said Boone, "more creatures. What's a Baboon Man?"

"I call 'em monkey men," said Lewis. "They come out right before election time, looking for victims to feed to their medicines. African gangsters wearing chimpanzee heads and skins."

"I thought you said they were baboons?"

"They are. In Krio, baboon means chimpanzee."

"Oh," said Boone, frowning into his beer. "Well, then, what do they call baboons?"

"Gorillas," said Lewis, firing off a bottle cap and drilling the kerosene can he had missed twice before. "Gorilla is Krio for baboon."

"Well, then . . ." Boone began.

"They don't have any," said Lewis. "There are no gorillas in West Africa. As for big apes, there's just you and me."

"You know, if we rounded up all these devils and witches and Baboon People in a zoo, we could charge admission and make a killing."

"Your friend had run-ins with Moiwo," said Lewis. "That's known. Not that Moiwo would ever do anything to a white man. Not directly anyway. Not even he would be that greedy. But the scary part would be if your buddy crossed Moiwo, and Moiwo decided to use some witch medicine or Baboon medicine on him. That would be . . ." Lewis stopped for a breath and a serious look into Boone's eyes. "Bad. Real bad. Worse than thunder medicine. Maybe even worse than witchcraft and *ndilei*."

"I've read about that," said Boone, "in a book about the Mende I found in Paris. What is it?"

"*Ndilei* is a bundle of rags or animal skins with a piece of red mineral substance called *tingoi* stuck into it. It's buried or planted in a person's house, and then later it turns into a bat or a boa constrictor . . . It's *bad* medicine. Ask old Sisay about *ndilei* medicine for Christ sake, or how about . . ." Lewis leaned over and whispered, "*Bofima*." His lips opened in a wicked slit. "Yeah, lay that one on him. See what he has to say about *bofima*."

Someone started a boom box going with *poo-mui* music at the next table, and the Thirsty Soul rang with the sounds of Talking Heads, *Once in a Lifetime*.

The ruckus caused Lewis to whirl and fire a bottle cap at the offender.

"I'm having a conversation here," he hollered over the lyrics.

A diamond miner stooped over the table and motioned at Lewis. "There are some girls waiting for us," he said, motioning toward the entrance, where a cluster of smiling young women in lappas hissed and waved at the white men. "How many do you want?"

"Whaddaya mean, how many do I want?" Lewis roared, Star foam flecking his lips. "As many as hell will hold and the devil will ask in for a drink! Round 'em up! We'll pay the freight! When inflation gets to where I have to think about how many women we're getting for the night, it's time to leave this country!"

Someone sneaked the volume back up on Talking Heads.

A piercing shriek rent the air and silenced the clamor of bottles, the buzz of conversation, and the boom box.

"WHY DON'T YOU DISGUSTING ANIMALS LEAVE THOSE POOR WOMEN ALONE!!" The voice sounded like one of the Erinyes fresh from the long ride out of hell.

It was Helen, on her feet and ready to draw male blood.

Lewis staggered off of his bench and gestured expansively at Helen, as if he were about to ask her for a dance.

"Helen, my dear," he slurred, "honey, darling, sweetie. You misunderstand me. I am a feminist. I'm defending these women's rights! I'm talking about *choice*, Helen! I don't have to tell you how important that is! As I understand our previous conversations," he said, with a drunken flourish of a Star, "these women have the right to control their own bodies. They have the right to choose when and whether to bear children, without any interference from me . . . or you, correct?"

Lewis staggered over to the entrance and led one of the African prostitutes into the Thirsty Soul. The woman smiled, then looked back at her companions and laughed.

Lewis stood her at the head of Helen's table and said, "Evening-O, missy. Whay your wife man?"

"Ah no get wife mahn," the woman said.

"You no get wife man?" said Lewis. "I no get wife. Whatin you come find na hya?"

The woman smiled and again looked back at her companions. "Ah come na hya foh make you me friend."

"Ahh!" Lewis said, winking at her. "You go want make me your friend?"

"Yes," she said. "Ah go want make you me friend too much. Let we go now," she added, holding out her hand.

"Wait, small-small, missy, do ya," he said. "Whatin go happen if you make me your friend, and one small peekin come out?"

The woman raised her hand and smiled behind it. "Ah want one small peekin too much," she said with a giggle.

"Thank you, missy!" howled Lewis. "That will be all! I'll be along shortly!"

He showed the woman back to the door and then waltzed by Helen.

"It's different, you pig," she said, "and you know it."

"You're right, Helen, it is different. In your case, we're talking about your right to control your own body, and in her case, we're talking about her right to control her own body. That is different."

Helen threw money on the table and headed for the door.

"Fortunately, my fellow Americans," said Lewis, raising his voice so Helen could hear him on the way to her dirt bike, "we are staying in a country that does not put any laws on this woman's body. So if anybody has a video camera, you might want to bring it along, and I'll see if she chooses to control her own body and use it to make some first-class porno movies."

More Star beer arrived. Lewis took his seat and banged the table with a new Star.

"How'd I do?" he said, drooling out of one corner of his mouth.

A crowd of Africans ran up Tikongo Road, laughing and clapping their hands, leading a jeep filled with uniformed Africans.

"Well, look at that," said Lewis. "The villagers always warned me that if you tell a story about a snake and use its name, it will answer the call and eventually appear."

"Who's that?" asked Boone.

"Section Chief Moiwo," Lewis said, "and his entourage. Don't worry, you won't have any trouble picking him out. Just look for the guy who gets the most food out the deal."

Boone rose to peer over the tops of the beggars, who began hissing and gesticulating, trying to pull his gaze down a notch.

Moiwo stood on the haunches of a well-fed pachyderm that rolled under his khaki shorts. As he waved and smiled, his belly strained at the seams and buttons of his safari suit. A policeman's cap heavily gallooned with gold braids rode low over a pair of black lenses and rims that hid his eyes from the sun and the world. He had an oversized head that seemed to be unevenly swollen, as if his skin had been upholstered to his skull and the fat had swollen into his face, featuring it with curious lobes and pouches. When he smiled, he showed a row of perfect white teeth. He gestured expansively with his arms, while shouting into a megaphone. Gold pinky rings set with stones flashed in the sunlight.

"Electioneering," said Lewis.

Other uniformed men stood on the running boards of the jeep and appeared to be scanning the crowd, like nervous Secret Service men. Finally one of them raised his arm, then several others followed, talking excitedly and pointing into the gathering crowd.

A commotion arose beyond the steel mesh, in the direction the men were pointing. A table of wares clattered to the ground, the woman with cakes and the groundnut girls scooped their products into basins or aprons and protected them against the developing fray. Citizens of all ages converged on the intersection where a knot of people were engaged in a heated argument.

"Tiefmahn!" someone hollered from the shops opposite the saloon, off in the direction where Moiwo's men were pointing. "Tiefmahn!"

A young man leapt from the tailgate of Moiwo's jeep and raced by one of the saloon's archways, pausing just long enough to shout "Tiefmahn!" to the patrons within. Another young man in rags stepped off the tailgate with a covered birdcage and joined the press of vendors at the entrance to the saloon.

The cry went up from the perimeters of a gathering throng of people who had restrained one young man and were beating and kicking him.

"Hmm," said Lewis, turning his sweating Star in his fingers. "Looks like one of Moiwo's boys spotted a tiefmahn. You're in for a show now."

"Tiefmahn!"

An old ma in a headwrap, whom Boone took to be the aggrieved party and victim of a petty theft, was administering blows about the thief's head with a porcelain basin. When the thief raised his arms to block her blows, men on either side of him pinned them to his sides. Several other adults pushed the thief and his captors back and forth, giving him a box to the ears or a poke in the eye when he was passed over to their side of the gauntlet.

"Tiefmahn!" shouted the little children who ducked under the legs of the adults and kicked the thief's shins or poked his legs with sticks.

The white Volunteers in the saloon rose and idled at the vacated archways of the saloon, taking in the spectacle with the halfhearted interest of football fans watching a preseason baseball game.

Lewis did not move from his seat at the table.

Boone half stood in a crouch, long enough to see the thief fall from view.

"Will they kill him?" Boone said, trying to be nonchalant like everyone else.

"Sometimes," Lewis said with a yawn, "but not usually. It depends what he tried to steal and if he's ever been caught before. If he's a repeat offender, they'll probably beat him up so bad he'll look dead, but he'll still be breathing. Sometimes they play possum on you too, because they know there's no fun in beating a dead thief. Then the police will come and take him to jail. If somebody in his family has money, they'll send along a bribe, and in two or three days' time, the thief will mysteriously escape. If no one in his family has money, the police will beat him to death out of sheer boredom and irritation."

Boone wondered for a moment what impact he might have if he left the saloon and tried to stop the beating. The crowd was now well into feeding on its frenzy and so large that he would succeed in getting nowhere near the action, nor would he even be heard above the furor.

As he watched, the crowd hoisted the thief back onto his feet and held his arms and legs, which emboldened the more timid members of the crowd to surge forward and deliver the blows they had been saving in their fear of getting too close. Soon, a ring of people formed, looking almost like dancers at a hoedown, except for the violence breaking out in their faces, balancing themselves with interlocked arms, freeing their legs and feet for kicking.

"It's a great country," Lewis said. "Instant justice. No lawyers, no judges, no wasted tax money."

"Instant brutality," said Boone.

A flatbed truck fenced with slats of wood and barbed wire made its way through the crowd, beeping its horn and gently nudging bodies aside with its bumper, until it ground to a halt in front of the saloon. Two uniformed Africans dismounted from the truck bed, rolled the limp thief onto his belly, bound his arms and legs behind him, and hoisted him up to two other uniforms reaching over the slats of the truck bed. As soon as the body cleared the barbed wire, it was dropped like a sandbag onto the truck bed, and the truck commenced beeping its horn and crawling through the dispersing crowd.

The proprietor showed the two groundnut girls and the woman with cakes out, and admitted a woman selling paste jewelry and the boy with the covered birdcage.

"About these medicines," Boone said, still sickened by the sight of the beating. "Is there any way to make sense of them?"

Lewis blurred in Boone's vision and slurred his speech. "There are two kinds of medicine. Legal and illegal. The most powerful legal medicine is thunder medicine. You can have a medicine man put thunder medicine on your house to protect it from thieves and to let everyone know that they'll be struck dead if they harm your property. That's legal, but it's expensive, and it requires the attendance of the Paramount Chief to make certain that it's properly controlled and not misdirected against innocent people. But if you're up against illegal medicine, the really bad stuff, you won't get anywhere, unless you get some of your own that's badder than the stuff they have. The most powerful illegal medicine is *bofima*. But it's a dangerous business, because you can't use the *bofima* unless you *own* it, and once owned, it enters into a kind of relationship with its owner. The owner has to 'feed' the medicine every so often to 'recharge' its powers. But it can get out of hand."

"What does the medicine eat?" asked Boone.

"Human fat," said Lewis. "*Bofima* is a pouch containing skin from the palms of the hands, the soles of the feet, and the forehead, best obtained while the victim is still alive. Then you add a cloth from a menstruating woman, some dust from the ground where a large number of people are accustomed to meet, a needle, a piece of fowl coop wire, a piece of rope used in a trap from which an animal has escaped, and whatever else is in the Baboon cookbook that year, and you have *bofima*. But, as I said, it only lasts so long before it needs to be fed again."

"What do they do with the *bofima*?"

"Anything they want," said Lewis, "because as soon as people hear about it they are thoroughly terrorized and will pay any amount of money or offer any privilege to escape the medicine's power. But aside from using it to put curses and swears on your enemies, it's used to guide men through difficult or dangerous endeavors, like getting elected to high office. The pouch has seven strings on it with a hook attached to each string. It's cast into the bush on a moonless night and pulled slowly back out. The head Baboon Man then interprets the tug of the thing and studies whatever snagged in the hooks, and the group conducts itself according to the omens. Every time a new member joins, he must provide the next victim to feed the *bofima*."

"Did Killigan tell you about *bofima*, the way he told you about Poro?"

"Actually, no," Lewis said, looking down the neck of his Star. "I had a spot of trouble last year up around Makeni. Some pretty bad trouble and . . ."

"You used *bofima*?"

"Only once," he said, "I got it from somebody else, and I unloaded it, without any ill effects, before it was feeding time."

"You consulted it by casting it in the bush?"

"Not really," said Lewis. "A guy working on one of my farm projects tried to poison me. Twice. Some unreimbursed woman damage he claimed I'd done on him. The second time he poisoned me, I was medevacked back to the States for three weeks. He was having one of the women in my cook's *mawe* put insecticide in the sauce for my rice chop. As you know, the stuff is so hot you'd never know if it was laced with cyanide. I was as sick as a dead dog for weeks."

"So you used the *bofima* to . . . get revenge?" Boone asked.

"What would you do? I killed the son of a bitch. Internal hemorrhage. Just what the doctor ordered. They brought him to me on a pallet. He had blood coming out of him every which way. It was leaking out around his eyeballs, for Christ's sake. He lived just long enough to tell everybody that I had killed him with bad medicine, which was just fine, because nobody else has tried to poison me since."

The beggars returned to the archways, fresh from the momentary diversion of the thief's beating, pleading for money and attention from the white people. The bobo with the covered birdcage negotiated in thick Krio with Volunteers at the next table. Lewis was getting so deep into Star he would soon need diving equipment. He glowered, then waved off the beggars.

The bobo stood between Boone and Lewis at the head of their table and set the covered birdcage between them.

"We don't want no tropical birds," said Lewis.

The boy wore a Muslim skullcap and rags. His teeth were stained orange by kola-nut paste, and one eye stared blank white, unsighted by river blindness.

The boy bartered with Lewis.

"Hah!" shouted Lewis. "That's one I haven't heard before. He says that in this cage he has a captured human soul, which he will allow us to see for the modest price of five hundred leones."

Boone felt something stir under the cover. The boy showed orange teeth in a smile, and cajoled Lewis.

"He says that inside this cage is the soul of a twin who did not properly bury his father or honor his father's memory. When the twin died, his soul flew through the bush in search of his father's grave, which of course he could not find because he had not properly buried his father and had not visited the grave or left food or libations there for his ancestor."

The boy smiled again and the white eye seemed to roll in its socket and develop a bluish cast.

"I'll pay half, if you pay the other half," said Lewis to Boone. "It's about five bucks American."

"OK," said Boone, watching the cage shudder with the movement of whatever was inside.

The boy removed the cover of the cage with the flourish of a magician. Inside, Boone saw what looked like a small human skeleton wrapped in white fur, with waxy, fingered wings spread-eagled and the pinions clipped to the bars of the cage. The white wings met at a torso that was pale and almost translucent, marbled with blue veins. The head, too, was pure white, with large oval ears ribbed in pearl gray. The snout was a wrinkled bivalve of bone-white cartilage, the mouth pink with small, sharp teeth open in a violent, silent shriek.

"That's no fucking soul," scowled Lewis. "It's an albino bat. I've seen that before. Soul of a twin. My ass! Deal's off."

The boy protested loudly and held out his hand, demanding payment, first from Lewis, then from Boone.

"Don't pay him," shouted Lewis. "Listen, bobo, I ain't no exchange student out here for the weekend from Freetown. I've been here two fucking years too long to get clipped by some bobo with a bat in a birdcage. Out!"

The proprietor hurried over with his golf club and threatened the boy, who gathered up his cage and shouted at Lewis and Boone. The boy fixed his one good eye in a baleful stare, first on Lewis, then on Boone, spitting words at the white men with teeth and tongue.

"Oh, shit," Lewis howled facetiously. "We're in trouble now. He's cursing us. He's putting a West African swear on us. I'm terrified! Yeah, right, if we travel in the bush we will be lost forever, if we try to eat we will choke on our food, I've heard it all before. Here," he shouted. "Try this one! Fuck you! How's that for a curse? That's an American curse for you, you little shit!"

The proprietor drove the boy and his covered cage through the entrance and shook the golf club after him.

"I could swear that was one of Moiwo's bobos," said Lewis. "I'm sure of it. What's he doing conning white men?"

The caged walls of the Thirsty Soul rattled with renewed vigor. The beggars had watched a prize of five hundred leones almost get paid over for nothing more than a glimpse of a white bat; now, to their minds, the money was up for grabs as surplus cash burning holes in the pockets of reckless *poo-mui* speculators.

Lewis banged the table in a rage.

"Do you think I could have just five minutes of peace and quiet?" he yelled, shooting a bottle cap into the steel mesh. "Seven days a week I live out in a village hovel listening to the ageless whine of poverty, the despair, the stupidity, the fantastic superstitions, the squalor and the misery. Once, just once a week, I come to this modest establishment to spend a short while with my fellow Americans, tasting libations and sharing our common heritage."

The saloon crowd fell silent, with only scattered chuckles. The chorus from the beggars lulled to a murmur of do-ya's.

"You know, the Americans have a saying that describes this," shouted Lewis. "It's called invading my space. That's what you people are doing, that's right, an invasion of my space, this space you see here where I'm settled in on my duff trying to enjoy myself has been invaded. An invasion by you, the invaders, exhibiting invasive and invasionary behavior and brimming with invasiveness. The Lord said the poor have always been with us, but do they have to invade my space? Do they have to dun me night and day for money? And after I get home to America, I'll probably turn on the TV, and there you'll be! Starving all over my living room. And you know what I'm going to do? I'm going to change the channel, that's what. You know why? Because I don't like looking at you. Go starve somewhere else. I am not starving, and I don't want to sit around imagining what it would be like. So get lost!

"May I hollow out just one patch of land here? Just these hundred or so square feet? I'll call it Little America. Do you suppose I could come once a week to *Poo-mui* Night, in the Thirsty Soul Saloon, in this Little America I made, kick back, and relax for a few hours? Is that asking too much? I guess so! That's going overboard! I'm set upon by beggars! Go away! Sure, I've got money, and guess what? You can't have any of it!

"You know what you people need?" Lewis hollered. "Exercise and the right kind of breakfast. I'm not talking about living longer, that's pretty much out of the question anywhere on this blighted continent. I'm talking about *feeling* better. If you all jogged, ate more fruits and vegetables, and less fat, and got in touch with your inner child, you'd all *feel* a lot better about yourselves. I'm talking about self-esteem!"

"Mastah, I no sabby whatin this esteem you talk. Do ya, I beg, lemme have ten cent. Me wife get febah, de peekins get notting foh eat. To God I pray, mastah, help me small-small."

"You probably think you've got it rough, don't ya?" Lewis howled. "Sure, the wife's sick, the kids got nothing to eat. Tell me something new! How would you like to live in the poorer sections of some of our American cities? Some of those people have nothing but a black-and-white TV to watch. Everybody else has color TVs. What do you think of that?"

"Mastah, I no sabby whatin dese TV you talk. Do ya let we have ten cent."

"You no sabby is right," said Lewis. "You don't know how lucky you are!"

Boone's vision blurred again, and his stomach turned, either announcing another binge of dysentery or simply registering his opinion of Lewis's sense of humor. Just as he thought about heading back to the rest house for some sleep, the proprietor appeared at his elbow and pointed toward the entrance of the Thirsty Soul.

A groundnut girl in a headwrap held a folded piece of paper toward him. Boone walked over to the entrance and knelt down beside her.

"Moussa noto tiefmahn," she said, big tears forming in the corners of her eyes. "He say me give dese papers Mistah Gutawa Sisay."

"Who?" Boone said, gently touching her elbow.

"Moussa Kamara," she said. "Dey been beat ihn foh a tiefmahn. He noto tiefmahn. He been come nya hya foh give you dese paper. He no tief any person. Dat Baboon Man Moiwo lie and say Moussa a tiefmahn. Moussa noto tiefmahn."

"Lewis!" called Boone.

Lewis swaggered over, and the two of them took the groundnut girl outside, where it was quieter. Lewis and she spoke Krio at length. Finally, he took the paper from her and handed it to Boone.

"She claims that man was not a tiefman." Lewis scowled, almost falling over in his drunkenness. "She claims that was Moussa Kamara, Killigan's servant. He was coming to see you. She claims Moiwo's men fingered him for a tiefman, then stood around while the whole town beat him to death."

"Moussa Kamara is dead," said Boone.

"I know that," said Lewis. "I was sitting right next to you."

"No," Boone retorted. "That could not have been Moussa Kamara. He was killed several weeks ago. Sisay said they hung him from a tree outside Killigan's village and stuffed him with pepper. He had a live gecko sewn into his mouth."

Lewis stooped down for some more animated Krio with the groundnut girl.

"She says the man who was just beaten to death as a tiefman was Moussa Kamara, Michael Killigan's servant. And that he was coming to see you. As soon as he knew that Moiwo's boys had spotted him, he tried to get away, but they called him a tiefman and the crowd got him instead."

Lewis gave the girl money and asked her more questions.

Boone opened the paper and drew near the lights from the Thirsty Soul. In the handwriting he would recognize anywhere was a message that at once filled him with hope and crushed him with despair:

This bobo is my servant, Moussa Kamara. He will lead you to me. Do not cooperate with anyone else. Trust no one. Do not tell anyone about this message. Do not tell anyone where you are going. Make sure you are not followed.

M.K.

(12)

Randall arose before Dweeb's ally and went out to his front lawn for *The New York Times*, national edition. His head still throbbed with visions of the bloody bundle. What passed for sleep had been no more than a vacillation between waking and sleeping nightmares. He had unconsciously lived his whole life assuming there was an external world, an internal life of the mind, and between them, he guessed, were his eyes. Now the boundaries were dissolving. Either his imagination was gushing out of his eye sockets and filling the external world with phantoms, or freaks of nature were freely swooping in through the open windows of his soul and taking over.

On his way outside, he half expected to float like an astronaut or see all the clocks in the house melt. He spied the sky-blue sleeve of the *Times* nestled in its usual spot next to the silver maple. Maybe the headline would read: "Bloody Bundle Shocks, Confounds Prominent Midwestern Bankruptcy Lawyer."

He read the paper at the kitchen table and tried to remember the Our Father, but he kept getting the words mixed up with the Hail Mary. He skipped the business section, ignored a lingerie ad, and lingered instead on a story about ragpickers living on the streets of Calcutta. They made their living by scouring garbage dumps all day for bits of plastic and paper, which they collected in bundles and sold for pennies to middlemen. A woman wrapped in a sari squatted on a patch of concrete with her two children—they stared out of the news photo with weary, soulful eyes.

Randall felt a sudden kinship with them, now that he too had been touched by despair. He asked himself if he would be willing to live under such conditions in exchange for having his son returned to him safe and sound, in exchange for not having a brain tumor, in exchange for having the world returned to a stable, predictable place. He concluded that, even if he did find his son, it would only be a matter of time before Michael would get wind of the pavement people in Calcutta and would then run off to join them. He tried to imagine himself cleansed of tumors and sitting in front of his hovel in Calcutta.

Maybe saying prayers would help. Maybe he should cross his fingers, bless himself, throw salt over his shoulder, knock wood. Maybe he should get down and crawl on his hands and knees in case there was some supernatural being in charge of the universe who might notice Randall's abject humiliation and dispense a little pity his way.

A brain tumor would, in all likelihood, kill him in less than a year, to say nothing of ruining his chances for being elected Chairman of the American Institute of Bankruptcy Lawyers.

Maybe he should forget the formalities and just go to church. St. Dymphna's was less than three blocks from his front door. *Do they even have daily mass anymore? Does anyone go these days?* Even if they didn't have mass, he could throw himself on the flagstones of the unfamiliar temple, a revenant altar boy trying to relearn the syntax of prayer, clawing at the floor of his thoughts, pleading for the love of God for the strength to bear whatever was happening to him.

•

The main door to the cathedral was locked, so Randall drew the collar of his coat closer and walked the long journey around the nave, up and down wheelchair ramps to the side door and into the soaring interior of St. Dymphna's Cathedral. It was a Gothic replica, designed to tip the head of the visitor back and lift the eyes to heaven. Light and harmonic shadows filled the ribbed, groined ceiling vaults, creating patterns almost as beautiful as the internal cohesion of the Bankruptcy Code, or the symmetrical ribbing of a bat's wing.

Twenty-seven years ago, Father Macaunahay had presided over the sacrament of matrimony marrying Randall Steven Killigan to Marjorie Cecilia Newstead. During the ceremony, Randall had let his eyes drift up to fingered vaults tinted pink by the rose windows of the transept, and had recalled how nothing had changed since his First Communion, since his Confirmation, since his altar boy days, when he had served mass at least once a day, with funerals and weddings thrown in to boot. The building was exactly the same, relentlessly and eerily just as he had left it, redolent with beeswax and incense, odors still lingering after forty years.

Randall Killigan in church! Perhaps it is possible to be wide awake and dreaming at the same time. Maybe it wasn't real, maybe it was only a place in his mind, which would explain why it never changed. On a bet, he could probably go up the stairs behind the sacristy and find the cavernous, marmoreal lofts of rosewood closets, probably still strung with cassocks and surplices, and fitted out with kneelers, where he had bowed his head and practiced reciting his Latin responses: "*Confiteor Deo omnipotenti . . .*" The same ornate marble railing where he had knelt to receive his First Communion still spanned the front of the cathedral. The small brass gate through which he had walked up onto the altar for his Confirmation, the beginning of the natural progression from Soldier of Christ to bankruptcy lawyer.

Everything was almost exactly the same, and would be the same, even if he came back in his sixties looking to bury his mother, or a friend, or looking to have his marriage annulled. On Judgment Day, he would probably find the place pretty much as is. He would be summoned from the grave by a voice of thunder, called to the pulpit, and ordered to proclaim his offenses against humanity to a congregation of friends, family, lawyers, and judges. Maybe an archangel would stand at the pulpit and summon Randall Steven Killigan forward to read his bankruptcy briefs aloud to the congregation of souls.

"Could you tell us a little bit more about debtor-in-possession financing?" the angel would say. "We would love to hear all about it."

His next thought was: *Where is everybody?* The early-morning masses in his altar boy days drew a crowd of at least a hundred. Here, scattered far and wide in the vast echoing expanses of the nave, were maybe ten or twelve elderly citizens—the men with bald heads and canes, the women with curved spines and tinted hair. To the last man and woman, they looked as if they might not show next week.

Faces mottled with age spots and frail, gray heads fitted out with flesh-colored hearing aids briefly glanced up at his passing. In small smiles and polite glances they showed him they knew why he had come: He was nursing some private tragedy—could they see it in his face?—cancer, or the loss of a loved one. Otherwise, why would an outwardly healthy, middle-aged man in a tailored suit show up at six o'clock mass on a Tuesday? Then again, if the church was not real, then the beings standing around him were apparitions from his dreams, spectral incarnations of his impulses and fears: faceless authority figures, former lovers, friends he had betrayed under extenuating circumstances, his son, his wife . . . His grandparents. Teachers who had expected better things of him.

He sensed his presence being noted as someone no one recognized, and as the only member of the congregation under sixty-five and still able to safely operate a can opener. The priest was bound to notice him too, as someone who had never been there before. Maybe Randall could talk to the priest afterward. He was in fine shape: *wanting* to talk to a priest? What do these guys *make* a year? Poverty? Chastity? Obedience? A place to sleep and eat, free scotch, and the respect of the community, in exchange for preaching to the converted—stand up there saying things people already knew, but didn't quite want to believe. Their job was to talk to guys like Randall, who were falling apart.

He knelt, bowed his head, and tried to pray. Then he heard everyone stand and the priest—a man Randall had never seen before (he was half expecting Father Macaunahay)—began:

"In the name of the Father, and of the Son, and of the Holy Spirit."

Randall said "Amen" along with everyone else, and promptly felt like a fraud.

He imagined that the entire congregation had heard his Amen and knew by its wavering tone and its uncertain enunciation that it was the Amen of a man who last went to mass twenty-seven years ago, at his wedding.

The priest was overweight. For some reason, Randall wanted him to be discalced and wearing a coarse garment, gaunt and haunted, gentle, with big moist eyes, just this side of a hallucination, nourished only by locusts and honey. Randall saw a mystic, a gentle teacher, who would place a hand on Randall's head and cast out his raging anxiety, maybe send it into a herd of plaintiffs' lawyers, who could then charge down the hill and throw themselves into the river.

Instead, the priest was stout and portly, and spoke of God's love with the stolidity of an estate-planning lawyer.

The priest and the congregation then began to pray together:

> *"I confess to almighty God,*
> *and to you my brothers and sisters,*
> *that I have sinned through my own fault*
> *in my thoughts and in my words,*
> *in what I have done, and in what I have failed to do . . ."*

Of course, he knew none of the words. And he could not find the prayer in the daily missalette, because they didn't call it the *Confiteor* anymore, so he mumbled along, slurring and humming the words in a rough approximation of what was being said. His eyes followed bundles of pilasters aloft to the soaring vaults again, until a yawn blurred his vision with tears of exhaustion.

The man standing several yards down in the same pew bore an uncanny resemblance to Randall's grandfather, may he rest in peace. Randall had a sudden premonition that he would come and help him find his place in the missalette. With a benevolent smile, the man would gently thumb through Randall's book, and stop at the appropriate page. There, in the ornamented initials of an illuminated manuscript, it would say: THIS IS NOT A DREAM.

> *"Glory to God in the highest,*
> *and peace to his people on earth*
> *Lord God, heavenly King,*
> *almighty God and Father,*
> *we worship you, we give you thanks,*
> *we praise you for your glory."*

Maybe figures in the congregation would begin turning in groups of two or three, studying the bankruptcy lawyer with looks of solemn disgust, abhorring him for the monsters he had raised in the privacy of his own soul, predatory creatures he had husbanded, then turned loose on the world. The people wanted to stay as far away as possible, but close enough to get a look at what sort of man could take such delight in the misfortunes of others . . .

The priest began the reading of the Gospel:

"Just then the disciples came up to Jesus with the question: Who is of greatest importance in the kingdom of God? He called a little child over and stood him in their midst and said: I assure you, unless you change and become like little children, you will not enter the kingdom of God. Whoever makes himself lowly, becoming like this child, is of greatest importance in that heavenly reign.

"See that you never despise one of these little ones. I assure you, their angels in heaven constantly behold my heavenly Father's face."

Change and become like little children, he thought. That's rich. He had a pretty good idea what would happen to child Randall if he was representing the bank in a nasty single-asset case, where the loans were guaranteed personally by the husband and wife, and the bank was after the house, the car, bank accounts, stock, the playground equipment in the backyard . . . and child Randall would come in advising everyone that they must all become like little children.

"We must love and trust each other," he might advise. "Aren't we all brothers and sisters?"

"You hold him down," one of the other lawyers would say, "I'll cut the meat off of him."

His remains would be bezoars in the intestines of his predatory opponents. Ritual cannibalism. The Rite of Spring Lawyering. He'd be tied down on an altar somewhere, listening to them discuss methods: "Do you think we can get his heart out fast enough, so we can see it beat a couple of times before it stops?"

Making himself lowly and loving his neighbor were out of the question. Randall could no more go around loving his neighbor in bankruptcy court than Hector could have kissed Achilles on the cheek at the gates of Troy and invited him to go skinny-dipping in the wine-dark sea, while rosy-fingered dawn broke in the east . . . Let compassion pop into his head just once, for even an instant, and his head would be off and rolling around the courtroom, and some other warrior of the Code would be astride his vanquished Christian remains, washing his hands in Randall's blood, and filling his lungs with a cry of victory.

The priest interrupted Randall's thoughts with a sermon. Smiling down from the pulpit, with his thumbs tucked into his cinctured alb, the priest looked out over the congregation and rested his eyes on Randall Steven Killigan.

He knows, thought Randall.

"You must *change*," the priest said, taking in the believers with his arms, "and become like little children. Make yourselves *lowly!* Most of us look to the scriptures for comfort and understanding. We would rather understand our lives than change them. Changing them takes work. We would rather mull over scriptural platitudes, things we can nod along with and go home saying, 'It's just as I thought. I was right all along.' But that's not the message here. The message is *change*. Lower ourselves. Become like little children, full of wonder and awe."

Change? For forty years he had been thinking through the wilderness of being. The paths and convergences that had brought him here were as various and complex as the nerves in his brain. At each juncture, he had made a selection, and each selection became a part of his being, as if living in the world a certain way could actually alter the synaptic structures of his brain; could maybe even rearrange or alter the constituent elements of the soul. So that in the afterlife the soul of a gambler would actually "look" different than the soul of Mother Teresa, and different than the soul of a bankruptcy lawyer.

Having selected the life of a bankruptcy warrior, he was now capable of certain thoughts, and not others. Quite without thinking, he had succeeded too well at self-discipline, producing an irreversible state of being. Happiness and peace of mind were no longer feasible, for instance, unless he was billing out at least 2,200 hours a year. If an angel of the Lord showed him the death of his son, the betrayal by his wife, eternal damnation self-selected by the warlord, showed him how each decision had led him willy-nilly down each juncture in the paths of being, he would still be helpless to change himself and go back.

He had no idea where these thoughts came from; he knew only that they were symptoms of weakness, of possible mental instability, of an organic disturbance, possibly a neoplasm, or some other bright object in his deep white matter. If he did not resolve this problem soon, he feared that the daily, obsessive anxiety would permanently alter his brain chemistry. Maybe he would wake up endowed with an ability to hear the high-frequency sonar screams of bats. Soon he would start to make crucial mistakes. He would mishandle one major bankruptcy, and that client would go away mad. A year later they would all be gone. "*He used to be the best goddamn bankruptcy lawyer in the Seventh Circuit,"* they would say. *"Then things took a bad turn. You were hearing about personal problems. It's always chicken and egg when drinking's involved, but I think he lost a son, his only son."*

He turned his attention back to the priest's sermon.

"Those here who are parents have a special knowledge of what it means to become like little children," said the priest. "We were children once. And now we are mothers and fathers, grandmothers and grandfathers. And how desperately we love our children. Not more than our spouses, but with an equally powerful love of a different kind. And when that love is returned, we are filled with joy, with the happiness known only to mothers and fathers.

"But when that love is not returned. When our son or daughter turns away from us in hatred or selfishness. How bitter our hearts! For then we become like the shepherd Jesus told us about who had ninety-nine sheep to watch over on the hillside and left them all to find and rescue the one helpless stray . . . Think of your pain if you were spurned by your own son or daughter, or maybe one of your children has been seriously ill, to the point where their life was endangered. How desperate and helpless your pain. How choked with bitterness and fear of losing your precious child forever!

"Let us imagine now in our hearts that desperate pain of love we have for our children when they are lost, or they have turned from us in anger. That is how your Father in heaven feels each time you turn away from him, or speak in anger to your brothers and sisters on earth, or take advantage of them in their weakness or ignorance. You spurn our Father in heaven, showing him only your hatred and selfishness!"

Did he see a bat a few nights ago? A huge bat! With his own two eyes, by the light of four light bulbs, in his own bedroom? Did he hold some bleeding freak of nature in his own two hands last night? And was he now hearing a sermon that was clearly written for him? He looked again into the soaring vaults, now washed in the pastel tints of morning sunlight diffusing through stained glass, maybe coming in through the north windows like the divine light in paintings of Gothic cathedrals.

His eighth-grade teacher—a shriveled, meanspirited nun with dentures that looked like a linebacker's mouth guard—had told him that the universe was one big miracle, one big expression of God's will, as if God had exhaled, and out came the universe in a storm of spectacular cosmic events. But because people lived, breathed, ate, and saw the miracle every day, all day, they thought it was routine. They could no longer look at the world with the eyes of the first human. (Think of what that first human saw! And with no words to help him!) Everything had been poisoned by preconceptions and expectations. They imagined it was subject to the pathetic laws and theorems they imposed upon it. Soon miracles consisted only of the unexpected, instead of the inexplicable—for ultimately nothing can be explained . . . she had said. And even if they could see Creation with the eyes of the first human, their heartbeats would rise (like Rilke's thunder!) and kill them.

He was here only because he could not bear to think that his son's disappearance was just another accident in a universe of colliding molecules. His own perceptions had so terrified him that he had sought shelter in the refuge of the weak. He was regressing to an earlier stage of psychological development. Half Catholic. Once the good nuns installed the basic components, no matter how many times he redid the wiring, there would always be certain phantom circuits that still carried religious impulses, cryptopsychic filaments extremely sensitive to the least . . . vibration or disturbance: deaths, times of sorrow, life-threatening illnesses . . . prompting a reversion to ritualistic processing behaviors . . .

> *"We believe in one God,*
> *the Father, the Almighty,*
> *maker of heaven and earth,*
> *of all that is seen and unseen."*

Randall was able to find this prayer, entitled "Profession of Faith," which long ago he had learned as "The Creed." He read it with feeling and sentiment for his schoolboy days.

"God from God, Light from Light, true God from true God, begotten, not made, one in Being with the Father."

Maybe Judgment Day would be like a section 2004 examination of the creditors in a Chapter 11 bankruptcy. Maybe he was deteriorating mentally. That's why he had turned to prayer, night hallucinations, and other symptoms of mental instability.

"On the third day, he rose again in fulfillment of the Scriptures: he ascended into heaven and is seated at the right hand of the

Father. He will come again in glory to judge the living and the dead, and his kingdom will have no end."

The priest began a litany of prayers for various parishioners and special causes, paying special attention to people who had *tithed*, or given a tenth of their incomes to the Church.

"And we pray, O Lord," the priest added solemnly, "for our President. We do not know the exact state of his health at this time. But we ask you, Lord, for his safe recovery."

What happened to the President? Randall almost said aloud. The President was abroad, Randall knew. He was halfway across the world with an entourage of American watch manufacturers. They were all in Switzerland demanding that Swiss people buy American-made watches, instead of unfairly selling Swiss-made watches to American consumers, while refusing to open Swiss markets to American watch manufacturers. Randall had seen the President on the six o'clock news, in high dudgeon with several American watch-manufacturing executives. "This is the very essence of an unfair trade practice," the President had said. "Americans buy quality Swiss watches; but the Swiss do not reciprocate by buying American-made watches, even though watches made in America are priced competitively."

Randall had seen the morning *Times*, but something must have happened after last night's printing of the national edition. He stifled the impulse to lean over the two empty pews and tap the shoulder of an elderly parishioner on the off chance that maybe she was picking up the news on those hearing aids that were squeaking with feedback.

The President had a heart condition. He must have had a coronary. That's it! A heart attack was the most logical explanation! The Merck! In two hours, the stock market was going to open in New York and plunge straight down a steep slope to hell. Maybe he could slip out and call his broker at home. Maybe he could buy options to cover his position, a basket of puts, or maybe even a straight short sale. Would that be easier or harder than just trying to dump the stock? If he tried to dump it, there would be no buyers, and he would end up getting a sale after it had dropped 30 percent in price. No, he was better off getting in line to buy options and betting on a fall.

Could he go any lower? Thinking about money at a time like this?

He should simply trust God, he realized, and calmed himself. After all, he was in church. God would take care of him, his Merck, and his son. What if he was a ragpicker in Calcutta? What if he grew a brain tumor? Would he care about the Merck then? Of course he would, because if his time was up, then his wife and his son were going to need all the money they could get. No more fat checks from the law firm. But God knew that, didn't He? God would take care of that.

Maybe Randall was remembering how to pray. Yeah. He should just kind of . . . let go and trust God. Just become . . . like a child. Just place himself at the mercy of his Father in heaven.

Maybe a straight short sale? No way. Who would be stupid enough to buy it?

> *"And so, Father, we bring you these gifts.*
> *We ask you to make them holy by the*
> *power of your Spirit,*
> *that they may become the body and blood*
> *of your Son, our Lord Jesus Christ . . ."*

Maybe God would help him find his son if he sold all the Merck and gave the money to the poor.

> *"On the night he was betrayed,*
> *he took bread and gave you thanks and*
> *praise.*
> *He broke the bread, gave it to his*
> *disciples, and said:*

> *Take this, all of you, and eat it:*
> *this is my body which will be given up for you."*

How many times had he rung the handbell as an altar boy at just this moment: the elevation of the Host? No bells rang now. There were no altar boys. These days they were probably all gang members. They went to rock concerts and knew all about sex, violence, and alcohol, instead of the consecration of bread and wine into the blood and body of Christ.

Take this, all of you, and eat it, he repeated silently. He felt like a person from a foreign country who had never been to mass, had never even *heard* of mass. The Eucharist suddenly struck him as a primitive, savage ritual. He imagined what it would sound like to have an American Catholic explain it to him. *It's like a sacrifice, an offering. But it's a mystery too. See, the priest changes the bread and wine into the body and blood of Christ. Then we eat it and drink it. But the bread and wine, they aren't just symbols, they BECOME the body and blood of Christ. Trans . . . Transmutation? No. Transubstantiation. Yeah, that's the word. There's another word that means you're eating God. Theo . . . Theophany? No, that's mystical experience. Theophagy, that's it. It means the sacrificial eating of a god. Sounds like a term paper*: The Central Role of Eating in Sacrificial Rituals. *Primitives used to do it, to get power, which the Catholics call grace. But wait?* he thought, interrupting his own imaginary explanation. Christ was a man too. He was sitting at the table with other men when he broke the bread. Eat my body. Drink my blood. He was telling other men to take his body and eat it. That's not theophagy, that's . . . And his thoughts came full circle to his son, probably chased through the bush by cannibals, heathens in loincloths, with bones through their noses. Why couldn't his son have just stayed home and gone to law school? On the other hand, what if Michael had gone to law school and had not graduated in the top 10 percent of his class? Cannibalism might look pretty good . . .

> "When supper was ended, he took the cup.
> Again he gave you thanks and praise,
> gave the cup to his disciples, and said:
>
> Take this, all of you, and drink from it:
> this is the cup of my blood,
> the blood of the new and everlasting covenant.
> It will be shed for you and for all
> so that sins may be forgiven.
> Do this in memory of me."

Randall decided to risk Communion, even though he knew he could be committing a mortal sin if he was not absolutely convinced that he was eating the body of Christ. He was not eating *symbols* of the body and blood of Christ as the pagan Episcopalians believed. No, the bread and wine actually *changed into* the body and blood of our Lord Jesus Christ. Not the historical Jesus, but the entire Person just the same. He remembered actually believing this with all his heart, and thought he might manage to do so again, if it would help him regain control . . .

He hurried to the front of the church, so he would be among the first in line, leaving only two elderly women between him and where he knew the priest would stand to distribute Christ's body in pieces of bread and his blood from communal cups of wine. Neither of these elderly women, Randall reasoned, could have any fatal viruses, and thus he could safely share the cup of the new and everlasting covenant with them.

"Body of Christ," said the priest, placing the Host in Randall's hand.

"Amen," said Randall, wondering when they'd stopped just putting the Host in your mouth for you. For he recalled it used to be a sin to touch the Host. He had done it once as a boy, quite without thinking, and had held the finger and stared at it for days, expecting it to wither. They probably had to change the method for distributing the Host after they lost the altar boys to gangs and rock concerts. Nobody to hold the silver paten under your chin.

"Blood of Christ," said a layperson, wiping the lip of the cup and offering it to Randall.

"Amen," he said, appreciating the hygienic efforts of the wine distributor, surprised by the taste of wine this early in the morning.

Randall knelt, bowed his head, and prayed that his son would be found. That he did not have a brain tumor. That there was some perfectly harmless explanation for the night disturbances. That God would convince Marjorie not to turn against him. That God would please keep the President healthy. Or if that was not to be granted, then that the stock market would not crash, or if that was not to be granted, then that the Merck miraculously would not fall along with the rest of the market. Or, failing all of the above, that he would be able to place an order for a whole bunch of puts and calls and other stock options to protect his Merck holdings, in which case, his prayers would require some modification, because he would then be asking for the Merck to precipitously decline, then stabilize long enough for him to sell his puts, whereupon it should then rise to above its present level, so he could sell his calls.

We ask this through Christ Our Lord, Amen.

But if God was hearing all of this, would He be quite annoyed and disappointed in Randall's preoccupation with money? Would He be insulted that the celebration of the mass had reminded Randall of cannibalism? Maybe God would think it was funny? Probably not. Laughter is satanic. It was invented after the Fall. God cannot laugh. Nowhere in the scriptures could Randall recall it saying, "God laughed and said, 'Why, that's the funniest thing I ever heard!'" The scriptures are full of desperate half-wits, birdbrains, madmen, tax collectors, con artists, and obtuse fishermen. Every page contains at least one gaffe by some thick-witted apostle, but nowhere do the scriptures say, "Jesus laughed and said, 'Oh, horse-feathers, Peter! Go jump in the Dead Sea!'" Maybe God cannot laugh because everything makes perfect sense to Him. No nonsense, no irony, no absurdity, no contradiction . . . To God, Groucho Marx was just another human thing making noises with his mouth. No wry, divine smiles, no sloppy raspberries. Not a day goes by without Him thinking: *That's not funny.*

"Let us pause for a moment," the priest said, "and contemplate God's love, accepting it into our hearts. For if we can do that, it will give every second of our short lives a divine purpose: serving Him."

This, Randall realized, was true. The overfed priest spoke the truth. Randall had lived his life indirectly serving God as a bankruptcy lawyer. By enforcing the law of the U.S. Bankruptcy Code, Randall was helping the world to be a stable and fair place. For what was the Code but a means to wipe the slate clean of failed endeavors, to assign any assets to the most deserving creditors, according to strict rules, and start anew? It was a law passed by Congress and the President, and Randall's job was to make sure that his clients understood what they were entitled to under the Code and that any debtors guilty of fraud were caught and punished. Would God tolerate fraud? No way! God hated swindlers and money changers. And Randall served God by making damn sure that fraudulent debtors paid in this life and the next. He might as well be a missionary for Christ's Church and get credit for all the good he's doing in the world.

Randall would serve God by making enough money so that his grandchildren would one day bear witness to Christ's love, privately educated, and raised in the glory of His love.

"The mass is ended. Go in peace."

"Thanks be to God."

Refreshed and full of grace, Randall was ready to go back to work casting lots for garments.

On his way out, he walked by an arrangement of three wooden closets, which he instantly recognized as the confessional, where he had knelt as an eight-year-old and confessed his sins, courageously admitting to crimes against humanity like telling a lie or hitting his sister.

Randall noticed a small green light over the priest's door, looking like a console light on a heavy appliance indicating the power was on; he realized that a priest was in there waiting to hear confessions.

On impulse, he opened the door and found the same red leather kneeler, the same cedar closet, a little wider than an upright coffin, upholstered in velvet instead of satin, the same purple curtain covering the sliding panel, closed when the priest was hearing the sins of the penitent in the other booth.

Randall went in, shut the door, and sat in darkness, staring into the shadowy veil in front of him. The hatch slid open.

"Bless me, Father, for I have sinned," said Randall, saying the words, almost without remembering them. "My last confession was . . . about forty or so years ago. I can't remember exactly."

He paused and heard the priest clear his throat.

"I also don't remember the exact words I'm supposed to say," said Randall, "but I'm in trouble, and I think my son's in trouble, and I may need help . . ."

"Do you want to reconcile yourself with God?" asked the priest, his voice textured with age and compassion.

"Yes," said Randall. "I think so, but I'm not sure about the sacraments, you understand. I think I just need help, because I'm so . . ."

"Do you intend to confess your sins to me and to God?" asked the old priest quietly.

Intend? thought Randall, seizing upon the word, and realizing again the naive impunity with which laypeople use words that are fraught with complex legal implications. *Intent* was an essential ingredient of *fraud*, the F-word of bankruptcy parlance. *Intentional* fraud could wipe out assets, nullify safe harbors and the protection of statutes, result in punitive damages. Do I *intend* to confess my sins to you and to God? Was it permissible to request that certain terms be defined before he gave an answer?

"I think so," said Randall, privately wondering if the doctrine of unclean hands, which barred wrongdoers from seeking redress in the courts of equity, might also bar him from petitioning God for assistance.

"What are your sins?" asked the priest.

"I am unsure about the rules, so I don't know exactly which ones I may have . . . not abided by. Have they changed or anything in the last few decades?"

"Do you love God?"

"I do," said Randall. "I think I do. I haven't thought much about it, until recently. But once I started thinking about it again, I kind of thought to myself that if God exists, which He probably does, I would love Him. And maybe if there was even a small chance He could help me . . . Then I would need His help."

"Do you love your neighbor?"

"My neighbor?" asked Randall. "You mean, other people? Do I love other people? Yes, I do, I think, when it's permitted. I mean, you can't go around loving opposing counsel, for instance. That would be a violation of the Code of Professional Ethics, because it would not be in my client's best interests. But generally, in the theoretical sense, I would say that yes, I love others, in a manner of speaking, within certain limits, consistent with various statutes, codes, and rules of court.

"This loving business," he continued. "I know it's desirable in terms of long-range planning, but my problem is more immediate. My son is missing in Africa. My only son, and I . . . Well, I may have a very serious illness. A brain tumor. I might die, or if I don't die, then it's something psychological. I might go insane, because mysterious . . . things are happening to me."

"You are afraid," said the priest.

Randall held his breath and mastered a rogue emotion, which threatened to bolt from his stables and make an ass of him.

"Yes," he admitted, hearing his voice crack nonetheless. It was time to go. Crying in the presence of a priest was even more humiliating than a brain tumor. Pretty soon he would break down and look for consolation in the Beatitudes: *Don't worry about being poor in spirit and weak, it means you're blessed!*

"Fear of death," said the priest. "No one can face that alone."

Randall looked down where a shaft of dim light fell through the veil onto his vesseled hand. He moved his own fingers, watching them from afar, wondering what they would look like when they were attached to a dead man whose eyes were empty sockets.

"You won't be alone," said the priest. "No matter what happens to you or your son, God the Father will be with you. And if God is calling you away from this world, only your body will perish, your soul will be with Him . . . if you have faith."

"Faith," repeated Randall, "in . . ."

"In God," said the priest patiently, "in eternal life, in the resurrection of the body, in life everlasting."

If he had a soul, Randall was unsure about whether he wanted it to survive him, unless he could have control over it, some kind of estate planning, or perhaps a durable power of attorney. Would his soul linger about his body and reminisce? Would it flee in terror into an eternal hell of its own making? Would it attend the funeral and savor the heaving bosoms of women who had loved him? Or disappear into the aether, mixing it up with lower-order souls who had never been to law school or medical school? Would a soul so situated be able to receive supplementary updates to the Code and to the Bankruptcy Reporters?

And what would the afterlife be like? What parts of his interior life would survive? Maybe it was all the same, here and hereafter. Maybe on the other side the laws were even more complex, with statutory histories covering all of eternity. Computerized research could serve up parallel authorities from other galaxies. He could eternally update the software of massive computer systems, giving him access to all the information in the universe by doing term searches of infinite complexity.

Maybe bankruptcy would go on forever, and he would always be the best bankruptcy lawyer in the universe, alone and unchallenged, feared by all, unwilling to indulge himself in the pleasures of the afterlife, because they might compromise his concentration and his technique.

Nothing but fond hopes, he realized. Death would be the end of his career. He felt the unidentified bright object in his deep white matter swell with multiplying cells. They were reproducing in a deadly geometrical progression. The tumor was throwing off colonies of cells, which were migrating to his lungs, his liver, his bones . . .

Brain tumor or no, there was only so much time left in his life. It was measured in seconds separating him from death. He could spend them making war in bankruptcy court, looking for his son, taking a hot bath, eating cookies . . . or praying.

"Father, I . . . am afraid I might be dying," he whispered. "I guess I just need to know what I'm supposed to do."

The priest sighed gently. "First make a full confession," he said. "Then we will pray together."

"Confession of what?" pleaded Randall. "I haven't killed anyone or committed adultery or anything . . . so, I mean . . ."

"Have you intentionally *harmed* anyone?" asked the priest.

Of course, Randall thought, *that's my job!*

"No," he said, "only in bankruptcy court. Only if they tried to harm my client first. Self-defense, I guess."

"I'm sure you can help your clients without harming other people," said the priest. "Can't you?"

Sure, thought Randall, *and a guitar mass probably would have ended the Siege of Leningrad.*

How was he supposed to convey the unmitigated savagery of a contested fee-application hearing to this old man who sat in a box all day listening to people moan about sins?

"I suppose so," said Randall.

"When you use your talents to help other people, you are serving God the Father," said the priest. "When you use your talents to harm others, you are turning away from God. That's what sin is. So if you recall any specific occasions when you used your talents to harm others, those would be sins you should confess now."

Now? thought Randall. *How much time do we have? A definition of "harm" would help.*

Maybe he could expedite things by offering to make a sizable tax-deductible donation.

Randall coughed. "Nothing specific comes to mind, Father, but I see what you are saying. I should just try to *help* people more."

"Yes," said the priest. "Find Christ in others."

"Uh-uh," said Randall.

"Then death will hold no terrors for you," said the priest.

That word again, thought Randall. He recalled that, under the Federal Rules of Evidence, section 804(b)(2), a statement made by a declarant, while believing that his death was imminent, concerning the cause or circumstances of what he believed to be his impending death is not excluded by the hearsay rule. In other words, thought Randall, if, just before he died, or just before he *thought* he was going to die, he said, "This brain tumor is killing me," that statement could be admissible evidence in a court of law, even though the declarant, Randall Killigan, was dead.

But so what!? he realized, suddenly verging on tears. *Who cares?* He'd be dead! All of his knowledge would molder into gray pudding, six feet under in a bowl at the back of his grinning skull. Forty years of reading. Twenty-five years of billable hours. Gone! Twenty-five times three hundred and sixty-five times twelve, minus a few weeks off. At least 100,000 hours. Gone!

Randall swallowed hard to keep the emotion out of his voice. "Father," he said, "I'm ready to pray now."

The smell of cedar and musty velvet. The light again on his own foreign hand. Silence. A susurrus. Breathing. Air passing through a stricture.

"Father?" said Randall, hearing only the faint sound of another suspiration. *The wind blows where it will,* he suddenly remembered. *You hear the sound it makes but you do not know where it comes from, or where it goes. So it is with everyone begotten of the Spirit.*

"Father?"

The old man's vocal cords groaned softly in a delicate snore on the other side of the purple curtain.

Randall shuddered, alone in the velvet darkness. What if it happened now? He would never know how close he had come to making his confession, because the last person he had turned to for help, his confessor, had nodded off! What if death was coming now? And Randall, the penitent manqué, was a seed or an encapsulated soul lodged in a dark pneumatic tube. There would be a sucking of air, and he would be drawn down, and flushed into the bowels of eternal night, far, far below, where his body would be resurrected and plunged into the void. His hands and fingers, his muscles and nerves would lose all sense of themselves and melt in the liquid blackness. His eyes would be clotted with night, they would swell and burst in bootless attempts to see.

Maybe, at first, he would be happy to discover that his mind seemed to have survived. But what about its legendary cravings for knowledge and information? The darkness visible contained no reading material. His Code, his *Wall Street Journal*, his *New York Times*, his *Forbes*—all the pages were gone! Only the ink had survived, had somehow drained off the pages of history and pooled into an infinite blackness. His intellect became disembodied appetite, foraging for food, sifting the depths of sunless oceans through the fine mesh of reason, desperate for something—anything!—to devour. Never mind his Code then, anything to give him some small pleasure. How about a flyer advertising a sale at a grocery store in another century, or maybe the back of a Chinese cereal box? And a candle to read it by?

Instead, he would find only himself, and his awareness of himself, floating, and straining the still seas of nothingness. In a final act of desperation, his imagination would turn itself inside out and create a chamber for him to think in, a single room walled in blackness, furnished only with memories from the split second that had been his earthly life. Alone in the desolation of absolute solitude, his memories would disintegrate, one by one, from being handled too often by his intellectual powers, and the particles would slip through the mesh . . .

The priest snored softly on the other side of the screen. Randall stared contemptuously, listening.

Catholic superstitions! Phantom circuits, paleopsychic eruptions! Buck up! What if somebody had him on film? The best bankruptcy lawyer in the Seventh Circuit? Wringing his hands and sniveling in a cedar closet? This was all caused by some organic dysfunction. Had to be! But OK, then. Take it like a man! If death was coming, he would meet it on his feet, with his boots on, in bankruptcy court. Let them tell stories about how three months after they had told him he had three months to live, he had shown up in bankruptcy court with a battle-ax, cleaved the skull of his opponent, and poured despoiled brains into his briefcase! In death, they would say, he was even more fearsome!

The legend would live on!

(13)

Jenisa lay abed, grinding her teeth in fear and listening to the sound of wings slashing the night and wind whistling in the teeth of Luba, who had transformed herself into a fruit bat and was swooping through the village looking for children to eat. Luba and the other witches in her coven fluttered in the eaves of the compounds and made the loud *crawk-aw-aw-awk* of witch birds, announcing their hunger for fresh infant blood. She heard Luba and her coven of scavenging night creatures; she *knew* Luba was a witch, but she fled in terror from the thought. As everyone knew, if Luba was a witch, she would instantly sense any suspicion harbored by others—even total strangers—and would kill any potential accusers before they could reveal her true nature.

Instead, Jenisa desperately tried to think only of the clothes she would have to brook tomorrow, about how Yotta, the big wife, was fat, ugly, and smelled like a bush cow, about the palm oil she would sell tomorrow along the highway, about her mother, who was sick with fever and needed her help, or even, if she had to, about how her husband, the section chief, had not sent for her to share his bed for many weeks, about how he was probably angry, because the Sande women had said that adultery, and maybe even witchcraft, had caused her to lose two children, about two baby girls whom she could have taken out on the morning of the third day after their births, and announced, "Resemble me in all my ways and deeds, being named after me," and whom she would have taught so well to love and suffer without complaining of pain or hardship, about her *poo-mui* love man who was lost somewhere in the bush. She thought of anything and everything she could, to keep from thinking the one thought that pursued all the others like a leopard chasing prey in the bush at night.

Maybe Luba the witch had already sensed the danger lurking in the half-formed hunches racing to catch Jenisa's thoughts. Maybe that was why Luba was fluttering outside in the eaves. Maybe Luba knew what Jenisa had felt just this morning while she was drawing a bucket of water from the well. The sickness coming in waves to her belly, the flush of heat in the cool morning air. She was at once ecstatic that she might at last bring a son or daughter to her wife man, and terrified that Luba would learn of her condition and eat the child before it could be born.

Just yesterday, Jenisa had argued with Luba over some palm-oil soap that had been left at the washing place. It was Jenisa's soap, but Luba tried to claim it as her own.

As other women had gathered to watch the argument, Luba—dressed as usual in rags, with mud smeared onto her shaved head—had thrown the soap on the ground and had said, "Take it, then. I don't want it," and walked away.

"It wasn't yours to want," Jenisa had shouted after her, and instantly regretted her boldness.

Luba turned and marched back to the soap, now wedged in the sand. She stared into Jenisa's eyes and a wicked smile spread across her face.

"I think we should give your soap to the washing and probing man who prepares the dead for burial."

This shocked everyone. What could such talk mean? She was not only evil but insane as well.

"I don't need soap," she said, holding out her filthy arms, bedraggled with the tatters of a country cloth dress.

"You," she said with a grin, "need soap!" Then she jerked and scared the gathering crowd, laughing at them when they gasped and drew back. "Some night soon," she said, staring off over the treetops of the surrounding bush, where the rest of her coven was probably roaming in the shape of animals, "I will dream about the woman whose soap belongs to the washing man."

Jenisa went straight to her hut in the *mawe*. She made sure that the witch nets were properly hung over the doors; she made sure the bamboo witch guns were in place. Then she sank onto her mattress in despair. For now, maybe the witch gun or her prayers would keep Luba at bay, but soon Luba would assume the shape of whatever animal would carry her into Jenisa's hut, so she could settle her witch weight on the young girl's face, and suffocate her, or eat another one of her children before it could be born.

Jenisa's only hope was the medicine. She had given the white stranger's gift to the juju man, just as the looking-around man had instructed. The juju man had placed the small canister of mosquito medicine into his pouch, then had asked her many questions about what kind of medicine she wished to let loose in the world. Was she seeking only to protect herself from Luba's malignant powers or was she seeking to harm or destroy the author of her sorrows? Destroy or defend?

"Destroy," Jenisa had said through clenched teeth. "She ate my children, then she wiped her lips and laughed."

"The medicine I will make for you is illegal," said the juju man. "I would never make such a medicine or let such a swear loose on anyone, no matter what they did to me. But this person has torn your heart to shreds, has dashed your dreams, and has destroyed your children. Who is qualified to sit in judgment of this monster that has eaten your children? Who can know the agonies you have suffered waking each morning and knowing that two beautiful children would be frolicking at your feet, living and loving you, but for the wickedness of Luba? You alone are able to decide all that must be done. You have paid me money and purchased my confidence and my skill. I will make the medicine and give it to you, but I do not want to know what you do with this evil thing. You alone will know. You must not tell anyone. You will answer before your ancestors and before *Ngewo*."

Some days later, the juju man met her in the bush at night and gave her a small black bundle with the *poo-mui* medicine sticking out of it like a spout at the top. He did not want to know whether or when she intended to use it, but if she wished to destroy an enemy with the medicine, she should obtain something from her enemy's house—an article of clothing, a lock of hair—and then bury it, together with the medicine, near her enemy's house. If your enemy is a witch, the next time the witch's shade leaves on a night journey, the medicine will fly into the bush after it, catch it, and kill it. When the shade does not return, the human form will slip into a coma and die.

So many feared that all the deaths in the village were caused by witches, but none dared speak of it. Jenisa did not even discuss it with Amida, her mate and her closest friend, for fear of retribution. Jenisa knew it was Luba, Amida knew it was Luba, everyone knew that Luba the witch was eating all the children in the village, but no one dared accuse her, even in private, for fear that Luba would come for them at night, settle on their faces, and suffocate them.

The night before Pa Gigba was shot by the hunter, Mama Saso's twins died during childbirth. Their birth had been foretold in a dream, in which Mama Saso went down to brook clothes at the river and saw two snakes twining around the washing rock. For months, sacrifices of rice and fowl had been left at altars made from termite mounds, where twins are worshipped. An older twin from another village was summoned to pray at the altars. The twin told Jenisa that *Ngewo* made two kinds of people: twins and the rest of the human race. Twins have the power to foretell the future, to cure diseases, to protect entire villages from witchcraft, and to make farms bear rice.

But Mama Saso's twins would never enjoy such powers, or use them to bring health and prosperity to their parents. They were dead. One week ago, Jenisa's cousin, Fatmata, who lived in the *mawe* near the dyeing yard, suddenly lost an infant. A week before that, another child had died. Jenisa's children had died. Amida had lost a child. Mariamu, who had borne three strong sons and two daughters, also, inexplicably, lost her little Borboh. Now Pa Gigba was dead.

The women went to their men, the men went to the old pas, and the old pas went to Pa Ansumana and the chief. Pa Ansumana and the chief went to Kabba Lundo, the Paramount Chief, who carried a staff topped with a brass ornament bearing the British coat of arms and ruled his province from a wooden throne given to his father by the British in 1961.

The Paramount Chief and Pa Ansumana had both lived long lives. They knew that witches thrived in villages poisoned by suspicion, fear, and despair. It was meaningless to ask if the witches caused death and disaster or if death and disaster terrorized human hearts and allowed witches to exercise their powers over their victims. Somehow the cycle had to be broken before more plans were laid and more afflictions hatched. Once the hysteria engendered by several tragedies got its grip on the village, mothers all but gave up caring for their children. Why bother? Why care for a sick child? If the witches were eating it from the inside out, no medicine or nourishment would do any good. But Pa Ansumana and Kabba Lundo had seen witchcraft take hold every decade or so, and once a village fell under its thrall, nothing would free the people except the powers of a witchfinder.

•

Luba could see across the courtyard and straight into a *mawe* filled with children she would love to eat. The mother, Mama Amida, had witch nets and witch guns hanging everywhere inside the hut and kept the curtain drawn because she was afraid of Luba. Luba laughed and then giggled hysterically at the pathetic attempts of these solid citizens to protect themselves from powers so awesome their imaginations could not contain them.

She watched them huddle together in their *mawes*. "We are families," they said. "We have each other. This surely must be the highest good." Luba had no family. She lived alone; her neighbors considered this a state so depraved and unnatural that only a warped and evil creature could endure it without dying. "We are happy," said her neighbors. "We love each other. We live with our families. We don't live alone in the dark like . . ." They made her sick with their petty conceits, the paltry rewards of their labors, the miserable glee they took in the accomplishments of their children. They were all so smug in the bosoms of their families, blessed with children to love and parents to honor.

But being happy was not enough for them. They needed Luba to hate. They selected her because she lived alone and had no one to protect her. Those with no families, those who were old or infirm or lived alone, with no one to take their part—these were the hateable ones, those without others. They must be warped and strange indeed, for who would sit alone in a hut with no one? Only a deviant, only someone who must harbor an intense hatred against happy families.

They had all turned against her, shunned her, and had given her a shed on the side of her husband's house, and rags to wear. And after they had driven her into herself, after her many hours of solitude and fear, she had turned inward for the first time and discovered an entire world, a universe, of which she had known nothing. She found she could control her dreams, she could fly at night, she could change herself into shapes and go out into the bush. She discovered that at night, in the bush, *anything* was possible, *anything and everything.* There were no rules for her. She could eat infants as she pleased, she could sex their fathers, she could suffocate their mothers. The light of day was such a humdrum affair. Once night came, she closed her eyes and roamed free.

She drew designs on herself with a sharp stick. She never washed, so she could savor all of her wonderful odors. She discovered her smells one by one, rich bouquets that grew more pungent and varietal as each day passed, and she reveled in them. What is the difference between an odor and a fragrance, between a weed and a flower, between a diamond and any other rock? Only that others tell you one is valuable and the other worthless. But Luba had learned that they are all exactly the same; nothing was better than anything else, unless thinking made it so. She baked and sweated in her shed, and soon she discovered that her own smells were far more interesting to her than the company of others had ever been. What were people but engines in search of fuel, whether food to feed their bellies or the admiration of others to feed their self-absorbed cravings for belonging? What did she have to say to them except to laugh hysterically at their own pitiful vanities? Why did they hate her? Because she could see their thoughts; they knew their hearts were open to her.

If people in the village wanted nothing to do with her, then she would live with animals in the bush. When she laughed, bats swarmed out of her mouth and flew into the bush, where they took up her laughter, spreading it far and wide, until the night echoed with the cackles of Luba the witch. When she was angry, her wrath grew teeth and claws and leapt out of her in the shape of a powerful leopard who bounded through the bush on the limbs of trees, scanning the path below for humans to eat.

Luba sat in her shed with her head in her knees. She giggled deliriously into her kneecaps. She had heard about several infant deaths in the village of Jormu, and she searched her dreams, wondering if it was there her magic shell had taken her. She burped contentedly, and the bellyful of infant blood she had siphoned during her night travels made her sleepy. It was her turn to laugh. She, who wore rags and slept in a shed, now had the power to terrorize entire villages. She made them all pay for their sins against her. The most powerful chiefs and medicine men were helpless against her!

She closed her eyes and smiled, recalling the exhilaration of her night flights. She collected all the hatred and evil her neighbors had showered on her; she saved it in a big witch pot, and then she poured it back on their heads at night. She was a deep and dark reservoir of their malice and hatred, made in their image and likeness, and when they saw themselves reflected in that dark pool, it made them hate her even more! The infant deaths, the suffocations, the paralysis, the poisons she put in the wells at night, the crops she destroyed, the blood she drank, all this they had brought upon themselves. They had chosen her to punish them for their own evil deeds. She was their conscience! Did the poor childless mothers have something to say to her? Did Luba pity them as they clawed the dirt in their anguish over the loss of their infant sons and daughters? They killed their children as surely as if they had done it with a knife. Their fathers, brothers, sons, sisters, wives, and mothers had shunned her. They all but sent her flying into the skies at night. Let them blame themselves!

She felt the wings growing from the sides of her throat, opening like the gills of a fish that swims in the night. She soared into the moonlit bush and watched rodents scattering in terror beneath her. If she were wearing her human shape, she would laugh; instead she filled her lungs with the humid night air and screamed at them, paralyzing them with her *craw-aww-awwk!* Luba the witch done come, you pathetic little creatures. Which one shall I eat? Which one wants to die tonight?

The unborn children were her favorite dish, so tender and moist and unsullied by human hands. She could puncture them with her teeth and suck them like yolk from an egg. Sweet and succulent, the flesh and blood of innocence. And having tasted such delights, she could no longer live without wanting more and more, and the more she ate, the more powerful she became. The pitiful charms and amulets worn by the women were useless against her!

Sooner or later she would no doubt be killed by a witch gun, or caught and starved in a witch net. But what choice did she have? She could sit in her shed and rot to death, alone, or she could roam at night and enjoy power over the entire world, if only for a time.

She had revenge on her enemies and made men love her who would never have looked twice at her in the light of day. Men are the weakest creatures! If she touched them just so, they sexed her, no matter what the cost or penalty. They submitted to her, even though they suspected her of witchcraft and feared that she might capture their souls at the moment of orgasm. And after she sexed them, she ate their children for dinner.

She went out of her way to make herself as ugly as possible. She did not bathe. She covered herself in mud. And despite her filth, she could make men sex her. This was her proudest achievement. She touched them just so, or let them do things to her that a Mende wife would never allow, and the men succumbed. When it was over, she laughed at them, as they pulled up their pants and sheepishly sneaked back into the village. But on the path back to their families, the men had to listen to the bush ring with the taunts and laughter of Luba the witch: *"You did not want me enough to put a big gift in my funeral basket, but you sneak out here in the bush at night and sex me by the light of the moon! You spill your human seed on the land that feeds your family! Someday I will see you in the place of everlasting hunger, where we can gnaw on each other's knees!"*

(**14**)

A troop of monkeys in a stand of mango trees shrieked at Boone as he ascended the path back to Nymuhun, where he intended to collect his belongings and travel to Killigan's village. Dusk seeped into the rank hells of green on either side of the path, but aloft in the riggings of vines and plaited palms, he could see his biological ancestors crawling on all fours across the limbs and screaming down at him, throwing sticks and mangoes at him, probably warning each other that a white devil on hind legs was traversing their territory, maybe wondering if they all fell on him together, could they take him?

There but for the grace of some fortuitous prehistoric genetic mutation go I, thought Boone. If his ancestors had been born in the bush, instead of the village, he would be up there on all fours, baring his teeth and screaming at his rivals, anguishing over the more coveted females, and plotting his career as an alpha male. Instead of growing up in a mango tree, he had been to college, and he had his job as an insurance claims adjuster waiting for him back in Indianapolis, where he would end up walking on two legs in a nice little office, baring his teeth and screaming at his rivals, anguishing over the more coveted females, and plotting his career as an alpha male.

While climbing the path to the village, he reviewed his options. He had been to see the police in Bo, where he had learned that Section Chief Moiwo had thoughtfully taken Moussa Kamara's body back to the boy's family in Ndevehun. He could journey the next morning to Killigan's village, where, he had been given to understand by the Volunteers in Bo, he would be welcomed as Michael

Killigan's brother, and where he could perhaps seek an audience with the Paramount Chief, Kabba Lundo, who was Killigan's African father. Or he could wait in Sisay's village for Lewis, who had offered to pick him up in three days and companion him on the journey to find Moiwo and ask after Killigan. Boone was impatient to do his own investigating, but he had the barest understanding of Krio, and was able to pick out only the obvious English words, and then only when it was spoken slowly by a villager who had had some schooling.

When he arrived at his temporary home, the cooking fires were already smoking in the village *mawes* and courtyards. The harvest rice was laid out everywhere on mats, and there was singing and dancing, men and women shuffling in place in the Mende fashion and shaking seed-pod rattles and bangles. The children streamed in and out of the courtyards, thrilled at the prospect of another late night of games and songs, because the moon was out.

"Evening-O, Mistah Gutawa," the villagers shouted. "How de body?"

"I tell God tank ya," said Boone.

He turned down an invitation to join a game of *warri*, which was under way in the baffa of Sisay's courtyard.

"Mistah Aruna get febah," said one peekin, pointing at Sisay's compound.

Boone should have known something was up, because the boom box was playing African music—Johnny Clegg and Savouka—instead of Sisay's precious Grateful Dead.

"Kong, kong."

Boone found his host prostrate on the cot in his quarters, shirtless, and chewing on a wet rag. A sheen of sweat shone in the light of the hurricane lamp. A woman in a headwrap tended him, handing him oranges and daubing him with damp cloths.

"Febah done hold me," Sisay said weakly.

Boone, who had come prepared to rage at his host for providing him with misinformation and possibly withholding important knowledge about Poro and powerful medicines, was at a loss for words. Sisay's face was a pallid grimace splotched with fever rashes, and he squirmed, panting shallowly, and soaking the sheets of his cot with sweat.

"Oh sha," Boone finally managed, recalling the Krio expression of condolence and commiseration. "Can I get a . . . doctor for you. Is there one in Bo, or . . ."

Sisay turned his sweaty head and grinned. "Yeah," he said between pants, "I think I need a blood transfusion, and maybe a CAT scan." He laughed bitterly and shivered in a chill. "I take the chloroquine," he said. "Other than keeping your fluids up, that's all you can do."

He sucked an orange and curled up on his side. "Your time will come. It's the common cold of West Africa, but *poo-muis* seem to have a much harder time of it than Africans. Take a good look, this is mild compared to what a white man gets the first time."

"You told me Moussa Kamara was dead," Boone said.

"And he wasn't," Sisay said, his fevering eyes looking up into Boone's. "I'm sorry. Our esteemed chief, Bockarie Koroma, told me that he had received word from Section Chief Moiwo that Moussa Kamara had been found dead outside his village, hanging from a tree, as I told you. After you left, I learned this was not true. I heard about the tiefman business in Bo."

Sisay put the rag back into his mouth. He turned on his side and shook with the rigors of fever. The woman wrung the cooling cloths into a bucket and touched them to him.

"Tell me more about this Moiwo character," said Boone. "His wife brought me food as a gift from him. He lives here?"

"He's got farms, houses, and wives in several villages, and apartments in Bo and Freetown. He went to an American University and studied somewhere in England. Then he came back here and made a 'gift of himself,' as he puts it, to the people of Sierra Leone. That's why he came back out to the bush, so he could reestablish his tribal roots, even though he was the son of a minister and raised in Freetown. He needs tribal roots because he's taking the long view: President Moiwo. When he talks to the Temne, he's a Temne man, because his mother was a Temne woman and his father was nearly half Temne. When he talks to the Mende, he's a Mende man, because his father was a Mende man and his mother was nearly half Mende. First he'll make a run at being an elected Paramount Chief, then he'll shoot for a vice presidency, then . . . who knows? Maybe he'll make *Time* magazine.

"He knows your friend is missing. He's probably doing everything possible to find him, because it would only add to his popularity at election time."

"It was one of Moiwo's men that started the tiefman beating in Bo," said Boone, stopping short of telling his host about the note.

"Some of the people in the street said that Moussa Kamara was not a tiefman, and that Moiwo had falsely accused him of stealing, then stood by while the mob did its work."

Sisay groaned and shook his head into the pillow. "Election business," he said. "Why did the white man bring elections to West Africa? It was so much easier when the chief with the most strong war boys was the headman. Now we put on a skit for the West every five years called 'democracy,' which means we have six months of secret society intrigue, witchcraft, bad medicine, riots, and ritual murders, followed by something called an election. If Moiwo is mixed up in this, then it's politics, it's control of smuggling and the mines, it's development money, and it's bad medicine."

"I'm going to go talk to Moiwo," said Boone. "I went to the police in Bo and found out he had left to take Moussa Kamara's body back to Killigan's village."

"At least consult the looking-around man here," said Sisay, "where I can translate for you. I've also asked Pa Ansumana to come and talk with us. Sam-King Kebbie, the looking-around man I told you about from Kenema, is here. Maybe tomorrow we should consult with him, and then hang heads with Pa Ansumana."

"I also saw Lewis in Bo," Boone ventured. "He didn't think much of the idea of a looking-around man. He thought we should hire someone to threaten Killigan's village with thunder medicine."

Sisay shook his head. "Lewis is so white," he said ruefully. "Just another *poo-mui* gangster come to plunder the dark continent."

He sucked an orange and sipped water from a ladle the woman held to his lips.

"The people in Killigan's village love him like a son. His disappearance has already caused them untold anguish and shame. They've combed the bush and the surrounding villages. Thunder medicine would only draw even more attention to their failure to find their favorite white stranger."

"But Lewis keeps talking about illegal medicines, pouches or bundles of stuff we could use to terrorize Killigan's enemies, if he has any, and maybe force them to turn him over."

Sisay shook his head again. "Well," he said weakly, "the first problem you will have using illegal medicine is that it is *illegal*. The jails here are a lot like hell, only the humidity is worse."

"He told me about a medicine called *bofima* that is fed with human fat . . ."

Sisay pointed a finger at Boone. "*Bofima* is *the* most illegal medicine in the country. You can swing from the gallows in Freetown for even talking about it. It is illegal, antisocial, and evil. To make the medicine, men dressed as leopards or baboons capture victims and silence them by breaking their jaws with metal claws. Then the victim's body parts are used to prepare or replenish the medicine. New members, or hapless travelers who stumble upon the meetings in the bush, are forced to join in the ritual cannibalism, then they are required to provide the next victim, usually a member of the initiate's own family. As I said, I would not even use the word, unless you're looking to get arrested and deported or executed."

"His suggestion was that you perhaps had used illegal medicine, and that you might know something more about it than you were saying."

"If I were ever going to use illegal medicine, I think my first victim would be Sam Lewis," he said weakly, closing his eyes in disgust.

"He also said you were high up in this Poro Society," Boone said, and paused.

"Well, then I'm sure he also told you that once a man is initiated into Poro, he is forbidden to speak about Poro matters to those who aren't members."

"He did," said Boone.

Sisay irritably cast an orange aside.

"Don't forget that you are a 'strangah,' " he said, emphasizing the Krio pronunciation. "It translates not so much as stranger but as 'guest.' A guest living temporarily with men who are almost all members of the men's society and women who are almost all members of the women's society. Both sworn to secrecy about their respective activities. Death or miscarriage will befall any woman who dares peek in the Poro bush. Elephantiasis and hernias the size of watermelons are what happens to the Mende man who dares peek into the Sande bush to observe the women's initiation rituals or Sande business. I'm not sure I know what would happen to a white man who went snooping into the Poro bush, but I can ask around."

"And are you forbidden to speak about Poro matters?"

"Of course," said Sisay.

"Because you are a member," said Boone.

"I am," said Sisay, without hesitation. "So is your African grandfather and most of the adult males in the village. But you are *not* a Poro member, and this fact is never far from your neighbors' thoughts."

"I respect their secrets," said Boone, "and I am grateful for their hospitality, but if Poro business has anything to do with Michael Killigan's disappearance, then I don't have much choice but to ask about it, do I?"

Sisay allowed a long silence to intrude, while Boone waited, not caring if his host ordered him to leave the village or berated him for his investigatory methods.

"As long as we're on the subject of manners," he said at last. "There's another question of etiquette that needs discussing. You've been a guest in this village now for almost ten days. The people have welcomed you into their community, but they aren't sure if you are happy or comfortable here."

Boone studied his host's sweaty face in the firelight.

"My best friend is missing," said Boone. "I'm in a foreign country where I don't speak the language. The climate is fetid. I have sores, dysentery, no leads so far. Yes, I'm uncomfortable."

"That's true," said Sisay, "your best friend is missing. I have a fever, and I left my American family long ago. I may never see them again. God gives every person his burdens to carry. But that doesn't mean that we turn away from the rest of the village, just because we are asked to bear a serious misfortune."

"Now, I'm not bearing my misfortunes correctly," Boone said, "is that it?"

"I'm saying there was much discussion of village business while you were in Bo. The elders, including your African grandfather, hung heads in the court *barri* for many hours, discussing the death of Pa Gigba and the deaths of children in the village, the election turmoil, your search for your American brother, and you were . . . discussed. Your name was mentioned several times, and I tell you this, not to impugn you or your ways in the least, but just to tell you that your behavior affects the village. Some even suggested that you had brought misfortune with you, though this was disputed by others, most notably your grandfather."

"What are you saying?" Boone asked. The guy seemed to be insinuating something and reassuring him at the same time.

"The Mende are very sensitive to a person's *social* personality. Let me regress to anthropology for an explanation. Where you come from, individual personalities happen to have relationships with others. Here, in Mendeland, and in most African villages, your relationship with others *is* your personality. People are never alone. People who enjoy spending time alone are suspect, because they seem to be developing some kind of marginal, extrasocial personality."

"What does all this have to do with me?" asked Boone.

"Your neighbors sense that you are the kind of person who enjoys spending time alone," said Sisay. "And they take it personally."

"Alone?" said Boone. He was suddenly angry. After he had gone out of his way to accommodate their insatiable curiosity about the contents of his backpack, their nagging questions about how things worked in the land of *Poo*, their insistent desire to see just how he did everything, from taking a crap to reading a book, from sneezing to picking wax out of his ears, now he was being criticized for spending too much time alone. He had patiently allowed them almost constant access to his company, allowed their children to squeal *poo-mui* at him the livelong day, let them touch the yellow hair on his arms, let them touch his boots, and marvel over his fingernail clippers. Now this? He was being accused of selfishness and ingratitude. He should spend *more* time with them. He should behave like his host, who rose at dawn, began talking Mende, continued talking Mende as the sun journeyed across the sky, paused just enough to gorge himself at dinner, and then resumed yacketing until the wee hours.

"You can't get two seconds alone in this hothouse of humanity," Boone protested. "The veranda is crammed with villagers all day, and if I go to my room at night, the *National Geographic* crew comes in to talk. Don't get me wrong, I *like* these people. But I'm a private person."

"That's the problem," said Sisay levelly. "Private people in Africa are . . . unusual. Most houses and huts have one large room, which sleeps ten or more. So the only way to spend time alone is to spend time in the bush. Hunters, travelers, farmers with farms deep in the bush, all of them spend time alone in the bush. They are marginal people. The villagers may admire them, but they also suspect them, because they move too easily and comfortably about in the bush, and because they enjoy being alone, something no villager understands."

"They think I'm antisocial?"

"All Americans are antisocial compared to Africans," said Sisay. He waved him away irritably. "You're making a bigger deal of it than I intended. It's just something you should be aware of. It was mentioned. I reported the mention. End of story."

End of stay, thought Boone.

"Tomorrow we will consult the looking-around man. Then we will ask our father about these things."

"I have to warn you," said Boone, "I don't believe in fortune telling."

"It's not fortune telling," said Sisay. "Think of it as protection. It's like insurance. Didn't you say your family was in the insurance business? Insurance is looking around out in the future for the most likely risks. Your insurance man identifies the most likely risks, then protects you from them. In exchange for his protection, you pay money. It's exactly the same here. Insurance men get their power at college; over here, the looking-around men receive their powers in their dreams, usually after being visited by one of their ancestors.

"You should do a good job of hiding one of your personal belongings, so you can test the looking-around man by making him find it for you."

"I have a better idea," said Boone. "I'll tell him I hid my buddy in the bush and please go find him."

Sisay shuddered and chewed into his rag.

"Are you sure there's nothing I can do?" Boone asked.

"Mix me up some rehydration salts," he said weakly. "Then I'll try to sleep. If I start hollering and seeing things during the night, come in and tie me down. I don't know if it's the chloroquine or the fevers or both, but white men with malaria can get the screaming meemies. Voices, shapes, delusions . . . One time I watched *Butch Cassidy and the Sundance Kid* from start to finish. No VCR, no movie, nothing. Just a high fever and a loading dose of chloroquine. The Volunteers claim it's the chloroquine. You take only one tablet a week as a prophylactic, and, as you may have noticed, even that lends a certain vividness to your dreams. If you wake up at night, it takes longer to decide whether you are awake or dreaming. Once you actually come down with malaria, you take two tablets for a loading dose and one every twelve hours after that. If the fevers don't make you see things, the loading dose of chloroquine will."

"If I hear you howling," said Boone, "I'll come in and bark at you."

He mixed the salts for Sisay and returned to his room, only to feel the familiar tug in his small intestine.

·

While he waited for sleep, night fell, and the moon rose like a glowing orange in the palms, casting huge shadows in the courtyards. Boone wearily clambered out of bed and into his plastic thongs to revisit his hut with the hole in the ground. It was a homecoming of sorts, noting that his old friend the spider had been productive in his absence; there were several captured cockroaches bound and wriggling like bandaged mummies, kept alive so they would be fresh at mealtime. He lit the hurricane lamp and hid his Swiss Army knife in a chink above the spider's web, then plugged the hole with a clod of dirt.

The dark hole in the wooden platform again seemed to emanate some infrasound from the underworld. Maybe the shock of Third World travel had endowed him with a certain clairaudient perception of spirits. When he lifted the lid and shined his flashlight into the hole, he half expected to find a scene from a Hieronymus Bosch painting.

It occurred to Boone that, unlike American toilet bowls, which are protected by pure and diaphanous beings, the outhouses and latrines of the Third World are probably inhabited by creatures with darker intentions—slithering around somewhere down there, clapping their warty hands with glee whenever a traveler from the First World staggers in to drop another payload of gastric acids. If he dared peer again into the black hole, he could probably see them, gnarled, ratlike apparitions, about the size and shape of a mongoose or a subterranean gargoyle, rooting around in the dark pit, feeding like duck-billed platypuses, sifting microorganisms with the membranes in their snouts. Little turd urchins, he suddenly thought. If they existed, they would probably wear fetid leather jerkins and britches, stained by fecal spume that splashed up under the latrine boards. They would have bulging brown eyes, weepy with thick mucus to protect their eyes during their burrowings, and they could curse in a dozen Third World languages. They would come and go between the visible and the invisible world as easily as Boone covered himself with a sheet. They would manage to stay one step outside the periphery of human sight, even though they were a tad clubfooted and not nearly as agile as the fairies and pixies of European folklore. At times, they popped up out of their shit swamps and went to work with wood-burning tools on afflicted assholes of travelers, snickering as they etched hexagrams, pentagrams, and other magic or satanic figures on swollen rosebuds.

Maybe the turd urchins would not fancy American bathrooms, because their food supply would be repeatedly wiped out by antiseptic blue fluids and abrasive cleansers. Maybe the turd urchins of America would evolve into little well-dressed maids and butlers in starched white morning dress, with whisk brooms, basin-tub-and-tile cleaners, and puffed silk wipe-ettes for daubing the pampered assholes of the First World, five or six times, until the sixth wipe-ette comes back snowy white. And the delicate, wholesome First World asshole would be given a light mist of perfume from an atomizer.

"That should do it, master," the conscientious First World maid would say. "You're ready for another day of eating as much as you want."

Boone settled wearily onto his heels and dropped another cataract of shit water aft. *God is very big*, he prayed. *Bigger*, he thought, than the wicked little mole creatures hissing from the shadows below; bigger than the carnivorous flies circling and waiting to lay their eggs under his skin.

He picked up a stray section from what once was a hardback book and discovered he held the preface to something called *Human Leopards: An Account of the Trials of Human Leopards Before the Special Commission Court*. Somebody—Sisay?—had made a slash in the margin, next to a passage describing the bush:

I have been in many forests, but in none which seemed to me to be so uncanny as the Sierra Leone bush. In Mende-land the bush is not high, as a rule it is little more than scrub, nor is the vegetation exceptionally rank, but there is something about the Sierra Leone bush, and about the bush villages as well, which makes one's flesh creep. It may be the low hills with enclosed swampy valleys, or the associations of the slave trade, or the knowledge that the country is alive with Human Leopards; but to my mind the chief factor in the uncanniness is the presence of numerous half-human chimpanzees with their maniacal shrieks and cries.

The bush seemed to me pervaded with something supernatural, a spirit which was striving to bridge the animal and the human. Some of the weird spirit of their surroundings has, I think, entered into the people, and accounts for their weird customs. The people are by no means a low, savage race. I found many of them highly intelligent, shrewd, with more than the average sense of humour, and with the most marvelous faculty for keeping hidden what they did not wish to be known—the result probably of secret societies for countless generations. But beyond such reasoning powers as are required for their daily necessities their whole mental energies are absorbed in fetish, witchcraft, "medicine" such as the Bofima and the like. What they need is a substitute for their bottomless wells of secret societies, for their playing at being leopards or alligators and acting the part with such realism that they not only kill their quarry but even devour it. In my opinion the only way to extirpate these objectionable societies is the introduction of the four R's—the fourth, Religion, being specially needed to supply the place of the native crude beliefs. No doubt the energetic action of the Government, and in a lesser degree the labours of the Special Commission Court, will have a good effect; but, I fear, only a temporary effect. The remedy must go deeper than mere punishment: the Human Leopard Society must be superseded by Education and Religion.

W. Brandford Griffith

2 Essex Court, Temple, September 1915

In the midst of his fanciful reading, he heard a sudden rustle of leaves, then a whisper, coming from somewhere behind him and outside the latrine. Again the whisper, and a horripilating chill swept through him.

"Will you feed the medicine?" a voice hissed at his back.

He whirled on the balls of his feet and almost dropped a leg into the hole. He searched behind him, the lamp's flame bobbing and making the mud walls dance with shadows. He peered at several chinks and thought he saw black skin move behind a crevice. A cheek? A woman's forearm?

"Will you feed the medicine?" the whisper asked, the sex of the speaker masked in sibilance.

Boone hitched up his drawers, grabbed the lamp, and went outside, realizing at once that he would have been better off with only the light of the nitid moon, for the lantern bathed the ambits of the latrine in a nearsighted glare and turned the bush into an army of warring shadows. From the village at his back, he heard the songs of dancing children, and more African music on the boom box.

He dialed down the wick and waited for his pupils to swell in the moonlight. Ahead of him, at a distance impossible to estimate, two orange pinpricks of light, as fixed as the bush itself, stared eyelike in the night, like distant bifocals reflecting the light of a fire.

"Scat," he said, instinctively hissing at the thing, thinking that if it was the eyeshine of a bush cat, he could startle it into movement.

"Scat," he said again, and hissed.

He took one step forward and promptly realized that to reach the lights, he would have to leave the path and make his way through overgrown bush.

Then it whispered, and he froze again.

"Will you feed the medicine?" it hissed.

"Who are you?" Boone whispered hoarsely.

"Will you feed the medicine?"

"Yes," said Boone, trying to raise a different response from whatever was hissing at him.

"If you keep me secret, I will teach you how to feed the medicine."

"Tell me your name," Boone said, scanning the bush shadows for a shape he could seize with his eyes.

This time the thing adopted Boone's intonation and hissed, "Scat." The orange eyes moved soundlessly away from him, appearing to recede into the bush without rustling the surrounding vegetation.

Boone returned to the latrine for his flashlight and tore out the marked page he had read. He took it back to Sisay, and found him still burning up, his sweat glistening in the light of a hurricane lamp.

"Is that your mark next to this description of the Sierra Leone bush?"

Sisay studied the page and smiled, then chuckled sentimentally. "It is. I read that passage before I came here, when I was still a graduate student. At the time, I thought it was a good description of the Sierra Leone bush, but I didn't mark it then. After I had lived here a few years, I found it again, and I marked it, because I thought it was a good example of a white man setting out to describe West Africa and winding up describing his own unconscious instead."

•

Boone rose at dawn to the tune of "Allah akbar" and found mold in his boots. The shirt he had hung up to dry the night before had simply absorbed more humidity. His tropical sores ached, his hair was sticky with sweat, and he realized for the tenth time that he was living in a climate where nothing ever dried: wounds, damp clothes, hair, navels, armpits, and underwear (if one was silly enough to wear it).

He found Sisay propped in bed and skipping morning prayers.

"I'm much better this morning," said Sisay, lifting himself onto one elbow. "But that doesn't mean anything. The fevers come in cycles, depending on which strain of malaria has been injected by the mosquito, and sometimes you're lucky enough to have more than one strain."

"Oh sha," said Boone.

As if to illustrate his anthropology lecture of the night before, Sisay hailed a corps of well-wishers, who were assembled on the veranda, and asked them into his rooms to cheer him up during the respite of his fever.

Boone grinned as conspicuously as possible and resisted the urge to go to his room.

After breakfast and the best wishes of half the village—including Pa Usman, who appeared with his *nomoloi* and served it a cola—the looking-around man arrived with his assistant and the paraphernalia needed for the ritual. Sam-King Kebbie and his assistant introduced themselves and engaged in the usual verbal waltz of greetings and inquiries after one another's wives, families, farms, and livestock, tales of recent journeys undertaken, the state of the economy, the upcoming elections—during which time Boone stared vacantly at the paraphernalia the looking-around man had brought with him: a bundle of sticks, a mat, a bag of pebbles, and kindling and herbs for building a small fire.

The assistant wore the usual leggings, sandals, and cotton shirt, topped off with a clay pipe and a skullcap. Sam-King Kebbie sported a shirt of country cloth studded with Koranic amulets and inked with symbols. Whenever he caught Boone looking at him, Sam-King promptly stared off into space, his eyes glazing in the throes of some psychic revelation.

After introductions, the looking-around man, who spoke only Mende, asked Sisay what Boone had hidden for him to find, and Boone described the Swiss Army knife. Then Boone was interviewed about the purpose of his visit to Sierra Leone and his stay in the village, which he reported was a happy one, except for runny belly, tropical sores, and the lack of cold beer. He was asked about steps he had taken to find his brother and about his journey to Bo.

Then Sam-King and his assistant rose, thanked the white men, and said they would return shortly with the Swiss Army knife.

After they had gone, Boone asked his big brother, "Do these guys go to school and get a degree in the looking-around sciences, or what?"

"Usually a looking-around man receives his powers in a dream, but he may also serve an apprenticeship to another looking-around man. Sam-King's grandfather was a very powerful looking-around man and later became one of the famed Tongo Players, who once traveled the country exposing and exterminating cannibals. His grandfather was able to detect them by having suspects in every village pick up a stone and hold it. Then he took the stones to a cotton tree and prayed over them until he was able to tell which of the stones had been handled by a cannibal.

"When Sam-King Kebbie was still a boy, and after his grandfather had died, a female genie came to him in a dream and began bargaining with him. His grandfather had taught him all about genies, so Sam-King knew he was involved in perilous negotiations. Either one acts boldly and assumes control over the genie or the genie takes control and makes a slave of the person, demanding exorbitant sacrifices, sexual favors, and constant attention. Sam-King bested the genie and was shown seven ranks of river pebbles spread on a mat. The genie also showed him the leaves of a plant and told him that the leaves and the pebbles were gifts from his grandfather, the Tongo Player.

"Next day, Sam-King picked pebbles from the river and scattered them in seven ranks on the mat. Then he went into the bush and obtained the leaves of the plant the genie had shown him in the dream. Sam-King washed his eyes in a lotion made from the leaves, and ever since he has been able to read the stones. People consult him when they are anxious or confused, sick, or about to undertake a journey or a project of importance. Sam-King then reads the stones and recommends a sacrifice, which will either protect his client from evil or help a favorable prediction come true."

"For a fee," Boone inserted, and made a face.

"Valuable services are seldom provided free of charge," said Sisay, "especially where you come from."

"And I'll bet he's never wrong about his predictions," said Boone sarcastically.

"Errors of cure and prognosis occur in every profession," said Sisay. "What if a devil or a witch or an angry ancestor interferes with the divination process for its own purposes, maybe to mislead the client with a false message? What if a swear or a curse from another source affects the diviner's prediction without his knowledge? What if the prescribed sacrifice fails to ward off evil because those participating in the offering are guilty of adultery or of other failings in their duties to their ancestors?"

"How convenient," said Boone acidly. "So it's never the looking-around man who's at fault, there's always another explanation."

"There's no malpractice insurance in these parts," Sisay said with a smile.

"Will he be able to tell me who is responsible for Michael Killigan's disappearance and whether bad medicine is the cause of it?"

"Possibly," said Sisay. "Names are almost never used. The looking-around man typically describes individuals whom one eventually recognizes, or who later reveal themselves."

"And if it's bad medicine, as your bosom buddy Lewis suspects, will he give me a counter-swear, or some kind of remedy, or what?"

"It would depend on what kind of illegal medicine is involved," said Sisay. "If it's witchcraft, Sam-King would send you to the *kondobla*, the antidote people. If it's bad medicine rather than witchcraft, he may very discreetly send you to a *hale nyamubla*, a bad medicine man or juju man. But, as I said, this would be illegal medicine. If it's simply ancestral displeasure, he would handle it himself by prescribing a suitable sacrifice. Think of Sam-King as a general practitioner, or a family physician, who would refer you to various specialists if your problem warranted such attentions."

Think of Sam-King as a mountebank or a palm reader, thought Boone. *Money inspires him with visions into the future.*

"Kong, kong," said a voice at the door, and the looking-around man's assistant entered alone, without speaking to Boone or Sisay.

"Where's my pocketknife?" said Boone.

Sisay put his finger to his lips and frowned.

The assistant built a small fire and spread a woven mat on the floor. On the mat, he placed the bundle of sticks and the bag of pebbles.

Sisay deferentially whispered a question in Mende, and the assistant gave a curt nod.

Sam-King appeared at the door and seated himself at the stick fire, placing herbs on the coals, closing his eyes and inhaling the smoke slowly and deeply. After a few minutes, one of his feet began twitching. Soon after, a hand did the same, and the tremblings spread to his limbs, torso, and head, mild at first, but gaining in intensity, until Sam-King's entire body was in convulsions, which appeared to be involuntary. The assistant solicitously prevented Sam-King from hurting himself on the furniture or extending his feet into the fire.

The convulsions gradually subsided, and the looking-around man opened his eyes in a blank stare. He reached down and picked up the short bundle of sticks and stared into it, squinting one eye, as if peering into a telescope of sticks. Then he set the bundle aside, burned more herbs, breathed more smoke, went into even more violent convulsions, and peered again into the stick bundle, this time with the astonished expression of an astronomer discovering a new planet.

He lowered the stick bundle and cried, "*Koli-bla!*"

Sisay stared aghast at Sam-King, then slowly moved his eyes to Boone.

"What'd he say?"

Sisay glanced again at the looking-around man, who was staring off in an amazed altered state.

"Baboon People," he said.

Sam-King chanted and turned toward the mat and the bag of stones. He selected seven pebbles and held them out toward Boone in his cupped hand and said something in Mende.

"Hold the pebbles in your right hand," said Sisay, "and think about what you want to know."

Boone did as instructed and returned the pebbles.

Sam-King placed the pebbles in ranks on the mat, murmuring and chanting as he worked. Boone looked at Sisay for translation, but he only shook his head.

Sam-King studied the stones for at least a quarter of an hour, occasionally speaking to them, singing or chanting. Then he closed his eyes, and again the convulsions set in. After they subsided, he opened his eyes and stared at the wall in a trance and began speaking in a monotone with an unblinking, expressionless face.

"Your brother is in the bush," said Sisay, "hiding from bad men. Your brother used very bad medicine against his enemies, and now the men who keep the medicine say it needs to be fed. Your brother must feed the medicine, or they will turn it against him."

Sam-King stopped talking and stared again, off in another transported vision.

"What does that mean?" Boone shouted in exasperation. "What kind of medicine? How's he supposed to feed it? Where *is* he? And how can I *find* him? That's what I'm paying twenty bucks for. Make sure he understands that!"

Sam-King collected all the stones and placed them in his hands, chanting again and gently tapping the back of his hands against the floor, like a dice thrower tapping the table for good luck. Again the stones were placed and studied. Again the convulsions, and the subsequent trance, monologue, and translation.

"A big man is going to ask you to offer a sacrifice. One of this big man's wives will take you to a holy place where the sacrifice will be offered. You must go with her to the holy place. If the sacrifice is offered according to instructions, your brother will return safely."

At the conclusion of this pronouncement, Sam-King curled up on the floor and appeared to sleep, except that he whispered and hummed, and occasionally gestured or sighed without opening his eyes. After a few minutes, he rose slowly, as if awakening from a deep sleep, uncertain of his whereabouts and of how he had arrived in Sisay's house.

"Ask him where I can find my brother now!" Boone said.

"It's not like that," said Sisay. "Once he's out of the trance, he has no memory of what was said, or what the stones said."

"Really!" yelled Boone. "I have no memory of my twenty bucks either! It's gone!"

Sam-King rubbed his eyes and looked genuinely confused, until his assistant apparently gave him a report of what had transpired. After more conversation, the two men rose to leave.

"Hey," called Boone. "What about my pocketknife?"

Sam-King paused on the threshold and smiled back at Boone. He patted the pocket of his pants, then pointed at Boone's pants and left.

Boone felt a smooth lump in his pocket. He refused to believe his fingers and brought the Swiss Army knife out where his eyes could do the job. He looked askance at Sisay and received only a wry smile.

Somehow these two con artists had found his knife and slipped it back into his pocket during the ceremony. Then left with his money.

"Where did you hide it?" asked Sisay.

"In the latrine," said Boone. "Above the spider's nest. I put it in a hole and plugged it with a dirt clod."

"Kong, kong," called Pa Ansumana, poking his head in the door and bestowing greetings on his sons with the gusto of a fraternity brother.

Sisay promptly described the session with the looking-around man, provoking the old man first to laughter, then to grave concern, then to laughter again when the narrative apparently concluded with the pocketknife.

Pa Ansumana chuckled loudly, rocked back onto his heels, and then erupted in outright laughter.

"What's so funny?" asked Boone.

Sisay covered his mouth, then explained. "He says a white man hiding something in the latrine is like a woman hiding something in her kitchen, or a peekin hiding something under its pillow. Where else do white men spend their time in Africa except in latrines? Next time you test a looking-around man, he says you should pick a better hiding place than the latrine you've been sitting in for ten days."

He seemed not the least troubled by the tragic death of Gigba, the disappearance of Killigan, Sisay's illness, the rumors of witchcraft in the village, or the unrest attending the elections. He placed a hand on Sisay's brow and pretended to burn himself, blowing on his fingers and shaking them, while merrily winking at Boone. Finally he flexed his arm and made a fist, the same "Be strong" signal he had made for Boone.

He settled on the floor and tended his pipe, remarking, according to Sisay, on the frail constitutions of white people and their almost continuous infirmities.

"I will explain all of this business to him," said Sisay. "The false news of Moussa Kamara's death, the beating in Bo, the report Pa Gigba gave us before he changed himself into a leopard and was killed in the bush, Sam-King's looking around."

Sisay spoke Mende, pausing now and again for deep feeble breaths, careful not to show his father pain or weakness. Pa Ansumana listened quietly, deliberatively sucking on the pipe Boone had given him as a gift on his naming day; occasionally his father interrupted Sisay with a brief question or a chuckle.

"He says Pa Gigba was not a sorcerer," said Sisay. "The leopard ear the hunter showed him was at least two days old. Pa Gigba was killed while traveling in the bush in his human shape."

"I've been hearing about all kinds of weird shit for the past two weeks," said Boone. "But nobody is going to convince me that a man can change himself into an animal."

As soon as the translation cleared Sisay's lips, Pa Ansumana gave a merry "so what?" shrug, and waited patiently for something more entertaining to talk about.

"I came here to find my brother," said Boone, "who is lost in the bush and may be in serious danger."

Sisay cleared his throat and translated. Boone twiddled his thumbs. Pa Ansumana tamped his pipe, using a shiny new *poo-mui* pipe nail, which also had been given to him by his new son, and which he used like a new broom.

"He says you will find your brother if God wants him to be found. In the meantime, he thinks you should learn to talk about something else. You talk only about your own misfortunes. And you never ask about the misfortunes of others."

"Ask him to tell me what he knows about Moiwo," said Boone. "Please," he added in the interest of being mannerly.

"He says Moiwo is a powerful man with a lot of land, many wives, and the ability to read *poo-mui* books. He has seen men like Moiwo only once or twice in his life, so powerful they are almost sorcerers, or forces from God. But he says Moiwo is a force that is trying to decide whether it should be good or bad. Like many powerful men, Moiwo asks himself whether it would be really wrong to do something bad on the way to doing something good. I have a son who is sometimes like that," which caused Sisay to blush afterward, almost as if he had translated it without understanding.

"Ask him if he thinks Moiwo had anything to do with Michael Killigan's disappearance."

"He says the Americans and the other *poo-mui* countries are giving Moiwo money because he gives them access to the diamonds and the minerals. So Moiwo has more money and men than the current Paramount Chief, Kabba Lundo, who sits on a wooden throne given to him by the British to commemorate Sierra Leone's independence. Kabba Lundo carries an elephant-tail fan, given to him by a Koranko chief, and he carries a staff topped with brass given to his ancestors by the British, and wears a tunic made of woven country cloth, which has been boiled in medicines, stamped with motifs that have secret meanings, and then adorned with Koranic amulets, called *sebeh*—all of which protect the chief from evil forces. He can barely move he is wrapped in so much power. Pa has seen bullets bounce off the garment."

Pa Ansumana paused and stuffed more tobacco in on top of the ashes in his pipe.

"But Kabba Lundo is getting old," Sisay said, resuming when Pa did. "Some say he is getting weak. Some say he is backing the wrong men in Freetown. Now Moiwo wants to be a Paramount Chief, and maybe it is his time, but sometimes old men do not give up power easily. They sometimes hold themselves in office by trickery instead of force, for old men can be extremely clever. Because they have lived longer, they know more tricks," he said, tamping his pipe and smiling smugly.

"Your brother was a particular favorite of Kabba Lundo, who was forever trying to get him to forget the American secret societies and join up with him as a Mende man. If your brother was openly supporting Kabba Lundo in the elections, that could make Moiwo angry. But not angry enough to humbug a *poo-mui*, that would take something much more serious. But just yesterday I have heard that when the *poo-muis* learned of your brother's disappearance, they contacted Section Chief Moiwo for assistance, not Kabba Lundo, who knew nothing of the disappearance until only recently. This was an insult to the Paramount Chief, and a tribute from the *poo-muis* to Moiwo, who lets them take the stones and metals from the mines without paying taxes on them. Kabba Lundo makes them pay the taxes.

"He went to see Kabba Lundo himself a short time ago, because of all the infant deaths in the village and all the talk of witchcraft. He and Kabba Lundo have their own plans for finding your brother and finding out if Moiwo had anything to do with your brother disappearing. You will see how two old men can outsmart a more powerful young one."

Pa giggled and appeared to be turning his and Kabba Lundo's plan over in his mind, savoring its ingenuity.

"Maybe Moiwo has been to see the Baboon Men," Sisay translated. "He can't say, but he would not be surprised. Who knows why people change themselves into animals and put their faith in bad medicines? Moiwo is probably changing himself into a baboon right now . . . a fat one, he suspects."

"Ask him if he *personally* has ever witnessed a person change into an animal, or an animal change into a human," asked Boone derisively.

When Sisay translated this question, Pa Ansumana snorted and spouted ash from his pipe, which swung dangerously off-beam, until his ragged molars reasserted themselves. He spoke in Mende, with the expression of a Brooklyn subway attendant telling somebody from Nebraska where to deposit the token.

"Sorcerers only change into animals when they are alone," translated Sisay, "so it is impossible for someone to see them change. Even if someone saw a person changing into an elephant or a baboon, they would never speak about it, or even admit it, because the witch or the shape-shifter would instantly kill the witness before the secret could be revealed."

"How convenient," said Boone.

Pa Ansumana interrupted Sisay before the latter could finish the answer, and the two of them spoke in Mende, Sisay gesturing periodically at Boone, while apparently explaining his skepticism.

"He says you don't believe people can change into animals because you come from the land of *Poo*. He has been told that in *poo-mui* land, the villages are no longer surrounded by bush, so the people there have no need of changing into animals. The *poo-mui* villages grew so big that they swallowed up all the bush, so in the land of *Poo* it is the animals who must learn shape-shifting, so they can assume human form and live in villages that cover the entire country."

Pa Ansumana tugged on the pipe Boone had given him and chuckled mischievously, then continued.

"He says white men have magic boxes with windows that contain stories, and if they see a story in the box, then they believe it, but if someone tells them what they saw with their own eyes, they don't believe it.

"He says I should ask you if you believe that *poo-muis* really walked around up on the moon, and if so, did you actually see them do it? Personally, he does not believe that *poo-muis* walked on the moon. He believes it was just a story *poo-muis* saw in the window of their magic box. When all the people in Sierra Leone were talking about how *poo-muis* were supposedly up walking on the moon, there was an outbreak of eye infections." Sisay stopped. "What you would call 'pinkeye.' And to this day, the people in Sierra Leone call pinkeye, or conjunctivitis, 'Apollo,' because they believe that when the *poo-muis* were up walking around on the moon, they shook so much moon dust loose that it irritated the eyes of people all over Sierra Leone. He himself does not believe this, because he has lived long enough to know that there was an even worse outbreak of pinkeye long ago, before people were claiming that *poo-muis* could walk on the moon."

"Tell him it's made of cheese," interrupted Boone. "And if he turns himself into a cow, he can grab a bite on the way over."

Sisay glowered at Boone and nodded for Pa to continue.

"All over Sierra Leone, hunters quickly cut the ears off the animals they kill for just this reason. If they kill a witch or a sorcerer traveling in the shape of an animal, the animal will change back into its human form, and they will be accused of murder. Do you think every hunter in Sierra Leone would cut the ears off their prey if they did not know as sure as we are sitting here that they may have killed a human in the shape of an animal?"

"That's like saying Sun Myung Moon must be God because there are so many Moonies," snapped Boone.

"When he was a young man," Sisay continued, "his first big wife was suspected of witchcraft because she had dreamed about a woman and caused the death of the woman's son. One morning when he went out to his farm, he found the big wife had been caught and killed in one of the traps they had made together on the farm. Do you think that if she was wearing her human shape she would be stupid enough to walk into a bush pig trap that she herself had helped build? No, she had obviously been traveling on the farm in the shape of a bush pig and had been caught and killed, which of course had changed her back to her human shape."

Boone took his weary head in his hands and shook it, groaning, "Ask him—please!—does he have *any* idea what happened to my brother?" said Boone.

Pa Ansumana made a comment, then laughed through his clenched teeth.

"What?" said Boone.

"He said maybe another white man has gone and killed himself."

Boone looked at his grandfather's face, which was a map of laugh lines, his eyes a-twinkle with amusement. "Real funny, I guess," said Boone.

"It's an inside joke," said Sisay. "Don't be offended. As far as I can tell, the Mende don't believe in suicide."

"You mean, they discourage people from killing themselves?" said Boone. "What a sound social policy."

"No," said Sisay, "I don't think they believe that anyone has ever committed suicide. I can't explain it to them. After I'd been here a year or so, a Peace Corps Volunteer up north in Koranko country killed himself, and the whole northern province went into shock. Word spread and soon the entire country was talking about it. The Mende men in the village came to me laughing uproariously, expecting me to tell them that this was an elaborate *poo-mui* prank. What would these *poo-muis* think of next? Not even a *poo-mui* would be crazy enough to kill *himself*. I tried to tell them that it was more a question of despair or depression, not simple craziness. They laughed uproariously.

"I tried again, and they laughed even harder. To them I was just carrying on with an outlandish farce. Why would a man kill *himself*, they wanted to know, and not his enemy, mind you, who probably had caused his despair by fraud or witchcraft? This was too rich for them. They could never swallow it. They forced themselves to admire the ingenuity of the story, but it was time to come clean.

"I was up half the night in a roundtable discussion in the *barri*. No African man would think of killing himself, they said, and certainly no *poo-mui* who came from a country where there was food everywhere and everyone was attractively plump, well fed, and protected by powerful medicines. I said that in the land of *Poo* quite a few *poo-muis* considered killing themselves from time to time, and some of them actually did it; that this was something that everyone in America had heard of or had seen. I told them that I personally had a friend who had lost his child and had become so sad that he had tried to kill himself, but someone had stopped him, just in time.

"The Mende men all looked at themselves and held their breath, as if to say, 'Shall we let this king trickster get away with this monkey business or shall we call him on it?' They laughed again and refused to hear any more.

"So now, whenever we reach a point in our conversations where there seems to be no conceivable explanation for what has happened, the people in this village throw up their hands and say, 'Well, maybe another *poo-mui* has gone and killed himself.' It's a standing joke. The way you or I would say, 'Once in a blue moon . . .' "

(**15**)

"**B**at shit," said Mack over the speakerphone. "Let me see, I think the technical term is 'guano.' So says the lab analysis report, which they just faxed to us. And the black strips holding the whole mess together are strips of cured boa constrictor skins. The red spout is some kind of mineral found over there, and," he added, "something a little weird here . . . Human blood. AB negative. They said it's a very rare blood type." Mack snickered. "That's your blood type, right?"

"How did you know that?" Randall demanded.

"I didn't know it," Mack said quickly. "I didn't. It was a joke. I was kidding."

"So was I," said Randall. "Mine's type O," he lied. "Must be African blood."

"Yeah," said Mack.

"So that's it? Nothing else?"

"That's it," said Mack. "Bat shit, boa constrictor skin, a mineral, and human blood. The people at the lab said they would put it back together as best they could and mail it back to you."

"Blood, bat shit, and boa constrictor skins," Randall muttered under his breath. "Somebody sent me blood and bat shit from Africa."

"How's our search for an anthropologist who knows about . . . what tribe?"

"The Mende," said Mack. "He returns from sabbatical today. I left a detailed description of the . . . bundle with one of his graduate students, and told him you needed an expert witness or a consultant. Professor Harris Sawyer, University of Pennsylvania. And the

Comco people are waiting for you down the hall on the Beach Cove foreclosure."

Randall left his notebook computer and drifted down the hall to conference room A. He wondered momentarily how it was that he was walking on the floor. What if since birth he had seen people walking only on the ceilings? Then walking on the floor would be the odd thing to do. What if these walls were not solid at all, but laser holograms that looked exactly like wallpaper patterns?

In the conference room, Randall found two in-house flunkies from Comco flanking the bank's lead counsel, Mr. Lance Buboe, a senior VP and old friend of the name partners of Randall's firm. Buboe was known chiefly for a nine-inch flap of hair that grew out of the left side of his head, just above his ear, and was trained and pasted up and across the glowing pink convexity of his head, all the way over to his right ear. Flap, the associates called him. Flap and company were wearing ties. Randall was also wearing a tie. And he was suddenly struck by the absolute uselessness of ties. Where did they come from? Who wore the first one? Why? Are these things vestigial bibs? Are they symbolic yokes? Tethers? Ornaments? They are not worn by the kind of people who are concerned about adding a splash of color to their wardrobe. Were they meant to cover cracked shirt buttons? What kind of costume had they all dressed in that day without even stopping for a second to wonder why?

"There he is," said Buboe, rising from his chair with a warm smile. "Genghis Khan. Look at him, boys! There are a lot of young associates vying to hold this man's armor! Great work on that lift stay," said Buboe extravagantly. "Brilliant work. Chuck is very pleased also," he added, giving Randall a knowing look. "Very pleased. And he controls all the work coming out of Chicago."

"I want to suggest something," said Randall, wondering if he would be able to go through with what he had in mind. "It's about this Beach Cove deal."

"What's there to discuss?" said Buboe. "Thanks to you, the stay's lifted. We foreclose, take the property away from these assholes, and sell it."

"I just want to propose something," said Randall.

I went to church this morning, Randall could say. He could tell Buboe and his boys what had happened. *I haven't told you,* he could say, *but I may be very sick. If I have cancer, it's in my brain. It could kill me very quickly. Within months. If it's not cancer, it's*

*something else that's . . . affecting me. So I went to church, and I
was trying to pray, because I've been so . . . desperate lately. So
helpless. So afraid. It changes you. I was praying. I was trying to
pray, because I had no choice. I had nothing else left. I was alone,
and I was afraid that I could be dead soon, or maybe that I was
having some kind of breakdown. And after I started praying, it
occurred to me that if God would let me go on living, I would do
more good. I could at least try to do more good. Instead of looking
for fights, I could bring people together and help them resolve their
disputes. I was wondering if Comco would be willing to give the
Beach Cove partners another chance?*

And if he actually said that, how long would he have to stare into
their open mouths? News of the psychotic break would make it
around the firm and out to the coastal offices within an hour. Every
lawyer in the place would be behind closed doors talking about how
Randall Killigan hosted a prayer breakfast and then tried to give
away the store to an adverse party. *Get a straitjacket. Get some
sedatives. Who knows what he'll do next?*

Instead, he regained his composure and said, "I was just making
sure there was absolutely no question of a deal."

"If you suggested that we should deal with those assholes," said
Buboe with a horse laugh, "I'd find a new lawyer."

"If you *wanted* to deal with them," Randall said jovially, "I'd get
a new client. As it is, I'm charging Mr. Bilksteen tuition and trying
to find him work in estate planning."

Once the Comco business was wrapped up, he stormed back to
his office and tried to act warlike. Maybe all this tumor business
was interfering with him. Maybe he was walking around thinking
about dying without even realizing it. Maybe he needed a designated
driver to run over people when they got in his way.

A messenger from a firm across town and a phone slip on his
computer desktop program told him that someone had pulled a fast
one on him over in Judge Baxter's court. The hearing he had spent
two weeks preparing for had been continued, and the continuance
had the potential for sending the whole case to hell's basement. He
had his Code in his hands looking for a section he could pull out
of his shoe like a razor blade.

He fed the messages to Benjy and swore. *See what happens if
you as much as look the other way to take a pee? Wham, they fuck
you!*

The speakerphone buzzed. Randall drew his broadsword as in days of yore and stabbed the blinking button.

"Indiana Jones on line three," said Mack, "back from Africa and ready to consult. Harris Sawyer, professor of anthropology, University of Pennsylvania."

As he introduced himself and was acquainted with the professor's qualifications, Randall calmly reminded himself that he was about to speak with a person who was not a bankruptcy attorney—was not even a lawyer—which meant he could not terrorize or annihilate the person, but instead had to be nice to him. Getting something out of somebody by being nice to them took at least three times as long as a simple threat to destroy their careers and seize all their tangible assets, which was why he gritted his teeth and looked at his watch whenever he was forced to be nice.

"I have a client who is a wealthy, eccentric collector, whom I shall not identify, but let's call her Colette. Colette married an entrepreneur in the import-export business. Let's call him, I don't know, Trader Vic, how's that? Trader Vic travels to West Africa a couple times a year and mails back African art, cloths, carvings, that sort of thing, to Colette. Anyway, on his last trip, Vic went to a place called Sierra Leone to buy some art from a tribe called the Mende tribe, which my associate tells me you know a lot about."

"I do," said Sawyer.

"We're, of course, prepared to pay a reasonable consultation fee, by the way," said Randall, "but on the last trip, the one to see the Mende, Vic disappeared . . . vanished! The next thing Colette knows, she gets a parcel from Freetown, Sierra Leone, and inside is a little black bundle, shaped like a big egg or a little football, and it has this red spout sticking out of it. And here's the funny part: She knows Vic didn't send it because the label on the package was not in his handwriting and whoever sent the thing misspelled her name."

Professor Sawyer cleared his throat. "A Mende person wishes to harm your client," he said, "or, more likely, someone wants to kill her. I suppose the other possibility is that they want to harm Trader Vic by harming his wife. The red spout is called *tingoi*; together with the black bundle, it's called *ndilei*, a powerful, malignant, illegal medicine, which is created by a witch or a juju man and is used to harm people."

Randall's scalp pringled and his heart jumped a notch, stalled, then sped onward.

"Why would witches or juju men want to harm my client?"

"My guess is somebody hired them to do the job," said Sawyer. "I hope you don't take umbrage at the comparison, but villagers hire bad medicine men, or *hale nyamubla*, to harm an enemy with witchcraft or bad medicine the same way an American would, say, hire a lawyer to sue somebody."

"A *medicine*?" asked Randall.

"Yes," said Sawyer, "but in the broad African sense of a charm, or a talisman. *Ndilei* is especially associated with witches and witch-craft, or 'witch business,' as the Mende call it. Once the bundle is placed in or near the victim's house, the person who planted it selects a night to dream of the victim, and on that night the medicine transforms itself into a witch spirit, takes on the shape of a bat or a boa constrictor, and attacks."

"Attacks?" said Randall hoarsely, flushing to his ears and breathing harder. "What would it do to, uh, Colette?"

"You get different opinions on the subject," said Sawyer, "depending on whether the bundle was created by a witch or a juju man. But most Mende would say that the *ndilei* assumes its animal form at the appointed hour and then sucks blood from the neck or a limb of the victim, and later the victim sickens and dies, or one of the victim's limbs withers or becomes paralyzed. What we call polio the Mende believe is caused by a boa constrictor swallowing the limbs of its sleeping victims. But more often the victim simply gets sick and slowly dies. Hemorrhage seems to be a favorite, fever followed by coma, hallucinations, seizures . . ."

"Hallucinations?" asked Randall hoarsely. "Coma?"

"Yes," said Sawyer, "but remember, these are physical symptoms, part of the physical world. In the spiritual realm, what's happening is that the witch spirit has attacked the soul, or *ngafei*, the vital force of the human victim while he or she is asleep."

"But, but . . ." said Randall, violently loosening his tie, "if, uh, Colette claims she *saw* a bat one night, but it was some time ago, and . . . Well, nothing happened to her. I mean, she doesn't have any withered limbs . . ."

"Another favorite," interrupted Sawyer, "is pulmonary tubercu-losis, in which case the witches are believed to have poured hot witch water on the person's soul, *ngafei*, causing blisters and the burning sensation one feels after a spasm of violent coughing."

"Witch water?" repeated Randall, struggling for air and planting his fist on his chest.

"But any physical manifestations are almost beside the point, because, as I said, what's happening takes place in the supernatural realm. The attack is on the person's *ngafei*, or soul, which is an inseparable counterpart of the victim's human form. But in Africa the supernatural *is* the physical, so it is described in physical terms, as the witch giving the victim witch meat to eat, or the witch spirit eating the victim's belly, or the witch spirit sucking blood from a vein, or . . ."

"Blood?" said Randall. "That's significant? You said that before. I mean, Colette did say something about blood, like, I think, once she said there was blood coming out of the bundle. Does that mean anything?"

A long silence filled Randall's ear.

"When my students ask me these questions," said Sawyer, "I use the two-hat method. First I'll put on my Caucasian anthropologist hat. Some anthropologists who have studied the Mende speculate that the *ndilei* or witch bundle has bladders or small bottles of blood inside of it, so that when the witch doctor finds it and accuses its owner of witchcraft, he can prove that it has been used to harm people. Now, off with the anthropologist's hat, and on with my villager's cap. As a person who lived in a Mende village for four years, I would say that a witch bundle containing blood is one that has obviously already taken on its animal form and attacked at least one victim, from whom it had siphoned blood. As we've discussed, a villager would now expect the victim to sicken and die."

Randall tore his tie completely off and threw it on the floor.

"But if he, if she, let's say Colette," Randall said, stuttering and having difficulty breathing. "Even if she was silly enough to believe in this wacky stuff. I mean, if the witch spirit had *entered* her, she'd know about it, right?"

Sawyer chuckled in Randall's ear.

"WHAT'S SO GODDAMN MOTHERFUCKING FUNNY?" Randall screamed, hurling a glass paperweight commemorating the Marauder Reorganization at the wall and backhanding a picture of Marjorie on her horse off his desk.

In the hallway, paralegals and secretaries scurried by, giving Randall's open door a wide berth, and once safely out of range rolled their eyes with looks that said, *Steer clear! He's at it again! Somebody must have queered another deal on him.*

"I didn't mean to be flip, Mr. Killigan," Sawyer hurriedly explained. "I was just amused that our conversation was touching upon one thorny anthropological conundrum after another, and that these enigmas are almost impossible to explain in a single sentence. But even more than that," he quickly added, "I was impressed at how a man of your intellectual prowess intuitively poses the very questions that anthropologists argue over for decades without resolving."

"And?" Randall said. "So? If a witch spirit had, I don't know, *gone* into her, then maybe she wouldn't know? It would just be there, hiding, or something? Talk! TALK TO ME! Don't giggle into the phone about conundrums! Sure it's a big puzzle for you. I've got a client who wants to know if this *thing* did anything to her. She's quite superstitious. Yes, very superstitious! So I would like to explain the entire matter to her, the way the Africans think of it, so I can put her mind at ease."

"I don't think the African explanation will put her mind at ease," said Sawyer, "because it is changeable and, by definition, mysterious. It is tempting to always talk about the *honei*, or witch spirit, as traveling in the shape of a witch bird or a voracious wild animal, in short as a foreign power operating at night, *outside* of its host. But the Mende also talk of the witch spirit as an *extension* or a replica of the host.

"I always use the example of cancer," said Sawyer.

"Cancer!" shouted Randall. "Witches cause cancer!?"

"No, no," said Sawyer. "Well," he added, "maybe. But no. It's a comparison I use in class. People in our country like to describe cancer as an invader attacking a victim, even though most cancers come from a single mutation of the person's *own* cell. There is no invading virus or bacterium. Cancer *is* the person, but it is also a deviant . . . *force*, which grows until it takes over . . . and kills the person."

"But she's not dying!" Randall argued, verging on a desperate whine. "Nothing's happened to her. She hasn't coughed up any witch meat, or gone into a coma, or gotten polio. So what I want to tell her is, that if this witch *thing* attacked her, she would know about it, because she would get sick. Right?"

"If your question is, do the Mende believe that the *ndilei* will *always* kill or maim its intended victim, the answer is no."

"I would hope so," said Randall. "I mean, the whole thing is completely fucking ridiculous to begin with. But I guess I was asking my question with an eye toward reassuring her that, even if she thought there was something to this witch or juju stuff, I could tell her that it doesn't always make you sick, or paralyze you, or kill you. I could tell her that not even the Mende believe that."

"That's correct," said Sawyer. "Because sometimes the witch spirit sets out to kill its victim and discovers, instead, that the person harbors a kindred spirit, or that the victim would be more useful to the witch as a host."

"A host," Randall repeated, feeling his throat tighten. "What do you mean, a host?"

"A witch host," Sawyer said. "Instead of killing or injuring the person, the witch spirit—or *honei*, in Mende—enters the person's belly and sets up housekeeping, turning him into a witch host, or witch person—a *honei-mui*. The two then spend the rest of their lives together destroying farms, eating children . . . feeding on the spirits of others."

•

The people in Ndevehun were accustomed to seeing a vehicle arrive every month or so, with supplies for the midwife including Guinness stout, which she sold on the side, and sometimes aspirins, or if fever was rampant, perhaps some *poo-mui* fever medicine. But no one could remember the last time a real medical doctor had seen patients in the village itself. The clinic was fifteen miles down the road in Mattru, where it was not unusual, after waiting in line in the sun all day, to be turned away in the evening without getting in to see the doctor.

On this particular day, one of the missionary doctors, a Krio from Freetown who had been to medical school in England, was receiving patients inside the midwife's quarters. All the women of the village had lined up outside—alone or with their children—chatting excitedly about the prospect of *poo-mui* medicine, free and in their own village! As each woman emerged from her visit with the doctor, she was closely interrogated by the women standing in line about the symptoms she had described to the visiting physician and the treatment she had received. The first four women had received only tablets of medicine for their treatment. At last, a woman emerged who had been given an injection, which, as all the women knew, was the most powerful medicine dispensed by doctors of white medicine. The woman said she had complained of fevers and headaches at night and nausea after eating.

One after another, the women in line went into the hut and complained of fevers and headaches at night and nausea after eating. Sometimes the gambit worked, and the patient emerged, holding a cotton swab over the injection site and beaming with satisfaction, but other times they emerged downcast, with only pills or lotions to show for their pains.

While the clinic was in progress, two Land-Rovers pulled into the village, containing *poo-muis* from Freetown and several Africans, one of whom the villagers recognized as Section Chief Idrissa Moiwo, along with other African big men, who wore the epaulets and military chapeaus of various ministries in Freetown. Section Chief Moiwo's speaker stood on a bench in the court *barri* and addressed the village through a bullhorn. The doctor had been hired by Mistah Randall Killigan of America. The medicine was being provided as a gift from Mistah Randall Killigan, father of Michael Killigan, also known to the villagers as Lamin Kaikai, who recently could not be found in his village, and whose father was desperate to find him. More medicine would be provided as a gift, including injections, vaccinations, rehydration fluids, infant formula, and all the most powerful *poo-mui* medicines. In addition, a pump was to be installed at one of the village wells, courtesy of Mistah Randall Killigan, as a gift to the people of this village, who it was hoped would provide any information they might have on the whereabouts of Lamin Kaikai to their chief, or to the speaker of Section Chief Idrissa Moiwo, who, though he had been to England and America for schooling and could read *poo-mui* books, had come back to the land of his birth and made a gift of himself to the Mende people. He was a Mende man. His mother was a Mende woman. His father was part Temne, but his father's heart had been with the Mende people. He loved his people and he knew his people loved Lamin Kaikai, so he was doing everything in his power to find brother Lamin. All rumors of Lamin's whereabouts should be reported to the speaker of Section Chief Idrissa Moiwo as soon as possible.

Also, if a villager or anyone else could provide information that would lead to the discovery of Lamin Kaikai, that person or persons would receive cash in the amount of five thousand United States dollars, or the exchange equivalent in leones.

Next, Section Chief Idrissa Moiwo was introduced, a stout man with the haunches and bulbous behind of a man who did a lot of sitting and eating, bound up in safari shorts and jacket, with black sunglasses and a quasi-military beret, complete with a medallion commemorating his service as a Minister of Finance for the former President in Freetown. Section Chief Moiwo effusively paid tribute to the absent American, Mistah Randall Killigan, for his generous gifts to the village, and refrained from mentioning that he himself had received an air-conditioned Land-Rover as a gift from the American to assist him in his investigation of the disappearance of the fine young Peace Corps Volunteer, Mr. Michael Killigan, the friend and counselor to the people of the village, whose disappearance had so saddened the people of his village, and whose hearts have been filled with sorrow and anguish since his disappearance. Construction of the pump for the well would begin as soon as parts arrived from Freetown. And the doctor would remain in the village, operating out of the midwife's quarters, until the people had received all the medical care they needed or desired.

A truck would arrive shortly bearing fifty bags of rice, also a gift from the generous Mistah Randall Killigan, who was desperately seeking information about the whereabouts of his son, Michael Killigan, Lamin Kaikai.

When the rice arrived, it was emblazoned with the logo of USAID, along with the warning in big red letters, which no one could read: "THIS RICE IS A GIFT FROM THE PEOPLE OF THE UNITED STATES. IT IS NOT TO BE SOLD IN WHOLE OR IN PART." The bags of rice had been turned over to the government at the docks in Freetown, and sold in the usual fashion to various wholesalers, who then normally transported it to the outlying town markets, where it was sold again, and on down to the villages, where it was sold by the cup to other villagers. In this case, Randall Killigan had arranged from Indiana for the purchase of fifty bags of the USAID rice from the Ministry of Agriculture, before it was sold to the wholesalers. Then he arranged to have it delivered to Killigan's village. Moiwo graciously arranged for the delivery of the rice to the village, and even allowed it to be given away. But he charged the chief a healthy tariff, and permitted him to tax any resale of the rice in the markets or along the roadside.

The injection of free rice into the village economy cut the going rate for a bag of rice by half. The farmers who had worked all year to bring in rice crops were forced to compete with traders who had paid nothing for their rice.

The offer of a reward amounting to an unimaginable sum of money threw the village into a turmoil and started a bull market in black magic and divination, for everyone knew that a looking-around man or a juju man was the best way to find someone or something that was lost. Within a week, the offer of the reward drove the village insane with greed. First off, all of the medicines dispensed from the midwife's hut by the Krio doctor were collected in a pail, and the pharmacopoeia of multicolored pills was hauled off and sold to the citizens of other villages, who randomly selected pills, paid outrageous sums, and took them to remedy everything from hernias to gas to gangrene. The money from the sale of the pills was then paid to looking-around men who advised their clients on how to find the missing *poo-mui*.

Back in Ndevehun, the crime rate soared as people stole radios, tape decks, farm implements, batteries, medicines, kerosene, and anything else that wasn't nailed down to raise money to consult the best diviners and find the missing *poo-mui* before someone else did. But consulting diviners was not good enough to ensure the success of the various search teams comprised of eager young men who left their farms and mines in hopes of winning the reward. With such money at stake, they also had to hire juju men to sabotage the efforts of their neighbors and thwart the competition. Before long the village of Ndevehun was a hornet's nest of swears, counterswears, juju, witch business, and sorcery.

Next, the first woman who had received the injection on the first day became quite ill with a terrible gastritis. When the other women who had received injections heard of her illness, they too fell sick, convinced that it was the injection that had caused their neighbor's illness and equally convinced that they were similarly afflicted. Some of the medicines being sold out of buckets aggravated the conditions of patients who took them, and the overall health of the village plummeted. After the pump was mounted on the well and cemented in place with concrete, a bolt which had been improperly secured to the plunger snapped, and no water could be pumped or drawn from the well because it was now sealed shut by the fixture.

And that was only the beginning, for rumor had it that even more money was on its way.

(16)

Following the session with the looking-around man, Sisay took to his quarters with another bout of fevers, and sent the women, children, Boone, and the other helpless, dependent relatives to eat at Pa Ansumana's house. With no translator, conversation consisted of short guttural sentences followed by exaggerated nods when Pa and Boone pretended to understand each other.

After dinner, Pa took a gnawed drumstick bone and placed it in front of Boone. Then the old man selected one for himself and bit it in half, chewing contentedly and pausing to suck marrow from the bone, until it was as hollow as a whistle.

"*Nyandengo!*" said Pa, again nudging a bone in Boone's direction.

Had Boone known this meal would have to last him three days, maybe he would have tried a chew and tasted a little bone marrow, which Sisay had told him was a delicacy in these parts. Instead, he thanked his father, but declined the bone, patting his belly repeatedly and saying, "Belly full too much."

After dinner, he went back to his room, extinguished his hurricane lamp, and sat in the moonlight streaming in through the cracks of his shutters. He threw open the shutters and peered up into the blue-jeweled vaults overhead. Was *Ngewo* up there somewhere in His cave, frolicking every now and again with the ancestors, who lived across the river in the village of white sands? Did He like to receive a chicken and a big pot of sweet upland rice? Did He call Himself Allah and demand that men face the east, bow, and pray to Him five times a day? Did He thrive on devotion, as the Catholics believed? Did He annually like to watch while a heart was cut out of a victim's chest and offered up to Him at dawn, as the Aztecs and thoracic surgeons believed? Did it really bother Him if people didn't worship on the Sabbath?

Maybe only His name changes through the ages, and every person's conception of Him is correct, as in the parable of the blind men feeling the elephant, with each blind man describing a different animal, depending upon which part of the beast they had hold of at the time. And to the Mende? *Ngewo mu gbate mahei:* God is the chief who made us. *Na leke Ngewo keni ta a lo ma:* Nothing happens, unless God agrees (to let it happen). *Ngewo lo maha le:* God, the chief, has the last word.

A chill swept through him, and nothing resembling a breeze occurred at this time in the dry season. He steadied himself, saw his friends the diamond maggots spinning again, then fell to his knees. He operated his heavy, cold limbs from afar, like a puppeteer in charge of a man-sized dummy. He could feel his blood—cold as crimson slush—coursing under his skin and flushing through his organs.

He took two of the chloroquine pills and lay down in the moonlight, waiting to see if he indeed had malaria. After the cold came heat and hot sweats. The next bout of fevers rattled his teeth and confirmed his suspicions. Borrowing Sisay's technique, he knotted a T-shirt and used it as a safety mouthpiece. Soon his lower back glowed, a rack of inflamed meninges, simmering like an order of large-end ribs on a bed of coals.

Pa Ansumana sent a woman to dab him with cool rags, but otherwise he was alone, listening to Sisay groan from time to time in the next room, hoping he would not die an ignoble death stranded in a village in West Africa. *Would they send his body home?* he suddenly wondered. Maybe the Mende would just inter him somewhere in the bush, where his flesh would keep for at least a week before microorganisms would chew him back into topsoil and loam.

He curled up in bed and waited for Missus Sickness. Soon he would be studying the ebb and flow of his fevers, charting the complex reproductive cycles of the malarial parasites, multiplying feverishly into hordes, then lysing into cellular debris at the hands of his immune system. He had read enough to know that he was now what parasitologists called an *intermediate host* for the malarial parasite, genus *Plasmodium*, a microscopic creature with the most complicated reproductive cycle in all of microbiology. The *definitive host*, the anopheles mosquito, had drunk blood from some other malaria victim, probably Sisay, containing cells that then multiplied sexually with other cells in the mosquito, until they were injected into Boone—the intermediate host—who was now providing a breeding reservoir for another batch of parasites that would infest his red blood cells and reproduce asexually. The furious reproductive cycles coincided nicely with the quartan fevers, until his blood was awash in toxins and the debris of his own exploded red blood cells.

If he had the sometimes fatal *falciparum* malaria, the parasite-infected red blood cells could choke off the supply of blood to his brain, leaving brain stew (simmer on low, until it thickens, then remove . . .).

When he wasn't shaking with chills, he warmed to his new ecological role of intermediate host. It occurred to him that perhaps humans were parasites breeding in the definitive host of the earth. While on earth, they multiplied sexually, until they were transformed by death and injected into some cosmological intermediate host, where they reproduced asexually, until they were returned to the earth again as gametocytes with a fresh urge to mate.

After the first set of high fevers, he slept until dawn and woke in a profound lethargy, at once depressing and peaceful. He heard an internal-combustion engine, which charged through his dreams like some freakish metal bush creature powered by fire and explosions. Eventually, he woke up without moving a muscle, stared out his window, and watched the world, of which he was no longer a part. If death came, he could not care; death's fevers could not be any worse than the ones he had already thrown off. And if life continued, what future terror could disturb him now, in this resting place of exhaustion and euphoria? He was spent and utterly passive, a heap of organs and bones in a sack of membranes, with limbs that moved self-consciously through space.

He spent the tropical morning sucking oranges, and after sucking them he looked at the mangled green rinds and thought about himself—empty, feeble, dehydrated, sticky, and sick to death of Africa. He would leave, if leaving were not so difficult; and if the woman at the Peace Corps information desk had been there, she could have said, "I told you so." It would be a twelve-hour trip into Freetown, another day or two lining up a plane ticket, a day or two waiting for a plane that would be scheduled and rescheduled without ever leaving. WAIT. Even then, he would first have to fly to Europe or North Africa, and make more arrangements. The first day after recuperating, he would wake up and wonder what had possessed him to leave Sierra Leone without first finding his best friend.

A servant girl tapped at his door with a fresh batch of rehydration salts and more sucking oranges. Behind her came another "Kong, kong" and the shaggy head of Sam Lewis appeared.

"Ain't it funny how white people run into each other in this country?" he said. "Oh sha about the fever business," he added. "Do you have plenty of the pills?"

Boone nodded. Lewis pulled up the lone chair.

"I got a ride here with Moiwo," he said. "After I left Bo, I had agriculture business down in that neck of the bush, so I stopped in Killigan's village to nose around for you. I ran into Moiwo and chewed the fat with him. He's in touch with Killigan's dad," Lewis explained, "and Killigan's dad is bankrolling a manhunt. As for Moussa Kamara, the guy was a thief from the get-go. His own father admitted as much to me. I talked to them after Moiwo dropped the body off. The groundnut girl was his kid sister, who always stuck up for him, even when he was caught red-handed, so I wouldn't put much stock in her version of the story. Moiwo's hot to find your buddy, though. He's got three Land-Rovers on the job, staffed with his own men, and doing a thorough job of it."

"What about the body parts and the Baboon business you were telling me he was into?" asked Boone weakly.

"That's election business," Lewis said. "Probably rumors started by his opponents. That's got nothing to do with your buddy. Though there are those in his village who say that your buddy was into illegal medicine himself and got in over his head. Again, pure gossip. *Congosa*, as they say in Freetown talk. As near as I can tell, Moiwo's got nothing against your friend. In fact, if he finds him it will bolster his reputation with the government men and *poo-mui* embassies in Freetown, and there's money. There's a five-thousand-dollar reward out for information, and Moiwo gets more on top if he gets the job done right. I think Killigan's old man has found the right guy for the job. Moiwo will find your buddy, if he can be found."

"Where's Moiwo now?" asked Boone.

"Here," said Lewis, "over in his compound, probably working over one of his young wives. He's been on the road, you know. He wants to take you back to Freetown with him, so you can meet with the embassy people."

They were interrupted by people banging pots in the courtyard. And from the direction of the *barri*, where the woman-damage cases were argued, Boone could hear an announcement being made.

"Everybody come out dae houses! Everybody listen! Everybody come out! Witchfinders done come just now! Paramount Chief Kabba Lundo he done bring witchfinders for cleansing our village. Everybody come out dae houses! Everybody listen!"

Boone's door opened, and a wan and haggard Sisay appeared. He barely acknowledged Lewis with a nod of his head, and summoned Boone out of bed.

"Is that a real witchfinder they got out there?" Lewis asked.

Sisay nodded. "So I'm told. I was also told that we all must go to the *barri*."

"I've heard about these witch cleansings," said Lewis. "Never seen one, mind you, but I've heard. They take three days, and there's no eating or sleeping allowed. If it's all the same to you boys, I'm leaving. And my advice to you," he said in Boone's direction, "is to get out of here while you still can."

"It's too late," said Sisay, weakened by fever and fatigue, and not liking Lewis any more for it. "The witchfinder has sealed off the village. No one may leave until it's over."

"We'll see about that," said Lewis. "I'm taking the first *podah-podah* into Bo town."

Lewis marched out the door first, followed by Boone and Sisay, who walked stiffly and gingerly out to the *barri* and seated themselves on a mud wall. Lewis went to Moiwo's Land-Rover and grabbed his daypack out of the back. He spoke briefly to the section chief, who was ensconced in the passenger's seat conferring with other uniformed men. Then he headed across the courtyard for the path that led from the village.

Villagers were assembling in the *barri* and gathering around a slight man in a simple powder-blue burnoose. His head was shaved or naturally bald, and the flesh of his face followed the contours of his skull, throwing huge black eyes that seemed to be all pupil and no iris into high relief. If this was the witchfinder, he did not go in for the amulets, cowrie shells, animal teeth, and medicine pouches that adorned the hunters, the looking-around man, and the chiefs. Instead, he held a wooden staff, with animal totems, figurines, and designs carved into it. The top of the staff was notched, and lashed in the notch was a wooden hand mirror. Except for the staff and the shaved head, the witchfinder looked like a typical old pa on his way to morning prayers.

Another speaker stood and announced that the witchfinder had completely surrounded the village with a white cotton thread, and that if anyone broke the thread or crossed the boundary, he or she would surely sicken and die.

Several of the villagers pointed at Lewis and shouted, alarmed at the prospect of anyone attempting to leave the village. The man in the blue burnoose rose to his feet and called out to Lewis, then set off after the *poo-mui* fool, twirling his staff and summoning two assistants to follow him. Lewis waved off the witchfinder. The crowd rose to its feet and talked excitedly among themselves.

As Lewis made for the path out of the village, the witchfinder called out to him that if he crossed the boundary marked by the white thread, he would die. As the witchfinder drew abreast of him, Lewis turned and spoke in Krio, telling his pursuer that he did not live in this village and did not intend to partake in a witch cleansing, which, he had heard, could last as long as a week. He was leaving, and the witchfinder could take his white cotton thread to hell and rot with it.

While Lewis explained himself, the witchfinder skillfully and unobtrusively positioned his staff so that the mirror showed Lewis his own reflection as he spoke. At least twice, Lewis noted his own annoyed reflection in the glass and irritably waved it off.

Boone and Sisay and the rest of the villagers had left the *barri*, where they had been assembling, and were now gathering around the witchfinder and Lewis, anxious to see if this reckless *poo-mui* would ignore the warnings of a real witchfinder.

As Boone brought up the rear of the crowd, he saw that, indeed, a cotton thread crossed the path and had been fastened to the twigs and branches of the bush fronting the village, continuing along the perimeter until it was obscured by the huts and compounds it surrounded. He was relieved to see that the thread seemed to pass behind the row of pan-roofed outhouses, preserving access to the latrines.

Lewis stopped at the boundary, turned, and apologized to the witchfinder for his previous rude remarks, but again explained that he did not live in this village and that he would not be staying for the witch cleansing. Again, the witchfinder twirled the mirror just so, and annoyed Lewis with his own reflection.

The witchfinder allowed the crowd to gather. He was a frail man with innocent eyes and a tender, soothing voice. He seemed earnest, but at the same time amused, as if he knew that he made his living off the folly of the human race, but somebody had to do the job, and fate had appointed him with the best qualifications. This confrontation with a pompous *poo-mui* seemed to put a little fun into the otherwise humdrum task of purging witches from villages.

As the witchfinder spoke, Sisay weakly translated almost in monotone, clearly wanting only to go back to the *barri* and sit down, but—along with everyone else—he was engrossed in the high-wire daring of Lewis, and translated the witchfinder's words for Boone.

"The witchfinder has sealed off the village with a white cotton thread. Witches may no longer enter the village, and all the witches and bad medicines within the village will be purged when his work is done. Here is a white man who thinks he can cross the boundary set up by the witchfinder. White men have many powerful medicines, but they are nothing compared to the powers of the witchfinder."

Lewis grimaced and politely waited for the witchfinder to finish, to minimize the disrespect he was about to show in leaving.

The witchfinder summoned one of his assistants from the crowd. A young man in an embroidered African shirt came forward bearing a platter with a knife on it, the blade curved and gleaming like a small scimitar, the handle made of carved bone or ivory, with diagonal, stylized masks or faces carved into it. The witchfinder handed his staff to the assistant, took the knife from the platter, and continued his announcement.

"If this man leaves the village he will never eat food again," Sisay translated. "If he tries to eat food, he will choke on his own tongue and die."

At the conclusion of this speech, the witchfinder smiled at Lewis and opened his mouth so wide the skin stretched even tighter against his skull. Then he stuck out his tongue, unfurling it in a single sinuous gesture, like a reptile stretching and tasting the air while sunning itself on a rock. The witchfinder laughed and wagged his tongue at Lewis in a display that, under other circumstances, might have been grotesquely humorous. With a careful, elaborate gesture, and with one eye on the crowd, the witchfinder made a pincer out of his first two fingers and his thumb and seized his own tongue. He brought the knife to his mouth, inserted the blade, and with a single quick flick sliced his tongue out of his mouth and threw it on the platter, which was still patiently being held by the assistant.

The crowd gasped and gagged. Children threw themselves on the ground. Adults backed away, terror and disbelief competing for expression on their faces. Boone trembled with nausea, and a new fever roared through his veins.

Lewis stared dumbfounded at the tongue, which was covered with blood and appeared to be writhing as the assistant tilted and rotated the platter, allowing the white man every opportunity to inspect it. The witchfinder opened his mouth, which was filled with blood, and showed Lewis the stump of his tongue, covered with blood and rhythmically spurting more with each beat of the witchfinder's pulse.

Boone stared in shock, long enough to confirm that either he had just watched a man cut his own tongue out of his mouth or he had seen the best magic act of his life. Using the same elaborate pincer gesture, the witchfinder calmly picked up his tongue from the platter by its tip and reinserted it in his mouth. Another assistant appeared with a white cloth, which the witchfinder used to pat his face and wipe his mouth. Then he smiled at Lewis, opened his mouth, and again wagged his tongue at the white man, sticking the thing out as far as he could, so that all could see that the tongue was seamlessly intact and unscathed, with no trace of mayhem except for a little bloody saliva.

After this display was over, the crowd's gasps of horror and wonder had subsided. The witchfinder closed his mouth and assumed the same mild manner he had used to address them at the outset. He quietly reiterated the curse, then, according to Sisay, said, "If the witchfinder can cut out his own tongue and then put it back into his mouth, think what a simple matter it would be to make another man choke on his."

Lewis looked sheepishly at the witchfinder, then at the crowd, until his eyes fell on Sisay.

"Maybe I should stay long enough to talk this over," he said. "Maybe I could pick a better time to leave." Then walking back to join his fellow *poo-muis*, he added, "I wouldn't want you guys to worry about me after I left."

Boone had another cold shudder of fever and nausea and headed back to the *barri* with Sisay, pondering what was either some incredible breach in the laws of nature or a trick of consummate skill. Had the witchfinder concealed something in his mouth before addressing the crowd? Had he simply cheeked a bladder or plastic bag of blood, along with an animal's tongue, which he then had removed and thrown on the platter? Boone tried to replay the scene in his imagination, but the crucial details were eclipsed by the horror of the performance.

Back at the *barri* all were seated and everyone's attention was devoted to the witchfinder, who was now being introduced by the Paramount Chief, Kabba Lundo, the latter in full ceremonial dress, bearing an elephant-tail fly whisk, the staff of office, and covered in cowrie shells, amulets, and pouches. The witchfinder looked almost monklike when escorted by the chief in such regalia.

The *poo-muis* sat together in one corner and the rest of the village grouped themselves roughly according to *mawes* around the *barri*. Moiwo and his men stood outside the *barri* attending to the proceedings, but periodically conferring among themselves, as if they were deliberating about the proper protocol for a section chief confronting a witchfinder brought into the village by the elected Paramount Chief.

"Brothers and sisters," said the witchfinder, according to Sisay, who translated for Boone. "The great Kabba Lundo has asked me to cleanse all the villages in his great chiefdom. I recognize faces that were here when I came to this village many years ago. When last I saw this village, it was cleansed of witchcraft and every villager had a pure and open heart. Now I see witch business has come again. I see dark hearts and sad faces. I see hatred and scheming, distrust and selfishness. No wonder the infants are dying! No wonder men are shot as animals in the bush! I smell malice and adultery, swear and counter-swear, bad medicine and sorcery."

The witchfinder dropped his arms and lifted his head, as if sniffing the air, or listening to some distant sound. He opened his large, innocent eyes and stared.

"There is witchcraft in this village. It has been overrun with witches."

The crowd gasped and whispered frantically.

Instead of the righteous, hysterical preacher one would expect, the witchfinder seemed saddened by the discovery of witches and touched by the frailty of human nature. He opened his eyes even wider and stared over the heads of his audience.

"But now all these witches are trapped in this village, and I will find them for you. When my work is done, this village will be cleansed of witches and witch medicine, and all those witches with black hearts who walked among you every day in seeming innocence, with friendly glances and outward smiles, will be exposed. Then you will see that when these witches patted the heads of your children, they were secretly thinking about eating them; when they heard about the rice pods swelling on your farms, they went out at night to destroy them; and when they learned that your wives were in labor, they trapped the babies inside their mothers and ate them before they could be born.

"All of the pregnant women and nursing mothers will be taken to a compound that I have already purified. They will remain there until my work is done. There they will be safe when the witches come out at night. Each person in this village must pay me two thousand leones, and the money must be given to Chief Kabba Lundo before the sun goes down, or I will leave at dawn without doing my work. If the money is paid, this village will be cleansed of witchcraft. If not, I will leave you as I have found you, just as the proverb says, and I will go to the next village."

After finishing his speech, the witchfinder went to his guest quarters with Chief Kabba Lundo, and the *barri* erupted in fretful conversation. Sisay shambled unsteadily back to his compound, with Lewis and Boone tagging along, and a string of villagers anxious for Sisay's opinion of the witchfinder, and asking one another where they could possibly obtain two thousand leones before sundown.

Sisay collapsed in his bed, while at least a dozen villagers gathered and sat on the floor, still gesturing and talking excitedly, turning occasionally and asking him questions, which he answered with an irritated wave of his hand. Pa Ansumana appeared in the doorway and beamed over the bowl of his pipe at Sisay, as if to say, "Nothing like a good witchfinding to really shake things up."

Boone shut himself in his room with Lewis, and the two of them mulled over the incident of the excised tongue. Both concluded that it had been a magic trick, but neither ventured that it was completely safe to cross the white thread and leave. Lewis shared what little knowledge he had of witchfinding, and Boone told him of his conversations with Sisay and Pa Ansumana on the subject. During the silences of their conversation, anxious chatter poured in from the neighboring compounds, and it was clear that the same discussions were being had all over the village, as the villagers weighed the tantalizing prospect of finally freeing themselves of witchcraft against the almost impossible demand for two thousand leones, nearly twenty dollars, or more cash than at least half of them had on hand.

After exhausting their own limited knowledge of witch cleansings, Boone and Lewis peeked into Sisay's quarters and found that the crowds had gone, leaving only Pa Ansumana in conversation with his *poo-mui* son.

"Take a seat," said Sisay. "There are things you should know."

Lewis and Boone gathered at the foot of the bed like children waiting for a bedtime story. Pa Ansumana sucked on his pipe and continued his conversation.

"This witchfinder is the most powerful member of the witchfinding cult called *kema-bla*. He is an old friend of the Paramount Chief, Kabba Lundo, and a very wealthy and respected witchfinder. I told you Kabba Lundo would make things tricky for Moiwo and he has done so, for now Moiwo is trapped in this village and cannot leave. Even if, as Pa Ansumana suspects, Moiwo does not believe in the witchfinder's power, he cannot leave, or the entire village would suspect him of being a witch, or of having bad medicine. Word would spread that he fled to avoid detection at the hands of the witchfinder. The same would have happened to that crazy *poo-mui* if he had left."

Pa Ansumana pointed at Lewis, then showed him a wagging tongue.

"Of course, he would have had to live as a suspected witch only until his next meal. For then he would surely have choked on his own tongue and died."

"The witchfinder's a magician," said Lewis. "If we hadn't been so freaked out at the sight of some old guy cutting out his tongue with a knife, we could have caught him in his magic act and showed everybody how it was done."

When this was translated for Pa Ansumana, his pipe spouted like a miniature volcano and covered his legs with ash and hot sparks. He brushed them away and laughed at the overweening arrogance of *poo-muis*.

"Leave now, then, *poo-mui* fool!" he said with a wave toward the door.

Lewis laughed nervously. "I think, uh, that would be . . . culturally insensitive," he said, with a glance at Sisay. "Wouldn't that be disrespectful or something? Besides, I've heard about these witchfinders. He'd probably make sure something bad happened to me. Then all the villagers would attribute it to his powers."

Pa Ansumana gave a perfect imitation of a chicken clucking and laughed, showering himself again in sparks and ashes. After he regained control of his risibles, he continued his conversation.

"In Bambara Chiefdom, where this witchfinder lives, there is a famous whetstone, a *yenge-gotui*, mounted in the middle of a clearing. For decades, maybe even centuries, many powerful warriors and prosperous farmers have sharpened their cutlasses on this stone, and though its shape has changed from years of sharpening, it is still the best whetstone in that chiefdom. The stone is now a memorial to the skill and foresight of the ancestors who selected it. The stone has its own memory, and it has absorbed the spirits of all the fathers and sons who have used it; it is impregnated with the prayers and dreams of the ancestors. The stone enshrines a spirit who visits people in dreams as an old man wearing a yellow gown. For generations, many, many people have been visited by this spirit."

There was a long pause, during which Boone suppressed a poisonous sneer. *More spirits! I should have guessed!*

"As you know, twins have very special cultic powers," continued Sisay, still translating for Pa Ansumana.

"You don't say," said Boone.

When this was translated, Pa Ansumana leaned forward, concern furrowing his brow, as he intently tried to explain the world to this *poo-mui* man-child, who seemed to know next to nothing about it.

"They can protect their families from witches and can foretell the future with ease," said Pa Ansumana, by way of Sisay. "The only person more powerful than twins is *gbese*, which means 'the sibling born after twins.' If Mende parents bear twins, they feel at once blessed and fearful, for the power of twins can be unruly and can disrupt the entire *mawe*. That is why the parents pray for *gbese*, who is the only being powerful enough to control the awesome, sometimes dangerous, powers of twins and mediate their disputes. *Gbese* are born with the ability to talk to spirits and to recognize witches."

Valuable skills, thought Boone. *I bet they call themselves consultants.*

"This witchfinder is a *gbese*. When he was still very young, the old man wearing a yellow gown appeared to him in a dream and gave him a beautiful wooden hand mirror, the one now fastened to the end of his staff. When the witchfinder looked into the mirror, he saw an old widow of his village hiding *ndilei* medicine in the rafters of her house. When he awoke from his dream, this young *gbese* witchfinder went straight to the whetstone and found the mirror the spirit had shown to him in the dream. He reported his dream to the chief and showed him the mirror.

"Not only was *ndilei* found in the rafters of the old woman's house, but the witchfinder soon discovered that he was also able to find lost or hidden objects, simply by looking into his mirror. After testing him, the chief and the elders of the village declared him a witchfinder. Since then, he has become a very wealthy and well-respected man by purging villages that have been overrun and paralyzed by witches."

Pa Ansumana chewed on his pipe. Sisay looked at Boone. Boone looked at Lewis.

Lewis said, "He's a charlatan, right?"

"He's an African psychiatrist," said Sisay. "Back in America, demons inhabit the mind. Here, they inhabit the bush."

"So what will happen now?" asked Boone.

"I'm not sure," said Sisay. "The last time a witchfinder was called into this village was before my time. Older villagers say that the pregnant women and young mothers will be separated and placed in a hut of their own, where they will be protected until all of the witches have been eradicated. Then there is fasting and no sleep and ceremonies, after which the witchfinder will find all the *ndilei* medicine in the village. *Ndilei* is always found and that means hysteria, for each bundle of *ndilei* medicine is believed to be filled with the blood of infants the witch has eaten. Sometimes there are cowrie shells sewn onto the bundle; each shell represents five infants the witch has killed and eaten with the help of the medicine."

"I should have left when I had the chance," said Lewis.

"You never had the chance," said Sisay.

·

That night, the witchfinder's assistants built a fire in the *barri*. Though the cost was dear, the money was collected. Some villagers sold possessions to get it; others sold interests in crops that were not yet harvested, asked for advances against dowries, borrowed from the Fula man, or begged from their neighbors, but everyone paid the money. No price was too high if paying it would stop the infant deaths and rid the village of witches once and for all. Even the white men paid the money, though what choice did they have?

The witchfinder and Kabba Lundo summoned the entire village to the *barri*, and all gathered around the fire. Stones were laid in a circle around the coals, and a huge cauldron was set over the flames. The witchfinder stared into the pot for a long time, and then looked out into his audience, his face lit from below and his huge eyes glowing with firelight.

"Tomorrow, anyone who knows in their heart that he or she is a witch may confess and be healed. Tomorrow, everyone must bring any bad medicine in their possession to this *barri*. *Any* bad medicine," the witchfinder repeated, "must be brought to me. If you do not bring the medicine on your own tomorrow, I promise you that the witchfinder will find it, and there will be no escaping the punishment of fines, or worse! The amnesty for witches ends tomorrow when the sun sets behind the palm trees. Go back to your houses, but do not sleep. Stay awake! Everyone in the village is in danger, except the nursing and expectant mothers, who have been secluded and protected. In these last few days of their freedom, the witches will be looking for new places to hide their medicines. They will be looking for new victims, because they know they will soon be caught and forced to confess, compelled to surrender their medicines and their powers. They also will be poisoning the food and water, so I have ordered the wells sealed and a ban on all cooking fires. Your chief will see that any food you have is collected and destroyed.

"Stay awake! Look around you. The person sitting next to you may be a witch hiding inside of a human being. You do not know when a witch will come for you, whether at dusk, at midnight, when the cock crows, or at early dawn. Let no one sleep tonight! Instead ask yourselves: Do I know of any witch business to confess to the witchfinder tomorrow? Do I have a pure heart, or do I have medicines I bought or made to harm my fellow villagers? Be on guard! Do not let a witch come suddenly and catch you asleep!"

(**17**)

"**A**re we all here?" Randall said into his speakerphone.

The hiss, howl, and cackle of international static gave way to the voice of Ambassador Walsh in Freetown.

"My political officer, Mr. Nathan French, is here with me," said the Ambassador.

"Hello, Mr. Killigan," said French.

"And our section chief?" said Randall. "He's there too, right?"

"Well, actually, no," said French. "He's not back from his trip to get the Westfall kid and bring him back to the embassy here in Freetown."

"Not back?" said Randall. "Our last conversation was four days ago, and he had already left!"

"Mr. Killigan," said the Ambassador. "It's the bush . . . The roads . . . Native matters. Once you get outside Freetown, things don't go according to plan."

"You said it's a day's journey out there and a day's journey back. That's two days. And two days is what I told the kid's father, who runs an insurance business not a block away from here. What am I gonna tell him? I told him I'd call him after I talked to you guys! The chief's driving *my* Land-Rover. What happened to the other two-plus days?"

"We don't know," said French, "because we haven't heard from the section chief. We trust that if there were some problem he would contact us, somehow, probably from Bo."

"There already is a problem!" Randall hollered. "A big problem! My son, an American citizen, an employee of the United States government, has been missing for two weeks! Two weeks! Two days used to make me crazy! Now it's two *weeks!* This alleged chief is already into me for a Land-Rover, fifty bags of rice, medicine, reward money, you name it! Am I supposed to buy him a fucking cellular phone so he can call home and tell us what he's up to? What's gonna happen if I spend another twenty thousand dollars and another eighty hours on the phone and we wind up having the same conversation after two *months!*"

"Mr. Killigan," said Ambassador Walsh, "I have to tell you that these delays aren't the fault of the United States government. We're dealing with rebel activity. We're dealing with excursions by the Liberians in the south and east. We're trying to get information about secret society business, which, as you know, is almost impossible to come by. Every other American in Sierra Leone is safe, accounted for, or evacuated. Your son's problems most probably have to do with the nature of *his* activities, not *ours*. I can't tell you what has happened. But, as we've discussed, the reports suggest that Michael involved himself in secret society matters, or worse, interfered with the Sierra Leone government's administration of its aid programs. That's not our fault. We are doing absolutely everything in our power . . ."

"Talk," shouted Randall. "Words! We're *talking* again! I *hate* talking! I have a passport, and it's stamped with a visa for Sierra Leone. If I have to, I'll bring Senator Swanson with me. When I get there, I want results! This conversation is already over, and guess what? *I have learned nothing new!* When you have results, call me! Until then . . . goodbye!"

He stabbed buttons on his phone and raised his assistant.

"Tell Judy to go ahead with the Freetown reservations. Once you get the dates, clear everything off the calendar and put it somewhere else, then bring me the court dockets and any meetings that can't be moved."

Randall disconnected the line and sat heavily into his leather recliner. A messenger brought him an envelope containing his passport and visa. He stuffed paper into his bear's gullet and swore. Twenty years of developing a nationwide bankruptcy practice had acquainted him with the limitations of telephones, and he instinctively knew it was time for him to show up in Freetown and clean out the barn. The United States government was having trouble finding one white man who was "lost" among four million black

Africans in a country the size of Indiana. It was giving him chest pains!

He held his fist against his sternum and tried to calm himself enough to venture forth and use the men's room. If a heart attack was coming, he wanted it to happen in the privacy of his own office, not in the public halls of power. He'd had nightmares in which he had seen himself grabbing his chest and faltering . . . What if it happened in front of the elevator banks? He would look up and see the lobby spored with the faces of paralegals and litigation support personnel, rushing toward him, marveling that the mightiest of all could have something as embarrassing as a heart attack. His enemies would use it as proof positive that he had failed to properly manage stress. It would suggest that he lacked the self-discipline necessary for good health; that he had failed to exercise or had overindulged in animal fat.

A beep and a squawk chorused from the speakerphone. He canceled them by pushing buttons, then hit the speed dial.

"Guaranteed Reliable Investment Mutual Trust," said a female computer voice. "Maximum protection at minimum cost. If you are calling from a Touch-Tone phone, press 1 now . . ."

"Fuck me!" shouted Randall. When would he learn not to *ever*, under *any* circumstances, make his own phone calls? He disconnected the line and told his administrative assistant to get Walter Westfall on the line.

"The insurance guy," Randall told her. "Guaranteed Reliable something and something."

It was just like Walter's kid to jump into one of Michael's brainless intrigues. Like the time they ate LSD and wound up on Interstate 70 trying to make a citizen's arrest of an Indianapolis police officer, who was, in the boys' own words, "unlawfully restricting our access to certain modes of being." And, as usual, if one of them was in trouble, there were soon two fools stomping all over places where Satan's own angels wouldn't think about treading.

He drew his toy broadsword and stabbed his keyboard, summoning his appointment calendar onto his computer screen.

"Walter Westfall, Guaranteed, Reliable," said his assistant.

"Randall?" said Walter over the speakerphone. "Is this business or pleasure?"

"It depends," said Randall. "Who's billing whom?"

"I take it this means you don't have any news for me," interrupted Walter.

"Nothing," said Randall. "Chief Send-Me-Bucks is still out there rounding up your boy and trying to find mine."

"Nothing on this end either," said Walter. "Nothing after the telegram from Paris. No phone calls, probably because he knows we would tell him to get his ass home, or at least keep it out of Africa."

"I'm going over there," said Randall. "Day after tomorrow."

"To Africa?" asked Walter.

"No, to Liechtenstein," said Randall. "I thought I'd look there first."

"If you're going to Africa," Walter said. "I'm adding endorsements to your policies. For you . . . and for Marjorie."

"What kind of endorsements?"

"Health," said Westfall, "life, travel, accident, disability. Anything could happen over there. I won't sleep unless I know you're protected. Your present policies probably exclude most of what goes on over there. For instance, I've never seen an endorsement for damage resulting from black magic or witchcraft."

"I'm covered healthwise, aren't I?"

"You will be when I'm through," said Westfall. "Your preexisting conditions are covered under the conversion option of your firm's old plan. That's a five hundred deductible preferred provider flex plan with 70 percent coverage to five thousand dollars, 80 percent coverage to ten thousand, and a cap of two-fifty. For non-preexisting conditions, you're covered under the firm's new flex plan, which is a one thousand deductible, nonpreferred provider with 80 percent coverage to five thousand, and a million-dollar cap. Of course, during the probationary period, the deductibles are separate and noncumulative, and the exclusionary provisions may overlap, creating a gap we can cover with a supplementary rider and an ancillary, preferred-subscriber premium, which will cover subordinate exclusions and limitations caused by a conflict between the two plans."

"What are you," said Randall, "a fucking lawyer?"

"No," said Walter. "I paid you guys to draft this shit up for me. It costs a fortune to create something this impenetrable. No jury in North America could possibly pretend to understand this stuff. And there's more. Let me see if I can simplify this for you. The long and short of it is, you'll be covered under one plan or the other for accidents and diseases incurred while traveling in the Third World, so long as any treatment you receive is preauthorized by Guaranteed Reliable Investment Mutual Trust Insurance Company, who will also have the sole discretion to determine if your care is obsolete, custodial, caused by a preexisting condition, rendered by a licensed health-care professional, medically necessary, experimental or investigational, or is inconsistent with the diagnosis and treatment of your condition. What do you think?"

"I have to be preauthorized?" asked Randall. "From West Africa?"

"Bring your calling card," said Walter, "that's my advice. No telling what will happen, I don't have a crystal ball on my desk. On the life end, I know you wanted the death benefit of your whole life kicked up. I can do that for you, but the underwriter wants blood, urine, vital signs, medical records, and another two-fifty a month in premiums. I sent you the paperwork. As soon as we get the forms, they'll send a nurse out to your house to collect the specimens."

"Blood?" asked Randall.

"It's not us," said Westfall, "it's the underwriter. You can imagine how careful they have to be with the AIDS thing and all."

"Pound of flesh," muttered Randall.

"Flesh?" said Walter. "They didn't send you a biopsy form, did they? That ain't right. They're not supposed to send you a biopsy form unless something looks funny in your lab work and they need more information. If they sent you a biopsy form, they made a mistake, or maybe they have cannibals working for them over there, I don't know. I'm just trying to jump you through the hoops so your boy and Marjorie will be taken care of if anything happens to you over there."

"Yeah," said Randall. "How much?"

"How much?" said Walter. "Don't ask me that. It gives me nightmares. It reminds me of Larry Banacek. Remember him? That's what he asked me. How much? And it was too much. He canceled his policy. I see his wife in church every Sunday with those four kids. They're in a condo now, and the kids are in public schools. I blame myself," he added. "I shouldn't have let him do it. I should've picked up the extra premiums myself."

Buzz went the intercom.

"Walter, I'll send the forms," said Randall. "I'll give them the blood and the urine, and I'll let you pick up the extra premiums."

"Yeah," said Walter, "and I'll send you a statement of services using your hourly rate."

One button banished Walter Westfall, another admitted Mack.

"Boss," said Mack over the speaker.

"What?" shouted Randall.

"No loaded weapons handy, I hope."

"None," said Randall. "Why? What happened?"

"Beach Cove," said Mack. "They're filing a lender liability suit against us. They're saying we forced them to adopt unsound management practices before we would qualify them for our loans."

Randall felt a cramp forming deep in his chest. At times like these, he could believe what his cardiologist had told him, that the heart is a muscle: it flexes, it cramps, it gets stronger . . . or weaker.

"Charlie," Randall said curtly, and smote the desk with his fist.

"What?" said Mack. "Who's Charlie?"

"Charles de Blois," said Randall, a thunderhead boiling just above his brow. "The Hundred Years' War. He was an ascetic warrior who sought spirituality by mortifying his flesh with knotted cords, wearing coarse garments crawling with lice, and making pilgrimages barefoot in the snow. He loved God, but he also knew how to take a town. One of the few useful things I learned before law school. It's time for the Charlie technique."

"We mortify our flesh?" asked Mack uncertainly.

"Negative," said Randall. "First we capture twenty or thirty prisoners and decapitate them. We roll our siege engines up just below the walls of Beach Cove, then we hurl the heads into the town. That's how Charles de Blois announced his intentions to take the city of Nantes. Nothing short of divine inspiration."

"I'll call Office Services and check on the siege engines," said Mack.

"We're going to countersue the Beach Cove officers individually, personally, for fraud," said Randall, gnashing his teeth and clutching his chest. "Call those financial investigators we have on retainer. I want individual assets—assets bought with Comco money borrowed from our client and paid out in salaries to enemy officers! I want that money back! I want family members. I want trust funds. Children's assets. Everything within a bloodline's reach. I want heady murder, spoil, and villainy! Tell them to watch the blind and bloody soldier with foul hand defile the locks of their shrill-shrieking daughters! With conscience wide as hell, mowing like grass their fresh fair virgins and flowering infants! Their fathers taken by the silver beards, and their most reverend heads dashed to the walls! Naked infants spitted on pikes!"

"Boss," said Mack. "Are you OK?"

(**18**)

Boone squirmed on his tick mattress, panting in the moonlit darkness, soaking his sleeping bag, and making love to Missus Sickness, wondering what would happen if he failed to satisfy her. He longed for an air-conditioned bedroom and a refrigerator filled with cold soda. If he could only rise and throw his legs over the side of a firm mattress, sink his toes into plush carpeting, totter into the bathroom, and draw crystal-clear water from a brass tap into a clean glass— water that had already been purified by filters and engineers in white lab coats—pure, sparkling, potable, treated water, with nothing but trace amounts of PCBs, insecticides, heavy metals, and radioactive substances—all monitored by government agencies and well below federally mandated levels, as measured in parts per million, billion, or trillion. For a glass of such water, he would do such things . . . He could drink as much as he wanted, until his belly was full of cold, clean, chlorinated, fluorinated water. And it would not make him sick, at least not right away.

Back in America, newspapers were coming out every day, and he was not there to read them. Food was being thrown into garbage disposals, and he had nothing but rice and pepper sauce to eat. Billions of megabytes of information were being transmitted by way of modems, fax machines, telephones, and computer screens, and not a single byte came his way. Back in America, his peers were sitting in graduate school classrooms, listening to lectures that would provide them with information and skills they could use to make more money. They were setting and achieving long-range goals. They were acquiring the computer equipment, the sound systems, and the home entertainment modules necessary for co-cooning. And Boone Westfall was absent without pay.

Instead of a one-bedroom apartment with access to a communal pool and tennis courts, he was occupying a cot on a mud floor in West Africa, trapped in a circle of white thread, waiting for an old man in a bathrobe to tell him what to do. He had nothing to eat or drink, and microbial parasites battened on his red blood cells. The never-ending journeys to the latrine had become a long march back and forth from the underworld. He pined for a clean linoleum floor, ceramic tiles, and a porcelain toilet he could fling his arms around, embrace, and be obliviously sick in.

About two in the morning, long after the witchfinder had gone to bed, a fruit bat or some other creature trying to take a mango back to its nest must have dropped its cargo onto one of the pan roofs, and the thunderclap of zinc sent Boone's heart clambering into his throat. The adjacent dwellings disgorged anxious villagers, who seemed convinced that witches were thronging just outside the periphery of human sight, waiting to suck a meal of salty blood from anyone who dropped off, even for an instant. Then a young girl actually saw a witch in the shape of an old woman with the eyes of a leopard, fresh blood dripping from her teeth. A bush spirit hissed at some children on their way back from the latrines. Grandma Dembe reported seeing a Baboon Man stalking the perimeter of the village, its pelt glistening with human fat, its metal claws clotted with human blood.

People assembled around the fire in the *barri* and sent the chief's speaker to rouse the witchfinder. They needed protection *now*. Tomorrow would be too late! The witchfinder sent back word that the villagers had no one but themselves to blame, for it was their own wickedness that had allowed witches to take over their village. Tomorrow, they would see who among them, even now, was pretending they were not witches, while secretly scheming to get at the sequestered infants and mothers.

Meanwhile, sleep was impossible, for it was said that the witches were trapped within the cylinder of cotton thread and swooping through the village, crawking in the shapes of fruit bats, unable to get out into the bush for their night rides, frantic for one last meal of human blood. Others, it was said, were slithering about in the shapes of boa constrictors, their eyes agleam with reptilian cunning, squirming in and out of the mud huts, looking to swallow and paralyze the exposed limb of a villager foolish enough to sleep.

Inside their huts, the villagers huddled around fires, keeping each other awake, and reproaching each other for having bad medicines in the house, which would have to be turned over to the witchfinder when the sun came up. Boone spent the night sweating and panting to the beat of banging pots and pans whenever hysterical villagers ran between the compounds trying to scare away the kaw-kaw witch birds with curses and loud noises. He dozed and dreamed of the African bush, where out on the farms the sky was swarming with flying creatures. A coven of witches soared overhead riding night birds and winnowing fans, suddenly spotting crops to eat, and landing as a pack of cutting grasses. Armies of them fell on the farms like locusts, devouring the rice pods and clustering under the fronded palms, sucking red palm oil from the palm nuts. He heard the savage cry of an ancestor who had never crossed the river to the village of white sands. Stone *nomoloi* sprang to life as fleshy dwarves with clubs and cutlasses, and a ferocious battle broke out over the crops. The dwarves hacked the cutting grasses, which were howling and gnawing at the ankles of their attackers. Soon the night was fraught with battles on land and air, for when the dwarves wrestled the cutting grasses to the ground, strangled them, and tore the carcasses open, out flew witch birds and fruit bats whose shapes darkened the face of the moon and whose wings thrashed the umbels of the palm trees.

Dawn found Boone anemic and weak as a wet kitten, fever still burning in his joints. The villagers guarded the doors, windows, and crevices of their homes with bamboo witch guns and nets, anxiously discussing whether their particular bad medicine was one of those covered by the witchfinder's decree.

By midmorning, the witchfinder's assistants had the fire going under the cauldron, and the villagers were staggering about in a stupor of exhaustion and anxiety. The two dozen or so innocents who had no bad medicines of any kind had assembled in the *barri* as instructed. The other two hundred or so citizens were still surreptitiously visiting respected elders, seeking opinions about whether the particular medicine in their possession would have to be turned over.

By noon, the guilty ones began coming forward. They approached the witchfinder with their medicines hidden in a paper, wrapped in cloths, or concealed in their garments. They tried to place the parcel on the ground next to the witchfinder's feet, or alongside the boiling cauldron, in the fond hope that they could scurry to their seats before being identified as the owners. But the witchfinder stopped each person with his mirrored staff. He tapped them gently with the meat of it, ignoring their whispered pleas for forgiveness and anonymity, turning them this way and that, until they faced the seated throng. Then, while the villager hung his or her head in a yoke of shame—the witchfinder held the reprobate's medicine aloft for all the assembly to see: bags of animal parts and bottles of putrefied concoctions, bundles of rags soaked in grume or excretions, balls of magic string, the dried claws or gizzards of fowls, bindles of herbs and vials of animal fat, horns of animals containing bits of ribbons, feathers, old razor blades, human hair and fingernail clippings, or pestled cowrie shells; Arabic writings sewn into cloths, pouches of gecko or snake heads, scrotiform bags of animal genitals, boa constrictor skins, even, at last, a petrified human foot.

The villagers came forward with their secret medicines and hung their heads in shame, sheepish old grandmas, once-dignified old pas, remorseful adolescents, distraught young wives, disgraced big wives—almost everyone had some pathetic fetish, which was held up for all the village to see. When the witchfinder was handed a particularly hideous talisman of bezoars, or animal offal, or a satchel of human body parts, he accepted it with a sad shake of his head, as if, no matter how many times he had seen such misanthropic confections, he still could hardly bear to imagine what dark thoughts and wicked intentions had spawned them. Affecting a wounded, anguished look, he paraded the pathetic mess up and down, as if to say, "See what human beings do when they are alone at night! See what ghastly deformities they pray over in hopes of bringing evil into the houses of their neighbors!"

Shaking the medicine in the face of its owner, the witchfinder then cast it into the cauldron, where a mound of accumulated rubbish was half submerged in a slow-boiling greenish broth. Then the witchfinder reached out with his staff and held the mirror in front of the culprit's face. "Na who dat?" he would ask. "Who dat you see?" The witchfinder came alongside and looked into the mirror, assuming a sad and piteous countenance almost matching the offender's doleful expression. Then, with a flick of his wrist, the mirror was used to show the reprobate the witchfinder's face, and, when he had the person's reflection in the mirror, he would say, "Look me face. See your mother," and tears would well up into the witchfinder's eyes as he assumed the sad face of a bitterly disappointed mother. Or he would say, "See me face. Look your wife," and put on a stricken mien, looking for all the world like the brokenhearted spouse of an unfaithful Mende man. "Look me face. See your father," he said to another, and cast his features in a patriarchal scowl.

If the villager cast his eyes down to avoid the accusatory stare, the witchfinder simply adjusted the mirror and patiently waited until the culprit opened his eyes. "Look me face. Your small-small peekin dae."

On it went into the tropical afternoon. The witchfinder took each amulet, greasy pouch, or bottle of poison and held it aloft, denouncing its owner and the social depravity which brought the bric-a-brac into being.

By day's end, the cauldron had a mound of charms, pouches, bundles, and balls of rags and string in it. And all the villagers were assembled, properly chagrined and afraid to look at one another. As evening fell, and the huge red tropical sun went down over the palm trees, the witchfinder stirred the pot and wept into it, sobbing and crying out against the darkness of the human heart.

"Soon," he said, "the real work will begin. Not one bundle of *ndilei* medicine has been turned over. But don't worry! The witchfinder will find each and every one! And last of all, the witchfinder will find the witch pot where the bundles of witch medicine draw their nourishment and strength."

The witchfinder stirred the pot and pointed at the setting sun. "Soon it will be too late for all witches!"

Moiwo and his men, who had all assembled as instructed but had turned over nothing in the way of medicine, fell into a hushed and heated discussion. Moiwo angrily rebuked one of his underlings, a man in a white military beret, who regarded the witchfinder with terror and quaked at his every pronouncement. The man's uniformed fellows steadied him and whispered urgently into his ear, but he pushed them away.

The assistants brought a long pole of the sort the women used for pestling rice, which had a pad or a bundle fixed to one end.

"This pestle will lead us to all the *ndilei* medicine in the village," the witchfinder announced. "And anyone who has not turned over bad medicine will be punished."

The witchfinder stirred the cauldron and looked over his shoulder at the setting sun. "Soon it will be too late for anyone who has hidden bad medicines!"

The man in the beret cried out, but was led over to the Land-Rover by Moiwo's men, resisting and pleading with his handlers.

Moiwo, who no longer wore his military uniform, but instead had donned a robe of country cloth and a necklace of cowries, stayed behind and addressed the witchfinder.

"Of course, I appreciate the great and good work the witchfinder is doing for this village. And although, as the witchfinder knows, I am quite busy with election business, I am happy to stay in this village, so that I and my family can participate in the witch cleansing. But my assistant is not a Mende man. He is from the Koranko tribe. He has no bad medicine, but he is still afraid, because he holds the witchfinder's powers in such high regard."

"If he is not a witch, and he has no bad medicine," the witchfinder said, "then he has nothing to fear."

"He is afraid the witchfinder might make a mistake and falsely accuse him of witchcraft or of bad medicine," said Moiwo.

"That," said the witchfinder, "is impossible. Bad medicine is either found in the person's possession or in his quarters, or it is not found. Mistakes are impossible."

Moiwo wandered closer to the *barri*, taking in the crowd with a sweep of his arm. "But I am sure that my Mende brothers and sisters have heard of instances where someone has been falsely accused of practicing witchcraft, or of having bad medicine, or even of cases," he said, pausing meaningfully, "where the witchfinder's powers were not real, but only illusions and trickery."

Moiwo nodded at the witchfinder. "I know that you are the most powerful witchfinder in Sierra Leone. I know you have only good and honest intentions and would never use simple tricks to make us believe you had certain powers we should pay money for," he said. "But some say that it is time for us to move beyond these superstitions and enter the modern world. Part of what I will try to do as Paramount Chief is free the people from this constant fear of witch business, of swear and counter-swear. Some say that even the most powerful witchfinder may sometimes use trickery and deception," said Moiwo with a smile, "if it serves his purposes," he added with a polite bow. "But of course I hope I know you better than that."

He bowed and grinned knowingly at the witchfinder.

Without breaking his gaze, the witchfinder put out his hand. His assistant brought the tray and the dagger.

"Come closer," said the witchfinder to Moiwo. "I want you to be sure of your eyes."

Moiwo shrugged his shoulders and half laughed, half sighed as he stepped closer to the witchfinder.

"Your eyes," said the witchfinder. "They are good eyes?"

"Of course," said Moiwo, holding the stare constant and smiling, "I have good eyes. My eyes would like to examine the witchfinder's mouth before he does any . . . work with the dagger."

"Good," said the witchfinder. "I want you to see inside my mouth." A pink cave hung with teeth opened, and he turned his cheeks out with his fingers.

The witchfinder seized the dagger from the tray and engaged Moiwo's eyes.

"You say, your eyes, they're good?"

"Very good," said Moiwo confidently.

Without a trace of rancor, the witchfinder said, "Something in my belly tells me that you do not believe in the witchfinder's powers."

The witchfinder held his robe against his stomach and placed the point of his dagger just below his sternum.

"But of course I do . . ." began Moiwo.

The witchfinder opened his mouth and screamed. One violent gouge of the knife opened his robe and his belly, allowing his assistant to catch intestines as they spilled out onto the platter, loops of viscera and membranes tumbling into a mound, followed by a fold of what appeared to be the omentum or the peritoneum.

The crowd in the *barri* screamed in terror, turning their faces aside and retching. Moiwo drew a sharp breath and put his hand over his mouth. Boone and Lewis jumped to their feet trying to inspect the opening in the garment, as the assistant pulled the last loops onto the platter, then hoisted the platter like a waiter in a restaurant and showed the pile of intestines to the crowd. The villagers gagged and clutched their children to their bosoms, struck dumb with wonder and fear. The second assistant brought a towel, which was inserted into the torn burnoose and used to wipe the witchfinder's belly. Boone shook with a hot flash and sat down, swallowing the gastric acid that had welled into the back of his throat.

The witchfinder smiled at Moiwo.

"I have removed the part that told me of your disbelief," he said innocently. Then, gesturing to the man in the white beret, who had been led away, the witchfinder said, "Perhaps you or your man would like to examine the witchfinder's belly and see that no trickery has been done."

He held open his rent garment, showing Moiwo and the crowd his smooth, thin, unblemished abdomen.

He clapped his hands, and one of the assistants provided him with his mirrored staff. "Perhaps I should ask the man questions now, so we can get a head start on our work and learn if he has anything to fear."

"That won't be necessary," Moiwo demurred. "I have never doubted the witchfinder's powers. I simply was remarking that sometimes mistakes have been made," he said with a nervous smile, "by other, perhaps less experienced, witchfinders." Then he bowed to the witchfinder and to the crowd and returned to his men.

The witchfinder dipped his staff into the cauldron and stirred. Dusk fell and the *barri* was lit only by glowing coals under the cauldron. The witchfinder sent his assistants to be certain that everyone in the village was assembled in the *barri*, except the nursing and expectant mothers. No one had slept the night before, and no one had eaten all day, as if the knotted stomachs of the villagers could have tolerated food.

When it was confirmed that all were present, the witchfinder sat in a chair with his back to the fire and to the crowd. He held his staff aloft, so he could look into the mirror and direct the firelight onto the faces of the villagers.

"Witches have been eating the children of this village," said the witchfinder calmly, the flames dartling shadows in the hollows of his face. "When mothers are sleeping at night, witches crawl from under the beds and poke their fangs into the soft skulls of the peekins."

A woman in the crowd cried out, then wept aloud for her lost child.

"It is time for us to identify witches," said the witchfinder gravely. "They are here with us. Right now! Hiding inside their human shapes! Why? Because they hope to eat more children. They want to suck children out of their mothers' bellies like the yolk of eggs, and eat the souls before they can be born!

"This pestle will find all the bad medicine in the village. We will find the witches," he said, smiling into his firelit mirror. "And after we find them, we will find the head witch and the witch pot! Woe to those who have hidden medicine from the witchfinder, they will be found out tonight!"

The huge tropical sun winked and sank below the bush. The witchfinder attended his pot, stirring with his staff and peering sadly into its swirling depths, as if he stared into the pooling oversoul of the village, a sinkhole where the lust, filth, hatred, and vengeance of all had collected. He wept into the cauldron, his tears glistening on his cheeks like tinsel in the firelight. He cried out against the wickedness of the human heart.

"Oh, mothers and fathers, grandmothers, grandfathers, sons, and daughters, this is what we have brought out from under our beds, fetched from our sacks and bundles, dug from holes in the earth, and stolen from animals in the bush. Listen to this wicked soup slap the sides of my pot! Hear this vile broth whisper with our dark desires! Smell the awful confections we prayed over in the hopes of destroying our neighbors! Look! Look what fearsome gruel has oozed forth from the wounds of our hearts!"

When darkness fell, the witchfinder sat with his back toward the crowd and twirled his mirror in the firelight. Everyone tried to avoid the witchfinder's reflection in the mirror and instead talked quietly to one another, or whispered about what might happen if witches were discovered in the village.

Boone could not see the witchfinder's face, because the mirror was aimed at the other half of the assembly. After a while, the mirror was completely still and the witchfinder stared into it for some time. Distressed murmurings erupted in the vicinity of the witchfinder's aim. The witchfinder stared without moving, then slowly raised his arm and pointed into the mirror. A hushed cry went up as Pa Usman, the man in the torn stocking cap whom Boone and Sisay had found in the bush with his stone dwarf, stood, loudly protesting and shaking his head. He quaked with fear, and strenuously shouted to those around him, throwing up his arms to proclaim his innocence of any witch business.

"The witchfinder has a suspect who needs to be interviewed," he announced.

Pa Usman? the villagers seemed to be saying in anxious disbelief.

The witchfinder showed the way with his staff, and led Pa Usman away to a neighboring courtyard, where they were hidden from the view of those in the *barri*. Small groups formed to debate the outrageous possibility that Pa Usman was somehow connected with witch business. Impossible, concluded most of the villagers. They had known him all their lives, and he was an infirm, slightly touched old man, who would not harm a driver ant, let alone a child.

Twenty minutes later, the witchfinder returned with Pa Usman in tow, the latter weeping and hiding his face in his stocking cap.

"This man has confessed to taking part in witch business," declared the witchfinder, showing Pa Usman to his seat.

The villagers gasped and stared, unable to look at the monster that had been masquerading as a kind old man for years. "There must be some mistake!" some still said. "How does the witchfinder even know what the old man is saying?"

The witchfinder summoned his assistants, who picked up the pestle and were immediately propelled, seemingly against their will, from one end of the courtyard to the other. They held on to it, throwing their heads back and gritting their teeth in their desperate efforts to control the headlong flight of the pestle. After a few minutes, the padded end of the pestle stopped at the door of Pa Usman's shed of zinc pan.

"I must have two witnesses who will come and prove that the *ndilei* medicine is indeed found," cried the witchfinder.

Lewis jumped to his feet and waved. "I am a witness!" Under his breath, he said to Boone, "I'll catch this runt in one of his tricks. Just watch."

The witchfinder summoned Lewis and another villager from the crowd. Together with the assistants and Usman himself, they entered the shed. A short while later, they emerged—the witchfinder bearing a small football-shaped black bundle of tightly wrapped rags or skins with a red tube sticking out of it and two cowrie shells sewn onto it.

As soon as the thing appeared the crowd gasped in horror.

"*Ndilei!*" the witchfinder cried, holding the bundle aloft in the light of the fire. "This pa was keeping *ndilei* medicine right under your very noses! Who knows how many infants this medicine has killed? Look at the cowrie shells and count the infant dead!"

The *barri* erupted in a clamor, some few still saying that Pa Usman, a man who had been born and raised in this village, could not possibly have a witch in his belly. But others shook their heads, whispered, and clucked their tongues, as if to say, "It just goes to show you, it's always those you least suspect!" Some reminded themselves about how Usman had started speaking nonsense some years back; how he seemed to be spending too much time in the bush with his *nomoloi*; how he was always sitting alone in his shed; and how some of these behaviors were suggestive. And if he was not a witch, why would he have a bundle of *ndilei* medicine in his shed?

Lewis returned to the *barri* and reported that, indeed, the assistants had actually discovered the black bundle inside Usman's pillow. Now the *barri* was filled with the wailing of women whose infants had recently died. Other old pas shouted reproachfully and pointed at the bundle the witchfinder still held aloft.

After things died down, the witchfinder displayed the *ndilei* once more, then dramatically hurled it into the simmering cauldron. A single cry issued from the impact: a mew of a cat, or the strangled cry of an infant, cut off. The sound brought the crowd's hysteria back with a vengeance, as people hugged each other in terror and stared into the cauldron in speechless awe.

The witchfinder sat with his back to the cauldron and the crowd. He twirled his staff and mirror, burnishing the upturned faces with firelight. People whispered anxiously and hid their eyes. The staff seemed to pause occasionally as the mirror searched and moved on. Then it came to rest. Another subdued murmur erupted in that vicinity of the crowd. The witchfinder raised his arm and pointed into the mirror.

This time, a feeble and skinny old woman rose to her feet, protesting weakly and attempting to wave the mirror away. Boone recognized her as the toothless old grandma with no fingers who had asked him and Sisay for medicine on his naming day. Grandma Dembe, the leper. She wept and shook her head, then held her arms and fingerless hands out to the crowd in supplication.

The witchfinder summoned her aside for the interview and returned with her a short time later, cordially showing her to her seat, then returning to his place next to the cauldron.

"This woman has confessed to taking part in witch business," announced the witchfinder.

The villagers moved away from Grandma Dembe and shook their heads in horror and disbelief, looking to her relatives for some explanation of how a kindly old grandmother, who had been singing songs to their children and grandchildren for as long as anyone could remember, was a witch. Was the world coming to an end? Had *Ngewo* and their ancestors left the village completely defenseless against the wiles of witches? How had this depraved witch so cunningly disguised herself? She had bathed their children, given them medicines, prayed, sang, laughed, and cried with them!

The witchfinder clapped his hands, the assistants picked up their pestle and were seemingly dragged about the village, as they dug in their heels and groaned with the effort needed to keep the powerful pestle under their control. No one was surprised when the club end of the pestle stopped at the door of the compound where Grandma Dembe lived and waited there, barely able to hold itself still long enough for someone to open the door and call the witnesses.

The witchfinder escorted Grandma Dembe, so she could be present for the search. After a few minutes, the assistants emerged with a red-spouted black bundle, and the mere sight of it filled the *barri* with squeals of horror and violent accusations. Small groups of bewildered and mortified villagers pleaded frantically with themselves, wondering how this could be so, that a gentle, sickly old woman who loved to tell the children stories in the baffas at night had been hiding witch medicine in her house! Had she turned the thing loose at night as a fruit bat or a boa constrictor to eat their unborn children!?

The witchfinder held the bundle aloft, and then, staff twirling and robe swirling, he flung it into the cauldron, whence the same stifled cry issued, sounding for all the world like the soul of an infant calling to its mother from some netherworld far out in the bush. More panic and frenzy, as the families of the witch people wept and implored their neighbors for forgiveness. "How were we to know? Would we let such a thing in our house?"

The crowd calmed itself down to a chorus of sobs and whispers reminiscent of a funeral or a deathbed vigil, and the witchfinder sat backwards and twirled his staff. This time, the blazing mirror traveled to the side of the *barri* where the *poo-muis* were sitting, and Boone was able to see the face of the witchfinder, which he had imagined would be focused in scrutiny on the faces of the crowd. He was surprised to discover that the witchfinder's expressions were quite animated, and that he seemed to change the look on his face each time he studied a different person, first sad to the point of weeping, then moving the mirror and silently laughing, then moving it, and looking askance at someone as if to ask, "Why are you looking at me?"

Then Boone realized with a shudder colder than his fever chills that he could see the witchfinder's face, because the witchfinder was staring at *him* in his mirror!

Boone quickly looked away, pretending to survey the crowd, or to watch the steam rising from the cauldron. But when he glanced back, the witchfinder was staring at him, this time wearing a look of absolute despair, as if the witchfinder were saying, "Why are you acting this way?" Boone looked up into the thatched roof of the *barri*, only to glance back and find a silent, uproarious laugh adorning the witchfinder's face. Boone pretended he had something to say to Lewis, and when he looked back into the witchfinder's flickering mirror, he found a face contorted with loathing and disgust: "How can a monster like you wear the shape of a human being?" the face seemed to be saying.

Then the witchfinder raised his arm and pointed at Boone in the mirror. Boone saw the eyes of the villagers turn on him and stare in horror.

"No," Lewis said. "You can't accuse a white man. That's impossible!"

"This is insanity!" cried Boone. He looked out over the crowd and shook his head into their reproachful stares. Heads turned together and whispered.

Sisay rose to speak, but the witchfinder silenced him with a gesture.

"The witchfinder will talk to the *poo-mui, alone*," he said in English. "The witchfinder lahrned his Engleesh," he added with a grin.

They went together to a neighboring baffa, where a solitary hurricane lamp burned on a rude table. The witchfinder sat at the table with his back to Boone and the mirror of his staff facing away from him. Boone could see blood pulsing in the vessels under the smooth scalp.

"What do you think about when you are alone?" asked the witchfinder in quite good English.

"What does that mean?" Boone retorted, staring at the back of the blue burnoose. "I think about how to find my best friend."

"Ah," said the witchfinder. "You think about your brother. If you found him, you would be happy, notoso?"

"That's why I'm here," said Boone.

"I see," said the witchfinder, twirling his staff until the mirror held a reflection of his huge eyes lit like dark pools by the hurricane lamp. "I see," he said, holding Boone's eyes in the mirror.

"You are here to find your brother," he said. "That is what you think about. If not for your brother, you would never have come to Sierra Leone. And if he cannot be found, or if he is dead, you will leave."

"I hope to find him," said Boone. "I don't like this witch interview or whatever it is," he added, with a shudder. "Those people back there think you brought me over here because . . . because I'm some kind of witch."

"Don't worry," said the witchfinder. "I did not bring you here because you are a witch. I must have words with you in private. I have a message from men who are holding your brother in the bush. If you want to see your brother alive, you must agree to feed certain powerful medicines."

The mirror swiveled slightly and the witchfinder stared at him.

"What is this *feeding* shit?" quavered Boone. "Is anybody going to tell me what it means?"

"You must bring a human victim to feed the medicine," said the witchfinder. "Then you must join the society and take the vow on the medicine. After that, both you and your brother will be allowed to return to his village, or even, if you like, return to America."

"That's nuts," said Boone, looking into the mirror, expecting to see the witchfinder's face but instead finding his own. "That's crazy. I'm supposed to give them a victim? A human being? I can't lead a human being off to be killed. Who am I supposed to give to them? You?"

"The victim has already been chosen," said the witchfinder. "You only must bring her and . . . prepare her. Others will do the feeding."

"Kill her?" asked Boone. "You want me to kill somebody?"

He could see the pupils of the witchfinder's eyes in the mirror, black contractile nodes, probing him like fingers.

"Her head will be covered," said the witchfinder. "You must only strike the blow."

"Oh," said Boone sarcastically. "Why didn't you say so! That makes it easy!"

"If you do not," said the witchfinder, "I assure you these men will kill your brother and use him to feed the medicine instead."

"I can't do it," said Boone. "Where I come from, that's called murder."

"This is Africa," said the witchfinder. "Things are different here." He chuckled. "And they are the same. Sometimes lives must be sacrificed for the good of the village. Lives are traded all the time, even in your country."

"I won't do it," said Boone.

"As you will soon learn," the witchfinder continued, "the woman Jenisa, the young wife of Section Chief Moiwo, is a witch."

He reached down beside him in the darkness, brought forth another one of the small black bundles of *ndilei* medicine, and set it on the table in the lamplight. Instead of a red spout this one appeared to have a white one, until Boone got a better look at it and saw that, sticking out of the top of the bundle, was the applicator of mosquito repellent he had given the woman named Jenisa.

"That's got nothing to do with me," Boone protested. "It's mosquito repellent."

"It *was* mosquito cream," said the witchfinder. "Now it's a very bad medicine. Now it is witch medicine."

"I gave it to her as a gift," said Boone. "Somebody else made it into this bundle. I told you, it's got nothing to do with me."

Sweat issued from his pores and fever gusted through him like a blast from a furnace.

"She had this bundle of *ndilei* medicine buried near the widow Luba's house. This woman Jenisa wants to kill the widow Luba because she is the head witch," said the witchfinder. "Neither of them would be a great loss to the village. You only must deliver the woman at the appointed place and at the appointed time. If you do not, your brother will be fed to the medicine. And then, later, when it is time for another feeding, one of the other members, or a new initiate, will deliver the woman Jenisa, and she will be killed anyway."

"This is impossible," said Boone, sweating with fever and agitation. "Even if I agreed, I barely know the woman. I can't ask her to go for a walk in the bush. She would never go."

"That is arranged," said the witchfinder. "You will be told to offer a sacrifice for your brother at a place not far from here where there is a huge cotton tree. The woman Jenisa's family offers sacrifice there to her ancestors. It will be suggested that she should lead you to the spot, and there you will feed her to the medicine."

"Murder her?" he said. "Impossible."

He ground his teeth and pondered his options. Maybe there was a way of doing this thing, he thought, desperately turning alternatives over in his mind. Maybe there was a way to play along with this, until he actually found Killigan. Then maybe they could all flee, or he could rescue the woman somehow. Maybe he should at least pretend to agree. Otherwise, it appeared, two lives would be lost instead of one.

He drew a breath to speak and looked up, only to find that the witchfinder had unobtrusively lifted his staff and was studying him in the lamplit mirror.

"Do you know that the witchfinder can see the thoughts of others?" he said with a smile. "Good, evil, humans in animal form, witches, I can see everything."

Boone stared at the witchfinder's face in the dark mirror.

"Don't worry about your conscience," the face said. "As long as you feed it, the medicine will let you believe anything you wish. It will speak to your conscience. Will you feed the medicine?"

Boone stared at the face and reconsidered.

"Sometimes you must be evil before you can be good. Notoso?"

"I am not evil," said Boone. "I'm just a visitor."

"Visitors can be very evil," said the witchfinder. "Besides, I don't care about good or evil. They are exactly the same to me. I've seen them poured into one soup after another, and they are both the same. I don't prefer one over the other. I'm paid to find witches. And do you know what? I always find them. Do you know why? My grandfathers and *Ngewo* gave me the power to see witches no matter where they are hiding."

The witchfinder flicked his mirror and spun it skillfully aloft.

"I look for witches in the bush. I look for witches in the village. And," he said, finding Boone's eyes with his mirror, "I look for witches inside other people."

The witchfinder smiled steadily into his mirror.

"I am *gbese*, the one born after twins. Nothing human or inhuman is hidden from me. I can see witches as plainly as you see me now," he said. "Can you see me?"

Boone swallowed and nodded his head.

"Witches think only of themselves. They are very easy to detect. They are so hungry for infants, especially unborn ones, that they are almost climbing out of their skins at the thought of eating infant flesh and drinking blood. They devour innocence."

The witchfinder stopped talking suddenly and flicked his mirror away, leaving Boone staring at the back of his head.

"Must I go on?"

"With what?" asked Boone.

"Are you hungry for innocence?"

"What are you talking about?"

"You are a witch," said the witchfinder. "You have three brothers. They also are witches, and your father is the head witch of the coven. There could be more brothers and sisters, but they were probably bargained away as victims for witch rituals."

"I am not a witch," said Boone, shaking suddenly and violently under the intense scrutiny of the witchfinder, because the witchfinder had somehow gotten the number of brothers right.

"I have been a witchfinder for a very long time. I must tell you that I have never heard a witch confess to witchcraft. A witch will *always* deny witchcraft," he said with a smile. "Until I force them to confess. Take you, for instance. You would probably never show yourself to the village. I would have to make you do it by telling you that unless you confess your true nature to this village, you will never see your brother alive again."

"I am not a witch," insisted Boone. "And if you want me to go back there and confess to witchcraft, I will not. And I will not take another person to be killed, not even for my best friend."

"Even white men must feed their medicines," said the witchfinder. "What about this *poo-mui* ancestor named Abraham? God's medicine was hungry. God asked Abraham to feed the medicine with the flesh of his own son. And Abraham was willing."

"That's not right," said Boone, "you're . . ."

"What about the first *poo-mui* ancestors? God told Adam and Eve they could eat all the food on earth, but not the fruit of a certain tree, because God used that fruit to feed His medicine. You see?"

"No," said Boone.

"I am told that white men build large houses with rods of powerful medicine in them. These rods make a fire that never goes out, and this fire heats the wires that make machines go. But I am also told that sometimes the medicine escapes from the rods and goes in search of people to burn and eat. I can tell you that if you would simply feed the medicine a victim from time to time, it would stop trying to feed itself.

"I am also told that *poo-mui* women feed their unborn babies to witches and white medicine men, so that medicines can be made from their bodies. And how about the medicines the white man puts on his crops to keep witches away and make them grow? Doesn't the medicine then go in search of human lives when it is hungry? Doesn't it put spells on the village wells and poison the children in the *poo-mui* villages? So what is to stop you from bringing one person who will soon be dead anyway?"

Boone almost said yes, just to see what would happen. Could he say yes, and still back out at a later time? Would he be setting something in motion that could not be stopped? Suppose he played along, telling himself he could back out of it if anything went wrong, until he got to the clearing with her and was forced to trade her for his best friend?

"Maybe I can do it," said Boone, catching a glimmer of himself in the mirror. "At least, I'll try."

The witchfinder gently rolled the staff in his fingertips and focused on Boone's reflection. He stared at Boone in the mirror, and Boone stared back. Then the witchfinder grinned so hard he showed his teeth and hissed through them, "Scat."

"It was you!" cried Boone, suddenly remembering the orange eyes in the bush behind the latrine.

"We must return," said the witchfinder. "We will talk later."

Boone looked toward the *barri*. "When we go back there," Boone said, "what will you tell them?"

The witchfinder focused on Boone's face by way of the mirror. "Don't worry. I will tell them nothing. I will simply move on to the next suspect."

The witchfinder held Boone's stare in the mirror and grinned. "You have a very strong want," whispered the witchfinder. "You want to find your brother. This want is a witch that has laid an egg."

The witchfinder jumped to his feet.

"Come," he said. "We are returning to the *barri*."

Boone's fever roared, his knees cracked as he walked. He had to go to bed before he died on his feet.

Once back in the *barri*, he saw their eyes look away from him.

They whispered, cringed, turned from him, everyone except Lewis.

"It's OK," Boone said to him. "I'll explain later."

When he looked up, he saw that the assistants had grabbed the pestle and were being pulled about the village, in and out of courtyards, in between the compounds, back around the *barri*, until they stopped in front of Sisay's house, then followed the tug of the pestle to the door of Boone's room.

"Come!" cried the witchfinder.

"Hey," said Boone. "You said we were just going to . . . move on. What are you doing?"

Boone, Sisay, and Lewis followed the witchfinder to the door, where they were allowed to go in first. Then, as the witchfinder held the door open, the pestle led the assistants straight to Boone's bed.

"Open it," said the witchfinder, pointing at the blue nylon sleeping bag.

Boone unzipped the length of the bag and flung it open, finding a black bundle of rags with the same white spout of mosquito repellent sticking out of the top. Either there were two identical bundles or somehow the witchfinder had moved the same one from the courtyard to his sleeping bag!

"You lied to me!" Boone said, shaking with fury and indignation.

"See this spout," the witchfinder said to Lewis and Sisay. "This is the straw that allows him to drink the blood of the infants he eats!"

The assistants blocked Boone with the pestle while the witchfinder snatched up the *ndilei* and marched out of the room, triumphantly holding it aloft as he strode back to the *barri*.

Boone collapsed on the bed, panting with fever.

"What a crock of shit!" cried Lewis. "You can't let him do this to a white man!" said Lewis, touching Sisay's elbow.

Sisay shook off Lewis and looked at Boone without expression.

"They don't believe I actually had witch medicine in here," Boone yelled at Sisay, "do they?"

"During your interview, most of them were saying they would not be the least surprised," he said levelly. "Because that would explain why you always wanted to be alone with it in your room. And why you don't care about anybody or anything except finding your own precious brother!"

"Christ!" screamed Boone, covering his face with his hands. "That son of a bitch conned me! He was trying to get me to deliver a victim to a bunch of murderers! He was telling me I had to feed some fucking medicine!"

"Quiet," snapped Sisay, cocking his head. "He's talking about you. He says that you not only killed Mama Saso's twins, who died the night after you came, but that you also offered to deliver a young woman of the village to the Baboon Men."

Boone leapt out of his bed and ran out to the *barri*, shouting and cursing the witchfinder, who was still displaying the *ndilei*, describing how it had surely siphoned the blood of Mama Saso's twins the night they died.

"Infant blood, my ass! You charlatan! If anybody's a witch, it's you!"

Before Boone reached the *barri*, the witchfinder spoke to his assistant, who stooped and produced a wooden mallet. The witchfinder faced Boone with the mallet in one hand and the *ndilei* medicine in the other. He set the black bundle on a stump in front of him and gestured for Boone to come stand across from him.

"You don't believe this *ndilei* medicine contains the blood of infants who died in this village?" asked the witchfinder.

"No, I don't!" raged Boone, ready to spit in the old man's face.

But before he could, the witchfinder lifted the mallet over his head with both hands and brought it down full force on the bundle, which splattered Boone and everyone else in a ten-foot radius with blood. The crowd screamed in horror and erupted in commotion, as people fled from the *barri*.

Boone was blinded by the sticky stuff and wiped his face with his hands, only to find that they were soaked and he was daubing more of it into his eyes. He turned and staggered back toward Sisay's compound, freezing when he felt a hand take him by the upper arm.

"Lewis?" he asked hopefully.

"Mistah Gutawa," said an African voice. "We take you to your brothah now. We must leave the village now."

"Who are you?" Boone asked, resisting the hands that were escorting him. "Where are we going? Did Michael Killigan send you?"

Boone managed to clear some of the grume from his eyes, and promptly saw he was walking between two men. He daubed once more at his eyes, but before he could open them, a heavy, foul-smelling sack was thrown over his head. It had the stench of a dead animal. When he opened his mouth to scream, a ragged husk was wedged into it, which allowed him to breathe and scream, but kept him from closing his mouth to form words. He raised his arms to fight, but they were seized by strong hands and pinned.

Men were now pulling the sack over his head and torso, while others were winding ropes or lashings of some kind about his waist and chest. He tried to throw himself on the ground and roll away from them, but the same strong arms and hands held him up.

"Tie claws on his hands," he heard someone say.

He screamed, vainly trying to form words; instead he was forced to shriek wordlessly from the back of his throat, like a raging primate, through jaws that were propped open. Hands seemed to be positioning the sack on his head, and he realized, as he opened his sticky eyes, that the head cover was fitted with eyeholes of some kind, for he caught a glimpse of firelight, or a torch. He continued struggling as his hands were individually bound. It seemed that his captors had placed a handle in each of his hands, and were tying it, binding it to him.

He shrieked as loudly as he could, but "Help!" came out "He-eh-ahhhh!"

Then he was suddenly set free. He could see out of one eyehole, and he spun around, looking for his assailants. But no one was near, only a crowd of villagers coming from the *barri* and pointing at him.

When he looked through the eyeholes at his arms, he saw iron claws. He looked down at his chest and found that he had been fitted, not with a sack, but with a pelt of some kind, which was lashed so tightly to him it pinched when he gasped for air.

He looked up in time to see the mob approach. He saw them snatch up cutlasses and farming implements, staves and rocks.

"Baboon Man! Baboon Man! Baboon Man!" they screamed, pointing at him and brandishing weapons.

"Baboon Man!"

He turned and fled, taking a path out of the village, breaking the white cotton thread in his flight, and lunging headlong down a steep incline into the bush.

(**19**)

The path fell beneath his feet and lowered him into darkness and the hush of vegetation.

He tore at the animal skin with his claws and promptly blinded himself by knocking the eyeholes askew. Without breaking stride, he batted at the hood until his eyes found the apertures; then he slashed and stabbed at the lashings on his torso, wounding himself instead of the bindings with his rude iron claws.

At the next rise, he stopped and strained to hear if the villagers had followed him across the boundary, but he was deafened by the sound of his own rasping struggles for air resounding inside the hood. The moon lit the top of the bush and showed him a dark slot where the path proceeded, but he had to grope for the contours of the terrain with his charging feet. Fever roared in his chest, and sweat stung his eyes. He failed in another attempted purchase on the hood with his claws. He tore what tasted like a palm kernel or coconut shell from his mouth, and sucked air into his lungs, coughing on debris, almost tasting the dead-animal stench of the hood.

He ran down into a hollow where the path widened, and the canopy of bush parted over a clearing of trampled grass. Streaming light at once gave him back his sight and made him feel suddenly visible. He took a step back into shadows and gasped for breath.

Trunks, stalks, and branches drooped lobes and blades around him. For one irrational moment, he wondered if he could look into the shimmering leaves and study his reflection, see the baboon hood they had tied on his head. He shivered and felt like a small human animal cowering at the edge of a cage of woven bush, illuminated from above by wanton boys and girls shining torches through the eye of a dome. Maybe, as the parables say, the moon and the stars are lamps lit by the ancestors so they can see what the living do under cover of darkness, hung in the sky so that the children of the dead will know that even at night their deeds are on display.

He stopped in the clearing and seemed to feel his auditory nerves growing out of his ears, through his hood, and into the bush in search of sound, stimulation, any auditory confirmation that he was a human being with the power to move through physical space. Next he felt hair growing, not only from his head, but from his body as well—the same fine hair that covered his arms and legs, the backs of his hands, and the tops of his feet now sprouted from his skin and unfurled in the night air, forming long silken tendrils that climbed like ivy into the overgrowth, innervating the bush with fibers attached to his skin.

If something stirred afoot, instead of being able to hear it, he would feel it, disturbing the threads of the web he had spun into the night. Maybe fever had burned out the hair cells in his inner ear, and now he was profoundly deaf, submerged in a sea of palpable soundlessness, breathing liquid stillness. The trampled grass seemed almost bioluminescent, lighting his way on his journey across the floor of the ocean bush, with noctilucas bobbing around him, waving their glowing flagella at him from the depths of the night.

He held his breath and listened to silence, shivering, though he could feel the heat of fever and flight coming off of him in waves. He drew a single deep breath and stood still, straining his ears and concluding with some relief that he was the only sentient being in the bush. Until he saw a glowing human figure move in the shadows and step into the clearing with him.

A naked African man painted entirely white stopped at the edge of the clearing and stared at Boone. He held a wooden bowl in both hands and walked slowly into the cylinder of silver light, his skin glowing, as if his entire body, including his genitals and his hair, had been dipped in whitewash. The roots of his hair were pale gray and pulled straight back from his face, pasted in place with the same white glue that coated his body. Only his eyes, black and glistening, were left unpainted, and seemed to shine brighter as the figure approached. When the man spoke, a dark hole opened in the chalk whiteness of his face and a soft voice filled the silent clearing like the roar of a waterfall in a box canyon. The figure crept forward, speaking in gentle masculine tones, as if he were a hunter or a shepherd soothing an animal while approaching it.

"Boa," said Boone, using the Mende greeting.

The man was slender and shorter than Boone, completely naked and weaponless, holding only the wooden bowl, but his whiteness seemed to have an occult and malevolent purpose. He recalled that, when someone died, naked runners painted white carried news of the death to the surrounding villages.

"I'm a man," Boone stammered, tugging again at his hood and resisting the urge to run away. "You sabby Krio talk? I am a man. Somebody tied this animal skin on me."

The white figure stooped slightly as it drew near, peering into the holes of Boone's mask, searching for and finding Boone's eyes.

"I'm a man," he repeated, terrified that he had blundered into some kind of hunting ritual and was being mistaken for a baboon.

The pale figure spoke again. The words sounded nothing like Mende, but Boone was no expert, and so tried several more Mende greetings. Without uttering a single familiar word or syllable, the man pleaded, then berated him. Boone feared that he was being asked or ordered to do something, and his inability to understand was being interpreted as willful disobedience.

Boone helplessly watched sadness fill the eyes with tears. In the profound hush of the bush, the alien voice acquired the dimensions of an orchestra, filling the clearing with the sounds of human desolation and the abstract music of speech. The figure groaned and lifted the bowl, holding it up to the moon, then threw back its head, and a single groan erupted into wailing. The man's wordless despair was so contagious that Boone suddenly felt they were the last two human creatures on the planet; their families, friends, and lovers had been slaughtered by bush spirits and fed to animals. Now it was their turn to die, and this figure—chalk-white with grief—was delivering the final lamentation of the last human, through infinite space, to an empty heaven.

The figure shuddered, presented the bowl to Boone, and motioned for him to take it. Boone balanced it on his iron claws and lifted it nearer the eyeholes, tilting it until the moonlight fell on a small silvery square in the bottom of the dish and a photographic image of Michael Killigan stared up at him—a frontal head shot from a passport photo or a driver's license.

"Where is Michael Killigan?" asked Boone. "Usai Lamin Kaikai?"

he asked, seized with the fear that the photo came from the personal effects of a dead man, that the cries to heaven were part of some bush mass for the dead.

The painted man continued speaking, meaningless sounds that were at once soothing and disorienting, as if Boone and this white figure would be able to express themselves and understand each other using pure speech.

Boone handed the bowl back to the painted man, so he could point at the photo with one of his claws.

"My friend," he said. "My brother. Lamin Kaikai. Where is he?"

Without responding, the painted man gestured at Boone to follow him, or go away, he couldn't tell which. Then the figure drifted off into the bush. Boone could not find the path that had brought him into the clearing; he was able only to discern the one the white figure had taken. The first live clue of his entire visit was walking away from him in one direction, while back in the direction from which he had come, villagers carrying clubs were looking to kill him for a witch or a Baboon Man.

Another chill shook him in his sweaty pelt. He felt a tug in the still air, as if ripples were passing above him on the surface of the night, and down below the current was flowing through him. The air was so humid here, someone had once told him, that radio waves leave tracks. He crept the rest of the way through the clearing, an animal slinking through the humid night.

On the trail just outside the clearing, the path forked and the white figure veered left, nimbly scaling an embankment choked with roots.

"I may have trouble keeping up," Boone called out, as if it would do any good. "I no able for keep up," he added, in the fond hope that Krio might improve his chances of being understood. He wheezed and flushed with fever, steadying himself in a bout of giddiness. "Febah done catch me bad," he called weakly. "Food no dae inside me belly for three days. I no eat nothing. Thirsty dae 'pon me. You sabby usai foh get water foh drink?" he cried.

The white figure called back to him and passed from view over the top of the hill.

When he crested the same hill, he looked down into a shrouded clearing where paths converged, pale and barely visible in the ink of night, hanging in the shadows like vapor trails left by clay ghosts.

He barely caught sight of the whiteness moving away from him in the moonlight, down another fork in the path.

"I say, I'm weak!" called Boone. "Hold up, please!"

An explosion of vegetation overhead stopped his heart with fear, as a nest of birds or bats slashed leaves and dispersed in the canopy of bush, where he heard them perch at a safer distance from him, then felt them watching him with the pin-eyed desire of vultures.

There was probably a very good reason for all these legends, he thought, following the pale figure into yet another fork in the path. The bush had no beginning, and no end. The villages were little pockets of human civilization in a galaxy of bush. For centuries, human feet had worn the paths of least resistance. Once a year or so, one of the villagers probably took the wrong fork, or chose the wrong trail out of a clearing, and before dark, they were lost, leaving nothing but their names and a few bush devil stories for posterity. If he got lost, how long could he last out here? Without water?

At the next rise, Boone saw an orange light flickering in the gully below him, where his guide had disappeared. Then another smear of fire or torchlight, and human voices. For one terrible instant he feared he had been led in a circle, and it was the village search party assembling in the clearing. But the voices neither advanced nor receded. He heard ringing metal and the cheerless laughter of men.

He descended slowly, freezing each time a silhouetted palm or a ghostly albedo of moonlight emerged like a human shape in his path. He searched ahead for the painted figure, but only the orange lights appeared before him, resolving into streaks from the slots of shuttered windows.

A low dark structure and two huts formed a compound in a clearing, with a baffa and a porch screened in by the sort of mesh petty traders used to protect their unattended shops after market hours.

He took a narrow, overgrown trail, which broke from the path and seemed to lead to the rear of the windowed structure, where shadows moved in the firelit interior, voices muttered, and the spanging of metal hammerblows issued. A roof pipe vented smoke and filled his nostrils with the smell of cooking meat. Hunger overpowered his fear, and he crept along the wall to one of the glowing windows.

The cracks in the shutters afforded him a view of embers glowing in an open hearth under the window, and in front of it a stone table littered with tools. He held his breath, adjusted his hood, and put his eye as near as he dared to the space between the shutters and squinted.

A huge shirtless blacksmith with a pipe clamped in his teeth tended the fire and worked the handle of a canvas bellows. He pounded a piece of leather or cloth studded with metal amulets and called out in a tribal language to someone working alongside of him. Illumined by firelight from the forge, the muscles of his upper body bulged in swollen arcs, like bundles of serpents writhing under his black skin. Sweat glistened on his chest and arms and dripped off of him, sizzling on the stones around the hearth. An aproned apprentice in a skullcap appeared at the blacksmith's elbow and handed him an iron cleaver. Through one eye, the young man watched his master work, the other socket an eyeless pink scar.

The blacksmith poked a stick into the embers and used it to relight his pipe, filling the air about his head with wraiths of white smoke. Then he turned away from Boone and lurched over to another table, dragging one apparently lame leg behind him. There he lifted something and the muscles of his upper back bloomed like the hood of a huge cobra. When he turned around, he hoisted the head of a hog or a bush pig in his arms and tossed it onto the anvil with a thud and a crack of bone muffled by flesh.

He joked with the apprentice and the two laughed quietly, talking softly as they worked.

Boone angled for a different view by squinting through another crack in the shutter and saw ridgepoles strung with dozens of animal heads and masks: the raffia headdresses he had seen worn by dancing devils, the grotesque mask of Kongoli, the clowning prankster whose buffoonery sometimes turned violent, a Poro devil's mask, heads of animals fitted with collars and vests of pelts, with holes for the arms of men. Masks of bush pigs, bush cows, baboons, alligators—all suspended in the flickering shadows of the firelight, staring back at Boone with huge glass eyes, lit somehow by reflective stones or minerals set deep in their sockets.

The head on the anvil was fresh and bloody. The blacksmith rolled it sideways, and one swollen pig eye, marbled with crimson veins, stared at Boone with the innocence of a Chagall horse head. The blacksmith abruptly upended the head on the anvil and began gouging an excavation where the head had once been joined to its body, ripping muscle, cartilage, and veins from the neck with an iron claw.

The apprentice began working at his side, stitching a pelt on a table strewn with metals, gems, bones, and a carcass spilling offal onto a wooden platter.

Boone heard the hiss of footsteps in the grass behind him, but before he could turn, something hard jabbed the back of his head through the hood, and a human voice sang through his nerves.

"*Poo-mui* Baboon Man, you like bullets too much?" Boone stiffened and decided not to turn. The voice belonged to a teenager, a mere bobo from the sounds of it, and Boone was unsure whether this made matters better or worse.

"Bullets dae beaucoup inside me weapon. Her name Lady Death. You want Lady Death sing bullets foh you?"

He was pushed along the wall by a barrel in the nape of his neck.

"Try something small, Mr. Baboon. Lady Death go sing you to sleep," said the boy. "Look the door."

Inside was a room off the blacksmith's quarters, lit by a thin tongue of copper light from a hurricane lamp. The stench of something that had been dead even longer than his hood nearly suffocated him. On a whiskey stool next to the lamp sat a boy in wraparound mirror sunglasses, his legs crossed, jauntily cradling an automatic rifle. He wore a pink bandanna pirate-style, and his skinny chest was covered by a heavy necklace of cowrie shells, lashed pouches, animal claws, amulets, Duracell batteries, and what appeared to be a TV remote control attached by an eyebolt to a feathered talisman.

"Boone," said a voice he instantly recognized in the shadows to his left.

"You mean *Ba*-boon," said the pirate in sunglasses, grinning with teeth stained orange by kola nuts and training the automatic weapon in the vicinity of Boone's neck.

"Killigan . . ." Boone said, before he was pushed by the neck to a stool in the opposite corner.

He turned to see his escort through the eyeholes of the mask, a youth of no more than fifteen or sixteen, with bloodshot eyes and a mane of dreadlocks swept back and held in place by sponge-tipped headphones, wired to a small cassette player strapped to his left biceps. He too wore a yoke of amulets and juju; on closer examination, Boone saw—festooned among the shells and animal teeth —a stick applicator of Arrid Extra Dry, a rusted hemostat, and a toy magnifying glass. The boy's rifle drooped in his right hand as he sucked hard on a spliff, then passed it to his seated comrade.

"I am Double O Seven," said the seated boy in the bandanna and mirror shades, filling the room with marijuana smoke. "This is Black Master Kung Fu." He handed the spliff back to Boone's guard.

"Are you OK?" Boone asked Killigan.

His friend's upper body was cloaked in shadows; his lower half striped in black patterns thrown by moonlit mesh from a window. His clothes were dark with sweat . . . or blood.

Under the window between Boone and Michael Killigan was a table strewn with human skulls spray-painted in neon colors and adorned with sunglasses and caps.

"Everything was fine," said Killigan tonelessly, "until you came to Sierra Leone to save me."

The resignation in his voice snuffed any chance of their leaving alive.

"Blacksmith!" yelled the seated pirate.

A single blow sounded, and a heavy door slid open, grating across the dirt floor. The swollen torso of the blacksmith appeared, backlit by the glowing forge. He set a calabash and a mounded platter of rice topped with meat sauce next to the boy in the bandanna.

Double O Seven handed the huge figure a cutlass.

"Take off his head."

Boone glanced at the pile of spray-painted skulls and drew his legs under his chair, preparing for one last feckless lunge.

The blacksmith brushed the cutlass aside.

"I go able use me hands," he said, advancing on Boone, a black sternum and buckling pectorals filling the eyeholes of the mask.

Boone tried to charge out of his chair and was firmly pushed back into it by powerful arms.

"Sit, small baboon," said the blacksmith with a chuckle, prying the knots of the lashings apart with his fingers.

The blacksmith grabbed the hood, lifted Boone out of his chair, and shook him out of the pelt, then threw the headpiece over his shoulder and returned to his quarters.

Suddenly Boone was able to see the whole room with eyes that had grown accustomed to the dimness. Medicines, fetishes, weapons, body parts, and animal masks hung from the rafters and cast huge shadows on the mud walls. A third boy was prostrate on a mattress opposite under the only other window, groaning and curled in the fetal position, his eyes fever-bright and staring at Boone.

The air was close and humid, reeking of sweat, cooked meat, and decay. The top of an upended crate near Boone was painted in black and white squares, with chess pieces in place, ready for a new game, if someone would only move the .45 pistol that occupied the center of the board.

The pirate named Double O Seven poured water from the calabash into a tin cup. Boone's lips stuck together in a dry swallow. He watched the mound of rice chop steaming in the copper halo of light.

"Hungry?" asked the boy, smiling through orange teeth. "I get fine chop," he added. "Tarsty?"

"Some water," said Boone, "would be good."

"I nevah see white man begging," said Double O Seven. "This one," he said, jerking his gun at Killigan, "he no beg. *Poo-muis* get begged from, but I think say, dey no beg self. Maybe put gun dae inside dey mouth, den maybe dey go beg. I no know. Pass we find out?"

The boy with dreadlocks picked up the calabash and poured water in a prolonged, seductive trickle into a cup.

Boone watched and swallowed reflexively.

"Who are these guys?" he whispered.

"They used to be soldiers," said Killigan in the same weary tone, "who were paid six dollars and a bag of rice per month, but when the government stopped paying them, they went to work for Moiwo."

"What do they want?"

"They're holding us until Moiwo gets here," said Killigan. "Moiwo wants photographs . . . and negatives."

The boy with the dreadlocks looked at Boone with bloodshot eyes and said, "Stinken sie Deutsch?"

The bobos looked at one another and laughed.

"Stinken sie Deutsch?" repeated Double O Seven, turning his head toward Boone. The wraparound shades were opaque, holding only twin reflections of the hurricane lamp's flame.

"I'm American," said Boone.

Double O Seven laughed and adjusted his shades. "He say you smell like Jarmahn," he said with a grin, accepting the spliff from his companion. "The last *poo-mui* who been sit down dae," he said, pointing at Boone's stool, "was a Jarmahn *poo-mui* from Jarmahnay. He say you smell Jarmahn."

"I'm not German," said Boone quietly. "I'm American."

"Aftah we kill dat Jarmahn from Jarmahnay," Double O Seven said, "ihn smell too much!"

They laughed uproariously and slapped the stocks of their weapons with glee.

Finally Double O Seven touched his comrade's elbow. "Hey, Black Master Kung Fu, whatin go happen if American *poo-mui* stink past Jarmahn *poo-mui*?"

They held their noses and laughed.

"Rotten fish bonga!" said dreadlocks. "Ih rank past rank. Smell dae go 'pon person's clothes, tae ih no dae come out!"

Boone shuddered with fever and fought the urge to vomit.

When they stopped laughing, the boy in the dreadlocks held the cup of water out to Boone, and nodded for him to take it. When Boone reached for it, the boy pulled it back and drank.

"Drinken sie Deutsch?" he said, and the two of them fell to laughing again.

"Why didn't you go with Pa Gigba the first night?" whispered Killigan, under cover of their merriment.

"The old guy said he didn't know anything," said Boone.

Dreadlocks kicked the chess table a foot closer to Boone, picked up the pistol, and tucked it into the rope belt of his britches.

"You chess player?" the boy in dreadlocks asked Boone.

"Yes," said Boone, at the same instant that Killigan said, "He doesn't play."

A single click came from the weapon cradled in the pirate's lap, as he swiveled and pointed the barrel at Killigan.

"I am Black Master Kung Fu," said dreadlocks. "I take black. Your move."

"We can get some water first?" asked Boone. "Do ya, I beg," he added, sliding a dry tongue across his lower lip.

"You win, I give you water," said Black Master Kung Fu. "You lose, I kill you."

The pirate laughed so hard he rattled the shells and animal teeth of his necklace. He pointed at the table of skulls. "Those people played chess no better!"

The boy on the floor mattress groaned and panted with fever.

"I don't want to play chess," said Boone.

"Move," said the pirate, pointing the dark eye of the gun barrel at Boone's head.

"Move," said Boone's opponent. "No passant."

"What?" asked Boone.

"He doesn't like the en passant rule," said Killigan. "He doesn't allow it."

"No en passant," said Boone. "Anything else?"

"Well, sometimes he won't let you castle. And even if he lets you, it puts him in a bad mood. He doesn't like castling; I'd avoid it."

"Move!" said Boone's opponent.

"QP4," said Killigan. "I've won three times using the Queen's Gambit. I'm a little reluctant to experiment with anything else. How's your game?"

"The last time I played was with you."

"Yeah," Killigan said quietly, and cleared his throat.

"Move!" said Black Master Kung Fu, bobbing his head to tinny music from his Walkman.

The boy on the mattress went rigid and appeared to have a small seizure, his head ticking slowly in spasms. Then he swallowed and stared at Boone again.

"Febah," said the pirate, handing the boy a tin cup of water.

The sick boy drank, then watched Boone's eyes.

"That chess game we were talking about," said Killigan, "the last one we played, where I told you I sent my knight to . . . capture you . . ."

"What game?" said Boone, watching the mane of dreadlocks, while he tried to remember the sequence of the Queen's Gambit declined.

"Gigba," he whispered.

"Oh," said Boone, "that game."

"I sent my black knight to take you," said Killigan, "but you resisted. I moved him back because you would not let him take you. When I moved him out to get you again, he was—taken."

"Your knight never tried to take me," said Boone. "I gave him the chance at least three times, but he said nothing about it. He said he didn't know where you were. Only that your—castle was attacked. And you disappeared."

"The white bishop," said Killigan, "he was there too, translating?"

"He was there," said Boone, "translating. The black knight lied to you."

"No," said Killigan. "Something lost in translation, I think. Something the white bishop hopes to find in a black king, or a future Paramount Chief."

"Hey," said the pirate in sunglasses, waving his gun at Killigan. "Your mouth makes noises too much."

The pirate rested his gun in his lap and began shoveling chop into his mouth with his hand.

"These two black pawns," said Killigan. "No real threat, until the king comes. They won't take pieces on their own, unless white tries for an opening."

The boy in dreadlocks puffed on another spliff, and sang softly to music no one else could hear. He moved his bishop.

"Mr. Baboon," said Double O Seven. "Why dat white runner we done send been find you on your way here and not inside Nymuhun village? Den say dat famous *gbese* witchfinder come out Bambara Chiefdom and done close Nymuhun foh witchfinding."

"Witchfinder done close off Nymuhun," said Boone. "But someone put a hood on me. I was chased out."

"Witchfinder done find witch business and witch medicine dae inside the village?" asked the boy. "*Honei-mui* dae inside the village?"

Boone looked at Michael Killigan, and saw the dark silhouette of his friend's head slowly nod.

"Yes," said Boone. "An old man. And an old woman. Witchfinder done find witch medicine dae inside they house."

"And you come out the village before the witchfinding done-done?" asked the boy incredulously. "You carry on go with a witchfinder's swear 'pon your head?"

"I—"

"You broke the boundary?" asked Killigan.

"Yes," hissed Boone. "I had no fucking choice."

"You carry on go with a witchfinder's swear 'pon you?" asked the boy. "I done see that *gbese* witchfinder put his hand into a bucket of boiling palm oil," said the pirate. "I done see that *gbese* witchfinder kill a man dead with his fingertip," he said, touching his companion with the ball of his index finger. "Dat *gbese* witchfinder put swear on you, his swear go kill you dead past dead. No lie! Unless we kill you first."

"I don't believe in swears," said Boone.

Double O Seven laughed and slapped his friend on the back. "He no believe in swear! Whatin I done tell you, notoso? Whatin I been say? Dis *poo-mui*, he no believe in swear!"

The boy snatched his gun out of his lap and flourished it aloft, jostling bundles and implements hanging from the rafters.

"You no believe in swear?" He laughed. The mirrored shades tilted upward and he poked the barrel of his gun up into the rafters, stirring huge shadows thrown from hanging medicines and masks. Finally he pushed a birdcage into view with his gun, turned it sideways and shook it, until the cloth cover fell to the floor.

"Swear done bring you to this place!" said the boy triumphantly. "*Poo-mui* fool!"

The pinioned albino bat writhed violently in its cage, its white wings straining, its bony snout and teeth open in a pink, soundless shriek.

Double O Seven pulled off his mirrored shades, smiling through the same orange teeth Boone had seen in Bo at the Thirsty Soul. He stared at Boone with one good eye, the other swirling milky white and opalescent in the lamplight.

"Swears work best on those who don't believe in them," he boasted. "Past now you believe in swear!"

The sound of banging metal came from the blacksmith's quarters. "Runner done come! Runner done come just now," the blacksmith's voice boomed from the smithy.

The pirate kicked at the stool under Boone's opponent. Dreadlocks scowled, shook his head, shouldered his weapon, and left the room.

Outside the window, over the bed of the sick boy, the chess player's voice greeted the messenger.

"What's gonna happen to us?" whispered Boone, suddenly imagining himself a silent, throbless carcass on the floor of a clearing in West Africa. When the bullet entered his brain, the images of this squalid room and the fever-bright eyes of the boy across from him would fade from his retinas—his powers of vision evanescing like steam from his lidless, sightless eyeballs. It seemed impossible that death—as random and banal as bad weather for the villagers —was now coming for a *poo-mui* from the wholesome state of Indiana.

"We will be . . . invited to join the society," said Killigan. "We will provide and prepare a human victim to feed the medicine, or we will *be* victims and the medicine will be turned against our families."

The voices outside the window fell into whispers. Killigan straightened in his chair and leaned toward the window. The eyes of the sick boy widened. The voices seeped into the dimness, urgent, tense, fearful.

"That messenger is from your village," said Killigan. "He brings news of the witchfinding. He says the *gbese* found a bundle in your room. He says you are a—"

"*Honei!*" the sick boy screamed, his eyes widening in sudden fright, staring at Boone. "*Honei-mui!*"

The pirate jumped off his stool and trained his weapon first on Boone, then on Killigan.

"You move small-small," he said uncertainly, his hands trembling for a grip on his gun. "I go kill you dead past dead!"

The pirate jerked his head in the direction of the shuttered window over the sick boy. "I dae come!" he shouted. "I dae come!"

The door banged open and shut. The sick boy's gaze was fixed on Boone.

"*Honei-mui!*" he yelled, his eyes lit with terror.

"You're a witch!" urged Killigan. "Stare at him!" he shouted in a sudden, savage voice.

"Witch?" Boone sputtered, wondering if his friend's ordeals in the bush had pushed him over the edge. "I'm not a witch!" Killigan's face was still obscured in the shadows. Boone looked back at the sick boy.

"You're a witch!" Killigan insisted, snarling through clenched teeth, his silhouette lunging in the shadows. "He knows you're a witch. Look into his eyes," he exhorted. "Find his soul!"

The boy screamed and raised his hands, transfixed by Boone's eyes, his mouth open in an empty scream.

"Stare!" roared Killigan. "Crawl inside of him!" he cried savagely. "Down his throat! Into his belly! Kill him!"

"Eyes!" the boy screamed. "Eyes! I no able for see!" he shrieked, holding his hands in front of his face. "*Honei-mui!*"

"Kill him!" Killigan commanded, his voice blaring cruelty and bloodlust.

The door to the veranda opened slowly and the pirate reappeared with his comrade close behind. They stepped uncertainly into the room. The boy went rigid on the bed, his hands still in front of his face.

"*Honei-mui!*" The boy convulsed, his mouth stuck open in a drooling grimace.

The pirate glanced at Boone and averted his eyes.

"Stare at them," Killigan urged menacingly. "Look dae eyes!"

The boy in dreadlocks tried to ready his weapon with shaking hands, pointing it at Boone.

"No," screamed the pirate, knocking the barrel down. "You no go kill a witch! You kill ihn and ihn shade come back 'pon you and smother your face at night! You no go kill a witch! Fool!"

The sick boy went into a full-blown seizure, his mouth forming a horrible, foaming rictus, his head jerking in slow, rhythmic tics, while clonic spasms gusted through his limbs.

"Suck out their souls!" hissed Killigan. "Look dae eyes. Open holes for you to crawl inside! Down their throats!" he coaxed. "Witch done come!" he screamed.

"I dae go!" yelled the pirate, banging open the door.

The boy in dreadlocks looked wild-eyed about the room, the muzzle of his weapon following his eyes, finally settling on the chessboard, which he demolished with a burst of gunfire, filling the air with wood splinters and reeking smoke. He followed his companion out the door, where terrified voices called out to one another.

"*Honei-mui!*" someone cried from the blacksmith's quarters, followed by the sound of tools falling to the floor and another door banging open.

"*Honei-mui!*" someone screamed, banging a pot with an iron tool and cursing. "*Honei-mui!*"

"Untie me," said Killigan curtly.

The boy on the mattress covered his eyes and moaned in terror.

Boone fumbled in the dark with the twine knotted around his friend's wrists. Killigan shook the twine free, then grabbed the cutlass and the calabash of water from the table. He kicked open the door and waited.

In the courtyard, the bald earth shone with a lunar glow. The well was capped by a weathered lid draped in fetishes and protective medicines, and padlocked to a ringbolt in the concrete lip. The sound of curses and metal banging receded into the bush.

"Let's go," pressed Killigan, and they lit out, running away from the voices and banging pots, up the same trail Boone had arrived on.

Boone's chest heaved as he clambered up the path behind Killigan's bobbing silhouette. At the top of the swell, they rested, sweat dripping from their faces and hands.

"Do you know where you're going?" pleaded Boone, gasping for air.

"Yes," said Killigan.

"How far is it to the border with Guinea?" Boone asked.

"Four hours by bush path," replied Killigan, "assuming we find the way."

"Then we should just plain leave, like *now*!"

"Just like a *poo-mui*," panted Killigan. "Come in, fuck everything up, then leave."

Boone grabbed his friend and searched his face for some semblance of sanity. "Where are we going?"

"Back to the village." Killigan pushed Boone away and turned, as if to continue on his way.

"The village!" Boone screamed on the verge of hysteria, grabbing his friend's arm. "We'll get killed! No way I'm going back to the fucking village!"

"This is Sierra Leone," said Killigan. "I've been risking my life here for three years. I'm not about to run away and let Moiwo take over because you've risked yours for two weeks."

"*You'll* die," yelled Boone. "Not me," he said, as if reassuring himself.

"No," Killigan shot back. "You'll get yourself killed, unless you go back with me and submit to the witchfinder. That I know for sure."

"The witchfinder?" Boone stopped, speechless with rage, as the import of his friend's words sank in. "Trust my life? To a bald quack in a bathrobe?"

Killigan turned and faced him down. "I can't explain Africa or witch business to you in fifteen minutes," he said bitterly. "So let's forget about witch business for a minute, OK? Let's pretend we're just *poo-muis* from Indiana," he said sarcastically.

"Good idea," said Boone.

"Now, let's reason," continued Killigan, "like good white men with good white logic! This is the bush!" he said, barely containing his rage. "There are no signs or maps! Even Africans get lost in the bush. Stoned teenage mercenaries are running around with automatic weapons. You heard them talking! The only thing they're afraid of is bad medicine and the witchfinder. I'm going to the village for protection; you're going to see the witchfinder!"

"Moiwo's in the village," said Boone.

"So's Kabba Lundo, the Paramount Chief. So's the witchfinder, who will protect us, and who apparently saw something in your nature."

Boone threw his head back and screamed in exasperation, "What the fuck are you talking about?" He studied his friend's face in breathless horror. "You believe this juju shit?"

"The African way is the only way out," insisted Killigan. "That means back through the village, not out in the bush. You'll have to take my word for it . . . or die."

Killigan turned and walked up the path without looking back.

"You too!" Boone hollered into the canopy of vegetation overhead. "I stick my fucking neck out for you! And when I finally find you . . . You're psycho too! White men go crazy here, is that it? White men go crazy?"

(**20**)

By the time the thatched huts of Nymuhun appeared on the bluffs ahead of them, dawn was oozing into the bush. Fogbows shimmered in the morning mist, and a low-rolling brume clung to the tops of the vegetation. Boone trudged along, starving and thirsty, fever glowing in his joints, and helpless rage pouring out of his mouth at his friend and his fate.

"Tell me what happened," Boone demanded between breaths.

"I told you all I can," said Killigan. "Moiwo is into bad medicine. He's smuggling. He's letting chemical companies dump all over the country. If he could sell slaves again, he would. He's got to be exposed and tried for his crimes, before he takes over the whole country and runs it even farther down the shit hole of West Africa. That's why the witchfinder is here, and why you shouldn't be."

"But why would Sisay help Moiwo?"

"Why not?" said Killigan. "It's no different here than anywhere else. Sisay's placing bets on who's going to win the election. Moiwo *lives* in Sisay's village. What do you suppose would happen if Moiwo asked him for help, Sisay said no, and then, next week, Moiwo is suddenly Paramount Chief?"

"OK, then what about this raid on your village? What was that? And why disappear into the bush? And what are these photographs?"

"I told you," said Killigan. "I went to Freetown. I had to go by bush paths, or I would have been taken. I took proof of Moiwo's doings to the proper authorities."

"To the embassy?" asked Boone.

Killigan laughed harshly. "That would be smart. Take proof of Moiwo's shit to the people he's in bed with."

"I don't understand," said Boone.

"That's right," snapped Killigan, "you don't."

"You're an American, right? You work for the United States government."

"I *used* to work for the Peace Corps," said Killigan. "Now I work for . . . other people."

"What other people?"

"No can say," said Killigan.

"Secret society mumbo jumbo, right? You can't tell me. I'm your best friend," said Boone, "I came all the way down here . . ."

"And almost got us both killed," Killigan interrupted. "My plan was perfect," he muttered. "I calculated absolutely every African variable down to the last villager. I delivered the goods on Moiwo, bought my ticket for Paris, and then I learned that a *poo-mui* green- horn by the name of Westfall was out in the bush looking for me, just waiting to fall into the clutches of Moiwo. I forgot how effort- lessly one misguided *poo-mui*—fresh off the plane—can destroy everything and anything in Africa!"

"You talk big," Boone hollered ahead. "But if I wasn't a witch, you'd be dead!"

Killigan turned to face Boone. He wiped his forehead with his bare hand, shaking sweat off of it into the bush. Then he pointed a finger into his friend's face. "I'll say this once, and then we won't discuss it again. Agreed?"

"No way," said Boone. "It depends what you say. For instance, after you're done, I might want to tell you to get fucked."

"If you had stayed in Paris," said Killigan, "and had waited ac- cording to plan, I would be there by now. I would be sipping espresso in a nice little café off the Place de la Concorde, fondly recalling the guillotine and the simple pleasures of civilized white people. Moiwo would be in jail waiting to swing from the gallows at the stadium in Freetown. My African father, Kabba Lundo, would be assured of his Paramount Chieftaincy, OK? And after our little va- cation, I could come back to Sierra Leone, marry the woman I love, and settle down to a long and happy life. It's all true. Just take my word for it. But, instead, you came to Sierra Leone and threw a tenderfoot *poo-mui* into the mix."

They continued marching. Boone slogged along behind, trying to console himself with the knowledge that each step was taking him closer to a tick mattress, where he could lie down and die in peace.

After a few minutes, he decided to attempt a truce.

"Is she African?" he asked.

"No," Killigan muttered sarcastically, without turning around. "She's a headhunter's daughter from the Iban tribe of Sarawak, in Borneo, just a few thousand miles from here."

Boone cursed himself for his choice of friends, his physical weakness, the fear and exhaustion that were making him dependent on yet another abusive white man.

After a long trek uphill, they reached the village boundary, stooped under the thread, and entered unannounced. A crowd was assembled in the *barri* after what had been—from the looks of the shriven and haggard faces of the citizens—another harrowing night of witchfinding.

An old woman put a padlock back on the lid to the well and struggled to her feet, balancing a bucket of water on her head for the nursing and expectant mothers.

Water dripped from the seams of the bucket and stirred deep cravings in Boone, who considered grabbing the pail from her without so much as a by-your-leave.

She greeted Michael Killigan, and then she recognized Boone. Her eyes and mouth froze open in horror, and the bucket tumbled off of her head. She fled the clearing and ran to the *barri*, waving her hands over her head, announcing the return of the white witch.

Boone walked backward, eyeing the thread boundary and the path back out of the village.

While his friend went ahead, Boone watched the crowd rise to its feet, all but Lewis, who sat holding his head, apparently sick to death of witches and witchfinding. The witchfinder appeared, with Kabba Lundo and the elders. They met Killigan at the well and greeted him, but the exchanges seemed subdued, almost staged. Several elders glanced at Boone, but no one greeted him.

Another Land-Rover had arrived in his absence. Four soldiers in red berets sat on the roof of it, their weapons slung carelessly around their necks as props for their elbows. They were well-paid Krios from the President's special forces, and they regarded the superstitious festivities of the villagers with bemused detachment. A middle-aged African in a blue uniform and a military chapeau sat inside, hiding the kola nut he was eating from the view of the witchfinder and the villagers.

Boone watched as Killigan paid homage to the deceitful witchfinder, stooping and giving Kabba Lundo two-handed handshakes. For all the world, his best friend looked like Sisay, kissing African ass, bowing, showing respect for elders, pretending everything made perfect sense. *How nice. A witchfinding! May I bring a friend and some bad medicine along?*

The muscles in Boone's legs twitched with fatigue, his knees nearly buckled. Killigan was suddenly transformed before his eyes into a stranger. His manners, his demeanor, his posture, the way Mende rolled off his tongue, just like an African! And he was surrounded by a gathering horde of Africans in headties, burnooses, skullcaps, safari shirts, robes, and lappas. Boone felt like a deaf man in a room full of writhing dancers, and nobody had taken the trouble to explain the phenomenon called music.

"Come," beckoned the witchfinder with a smile for Boone. "Let us finish this witch business so the village will be safe again."

He had only bitter choices. Leave and go tearing through the bush until he fell over dead. Or stay here and place himself in the keeping of secret societies and jungle cults, headed up by a wacko septuagenarian with a broomstick and a mirror.

"Boone," called Killigan. "Come to the *barri*."

"Let's wind it up," begged Lewis. "The midwife has Guinness, and I am ready to eat my fucking hands I'm so hungry!"

Boone staggered forward, joining Killigan and the elders. He dragged his feet on the way across the courtyard, unwilling to trust anyone, but he had no other options.

The crowd opened and admitted them into the *barri*. Through the shifting bodies of the villagers, Boone saw a short row of chairs and a cot of some kind where a woman slept under a blanket.

"Take seat," said the witchfinder.

Killigan showed Boone one of the chairs. Boone dropped into it, only to rise to a crouch when he saw Moiwo enter, a billowing country cloth robe covering necklaces of medicines and cowrie shells.

"Brother Lamin Kaikai," Moiwo said, his face cracking open in an ugly fleer.

"Greetings," said Killigan. "My regards to the section chief," he added grimly.

Someone sat next to Boone, and the crowd began shuffling into a new formation. Instead of seating themselves in the *barri*, they remained standing, fanning out, circling.

Boone looked at the chair next to him and recognized Grandma Dembe, and next to her Pa Usman and his *nomoloi*, and, on the other side of Usman, Jenisa. He was sitting with the other accused witches. And next to them the cot, with the witchfinder's assistants on either side of a woman whose face Boone could not see. When Boone looked up to find Killigan, he found instead a ring of crowded heads staring down at him, pressing in, rank on rank, leaving just enough room for the witchfinder and those accused.

Air shuddered in and out of Boone's lungs, as he looked out at eyes which seemed to stare back at him from the bobbing appendages of a single organism, a massive hydra arrayed with human heads and hateful stares.

The witchfinder banged the cauldron with his staff and surveyed the crowd.

"I have found all the witches!" he cried.

The villagers jeered and hissed, jostling one another for better views. Boone labored for air, his chest heaving, as if he had run a great distance, only to be trapped.

"We have them all here!" shouted the witchfinder. "And, as you already know, the head witch, the creature who ate your children, the leader of the coven, and keeper of the witch pot, is dead!"

The assistants hoisted a body from the cot and held it up in the center of the crowd by its shoulders and its hair. Boone recognized the sagging, lifeless face of Luba, before it was covered with flying spittle and wounded with jabbing sticks. He gagged and covered his mouth.

The witchfinder waved his staff and spread his arms.

"The old ones here remember hearing stories of my grandfather," he said. "Kenei Lahai was one of the Tongo Players, famous for finding witches and exterminating cannibals. In those days, witches and cannibals were killed and thrown on the fire!"

The crowd cheered. Boone shook violently, looking for Killigan or Lewis, but to no avail.

"Those days are no more!" cried the witchfinder. "We no longer kill witches, we cure them, and then we fine them. This witch died only because her shade left her body while she was asleep. When it tried to escape into the bush, it was trapped in a witch net. Now she sleeps forever. But don't worry! Her shade will not return to haunt the village," he said, reaching into the folds of his robe, "because I have it here."

The witchfinder drew his hand from his loppy sleeve and held a writhing serpent over the heads of the villagers, who cried out and stumbled back in terror.

Boone tried to stand, only to be knocked back into his chair by the seething crowd.

The assistants dropped the body of the witch and covered it with a blanket, then handed the witchfinder a pouch. He poured the undulating reptile into the leather bag and tied it with a string.

"Listen to the shade die!" said the witchfinder, flinging the pouch into the cauldron and stabbing it into the mire with the butt of his staff.

A distant cry came from the bush, and the people stared in wonder, listening to the shade's death rattle, which somehow came to them from far out in the bush.

The witchfinder tended his pot, peering into the swirling morass of bad medicines and witch bundles, poison and infant blood, which had stewed for three days and now gave off the acrid scent of burning hair.

The crowd pressed in around Boone and the accused.

"Section Chief Moiwo," said the witchfinder with a nod.

"Yes, witchfinder," said Moiwo.

Boone leaned forward in his chair when he heard the chief's voice immediately behind him.

"I will now deal with the more serious charges we spoke about."

"Fortune has brought them back to us," said Moiwo. "The time is ripe."

"As I said," continued the witchfinder, "we no longer kill witches, we cure them. Sometimes we forgive them. But other very serious charges have been made. That is why Vice President Bangura has sent members of the government's special forces here. As you all know, certain bad men make very bad medicines from the bodies of human victims. These men want power so badly, they feed women and children to the medicine, and then use it to terrorize their enemies. These men are far worse than witches! They are cannibals! These we do kill. The British hanged them from the gallows in Freetown! And so shall we!"

The crowd murmured its approval.

"Now," said the witchfinder, "you will all help me find these cannibals."

Boone watched a forest of trunks and limbs crowd closer around him, stifling him with the heat of their bodies and the smell of sweat.

"Everyone close your eyes! Do not open them until I say the word."

Boone looked up at the witchfinder, who smiled down at him and winked, pulling one eyelid down with his finger and pointing at Boone. Boone tried to close his eyes, but they fluttered open and shut in nervous terror.

"Grandfather! I pray to you and *Ngewo*," cried the witchfinder, "help me teach these people to find cannibals. Teach them to see cannibals without their eyes! Teach them to see with their hands!"

Boone hunched into a ball on the chair, nauseous with terror.

"A powerful section chief tells me that certain *poo-muis* among us are cannibals in love with bad medicines. Certain *poo-muis* among us tell me that a certain section chief makes bad medicines from the bodies of young boys."

"Witchfinder," said Moiwo in a shaking voice, "this is not the . . . method we discussed."

"Grandfather! Help the people see with their hands! Find the cannibals!"

Boone's heart crawled into his throat when two heavy hands fell upon his shoulders. He kept his eyes closed and sobbed helplessly into his kneecaps, waiting for other hands to fall on him and carry him off.

"You lied!" cried the voice of the section chief. "You lied to me!"

Boone looked up to see Moiwo's fat limbs held by masses of fingers and hands.

"Lying is part of my job," said the witchfinder flatly.

He raised the butt of his staff and slowly extended it under the nose of the restrained Moiwo, tapping one of the chief's shoulders, then the other. Moiwo's limbs surged against the grip of the villagers, who held him fast.

The witchfinder tapped the chief's collarbones, gently, thoughtfully, smiling and watching the fat chief's cheeks quiver with rage.

"My grandfather taught me that a cannibal almost always shows himself by accusing others of cannibalism."

Moiwo snarled, "Be careful not to exceed your powers, witchfinder."

The witchfinder poked his staff into the necklaces around Moiwo's neck, pressing the knob of it under the cords and drawing bags, shells, and pouches out from under the country cloth robe, sifting and poking with his staff, flinging shells and animal teeth aside, until he exposed seven iron hooks sewn to a heavy pouch, swollen and gleaming with blood and fat.

"*Bofima!*" screamed the villagers, gripping the swollen limbs so tight that blood appeared around their fingernails.

"*Bofima!*" shrieked the women and children, gathering weapons and sticks in a frenzy.

An old woman with a big spoon stepped between the witchfinder and Moiwo. "Eyes!" she screamed. "Let me take them!"

"Monkey works!" someone cried. "Baboon eats!"

Cutlasses, pestles, and sticks rained blows on the section chief's head and shoulders.

The witchfinder hooked the cords of the bloody charm with his staff, lifted it from the neck of the chief, and hoisted it aloft, over the heads of the villagers.

"Stop!" cried the witchfinder, twirling the gruesome bladder overhead, its hooks spinning shadows on the ground. The fringes of the crowd fell back, cowering under the whirling medicine.

"The good people of this village don't bloody their hands killing Baboon Men!" called the witchfinder. "This one goes to the gallows in Freetown!"

The mob swarmed around Moiwo. The witchfinder flung the *bofima* into the cauldron with a splash and a swirl of his sleeves.

"Come!" he cried, marching across the courtyard toward the Land-Rovers.

The crowd surged out of the *barri*, pushing and pulling the section chief with them, sucking their teeth and cursing him.

"Witnesses!" cried the witchfinder, summoning the soldiers and the official from the government vehicle.

At the rear of Moiwo's Land-Rover, the witchfinder hooked his staff under a tarpaulin and pushed it back. Shrieks of terror rang in Boone's ears when the villagers saw the bloody cargo in Moiwo's Land-Rover: a mound of baboon pelts and masks, iron claws clotted with blood, and jars of human fat. Flies rose from lidless cardboard boxes of bones and skulls.

"Stop!" cried the witchfinder, parting the crowd with a wave of his staff.

Bloodied, covered with spittle and streaked with tears of rage, the chief fell forward, weaving and reeling in his torn robes.

"Section Chief Moiwo," said the man in the blue uniform, placing a hand under the chief's arm and turning him over to the guards.

"Monkey works!" someone shouted.

"Baboon hangs from gallows!" yelled another.

The crowd sang with infernal glee, joyfully cursing Moiwo and his men.

Kabba Lundo and the soldiers escorted Moiwo to the waiting vehicle. The African elders hung heads with the witchfinder, conferring about how to wind up the proceedings and restore the peace of the village.

Boone felt more fever radiate through him and saw the familiar fur crowd his vision. He heard the government vehicle pulling out of the village. Maybe next, the mob would come for him, but he was suddenly so numb he did not care. Death seemed about as ominous as a summer storm brewing. If Charon himself showed up to ferry him off to the underworld, Boone would have jumped aboard, convinced that he was going to a better life.

He plodded back to the *barri* in search of his chair. There he found Jenisa, her back to him, bowing over Luba's shrouded body.

"Was it a bad sickness?" she whispered. "Meestah Sickness done come for you. I hope you take him with you to the bad place." She stooped and put her mouth close to Luba's ear. "I found you in my dream."

Boone took his seat, and startled her.

"She done die," Jenisa said with a smile.

"Because she was a witch?" Boone asked.

She averted her eyes. "I no know. She fell sick." She shrugged.

"Because of witch medicine?" he asked.

"I no know," she said. "I am only a mother with small peekin dae inside. I do what I must to keep it safe," she added, looking down at her waist. "Kill, if I must."

The witchfinder banged his staff on a pot and one of his assistants cried, "Everybody listen! Everybody listen! Bad medicine done-done! All bad medicine dae inside the witchfinder's pot!"

"At last," said Boone, rising from his chair. "This fucking bullshit is over." He trudged wearily away from the *barri*, hoping to put one foot in front of the other until his head found his sleeping bag.

"The village is almost rid of witch business!" cried the witchfinder.

"As soon as the *poo-mui* witch confesses, the village will be cleansed! Come to the *barri* and rejoice!"

Boone continued stumbling toward Sisay's quarters.

"Boone," hollered Killigan. "Where are you going? Moiwo's gone. We're safe."

"Hey," said Sisay. "Get back here, or you'll be showing disrespect to the witchfinder."

Boone stopped in his tracks and shook with rage. Then he walked to Sisay's house, into his room, closed the door, and fell forward onto his mattress, hearing distant murmurings, like wasps buzzing under the eaves during a summer nap.

The door opened.

"Kong, kong," someone said.

"Wrong, wrong," Boone muttered. "Get the fuck out. I'm sick. No, wait. I'm dead. Tell them I died."

He heard African and American voices, entering his quarters, discussing him.

"It makes no difference," he heard the witchfinder say. "Yes, he is a *poo-mui*, but he is also a witch. He is a danger to the village until he confesses. Until then, all of our work is for nothing."

"Boone," said Killigan. "Listen, we have to go back out to the *barri*. You have to . . . confess."

"Fuck you," said Boone into the sleeping bag.

"He is more dangerous than all the others," said the witchfinder. "Unlike the other witches, he was allowed out on his night ride. He probably fed his medicine, and now he is waiting to use it again. Why else would he come in here alone?"

Boone covered his head with the sleeping bag.

"Boone," said Killigan. "Pa Ansumana is here. He wants you to go back to the *barri* and confess. He asks you, please, do not disgrace him after everything he has done for you."

"Someone should explain to him," said the witchfinder, "that a forced confession is very, very embarrassing and degrading for a witch. Other than being a witch in the first place, a forced confession is probably the worst thing that can happen to someone."

"Boone," said Lewis. "When in Rome, man. You know what I'm saying? Just go out there, make words with your mouth, do what they tell you, and forget about it, OK? I'm starving, and this old geezola isn't gonna let anybody eat until you confess to witch business."

Boone rolled over and sat up. "How long does it take?" he demanded, nervously running his hands through his hair.

"Not long," the witchfinder assured him. "Once we have a confession."

"OK," said Boone, without opening his eyes. "I'm a witch. I like to eat babies at night."

He turned around and flopped back onto his mattress, burrowing deeper under the sleeping bag.

"Very good," said the witchfinder. "At least now he admits it. But the confession must be made in public, before the entire village."

Boone ground his teeth and swallowed a curse, a creative one that would have insulted the witchfinder, his ancestors, and his offspring, and withered the family tree in both directions.

"Boone?" said Killigan. "Come on, man."

Boone sat up again. Lewis and Killigan stood on either side of him and helped him to his feet.

"Five minutes?" asked Boone. "Will it take longer than five minutes?"

"Probably less," said the witchfinder. "Let us go now."

In the *barri*, the villagers whispered and taunted him as he took his seat. Boone scowled and watched as the witchfinder picked up his staff, summoned his assistants, and stirred his pot. He spread his arms and embraced the community.

"I stir a wicked broth of bile and venom, of bitterness and tears, of malice and jealousy," he said, weeping again and dribbling tears into the pot. "My ears are deafened by the cries of our ancestors, who want to know how and why their children have wished these terrible things upon each other! What possessed us to turn these hideous curses loose on the world? What dark and selfish desires prompted us to visit misfortunes on our brothers and sisters? How can our eyes behold each other's faces after tonight?

"Like brings out like," he said solemnly. "We plant hate, and hate we will harvest. Now the last witch has come forward. A white witch, who came here to eat your unborn children!"

The *barri* erupted in a clamor of rage. The parents of dead children cried out for vengeance.

"Last night," said the witchfinder, "when this *poo-mui* witch was out on his night ride, we found the witch pot where he feeds his medicines. You saw with your own eyes the remains of the infant dead. Their limbs were scattered all around like the bones of slaughtered chickens! We saw infant skulls that this witch had eaten while praying over his witch medicine in his room!"

Cries of horror and condemnation assaulted Boone's ears. He spit on the ground between his feet, and gnashed his teeth.

"Now this witch has come forward and will confess his crimes. You will hear from his own lips how he ate your children and smothered the unborn babies while their mothers slept, so he could crack their skulls and suck out their brains! Now you will hear his confession!"

Boone stood unsteadily amid the insults and cries for revenge. He faced the ranting crowd, staring down every pair of eyes that dared meet his. He had already given himself up for dead. Malaria or the volatile passions of the community would probably kill him before dawn. A quirk of fate had fetched him up in this dusty thumbprint called a village, and another quirk would soon finish him. These were his last words, a deathbed speech to a ragtag assortment of human beings, who happened to be standing in the same clearing with him when God reached out of the sky and touched him.

He stared at his best friend, at Sisay, at Pa Ansumana, then walked down the file of his fellow witches. Funny, how they all looked the same. Funny, how a single blow properly administered, a stray bullet, a random virus, a bite from the right mosquito, a bucket from the wrong well, a snake slumbering in the path, a rabid dog, a swear, an enraged ancestor, or a witch's bad dream could snuff the life out of him, or any one of them.

He bowed to Kabba Lundo, and lastly fixed his gaze on the witchfinder, who smiled broadly at the prospect of finishing his work once and for all.

Boone turned to the villagers.

"I have something to say," he began, then choked, swallowed, and fell silent. He shuddered with emotion and found his tongue. "OK, listen. I have tried to be—sensitive. I'm a white man in Africa. I'm a stranger in a foreign country. I tried to be—polite. I thought I was open-minded. But now, I don't know what kind of village you people are running here. I don't know if this is folie à deux, folie à trois, folly de village, African follies, or JUST A FUCKING TROPICAL INSANE ASYLUM!"

He filled his lungs with rage and screamed into the sky, slinging spit and curses over the heads of his audience, as they recoiled from his raging hands and face.

"YOU PEOPLE ARE ALL INSANE!" he screamed. "You're human beings, I guess, but YOU'RE ALL FUCKING INSANE! ESPECIALLY THE WHITE ONES! THEY SHOULD KNOW BETTER! White, black, *poo-mui*, Mende, you're all lost in some fantastic, contwisted delusional system! Your lives are run by witches, bush devils, Baboon Men, ancestors, leprechauns, fucking genies, Leopard People, shape-shifters, mermaids, juju witch shit, bush devils, and I don't know what the fuck else!"

He marched in front of the crowd, shaking his fist in their faces. "You look like human beings!" he hollered. "I'm a human being too! Look at me! Flesh and fucking blood, just like you! But guess what? Once I got here, I had to forget *everything* I thought I knew about human beings! I forgot! Now all I know is one thing. One fucking thing!"

He strode over to where his best friend and the other *poo-muis* had collected.

"West Africa has obliterated everything I know, except for one thing! Do you know what that one thing is?" he shouted into Sisay's face. "The only thing I know," he said, drawing a huge breath and flailing the air with his arms, "is that I AM NOT A FUCKING WITCH! Does everyone understand that!? One more time: I AM NOT A FUCKING WITCH!

"Where's the bald carnival barker in the bathrobe?" cried Boone. "I want to make sure he hears this!"

The witchfinder appeared next to the cauldron wearing the expression of a homeowner who just found a household pest after an exterminator's visit.

"I am not a witch," said Boone. "I am not a Baboon Man. I am not a colt pixie, a wood nymph, a hippogriff, or a hamadryad! I am not a tooth fucking fairy! Nor am I one of Santa's elves. I'm not a worricow, a urisk, a salamander, or a goddamn bush devil! I'M A FUCKING HUMAN BEING!"

The witchfinder sheepishly crept forward and bowed his head, hoping to end the spectacle as quickly and as politely as possible.

"You say you are not a witch," said the witchfinder quietly.

"NO!" shouted Boone, so loudly that the villagers winced and covered their ears. "That's not what I said! I didn't just *say* I'm not a witch. That doesn't seem to do any good around here! I am describing a FACT! Rational people believe in something called objective reality, OK? Objective reality contains empirical data, which rational people call FACTS!"

The eyes of the villagers glazed over. Pa Usman yawned and patted his *nomoloi*.

"FACT!" screamed Boone. "I am talking about a FACT! A verifiable, incontrovertible, accurate, completely valid FACT, namely, THAT I AM NOT A FUCKING WITCH! UNDERSTAND?"

The witchfinder shook his head and sighed, dreading the thought of the extra work this lunatic *poo-mui* was creating for him.

"May I speak now?" asked the witchfinder.

"Yes," said Boone, "but please confine yourself to discussing FACTS."

"Facts," said the witchfinder with a nod. "I will try, but facts are very boring. Let me say that I have been finding witches in Sierra Leone since before you were one small peekin," said the witchfinder wearily. "One fact is that I've never found a *poo-mui* witch before. But I should have known that a *poo-mui* witch would be full of disrespect and too proud to confess."

"I'm not listening," said Boone, covering his ears.

"Very well," said the witchfinder. "Pa Ansumana, you are responsible for this *poo-mui* witch?"

Pa shrugged his shoulders and shook his head.

"Mistah Lamin Kaikai," the witchfinder said to Killigan. "This witch is your stranger? Your small American brother? He doesn't have better manners?"

Killigan grimaced sheepishly and looked at his feet.

"Mistah Aruna Sisay?"

Sisay did a mime of washing his hands.

"Well then," said the witchfinder, looking innocently around him, as if he had been insulted and wounded by this offensive challenge to his powers. He clapped his hands, and his assistants brought forth another platter, this one with two small balls of dough in the center.

"Oh no!" shouted Boone. "No more sideshow mutilations. I don't care if you cut your own fucking head off and put it back on again. That doesn't mean I'm a witch. I AM NOT A FUCKING WITCH!"

"You said you could prove to us that you are not a witch," said

the witchfinder gently. "Here is your chance. This is witch poison,"
explained the witchfinder. "If a person eats it, no harm will come
to him. If a witch eats it . . ." he said. "Well, we will see soon enough
what happens when a witch eats it. That is, if you are still willing
to prove that you are not a witch."

"I have a better idea," said Boone, with a malicious grin. "Let's
see what happens when a non-witch eats it first."

"As you wish," said the witchfinder. He picked one ball from the
plate and opened his mouth.

"Stop!" yelled Boone.

The witchfinder held the ball of dough in front of his open lips.

"I'll take that one," said Boone, holding his hand under the witchfinder's fingers.

The witchfinder shrugged and pursed his lips, then dropped the
dough into Boone's palm. It was the size of a marble or a grape.
Boone flattened the dough with his thumbs, inspected it for foreign
objects, and sniffed it. It was as pale as bread dough, but firmer
and greasier, like putty. He held it between his lips, while he seized
the other ball and examined it in the same way, satisfying himself
that they at least appeared to be identical. Then he rolled the second
one back into a ball and placed it on the witchfinder's platter.

The witchfinder plucked the dough from the platter and popped
it into his mouth, opening his teeth, and showing Boone that it
indeed sat on his tongue. Then he closed his mouth and swallowed.

Boone rolled his dough back into a ball and looked at it.

"Please, wait," said the witchfinder, handing the empty platter to
his assistant, and walking toward Boone. "I want you to understand
what is about to happen to you."

The witchfinder held up his arms and pulled back the baggy
sleeves of his robe, twisting and curling his arms, then spreading
his fingers and turning his hands over for Boone to examine.

"See anything?" he asked. "Here," he said, standing close to
Boone. "Under my robe," he said, guiding Boone's hands over the
contours of his chest, waist, and back. "Feel anything?"

Boone reluctantly shook his head.

"Please," said the witchfinder to the crowd. "Everyone stand back
from this witch, for there is no telling what effect the poison will
have!"

The villagers, *poo-muis* included, stepped well away from the
witchfinder and Boone.

"Please," shouted the witchfinder. "I want this witch to understand that no one and nothing was near him when he ate the witch poison. Please!" he said, summoning his assistants to help move the crowd back.

A circle with a radius of at least twenty feet opened around Boone and the witchfinder.

The witchfinder opened his mouth and turned out his cheeks. "The witch poison is gone," he said. "I ate it. Now it's your turn."

Boone resolutely threw the dough into the back of his throat, wetted it with spit, and swallowed. He felt it clear his throat and lodge somewhere under his sternum. He swallowed again, expecting to push it on through to his stomach. Instead, it stuck again and slowly erupted in a searing internal explosion, as if someone had lit a book of matches at the juncture of his esophagus and his stomach. He fell helplessly to his knees and gagged, then retched again and went down on all fours, feeling as if he had vomited, but the contents had lodged somewhere between his stomach and his throat. He heaved, and the foreign object worked its way into the back of his throat.

The witchfinder knelt down next to him and held him by the back of the neck.

"It's coming!" cried the witchfinder. "It's coming out!"

Boone gagged and saw a black hand pass under his eyes. He retched, and felt the witchfinder stick his hand into his mouth, then felt the fingers squirm and wriggle, clawing at his tongue and the back of his throat, as if the fingers were the limbs of a small animal desperately searching for a foothold inside his mouth. He heaved, one gag reflex triggering another.

"I have it!" cried the witchfinder. "I have hold of it now. I'm bringing it out!"

Boone violently retched and cleared his airway, vomiting around the witchfinder's hand and soaking the ground in front of his knees.

With the scrabbling fingers of his right hand still inside Boone's mouth, the witchfinder said, "Are your eyes open? Open your eyes," he said patiently. "I want your eyes to be open before I pull it out."

Boone wept and trembled, unable to tear the hand out of his mouth. He opened his eyes, and watched the witchfinder's hand emerge with something dark and wriggling. He blinked once and stared at the darting head and waving forelegs of a gecko, wriggling in the grip of the witchfinder, and clawing for purchase on his fingers. The witchfinder made a circlet of his thumb and forefinger, collaring the lizard and closing his hand around it. One black eye set in a streak of orange peered from the side of the head, and a red tongue flicked the air.

One of the assistants produced a small leather pouch. The witchfinder slipped the lizard inside and bound the bag with a cord.

Boone hung his head and coughed. When he stopped for a breath of air, he felt the witchfinder's lips touch his ear.

"Witchman," the voice whispered, "I have captured your shade."

(**21**)

Randall Killigan took his seat in Ambassador class on a wide-body out of Paris bound for Freetown, Sierra Leone. He pulled a shaving kit out of his carry-on bag and inventoried his medicines for the fourth time since leaving New York. Dramamine, Zantac, Lomotil, Advil, and Tylenol in one compartment. Antimalarials, antibiotics, and antihistamines, in another. Procainamide, quinidine, digoxin, beta blockers, calcium blockers, and assorted cardiac antiarrhythmics in yet another. He also had a printout from his computer detailing dosages and contraindications, along with boldface warnings about which ones should not be taken with certain others. Tricky business, because he kept cardiologists the way other men kept mistresses, and he had to make sure they didn't find out about each other. This assured him that second and third opinions were reliable and independent, but it also exposed him to dangerous synergisms whenever he took two separately prescribed heart medications that didn't belong together in his bloodstream.

After checking his medicines, he went to work connecting his notebook computer to the plane's cellular phone system, hoping to get stock quotes in real time. He had a stop loss order set to go off on his Merck if it fell more than 8 percent, but his newest fear was that it might sink just enough to trigger the sell order, then rebound to new highs.

When the hookup failed, he had words with the flight attendant, then stared out the window, grimly and stoically preparing himself for this adventure into the primitive world. What if he was making a mistake? Rushing off like this to a place where basic necessities, like patching a modem to a cellular phone network, were major ordeals?

At Lungi airport in Freetown, Randall was met by a host of special travel assistants, cheerful and knowledgeable fellows who expedited his passage through the immigration office for less than twenty dollars. For another twenty, they protected his luggage from sticky-fingered customs agents, and stoutly defended his rights to bring currency and medications into Sierra Leone. For forty dollars, they processed his papers, changed money for him, and solicited bids for transportation into Freetown. The normal price of $150.00 for a taxi and a ferry ride was halved by a robust and skillfully conducted auction. He tipped them all and took his seat in a private car, a contented white man, grateful for the attentions of the special travel assistants.

The taxi and ferry crossing took him to Freetown proper, where his car was promptly engulfed in a mass of black, half-naked human beings spilling out of shacks and open-sided markets with trays and parcels on their heads. He nearly gagged on the smell of rotten produce and drying fish. A press of naked children thrust a bouquet of flowering hands and open palms into his face. When he tried to roll up his window, the handle came off in his hand.

"White mahn, let we have ten cents. Do ya, I beg."

The crowd was loud, volatile, dressed in rags, covered with dust from unpaved streets, and streaked with mud made from their own sweat. Mouths laughed and shouted at one another, cursed and prayed. In the tangle of writhing bodies, his eyes seized upon crippled and withered limbs, raw patches of skin disease, missing digits, wounds crawling with flies, eyes clotted with ghostly white growths, unrepaired birth defects that had ripened into adult facial deformities.

"Keep you money inside you pocket," his driver warned him. "Tiefmahn dae beaucoup."

"I beg your pardon?" asked Randall.

The driver sucked his teeth and patiently urged his vehicle forward through the crush of flesh, gently nudging human beings aside with his front bumper.

In a wave of nausea and revulsion, Randall realized he had come too far; he had crossed a forbidden threshold into another dimension, had rashly charged into a realm of human chaos, where his life was suddenly as cheap as those of the beggars and urchins swarming around him.

He heaved a sigh when the crowded market slums gave out onto a main boulevard, which his driver explained would take them past a famous landmark, a five-hundred-year-old cotton tree in the center of town, in the same roundabout occupied by the American Embassy.

And what a spectacle! The tree itself was the biggest living thing he had ever seen, with massive limbs dwarfing the surrounding structures and soaring into the sky above the traffic roundabout. But even from a distance, he could see that the people of Freetown had adorned the tree with the most beautiful garments imaginable!

Spectacular capes hung from every limb and shone in the sun like pelts made of rainbows. And as he drew nearer, he could see that the capes changed colors in the breeze, like the skins of huge hooded chameleons. He had never seen such radiance in a garment, and promptly supposed that these tie-dyed wonders were probably even more beautiful than the coat of many colors worn by Joseph in the Bible.

He decided at once that he had to have one and made a mental note to ask the people at the embassy how he could arrange to buy such a beautiful cape and take it home.

By midmorning he was in conference, having his eyes peeled open with stories about his son's doings in Sierra Leone. Michael had turned up, but the explanations did not seem to fit the episodes.

"These are the kind of people your son is working to keep in power," said Ambassador Walsh, pushing a stack of photographs across the table to Killigan.

The lights flickered and the air conditioners recycled, as the power failed and the generator kicked in.

Randall looked up at the lights.

"Don't worry," said the Ambassador. "The power goes out three or four times a day. But we have our own generators, and plenty of fuel."

Randall grimaced as he studied the photographs. "They're wearing animal skins. One's a white man. You're not telling me that's my son, I hope."

"We don't know," said Walsh, with a glance at his political officer, Nathan French. "There are two other photos where one of the

African participants has his mask off, but the light and the resolution are so poor that identification is impossible."

"Are those headdresses or what?" asked Randall, all but holding his nose. "Are they killing someone? This is a human being, with holes cut into him. Are they skinning him?"

"Ritual cannibalism," said French. "They make medicines and charms out of human body parts."

"Disgusting," muttered Randall, flicking the photographs away with his finger.

"Probably the same people who sent you your package," added Mr. Moiwo with a shake of his head.

"You see the kind of benighted superstition we are dealing with, Mr. Killigan," said Walsh. "These chiefs are keeping the villages in the dark ages, so they can control the people with witchcraft and swears. They resist every attempt at rural and industrial development, because they have vested interests in the status quo. Land cannot be developed or put to commercial use because the chiefs insist the ancestors own it all, meaning that no one can buy it. Imagine trying to convince a mining or timber company to invest millions of dollars developing land they can't own."

"Under the current Paramount Chiefs," said Moiwo, "the land will be devoted only to subsistence-level farming."

"But after the election," said Randall, "you'll be in a position to change things, at least in your part of the country. Isn't that what you said?"

The other men drew breaths and looked at one another.

"There was a problem with the election," said Walsh. "It had to be postponed until we could be certain of a fair result. This Paramount Chief, Kabba Lundo, who has the devotion of your son, is devious and resilient. Somehow he has managed, through demagoguery, trickery, and intimidation, to convince the people that Section Chief Moiwo is involved in these secret, illegal societies. The symbols and activities of these cults have so infected their thinking that even presumably rational people, like your son, now accuse Chief Moiwo of certain unspeakable human sacrifices and cannibalistic rituals that have been outlawed since the turn of the century."

"It's an old trick," added French. "When the British made this kind of thing illegal, it did nothing to discourage the cannibalism, but it did allow practitioners to have their ghastly medicines and frame their opponents at the same time."

Ambassador Walsh filled a water glass from a canister at center table.

"Kabba Lundo is quite jealous of our relationship with Section Chief Moiwo, who has been a loyal friend to U.S. interests. It is no secret in the bush that we feel Moiwo is the most qualified man for the office of Paramount Chief. Our evidence suggests that Kabba Lundo—clearly from the old black magic school of African leaders—committed a so-called Baboon murder and then tried to eliminate Mr. Moiwo, his rival, by framing him with the crime. Your son, Michael, gullibly succumbed to the circumstantial evidence carefully arranged by Kabba Lundo, and was goaded into joining ranks with the old guard."

"When you do hook up with your son," said French, "don't be surprised at the vividness of his delusions. You cannot imagine the stress and privations of these initiations in the bush. All of these secret bush societies use brainwashing techniques to indoctrinate their members. After one of these sessions, your boy traveled by bush path all the way to Freetown and delivered these photographs to Vice President Joseph Bangura of the Sierra Leonean government, who himself has recently been tried and found guilty of high treason. Your son tried to tell Bangura that these photographs were pictures of Section Chief Moiwo's men."

Moiwo smiled and shook his head in disbelief. Walsh rolled his eyes, and French snorted at the absurdity of the idea.

"As you can see for yourself," said French, "identification is absolutely out of the question, and we have reason to believe that all of this was staged by Kabba Lundo and his men."

"The Peace Corps will not tolerate political activity," said Walsh. "We have reports that your son is leaving Sierra Leone and is headed up to Mali on holiday with his American friend. If you would like to go out to his village and see for yourself if he's left yet, we can provide you with a vehicle, a driver, and a translator. It's about a day's journey into the bush."

"You're offering to send me out to where those photographs came from?" Randall asked hoarsely, making an ugly face at the photos. He recalled the reckless filthy humans he had seen in the markets and realized that they were probably exemplary citizens of the country's comparatively civilized capital city. He could just imagine what kind of desperate brutes were waiting to greet him out in the bush!

"Gentlemen, I'm a lawyer from Indiana. My kid has some metabolic disorder of the brain that makes him want to go live in mud huts with superstitious Africans. He was crazy enough to go out to this jurisdiction you all call the bush, but his dementia is neither genetic nor contagious. What I want is for you to get him out of there and send him home."

The import of his own words startled him. He tried to imagine a normal, healthy college graduate from Indiana wanting to live in this cesspool of human deprivation and despair. Impossible. Next he imagined what kind of insane, ostensibly civilized person would not only venture out to the bush but live there, for three, four years! Maybe his kid was seeing bats at night. Maybe his kid had a bright object in his deep white matter. What if he went out to the bush looking for his son and found a psychotic white man sitting around a fire chanting with a bunch of secret-society juju men?

The generator stalled and the lights went off, shrouding the conversation in a full second of darkness.

"OK," someone called from another room, and the clatter resumed in a flicker of lights.

More likely, it was a case of too much privilege. And if Dad risked his neck following the kid into no-man's-land and paid his way out, what then? Treat an overdose of privilege with a bolus of protection? No, he had already done enough.

"If we find him," said the Ambassador, ignoring the lights, while Randall stared irritably at the flickering bulbs overhead, "he will be discharged from his service and forced to leave Sierra Leone. If he has already left the country, he will not be allowed to return. We can promise you that. Whether he will return to the United States is not for us to decide," said Walsh. "Maybe not even for you to decide," he added.

Randall stabbed the table top with his index finger. "You just make sure he gets out of Sierra Leone safely," he said, "and don't give him a job anywhere else. When he runs out of money, he'll come home."

"Gentlemen," said Moiwo, putting his hands on the table. "It's been my experience that difficult matters are more easily digested when accompanied by a meal. The hour is here, and I have a fine place in mind."

"If you'll excuse us for a moment," said the Ambassador as the men rose from the table, "while we advise our personnel of our plans."

After the Americans had left, Randall shook Moiwo's hand. "I can't thank you enough for your help," Randall said. "I'm sure things could have turned out much worse."

"Please," said Moiwo. "After all your country has done for us, it's the least I can do."

Randall strolled to the windows for a view of Freetown through the bars of the embassy windows. A haze of harmattan dust settled on the city. Again, he saw the magnificent capes of the cotton tree shining in the setting sun. Then he was startled to see them breaking away from the tree in pairs, and flying, flocking. Swarming around the tree. They were birds! Spectacular, beautiful birds!

"I thought those were capes of some kind," said Randall uncertainly, turning to his African host. "I thought they were beautiful garments when I saw them from the taxi. The colors were so vivid. Extraordinary!"

His heart squirmed in a momentary panic. What if this was just another vision? What if he was seeing things again? Before he left home, he had scheduled another MRI with Bean, then changed his mind and decided he would have the MRI done at the University of Chicago.

"Ah, the cotton tree capes," said Moiwo, with a wink and a laugh. "Aren't they lovely? I must warn you not to mention them to your American friends, or to anyone for that matter. The superstitions and taboos associated with them are a very painful subject locally."

"Why am I not surprised?" said Randall, sighing with relief. "Still, they are absolutely beautiful."

"The tourists who appreciate fine garments often want to buy them, when they see them in the daylight. But as you can see, it's impossible. They are not for sale."

"I'll admit that buying one was my first thought," said Randall, "and I thought to myself they must be very valuable," he added with a laugh, "until I saw them flying. What kind of bird are they?"

"The citizens call them witch birds," said Moiwo, "but if you check with your zoologists over at USAID, you will find that they are fruit bats. Giant fruit bats that have been nesting in that tree since the land was sold to the British."

Randall stared at the swarming forms, now dark in the setting sun, and settling on the limbs of the tree, their silhouettes filing slowly across the limbs like hooded figures filling pews. He heard loud sounds, like a huge percussion orchestra of boards and blocks of wood striking other pieces of wood.

"Shall I arrange for you to have one?" asked Moiwo with another wink. "But," he added with a facetious grin, "I will only get it for you if you will keep it absolutely secret. The legend says that once you own one, it is fatal to tell anyone about it, or to give it away."

"Fruit bats," said Randall dully. "Witch birds."

"And I won't accept a penny for it," said Moiwo with a chuckle. "It is a gift from me. After all your country has done for me, it's the least I can do."

(**22**)

Well-fed poets may dream of finding the world within a grain of sand, but a starving man can find the entire universe and all the ecstasies of eternity in a mouthful of groundnut stew and a tin cup of well water. Boone and Killigan sat in a circle with their extended African families in the single huge room of Pa Ansumana's house. A candle cast a blood-colored aureole over a mounded platter of food. Pa apportioned beef to the men, then gave the signal, and the scrimmage was on. Dark arms, hands, and fingers reached from the shadows and scooped up gobbets of chop. Boone gouged softball-sized wads of rice from the tray with his right hand and stuffed them into his mouth, licking orange palm oil from his fingers, and finally mastering the art of the chewless swallow.

Nyandengo!

Soft laughter, grunts of pleasure. He had come down off another roaring fever and landed in the familiar post-febrile euphoria. Cold cups of well water soothed burning nerves at the back of his throat. There was no rust on God, no rust on the human beings who sat with him in the dark, feeding themselves, as if the food all went to a communal tongue, gullet, and belly, aglow with the elemental pleasure of nourishment.

Yesterday they would have crushed his skull at a word from the witchfinder, today they were praising God and feeding the ancestors in his name. Once the *honei* had been removed from the *mui*, it seemed he was again a harmless figure of fun. To the immense delight of his brothers and sisters, the after-dinner conversation consisted of resurrected latrine jokes and puns about a white belly running back and forth from the outhouse at night. He was told for the first time that his name, Gutawa, meant "great ass." Gales of laughter greeted each rendition of the line: "I am not a fucking witch." He was the same white-skinned doofus who had stumbled into their village two weeks ago not knowing enough to cover his head in the midday sun, lacking even a peekin's knowledge about how to protect himself from witchcraft, vulnerable to the mildest fluctuations of diet and climate, prey to the most obvious wiles of God, men, and witches. Now it seemed his helplessness had endeared him to them. He was their feeble-minded charge, who, for some reason known only to God and the ancestors, had been born in a white skin, grew up in a cave with heaps of money, treasures, food, disposable pipe cleaners, and medicines, went to *poo-mui* schools for twenty-some years, and came out a middle-aged, white bobo, barely able to feed himself.

After dinner, Killigan and Boone retired to Boone's shed next to Sisay's house and stood each other go-downs of palm wine.

"Here's to my small *poo-mui* brother," said Killigan, giving his friend a long, tender look and clinking his tin mug against Boone's. "I tell God tank ya."

Boone looked into a face he had first seen twenty-three years ago in kindergarten. The lineaments and expressions were still there, but now they were stubbled with a beard that looked as if it had been trimmed with a blunt cutlass. The eyes flashed with the same slightly deranged intelligence that had once shown his kindergarten classmates how to occlude a drinking straw full of chocolate milk and carry it over to the aquarium, but now those eyes were flanked by pale tribal scars on his temples. The cheerful disregard for the opinions of others and the expectations of his father that had gotten Michael Killigan in trouble as a teenager had brought him to West Africa and had seen him through the privations of the bush as well as the treachery of his political enemies.

"I'm bigger than you," said Boone. "I'm older than you, and I'm smarter than you. If we have to be brothers I'll be the big brother."

"But you came to Africa after I did," chided Killigan. "Any Mende man would call you my small brother. I am your host. You came here to visit me. I am responsible for you."

"I didn't come here to visit," said Boone. "I came here to find your ass. Instead, I ended up being had by some African mountebank."

"In the words of a *poo-mui* proverb no African would subscribe to," said Killigan, "it's the thought that counts. You took big risks to come here and endanger my life. I owe you." He smiled. "But you should have stayed in Paris and thought about coming."

"All I want to know is how the old guy did it," said Boone, scowling and refilling his cup from another Esso oil jug, which apparently was the preferred method for storing palm wine.

"You mean how he captured your shade?" asked Killigan.

Boone spat and clenched his teeth.

"You mean, how he knew you were a witch?" Killigan asked. "Simple. He is a *gbese*, the one born after twins, and the most respected witchfinder in Sierra Leone. He can see everything. Who else would suspect a witch spirit of hiding inside of a *poo-mui*?"

Boone waited for a smile, but none was forthcoming. His best friend stared implacably into his eyes as if he were discussing Boone's recent recuperation from a nasty case of poison ivy.

Boone made a mental note to settle this thing with fisticuffs once they got back to civilization. For the moment, he ignored the superstitious misfit seated next to him, and instead talked aloud to himself. "His robe probably has more pockets than a fishing vest. He told everybody to move back, and that's when he pulled the gecko out of his robe, or had one of his assistants hand it to him."

"Still trying to find your way around Sierra Leone with a map of Indiana?" asked Killigan.

"Look," said Boone irritably, "why don't you and Sisay go off somewhere and start a village for culturally sensitive white people. You could spend the rest of your lives pretending you believe in witchcraft and native medicine." He stamped his spittle into the floor with the sole of his boot. "Hey, speaking of Sisay, where is old Machiavelli anyway?"

"They don't call them woodsheds over here," said Killigan, "but I suspect that's where he is, with Pa Ansumana and Kabba Lundo."

"And Lewis? Where'd he go?"

"To do me a favor," said Killigan. "He took Jenisa to Freetown. To immigration. Do you mind?"

"Mind what?"

"If she comes with us?" said Killigan. "I can't take the chance of leaving her here. Moiwo might get loose. Or what if they won't let me back into the country after our travel?"

"I take it this means you like her more than Mary Lou Cratville?"

"Small brother," said Killigan. "This woman is fine-O. Size one.

Woman past woman. And," he added with a taut smile, "one small peekin is on its way."

Boone's momentary considerations of cultural barriers and practical difficulties were eclipsed by the force field emanating from his best friend's passion.

"Will the government let her leave the country?" he asked.

"Mas-mas," said Killigan, rubbing imaginary bills between his fingertips. "The 'sweet of office.' I gave Lewis the money. She'll get the papers."

"Well then," said Boone, "bring her along. The two of us can start another coven. Maybe paralyze one of your limbs one night while you're sleeping. I won't say which one. And where are we going?"

"Mali," said Killigan. "The Dogon country, beautiful villages built into the Bandiagara cliffs. After that, Timbuktu. There's a flight every other day from Freetown to Bamako, Mali. Air Mali," he added, "also known as Air Maybe. After that to Niger by bush taxi, across the Sahara on trucks to Tunisia, and then a ferry to Sicily. For the next few months, we'll be four world travelers in search of a place to raise one small peekin."

"Kong, kong," said a voice at the door.

"Here they come," sighed Boone. "What have they been doing with themselves all night?" He poured Killigan another slug of palm wine. "We've been in here alone for at least fifteen minutes."

Pa Ansumana came first, pipe stoked and spewing smoke. Next came one of the witchfinder's assistants, with a live white chicken swaddled in his arms.

Pa and Killigan spoke Mende.

"I don't mean to interrupt," said Boone, "but why is there a chicken in my bedroom?"

"I was hoping to talk to you about it before they got here," said Killigan. "You are leaving on a long journey. Your grandfather wants to be sure that all is 'right' between you and your ancestors, and that you will reach your destination safely."

"OK," said Boone.

"So," continued Killigan, glancing at the assistant and the chicken, "it's kind of like a diagnostic procedure. You're nothing but a passive participant. It's painless, I promise. Your grandfather has pulled *sara* for you, meaning he has offered sacrifices for you, to make sure that none of his ancestors are angry about you and your witch business, and that your many transgressions against them have been forgiven."

"This is something I have to do, right?" murmured Boone, looking up and seeing his grandfather's face frowning down at him from a cloud of smoke.

"I'm afraid so," said Killigan. "The assistant will prepare you and then put grains on your palms and your tongue. If the chicken eats the grains, then the ancestors are happy, they have accepted Pa's gifts, and they will watch over you on your journey."

"What happens if the chicken doesn't eat the grain?" asked Boone.

"Then we turn you into a chicken," said Killigan. "Just kidding. It means Pa will have to offer more sacrifices and spend more money on looking-around men until the ancestors are satisfied."

"OK," said Boone. "What do I do?" he asked, regarding the assistant with a wary eye.

"Take off your boots and sit up with your bare feet in front of you."

The assistant handed the chicken to Pa and approached Boone with a ball of cotton thread. He spoke Mende to Killigan.

"Turn out your palms," said Killigan.

Boone sat on the floor and opened his hands.

The assistant unraveled a length of white thread, wrapping one end of it around his left big toe, then stringing it up to his left thumb, where it was wrapped again, then to his left ear and wrapped, behind his head, over to his right ear, down to his right thumb, then to his right big toe.

"I'm Gulliver, right?" said Boone, relaxing his hands slightly.

"Palms up," said Killigan. "And stick out your tongue."

"Can't we just do the palms?" said Boone. "I'm not sure I want to be pecked in the tongue by a chicken."

Pa muttered gravely, as if he had all but written off this *poo-mui* son of his but was giving him one last chance to redeem himself.

Boone stuck out his tongue.

The assistant drew a pouch from his shirt and sprinkled grains onto each of Boone's hands, then placed grains on Boone's extended tongue.

Pa handed the chicken to the assistant, nodded, and spoke Mende to Killigan.

The assistant cradled the hen and approached, holding it between Boone's supine palms.

The head tilted and one beady eye glinted with orange lamplight. The hen pecked the grains out of his right hand, then his left.

The feathered head cocked an eye for a gander at the food on Boone's tongue. Its head tilted and the other eye probed furiously, sparkling with hunger.

"Fathers and grandfathers," said Killigan, translating for Pa, "please accept our gifts and look with favor on our son."

Boone stared into the firelit eye and saw himself sitting on a dirt floor in West Africa, sweating, slightly addled by palm wine, covered with tropical sores, woozy from malaria—a human being, an organism breathing, eating, and aging in the bush. The chicken's eye blinked open like a small tear in the material world fitted with a tiny, convex monocle. When Boone peered inside, he saw a fire burning in a huge dark room on the other side of the lens. Thronged around the hearth were his ancestors—hordes of them silhouetted and staring out at him, thousands of eyes on bobbing heads, watching his every gesture, hearing his every word. They were telling each other stories about how he had lived his life. When the ancestors saw him hurt their living relatives or take advantage of them, they shook their heads and disowned him, an adopted *poo-mui* with no training, a spoiled and selfish son raised by greedy people in the land of *Poo*. When the ancestors saw him help their relatives on earth, they were proud of him and boasted about how much he resembled them, how their strength of character had been successfully passed from one generation to the next, and had even managed to find its way into an adopted *poo-mui*.

The head darted, stopped, and cocked.

Boone seemed to hear his audience draw breaths and hold them.

The hen pecked the grain from his tongue.

(23)

"**N**othing," said Bean, walking out of the radiology booth and tucking a ballpoint pen into the vest pocket of his lab coat.

Randall sat up on the scanning table.

"You're clean," said Bean. "No unidentified bright object in the deep white matter. No tumor. No arteriovenous malformation. No cyst. Nothing. You're cured. More likely, you were never sick. False positive."

"Nothing," repeated Randall, sitting on a stool next to the MRI machine. "If something was there, you could see it?"

"We could see it," said Bean clapping him on the back. "You get the best pictures in the universe out of these things. You can see everything. There's nothing there. The UBO was a false positive. And you saved yourself a trip to Chicago."

"Yeah," said Randall, putting his tie back on and looking around for his suit coat.

"Well?" said Bean. "You're happy, right?"

"I'm . . . happy," said Randall vaguely, avoiding his buddy's stare. "But . . ."

"But what?" Bean demanded.

"But . . . now there's no . . . explanation. I just saw a huge, ugly West African bat flying over my bed at three in the morning, and—"

"You are *impossible* to please," said Bean, throwing up his hands. "Never mind! Forget what I just said! I was *hiding* things from you again!"

"You were?" asked Randall, in a single instant of panic.

"Yes," howled Bean. "I was trying to *deceive* you. That's my job!

I'm a doctor! I'm a master of deception! I didn't want you to know that the MRI shows a malignant brain tumor the size of a grapefruit! That's right! And that's why you saw the bat, OK? There! *Now are you happy?*"

Randall hung his head.

"You've got six weeks to live," shouted Bean, throwing the MRI films into a rack. "But don't worry, we'll get you in downstairs! We'll cut that massive brain tumor right out of there!" he hollered. "And the next time you're in the decathlon, you can use it in the fucking shot put!"

•

He drove back downtown, trying to develop an appreciation for the newly discovered purity of his deep white matter. He was healed. He was an American citizen. He was well into the top 1 percent in terms of disposable income. Life had laid out a banquet for him. He was not huddled in some mud hut in a backwater Third World country, where he would have to think about drinking water and food every day.

Maybe the bat was just a freak illusion. But what about the bloody bundle? Was *that* real? And what about the capes? What about this peculiar . . . aura around everything, almost as if objects—reality —*radiated* light, instead of just reflecting the sun's? Even in the middle of the morning, everything seemed to glow with swamp gas, or St. Elmo's fire, or the phosphorescence of the sea at night . . .

He rode up the elevator with two junior partners who were talking golf and going nowhere as lawyers. Just *having* the huge chunk of time available for a golf game was indicative of a floundering career, and these profligates had wasted it twice by playing with each other, instead of with clients.

At his floor, Randall got out, and firm personnel streamed through the lobby, greeting him by name, asking him how was his trip to Africa, telling him how glad they were that his son had turned up OK.

He suddenly realized that these people knew everything about him, even though he didn't even know their first names! Until today, this had always seemed normal. With a hundred and twenty partners and eighty-some associates, it was enough to keep track of the lawyers' names. And he had far too much on his plate to be chatting about people's families or how they had spent their weekends. Now he realized that he had walked past these people twenty times a day for years, decades! And he didn't know their names!

At the reception area, he received swatches of pink message slips stacked according to days. He turned to walk from the marble floor of the reception area onto the carpeted hallway that led to his office, and almost paused. The chocolate-colored carpeting looked firm and plush. He had never once noticed the color, or thought of it as having anything but a solid floor underneath it. Now he wondered. What if it was actually . . . insubstantial? What if he stepped onto it and sank up to his knees in some frosting-like substance? Or worse, found himself swimming in institutional-colored quicksand?

He hurried to the familiar surroundings of his desk and work-tables, switched on his computer, and stabbed the intercom.

"Commander," said Mack with a giggle.

"I'm back," said Randall.

"First, good news," said Mack. "Remember that motion to dismiss the Beach Cove lender liability suit that Spontoon drafted up for us? Judge Hamilton granted it. Case dismissed."

"That's great," said Randall. "Did you tell Comco?"

"I sent Flap a copy of the judge's order, with a note over your signature. He's thrilled. I think he left a tribute to your awesome powers on your voice mail."

"What's the bad news?" asked Randall, flipping through faxes stamped URGENT.

"Real weird," said Mack tonelessly. "Our friend Mr. Bilksteen argued the Beach Cove motion before Judge Hamilton. Spontoon demolished him; the judge reamed him a new asshole and dismissed the case. Then Bilksteen went back to his office and had some kind of . . . coronary event."

"A what?" said Randall, throwing the faxes aside.

"They said it was a . . . coronary event," said Mack. "He's in intensive care over at St. Dymphna's Medical Center. Not doing real well, from the sound of it."

"Bilksteen had a heart attack after he argued the Beach Cove motion?" asked Randall, looking around his office, wondering if the walls and ceiling were collapsible, or maybe porous, or inflatable, or maybe . . . they were breathing, or billowing softly, like swamps of viscous paint somehow defying gravity . . .

"Well," said Mack uncomfortably, "they didn't *call* it a heart attack."

"That's weird," said Randall. "Uh, I'll get back to you on some other stuff, after I . . . take care of some . . . matters . . ."

"Yes, boss," said Mack.

"But wait a second," said Randall. "I need something, kind of right away."

"Yeah," said Mack eagerly.

"I need that anthropologist. The Mende expert. His name . . ."

"Harris Sawyer," said Mack. "University of Pennsylvania."

"Yeah," said Randall. "Get him for me again. Tell him it's important."

"Righto," said Mack.

Randall started feeding pink slips and faxes to his bear. He saw a messenger come in and add another hateful piece of paper to the miasm engulfing his desk, his life, his ability to . . . think clearly.

When he turned back to begin clearing the stuff, he found a mound of crawling white membranes scored with ancient writings and cryptograms. The pages multiplied like cells under his fingers, spilled around him like white leaves encrypted with occult symbols, cuneiform script and insignias in ogham, alchemical equations and ancient Hebrew from the Dead Sea Scrolls. The pile heaved under his hands like a white-skinned animal shedding reams of papyrus scored with runes and hieroglyphics. Paper! Words! Symbols!

Out of the swimming print, he spotted a fax bearing today's date and the style of the Beach Cove lender liability suit. Under the style of the case, in bold caption, it said: NOTIFICATION OF CHANGE OF COUNSEL, followed by two sentences advising all attorneys of record and all named parties that Attorney Thomas R. Bilksteen, of McGrath, Becker & Warren, was deceased, and that representation of the debtor would be assumed by the surviving partners of the firm.

Beep went the intercom.

"Line one," said Mack. "*Dr.* Harris Sawyer, University of Pennsylvania."

"Dr. Sawyer," said Randall, clearing his throat and setting papers aside, "I appreciate your promptness. I'm just back from . . . being out of the office. My . . . client . . . What was it we called her? Colette? Yes, Colette's having problems again. Serious ones, I think."

"I'm sorry to hear that," said Sawyer. "I hope I can be of some help."

"Yeah, well, as I told you, she's very superstitious," said Randall. "Yes, very superstitious. And now she believes this bundle thing may have . . . I don't know . . . *done* something to her. Things actually *look* different to her. Things are happening to her which she cannot explain. Certain unusual perceptual phenomena . . ."

"How unfortunate," said Sawyer.

"Yeah," said Randall. "I guess, well, let me share with you what I'd like to do. I really need to tell her that if this bundle turned into a witch spirit and, I don't know, *entered* her, or *bit* her, or *infected* her, or whatever it's supposed to do, she would *know* about it, wouldn't she? I mean, even the Mende would say that if she was a . . . Whaddaya call it? Witch host? Or witch person? Then she would *know* she was a witch host. Right? I mean, let's face it," said Randall with a hoarse laugh, "this is all superstitious shit! It's not real! I can tell her that! I can tell her it's not real. I can tell her that even if she believed in this kind of *silly shit*, the juju or whatever, then something would have happened to her by now. Do you follow me? I mean, even one of these African tribesmen would say that if she's not dead, or, or sick . . . then the thing didn't work, if you know what I'm trying to say. Blood or no blood! *It didn't do anything!*"

"I trust you recall the two-hat method," said Sawyer. "And I think you know that the Caucasian anthropologist might suggest that Colette avail herself of some counseling, or maybe psychological help, but that's not why you called me."

"No," said Randall quickly. "See, it's as I said before, she's so superstitious she likes to have these things explained to her from the African point of view, so she can be absolutely sure she understands the entire phenomenon, from every perspective . . . You follow me?"

"Of course," said Sawyer. "The issue, then, is whether a witch person, or witch host would always know he or she had a witch spirit. The Mende disagree on this point, and so do the anthropologists. Some say that when a witch enters a village, it is like a powerful sound in a room filled with tuning forks. Or let's use a Mende proverb: *Hinda a wa hinda.* 'Something brings something,' or, even better, 'Like brings out like.' In the Midwest, they might say, 'If you plant corn, you get corn,' something like that. Anyway, some forks respond to the frequency, others don't, and those responding can 'feel' the frequency—they *know* they are witches, even though they will always deny it. But that's not Colette's case, I take it," said Sawyer.

"No," said Randall with a dismissive laugh, "she doesn't know. At least she's not telling me," he quickly added.

"But others say," Sawyer continued, "that often a witch host sees only malice, chaos, destruction, and evil all around him. As time goes on, he senses that the evil seems always to be linked to him. Then, perhaps, he has a dream, or is skillfully questioned by a looking-around man or a witchfinder. And then," said Sawyer, pausing.

"Then what?" Randall urged.

"Then suddenly," he said, warming to his role as a Mende villager. "Suddenly the witch host realizes that the darkness he always so quickly saw in others is really only his own dark powers reflected in the looking glasses of their innocent hearts. He discovers that the evil he had always ascribed to human nature is really the fruit of his own wicked labors. He planted seeds, and now the harvest has come in. His life is filled with evil people, because they are his converts, members of his coven. In one horrible instant, he sees that he is the *cause* of much of the despair, destruction, and evil in his life. He may have convinced himself that he was only using bad medicine to protect himself—so-called defensive medicines, or counter-swears—but before long, he discovers that he has a witch spirit, and the witch spirit has gradually . . . taken over."

The line fell silent.

"Mr. Killigan," said Sawyer. "Mr. Killigan, are you there?"

ACKNOWLEDGMENTS

In the early 1980s, I lived in villages and towns in Sierra Leone for approximately seven months. The Mende people of Sierra Leone generously shared their homes, their food, their conversation, and their way of life with me. Most often, my hosts were very poor villagers who refused to accept any compensation for their hospitality.

White Man's Grave is a work of fiction. Although it purports to describe the rituals of several secret societies, legal and illegal, these descriptions were not provided by any member of a secret society, nor did any member of any secret society, legal or illegal, ever reveal any society secrets to me.

I returned from Sierra Leone and invented the story *White Man's Grave* after studying several books on the Mende and Sierra Leone, including the following texts.

The mysteries of the Mende culture are set forth with poetic grace and scholarly clarity in two books: W. T. Harris and Harry Sawyerr, *The Springs of Mende Belief and Conduct* (Freetown Sierra Leone University Press, 1968). Kenneth Little, *The Mende of Sierra Leone* (Routledge & Kegan Paul, 1967).

The character of the witchfinder was inspired, in part, by the captivating eyewitness accounts contained in Anthony J. Gittins's *Mende Religion* (Steyler Verlag—Wort und Werk Nettetal, 1987).

Michael Jackson's *Paths Toward a Clearing* (Indiana University Press, 1989) is denominated as "anthropology," but is actually poetry, philosophy, literature, psychology, and anthropology all set forth in one excellent book about human nature and the Koranko tribe of Sierra Leone.

Sierra Leonean Krio is a very beautiful spoken language containing more wit, proverbs, and human wisdom than all of Shakespeare. However, its various written manifestations are almost impossible to decipher unless one already knows the language. I have attempted to invent a printed Krio, which I hope "sounds" like Krio but is also quickly apprehended by the English-speaking reader.

I am grateful to Michael Becker, Gregory Willard, and Dr. John Adair for their advice and technical expertise.

Finally, the *Grave* was shallower and a lot narrower until Jean Naggar placed the manuscript and its lazy author in the keeping of editor John Glusman.